The Coroners Jury Report of Billy The Kid

The Inquest That Sealed the Fame of Billy Bonney and Pat Garrett

By
Gale Cooper

GELCOUR
BOOKS

OTHER BILLY THE KID BOOKS
BY GALE COOPER

THE HISTORY

BILLY AND PAULITA: THE SAGA OF BILLY THE KID, PAULITA MAXWELL, AND THE SANTA FE RING

BILLY THE KID'S WRITINGS, WORDS, AND WIT

THE LOST PARDON OF BILLY THE KID: AN ANALYSIS FACTORING IN THE SANTA FE RING, GOVERNOR LEW WALLACE'S DILEMMA, AND A TERRITORY IN REBELLION

THE SANTA FE RING VERSUS BILLY THE KID: THE MAKING OF AN AMERICAN MONSTER

THE HOAXES

CRACKING THE BILLY THE KID CASE HOAX: THE STRANGE PLOT TO EXHUME BILLY THE KID, CONVICT SHERIFF PAT GARRETT OF MURDER, AND BECOME PRESIDENT OF THE UNITED STATES

THE COLD CASE BILLY THE KID MEGAHOAX: THE PLOT TO STEAL BILLY THE KID'S IDENTITY AND DEFAME SHERIFF PAT GARRETT AS A MURDERER

CRACKING THE BILLY THE KID IMPOSTER HOAX OF BRUSHY BILL ROBERTS

BILLY THE KID'S PRETENDER JOHN MILLER

BLANDINA SEGALE, THE NUN WHO RODE ON BILLY THE KID: SLEUTHING A FOISTED FRONTIER FABLE

COVER AND BOOK DESIGN BY GALE COOPER

For Billy Bonney,
named by his
Santa Fe Ring enemies,
"Billy the Kid;"
and called "Kid" by his
freedom fighting
compatriots

SECOND EDITION

ISBN: 978-1-949626-28-5 HARDCOVER
ISBN: 978-1-949626-29-2 PAPERBACK
LIBRARY OF CONGRESS
CONTROL NUMBER: 2020906545

GELCOUR BOOKS.
ALBUQUERQUE, NEW MEXICO

ORDERING THIS BOOK:
Amazon.com, BarnesandNoble.com, bookstores

WEBSITE:
GaleCooperBillytheKidBooks.com

YOUTUBE CHANNEL:
Gale Cooper's Real Billy the Kid

Printed in the United States of America
on acid free paper

CONTENTS

PART I:
THE OLD WEST'S
MOST FAMOUS KILLING

CHAPTER 1:
THE OUTLAW-LAWMAN SAGA
THAT EXCITED AMERICA

CHAPTER 2:
IMPOSTER HOAXES'
IMPASSABLE HURDLE

CHAPTER 3:
THE WITNESSES
AND THE DEATH SCENE

CHAPTER 4:
BILLY BONNEY'S LIFE

CHAPTER 5:
BILLY BONNEY
IN HIS OWN WORDS

PART II:
THE "BRUSHY BILL" IMPOSTER HOAX AND ITS FAKED DEATH SCENE AND DENIED CORONER'S JURY REPORT

CHAPTER 1:
THE "BRUSHY BILL" IMPOSTER HOAX

CHAPTER 2:
THE MAKE-OR-BREAK DEATH SCENE

CHAPTER 3:
TRUE-BELIEVERS CONTINUE THE "BRUSHY BILL" HOAX'S FAKE DEATH SCENE AND CORONER'S JURY REPORT DENIAL

PART III: THE JOHN MILLER IMPOSTER HOAX AND THE FAKED DEATH SCENE AND DENIED CORONER'S JURY REPORT

CHAPTER 1 :
JOHN MILLER'S IMPOSTER HOAX'S DEATH SCENE AND CORONER'S JURY REPORT FAKERY

PART IV:
THE "BILLY THE KID CASE" HOAX AND THE FAKE DEATH SCENE AND DENIED CORONER'S JURY REPORT

CHAPTER 1:
THE "BILLY THE KID CASE" FORENSIC DNA HOAX

CHAPTER 2:
"BILLY THE KID CASE" HOAX'S FAKED DEATH SCENE

CHAPTER 3:
"BILLY THE KID CASE" HOAX LEGAL FILINGS

CHAPTER 4:
"BILLY THE KID CASE" HOAX TV DOCUMENTARY WITH THE FAKE DEATH SCENE AND CORONER'S JURY REPORT DENIAL

CHAPTER 5:
"BILLY THE KID CASE" HOAX FAKE FORENSICS WITH DR. HENRY LEE

CHAPTER 6:
ILLEGAL EXHUMATIONS OF JOHN MILLER AND WILLIAM HUDSPETH BASED ON THE FAKE DEATH SCENE AND NO CORONER'S JURY REPORT

CHAPTER 7:
TRYING TO DIG UP "BRUSHY BILL"

PART V:
THE RETURN OF THE "BRUSHY BILL" HOAX'S FAKE DEATH SCENE AND DENIED CORONER'S JURY REPORT WITH FIX-UPS

CHAPTER 1:
RETURN OF FAKERY IN *BILLY THE KID: BEYOND THE GRAVE*

CHAPTER 2:
FURTHER FAKERY IN
BILLY THE KID: THE LOST INTERVIEWS

CHAPTER 3:
ACCUSING GARRETT IN
PAT GARRETT: THE MAN BEHIND THE BADGE
OF A FAKED DEATH SCENE
AND NO CORONER'S JURY REPORT

PART VI:
"COLD CASE BILLY THE KID" MEGAHOAX WITH FAKED DEATH SCENES AND DENIED CORONER'S JURY REPORT

CHAPTER 1:
FUSING OF ALL THE IMPOSTER HOAXES
AS A MEGAHOAX WITH A FAKE DEATH SCENE

CHAPTER 2:
FAKING NO INQUEST

CHAPTER 3:
THE RETURN OF FAKE FORENSICS

CHAPTER 4:
RETURN OF THE "BILLY THE KID CASE'S" EXHUMATION FAKERY

CHAPTER 5:
FOREGONE CONCLUSION

PART VII:
SUMMARY AND CONCLUSIONS

CHAPTER 1:
IMPASSABLE HURDLES ARE IMPASSABLE

PREFACE

I tell you what: Billy Bonney, called “Kid” by his pals, and “Billy the Kid” by his enemies, had as much chance as a one-legged man in a kicking contest of dying in bed. But he died like he wanted: standing up and free; cause he wouldn’t high-tail it out of New Mexico Territory after his jailbreak, just before the Ring was fixing to hang him by that Lincoln County Sheriff, Pat Garrett. By Ring, I mean Santa Fe Ring: politician varmints controlling the Territory back then - same as today.

Well, this here book is just about that boy’s dying, cause years after it, a passel of fellas just airing their lungs in a campaign against the truth, claimed to be him, by spinning yarns that Garrett never did kill him, and lied bout it to get the reward. Truth is, those long-in-the-tooth old-timers with wasted lives was pretending that they never did die that July 14, 18881 night of his killing, cause they wanted the bragging rights of being Billy. And they got them authors slick as calf-slobbers hoping to get rich by putting their lies in books calling them Billy the Kid - which Billy hisself never would have called hisself, with it being the name he got from the Santa Fe Ring’s branding him an outlaw stead of the Lincoln County War freedom fighting hero that he was.

Now, I’m an old-timer myself, who always starts this here author’s books, and usually feel good about being fictional myself, since her books are always fighting crooks messing with Billy’s real history; and they’s crooks dangerous as poked rattlesnakes, making your neck hair stand up to face them. So I ain’t complaining bout being fictional - unlike her.

This here book is on the simple side, just letting folks know bout poor Billy’s Coroner’s Jury Report - what the Justice of the Peace and some good citizens wrote in them days to get the facts straight when somebody killed somebody, to decide if it was on the up-and-up, or needed a murder trial. And it was binding as a hangman’s knot. And that there Report shows those old-timers’ yarns about being Billy was worthless as a pail of hot spit.

You may be cogitating on how those old liars got around that Report. Well, it was as surprising as a fifth ace in a poker deck: they said it never did exist. So this book shows it did. Some fights is easier then others.

Vern Blanton Johnson, Jr.
Lincoln, Lincoln County, New Mexico

AUTHOR'S FOREWORD

Because of its tremendous fame, Billy the Kid history has been plagued by profiteering hoaxers riding on its coattails. Most dramatic were old-timer Billy the Kid imposters in the second quarter of the 20th century, claiming survival of Sheriff Pat Garrett's shooting on July 14, 1881. From their lies, arose attention-seeking hoaxers, into the 21st century, backing the scams with misinformation and faked forensics. All were rooted in antiquated ignorance of the impersonators, forced to build their tales on dime novel-like productions available before the scholarly research of the late 20th century. So they all gave themselves away by glaring errors. And the most recent pretender-backers even attempted dishonest fix-ups of the original old-timers' fabrications, by slipping in facts discovered long after their deaths.

My revisionist writings over the past 20 years make fakery even harder, since my research and books have clarified the role of the Santa Fe Ring, the dominating Territorial force shaping Billy Bonney's 1970's period. Leaving out the Ring, as has been done by past historians, was like recounting the Civil War and omitting slavery. And factoring in the Ring explains the causality of events and the motives of participants. Comprehensible are the grass-roots anti-Ring uprisings of that decade when the Ring's rapacious take-over was lethal and unchecked. For the history of Billy Bonney, it explained the lost Lincoln County War Battle as the culminating freedom fight; showed him as its charismatic, political zealot hero; clarified his lost, but deserved, pardon; and revealed the use of the Secret Service in his politically motivated elimination. Of course, none of this was known by the old Billy the Kid pretenders. And the modern charlatans cannot use this reality, which is totally alien to their hoaxes derived from the Ring's own outlaw mythology going back to Billy's own day.

But all the elaborate fakery, now spanning about 70 years, is eliminated by the single fact that Pat Garrett killed Billy Bonney. And one document irrefutably proved it: Billy Bonney's Coroner's Jury Report of July 15, 1881. So this book focuses on it, and on the hoaxers' twisted lies attempting to escape its fatal reality.

Gale Cooper, M.D.
Sandia Park, New Mexico

METHODOLOGY

PRIMARY DOCUMENTS: Primary documents have italics for handwriting, two columns for articles, and special font for books.

COMMENTARY: Boldface is for author's comments or to highlight hoaxers' claims. Underlings and italics add emphasis. Page numbers are given for cited books or for navigation in this book. And the "Appendix" and "Bibliography" are annotated.

ACKNOWLEDGMENTS

Overriding is my debt to Billy Bonney, whose cause, courage, intelligence, and joie de vivre are my inspiration.

Special thanks goes to government employee, Harold Abbott, who, in 1932, found the July 15, 1881 Coroner's Jury Report of William Bonney in the old Capitol Building in Santa Fe, New Mexico, and had the foresight to make copies to preserve this historic document.

Historical bedrock is from books by Frederick Nolan on Billy the Kid, the Lincoln County War, and John Henry Tunstall. As valuable is Leon Metz's Pat Garrett biography and Jerry (Richard) Weddle's book on Billy Bonney's early adolescence.

National Archives documents used were in the Justice Department, and the Department of the Interior.

Collections used were at the Las Cruces, New Mexico State University Library's Rio Grande Historical Collections' Herman B. Weisner Papers, ca. 1957-1992 and Blazer Family Papers, 1864-1965; the Albuquerque, University of New Mexico Center for Southwest Studies, University Library, Catron Papers; the State of New Mexico Office of Cultural Affairs Historic Preservation Division; the Office of the New Mexico State Historian; the Silver City Museum and Library; the Midland, Texas Nita Stewart and J. Evetts Haley Memorial Library and Historical Center; and the Canyon, Texas Panhandle-Plains Historical Museum. Collections used for William Bonney's and Lew Wallace's documents were the Santa Fe, New Mexico, Fray Angélico Chávez Historical Library; and the Indianapolis, Indiana Historical Society's Lew and Wallace Collection.

PART I

THE OLD WEST'S MOST FAMOUS KILLING

CHAPTER 1
THE OUTLAW-LAWMAN SAGA THAT EXCITED AMERICA

OVERVIEW

One can never underestimate the public's ability to recognize a great story. And the outlaw-lawman saga of Billy the Kid and Sheriff Pat Garrett was on the level of high drama and great tragedy. In its own day - the late 1870's to 1881 - it had already captivated New Mexico Territory, and penetrated national media. The trajectories of both men, aged almost a decade apart, and larger than life, collided near midnight on Thursday, July 14, 1881, when Garrett fatally shot unsuspecting 21 year old Billy in a dark room ambush in the mansion bedroom of Billy's young lover's brother, in their family-owned town of Fort Sumner.

This killing played out against the Territory's blood-soaked decade of grass-roots uprisings against the lethal, land-grabbing, political-economic cabal of the Santa Fe Ring. In the most famous anti-Ring rebellion, the 1878 Lincoln County War, teenaged Billy Bonney emerged as the people's hero, and the Ring's vilified opponent: outlawed and hunted as Ring-named "Billy the Kid." The Ring's attempt to eliminate him with legal guise of hanging for Lincoln County War murders failed with his dramatic escape on April 28, 1881 from Pat Garrett's custody in the Lincoln County courthouse-jail. So Garrett was just completing his killing task 78 days later. And Billy died as he would have wished: while living free.

One document encapsulated this famous Old West event: the July 15, 1881 Coroner's Jury Report of William Bonney alias "Kid," in legal Spanish typical of the times, the day after the killing, and after the night in which shocked townspeople held a candlelight vigil for the boy they thought was safe in their midst.

GROWTH OF THE OUTLAW MYTH

Billy Bonney's story began with mythology fabricated by the victorious Santa Fe Ring, which had succeeded in theft of the vast Hispanic land grants retained after the Mexican-American War's 1848 treaty of Guadalupe Hidalgo. That Ring had crushed rebellions precipitated by its infiltration of executive, judicial, and legislative branches; leaving the Territory as its fiefdom. Opponents not intimidated by its terrorist threats or destroyed by its malicious prosecutions, were assassinated.

Billy had been inspired by his few months of employment by murdered merchant-rancher John Tunstall; then by local attorney, Alexander McSween, who led the Lincoln County War anti-Ring resistance. Billy became a political zealot, whose atypical bi-culturalism made him the Ring's feared precipitant of a future Hispanic uprising. So he was outlawed with the made-up name "Billy the Kid," and marked for killing.

Before this, in 1872, legislators in Santa Fe had risen up against the increasing Ring stranglehold, and were suppressed by the Ringite Governor. In 1876, to the southwest, was the Grant County Rebellion, with its "Declaration of Independence" and attempt to secede to Arizona Territory. From 1875 to 1877, Ring atrocities to the north precipitated the Colfax County War, with assassination of the leader and citizens' futile exposés to Ring-biased President Rutherford B. Hayes. The culminating defeat was the 1878 Lincoln County War, where Ring-beholden troops illegally enabled opponents' murders; and in which Billy Bonney emerged with name recognition and refusal to leave the Territory.

Billy's outlawing was magnified by his 1879 pardon bargain with Governor Lew Wallace, to free himself from his Lincoln County War murder indictments. Wallace reneged under Ring pressure, and hid his moral failure by publishing self-justifying additions to the outlaw myth of Billy the Kid.

By 1882, Pat Garrett capitalized on his fame for killing Billy the Kid the year before by working with a ghost-writer to publish his own outlaw myth rendition. That mold was not broken by the scholarly historians of the latter half of the 20th century, who merely plastered new findings onto that antique armature.

It has taken my research, analyses, and books to restore Billy Bonney and his compatriots to freedom fighter glory. Likewise, I exposed the modern Ring's corruption; all made possible because Billy's extreme fame kept alive memory of his times.

EMERGENCE OF HISTORICAL PARASITES

There was a peculiar side-effect of Billy's posthumous fame: emergence of mentally disturbed, attention-seeking old men, in the second quarter of the 20th century, who claimed to be him. Since he was fatally shot in Fort Sumner on July 14, 1881 by Pat Garrett, that necessitated these imposters' second fabrication: accusing Garrett of killing the wrong man and covering it up.

Additionally, fascination with Billy the Kid was so insatiable that his old-timer contemporaries got autobiographies published merely my adding him. And the most glib impersonators followed suit by attracting hoaxing profiteering authors.

The obstacle faced by hoaxing historical parasites was that scholarly history books about Billy Bonney's life had not yet been written. There was only the antiquated outlaw mythology of the 19th century, with its seepage into the early 20th century. So the cribbed fake fables became their "memories" as Billy, and exposed their chicanery. They were saved only by the equally benighted public, unable to distinguish fakery from truth.

But the imposters' development of a duped market for their productions, spawned a bottom-feeding industry of hucksters promoting them to the present day - with updates like faked DNA forensics. And I have exposed these charlatans too.

PUBLICIZED IMPOSTERS

One Billy the Kid imposter outdistanced the others because he got a huckster promoter, a publicity hook, and a book. Named Oliver Pleasant "Brushy Bill" Roberts, his delusions and attention-seeking yielded his multiple Old West identities, among them Billy the Kid. His discoverer was a traveling salesman named William V. Morrison, who impersonated a lawyer, and got Old West mileage from his descent from Lucien Maxwell's brother. He was a hardworking showman, who researched Billy the Kid. And he saw the publicity hook: Billy's lost pardon for Lincoln County War indictments. He would seek it for "Brushy" from New Mexico's governor. Though this scam ultimately failed; it kindled public imagination, yielded his book on "Brushy," and rippled out over time to get true-believer converts, who doggedly peddled the lies and held dear conspiracy theories as to "Brushy's" rejection.

A second imposter, named John Miller, had no believers and a lethargic author. But Miller burst into public awareness as part of the biggest historic-forensic hoax ever perpetrated: the 2003 "Billy the Kid Case." And it thrust to the present the imposter claims.

THE "BILLY THE KID" CASE HOAX

The "Billy the Kid Case," beginning in 2003, was a self-serving publicity stunt of corrupt New Mexico Governor Bill Richardson and his major political donor, who was a "Brushy Bill" believer. Using that imposter's claim of surviving the Garrett shooting, it was a real Sheriff's Department murder case against Garrett as killing an innocent victim. That this stranger lay in Billy's Fort Sumner grave was to be proved by faked DNA matchings, to make "Brushy Bill" Billy the Kid. I fought this hoax in district courts, stopping the exhumations of Billy and his mother; then revealed its DNA fraud in open records litigation and books. That saved the history from destruction, beyond retrieval, by these rogues.

THE "COLD CASE BILLY THE KID" MEGAHOAX

In 2018, "Brushy"-believer and author, W.C. Jameson, partnered with past "Billy the Kid Case" hoaxers, to combine the "Brushy Bill" and "Billy the Kid Case" hoaxes in his book: *Cold Case Billy the Kid.* Its pernicious result was resuscitating both scams in the public forum.

THE HOAXERS' MIGHTY OBSTACLE

Though scholarly history books had been written since the days of the old-timer imposters, which laid to rest their fables, frivolous media productions using the outlaw myth - like the movie, "Young Guns II" - had maintained public ignorance sufficiently for modern hoaxers to ply their lies. But there was one impassable hurdle to their chicanery: the July 15, 1881 Coroner's Jury Report of William H. Bonney, the Kid.

CHAPTER 2
IMPOSTER HOAXES' IMPASSABLE HURDLE

THE CORONER'S JURY REPORT

On July 14, 1881, Billy Bonney had a particularly dramatic death scene in the Fort Sumner mansion of the Maxwell family - with the bedroom ambush by Sheriff Pat Garrett in the place he felt safest - with multiple witnesses of it and of his corpse.

At the inquest the next day, an air-tight Coroner's Jury Report was generated, confirming his identity as the victim. It was then filed with the correct authority to concur that murder prosecution was unwarranted in the homicide: the District Attorney of the First Judicial District, which included Fort Sumner's San Miguel County. And because of the additional issue of Pat Garrett's claiming the reward on Billy the Kid, that Coroner's Jury Report was further scrutinized by the Territory's highest public officials before the reward was granted to Garrett as justified.

But the later Billy the Kid identity thieves' were forded to fake a death scene for their "survival" of that Pat Garrett shooting. And that required denying the existence of the Coroner's Jury Report that identified the victim as Billy Bonney, as well as forcing their denying that Garrett got his reward for his fatal encounter with Billy Bonney. That level of lying in the face of stark reality necessitated betting on bottomless public ignorance and gullibility. It was a bet bound to be lost.

Nevertheless, the pretenders and hoaxers, of necessity, tried hard to discredit the Report, to defame Pat Garrett, to denounce the coroner's jurymen, to claim it never existed, and to fabricate conspiracy theories to explain it away - all to enable continuation of their lies, profiteering, and self-publicizing.

So a book is justified on the Coroner's Jury Report of William H. Bonney as the one document alone that ends the disreputable industry of fakery, and its abuse of its audience.

THE DEFINITIVE CONCLUSIONS

Billy the Kid's imposters' survival hoaxes were ended, before they started, by the Coroner's Jury Report, in Spanish, for the July 15, 1881 inquest on the victim, William Bonney, fatally shot by Pat Garrett on July 14, 1881. **[Figure: 1]**

It confirmed its proper filing with the District Attorney of the First Judicial District, William Breeden:

"To the District Attorney of the First Judicial District of the Territory of New Mexico, Greetings."

It showed proper action by San Miguel County Justice of the Peace Alejandro Segura, as *ex officio* coroner:

"[I]mmediately upon receiving said information [of a murder] I proceeded to the said place and named Milnor Rudulph, Jose Silva, Antonio Saavedra, Pedro Antonio Lucero, Lorenzo Jaramillo and Sabal Gutierres a jury to investigate the case."

The body was identified:

"[The jury] found the body of William Bonney alias "Kid" with a shot in the left breast."

The eye-witness was interviewed:

"[The Jurymen] examined the evidence of Pedro Maxwell [Peter Maxwell, owner of Fort Sumner], which evidence is as follows: 'I being in my bed in my room, at about midnight on the 14th day of July, Pat F. Garrett came into my room and sat down. William Bonney came in and got close to my bed with a gun in his hand and asked me "who is it" and then Pat. F. Garrett fired two shots at the said William Bonney and the said William Bonney fell near my fire place and I went out of the room and when I came in again about three or four minutes after the shots the said William Bonney was dead.' "

The jurymen's verdict stated:

"[T]he deed of said Garrett was justifiable homicide."

The recommendation was for merited reward:

"[G]ratitude … is due to the said Garrett for his deed and [he] is worthy of being rewarded."

THE TRANSLATED CORONER'S JURY REPORT

Territory of New Mexico) Precinct No. 27
County of San Miguel)

To the District Attorney of the First Judicial District of the Territory of New Mexico,

Greetings:

On this 15th day of July, A.D. 1881, I, the undersigned, Justice of the Peace of the above named precinct, received information that a murder had taken place in Fort Sumner, in said precinct, and immediately upon receiving said information I proceeded to the said place and named Milnor Rudulph, Jose Silva, Antonio Saavedra, Pedro Antonio Lucero, Lorenzo Jaramillo and Sabal Gutierres a jury to investigate the case and the above jury convened in the home of Luz B. Maxwell and proceeded to a room in the said house where they found the body of William Bonney alias "Kid" with a shot in the left breast and having examined the body they examined the evidence of Pedro Maxwell, which evidence is as follows:

"I being in my bed in my room, at about midnight on the 14th day of July, Pat. F. Garrett came into my room and sat at the end on my bed to talk with me. A little while after Garrett sat down, William Bonney came in and got close to my bed with a gun in his hand and asked me "Who is it Who is it?" and then Pat F. Garrett fired two shots at the said William Bonney and the said Bonney fell near my fire place and I went out of the room and when I came in again about three or four minutes after the shots the said Bonney was dead."

The jury has found the following verdict:

We the jury unanimously find that William Bonney has been killed by a bullet in the left breast in the region of the heart, the same having been fired from a pistol in the hand of Pat F. Garrett, and our verdict is that the act of said Garrett was justifiable homicide and we are unanimous in the opinion that the gratitude of all the community is due to the said Garrett for his deed and is worthy of being rewarded.

M. Rudulph, President
Anto Sabedra
Pedro Anto Lucero
Jose x Silba
Sabal x Gutierrez
Lorenzo x Jaramillo

All which information I put at your disposal.

Alejandro Segura Justice of the Peace

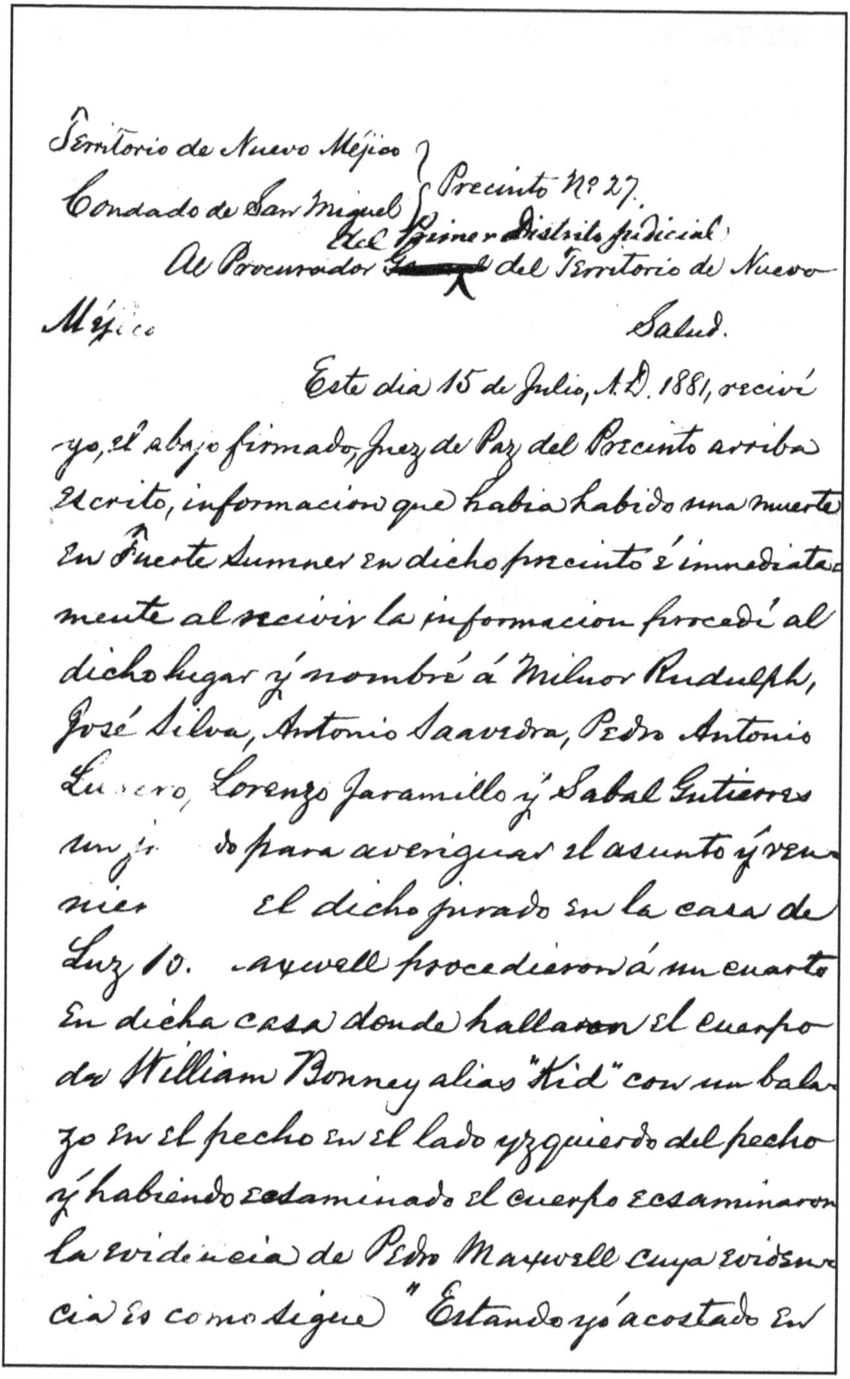

Territorio de Nuevo Méjico }
Condado de San Miguel } Precinto No. 27.
Del Primer Distrito Judicial

Al Procurador [struck] del Territorio de Nuevo Méjico

Salud.

Este dia 15 de Julio, A.D. 1881, recivé yo, el abajo firmado, Juez de Paz del Precinto arriba escrito, informacion que habia habido una muerte en Fuerte Sumner en dicho precinto é inmediatamente al recivir la informacion procedí al dicho lugar y nombré á Milnor Rudulph, José Silva, Antonio Saavedra, Pedro Antonio Lucero, Lorenzo Jaramillo y Sabal Gutierres un jurado para averiguar el asunto y venier. El dicho jurado en la casa de Luz B. Maxwell procedieron á un cuarto en dicha casa donde hallaron el cuerpo de William Bonney alias "Kid" con un balazo en el pecho en el lado yzquierdo del pecho y habiendo ecsaminado el cuerpo ecsaminaron la evidencia de Pedro Maxwell cuya evidencia es como sigue " Estando yo acostado en

FIGURE: 1. Original Spanish Coroner's Jury Report of July 15, 1881 for William H. Bonney aka Kid (Courtesy of the Indiana Historical Society, Lew Wallace Collection)

mi cama en mi cuarto a cosa de media noche el dia 14 de Julio entró á mi cuarto Pat. F. Garrett y se sentó en la orilla de mi cama á platicar conmigo. A poco rato que Garrett se sentó entró William Bonney y se arrimó á mi cama con una pistola en la mano y me preguntó "Who is it? who is it?" y entónces Pat. F. Garrett le tiró dos balazos á dicho William Bonney y se cayó el dicho Bonney en un lado de mi fogon y yó salí del cuarto cuando volví á entrar yá en tres ó cuatro minutos despues de los balazos estaba muerto dicho Bonney."

El jurado há hallado el siguiente dictámen "Nosotros los del jurado unanimente hallamos que William Bonney há sido muerto por un balazo en el pecho yzquierdo en la region del Corazon tirado de una pistola en la mano de Pat. F. Garrett y nuestro dictámen es que el hecho de dicho Garrett fué homicidio justificable y estamos unánimes en opinion que la gratitud de toda la communidad Es devida á dicho Garrett por su hecho y que Es digno de ser recompensado."

W. [illegible]

Presidente

Ant.º Salbedra

pedro Ant.º Lucero

Jose + Silba

Sabal + gutierrez

Lorenso + Jaramillo

Todo cuya información pongo á conocimiento de V.

Alejandro Segura

jues de paz

CONFIRMATION OF JURY PRESIDENT MILNOR RUDULPH'S SIGNATURE

A thrust in the "Brushy Bill" hoax was fabricating that Jury President, Milnor Rudulph, was not present, so the Report was fake. But his signature, with unique Spencerian flourishes, on the Report matches the one on his May 18, 1879 letter to Territorial Secretary William G. Ritch **[FIGURE: 2]** proving his presence.

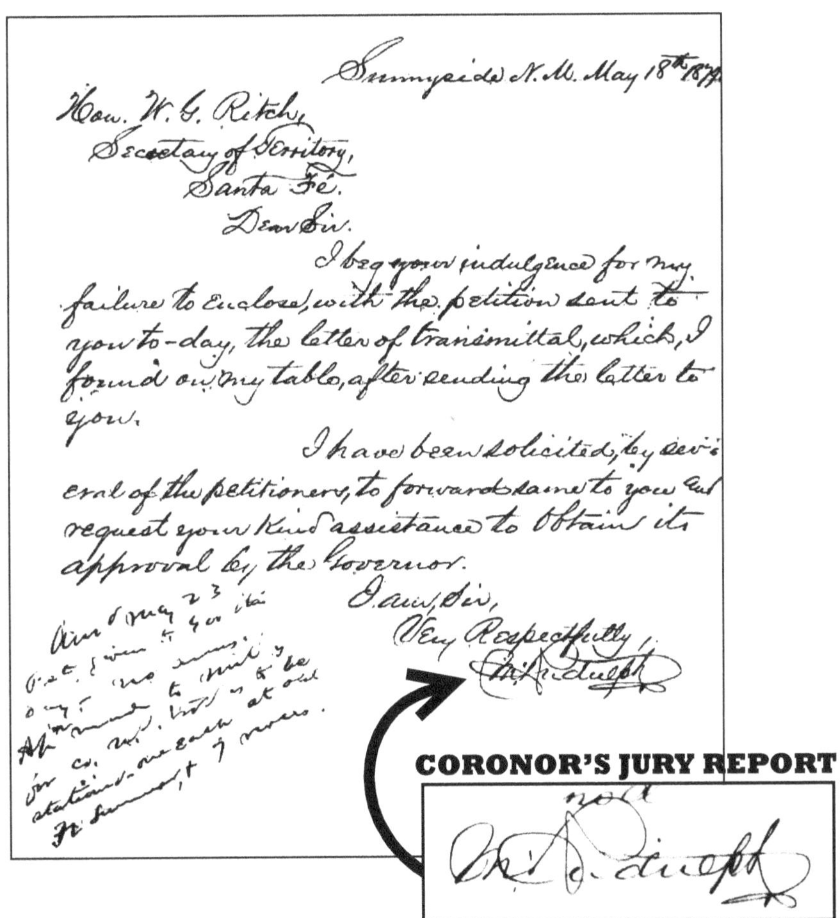

Sunnyside N.M. May 18th 1879

Hon. W. G. Ritch,
Secretary of Territory,
Santa Fe.
Dear Sir.

I beg your indulgence for my failure to enclose, with the petition sent to you to-day, the letter of transmittal, which, I found on my table, after sending the letter to you.

I have been solicited, by several of the petitioners, to forward same to you and request your kind assistance to obtain its approval by the Governor.

I am, Sir,
Very Respectfully,
M. Rudulph

FIGURE: 2. Letter of May 18, 1879 from Milnor Rudulph to Territorial Secretary William G. Ritch to show that his signature matched the one on the Coroner's Jury Report. (Courtesy Territorial Archives of New Mexico Microfilm, Albuquerque Genealogical Library Microfilm)

THE CONFIRMATION OF THE JURYMEN

Another ploy of the "Brushy" hoax was claiming the Coroner's Jury Report's signers did not exist or were not local men. They were Milnor Rudulph, as President; Antonio Saavedra; Pedro Antonio Lucero; Jose Silba; Sabal Gutierrez; Lorenzo Jaramillo; and Alejandro Segura, as Justice of the Peace.

But checking the census for 1880, the year before they signed, shows all in San Miguel County. In Cabra Arenoso, were Alejandro Segura and Sabal Gutierrez. In Sunnyside, were Milnor Rudulph and Jose Silba. In Fort Sumner, were listed Lorenzo Jaramillo and Antonio Saavedra. In San Miguel, was listed Pedro Antonio Lucero.

THE SPANISH STYLE WAS COMPATIBLE WITH AUTHOR, ALEJANDRO SEGURA

Justice of the Peace Alejandro Segura identified himself as the author of the Coroner's Jury Report; writing it in the first person, as translated: "On this 15th day of July, A.D. 1881, **I, the undersigned, Justice of the Peace** of the above named precinct, received information that a murder had taken place in Fort Sumner ... and immediately upon receiving said information **I proceeded to the said place and named [the jurymen]** ... The jury has found the following verdict [which he gave as justifiable homicide] ... All which information **I put at your disposal**. Alejandro Segura Justice of the Peace."

But the "Brushy" hoax also attempted to dismiss the Coroner's Jury Report by claiming it was written by Pat Garrett himself, as part of his faking the killing.

But expert analysis of its handwriting by Dr. Aaron Taylor of Taylor Translations, Albuquerque, New Mexico, noted its formal and sophisticated Territorial Spanish compatible with late 1800's script by a native-speaking writer, like Alejandro Segura. It would have been unknown to Pat Garrett, then in the Territory only three years and not yet even able to *speak* Spaniah. And by the first half of the 20th century these tell-tale stylistic elements were abandoned, further confirming dating. Annotation of the Report shows its Spanish-specific features. **[FIGURE: 4]**

Dr. Taylor found the following tell-tale stylistic examples of letter formations, accent marks, and spelling:

1. The capital “G” looks like an upside-down number five.

2. The lower case “e” is written like a little capital “E.”

3. The lower case “p” has an ascending line that makes it resemble a lower case “h.”

4. The capital “B” looks like a capital “R.”

5. The letter combination “ecs” in “escaminado” and “escaminaron” (“examined” and “they examined” respectively) was retained even in published texts, and not commonly changed to “ex” for the same sound until the 1930’s.

6. The letter “a,” when used as a lone letter meaning “to,” commonly had an accent as shown here.

7. The letter “y” with an accent was unusual in the 1800’s, indicating use of more old-fashioned colonial Spanish.

THE PAT GARRETT NAME

Also debunking Pat Garrett as the Report’s writer is the mismatch of his actual signature to the “*Pat. F. Garrett*” in the Report (page 2, line 8). Only an exceptional forger would alter his own written name to hide his authorship. **[FIGURE: 3]**

NAME IN THE REPORT

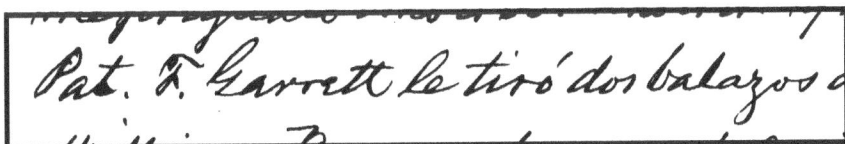

Pat. F. Garrett le tiró dos balazos

ACTUAL SIGNATURE ON LETTER

Your faithful Husband
P. F. Garrett

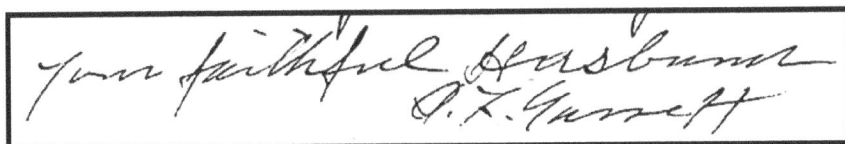

FIGURE: 3. Pat Garrett’s actual writing of his name in his December 13, 1901 letter to his wife, Apolinaria, does not match penmanship of his name in the Coroner’s Jury Report

ANNOTATED CORONER'S JURY REPORT

Annotation of the Report isolates examples of old-style Spanish, numbered to refer to Dr. Aaron Taylor's above list.

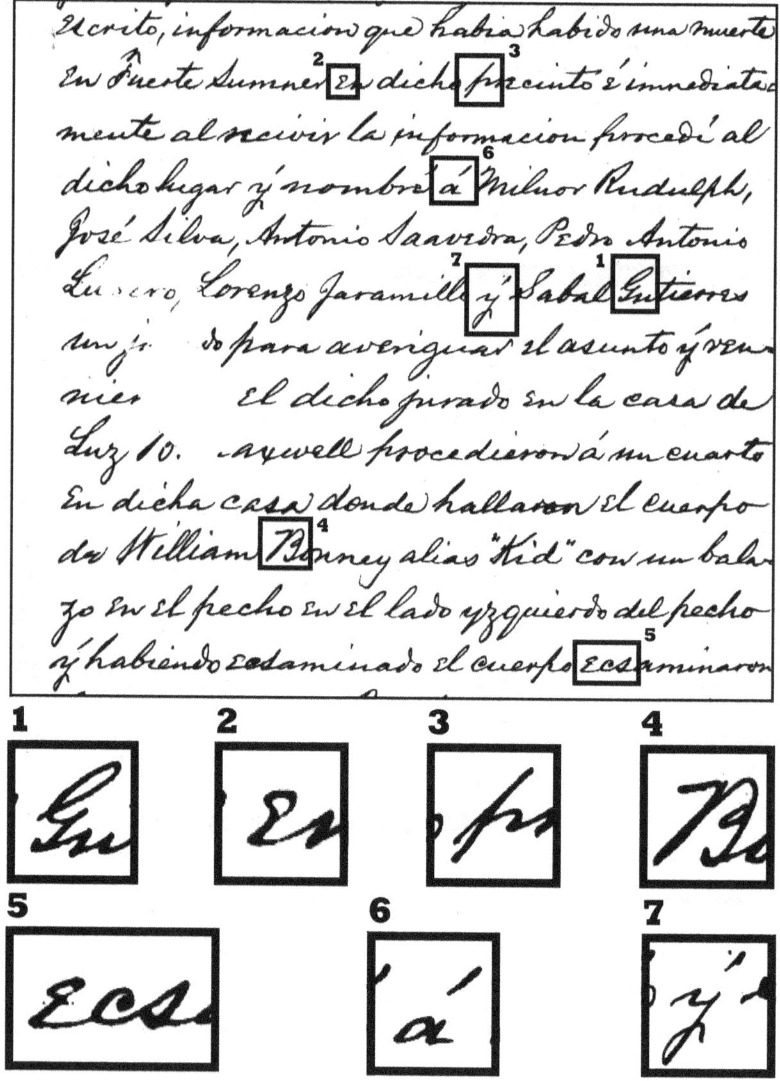

Escrito, informacion que habia habido una muerte
en Fuerte Sumner en dicho precinto é inmediatamente al recivir la informacion procedí al
dicho lugar y nombré á Milnor Rudulph,
José Silva, Antonio Saavedra, Pedro Antonio
Lu[illegible]ero, Lorenzo Jaramillo y Sabal Gutierres
un j[illegible]do para averiguar el asunto y ven-
nier [illegible] El dicho jurado en la casa de
Luz [illegible] [illegible]axwell procedieron á un cuarto
en dicha casa donde hallaron el cuerpo
de William Bonney alias "Kid" con un balazo en el pecho en el lado yzquierdo del pecho
y habiendo ecsaminado el cuerpo ecsaminaron

FIGURE: 4. Coroner's Jury Report annotated for antique Spanish style with reference to Dr. Aaron Taylor's list's numbering

STATUTE GOVERNING THE CORONER'S JURY REPORT

The Coroner's Jury Report was written in proper conformity to Territorial law, pointing additionally to Alejandro Segura's following Justice of the Peace procedures. Its statute, edited by L. Bradford Prince, Governor from 1889 to 1893, was in *General Laws of New Mexico; Including All the Unrepealed Laws From the Promulgation of the 'Kearney [sic] Code' in 1846, to the End of the Legislative Session of 1880, With Supplement, Including the Session of 1882.* It was under "Article XV, Chapter XL, Constables, Coroners, and Inquests." For Inquests, the Act of January 30, 1867 pertained; stating:

> SECTION 1. It shall be the duty of each justice of the peace within his respective precinct, to inquire into and investigate the cause of death of any human being that shall be found dead in the precinct of said justice of the peace, when it may appear that said death was caused by violence or any other illegal means, and it is hereby made the duty of every justice of the peace, when required so to do, in writing, by any two heads of families and voters in the precinct, to examine and inquire into the cause of death of any human being, be the cause of death what it may.
>
> § 2. The examination provided for in the foregoing section shall be held over the body of the deceased and with a jury of six men, voters of the precinct, which jury shall be summoned by the constable, verbally, by an order of the justice of the peace to that effect, and the witnesses shall be examined and their attendance compelled as in all other cases before a justice of the peace.
>
> § 3. Whatever the cause of death of any person shall have been ascertained in the manner prescribed in this act, the verdict of the jury shall be in writing, which shall be signed by the justice of the peace and each one of the jury, **and so recorded in the office of the probate judge of the county in which the inquest was held, and**, and the verdict of the jury shall be in the following form:

> "We the undersigned, justices of the peace and jury, who sat upon the inquest held this —— day of ——, 18 –, on the body of (here shall be stated the name of the deceased, if known, and if not, then state 'on the body of a person whose name is unknown'), found in precinct number —, of the county of ——, find that the deceased came to his (or her) death by reason of (here insert the cause of death, and by whom the crime was committed if ascertained)."
>
> A.B., Justice of the Peace
> C.Dd., &c.
>
> § 4. In the absence of the justice of the peace from his precinct, or during the sickness of such justice of the peace, then any justice of the peace of the county may hold such an inquest ...
>
> § 5. Every justice of the peace who shall hold an inquest as provided for in this act, shall receive from the county treasury of his county the sum of two dollars in full of all his services in such inquest, and the constable shall receive the fees allowed by law to persons in causes before justices of the peace, which fees shall be paid out of the county treasury, and the witnesses shall receive the fees now allowed by law, and the county shall also pay the necessary expenses of the decent interment if the said deceased over which an inquest has been held as herein provided, which shall be allowed by the probate judge.

Thus, it can be seen that Justice of the Peace Alejandro Segura followed proper procedure. By law, he did not retain the Coroner's Jury Report himself. It was to go to the proper probate judge. But that would be for a decedent's estate or assets. Billy had none. Segura chose the best disposition for this high-profile killing: the person to whom the Report was addressed: "To the District Attorney of the First Judicial District of the Territory of New Mexico" (whose jurisdiction was Fort Sumner's San Miguel County). That was the highest-ranking Territorial prosecutor, William Breeden; also Attorney General; thus, the correct prosecutor to assess the killing in light of the Report's verdict of famous Billy the Kid's justifiable homicide and Garrett's deserved reward. Furthermore, this disposition was also reported to Acting-Governor William Ritch by Pat Garrett himself.

PAT GARRETT'S LETTER TO THE ACTING-GOVERNOR

On July 15, 1881, the day after the killing, Pat Garrett sent a letter, **with enclosed copy of that day's Coroner's Jury Report**, to Territorial Acting-Governor, William Ritch, confirming his killing of Billy Bonney along with its circumstances.

The letter was quoted in July 23, 1881's Las Cruces *Rio Grande Republican* as "Kid the Killer Killed, Wm. Bonney alias Antrim, alias Billy the Kid, Fatally Meets Pat Garrett, the Lincoln County Sheriff." It stated: "Below is given Sheriff Garrett's report as made to Acting Governor Ritch which contains also the verdict of the coroner's jury [with English translation, but explaining: 'The verdict is given in Spanish in Garrett's report']." The article stated:

William Bonney, alias 'the Kid,' is dead. No report could have caused more general feeling of gratification than this, and when it was further announced that the faithful and brave Pat Garrett, he who had been the mainstay of law and order in Lincoln county, the chief reliance of the people in the dark days, when danger lurked at every hand, has accomplished the crowning feat of his life by bringing down the fierce and implacable foe single-handed, the sense of satisfaction was heightened to one of delight. The following is Sheriff Garrett's official report to the chief executive of the territory.

It is as follows. – Fort Sumner, N.M., July 15. - Fort Sumner, N.M., July 15, '81 - To his Excellency the Governor of New Mexico:

"I have the honor to inform your Excellency that I had received several communications from persons in and about Fort Sumner, that William Bonney, alias the Kid, had been there, or in that vicinity for some time.

"In view of these reports I deemed it my duty to go there, and ascertain if there was any truth in them or not, all the time doubting their accuracy; but on Monday, July 11, I left home, taking with me John W. Poe and T.L. McKinney, men in whose courage and sagacity I relied implicitly, and arrived just below Fort Sumner, on Wednesday, 13th [sic]. I remained concealed near the houses, until night, and then entered the fort about midnight, and went to Mr. P. Maxwell's room. I found him in bed, and had just commenced talking to him about the object of my visit at such an unusual hour, when a man entered the room in stockinged feet, with a pistol in one hand and a knife in the other. He came and placed his hand on the bed just beside me, and said in a low whisper, "who is it?" (and repeated the question) he asked Mr. Maxwell.

I at once recognized the man, and knew he was the Kid, and reached behind me for my pistol, feeling almost certain of receiving a ball from his at the moment of my doing so, as I felt sure he had now recognized me, but fortunately he drew back from the bed at noticing my movement, and, although he had his pistol pointed at my breast, he delayed to fire, and asked me in Spanish, "Quien es? Quien es?" This gave me time to bring mine to bear on him, and the moment I did so I pulled the trigger and he received his death wound, for the ball struck him in the left breast and pierced his heart. He never spoke, but died in a minute. It was my desire to have been able to take him alive, but his coming upon me so suddenly and unexpectedly leads me to believe that he had seen me enter the room, or had been informed by someone of the fact; and that he came there armed with pistol and knife expressly to kill me if he could. Under that impression I had no alternative but to kill him or to suffer death at his hands.

I herewith annex a copy of the verdict rendered by the jury called in by the justice of the peace (ex officio coroner), the original of which is in the hands of the prosecuting attorney of the first judicial district."

(The verdict is given in Spanish in Garrett's report, and upon being translated is as follows:

"We the jury unanimously say that William Bonney came to his death by a wound in the breast in the region of the heart, fired from a pistol in the hand of Pat F. Garrett, and our decision is that the action of said Garrett, was justifiable homicide; and we are united in opinion that the gratitude of all the community is due to said Garrett for his action, and he deserves to be compensated."

(Signed) M. Rudolph, Foreman,
Antonio Savedra,
Pedro Antonio Lucero,
Sabal Gutierres,
Lorenzo Jaramillo

I am Governor, very respectfully your Excellency's obedient servant,

Pat F. Garrett

THE ISSUE OF NO CULPABILITY

Pat Garrett's letter of July 15, 1881 to Acting-Governor William Ritch confirmed that proper legal procedure had been followed. The original Coroner's Jury Report had been sent by Alejandro Segura to the District Attorney for the First Judicial District, William Breeden, responsible for San Miguel County, in which was Fort Sumner, the homicide site. Garrett's letter to Ritch confirmed that he sent Ritch its copy; writing: "I herewith annex a copy of the verdict rendered by the jury called in by the justice of the peace [*ex officio* coroner, meaning by virtue of his position or status], **the original of which is in the hands of the prosecuting attorney of the first judicial district.**"

Breeden, also the Territorial Attorney General, would have checked the verdict: "[O]ur verdict is that the action of said Garrett was justifiable homicide." That meant the killing was deemed self-defense, as was subsequently confirmed by prosecutor Breeden by his not filing a murder charge against Garrett, and later by his assisting Acting-Governor Ritch in processing Garrett's reward payment for the killing.

GARRETT'S REWARD COLLECTION AND THE CORONER'S JURY REPORT

Garrett's letter to Acting-Governor Ritch also initiated the process of collecting his reward. The Coroner's Jury Report had presented no problem with its conclusion stating: "[W]e are unanimous in the opinion that the gratitude of all the community is due to the said Garrett for his action, and **he deserves to be rewarded**."

But issuing the reward to Garrett was complicated by two variables: its being a **private reward** offered by past-Governor Lew Wallace, and its **not being a dead-or-alive offer**.

The reward offer, published by Lew Wallace, in his own name, in December 22, 1880's *Las Vegas Daily Gazette*, and May 3, 1881's *Santa Fe Daily New Mexican*, had stated:

BILLY THE KID
$500 REWARD
I will pay $500 reward to any person or persons who will capture William Bonney, alias The Kid, and deliver him to any sheriff of New Mexico. Satisfactory proofs of identity will be required.
LEW. WALLACE,
Governor of New Mexico

Its stipulating that William Bonney was to be captured and delivered "to any sheriff of New Mexico," meant alive. To cover that Bonney was now dead (i.e., not deliverable alive), Garrett's letter to Ritch had explained that capture had been impossible, and killing the only option: "**It was my desire to have been able to take him alive, but his coming upon me so suddenly and unexpectedly leads me to believe that he had seen me enter the room, or had been informed by someone of the fact, and that he came there armed with pistol and knife expressly to kill me if he could. Under that impression I had no alternative but to kill him or to suffer death at his hands.**"

And the "Kid the Killer Killed" article showed public agreement; stating: "William Bonney, alias 'the Kid,' is dead. No report could have caused more general feeling of gratification than this, and when it was further announced that the faithful and brave Pat Garrett, he who had been the mainstay of law and order in Lincoln county, the chief reliance of the people in the dark days, when danger lurked at every hand, has accomplished the crowning feat of his life by bringing down the fierce and implacable foe single-handed, the sense of satisfaction was heightened to one of delight."

So death instead of capture presented no problem to all concerned in justifying the reward.

But the second issue of Lew Wallace's private reward offer presented a more complicated legal matter for issuing the reward payment to Garrett.

Importantly, the issue of corpse identity never arose, because the it was obviously Billy Bonney by confirmation of the coroner's jurymen and witness, Peter Maxwell.

GRANTING REWARD NEEDING LEGISLATIVE INTERVENTION

Acting-Governor William Ritch had an impediment in simply issuing the reward's payment: uneasiness about using Territorial funds to cover Lew Wallace's private offer. And Wallace had left the Territory and his governorship in May of 1881, before his term was completed. Lionel Sheldon had been appointed as his replacement, but was away from the Territory. So Ritch, as past Secretary of State under Lew Wallace, became Acting-Governor.

GARRETT'S MEETING WITH RITCH

Garrett, with his attorney, T.B. Catron, met with Ritch on July 20, 1881, as reported by the July 21, 1881 *Santa Fe Daily New Mexican*. Ritch was quoted as "willing to pay the amount, and would be glad to do so," but made clear that the delaying issue was checking the records about the nature of the reward. It stated:

Yesterday afternoon Pat. Garrett; **accompanied by Hon. T.B. Catron** and Col. M. Brunswick, called upon acting-Governor Ritch in regard to the reward offered by ex-Governor Lew Wallace for the Kid. The reward was fixed at five hundred dollars, and the offer was published in the papers. Governor Ritch announced that he was willing to pay the amount, and would be glad to do so, but that he would have to look at the records first. **He was not in the city when the [reward] offer was made, and had never received any notification of it, consequently did not know whether or not it was on record**. In consequence of the state of affairs, the question of the reward was not settled.

LEGAL CONSULTATION OF WILLIAM BREEDEN

To properly issue the reward, Acting-Governor William Ritch sought expert legal advice from William Breeden. Not only was Breeden the responsible prosecutor as District Attorney of the First Judicial District; but he had also received the original of the Coroner's Jury Report, and knew Garrett's killing of William H. Bonney was declared in justifiable self-defense. Breeden was also the Territorial Attorney General; and, thus, had ultimate authority to advise on proper legality for converting Lew Wallace's private reward to a Territorial one.

Ritch recorded his consultation with Breeden in his July 21, 1881 *Executive Record Book 2* entry as titled: "In the matter of the application by Patrick F. Garrett for a reward claimed to have been offered May-1881 for the capture of Wm Bonney alias 'the Kid.' " Quoting in this entry from Breeden's response to his questioning, Ritch confirmed that Breeden agreed that the reward was a private offer, since Wallace had not filed it with Breeden's office or that of the Territorial Secretary (then Ritch himself), formally converting it to a Territorial offer. Breeden had stated: "*In addition, we will add as fact that there was no record whatever in this office or at the Secretary's office of there having been a reward offered as set forth by Attorney General, nor was there any reward or file in said offices of a corresponding reward in any form.*" So the issue to be resolved was converting Wallace's private reward to a Territorial reward.

RITCH'S EXECUTIVE RECORD BOOK ENTRY ON BREEDEN CONSULTATION ON THE REWARD

Acting-Governor Ritch's July 21, 1881 *Executive Record Book 2* entry presented Breeden's opinion (here in boldface); stating:

Executive Department
Territory of New Mexico
July 21st 1881

July 20th 1881 Pat F. Garret [sic- throughout] Sheriff of Lincoln County appeared and presented a bill for $500. claiming it as a reward offered on or about the 7th of May 1881 by the late Governor Lew Wallace, for the capture of said Bonny [sic, throughout].

As evidence of said offer having been made the affidavit of publication thereof made by Chas. H. Green [sic – Greene] the editor and manager of the Daily New Mexican was presented with said bill, as also was presented a statement of the proceedings and verdict of a coroner's jury at Fort Sumner in San Miguel County upon the body of the said Bonny, captured as aforesaid, and a statement of Garret directed to this office of his doings in the premises.

Upon examination of said papers it was deemed important that the opinion of the Attorney General be taken thereon and they were at once transmitted to that office. On the following day the papers with the opinion of Hon. Wm Breeden Attorney General were filed.

Said opinion is quite full. We quote the closing paragraphs as sufficient in this connection, to with

"The offer by the Governor, or the notice thereof, which is all there is to show such an offer, is as follows –

Billy the Kid

$500 Reward

"I will pay five hundred dollars reward to any person or persons, who will capture William Bonny, alias the Kid, and deliver him to any Sheriff of New Mexico. Satisfactory proof of identity will be required.

Lew Wallace
Governor of New Mexico"

"This certainly appears to be the personal offer of Governor Wallace, and it seems he did nothing to indicate that it was intended as an executive act on behalf of, and to bind the Territory.

"If the reward should be paid, it is very probable that the Legislature would approve the payment if so desired, and that no objection would be raised, or that it will provide for its payment if it remained unpaid, at the next session thereof;

[AUTHOR'S NOTE: Breeden saw no problem with the Legislature's eventual approving of reward payment.]

but if the Governor [Ritch] should now direct the payment of the claim, he would doubtless expose himself to the charge of misappropriation of the Territorial funds, in case the Legislature should refuse to ratify or approve the payment."

[AUTHOR'S NOTE: So Breeden said if Ritch paid the reward himself *before legislative approval*, it could be criticized as misappropriating funds.]

[AUTHOR'S NOTE: Ritch then added commentary in his own words.]

In addition we will add as a fact that there was no record whatsoever; either in this office or at the [Territorial] Secretary's office of there having been a reward offered as set forth by Attorney General, nor was there any record or file in said offices of a corresponding reward in any form.

[AUTHOR'S NOTE: Ritch confirmed that Wallace had not converted his reward offer into a Territorial offer.]

The opinion of the Attorney General [Breeden] appearing to be consistent with the law and the facts, decision is rendered accordingly and the Governor [Ritch, speaking for himself] declines to allow the reward at this time. Believing however, that Mr Garrett has an equitable claim against the Territory for said reward, the action at this office will simply be suspended until the case can properly be represented to the next Legislative Assembly.

Ritch

Act Governor NM

[AUTHOR'S NOTE: Ritch confirmed that Garrett's reward was deemed justified by him and Breeden, but had to be converted to a Territorial reward, though that made action in his office "suspended," or delayed in making payment to Garrett until legislative action.]

RITCH'S FORGOTTEN RECORDING OF REWARD

It may be noted that Ritch had forgotten that he *had actually recorded* Wallace's reward eight months earlier, when he was Territorial Secretary! So Ritch had been overly cautious; though one could argue that the wording still looked like a private offer.

Wallace had informed Ritch about the reward by letter on December 13, 1880. That day, Ritch entered it into "Executive Record Book 2" on page 473. Wallace wrote:

Executive Office
SANTA FE., N.M.
Dec. 13______ 1880

Hon. W.G. Ritch
Loc. New Mexico.
Sir:
Be good enough to prepare a draft of proclamation of reward $500. for the capture and delivery of William Bonney, alias the Kid to the Sheriff of the County of Lincoln.

Yours, truly,
Lew Wallace, Governor

Ritch had then written in the "Executive Record Book":

Dec 13 [1880]
Reward
Territory of New Mexico) Indictment in
vs) Lincoln co. Dist. Court
William Bonney) for murder
alias "The Kid"
Executive Office
Territory of New Mexico

Whereas William Bonney, alias "The Kid" charged under indictment issued from the District Court in and for the county of Lincoln of the crime of murder committed in said county: And whereas the said William Bonney, alias "The Kid" is a fugitive from justice

Now Therefore Lewis Wallace, Governor of the Territory, by virtue of the power and authority vested in me by law and believing the ends of justice will be served thereby do hereby offer a reward of five hundred dollars ($500.) for the apprehension and arrest of said William Bonney, alias "The Kid" and for his delivery to the Sheriff of Lincoln County at the county seat of said county.

In witness Whereof I have set my hand and have caused the great seal of the Territory to be hereto affixed this 13th day of December 1880.

Lew. Wallace,
Governor N.M.

By the Governor
Wm Ritch, Secretary N.M.

REWARD GRANTED TO GARRETT BY THE LEGISLATURE

The February 18, 1882 legislative Act confirmed the delay as a mere "technicality;" stating: "Garrett is justly entitled to the above reward, and payment thereof has been refused upon a technicality." It stated:

AN ACT FOR THE RELIEF OF PAT. GARRETT
CONTENTS

SECTION 1. Authorizes payment of $500 reward for the arrest of "the Kid."

WHEREAS, The Governor of New Mexico did, on or about the 7th day of May, A.D., 1881, issue certain proclamation in words and figures as follows, to-wit:

"I will pay five hundred dollars reward to any person or persons who will capture William Bonney, alias 'The Kid,' and deliver him to any sheriff of New Mexico. Satisfactory proof of identity will be required."

(Signed) Lew. Wallace
Governor of New Mexico.

AND, WHEREAS, Pat. Garrett was at that time sheriff of Lincoln county, and did, on or about the month of August, 1881, in pursuance of the above reward, and by virtue of a warrant placed in his hands for the purpose, attempted to arrest said William Bonney, and in said attempt did kill said William Bonney at Fort Sumner, in the county of San Miguel, in the Territory of New Mexico, and wherefore, said Garrett is justly entitled to the above reward, and payment thereof has been refused upon a technicality. Therefore

Be it enacted by the Legislative Assembly of the Territory of New Mexico:

SECTION 1. The Territorial Auditor is hereby authorized to draw a warrant upon the Territorial Treasurer of the Territory of New Mexico, in favor of Pat. Garrett for the sum of five hundred dollars, payable out of any funds in the Territorial treasury not otherwise appropriated, in payment of the reward of five hundred dollars heretofore offered by his Excellency, Governor Lew. Wallace, for the arrest of William Bonney, alias "The Kid."

SEC. 2. This act shall take effect and be in force from and after its passage.

Approved February 18, 1882,

GOVERNOR SHELDON'S APPROVAL

And, once returned from traveling, Governor Lionel Sheldon even stated, in his February 14, 1882 letter to the Legislature, that *he* would have paid Garrett's reward outright: "*It is a claim which I think I should have paid if it had not been understood that the matter was to be referred to the legislature before it came into my hands.*" (Sheldon had been out of the Territory from July 3, 1881 to August 27, 1881, leaving more timid Ritch in charge).

Sheldon wrote:

Executive Office,
Territory of New Mexico,
Santa Fe, *February 14th* 1882

Hon Lewis Baca
President of the Council

In the matter of the claim of Sheriff Garrett Lincoln county for the reward offered for the capture of "the Kid" so called, I am of the opinion that he is entitled to payment. He could not technically comply with the terms of the reward because when he met the "Kid" in Maxwell's room it is very certain that one or the other would be killed. It was not a reward the payment of which depended on conviction. The Kid had been convicted and was under sentence to be hanged. Garrett was in pursuit with an intention to capture if it could be done normally but under the circumstances of their meeting capture was pout of the question. It will not do to the technical in this case because men will not be willing to take risks and
proper services in the protection of society against bad men if captious objections are interposed to avoid the discharge of public observations. The case under consideration is too notorious and remarkable to be made a precedent for the refusal to pay for services performed substantially in compliance with the provisions of high authority.

It is a claim which I think I should have paid if it had not been understood that the matter was to be referred to the legislature before it came into my hands.

Very Respectfully
Lionel A. Sheldon
Governor of New Mexico

UPSHOT OF ADDED SCRUTINY

Acting-Governor William Ritch's delaying payment of Pat Garrett's reward resulted inadvertently in the Coroner's Jury Report for William Bonney getting scrutiny and approval not only by himself and Territorial Attorney General William Breeden, but also by Governor Lionel Sheldon and the Legislature. And all agreed that Garrett killed Billy the Kid, and therefore deserved the reward. And the validity of the Coroner's Jury Report itself was never a matter of controversy.

THE RING AND THE REPORT

Another thrust of the "Brushy Bill" hoax's denial of the Coroner's Jury Report's existence was to make-up that the reward had been granted to Pat Garrett *without a Coroner's Jury Report* because the Santa Fe Ring controlled the Legislature.

That Ring was described in D.W. Meinig's 1998 *The Shaping of America: A Geographical Perspective on 500 Years of History, Volume 3: Transcontinental America 1850 - 1915.* Meinig wrote:

> In the 1870's ... the "Santa Fe Ring" ... emerged into full notoriety: "it was essentially a set of lawyers, politicians, and businessmen who united to run the territory and to make money of this particular region. Although located on the frontier, the ring reflected the corporative, monopolistic, and multiple enterprise tendencies of all American business after the Civil War. Its uniqueness lay in the fact that, rather than dealing with some manufactured item, they regarded land as their first medium of currency." "Land" meant litigation, and "down the trail from the states came an amazing number of lawyers" who, "still stumbling over their Spanish, would build their own political and economic empire out of the tangled heritage of land grants." ... "[E]ventually over 80 per cent of the Spanish grants went to American lawyers and settlers" ... [C]onsiderable resistance and violence [was] generated by this American assault ... To the Anglos land was a commodity to buy and sell, to exploit as quickly as possible, a means of profit and propellant of one's personal progress. Furthermore, "American land policy featured precise measurement and documentation, assumed individual ownership, and came out of a tradition that expected western land to be open for settlement" ... The most vulnerable parts of the Hispano system were the common lands, essential to the grazing economy, but often used without title ... that was readily challenged under American law and likely to be declared by the courts to be public land subject to routine

> survey and sale. This process of Anglo encroachment ... reached an important victory in an early court approval of the Maxwell Grant, an infamous case wherein the original 97,000 acres was inflated to nearly 2 million covering a huge county-sized area ... [T]he invasion of New Mexico had taken on a new momentum.

The "Brushy" hoax had lifted the Ring as corrupt politicians from Maurice Garland Fulton's editor's note in the 1927 edition of Pat Garrett's *The Authentic Life of Billy the* Kid. Fulton wrote:

> Garrett is one of the few writers of the Lincoln County War who has had the frankness and courage to mention Catron's name in connection with it. [Catron] is the figure that looms up behind the Murphy and Dolan faction. As the president of the powerful First National Bank at Santa Fe, he furnished the money needed by Murphy and Dolan in their business, of course taking mortgages which at the close of the War gave him possession of their store and its stock of goods. Catron was also a cattle raiser, and in some sense a dominating figure in that industry in the western part of the county. **Besides all this he was a powerful member of the clique of politicians and business men called in those days the "Santa Fe Ring," which largely controlled the Territory of New Mexico.** (Garrett, Page 59)

In fact, the reverse argument applied, confirming validity of the Coroner's Jury report: the Ring's political motivation would be to granting Garrett his reward *because of certainty that he had killed Billy Bonney*. The Ring wanted anti-Ring Regulator, Billy Bonney, dead as a hot-head capable of instigating a future Hispanic uprising, like the past Lincoln County War.

It is also noteworthy that the July 21, 1881 *Santa Fe Daily New Mexican* had reported that Ring head, T.B. Catron accompanied Pat Garrett, presumably as his legal counsel, to his June 20, 1881 meeting with Acting-Governor Ritch, himself a Ringite too; stating: "Yesterday afternoon Pat. Garrett; accompanied by Hon. T.B. Catron ... called upon acting-Governor Ritch in regard to the reward offered by ex-Governor Lew Wallace for the Kid."

THE FEDERAL INDICTMENT

Territorial Ring head, Thomas Benton Catron, when U.S. Attorney, had responded to the Regulators' (including Billy Bonney) killing of Andrew "Buckshot" Roberts, one of Sheriff William Brady's posseman murderers of John Tunstall, by attempting to take control of their prosecution (and guaranteeing their hanging) by issuing his own federal indictment of June 21, 1878: "Case No. 411, United States vs. Charles Bowdry [Bowdre], Doc Scurlock, Henry Brown, Henry Antrim - alias Kid - John Middleton, Stephen Stevens, John Scroggins, George Coe and Frederick Waite."

Catron's contention would later be proved false by Billy Bonney's loyal attorney, Ira Leonard, in Billy's 1881 Mesilla hanging trials. Catron's indictment was based on "Buckshot" Roberts having been killed *in* the Mescalero Indian Reservation, that being Indian Country and controlled federally. In fact, the killing was at privately owned Blazer's Mill, within the perimeter of the Reservation, making it a Territorial matter; causing Catron's indictment to be quashed for invalid jurisdiction.

Even more subtle, was the fact that Catron's having a federal indictment against the Regulators, including Billy, effectively prevented their pardoning by a future sympathetic Territorial Governor - as might have happened with Lew Wallace.

The indictment stated:

The United States of America)
Territory of New Mexico)
Third Judicial District)

In the United States District Court for the Third Judicial District of the June Term of 1878.

The Grand Jury of the United States of America from the body of the good and lawful men of the Third Judicial District aforesaid – duly empanneled sworn and charged to the Term of aforesaid to inquire in and for the body of the Third Judicial District aforesaid upon their oaths do present that Charles Bowdry [sic - Bowdre throughout], Doc Scurlock, Henry Brown, ***Henry Antrim – alias Kid –*** *John Middleton, Stephen Stevens, John Scroggins, George Coe and Frederick Waite, late of the Third Judicial District in the Territory of New Mexico on the fifth [sic - fourth] day of April in the year of our Lord Eighteen hundred and*

Seventy-eight ***at and in this reservation of the Mescalero Apache Indians in the Said Third Judicial District, Said Reservation then and there being a part of the Indian country,*** *with force and armed in and upon one Andrew Roberts then and there being in the Said Reservation feloniously, willfully, unlawfully of this malice aforethought and from a premeditated design to effect the death of the Said Andrew Roberts, did make an assault, and that the Said Charles Bowdry, Doc Scurlock, Henry Brown,* ***Henry Antrim – alias Kid*** *– John Middleton, Stephen Stevens, John Scroggins, George Coe and Frederick Waite certain guns then and there loaded and charged with gunpowder and divers leaden bullets, which said guns the Said Charles Bowdry, Doc Scurlock, Henry Brown,* ***Henry Antrim (alias Kid)*** *John Middleton, Stephen Stevens, John Scroggins, George Coe and Frederick Waite in their hands then and there had and held to, against and upon the Said Andrew Roberts there and then within the Said Reservation feloniously, willfully, unlawfully of this malice aforethought and from a premeditated design to effect the death of the Said Andrew Roberts – did shoot and discharge, and that the Said Charles Bowdry, Doc Scurlock, Henry Brown,* ***Henry Antrim – alias Kid*** *– John Middleton, Stephen Stevens, John Scroggins, George Coe and Frederick Waite, with the leaden Bullets aforesaid, out of the guns aforesaid, then and there by force of the gunpowder that discharged and sent forth as aforesaid and on Roberts in and upon the right side of the belly of him the Said Andrew Roberts then and there within the Said Reservation feloniously, willfully, unlawfully of this malice aforethought and from a premeditated design to effect the death of the Said Andrew Roberts, did strike, penetrate and wound, giving to the said Andrew Roberts then and there and within the said Reservation and with the leaden Bullets aforesaid, that discharged and sent forth out of the guns aforesaid by the said Andrew [Charles] Bowdry, Doc Scurlock, Henry Brown,* ***Henry Antrim – alias Kid*** *– John Middleton, Stephen Stevens, John Scroggins, George Coe and Frederick Waite in and upon the right side of the belly of him the said Andrew Roberts one mortal wound of the depth of ten inches and of breadth of one half of an inch of which said mortal wound the Said Andrew Roberts then and there at the said Reservation instantly died and so the Jury aforesaid upon their oaths as aforesaid do say that the Said Charles Bowdry, Doc Scurlock, Henry Brown,* ***Henry Antrim – alias Kid*** *– John Middleton, Stephen Stevens, John Scroggins, George Coe and*

Frederick Waite the Said Andrew Roberts in manner and form aforesaid feloniously, willfully, unlawfully of this malice aforethought and from a premeditated design to effect the death of the Said Andrew Roberts, did kill and murder against the form of the Statute in such case made and provided against the Peace & dignity of the United States. And the Jurors aforesaid upon their oaths aforesaid do further present that Charles Bowdry late of the Third Judicial District in the Territory of New Mexico on the fifth day of April in the year AD Eighteen hundred and Seventy-eight at and within the Reservation of the Mescalero Apache Indians said Reservation being then and there situate in the Third Judicial District aforesaid and then and there being Indian Country in and upon Andrew Roberts then and there being in the Said Reservation in the Said District, feloniously, willfully, unlawfully of his malice aforethought and from a premeditated design to effect the death of the Said Andrew Roberts did make an assault and that the Said Charles Bowdry a certain gun then and there loaded and charged with gunpowder and one leaden Bullet which gun he the Said Charles Bowdry in his right hand then and there had and held to at against and upon the Said Andrew Roberts then and there within the Said Reservation feloniously, willfully, unlawfully of his malice aforethought and from a premeditated design to effect the death of the Said Andrew Roberts, did shoot and discharge and that the Said Charles Bowdry with the leaden Bullet aforesaid out of the gun aforesaid then and there by force of the gunpowder aforesaid shot and sent forth as aforesaid the Said Andrew Roberts in and from the right side of the belly of him the Said Andrew Roberts then and there and in the Said Reservation feloniously, willfully, unlawfully of his malice aforethought and from a premeditated design to effect the death of the Said Andrew Roberts, did strike, penetrate and wound, giving to the Said Andrew Roberts then and there with the leaden Bullet aforesaid so as aforesaid that discharged and sent forth out of the gun aforesaid by the Said Charles Bowdry in and upon the right side of the belly of the Said Andrew Roberts one mortal wound of ten inches and of breadth of one half of an inch of which said mortal wound the Said Andrew Roberts then and there at the said Reservation instantly died and the Jury aforesaid upon their oaths aforesaid do further present that Doc Scurlock, Henry Brown, ***Henry Antrim – alias Kid*** *– John Middleton, Stephen Stevens, John Scroggins, George Coe and Frederick Waite of the Third Judicial District aforesaid and on the day and year aforesaid with force and arms at the Said*

Reservation in the Said District aforesaid feloniously was present aiding and abetting and assisting the [Said] Charles Bowdry the felony and murder aforesaid to do and commit against the form of the Statute in such case made and provided against the Peace & dignity of the United States and the Jurors aforesaid upon their oaths aforesaid do say that the Said Charles Bowdry Doc Scurlock, Henry Brown, Henry Antrim – alias Kid – John Middleton, Stephen Stevens, John Scroggins, George Coe and Frederick Waite in manner and form aforesaid feloniously, willfully, unlawfully of his malice aforethought and from a premeditated design to effect the death of him the Said Andrew Roberts, him the Said Roberts did kill and murder against the form of the Statute in such case made and provided and against the peace and dignity of the United States.

Thomas B. Catron
United States Attorney
for New Mexico

411 ...

C.P. Crawford
Foreman of the Grand Jury

Witnesses
Aurelius Wilson, John Patten, John Watts, J.H. Blazer, Sam F. Mills, [missing first name] Howe, William Gentry

Filed in my Office
the 21 day of June 1878
John S. Crouch, Clerk

THE SECRET SERVICE

More evidence of the Ring's determination to eliminate Billy was that from mid- September 1880, through December 1880, the head of the Secret Service, Chief James Brooks, sent one of his 40 Special Operatives to New Mexico Territory - in likely political assistance to T.B. Catron and his Santa Fe Ring co-boss in Washington, Stephen Benton Elkins - to eliminate the last of the Regulators in the Territory - especially Billy Bonney. A branch of the Treasury Department, the Secret Service was primarily concerned with counterfeiting, though could pursue any criminal investigation.

Pointing to that ulterior motive, is that the Ring knew Territorial counterfeiting was minor, and that Regulators were not counterfeiters. But the convoluted plot involved linking counterfeiters to Billy Bonney's post-Lincoln County War guerrilla rustling from Ringites. Key was local Ringites successfully duping the gullible and lazy Special Operative, named Azariah Wild. He facilitated Pat Garrett's election as Sheriff in November of 1880, then made him a Deputy U.S. Marshal for Territory-wide jurisdiction to capture Billy, who became the target of the pursuit.

It is arguable that Billy would not have been captured by Garrett on December 22, 1880 at Stinking Springs, had it not been for Wild's paying for spies and assisting with getting Texas possemen; since New Mexicans refused to pursue Billy.

WILLIAM BREEDEN

William Breeden, the man who received the original Coroner's Jury Report from Pat Garrett, would have recognized its significance, and would have been overjoyed that the last of the Regulators was finally dead. He was a very special member of the Santa Fe Ring.

Breeden had facilitated the Ring's 1866 founding by attorneys, Thomas Benton Catron and Steven Benton Elkins. At the time, Breeden was a politically powerful attorney and was founding the Territory's Republican party. Catron, a Confederate and Democrat, opportunistically switched to that party, and at his 1866 arrival, with Breeden's influence, was quickly appointed by Acting-Governor W.F.M. Arney as District Attorney for the Third Judicial District. Breeden then facilitated the appointment of Elkins as Attorney General the next year.

Breeden was born in Mason County, Kentucky, on February 18, 1841, and was related to President James Madison on his paternal grandmother's side. When he was 12, his family moved to Keokuk, Iowa. After briefly attending the Lexington Masonic College in Lexington, Missouri, he went west in search of Pike's Peak gold. Returning to Missouri in 1860, he taught school until his Union Civil War service. After the war and administrative work in Washington, D.C., he was appointed in 1867 by President Andrew Johnson as assessor of internal revenue for New Mexico Territory; and served to 1869.

In 1867, he founded the Territory's Republican party. In 1872, he began law practice in Santa Fe. **In 1874 he was appointed Attorney General by Ringite Governor Marsh Giddings, making him concomitantly District Attorney for the First**

Judicial District by a Territorial statute from 1863. And in 1876 and 1878, he was reappointed by Governor S.B. Axtell.

In 1875, he was elected to the Legislature's Council from Santa Fe County, and re-elected in 1878. In 1876, he was a Delegate to the national Republican convention, helping to elect Ring-allied President Rutherford B. Hayes. In 1879, he was one of the original incorporators of railroad companies controlled by the Atchison, Topeka, and Santa Fe Railroad Company.

From 1878 through 1880, Breeden's Ringite law partner, Henry Waldo, held the office of Attorney General, maintaining Ring control. **In 1881, Breeden was re-appointed as Attorney General by Lew Wallace's replacement, Ringite Governor Lionel Sheldon. His appointment made him also the District Attorney for the First Judicial District of Santa Fe, making him the proper recipient of the Coroner's Jury Report of William Bonney. He served until 1889.**

He was also U.S. Attorney for a total of 14 years. In 1881, he was President of the New Mexican Printing and Publishing Company (which published the Ringite *Santa Fe New Mexican*) and Vice-President of Catron's and Elkins's Second National Bank of Santa Fe. He was then in his law partnership in Santa Fe with Henry Waldo, originally in Catron's law firm, and the defense attorney in the Ring-biased Court of Inquiry for Commander Nathan Augustus Monroe Dudley, which shielded Dudley from deserved court martial for his Lincoln County War Battle Posse Comitatus violations. Breeden died on January 28, 1913, with a laudatory death notice in *The New York Times*.

On May 31, 1874, Breeden wrote as Chairman of the Republican Committee to Stephen Benton Elkins, newly elected as Delegate to Congress (in an allegedly rigged election): "*We all feel proud of you – You have distinguished yourself and the Territory ... Catron was well when I left him ... **Ben Stevens** has been very ill but is recovering.*" **[AUTHOR'S NOTE: In March of 1876, Second Judicial District Judge Benjamin Stephens had plotted with Governor S.B. Axtell, to kill Colfax County anti-Ring activists, having appointed Breeden as his Attorney General.]**

Breeden's participation in approving and processing the Coroner's Jury Report, thus, was at the highest level of Ring approval. Trying to fool him about the killing of Billy Bonney would have been lethal - as Garrett would have known!

GARRETT AND THE RING

Best known of Ring-beholden participants in Billy the Kid history, Billy Bonney's killer, Pat Garrett, had bridged the Ring's enforcers and its thug assassins, by getting a lawman's title.

Born on June 5, 1850 (almost a decade before Billy Bonney) in Chambers County, Alabama, he moved with his family to a Claiborne Parish Louisiana, plantation when he was three. His father died in 1868, and Garrett headed west. He may have had an illegitimate child in Texas and killed a black man there. In 1876, as a Texas buffalo hunter, he murdered a teenager named Joe Briscoe, who was part of their group. Though one of the partners claimed it was malicious, Garrett got off on self-defense.

Depressive, alcoholic, lacking in skills besides killing animals and people, he went to Fort Sumner, New Mexico Territory, where he worked as a wagon driver for town owner, Peter Maxwell, a bartender in the town's Hargrove Saloon, and as a helper in a local hog farm of a Thomas "Kip" McKinney.

His had the right profile for the Ring's choice to kill its foe, Billy Bonney. Backed for Lincoln County Sheriff, he won on November 2, 1880. He then joined Secret Service Agent Azariah Wild - also engaged by the Ring for that task - who made him a Deputy U.S. Marshall, with money to pay spies and a Texas posse.

Garrett tried hard to kill Billy. He ambushed him first on December 19, 1880 (killing Tom O'Folliard instead); then on December 22, 1880 (killing Charlie Bowdre instead). So he settled on capturing Billy at Stinking Springs that day. After a hanging sentence in Mesilla, Billy, however, escaped Garrett's Lincoln jail, 15 days before the hanging date. Garrett finally succeeded in killing him in the Fort Sumner ambush, 77 days later.

To profit from that famous killing, Garrett used ghostwriter Ash Upson for his dime novel-style 1882 book, *The Authentic Life of Billy the Kid*, to advance the Billy the Kid outlaw myth and to conceal his own Ringite participation.

Likely not reelected as Lincoln County Sheriff because of killing Billy, Garrett's employment woes continued. In 1896, living in Uvalde, Texas, with his large family, he was brought back to New Mexico Territory to find the February 2, 1896 killers of Attorney Albert Jennings Fountain and his son, Henry, near White Sands; and was made Doña Ana County Sheriff for arrests. Much like his Billy the Kid task, its intent was eliminating a Ring enemy - now Catron's political and ranching rival, Oliver Lee.

Garrett, accusing Lee and his ranch associate, James Gilliland, of the murder, tried his usual ambush tactic, but got his Deputy killed instead by Lee and his ranch hands. And when Lee and Gilliland were tried for the Fountain and deputy murders, they were acquitted.

Garrett killed again on October 7, 1899, assisting a sheriff George Blalock of Greer County Oklahoma, in New Mexico. The victim was an accused murderer named Norman Newman.

In 1901, based on Billy the Kid killing fame, he was made El Paso Customs Collector by President Theodore Roosevelt. But he was removed in 1906 by political enemies. He bought a New Mexico ranch, but its failure forced his return to El Paso for real estate company work. His accusation of living with a prostitute there, made New Mexico Territory Governor-elect George Curry withdraw on offer of a prison superintendent job.

Garrett's destitute family had rented his New Mexico ranch to a goat raiser named Wayne Brazel. Garrett's dispute about land use and lease with Brazel, led to both men arguing on a road to Las Cruces on February 29, 1908, while both were on their way to sell the goats and the Garrett ranch to buyers, Carl Anderson and Jim Miller. Brazel shot armed Garrett in claimed self-defense. The jury in Brazel's subsequent murder trial agreed and exonerated him.

Like other Ring-beholden enforcers, chronically indebted Garrett was on Catron's loan payroll. Garrett's biographer, Leon Metz, in his 1874 book, *Pat Garrett: The Story of a Western Lawman,* described Garrett being pressured by Catron for an unpaid $500 note signed on February 20, 1901. On May 31, 1904, Catron's collector wrote back that local banks told him that Garrett "was no good and that the endorser would have to pay. They did not even want to take it for collection as they had plenty of their own against him." (Metz, Page 260) By June 1, 1904, Catron wrote to Garrett with paternal benevolence reserved for his minions: "The time will come when there will be a reappointment, and then all these businessmen [to whom you are indebted] will turn loose against you, and you may find it somewhat difficult to get a party to stand by you." (Metz, Page 260) There was no record that Garrett paid Catron. He may have considered it a bonus fee for his services. And he was not incorrect.

LATER FINDING OF THE REPORT

The proper filing of the Coroner's Jury Report can be traced from its July 15, 1881 sending to Santa Fe to William Breeden - as District Attorney of the First Judicial District and its legal analyst as Attorney General - to its chance finding, in 1932, in stored public records by a government employee.

It had also been indirectly referenced in a 1935 book by a Frank M. King titled *Wranglin' the Past: Reminiscences of Frank M. King*, in his chapter titled "The Kid's Exit." King wrote that Garrett's July 15, 1881 letter to Acting-Governor William Ritch, which cited the Report's copy sent to Ritch, had recently been located in old files of the Secretary of State of New Mexico.

Its finder, in 1932, was a Harold Abbott, employed in Santa Fe's State Land Office from 1931 to 1933. It was with San Miguel County court records, in the state capitol's basement. He made copies of it for himself and others, including his brother George. Harold died in 1937; George in 2006.

So George Abbott lived to see his brother's finding of the Coroner's Jury Report becoming proof against the "Brushy Bill" imposter hoax. On November 30, 1950, the day of "Brushy's" pardon hearing, the *Alamogordo News's* front page declared "Sumner Jury Thought The Kid Had Been Killed." It stated:

Although the perennial controversy over whether the infamous Billy the Kid still lives, has again arisen, at least one Alamogordo man, Frank Phillips, 84, claims personal knowledge of his death in 1881 at the hands of the late Sheriff Pat Garrett, and George Abbott, also of Alamogordo has in his office at the Pioneer Abstract Co., a photostatic copy of the verdict of the coroner's jury which viewed the remains of the late Wm. Bonney

Some twenty years ago, when the late Harold Abbott, brother of George, was an employee of the state land office in Santa Fe, he, with other employees, were going over some old records in the basement of the state capitol. There they ran across, in the San Miguel court records, the original copy of the coroner's jury, dated July 15, 1881, and written in Spanish. The document covered three pages of which they made photostatic copies.

As the reader will see from the document, translated below, the six men serving on the jury and the Justice of the Peace who empanneled them, seemed convinced that Wm.

Bonney, known as "Kid," was quite dead, and that he had been killed by Pat Garrett.

The most recent controversy arose when a firm of El Paso lawyers appealed to Governor Mabry for a full pardon for Wm. Bonney, who claims that the man killed at Fort Sumner by Pat Garrett was another outlaw, and not the Kid at all; that the Kid left the country, assumed the name of ["Brushy Bill"] Roberts, and has lived in Old and New Mexico all this time.

The documentary evidence of the Kid's death is translated as follows:

Territory of New Mexico
San Miguel County
Precinct No. 27

To the attorney of the 1st Judicial district of the Territory of New Mexico:

Greetings: [The English Translation followed]

FROM BREEDEN TO HAROLD ABBOTT

One can trace the Coroner's Jury Report's storage in the state Capitol Buildings. First was William Breeden's Palace of the Governors office. Breeden apparently filed it in his capacity as District Attorney for the First Judicial District under San Miguel County court records, as he categorized this Fort Sumner killing in that county.

As Attorney General also, his office was in rooms 5, 6, and 8, according to Clinton P. Anderson in his 1944 *New Mexico Historical Review* article titled "The Adobe Palace." (Anderson, Page 110) **[FIGURE: 5]** Anderson noted that Breeden used that office till 1889. (Anderson, Page 112)

Next occupying Breeden's office area in that Capitol Building was the State Land Office's Commissioner.

A Jesse Nusbaum's 1909 journal recorded Palace of the Governor's rooms; being published in 1978 by Rosemary Nusbaum, as: *The City Different and the Palace, The Palace of the Governors: It's Role in Santa Fe History*. It stated that "the block of five rooms west of the Historical Society's quarters were occupied by Robert P. Ervin, Commissioner of Lands." (Nusbaum, 86)

Robert P. Ervin served as State Land Commissioner from 1907 to 1918. And though the Palace of the Governors was renovated from Breeden's period to the Ervin one, the general office location stayed the same. And apparently Breeden's old records were stored along with those of the State Land Office.

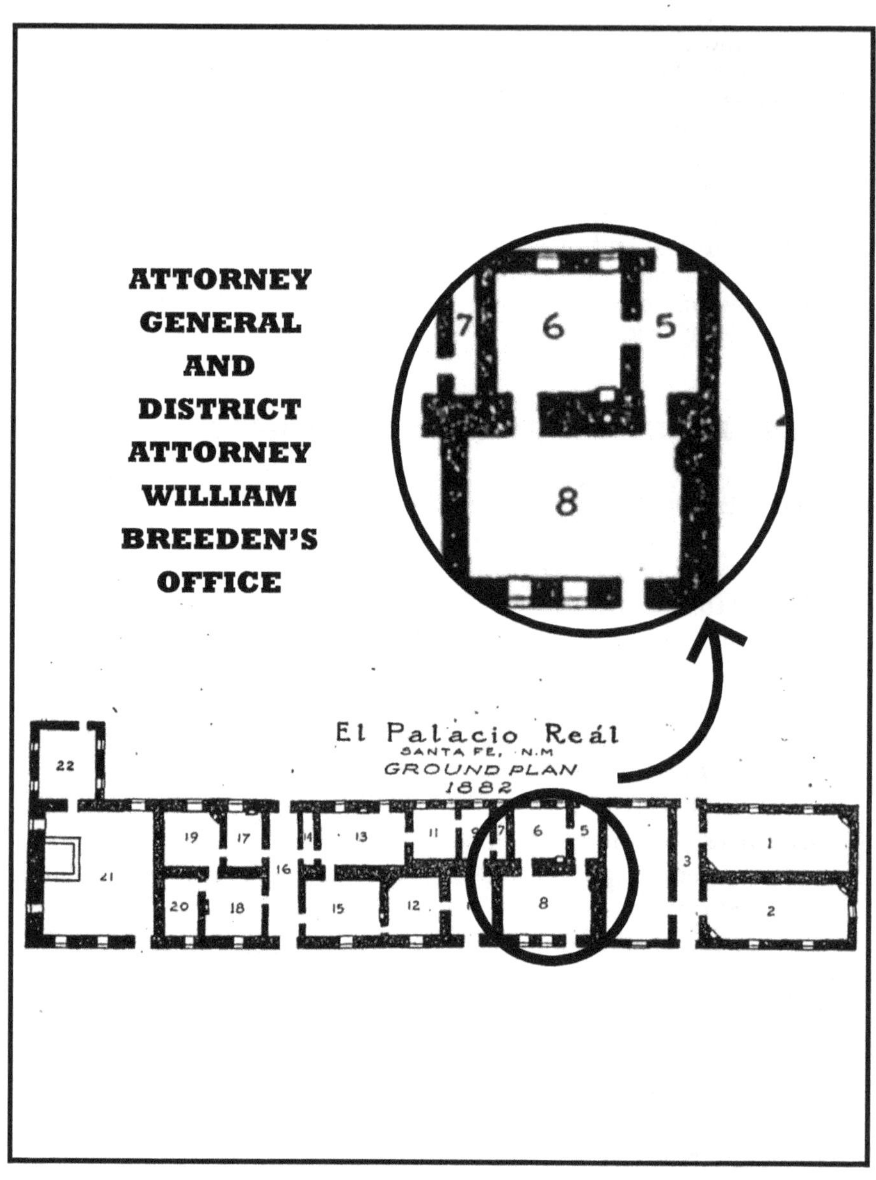

FIGURE: 5. Palace of the Governors in 1882, showing Attorney General William Breeden's office as rooms 5, 6, and 8. From Clinton P. Anderson's 1944 *New Mexico Historical Review*. Article: "The Adobe Palace" Page 110.

The State Land Office's combined records followed the Capitol Building's relocations. Harold Abbott had stated that in 1932 "he, with other employees, were going over some old records **in the basement of the state capitol**;" so those records presumably related to his Land Office job. But his finding of Breeden's **San Miguel court records"** with them indicates that they had stayed together since their first Palace of the Governors storage.

But the Capitol Building in Harold Abbott's day was not the one after the Palace of the Governors. From 1850 to 1886 one was under construction, but ended up as the Territorial Courthouse.

In 1886, another building became the Capitol, replacing the Palace of the Governors. But it burned down in six years, on May 12, 1892; though its archives were saved.

Then the Territorial Courthouse became the temporary Capitol Building until another was completed in 1900. That one was used for 66 years, until today's Capitol Building, "the Roundhouse," was dedicated in 1966. And the previous Capitol Building was renamed as the Bataan Memorial Building.

So by Harold Abbott's 1932 finding of the Coroner's Jury Report in the Capitol Building's basement (of the future Bataan Memorial Building), the old Palace of the Governors records might have been moved multiple times. Additionally, Frank M. King had reported in his 1935 book, *Wranglin' the Past*, that Garrett's July 15, 1881 letter to Ritch, with the Coroner's Jury Report copy, was found in old files of New Mexico's Secretary of State. And his offices were also in that Capitol Building, according to a 1932 article in the *Santa Fe New Mexican* titled "Call for Bids."

So the Coroner's Jury Report had provable and correct provenance.

RESURFACING OF HAROLD ABBOTT'S COPY

Harold Abbott's Coroner's Jury Report copy reappeared 19 years later in the February, 1951 edition of *New Mexico Magazine* under "Glimpses of History," in response to "Brushy Bill's" failed pardon attempt, with the reporter writing: "Interest in Billy the Kid - New Mexico's most notorious outlaw - was revived a few weeks ago when an old timer appeared on the scene to claim the identity of the Kid." The article addressed the "Brushy Bill" hoax's "assertion that a coroner's inquest report was not legally on file." But the reporter had dutifully located Harold Abbotts Coroner's Jury Report copy; writing:

However, a photostatic copy of the report has been located by New Mexico Magazine in Alamogordo. The photostat is owned by George Abbott, who said his brother had the copy made about 20 years ago. The report is reproduced on the left. Because part of the copy was badly faded, about a dozed lines were eliminated for this reproduction [in the article]." It concluded: "O.L. Roberts, of Hico, Tex., the man who claimed the identity of Billy the Kid, died late in December of a heart attack, while he was walking along the street in Hico. **He died without being able to make his claim stand**."

To be noted is that the "Brushy" hoaxers owned this article with its Coroner's Jury Report photostat, since it was in C.L. Sonnichsen's collected papers. But all proof of the existence of the Report was concealed.

MAURICE G. FULTON RELOCATES THE REPORT

The Coroner's Jury Report was independently relocated 19 years after Harold Abbott's find. That also proved that public employees had done a good job in keeping San Miguel County legal records together; albeit combined with State Land Office Records.

On August 5, 1951, historian Maurice Garland Fulton, having relocated the Report, used it to respond to William V. Morrison's working with C.L. Sonnichsen to write a book on "Brushy Bill" as the surviving Billy the Kid." Fulton published an article in *The El Paso Times* titled "Coroner's Report Proves Billy the Kid is Dead, Historian Asserts, Researcher Discovers Document." It had his photostatic copy of the Report, matching the Harold Abbott copy in *New Mexico Magazine,* six months earlier.

Fulton had struck at the heart of the "Brushy Bill" scam, in which Morrison claimed the Report was not real because it had not been "certified" or "recorded," so was not acceptable. So Fulton made clear that certifying was a modern procedure and irrelevant to 19th century documents. But he also responded by certifying the copy of it that he made! And it obviously matched Harold Abbott's copy.

The Fulton article stated:

Billy the Kid is dead. The famed outlaw met death at the business end of Pat Garrett's flaming pistol in July of 1881. So says Col. Maurice G. Fulton, of Roswell, N.M., former custodian of the Lincoln County Museum ...

A 91 year old man, claiming to be the Kid and represented by William V. Morrison of St. Louis, appeared last year before Gov. Thomas J. Mabry of New Mexico and appealed for a pardon [as Billy the Kid and was rejected].

According to Colonel Fulton, "William Bonney, alias Kid, alias William Antrim" could not possibly be alive. He offers, as part of his proof, the coroner's report on the killer's death and a reward believed to be paid to Sheriff Pat Garrett for effecting that death.

Colonel Fulton recently said:

"**Morrison's contention that the coroner's report was not 'recorded' is taking the modern practice rather than the older one [about certifying copies]**. We are lucky to have a report in this instance, for coroner's jury reports are hard to find, even when they happen to have been made."

Fulton also donated a copy of the Coroner's Jury Report to the Indiana Historical Society's Lew Wallace Collection, with each of its three pages certified on January 18, 1951 on the back. **[FIGURE: 6]**

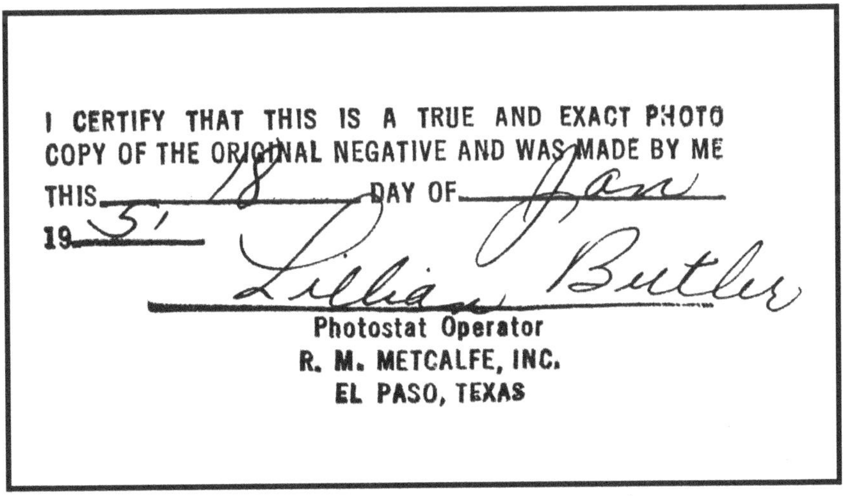

I CERTIFY THAT THIS IS A TRUE AND EXACT PHOTO COPY OF THE ORIGINAL NEGATIVE AND WAS MADE BY ME THIS 18 DAY OF Jan 19 51

Lillian Butler
Photostat Operator
R. M. METCALFE, INC.
EL PASO, TEXAS

FIGURE: 6. Certification on January 18, 1951 of Maurice Garland Fulton's Coroner's Jury Report copy donated to the Indiana Historical Society. Courtesy of the Indiana Historical Society.

GARRETT'S PROSECUTION IMMUNITY BY STATUTE OF LIMITATIONS FOR MURDER

Besides the imposter hoaxs' denial of the the Coroner's Jury Report, was making-up an "innocent victim," killed by Garrett as a "cold case" murder needing investigation.

But that was an impassable hurdle too. New Mexico Territory had a Stature of Limitations for murder. The 1876 *Acts of the Legislative Assembly of the Territory of New Mexico* established a **10 year limitation on prosecution for murder** in the 1882's *The General Laws of New Mexico* Edited by L. Bradford Prince, under "Limitation of Criminal Actions." **With the killing in 1881, the possibility of Garrett's prosecution ended in 1891**. The statute stayed in effect as (NMSA) 1953, 40A-1-8(3). It stated:

CHAPTER XIII.

AN ACT to provide the limitations of criminal actions.

CONTENTS

Sec. 1. Limitation; - murder, within ten years; 2d, manslaughter, six years; 3d, perjury and other felonies, three years; 4th, misdemeanors, two years; 5th, violation of revenue laws, three years

Sec. 2. Provides if defendant absconds or secretes himself the limitation shall not hold for that time.

Be it enacted by the Legislative Assembly of the Territory of New Mexico:

SECTION 1. No person shall hereafter be prosecuted, tried, or punished, in any court of this Territory; unless the indictment shall be found, or information filed therefore as hereinafter limited and provided.

First. For murder, within ten years from the time of the offence or act was committed.

Second. For manslaughter, or any other killing of a human being, except murder in the first degree, within six years from the time the offence was committed.

CHAPTER 3
THE WITNESSES AND THE DEATH SCENE

It took delusional disorders of Billy the Kid imposters, and sociopathic scorn of public intelligence by their hoaxing promoters, to claim that the most documented death in the Old West never happened. It was not only the Coroner's Jury Report that was an impassable hurdle. A huge number of people saw the corpse, besides the Report's witness, Peter Maxwell; and they documented their experience. In addition, killing Billy the Kid was a major media event, with national reporting.

PAT GARRETT WROTE A BOOK

The 1881 killing of Billy the Kid had viral fame, inspiring Pat Garrett to ally with his journalist boarder, Ashmun "Ash" Upson, to create his ghostwritten book, issued the following year: *The Authentic Life of Billy the Kid The Noted Desperado of the Southwest, Whose Deeds of Daring and Blood Made His Name a Terror in New Mexico, Arizona, and Northern Mexico.* Though it used that period's popular and lurid dime novel style, and though the history of Billy Bonney had not yet been researched, so was fictionalized, both men knew Billy. Upson had been a border with his family in Silver City; and Garrett, having met him in 1878, when both spent time in Fort Sumner, certainly knew the specifics of his own tracking, capturing, jailing, and killing of him. Garrett's lethality was undisputable, with first killing two of Billy's companions in his attempt to kill him. On December 19, 1880, he and his Texan posse ambushed Billy's group returning to Fort Sumner. Tom O'Folliard was fatally shot. In the early morning of December 22, 1881, with Billy and his group attempting to escape the Territory and having spent the night in a rock line-cabin at Stinking Springs, Charlie Bowdre emerged first wearing either Billy's hat, or one that looked like it, and was immediately killed by Garrett, as mistaken for Billy. Only then did Garrett settle on capturing Billy for certain hanging trials.

As to Garrett's finally killing Billy, his book described his coming to Fort Sumner with his Deputies John William Poe and Thomas "Kip" McKinney; and, late that moonlit night of July 14, 1881, stationing them on the porch of the Maxwell family mansion, while he went inside to check with the town's owner, Peter Maxwell in his dark bedroom. The book stated:

> I left Poe and McKinney at the end of the porch, and about twenty feet from the door of Pete's bedroom, while I myself entered it. I walked to the head of the bed and sat down near the pillow and beside Maxwell's head. I asked him as to the whereabouts of the Kid. He replied that the Kid had certainly been about, but he did not know whether he had left or not. At that moment, a man sprang quickly in the door, and looking back, called twice in Spanish, "Quien es? Quien es? (Who comes there?)" No one replied, and he came into the room. I could see he was bareheaded, and from his tread I could perceive he was either barefooted or in his stocking feet. He held a revolver in his right hand and a butcher knife in his left.
>
> He came directly towards me while I was sitting at the head of Maxwell's bed. Before he reached the bed, I whispered, "Who is it, Pete?" but received no reply for a moment. It struck me that it might be Pete's brother-in-law, Manuel Abreu, who had seen Poe and McKinney on the outside and wanted to know their business. The intruder came close to me, leaned both hands on the bed, his right almost touching my knee, and asked in a low tone "Who are they, Pete?" At the same instant Maxwell whispered to me, "That's him!"
>
> Simultaneously the Kid must have seen or felt the presence of a third person at the head of the bed. He raised quickly his pistol - a self-cocker - within a foot of my breast. Retreating rapidly across the room, he cried, "Quien es? Quien es? (Who is that? Who is that?)" All this happened more rapidly than it takes to tell it. As quick as possible I drew my revolver and fired, threw my body to one side, and fired again. The second shot was useless. The Kid fell dead at the first one. He never spoke.

> A struggle or two, a little strangling sound as he gasped for breath, and the Kid was with his many victims. (Garrett, Pages 215-216)

Garrett's description matched Peter Maxwell's witness statement to the Coroner's Jury the next day: "I being in my bed in my room, at about midnight on the 14th day of July, Pat F. Garrett came into my room and sat down. William Bonney came in and got close to my bed with a gun in his hand and asked me "who is it" and then Pat F. Garrett fired two shots at the said William Bonney and the said William Bonney fell near my fire place and I went out of the room and when I came in again about three or four minutes after the shots the said William Bonney was dead."

DEPUTY POE WROTE A BOOK

John William Poe, Kentucky-born and a past buffalo hunter, like Pat Garrett, was a Deputy U.S. Marshal and a Deputy Sheriff in Texas. In late 1880, he was hired by the Canadian River Cattlemen's Association to combat rustling centered in New Mexico, and had moved there to White Oaks. He was deputized by Pat Garrett, who was then Lincoln County Sheriff and a Deputy U.S. Marshal, to hunt Billy Bonney following his April 28, 1881 jailbreak in Lincoln while awaiting hanging. After participating in the killing, Poe was elected Lincoln County Sheriff the following year, serving until 1885; then did ranching and later moved to Roswell in the Territory, operating a store and founding both the Bank of Roswell and the Citizen's Bank of Roswell.

Poe's book, *The Death of Billy the Kid*, was first printed as a long article, *The Killing of Billy the Kid*, then as a booklet by an E.A. Brininstool in 1922 and 1923. It was published as a book by Houghton Mifflin in 1933. Though Poe had never met Billy until moments before the fateful encounter, he was the one who had urged Pat Garrett's recognizance of Fort Sumner because of Billy's rumored presence there. And his reporting of the shooting gives the multiple victim identifications that left him confident that Billy had been killed. His book stated:

> It was probably not more than thirty seconds after Garrett had entered Maxwell's room, when my attention was attracted, from where I sat in the little gateway, to a

man approaching me on the inside of and along the fence, some forty or fifty steps away. I observed that he was only partially dressed and was both bareheaded and barefooted, or rather, had only socks on his feet, and it seemed to me that he was fastening his trousers as he came toward me at a brisk walk.

As Maxwell's was the one place in Fort Sumner that I had considered above suspicion of harboring the Kid, I was entirely off my guard, the thought coming into my mind that the man approaching was either Maxwell or some guest of his ... He came on until he was almost within arm's-length of where I sat, before he saw me, as I was partially concealed from his view by the post of the gate.

Upon seeing me, he covered me with his six-shooter as quick as lightning, sprang onto the porch, calling out in Spanish, "Quien es" (Who is it?) – at the same time backing away from me toward the door through which only a few seconds before had passed, repeating his query, "Who is it?" in Spanish several times.

At this I stood up and advanced toward him, telling him not to be alarmed, that he should not be hurt; and still without the least suspicion that this was the very man we were looking for. As I moved toward him trying to reassure him, he backed up into the doorway of Maxwell's room, where he halted for a moment, his body concealed by the thick adobe wall at the side of the doorway, from whence he put out his head and asked in Spanish for the fourth or fifth time who I was. I was within a few feet of him when he disappeared into the room.

After this, and until after the shooting, I was unable to see what took place on account of the darkness of the room, but plainly heard what was said inside. An instant after the man left the door, I heard a voice inquire in a sharp tone, "Pete, who are those fellows on the outside?" An instant later a shot was fired in the room, followed immediately by what everyone within hearing distance thought were two other shots. However, there were only two shots fired, the third report, as we learned afterward, being caused by the rebound of the second bullet, which had struck the adobe wall and rebounded against the headboard of the wooden bedstead.

I heard a groan and one or two gasps from where I stood in the doorway, as of someone dying in the room. An instant later, Garrett came out ... He stood close by me to the wall at the side of the door ands said to me, "that was the Kid that came in there onto me, and I think I have got him." I said, "Pat, the Kid would not come to this place; you have shot the wrong man.

Upon my saying this, Garrett seemed to be in doubt himself as to whom he had shot, but quickly spoke up and said, "I am sure that was him, for I know his voice too well to be mistaken." This remark of Garrett's relieved me of considerable apprehension, as I had felt almost certain that someone whom we did not want had been killed.

A moment after Garrett came out of the door, Peter Maxwell rushed squarely onto me in frantic effort to get out of the room, and I certainly would have shot him but for Garrett's striking down my gun, saying, "Don't shoot Maxwell ..."

We afterwards discovered that the Kid had frequently been at his house after his escape from Lincoln, but Maxwell stood in such terror of him that he did not dare inform against him.

[Maxwell then got a candle from his mother's room and placed it on the window-sill from the outside.] This enabled us to get a view of the inside, where we saw a man lying stretched upon his back dead, in the middle of the room, with a six-shooter lying at his right hand and a butcher knife at his left. Upon examining the body, we found it to be that of Billy the Kid. Garrett's first shot had penetrated his breast just above the heart. (Poe, Pages 32-41)

Poe's description matched Pat Garrett's as well as the Coroner's Jury Report; which stated: "[The jury] found the body of William Bonney alias 'Kid' with a shot in the left breast."

A.P. "PACO" ANAYA BURIED BILLY AND GOT A BOOK

A.P. "Paco" Anaya was a Fort Sumner friend of Billy's. His 1991, posthumously printed memoir held the truth in his title: *I Buried Billy*. Anaya was one of the 200 Fort Sumner residents who held a candle-light vigil for Billy's body on the night of July 14-15, 1881, all having identified him. Real dead Billy ends the imposters' and "Billy the Kid Case" promulgators' hoaxes. Anaya wrote: "I, the writer, and my brother, Higinio Garcia, and several others of those that were there, dressed Billy with those clothes then we laid him on a high bed ... [A]nd on the next day we buried him." (Anaya, Page 132)

A TOWN IDENTIFIED THE BODY TOO

After his jailbreak on April 28, 1881, Billy had chosen Fort Sumner as a destination for two reasons: his secret young lover, Paulita Maxwell, was there; and he felt confident in the protection of the Maxwell family and Fort Sumner's over 200 residents, who had known him since early 1878, and would have been aware of his freedom fighter role. The response of the townspeople to this horrific killing in their midst, was described by John William Poe in his 1933 book, *The Death of Billy the Kid*. Once again, as an outsider, he was surprised. He quickly realized that this boy, who had been presented to his as a despicable outlaw-murderer, was beloved by the primarily Hispanic residents. Poe wrote:

> Within a short time after the shooting, quite a number of the native people gathered around, some of them bewailing the death of their friend, while several women pleaded for permission to take charge of the body, which we allowed them to do. They carried it across the yard to a carpenter shop, where it was laid out on a workbench, the women placing lighted candles around it according to their ideas of properly conducting a "wake" for the dead ...
>
> [The shooting] occurred at about midnight on the fourteenth of July, 1881. We spent the remainder of the night on the Maxwell premises, keeping constantly on our

guard, as we were expecting to be attacked by friends of the dead man. (Pages 41-42, 44)

So not only did multiple townspeople identify Billy as the corpse in the night vigil, but they were infuriated enough by his killing to present a risk its perpetrators.

As an aside, the townspeople's response put in perspective the Coroner's Jury Report's statement: "[W]e are unanimous in the opinion that the gratitude of all the community is due to the said Garrett for his deed and is worthy of being rewarded." The Coroner's Jury President was Milnor Rudulph, Postmaster of Sunnyside, seven miles north of Fort Sumner. Rudulph was a loyal Ringite who had helped Thomas Benton Catron and the Santa Fe Ring take over the Legislature in 1872 to block anti-Ring bills. His actions contributed to the first of the Territory's anti-Ring, freedom fights, which I named the 1872 Legislature Revolt. Ringite Governor Marsh Giddings's brought troops into the Legislature's hall, to suppress the legislators, enabling the Ring to keep their Ring-biased judges in power to continue malicious prosecutions of their opponents. Rudulph's dangerous bias apparently affected Alejandro Segura's writing of the Coroner's Jury Report. The frightened juryman had no alternative but to sign the conclusion the day after Ring terrorism invaded their town.

DELUVINA MAXWELL WAS THERE TOO

A Navajo woman, purchased as a nine year old child slave by Lucien Bonaparte Maxwell, the owner of the two million acre Maxwell Land Grant, then Fort Sumner, and never emancipated, was deeply attached to Billy Bonney, and laid wildflowers on his Fort Sumner grave for decades, until her own death.

Her own eye-witness confirmation of his being the corpse was given in a June 24, 1927 interview to historian, J. Evetts Haley, in Fort Sumner. She stated:

> I came here about [1869] and was here when Billy the Kid was killed. Billy the Kid was my compadre, my friend, poor Billy ... Pete Maxwell had told Billy he better go, as Pat Garrett was coming after him. Billy said he did not care, he was not afraid of Pat Garrett. The night he was killed Billy came in hungry, went down with a butcher

> knife to get some meat at Pete Maxwell's ... After passing the men outside, he went into Maxwell's room where Garrett was and he shot him. The story is told that I was there and went in with a candle to see if Billy was dead. I did not do it. Pete took a candle and held it around in the window and Pat stood back in the dark where he could see in the room. When they saw he was dead, they both went in ...
>
> Most of the native people (Mexicans) who lived in town went to his funeral ...
>
> I did not see Billy the night after he was killed, **but I saw him the following morning.**

To be noted is that Deluvina's description matched that of John William Poe about Maxwell placing the candle, and the Hispanic residents' vigil to view the body.

THE PRESS WAS PROFUSE

There was also massive, front page, national press about the killing of Billy the Kid; with no reason to fabricate the event; with Billy portrayed as a terrifying outlaw-murderer, whose death was a public relief. Already mentioned, has been the July 23, 1881's Las Cruces *Rio Grande Republican's* "Kid the Killer Killed, Wm. Bonney alias Antrim, alias Billy the Kid, Fatally Meets Pat Garrett, the Lincoln County Sheriff." which quoted from the Coroner's Jury Report itself.

Here are some other Territorial examples:

On July 18, 1881, *The Las Vegas Daily Optic's* headline was: " 'The Kid' Killed! He Meets His Death at the Hands of Sheriff Pat Garrett, of Lincoln County." It gave identification of the body, as confirmed in the correctly cited Coroner's Jury Report: "An inquest was held on his body today [sic] and the verdict of the jury was 'justifiable homicide' and that Pat Garrett ought to receive the thanks of the whole community ... and that he is truly worthy of a handsome reward."

The July 21, 1881 *Santa Fe Daily New Mexican*, in "Garrett Exonerates Maxwell," confirmed Peter Maxwell as a witness to the shooting, and addressed rumors that he had hidden Billy the Kid in Fort Sumner before the killing. Garrett, protecting

Maxwell, a possible traitor, was quoted: "[H]e does not think that Maxwell was in with the Kid ... He says that Pete acknowledged that fear kept him from informing on the Kid."

The July 22, 1881 *Las Vegas Daily Gazette*, in "Words of Commendation and Encouragement," stated: "Immediately on the receipt of the news of the killing of Billy 'the Kid' by Sheriff Garrett, prominent citizens of Roswell and the lower Pecos wrote us giving particulars and expressing satisfaction. [One wrote], 'God bless Pat Garrett for his good work' will escape many a lip, and people will never cease to love him for his great achievements."

Here are some national examples.

July 20, 1881's *The Chicago Daily Tribune* had "Account of the Manner in Which 'Billy the Kid' Was Killed, The Kid Killed;" stated: "[Garrett], who had taken advantage of the dim, uncertain light to get his weapon ready for use, brought it to bear on the Kid, shooting him through the heart at the first pull of the trigger. He died in two minutes without uttering a word. The [Las Vegas *Daily*] *Optic* to-night says of the affair: "Billy the Kid" was the terror not only of Lincoln County, but of the whole Territory; a young desperado who has long been noted as a bold thief, a cold-blooded murderer, having, perhaps, killed more men than any person of his age in the world ... All making rejoices ... It is now in order for Pat Garrett to be well rewarded for his services."

The Weekly Gazette (Colorado Springs Gazette) of July 23, 1881 had "Billy the Kid, At Last the Bullet Finds its Billet, New Mexico's Noted Outlaw Shot by a Sheriff." It stated: "The Gazette has positive information this morning from Fort Sumner of the death of 'Billy the Kid.' This noted desperado was killed at Fort Sumner on the Pecos river on the 14th by Pat Garrett, sheriff of Lincoln county."

On July 26, 1881, under "Champion Murderer," the *Fort Wayne Daily Gazette* stated: "The *Daily Optic* to-night give [sic] an interesting account of the killing of William Bonney, alias Billy the Kid, the noted desperado, at Fort Sumner on Thursday night."

That July 26, 1881 was also the *Savannah Morning News's* "Billy the Kid, A Youth With Nineteen Murders to His Account – The Inhabitants of New Mexico Overawed by a Boy of Twenty-One, Who Was Killed at Sight." It stated: "It is said that there was only one man in Lincoln county, Pat Garrett, who had the nerve to meet [Billy the Kid]. Pat was selected for this very purpose, and started on Billy's trail a few weeks ago, meeting with success ... as the telegraph informs us of Billy's death by his hands."

On August 10, 1881 *The New York Sun*, reprinted from the *St. Louis Globe-Democrat* "The Life of Billy the Kid. His Name Was Billy McCarthy, And He Was Born in New York."

That reprint was also in August 12, 1881's *The Lancaster Intelligencer* as "Billy the Kid, His Name Was Billy McCarthy and He was Born in New York, Murdering a Man at the Age of Sixteen – Made a Deputy Constable – Gen. Lew Wallace's Admiration for the Youthful Desperado, Under Sentence of Death – Killing Two Men in Thirty Seconds – The Kid Killed." It stated: "Billy the Kid was rapidly nearing the inevitable close of his blood-stained career ... Deputy Sheriff Pat Garrett with two companions started on his trail, swearing to capture or kill him or die trying ... Shortly before midnight Garrett went to Maxwell's, and had just seated himself in the dark on the side of Maxwell's bed when the door opened, and in walked the Kid ... [He] leveled his pistols, exclaiming: "Quien es? Quien es? But his delay of asking was fatal. Before the words were off his lips Pat Garrett's bullet was through his heart, and 'Billy the Kid,' the terror of New Mexico, lay a gasping, quivering corpse."

CHAPTER 4
BILLY BONNEY'S LIFE

REAL HISTORY

Billy Bonney's life was complex and traumatic He was an erstwhile juvenile delinquent and killer, who became a teenaged, bi-cultural, bi-lingual resistance fighter against the Santa Fe Ring. It fit amazingly into just 21 years.

* * * * * * * * * * * * * * *

In a hot, full-mooned, New Mexico Territory night as bright as day, the 21 year old, homeless youth, Billy Bonney, with trusting stockinged feet, approached the porticoed, two story, Fort Sumner mansion of the Maxwell family, at about a quarter to mid-night.

That day, July 14, 1881, was the third anniversary of the Lincoln County War's start, which had left him branded as the outlaw, "Billy the Kid;" though, to himself, he was a freedom fighter: the last Regulator and that bloody War's only participant to be convicted and sentenced to hanging.

That July night, he intended to cut a dinner steak from the side of beef hanging, at the patrón's generosity, on the mansion's north porch. But first he would check in, as requested, with that patrón and town owner, Peter Maxwell, at his south porch's front corner bedroom.

Asleep in that mansion was Billy's secret lover, Maxwell's sister, Paulita, seventeen, and just pregnant with Billy's child. Also there, lived a never-emancipated Navajo slave, Deluvina; purchased, as a child, by Peter's and Paulita's fabulously wealthy, deceased father, Lucien Bonaparte Maxwell. Then, the family had lived in Cimarron, a New Mexico Territory town in Colfax County, which Lucien had created on his and his wife's almost two million acre land grant; later named after himself.

That was before Lucien was cheated in the sale of that Maxwell Land Grant by unscrupulous lawyers, Thomas Benton Catron and Stephen Benton Elkins, who used their profits to propel their Santa Fe Ring. As Billy knew, that corrupt collusion of public officials still controlled New Mexico Territory. As a hero in the lost Lincoln County War of 1878, Billy had fought that Ring. If he thought about his mortal danger, he knew its source was the Ring. If he thought about injustice, he knew it was promised pardon withheld by past Governor, Lew Wallace.

That July of 1881 day was 2½ months since Billy's jailbreak escape from his scheduled hanging on May 13th. He knew that Lincoln County Sheriff Pat Garrett would be in pursuit. Garrett had captured him on December 22, 1880 at Stinking Springs for his hanging trial. And in Billy's April 28, 1881 escape from Garrett's Lincoln jail, he had shot dead his deputy guards: James Bell and Robert Olinger. Garrett would kill him on sight.

When first tracking Billy in late 1880, Garrett had killed Billy's friends, Tom O'Folliard and Charlie Bowdre - missing Billy only by accident. In fact, at the Stinking Springs capture of Billy and his companions, Garrett killed Bowdre by mistaking him for Billy: the prize for which the Ring had made Garrett a Sheriff.

To be near Paulita, Billy had recklessly chosen return to Fort Sumner, instead of fleeing to Old Mexico, the natural choice given his bi-culturalism. But he relied on the Maxwell family's protection, as well affection of the townspeople he had known since 1878. It would take betrayal to bring his death.

Billy's life had been traumatic. Illegitimate, he was a second son, born on November 23, 1859, in New York City, as William Henry McCarty. Raised in Indiana with his brother, Josie, by his mother, Catherine, he became "Henry Antrim" after she married an Indiana man, William Henry Harrison Antrim, in 1873, after they relocated to New Mexico Territory. Antrim became a miner; and the family lived in Silver City. But he evicted Billy at 14½ to homelessness when she died of tuberculosis in 1874.

In Silver City's school, he learned Spencerian script. He also became fluent in Spanish; and was atypically bi-cultural. By 1975, he was doing petty theft and butcher shop and hotel work.

By September, Silver City Sheriff, Harvey Whitehill jailed him for burglary, and laundry and revolver robbery; his adult accomplice having escaped. Facing ten years hard labor - the Kearny Code statutes making no provision for juveniles - he escaped through the chimney and fled across the border to Arizona Territory's little town of Bonita.

In Arizona, as Henry Antrim, Billy again combined work - as a cook at a small hotel - with crime: stealing military blankets, saddles, and horses; while fatefully developing shootist skills. In 1876, incarcerated at local Fort Grant's guardhouse with his older, thieving accomplice, John Mackie, he escaped through a roof ventilation space. But he defiantly stayed in Bonita, relying on his rustling charges being dropped on a technicality.

On August 17, 1877, Billy's life again changed horrifically. His argument at Bonita's Atkins Cantina with a bullying blacksmith, Frank "Windy" Cahill, escalated to his fatally shooting that unknowably unarmed man. He escaped on a stolen horse. The Coroner's Jury declared him - as Henry Antrim - guilty of homicide, ignoring self-defense. So at 17½, he was almost hanged for murder. He escaped back to New Mexico Territory with an alias: William Henry Bonney - Billy Bonney. "Bonney" was likely his mother's maiden name.

By the next month of September, 1877, Billy attached himself to familiar sociopaths in Jessie Evans's murderous and rustling Santa Fe Ring-affiliated gang.

But Billy had a conversion. He met kind, wealthy Englishman, John Henry Tunstall, a Ring competitor. By the next month, October of 1877, he left Jessie Evans's gang to become Tunstall's ranch hand. Tunstall's men affectionately nick-named him "Kid." Tunstall became the lost father found; even gifting him, under the Homestead Act, with a ranch on the Peñasco River in partnership with another employee, half-Chickasaw Fred Waite.

And Billy had stumbled into a noble cause: ending Ring oppression. His gunman skill now elevated him as a protector of the good. And the town of Lincoln, as well as Tunstall's ranch on the Feliz River, became home. But Billy's tragic destiny was unrelenting. After only 4½ months, this idyllic time ended with Tunstall's Ring assassination.

Lincoln, site of the future Lincoln County War, was oppressed by the Ring through the mercantile monopoly of "The House": a two-story adobe, general store run by its local Ring bosses, Emil Fritz, Lawrence Murphy, James Dolan, and John Riley for secret partner, Ring boss, Thomas Benton Catron. Terror reigned. In 1875, when rancher, Robert Casey, defeated Murphy in a Lincoln election, he was assassinated the same day. Three weeks later, Lincoln's anti-Ring, Mexican community leader, Juan Patrón, was shot by Riley; surviving as a limping cripple.

Hope for change began in late 1876 with arrival in Lincoln of English merchant, John Henry Tunstall; persuaded to settle there by a resident attorney, Alexander McSween, a Ring opponent, but once legal counsel to "The House." Tunstall planned to defeat the Ring by fair mercantile and ranching competition.

But Tunstall's plans coincided with boss Catron's monopolistic thrust into Lincoln County: secretly owning a Pecos River cow camp fronted by "The House," and creating his Carrizozo Land and Cattle Company from dying Murphy's ranch in 1878.

By 1877, Tunstall had built, just a quarter mile northeast of "The House," a general store and bank. And he began two cattle ranches to wrest from "The House" its beef and flour contracts to local Fort Stanton and the Mescalero Indian Reservation. He even exposed Ringite Lincoln County Sheriff William Brady's embezzlement of tax money to buy rustled cattle for Catron's ranches. So Tunstall and McSween got on the Ring's hit list.

Ringmen preferred to kill with guise of legality. So they entangled Tunstall in malicious prosecution of McSween, who was attorney for the estate of "The House's" partner, Emil Fritz, who died intestate in 1874, but had two local siblings and a life insurance policy. In 1877, McSween had successfully litigated to get its $10,000 proceeds from its withholding New York City insurance company, minus $3,000 to the collections firm - leaving $7,000 minus his fees. Knowing that the House faced bankruptcy from Tunstall's competition, and would extort that sum from Fritz's local heirs, he retained it while seeking heirs in Germany. But the Ring used that to make an embezzlement case.

In December of 1877, McSween left on business to St. Louis with his wife and with Tunstall's business associate, the cattle king, John Chisum, then also president of the Tunstall's Lincoln Bank. Ring boss T.B. Catron had McSween arrested as an absconding embezzler. Chisum was also jailed on faked debts in retaliation for backing Tunstall.

On February 4, 1878, McSween had his hearing in Mesilla under Ringite District Judge Warren Bristol (later Billy's hanging judge), who indicted him for embezzling; intending his incarceration and killing in Lincoln by its Ringite Sheriff, William Brady. McSween was saved by Deputy Sheriff, Adolph Barrier, from his Las Vegas, arrest site, who kept him in personal custody.

But Judge Bristol had set the Ring's traps for assassination of McSween and Tunstall. He set McSween's bail at $8,000, with approval only by Ringite District Attorney William Rynerson; who refused all bondsmen, so Sheriff Brady could arrest and kill him. And Bristol attached McSween's property to the sum of $10,000 - falsely deemed the embezzled total - to ensure the money if he was convicted by that April's Grand Jury. Then Bristol lied that Tunstall was in partnership with McSween, so his property should be attached too. And Bristol appointed Brady for the attachments, in the hope that Tunstall and his men would be provoked to violence to justify killing him in faked "self-defense."

But Tunstall merely said that any man's life was worth more than all he owned. Billy, with Tunstall three months, must have been overwhelmed by this novel idealism.

Also, Tunstall was winning. He had bankrupted "The House," making boss Catron emerge its mortgage owner. And McSween was likely to be exonerated by the April Grand Jury. So the Ring acted, using the embezzlement case's property attachment.

On February 18, 1878, when Tunstall was transferring his horses, which were immune to the attachment, from his Feliz River Ranch to Lincoln, Brady called evasion of attachment, and sent his big posse of Deputies, Seven Rivers Ring rustlers, and Jessie Evans's outlaw gang after Tunstall and his men, including Billy. Tunstall, becoming isolated, was murdered, his horse slain; with both corpses mutilated. This martyrdom, coupled with more Ring outrages, triggered the Lincoln County War.

Sheriff Brady refused to arrest the murderers. So anti-Ring Justice of the Peace John "Squire" Wilson issued warrants for his other possemen, appointing Billy and Fred Waite as Deputy Constables under Town Constable Atanacio Martinez for their service. But Brady shielded them by putting Billy, Waite, and Martinez in Lincoln's pit jail. And he confiscated Billy's Winchester '73 carbine - likely a gift from Tunstall.

Next, Wilson defied the Ring by deputizing Tunstall's foreman, Dick Brewer; who, in turn, made Tunstall's men, including now-released Billy, his possemen to serve the warrants. Billy, then 18, was still a lawman.

Meanwhile, Attorney Alexander McSween, in mortal danger from Brady and the Ring, went into hiding with Deputy Sheriff Barrier; mostly in the nearby Hispanic town of San Patricio.

By March of 1878, Dick Brewer's posse had captured Tunstall murder possemen, William "Buck" Morton and Frank Baker, who were shot attempting escape. Billy was in the firing group.

At that point, including "Windy" Cahill, Billy Bonney was now involved in three killings.

The Ring hit back. Ringite Governor Samuel Beach Axtell, by illegal proclamation, removed Wilson's Justice of the Peace powers to retroactively outlaw Dick Brewer's posse; then declared Sheriff Brady to be Lincoln County's only law enforcer.

Enraged, Tunstall's men named themselves "Regulators" after pre-Revolutionary War freedom fighters. Included were Tunstall men - Billy; Fred Waite; John Middleton; Jim "Frenchie" French; farmer cousins, George and Frank Coe; and homesteader, Charlie Bowdre - and a John Chisum cattle detective, Frank MacNab. Dick Brewer was chosen as leader. Only one month after Tunstall died, Billy was being schooled in politics of revolution.

The Ring's next chance to assassinate McSween was April 1, 1878, when he returned to Lincoln for his Grand Jury embezzlement trial. That morning, to save him, Regulators with carbines, and Billy with only a revolver, ambushed Brady and his three deputies from behind an adobe corral wall at Tunstall's store. Brady and Deputy George Hindman died. Recklessly, Billy, with Jim French, ran out to retrieve his confiscated Winchester '73 carbine from Brady's body. Both got leg wounds from firing surviving deputy, Jacob Basil "Billy" Matthews.

Three days later, on April 4, 1878, Deputy Dick Brewer, seeking stolen Tunstall horses, led Billy, John Middleton, Fred Waite, Frank Coe, George Coe, and Charlie Bowdre to Blazer's Mill - a privately owned, way station and grist mill within the Mescalero Indian Reservation. Accidently encountered was Tunstall murder posseman, Andrew "Buckshot" Roberts, for whom they had a warrant. Roberts fired his Winchester carbine at Bowdre, who shot him in the belly. Roberts's bullet had hit Bowdre's belt buckle, ricocheted, and wrenched George Coe's revolver, mutilating his trigger finger. Another Roberts shot hit Middleton, though he survived. Then Roberts killed Brewer, later dying himself from Bowdre's wound. Billy had not fired a shot. And the response to Roberts had been self-defense. But Ring boss Catron, as U.S. Attorney, seized on this killing to file his federal indictment against the Regulators, including Billy, claiming the murder site was the Mescalero Reservation, under federal control.

Billy's murder involvement now totaled six men; though only "Windy" Cahill was demonstrably by his hand.

At the April, 1878, Lincoln County Grand Jury, McSween was exonerated for embezzling. He continued his anti-Ring fight with the Regulators; though John Chisum had reneged on his promise to pay them. And Billy, their hot-headed fearless zealot, was becoming an inspiration.

McSween sought intervention, since murdering a foreigner elicited investigation. He filed a complaint with the British ambassador and to President Rutherford B. Hayes, accusing U.S. officials of murdering Tunstall. So investigating attorney, Frank Warner Angel, was sent by the Departments of the Interior and Justice. Arriving on May 4, 1878, Angel took 39 depositions. Billy, volunteering for one, entered the national stage.

And feeling empowered, Lincoln County Commissioners appointed neutral John Copeland, as Sheriff replacing Brady. He deputized Regulator, Josiah "Doc" Scurlock, to recover Tunstall's horses, stolen by the Ring. Still a lawman, Billy was on Scurlock's posse. And Wilson continued as Justice of the Peace.

Optimism was short-lived. New Regulator leader, Frank MacNab, was killed on April 28, 1878 by Ringite Seven Rivers rustlers. By May 28th, because John Copeland forgot to post his tax collecting bond, Governor Axtell, by another proclamation, removed him, appointing Ringite George Peppin as Sheriff.

War fervor built, with furious Regulators and Mexicans calling themselves "McSweens." Billy's affiliation with local, firebrand youth, Yginio Salazar, and Billy's closeness to Hispanic residents of nearby San Patricio and Picacho, arguably brought them all into the McSween alliance. By April 30, 1878, McSweens were skirmishing with Ring partisans, known as "Murphy-Dolans."

McSween again hid, often in San Patricio. In revenge, Sheriff Peppin, with John Kinney's Ring-rustler gang from Mesilla, on July 3, 1878 conducted a revenge massacre in San Patricio. In response, on July 13th, Billy sent his "Regulator Manifesto" letter to Catron's brother-in-law, then managing his Carrizozo cattle ranch, threatening retaliation against Catron himself.

The Lincoln County War's Battle began the next day: July 14, 1878. McSween, with 60 men - Regulators and Hispanic residents of San Patricio and Picacho - occupied Lincoln. Intending peaceful victory, he kept his wife, Susan, and her sister, Elizabeth Shield, with five children, in his double-winged house; along with the sister's attorney husband's law intern, Harvey Morris.

McSween's men took strategic positions in houses throughout the mile-long town, most of whose inhabitants had fled. When Seven Rivers and John Kinney outlaws joined James Dolan and Sheriff George Peppin, Billy, Yginio Salazar, Tom O'Folliard, José Chávez y Chávez, Ignacio Gonzales, Florencio Chávez, Francisco Zamora, and Vincente Romero rushed to McSween's house, joining guard, Jim French.

Though Ring men occupied foothills south of Lincoln, they were held at bay for five days by shooting McSweens. Regulators were about to win. But McSween did not realize that Fort Stanton's new Commander, Lieutenant Colonel N.A.M. Dudley, was beholden to the Ring. McSween was also reassured by the Posse Comitatus Act, passed the month before in Washington, barring military intervention in civilian disputes.

On July 16th, Commander Dudley sent to Lincoln, for "fact-finding," 9th Cavalry Private Berry Robinson, who was almost hit in the mutual gunfire. Next, on July 18th, James Dolan used Ringite townsman, Saturnino Baca, to lie that his wife and children were at risk from the McSweens.

The next day, July 19th, violating the Posse Comitatus Act, Dudley marched on Lincoln with 39 troops - white infantry, black 9th Cavalry, and white officers - two ambulances; a howitzer cannon; and a Gatling machine-gun. Panicked McSweens - except those in his besieged house - fled north across the Bonito River. Dudley himself threatened McSween with razing his house if any soldier was shot, then left three soldiers there to inhibit its defenders' shooting. He ordered three more to accompany Sheriff Peppin as a shield. Next, by death threats, he forced Justice of the Peace Wilson to write arrest warrants for McSween and his men for attempted murder of Private Robinson to feign reason for his intervention. Then he encamped at the east side of Lincoln.

All this enabled Sheriff Peppin's outlaw posseman set fire to McSween's house. His family was evacuated after Dudley refused McSween's wife's plea to save him.

By nightfall, the burning McSween house, worsened by an exploding gunpowder keg for bullet-making - left all trapped in the east wing. At 9 p.m., escape was made into fire-lit shooting Ringites. Billy saw law intern, Harvey Morris, fatally shot. And he saw Dudley's treasonous crime: three of his white soldiers, imbedded with the assailants, under orders, fired a volley at those escaping. Arguably, they had even killed Morris.

Then shot dead were Alexander McSween, Francisco Zamora, and Vincente Romero. Yginio Salazar survived with two bullets in his back. Symbolizing horror, McSween's starving, yard chickens ate the eyeballs of his corpse. Again was Ring murder and mutilation in Lincoln County to gain treacherous victory.

No one knew that Ring influence extended to Washington, D.C. Investigator Frank Warner Angel, after documenting crimes of Governor S.B. Axtell, U.S. Attorney Catron, and Sheriff Brady's posse, nevertheless concluded falsely in his report - likely under duress - that no U.S. officials were involved in Tunstall's murder. But Catron was forced to resign as U.S. Attorney. And President Hayes scapegoated Governor Axtell, replacing him with Civil War General Lew Wallace. But Angel secretly tried to get justice by writing for Wallace a notebook listing Ringites, and sending him an exposé on the Santa Fe Ring printed in 1877.

Though most Regulators fled the Territory, Billy stayed and carried out the "Regulator Manifesto's" guerrilla rustling with Tom O'Folliard and Charlie Bowdre - who had relocated to Fort Sumner with his wife Manuela. For his outlets, Billy used non-Ringites: Pat Coghlan and Dan Dedrick. Dedrick was a counterfeiter owner of Bosque Grande, a ranch 12 miles south of Fort Sumner. With his two brothers, he also owned a livery stable in White Oaks, a town about 45 miles northwest of Lincoln. Billy also sold rustled horses in Tascosa, Texas; where he wrote his subsequently famous, bill of sale to Henry Hoyt, for an expensive sorrel horse - likely dead Sheriff Brady's. He also got money by gambling. He was again a homeless drifter.

Amidst public hope, on October 1, 1878, Lew Wallace became Governor. A high-achieving elitist, he was the son of an Indiana governor; a Civil War Major General; an Abraham Lincoln murder trial prosecutor; author of best-selling novel, *The Fair God*; and was writing *Ben-Hur A Tale of the Christ*. He had wanted an exotic ambassadorship, like to Turkey, not that backwater position. So, to quickly end Lincoln County "troubles," without confronting the Ring, he issued, a month after arriving, an Amnesty Proclamation; though excluding those indicted. Billy had been indicted for the Brady, Hindman, and Roberts murders.

There were more sources of hope. The new Sheriff, George Kimbrell - having been appointed to replace Sheriff George Peppin, who resigned - was anti-Ring. And McSween's widow, Susan, had brought to Lincoln Attorney Huston Chapman to charge Commander N.A.M. Dudley with the Lincoln County War Battle's murder of her husband and arson of her home.

Those pressures elicited peace overtures by James Dolan, to Susan McSween, then to Billy - proof he was a Ring threat.

The Billy-Dolan peace meeting was fatefully scheduled on the February 18, 1879 anniversary of Tunstall's murder. It ended in calamity. As James Dolan; Billy; Jessie Evans and Jessie's new gang member, Billy Campbell; and Billy's Regulator friends, Tom

O'Folliard and Josiah "Doc" Scurlock, walked Lincoln's dark street after the meeting, they encountered Chapman. Dolan and Campbell fired at point-blank range, killing him, then ignited his clothing. Billy was again an eye-witness.

Chapman's murder forced Governor Wallace to go to Lincoln - after procrastinating for five months after arriving. Once there, he avoided Ring confrontation, using the Ring's own concoction of vague "outlaws and rustlers" causing trouble. The Ring had given him a list of Regulators as "outlaws;" with Billy on it as "the Kid."

Focus on Billy - likely through Dolan - made Wallace put the astronomical reward of $1,000 on his head. Billy responded with his pardon plea, writing on March 13, 1879, to offer Wallace his eye-witness testimony against Chapman's murderers in exchange for annulling his Lincoln County War indictments. It was Billy's bold and calculated risk to negate Ring power over himself.

His articulate pardon plea letter, in his personalized Spencerian script, led to his March 17, 1879, nighttime meeting with Wallace in Justice of the Peace Wilson's Lincoln house. And Billy believed Wallace agreed to his pardon bargain.

To avoid assassination before testifying, Billy requested from Wallace a sham arrest (He had already seen Ring assassinations of John Tunstall, Alexander McSween, Harvey Morris, Francisco Zamora, Vincente Romero, and Huston Chapman.) He was kept in the home of his Lincoln friend, Juan Patrón, the town Jailer. Wallace, housed next door, interviewed him and got his additional letter about Lincoln County War issues.

Billy fulfilled his pardon bargain the next month by testifying in the Grand jury. He got indictments for Chapman's killers, with James Dolan and Billy Campbell for first degree murder, and Jessie Evans as accessory. But Ringite District Attorney William Rynerson, colluding with Judge Bristol, had his trial venue for his indictments switched from Lincoln to Doña Ana County to guarantee his hanging. Still Wallace issued no pardon.

By that April of 1879, Alexander McSween's widow, Susan, retained Attorney Ira Leonard, Chapman's office-mate from Las Vegas, to prosecute Dudley. So Dudley, under likely advisement from Catron, who had represented him for past court martials, got defamatory affidavits to diminish her credibility. And he requested a military Court of Inquiry, where judges would be biased, and where he would be defended by Catron's law firm member, Henry Waldo. And on April 25th, the Ring tried unsuccessfully to assassinate Ira Leonard to stop the case.

Wallace, having removed Dudley as Commander, testified against him in the 1879 Court of Inquiry, though without confronting the Ring. Billy testified also, for his own anti-Ring agenda. He devastatingly reported the three white soldiers firing a volley at him and escaping others: meaning officers; meaning under Dudley's orders; meaning violating the Posse Comitatus Act and justifying court martial, and even hanging. His courage made Ira Leonard take him as client.

By July of 1879, the biased Court of Inquiry exonerated Dudley. And Billy, with no pardon and imminent transport to Mesilla for a hanging trial, exited his bogus jailing.

The Ring recouped. By October of 1879, Susan McSween lost her civil trial against Dudley in Mesilla, to which her venue had been changed by Judge Bristol. That month, Bristol also voided James Dolan's Chapman murder indictment because no witness dared to come for the trial. Dolan, certain of immunity, had even taken over Tunstall's store. Tunstall's ranch property was given by the Ring to Dolan, Riley, and Rynerson; and Billy's Peñasco River ranch went to Jacob Basil "Billy" Matthews, head posseman for Tunstall's murder. And there was a more subtle Ring victory: Lew Wallace's humiliation in the Court of Inquiry made him shun Lincoln County "troubles" and Billy's pardon.

Billy's future killer, Patrick "Pat" Floyd Garrett, had arrived in New Mexico Territory's Fort Sumner in 1878. Born to an Alabama plantation family, relocated to Claiborne Parrish, Louisiana, when 9½ - and Billy was just born - he had even been willed a slave. After the Civil War, he drifted to Texas, where he possibly murdered a black man, before becoming a buffalo hunter from 1876 to 1878 with two partners and a kid named Joe Briscoe. Garrett murdered Briscoe, but claimed self-defense. He never met fellow buffalo hunter, John William Poe; but later, his, Poe's, and Billy's histories would merge on the night of July 14, 1881.

In Fort Sumner, tall Garrett met transient kid, Billy Bonney, gambling at Hargrove's or Beaver Smith's Saloons. They were given townspeople's nicknames, "Big Casino" and "Little Casino," for their poker playing and height discrepancies.

The original Fort Sumner was built in 1865 by the U.S. government on desert flatlands east of the Pecos River for soldiers guarding Bosque Redondo: a concentration camp for 3,500 Navajos and 400 Apaches, until their scandalous starvation caused release of the Navajos to their homeland in 1868; the Apaches having already escaped. In 1870, Fort Sumner was purchased by Lucien Bonaparte Maxwell, one of the Territory's richest men. Converting it into a town around its parade ground, and using its thousands of acres for sheep raising, he settled there with his wife, Luz Beaubien; daughters, including Paulita; and son, Peter. Retained was the military cemetery for his family. Eventually it received Billy's body, to lie beside Pat Garrett's earlier shooting victims: Billy's Regulator pals, Tom O'Folliard and Charlie Bowdre. Maxwell died in 1875, leaving the town to his wife and son, Peter; who became the family's ruin through mismanagement. But when Pat Garrett and Billy Bonney gambled there, Fort Sumner was still thriving.

Before buying Fort Sumner, Maxwell's wealth came from his marriage to Luz Beaubien, an heiress of the almost two million acre Beaubien-Miranda Land Grant, buying its shares from her siblings. In 1870, he then sold it as the Maxwell Land Grant. But he was cheated by his robber baron attorneys, Thomas Benton Catron and Steven Benton Elkins, who resold it for double the money. That profit fortified their Santa Fe Ring, as they enriched themselves with railroads, banks, and mines. Catron eventually owned six million acres - more than anyone in U.S. history. In the Lincoln County War period, he was Billy's lethal enemy, with the Ring branding him as outlaw "Billy the Kid" to kill him. By 1912's New Mexico statehood, Catron was one of the two first senators.

By 1878, before the Lincoln County War, Pat Garrett and Billy Bonney led separate lives, though connected by Fort Sumner's Gutierrez sisters: Juanita, Apolinaria, and Celsa. Billy befriended Celsa, married to her cousin, Saval Gutierrez, a Maxwell sheep herder. Billy's July 14, 1881 death walk would start at their house. Garrett married Juanita, who died soon after of a possible miscarriage. Two years later, in 1880, he married Apolinaria, with whom he would father eight children. It was a double marriage with his Fort Sumner, best friend, Maxwell's foreman, Barney Mason, later a spy assisting Garrett's capture of Billy.

In 1878, Garrett had been desperate for employment. At Fort Sumner, he drove a wagon for Peter Maxwell; helped a local hog raiser, Thomas "Kip" McKinney; and bartended at Hargrove's Saloon. Then came 1880 and the opportunity of his life. For Lincoln County's November election, the Ring needed a compatible Sheriff. To qualify, Garrett moved with his wife, Apolinaria, to that county's town of Roswell; adding, as a boarder, an unemployed journalist named Ashmun "Ash" Upson. In 1882, Upson would ghostwrite Garrett's book about killing Billy the Kid.

By 1880, the Ring's outlaw myth propaganda had advertised Billy's gunman reputation. That almost succeeded in his killing on January 3, 1880 at Fort Sumner's Hargrove's Saloon. A Texan bounty hunter named Joe Grant tried to shoot him in the back. Saved by Grant's gun's misfiring, Billy retaliated fatally. Obvious self-defense, that killing was not legally pursued.

Billy was now linked to murders of seven men: Frank "Windy" Cahill, William Brady, George Hindman, Andrew "Buckshot" Roberts, William "Buck" Morton, Frank Baker, and Joe Grant.

That 1880, when his now-famous tintype photograph was taken in Fort Sumner, Billy may have heard first mythological whispers of his outlawry. The Ring was setting its legal trap for eliminating him. In addition to murderer and rustler, he would be accused of connection to counterfeiters to bring in the Secret Service, a branch of the U.S. Treasury Department, with funding to track him down. Catron's Lincoln County agent, James Dolan, initiated the investigation by reporting receipt of a counterfeit $100 bill in his Lincoln store. And Catron or Elkins were the likely contact to Secret Service Chief, James Brooks.

By September 11, 1880, Secret Service Special Operative Azariah Wild was sent to Lincoln. Dolan's received counterfeit bill, falsely linked to Billy, actually came from a Billy Wilson and a Tom Cooper, employed by the counterfeiter, Dan Dedrick. But they occasionally rustled with Billy and his regulars: Tom O'Folliard, Charlie Bowdre, and a "Dirty Dave" Rudabaugh.

Gullible Operative Azariah Wild was led to believe by James Dolan and Catron's brother-in-law, Edgar Walz - then managing Catron's Carrizozo cattle ranch - that Billy was in the country's largest counterfeiting and rustling gang. In December of 1880, the *New York Sun*, with leaked Wild reports, featured Ring propaganda of Billy in: "Outlaws of New Mexico. The Exploits of a band headed by a New York Youth, War Against a Gang of Cattle Thieves, Murderers, and Counterfeiters." He was alias "the Kid." The Ring had launched his national outlaw myth.

The Ring's plot almost backfired when Wild was told by Attorney Ira Leonard that his client, Billy Bonney, would testify against the counterfeiters. On October 8, 1880, Wild wrote in his daily report to Chief James Brooks that he himself would arrange a pardon for Billy in exchange for that testimony. But Wild confided that pardon plan to his Ringite minders, who convinced him that Billy, staying in Fort Sumner, was the gang's leader! In his report for October 14, 1880, Wild wrote that he intended to arrest him. But Billy was cautious. He held up the stagecoach with Wild's mail, read that report, and avoided the meeting with Leonard and Wild. But another pardon was lost.

The Ring was determined to eliminate Billy. The next option was getting a Lincoln County Sheriff willing do it. The current Sheriff, George Kimbrell, who had assisted in Billy's sham arrest, was a McSween-side sympathizer. The Ring chose Pat Garrett. Secretly, Wild worked with him to form posses to capture Billy and his "rustler-counterfeiter gang;" while, for the upcoming sheriffs election, Garrett was advertised as a law-and-order man to new gold-rush settlers in White Oaks, unaware of Lincoln County War issues, but a third of Lincoln County's voters.

In the November 2, 1880 election, Pat Garrett got 358 votes to Kimbrell's 141. Wild, convinced by his Ring contacts that Kimbrell protected the "Kid gang," also gave Garrett immediate Territorial power for the capture by appointing him Deputy U.S. Marshall. Unaware, Billy would have wrongly thought that Garret's authority was limited to Lincoln County, not Fort Sumner's San Miguel County, where he stayed.

And unaware of his locally publicized "outlawry," Billy still brought stolen horses to the Dedrick's White Oaks livery. On November 22, 1880, a White Oaks posse ambushed him, Tom O'Folliard, Billy Wilson, Tom Pickett, and "Dirty" Dave Rudabaugh at nearby Coyote Spring, shooting dead two of their horses before Billy's group escaped. Six days later, that posse attacked them again at the way station ranch of "Whiskey" Jim Greathouse, 45 miles northeast of White Oaks; accidentally killing one of their own men, Jim Carlyle, but blaming Billy.

That accusation prompted Billy's only letter of 1880 to Governor Lew Wallace. On December 12th, he wrote, denying his outlawry and murdering of Jim Carlyle. He even described his Robin Hood role of seeking justice for the downtrodden. Wallace never answered. Instead, on December 22, 1880, he placed a Las Vegas *Daily Gazette* notice: "Billy the Kid: $500 Reward." He would repeat it in the *Daily New Mexican* on May 3, 1881, after Billy's jailbreak. His betrayal of the pardon bargain was complete.

By December of 1880, dreadful days began for Billy. U.S. Marshall Pat Garrett, backed by Azariah Wild, had assembled Texan posses to ride after Billy, since New Mexicans, to whom he was an anti-Ring hero, refused. Garrett's first ambush was on December 19, 1880, when Billy, Tom O'Folliard, Charlie Bowdre, Billy Wilson, Tom Pickett, and Dave Rudabaugh rode into Fort Sumner. O'Folliard was shot dead. The rest escaped.

Billy's group tried to flee the Territory in a snowstorm; but stopped, about 16 miles from Fort Sumner, on December 21, 1880, at a rock-walled, windowless, shepherds' line cabin at Stinking Springs. There Garrett ambushed them the next morning, killing Charlie Bowdre, whom he mistook for Billy, his intended victim. The rest surrendered. It would be seven months before Garrett succeeded in his mission to kill Billy.

Garrett transported his prisoners by train, via Las Vegas, New Mexico, to the Santa Fe jail. Billy remained there from December 27, 1880 to March 28, 1881, because the Ring awaited completion of the railroad to Mesilla to avoid a rescue. But he almost escaped by tunneling out with fellow prisoners.

From his cell, Billy wrote four unanswered letters to Wallace, in 1881, pleading for his pardon: writing on March 4th: "*I have done everything that I promised you I would, and you have done nothing that you promised me.*" On March 2nd, he had threatened: "*I have some letters which date back two years and there are Parties who are very anxious to get them but I will not dispose of them until I see you.*" Wallace never got over that audacity or his own guilt, reworking the pardon obsessively till the end of his life in vindictive fictionalized articles on the outlaw "Billy the Kid."

Billy's first Mesilla murder trial, under Ringite Judge Warren Bristol, began on March 30, 1881, with jurors unaware of Lincoln County War's issues, and without any Lincolnites daring to be witnesses for his defense. Attorney Ira Leonard represented him for past U.S. Attorney Catron's June 21, 1878 federal indictment, Case Number 411, the United States versus Charles Bowdre, Josiah Scurlock, Henry Brown, William Bonney alias Henry Antrim alias the Kid, John Middleton, Steven Stevens, John Scroggins, Frederick Waite, and George Coe for the murder of Andrew "Buckshot" Roberts. It was first because the Ringites likely considered it unbeatable.

But, surprising everyone, Leonard got it quashed as invalid, since the federal government had no jurisdiction over Blazer's Mill, the murder site; because private property, like it, was under Territorial jurisdiction. Its being surrounded by the federally-controlled Mescalero Reservation was irrelevant.

Remaining were only the Sheriff William Brady and Deputy George Hindman Territorial indictments; and, though Billy been firing in the group of Regulators, he had only a revolver lacking accurate range.

But, suddenly, Ira Leonard withdrew, likely after a Ring threat. That was disastrous. Billy got Ring-biased, court appointed attorney, Albert Jennings Fountain, who considered him an outlaw; along with co-counsel John D. Bail, a Ringite Catron friend.

On April 8th and 9th of 1881, was Billy's Brady murder trial. His Spanish-speaking jury, given no translator, heard only prosecution witnesses - including James Dolan. After Judge Bristol's biased instructions (with translator) made Billy's mere presence equal to firing the fatal shot, the jury found him guilty of first degree murder; its sole punishment being hanging. On April 13th, Judge Bristol set Billy's hanging date for May 13th, to limit time for appeal. Billy was to be hanged in Lincoln by its Sheriff, Pat Garrett.

From the Mesilla jail, Billy wrote to Attorney Edgar Caypless - conducting his replevin case against Stinking Springs posseman, Frank Stewart for stealing his racing mare at Stinking Springs - hoping to get money from her sale to pay for an appeal.

Ironically, the new Lincoln jail, where Billy was incarcerated to await hanging, was in the past "House," which Catron had sold to Lincoln County for its courthouse, with second floor as jail.

On April 21, 1881, Billy arrived to Sheriff Garrett's custody. For his 24 hour guard, Garrett deputized a White Oaks man, James Bell, and a Seven Rivers man, Bob Olinger. Garrett's further precaution was shackling Billy at wrists and ankles, with securing to a floor ring - all to guarantee his hanging death.

But on April 28th, with Garrett away collecting White Oaks's taxes, Billy escaped. He used a revolver from an accomplice's putting it in the outhouse, or by seizing Bell's. A likely accessory was caretaker, Gottfried Gauss: Tunstall's past cook, and witness to the Ring's Lincoln County War atrocities. Billy shot Bell dead as the man fled down the jail's stairway to sound alarm.

Deputy Bob Olinger, across the street at the Wortley Hotel with jail prisoners, either heard the shot or was directed to the ambush. Billy was at the second-floor window, and killed him with his own Whitney double-barrel shotgun.

Billy then spent hours using a miner's pick, supplied by Gauss, to break his leg chain to enable riding; while gathered loyalist Lincoln townspeople, in passive resistance, did nothing to stop him. He finally rode away on a pony supplied by Gauss.

As of that April 28, 1881 escape, Billy was involved in the murder of nine men; James Bell and Robert Olinger adding to Frank "Windy" Cahill and Joe Grant as Billy's only provable killings.

Of the dead, Billy would have said that that Cahill's and Grant's killings were in self-defense; that he was a legal posseman at the group shooting of escaping arrested Tunstall murderers, William "Buck" Morton and Frank Baker; that his gun lacked range to hit Sheriff William Brady or Deputy George Hindman, and their killings by the Regulators were to save Alexander McSween from murder by them; that he had not shot Andrew "Buckshot" Roberts, a Tunstall murderer and murderer of Dick Brewer firing at his group, and killed solely by Charlie Bowdre in self defense; and that Deputy James Bell, after refusing to be tied, had tried to run for help, so was killed to save himself from unjust hanging (and Bell had been on the White Oaks posse, and possibly killed Jim Carlyle, then falsely accused him).

Only Seven Rivers rustler, Bob Olinger, would have been admittedly hated as being in each Lincoln County War period crime - Tunstall's murder, Frank MacNab's ambush murder, and the War's skirmishes and battle. Billy's rage was so great, that he smashed apart Olinger's shotgun to throw it on his corpse, delaying his own escape.

That count of nine killed men - with only four certain - remained as Billy's final true tally.

Billy's escape route was across the Capitan Mountains to the Las Tablas home of his friend, Yginio Salazar. He next went south, possibly intending to go to Old Mexico, and visited friendly rancher, John Meadows. But he reversed, going northeast to Fort Sumner and Paulita, where he hid in the Maxwell's sheep camps, confident of protection by the Maxwells and townspeople. He was unaware that Pat Garrett was paying Maxwell's past foreman, Barney Mason, as a spy, through Secret Service Operative Azariah Wild.

Garrett's two deputies for the pursuit of Billy to Fort Sumner - John William Poe and Thomas "Kip" McKinney - did not know Billy. Poe, a buffalo hunter, past Deputy U.S. Marshall in Texas, cattle detective, and recent White Oaks settler, had met Garrett during the Wild-assisted tracking of the "Kid gang." McKinney knew Garrett from their 1878, hog farming days.

Once in Fort Sumner, Garrett, doubting Billy's presence as too foolhardy, was urged by Poe to stay. On July 14, 1881, Poe, a stranger to the townspeople, did recognizance of the town; and also checked with Sunnyside postmaster, Milnor Rudulph, seven miles to its north. Poe became convinced Billy was nearby. That night, he, Garrett, and McKinney planned an ambush in Peter Maxwell's bedroom, with Maxwell as traitor. Unknown accomplices likely directed Billy to Maxwell's bedroom, where Garrett waited, with Poe and McKinney outside to kill Billy if he managed to escape through the door to the porch.

Near midnight, Billy proceeded from the converted barracks house of Celsa and Saval Gutierrez, carrying their butcher knife across the parade ground to cut a dinner steak in light of the almost-full huge moon, hovering at the horizon. But he first went toward Maxwell's bedroom. Seeing Poe, he asked in Spanish who he was, then entered.

Inside, to Maxwell, in bed as decoy, Billy asked again in Spanish who was there, possibly sensing Garrett in the darkness. Garrett fired. Next, he fired wild. But the first shot was fatal. In terror, Maxwell ran out, almost getting shot by Poe, primed for back-up killing. Then Garrett returned to the room, with Poe and McKinney, and made sure Billy was dead.

The townspeople held a night vigil for Billy in their carpenter's shop. The Coroner's Jury, the next day on July 15, 1881, had as President, Postmaster Milnor Rudulph, a loyal Ringite who had helped take over the Legislature in 1872 to block anti-Ring bills in the Legislature Revolt. His influence apparently led Alejandro Segura to write the Coroner's Jury Report with conclusion that the frightened juryman signed: "*[O]ur verdict is that the deed of said Garrett was justifiable homicide and we are unanimous in the opinion that the gratitude of all the community is due to the said Garrett for his deed and he is worthy of being rewarded.*"

Ring terrorism was now complete. Silence fell for a generation before any dared contradict the Santa Fe Ring's outlaw mythology of Billy the Kid, crystallized in Billy Bonney's Coroner's Jury Report.

CHAPTER 5 BILLY BONNEY IN HIS OWN WORDS

EVOLUTION OF THE RING'S DANGEROUS OPPONENT

Billy Bonney began life as illegitimate and named Henry McCarty. By 13½, with his mother's marriage, he became a Silver City, New Mexico Territory, violent tempered, juvenile delinquent, now named Henry Antrim. Finally jailed there in 1875 for burglary and robbery, he escaped to Arizona Territory, where his robbing and shooting obsession escalated to military horse and tack theft, culminating in a murder and escape back to New Mexico Territory in 1877 at 17. There he devised the alias Billy Bonney and joined the Jessie Evans outlaw gang, being identified in one of its stage hold-ups. He definitely lived the criminal life.

But his fate was surprising. Riding with the Evans gang only a month, in October of 1877, he was hired by merchant-rancher John Tunstall, an honorable idealist, and Santa Fe Ring opponent. Exposure to goodness and a cause was transforming. And Tunstall's horrific Ring assignation in less than five months, on February 18, 1878, catalyzed Billy's conversion to anti-Ring political zealot. This was enhanced by his bi-cultural identification with the Ring-oppressed Hispanic population.

His violent nature became anti-Ring zeal in the Regulator movement of Tunstall's other employees and sympathetic Lincoln residents. For the 3 years, 4 months, and 26 days remaining to him, he unwaveringly waged his own rebellion against the Ring, preserved in his brave and brilliant writings and interviews.

It was obvious to the Ring that he had to be eliminated. But even with its outlaw propaganda of Billy the Kid, and its success in killing him, the Ring failed. His dramatic end, confirmed by the Coroner's Jury Report, only guaranteed that some day the truth would emerge as to his freedom fighting cause.

AFFIDAVIT AND DEPUTIZING

A key factor Billy Bonney's history was his lawman status in pursuing John Tunstall's killers. On February 19, 1878, the day after Tunstall's murder, Billy and Tunstall's foreman, Dick Brewer, gave eye-witness affidavits to Lincoln Justice of the Peace John "Squire" Wilson, to enable his writing arrest warrants. It is the first time Billy's voice is publicly heard. He named Tunstall's killers as Sheriff Brady's possemen: "*James J. Dolan, Frank Baker, Jessie Evans, George Davis, A.H. Mills, W.S. Morton, [William] Moore, George Hindman, [Frank] Rivers, Pantaleon Gallegos, divers other persons unknown.*" It yielded Wilson's February 19th legal arrest warrants, stating:

Territory of New Mexico)
County of Lincoln)

Be it remembered that before the undersigned Justice of the Peace in and for the County and Territory aforesaid, personally came R.M. Brewer & ***W. Bonney*** *who being duly sworn according to law deposeth & saith that at the County and Territory aforesaid on the 18th day of February 1878 in and upon the [presence] of J.H. Tunstall, Robt A. Widenman[n], R.M. Brewer,* ***William Boney*** *[sic] & John Middleton, then and there in the Peace of the Territory an assault was made with divers deadly weapons to wit with Winchester Guns and Colts Revolvers, and divers other deadly weapons by James J. Dolan, Frank Baker, Jessie Evans, George Davis, A.H. Mills, W.S. Morton, [omitted first name] Moore, George Hindman, [Frank] Rivers, Pantaleon Gallegos, divers other persons unknown and did then and there as affiant believes wounded & killed J.H. Tunstall contrary to the statute in such case made and provided against the Peace & dignity of the Territory.*

R.M. Brewer
William Bonney.

After Sheriff Brady refused to serve them, Wilson concluded that "*there being then and there no officers to serve such warrant the undersigned as directed by law, in such cases specially empowered Richard H. Brewer to serve the same endorsing such deputation on said last mentioned warrant.*" Wilson wrote:

The Territory of New Mexico)
County of Lincoln)

I, John B. Wilson justice of the Peace in and for precinct № 1 Lincoln County, New Mexico, do hereby certify that on or about the 19th day of February 1878 ***W. Boney*** *[sic] and R.M. Brewer filed in my office affidavits charging John [James] J. Dolan, J. Conovair, Frank Baker, Jessie Evans, Tom Hill, George Davis, A. [Andrew] L. ["Buckshot"] Roberts, P. [Panteleon] Gallegos, T. Green, J. Awly, A.H. Mills, "Dutch Charley" proper name unknown, R.W. Beckwith, William Morton, [Deputy] George Hindman, J.B. Matthews and others with having murdered and killed one John H. Tunstall at the said County of Lincoln on or about the 18th day of February 1878, that on or about the 20th day of Feby 1878, I secured warrants on said affidavits for the arrest of the parties above named and directed the same to the Constable of for precinct № one in said County to wit: Atanacio Martines [Martinez].*

That on or about the 20th day of Feby 1878 said warrant was returned "not served" that on or about the said last mentioned day the undersigned issued an alias warrant for the apprehension of the above named persons, and there being then and there no officers to serve such warrant the undersigned as directed by law, in such cases specially empowered Richard H. Brewer to serve the same endorsing such deputation on said last mentioned warrant.

In testimony whereof I have hereinto set my hand at Lincoln Precinct № 1 Lincoln County, N. Mexico this 31st day of August 1878.

John Wilson, Justice of the Peace

This enabled Special Constable Dick Brewer to deputize Billy and Fred Waite as Deputy Constables under Lincoln Town Constable Atanacio Martinez to serve the warrants. To block the arresting, Sheriff William Brady then illegally locked them in Lincoln's pit jail, and confiscated Billy's Winchester '73 carbine.

DEPOSITION TO FRANK WARNER ANGEL

On June 8, 1878, Billy gave his eloquent eye-witness deposition, with characteristic meticulous attention to detail, on John Tunstall's murder, to Investigator for the Departments of Justice and the Interior, Frank Warner Angel, with Lincoln

Justice of the Peace John "Squire" Wilson, as witness. In it, Billy added perspective on Tunstall's generosity by referencing that Tunstall had gifted him and fellow employee, Fred Waite, a Peñasco River ranch. He also made clear the injustice of the legal case against Tunstall; and that Tunstall's horses, being herded back to Lincoln by him and other employees, were exempted from its property attachments. And he made real the terrorist act of the murder.

Also, Billy proved his Regulator fervor to attain justice. He was risking his life by coming to Lincoln to give that deposition after Ringite Governor Samuel Beach Axtell's illegal proclamation outlawing the Regulators, and after receiving his own April Grand Jury indictments for Regulator killings in the Lincoln County War. He then signed the document, as witnessed by Angel and Wilson; which Angel's transcriptionist recorded as follows:

Territory of New Mexico)
County of Lincoln)
)

William H. Bonney was duly sworn, deposand says that he is a resident of said county, that on the 11th day of February A.D. 1878 he in company with Robt. A. Widenmann and Fred T. Waite went to the ranch of J. H. Tunstall on the Rio Feliz, that ***he and said Fred T. Waite at the time intended to go to the Rio Peñasco to take up a ranch*** *for the purpose of farming. That the cattle on the ranch of said J. H. Tunstall were throughout the County of Lincoln, known to be the property of said Tunstall; that on the 13th of February A.D. 1878 one J.B. Matthews claiming to be a Deputy Sheriff came to the ranch of said J.H. Tunstall in company with Jesse Evans, Frank Baker, Tom Hill and [Frank] Rivers, known outlaws who had been confined to the Lincoln County jail and had succeeded in making their escape, John Hurley, George Hindman, [Andrew] Roberts and an Indian aka Ponceаro the latter said to be the murderer of Benaito Cruz, for the arrest of murderers of whom (Benaito Cruz) the Governor of this Territory offers a reward of $500. Before the arrival of said J.B. Matthews, deputy Sheriff, and his posse, having been informed that said deputy sheriff and posse were going to round up all the cattle and drive them off and kill the persons at the ranch, the persons at the ranch cut portholes into the walls of the house and filled sacks with earth, so that they, the persons at the ranch,* *should they be attacked or murder attempted, could defend themselves, this course being thought necessary* ***as the sheriffs posse was composed of murderers, outlaws, and desperate characters none of whom has any interest at stake in the County, nor being residents of said County****. That said Matthews when within about 50 yards of the house was called to stop and advance alone and state his business, that said Matthews after arriving at the ranch said that he had come to attach the cattle and property of A.A McSween, that* ***said Matthews was informed that A.A. McSween had no cattle or property there****, but that if he had he, said Matthews could take it. That said Matthews said that he thought some of the cattle belonging to R. M. Brewer whose cattle were also at the ranch of J.H. Tunstall, belonged to A.A. McSween, that said Matthews was told by said Brewer that he Matthews could round up the cattle and that he, Brewer, would help him. That said Matthews said that he would go back to Lincoln to get new instructions and if he came back to the ranch he would come back with one man. That said Matthews and his posse were then invited by R.M. Brewer to come to the house to get something to eat.*

Deponent further states that Robert A. Widenmann told R.M. Brewer and the others at the ranch, that he was going to arrest Frank Baker, Jesse Evans and Tom Hill said Widenmann having warrants for them. That said Widenmann was told by Brewer and the others at the ranch that the arrest could not be made because if it was made they, all the persons at the ranch would be killed and murdered by J.J. Dolan and their party. That said Evans advanced upon said Widenmann, said Evans swinging his gun and catching it cocked and pointed directly at said Widenmann. That said Jesse Evans asked said Widenmann whether he Widenmann, was hunting for him, Evans, to which Widenmann answered that if he was looking for him, he, Evans, would find it out. Evans also asked Widenmann whether he had a warrant for him; Widenmann answered that it was his (Widenmann's) business. Evans told Widenmann, that if he ever came to arrest him (Evans) he, Evans would pick Widenmann as the first man to shoot at, to which Widenmann answered that that was all right, that two could play at that game. That during the talking Frank Baker stood near said Widenmann, swinging his pistol on his finger, catching it full cocked pointed at said Widenmann.

The persons at the ranch were R. M. Brewer, John Middleton, G. Gayss [Gauss], M. Martz, R.A. Widenmann, Henry Brown, F.T.

Waite, Wm McClosky and this deponent. J.B. Matthews after eating started for Lincoln with John Hurley and Ponceano the rest of the party or posse saying they were going to the Rio Peñasco. Deponent started to Lincoln with Robert A. Widenmann and F.T. Waite and arrived at Lincoln the same evening and again left Lincoln on the next day, February the 14th in company with the above named persons, having heard that said Matthews was going back to the ranch of said J.H. Tunstall with a large party of men to take the cattle and deponent and Widenmann and Waite arrived at said ranch the same day.

Deponent states that on the road to Lincoln he heard said Matthews ask said Widenmann whether any resistance would be offered if he Matthews returned to take the cattle, to which said Widenmann answered that no resistance would be offered if the cattle were left at the ranch but if an attempt was made to drive the cattle to the Indian Agency and kill them for beef as he, said Matthews had been heard to say would be done, he, said Widenmann, would do all in his power to prevent this.

Deponent further says that on the night of the 17th of February A.D. 1878 J.H. Tunstall arrived at the ranch and informed all persons there that reliable information had reached him that J.B. Matthews was gathering a large party of outlaws and desperados as a posse and the said posse was coming to the ranch, the Mexicans in the party to gather up the cattle and the balance of the party to kill the persons at the ranch. It was thereupon decided that all persons at the ranch excepting G. Gauss, were to leave and Wm McClosky was that night sent to the Rio Peñasco to inform the posse who were camped there, that they could come over and round up the cattle, count them and leave a man there to take care of them and that Mr. Tunstall would also leave a man there to help round up and count the cattle and help take care of them, and said McClosky was also ordered to go to Martin Martz, who had left Tunstalls ranch when deponent, Widenmann and Waite returned to the town of Lincoln on the 13th of February and asked him said Martz to come to the ranch of said Tunstall and aid the sheriffs posse in rounding up and counting the cattle and to stay at the ranch and take care of the cattle.

Deponent left the ranch of said Tunstall in company with J.H. Tunstall, R.A. Widenmann, R.M. Brewer, John Middleton, F.T. Waite, said Tunstall, Widenmann, Brewer, Middleton and deponent driving the loose horses, Waite driving the wagon. Said Waite took the road for Lincoln with the wagon, the rest of the party taking the trail with the horses. ***Deponent says that all the horses which he and the party were driving, excepting 3 had been released by sheriff Brady at Lincoln that one of these 3 horses belonged to R.M. Brewer, and the other was traded by Brewer to Tunstall for one of the released horses.***

Deponent further says, that when he and the party has traveled to within about 3 miles from the Rio Ruidoso he and John Middleton were in drag in the rear of the balance of the party as just upon reaching the brow of a hill they saw a large party of men coming towards them from the rear at full speed and that he and Middleton at once rode forward to inform the balance of the party of the fact. Deponent had not more than barely reached Brewer and Widenmann who were some 200 or 300 yards to the left of the trail when the attacking party cleared the brow of the hill and commenced firing at him, Widenmann and Brewer. Deponent, Widenmann and Brewer rode over a hill towards another which was covered with large rocks and trees in order to defend themselves and make a stand. But the attacking party, undoubtedly seeing Tunstall, left off pursuing deponent and the two with him and turned back at the caño in which the trail was. Shortly afterwards we heard two or three separate and distinct shots and the remark was then made by Middleton that they, the attacking party must have killed Tunstall. Middleton had in the meantime joined deponent and Widenmann and Brewer. Deponent then made the rest of his way to Lincoln in company with Robt. A. Widenmann, Brewer, Waite and Middleton stopping on the Rio Ruidoso in order to get men to look for the body of J.H. Tunstall.

Deponent further says that neither he nor any of the party fired off either rifle or pistol and that neither he nor the parties with him fired a shot.

William H. Bonney

Sworn and subscribed before me this eighth day of June A.D. 1878.

John B. Wilson
Justice of the Peace

"REGULATOR MANIFESTO"

On July 3, 1878, during the multiple skirmishes in the Lincoln County War leading to the final Battle, there occurred a retaliatory Santa Fe Ring massacre at anti-Ring San Patricio: the Hispanic community which was like bi-cultural Billy's second home. On July 13, 1878, ten days after it, Billy took action: challenging the Ring, in what I named the "Regulator Manifesto." It is the anti-Ring declaration of the Lincoln County War Battle, starting the next day. It is signed only "*Regulator*."

Existing as a copy, it was first attributed to Charles Bowdre by early historian, Maurice Garland Fulton, who claimed implausibly that its recipient, Ring head, T.B. Catron's, brother-in-law, Edgar Walz, recognized Bowdre's handwriting. But I believe it was Billy's production, either dictated to Bowdre, or wrongly attributed to him by Walz. And it heralds Billy's future retaliative guerrilla rustling from Ringites, like Catron and Walz. It stated:

In Camp, July 13, 1878.

Mr. Walz. Sir: - We are all aware that your brother-in-law, T.B. Catron sustains the Murphy-Kinney party, and take this method of informing you that if any property belonging to the residents of this county is stolen or destroyed, Mr. Catron's property will be dealt with as nearly as can be in the way in which the party he sustains deals with the property stolen or destroyed by them.

We returned Mr. Thornton the horses we took for the purpose of keeping the Murphy crowd from pursuing us with the promise that these horses should not again be used for that purpose. Now we know that the Tunstall estate cattle are pledged to Kinney and party. If they are taken, a similar number will be taken from your brother [in-law, Catron]. It is our object and efforts to protect property, but the man who plans destruction shall have destruction measured on him. Steal from the poorest or richest American or Mexican, and the full measure of the injury you do, shall be visited upon the property of Mr. Catron. This murderous band is harbored by you as your guest, and with the consent of Catron occupies your property.

Regulator

HOYT BILL OF SALE

After the lost Lincoln County War, refusing to leave the Territory, like most Regulators, Billy earned money by gambling and retaliatory rustling from Ringites, conforming to his July 13, 1878 "Regulator Manifesto." Thus, he would not have considered himself a common rustler - as he later labeled Seven Rivers rustlers to Governor Lew Wallace in a March 23, 1879 interview.

Billy used non-Ring outlets for stock, and sold horses himself in Tascosa, Texas. There, on October 24, 1878, he "sold" to Dr. Henry Hoyt a sorrel horse - likely Sheriff William Brady's Dandy Dick stolen from Catron's Carrizozo ranch. He priced it high for its bill of sale, which demonstrated legalese he had possibly learned from Alexander McSween; and with proper witnessing by saloon owners, James E. McMasters and George J. Howard. That skill would be used in 132 days to write his first pardon plea letter to Governor Lew Wallace.

Billy impressed Hoyt, so he kept it. On April 27, 1929, he sent its copy to Wallace's grandson, Lew Wallace Jr.; writing: "I am one of the very few men living who was well acquainted with that famous outlaw 'Billy the Kid' and for many years supposed I had the only specimen of his handwriting in existence [until learning about the Lew Wallace letters], **a Bill of Sale for a horse he presented me with, and wrote out himself**, to protect me should my ownership ever be questioned, a very important matter in that part of the world at that period. This paper I have preserved all these years."

The Hoyt Bill of Sale stated:

Tascoso Texas
Thursday Oct 24th 1878

Know all persons by these presents that I do hereby Sell and deliver to Henry F. Hoyt one Sorrel Horse Branded BB on left hip and other indistinct Branded on Shoulders for the sum of Seventyfive $ dollars in hand received
W HBonney

Witness
Jas. E. McMasters
Geo. J. Howard

LETTER OF MARCH 13, 1879 TO LEW WALLACE

On approximately March 13, 1879, Billy began his pardon plea to Governor Lew Wallace, offering eye-witness testimony against Ringite murderers of Attorney Huston Chapman on February 18, 1879 in an exchange, since Wallace's November 13, 1878 Amnesty Proclamation had excluded those indicted, like him. Noteworthy is that Billy asked to "*annuly*" - meaning annul - his indictments for the murders of William Brady, George Hindman, and Andrew "Buckshot" Roberts. That was correct: a pardon is post-sentencing; annulment is before. He wrote:

To his Excellency the Governor.
General Lew. Wallace
Dear Sir I have heard that You will give one thousand $ dollars for my body which as I can understand it means alive as a witness. I know it is as a witness against those that murdered Mr. Chapman. if it was so as that I could appear at Court, I could give the desired information. but I have indictments against me for things that happened in the late Lincoln County War and am afraid to give up because my Enimies would Kill me. the day Mr. Chapman was murderded I was in Lincoln, at the request of good citizens to meet Mr. J.J. Dolan to meet as Friends. So as to be able to lay aside our arms and go to Work. I was present when Mr. Chapman was murderded and know who did it and if it were not for these indictments I would have made it clear before now. if it is in your power to Annully those indictments I hope you will do so so as to give me a chance to explain. please send me an annser telling me what you can do. You can send annser by bearer.

I have no wish to fight any more indeed I have not raised an arm since Your proclamation. as to my Character I refer to any of the Citizens, for the majority of them are my Friends and have been helping me all they could. I am called Kid Antrim but Antrim is my stepfathers name.

Waiting for an annser I remain
Your Obedient Servant
W.H. Bonney

LETTER OF MARCH 20, 1879 TO "SQUIRE" WILSON

Billy began a flurry of March 20, 1879 letters by writing to Justice of the Peace John "Squire" Wilson to check with Lew Wallace about his planned feigned arrest for his pardon bargain, since many of the men he was supposed to testify against for the Huston Chapman murder had escaped from their Fort Stanton imprisonment. He wrote from his safe-haven:

San Patricio

Thursday 20th 1879

Friend Wilson.

Please tell You know who that I do not know what to do, now as those Prisoners have escaped. So send word by bearer. a note through You it may be he has made different arrangements if not and he still wants it the same to Send :William Hudgins [Hudgens]: as Deputy, to the Junction tomorrow at three Oclock with some men you know to be all right. Send a note telling me what to do

WHBonney

P.S. do not send Soldiers

LETTER OF MARCH 20, 1879 TO LEW WALLACE

Wallace responded to Wilson with arrangements, and enclosed a vague "*note*" for Billy about their "*understanding.*" Billy responded with a precautionary scenario for his sham arrest:

San Patricio

Lincoln County

Thursday 20th 1879

General. Lew. Wallace:

Sir. I will keep the appointment I made. but be Sure and have men come that You can depend on I am not afraid to die like a man fighting but

I would not like to be killed like a dog unarmed. tell Kimbal [Kimbrell] to let his men be placed around the house and for him to come in alone: and he can arrest us. all I am afraid of is that in the Fort we might be poisoned or killed through a window at night. but You can arrange that all right. tell the Commanding Officer to watch)Let Goodwin(he would not hesitate to do anything there Will be danger on the road of Somebody Waylaying us to kill us on the road to the Fort. You will never catch those fellows on the road Watch Fritzes. Captain Bacas ranch and the Brewery they Will either go to Seven Rivers or to Jicarillo Mountains they will stay around close untill the scouting parties come in. give a spy a pair of glasses and let him get on the mountain back of Fritzes and watch and if they are there there will be provisions carried to them. it is not my place to advise you, but I am anxious to have them caught, and perhaps know how men hide from Soldiers, better than you. please excuse me for having so much to say

and I still remain Yours Truly
W H. Bonney

P.S.
I have changed my mind Send Kimbal [Kimbrell] to Gutieres just below San Patricio one mile, because Sanger and Ballard are or were great friends of Camels [Billy Campbell's] Ballard told me ~~today~~ yesterday to leave for you were doing everything to catch me. it was a blind to get me to leave tell Kimbal [Kimbrell] not to come before 3 oclock for I may not be there before

THE LEW WALLACE INTERVIEW

During Billy's sham arrest in Lincoln, Lew Wallace and Billy were housed next door to each other; with Billy in his friend, jailor Juan Patrón's, house, and Wallace at José Montaño's.

On March 23, 1879, Wallace interviewed Billy, asking nothing about the Lincoln County War. At this period, Wallace was collecting information about Territorial outlawry, and Billy seems to have responded to that quest by telling him about the Santa Fe Ring's network of cattle rustlers, who fulfilled the beef contracts for Fort Stanton and the Mescalero Indian Reservation; which were held by the local Ring front, "The House," then controlled by James J. Dolan and John Riley. Noteworthy is Billy's vast fund of local information and geography. The notes stated:

William Bonney ("Kid")
relative to arrangement with him.
Notes:

3-23-1879

Statements by Kid, made Sunday night March 23, 1879

1. There is a cattle trail beginning about 5 miles above Yellow Lake in a cañon, running a little west of north to Cisneza del Matcho (Mule Spring) and continuing around the point of the Capitan Mountains down toward Carrizozo in the direction of the Rio Grande. Frank Wheeler, Jake Owens and Dutch Chris are supposed to have used this trail taking a bunch of cattle over. Vansickle told K. so. They stopped and killed two beavers for Sam Corbett – hush money to Vansickle to whom they gave the beavers. Vansickle also said the Owens-Wheeler outfit mentioning "Chris" Ladbessor using this trail for about a year, but that lately their horses had given out, and of 140 head which they started to work they had only got through with 40. That now they were going to the Reservation to make a raid on the Indian horses to work on.

The Rustlers.

The "Rustlers," Kid says: were organized in Fort Stanton. Before they organized as "Rustlers" they had been with Peppin's posse. They came from Texas. Owens was conspicuous amongst them. ***They were organized before the burning of McSween's house****, and after that they went on their first trip down the county as far as the Coe's ranch and* ***thence to the Feliz where they took the Tunstall cattle.*** *From the Feliz they went to the Pecos, where some of them deserted, Owens amongst them. (Martin, known to Sam Corbett) was in charge of the Tunstall cattle, and was taken prisoner, and saw them kill one of their own party. On the same trip they burnt Lola Wise's house, and took some horses. Coe at the time was ranching at the house. On this trip they moved behind a body of soldiers, one company, and a company of Navajo Scouts. They moved in sight of the soldiers, taking horses, insulting women. Lorenzo Trujillo (Jus. Peder) Juan Trujillo, Jose M. Gutierres, Pancho Sanchez, Santos Tafoya, are witnesses against them. They stopped on Pecos at Seven Rivers. Collins, now at Silver City, was one of the outfit – nick-named the Prowler by the cowboys. At Seven Rivers. There joined them Gus Gildey (wanted at San Antonio for killing Mexicans) Gildey is carrying the mail now from Stockton to Seven Rivers – James Irvin and*

Reese Gobles, (rumored that their bodies were found in a drift down the Pecos) – Rustling Bob (found dead in the Pecos, killed by his own party) – John Selman (whereabouts unknown) came to Roswell while [Captain] Carroll was there –

The R's [Rustlers] stayed at Seven Rivers; which they left on their second trip via the Berenda for Fort Stanton. On their return back they killed Chavez boys and the crazy boy, Lorenzo – and the Sanchez boy, 14 years old. They also committed many robberies. They broke up after reaching the Pecos, promising to return when some more horses got fat.

<u>*Shedd's Ranch*</u>

The trail used going from Seven Rivers to Shedd's was round the S.W. part of the Guadalupe Mts. by a tank on the right hand of trail: from Shedd's the drives would be over to Las Cruces Jesse Evans, Frank Baker (killed) Jim [James] McDaniels (at Cruces, ranging between Cruces and El Paso) Reed at Shedd's bought cattle from them – also sold cattle to E.C. Priest, butcher in Cruces. "Big Mose" (at Cruces last heard from) and [blank], deserter from cavalry – (went to Arizona)

<u>*Mimbres*</u>

Used to be called Mormon City – situated 30 miles on the road to Cruces from Silver City south. A great many of what are known as "West Harden gang" are there. Among them Joe Olney, known in Mimbres as Joe Hill; he has a ranch in old Mexico somewheres near Coralitos. He makes trips up in this country: was at Penasco not long ago.

<u>*San Nicholas Spring*</u>

Is about 18 miles from Shedd's Ranch on the road to Tularosa, left hand road. There's a house at the spring and about 4 or 5 miles from it N.W. is another corral of brush and a spring, situated in a cañon. There Jim [James] McDaniels used to keep stolen Indian horses. McD. one of the Rio Grande posse. Kid says the latter is still used.

<u>*The Jones Family*</u>

Came from Texas. Used to keep saloon at Fort Griffin. The family consists of the father, Jim Jones, John Jones, boy about 10 years old, a girl about 13, and the mother. Marion Turner lives with the family, and he killed a Mexican man at Blazers Mill "just to see him kick." He had no cattle ***when the War started****. The Jones, John and Jim, killed a man named Riley, a partner of theirs, on the Penasco 3 or 4 years ago.*

THE "BILLIE" LETTER TO LEW WALLACE

On a likely March 24, 1879, Billy wrote a letter to Wallace about Lincoln County War events. It exists now as a one-page fragment, signed "Billie." I dated and authenticated it in my 2012 book, *Billy the Kid's Writings, Words, and Wit*. It stated:

... on the Pecos. All that I can remember are the So Called Dolan Outfit but they are all up here now. and on the Rio Grande this man Cris Moten I believe his name is he drove a herd of 80 head one Year ago last December in Company with Frank Wheeler Frank Baker deceased Jesse Evans George Davis alias Tom Jones. Tom Hill, his name in Texas being Tom Chelson also deceased, they drove the cattle to the Indian Reservation and sold them to John Riley and JJ Dolan. and the cattle were turned in for Beef for the Indians the Beckwith family made their boasts that they came to Seven Rivers a little over four years ago with one Milch Cow borrowed from John Chisum they had when I was there Year ago one thousand six hundred head of cattle. the male members of the family are Henry Beckwith and John Beckwith Robert Beckwith was killed the time McSween's house was burned. Charles [blank] Robert Olinger and Wallace Olinger are of the same gang. their cattle ranch is Situated at Rock Corral twelve miles below Seven Rivers on the Pecos. Paxton and Pierce are Still below them forty miles from Seven Rivers there are four of them Paxton: Pierce: Jim Raymers, and Buck Powel. they had when I seen them last about one thousand head of cattle: at Rocky Arroyo there is another Ranch belonging to [blank] Smith who Operated on the Penasco last year with the Jesse Evans gang those and the places I mentioned are all I know of this man Chris Moten at the time they stole those Cattle was in the employ of Dolan and Co. I afterwards Seen Some of the cattle at the Rinconada Bonita on the reservation those were the men we were in search of when we went to the Agency. the Beckwith family were attending to their own Business when this War started but G.W. Peppin told them that this was John Chisums War. and so they took a hand thinking they would lose their Cattle in case that he Chisum won the fight. this is all the information I can give you on this point

Yours Respectfully Billie

LOST GRAND JURY TESTIMONY

Billy fulfilled his side of the Lew Wallace pardon bargain by testifying against the murderers of Attorney Huston Chapman - James Dolan, Billy Campbell, and Jessie Evans - in the April 1879 Lincoln County Grand Jury. By doing that, he was also implicating the Santa Fe Ring and risking his life. His testimony achieved those men's murder indictments: James Dolan and Billy Campbell for murder; Jessie Evans for accessory to murder.

That testimony was confirmed in *The Grant County Herald* of May 10, 1879, as reprinted from the Mesilla *Thirty Four*: "At the recent term of court in Lincoln, about 200 indictments were found. Among them, Col. Dudley and George W. Peppin for burning McSween's house, **Dolan and Campbell for the Chapman murder, in which the Kid is the principal witness**."

TESTIMONY AGAINST N.A.M. DUDLEY

Proof of Billy Bonney's anti-Ring commitment was his testifying against the Ringite past Fort Stanton Commander N.A.M. Dudley on May 28th and 29th, 1879, since it was not part of his pardon bargain, and it risked his life. But he was seeking justice for Dudley's illegal military intervention in the Lincoln County War Battle, enabling the murders of Billy's compatriots: Alexander McSween, Harvey Morris, Francisco Zamora, and Vincente Romero. Billy twice made the unprotected, nine mile trip from his Lincoln sham custody to the courtroom in the Fort Stanton Adjutant's office for his court appearances.

His Regulator zeal, plus his courage and intellectual brilliance, made him unshakable under Dudley's lawyer's abusive cross-examination. Billy's precise and devastating testimony alone should have yielded a court martial after this interchange: "*How many soldiers fired at you? ... Three ... How many shots did those soldiers fire, that you say shot from the Tunstall building? ... I could not swear to that on account of firing on all sides, I could not hear. I seen them fire one volley ... Were the soldiers which you say fired at you as you escaped from the McSween house on the evening of July 19th last, colored or white? ... White troops.*"

A volley meant the three soldiers fired in unison. That required Dudley's order. "White" meant they were officers. That directly linked Dudley to ordering his soldiers to murder civilians. That was his treasonous Posse Comitatus Act violation. So dangerous was this evidence, that Dudley's lawyer's closing argument devoted a large part to a false attack on Billy.

Noteworthy, is that the Ring had already bestowed his outlaw moniker, "Billy the Kid;" and Billy was still uncertain about it under questioning. His transcript stated:

WILLIAM BONNEY, a witness being duly sworn, testified as follows.

Q. by Recorder. What is your name and place of residence?

Answer. My name is William Bonney. I reside in Lincoln.

Q. by Recorder. Are you known or called Billy Kidd, also Antrim?

Answer. Yes Sir.

Q. by Recorder. Where were you on the 19th day of July last and what, if anything, did you see of the movements and actions of the troops in that city, state fully?

Answer. I was in the McSween house in Lincoln, and I saw soldiers come from the post with the sheriff's party, that is the sheriff's posse joined them a short distance below there, the McSween house. Soldiers passed on by and the men dropped off and surrounded the house, the sheriff's party. Shortly after, the soldiers came back with Peppin, passed the house twice afterwards. Three soldiers came and stood in front of the house, in front of the windows. Mr. McSween wrote a note to the officer in charge asking what the soldiers were placed there for. He replied saying that they had business there, that if a shot was fired over his camp, or at Peppin, or at any of his men, that he had no objection to blowing up, if he wanted, his own house. I read the note myself, he handed it to me to read. I saw nothing further of the soldiers until night. I was in the back part of the house. ***When I escaped from the house three soldiers fired at me from the Tunstall store, outside corner of the store.*** *That's all I know in regards to it.*

Q. by Recorder. Did the soldiers that stood in front of the windows have guns with them while there?

Answer. Yes Sir.

Q. by Recorder. Who escaped from the house with you and who was killed at the time, if you know, while attempting to make their escape?

Answer. Jose Chavez [Chávez y Chávez] escaped with me, Vincente Romero, Francisco Zamora and McSween.

Q. by Recorder. How many persons were killed in that fight that day, if you know, and who killed them, if you know?

Answer. I seen five killed, I could not swear to who killed them, I seen some of them that fired.

Q. by Recorder. Who did you see that fired?

Answer. Robt. Beckwith, John Hurley, John Jones, ***those three soldiers, I don't know their names.***

Q. by Recorder. Did you see any persons setting fire to the McSween house that day, if so, state who it was, if you know?

Answer. I did, Jack Long, and there was another man I did not recognize.

Recorder stated he had finished with the witness.
Cross examination.

Q. By Col. Dudley. What were you, and the others there with you, doing in McSween's house that day?

Answer. We came here with McSween.

Q. By Col. Dudley. Did you know, or had you not heard, that the sheriff was endeavoring to arrest yourself and others there with you at the time?

Answer. Yes Sir. I had heard so, I did not know.

Q. By Col. Dudley. Then were you not engaged in resisting the sheriff at the time you were in the house?

Objected to by Recorder. The Court has already ruled that nothing extraneous from the actual occurrence that took place, and Col. Dudley's actions in connection therewith, should be further inquired into ... it cannot be a matter of defense of Col. Dudley or justify his actions however much the parties may have been resisting the sheriff or civil authorities.

Lt. Col. Dudley, by his Counsel, states he does not deem it necessary to make reply to the objection.

Objection sustained.

Q. By Col. Dudley. In addition to the names you have given, are you also known as the "Kid?"

Answer. I have already answered that question, Yes Sir, I am, but not "Billy Kid" that I know of.

Q. By Col. Dudley. Were you not and were not the parties with you in the McSween house on the 19th day of July last and the days immediately preceding, engaged in firing at the sheriff's posse?

Court objects to the question.

Lt. Col. Dudley, by his Counsel, asks, does the Court intend to rule here, that after once gone into this matter of firing into the McSween house by the testimony of this witness, it is not permissible to show all the circumstances under which this firing took place ...

Court cleared and closed.

Court opened and its decision announced ...

The Court directs the case to proceed calling attention to its previous rulings which were deemed sufficient by explicit.

Q. By Col. Dudley. Whose name was signed to the note received by McSween in reply to the one previously sent by him to Col. Dudley?

Answer. Signed N.A.M. Dudley, did not say what rank, he received two notes, one had no name signed to it.

Q. By Col. Dudley. Are you as certain of everything else you have sworn to as you are to what you have sworn to in answer to the last proceeding question?

Answer. Yes Sir.

Q. By Col. Dudley. From which direction did Peppin come the first time the soldiers passed with him?

Answer. Passed up from the direction of where the soldiers camped, the first time I saw him.

Q. By Col. Dudley. What direction did he come from the second time?

Answer. From the direction of the [Wortley] hotel from the McSween house.

Q. By Col. Dudley. In what direction did you go upon your escape from the McSween house?

Answer. Ran towards the Tunstall store, was fired at, and there turned towards the river.

Q. By Col. Dudley. From what part of the McSween house did you make your escape?

Answer. The northeast corner of the house.

Q. By Col. Dudley. How many soldiers fired at you?

Answer. Three.

Q. By Col. Dudley. How many soldiers were with Peppin when he passed the McSween house each time, as you say?

Answer. Three.

Q. By Col. Dudley. The soldiers appeared to go in company of threes that day, did they not?

Answer. All that I ever saw appeared to be three in a crowd at a time after they passed the first time.

Q. By Col. Dudley. Who was killed first that day, Bob Beckwith or McSween men?

Answer. Harvey Morris, McSween man, was killed first.

Q. By Col. Dudley. How far is the Tunstall building from the McSween house?

Answer. I could not say how far, I never measured the distance. I should judge it to be 40 yards, between 30 and 40 yards.

Q. By Col. Dudley. How many shots did those soldiers fire, that you say shot from the Tunstall building?

Answer. I could not swear to that on account of firing on all sides, I could not hear. I seen them fire one volley.

Q. By Col. Dudley. What did they fire at?

Answer. Myself and Jose Chavez [Chávez y Chávez].

Q. By Col. Dudley. Did you not just now state in answer to the question who killed Zamora, Romero, Morris, and McSween that you did not know who killed them, but you saw Beckwith, John Jones, ***and three soldiers fire at them****?*

Answer. Yes Sir. I did.

Q. By Col. Dudley. Were these men, the McSween men, there with you ***when the volley was fired at you and Chavez by the soldiers****?*

Answer. Just a short ways behind us.

Q. By Col. Dudley. Were you looking back at them?

Answer. No Sir.

Q. By Col. Dudley. How then do you know they were just behind you then, or that they were in range of the volley?

Answer. Because there was a high fence behind, and a good many guns to keep them there. I could hear them speak.

Q. By Col. Dudley. How far were you from the soldiers when you saw them?

Answer. I could not swear exactly, between 30 and 40 yards.

Q. By Col. Dudley. Did you know either of the soldiers that were in front of the window of McSween's house that day? If so, give it.

Answer. No Sir, I am not acquainted with them.

Redirect.

Q. by Recorder. Explain whether all the men that were in the McSween house came out at the same time when McSween and the others were killed and the firing came from the soldiers and others?

Answer. Yes Sir, all came out at the same time. ***The firing was done by the soldiers until some had escaped.***

Recorder stated that he had finished with the witness.

Q. by Col. Dudley. How do you know if you were making your escape at the time and the men Zamora, Morris and McSween were behind you that they were killed at that time, is it not true that you did not know of their death or the death of either of them until afterwards?

Answer. I knew of the death of some of them, I did know of the death of one of them. I saw him lying down there.

Q. by Col. Dudley. Did you see any of the men last mentioned killed?

Answer. Yes Sir, I did, I seen Harvey Morris killed first, he was out in front of me.

Q. by Col. Dudley. Did you not then a moment ago swear that he was among those who were behind you and Jose Chavez [Chávez y Chávez] when you saw the soldiers deliver the volley?

Answer. No Sir, I didn't think I did. I misunderstood the question if I did. I said he was among them that was killed not behind me.

Witness then withdrew ...

In Billy's second day of testimony on May 29th, he confirmed that Dudley's white officers fired at escaping McSweens, including himself; and that visibility came from the burning McSween house that made the area "*almost light as day*." The transcript stated:

Q. by Court. Were the soldiers which you say fired at you as you escaped from the McSween house on the evening of July 19th last, colored or white?

Answer. White troops.

Q. by Court. Was it light enough so you could distinctly see the soldiers when they fired?

Answer. The house was burning. Made it almost light as day for a short distance all around.

LETTER OF DECEMBER 12,1880 TO LEW WALLACE

After Governor Lew Wallace betrayed the pardon bargain, Billy was publicly outlawed in lurid press. On December 12, 1880, he wrote to Wallace to deny a December 3, 1880 *Las Vegas Gazette* article by J.H. Koogler, titled "Desperadoe's Stronghold."

Billy's letter made clear that he did not consider himself an outlaw. He wrote: *"I noticed in the Las Vegas Gazette a piece which stated that, Billy "the" Kid, the name by which I am known in the Country was the captain of a Band of Outlaws who hold Forth at the Portales.* ***There is no such Organization in Existence. So the Gentleman must have drawn very heavily on his Imagination.*** " In addition, the letter shows his self-assured legal knowledge, describing to Wallace that he considered the posse illegal, for lack of proper arrest warrants: *"I asked for their Papers [warrants] and they had none. So I concluded that it amounted to nothing more than a mob."*

By that December 12th, he had endured Secret Service pursuit, another lost pardon through a possible Secret Service bargain, two White Oaks posse ambushes, and a false murder accusation for Jim Carlyle. Seven days later, Garrett's posse would ambush Billy's group near Fort Sumner, killing Tom O'Folliard, intending to kill him. Ten days away was his Stinking Springs capture, where Garrett would shoot dead Charlie Bowdre when mistaking him for Billy. Billy wrote:

Fort Sumner
Dec. 12th 1880
Gov. Lew Wallace
Dear Sir

I noticed in the Las Vegas Gazette a piece which stated that, Billy "the" Kid, the name by which I am known in the Country was the captain of a Band of Outlaws who hold Forth at the Portales. There is no such Organization in Existence. So the Gentleman must have drawn very heavily on his Imagination. *My business at the White Oaks at the time I was waylaid and my horse killed was to See Judge Leonard who has my case in hand. he had written me to come up, that he thought he could get Everything Straightened up I did not find him at the Oaks & Should have gone to Lincoln if I had met with no accident. After mine and Billie Wilsons horses were killed we both made our way to a Station, forty miles from the Oaks kept by Mr Greathouse. When I got up the next morning The house was Surrounded by an outfit led by one Carlyle, Who had come into the house and Demanded a Surrender. I asked for their Papers [warrants] and they had none. So I concluded that it amounted to nothing more than a mob and told Carlyle that he would have to Stay in the house an d lead the way out that night. Soon after a* *note was brought in Stating that if Carlyle did not come out inside of five minutes they would Kill the Station Keeper)Greathouse) who had left the house and was with them. in a Short time a Shot was fired on the outside and Carlyle thinking Greathouse was Killed jumped through the window. breaking the Sash as he went and was killed by his own Party they think it was me trying to make my Escape. the Party then withdrew.*

they returned the next day and burned an old man named Spencer's house and Greathouses also

I made my way to this Place afoot and During my absence Deputy Sheriff Garrett Acting under Chisum's orders went to the Portales and found Nothing. on his way back he went by Mr Yerby's ranch and took a pair of mules of mine which I had left with Mr Bowdre who is in Charge of mr Yerby's cattle. he (Garrett) claimed that they were stolen and even if they were not he had no right to Confiscate any Outlaws property.

I had been at Sumner Since I left Lincoln making my living Gambling the mules were bought by me the truth of which I can prove by the best citizens around Sumner. J.S. Chisum is the man who got me into Trouble and was benefited Thousands by it and is now doing all he can against me There is no Doubt but what there is a great deal of Stealing going on in the Territory. and a great deal of the Property is taken across the [Staked] Plains as it is a good outlet but so far as my being at the head of a Band there is nothing of it in Several Instances I have recovered Stolen Property when there was no chance to get an Officer to do it.

one instance for Hugo Zuber Post office Puerto de Luna. another for Pablo Analla Same Place.

if Some impartial Party were to investigate this matter they would find it far Different from the impression put out by Chisum and his Tools.

Yours Respect

William Bonney

SANTA FE JAIL LETTER: JANUARY 1, 1881

After capture, Billy was kept in the Santa Fe jail, awaiting transport to Mesilla for his hanging trial. On January 1, 1881, four days after arriving, he wrote to Lew Wallace:

Santa Fe
Jan 1st 1881

Gov. Lew Wallace
Dear Sir
I would like to see you for a few moments if You can spare the time.
Yours Respect.
W.HBonney

SANTA FE JAIL LETTER: MARCH 2, 1881

On March 2, 1881, Billy sent his second jail letter, which Wallace considered "blackmail." Billy wrote:

Santa Fe Jail New Mex
March 2nd 1881
Gov. Lew Wallace
Dear Sir
I wish you would come down to the jail to see me. it will be to your interest to come and see me. ***I have some letters which date back two years, and there are Parties who are very anxious to get them but I shall not dispose of them until I see you. that is if you will come immediately***
Yours Respect
Wm H Bonney

SANTA FE JAIL LETTER: MARCH 4, 1881

On March 4, 1881, Billy wrote his third jail letter in tragic confirmation of the pardon's betrayal: "*I have done everything that I promised you I would, and You have done nothing that You promised me.*" Billy wrote:

Santa Fe. In jail.
March 4th 1881
Gov. Lew Wallace
Dear Sir

I wrote You a little note the day before yesterday but have received no annser. I Expect you have forgotten what you promised me, this Month two Years ago. but I have not, and I think You had ought to have come and seen me as I requested you to. ***I have done everything that I promised you I would, and You have done nothing that You promised me.***

I think when You think the matter over, You will come down and See me, and I can then Explain Everything to You.

Judge Leonard, Passed through here on his way East, in january and promised to come and See me on his way back. but he did not fulfill his Promise. it looks to me like I am getting left in the Cold. I am not treated right by [U.S. Marshal John] Sherman. he lets Every Stranger that comes to See me through Curiosity in to See me, but will not let a Single one of my friends in, not Even an Attorney.

I guess they mean to Send me up without giving me any Show. but they will have a nice time doing it. I am not entirely without friends.

I shall Expect to See you Sometime today
Patiently Waiting
I am Very truly Yours, Respect.
Wm H. Bonney.

SANTA FE JAIL LETTER: MARCH 27, 1881

On March 27, 1881, Billy wrote to Wallace for the last time, emphasizing the pardon bargain, possibly hoping that it would be issued after his sentencing in the Mesilla trial. He wrote:

Santa Fe New Mexico
March 27th/81
Gov Lew Wallace
Dear Sir

for the last time I ask: Will you keep Your promise. I start below tomorrow. Send Annser by bearer.

Yours Respt
WBonney

LETTER TO ATTORNEY EDGAR CAYPLESS

After Billy's unjust hanging sentence for the Regulators' killing of Sheriff William Brady, handed down by Ringite Judge Warren Bristol on April 13, 1881, Billy wanted to appeal.

Two days later, on April 15th, he wrote to Las Vegas attorney, Edgar Caypless, whom he had earlier hired on contingency to file his audacious replevin (rustling) suit for recovery of his bay mare from Pat Garrett's posseman, Frank Stewart, who had stolen her at Billy's Stinking Springs capture. Billy hoped to sell her to pay an appeal lawyer, with grounds that his Spanish-speaking jurymen had been deprived of a translator.

Caypless prevailed in the replevin case, but only after Billy's death; and he kept the mare's sales price as fee.

For his last known letter, Billy wrote:

Dear Sir. I would have written before this but could get no paper. My United States case was thrown out of court and I was rushed to trial on my Territorial charge. was convicted of murder in the first degree and am to be hanged on the 13th day of May. Mr. A.J. Fountain was appointed to defend me and has done the best he could for me. He is willing to carry the case further if I can raise the money to bear his expense. The mare is about all I can depend on at present so hope you will settle the case right away and give him the money you get for her. If you do not settle the matter with Scott Moore [to whom Frank Stewart sold the mare] and have to go to court about it either give him [Fountain] the mare or sell her at auction and give him the money. please do as he wishes in the matter. I know you will do the best you can for me in this. I shall be taken to Lincoln tomorrow. Please write and direct care of Garrett, sheriff. excuse bad writing. I have my handcuffs on. I remain as ever

Yours respectfully,
W.H. Bonney

NEWSPAPER INTERVIEWS

Billy Bonney's press interviews occurred after his Stinking Springs capture, and after his Mesilla hanging verdict. He was already nationally famous, and making ironic commentary like in his April 3, 1881's Santa Fe *Daily New Mexican's* "Something About the Kid": "At least two hundred men have been killed in Lincoln County during the past three years, but I did not kill all of them."

On December 27, 1880, the *Las Vegas Daily Gazette* published editor, Lucius "Lute" Wilcox's, article about the Stinking Springs capture and prisoner transport to Las Vegas, titled: 'The Kid. Interview with Billy Bonney The Best Known Man in New Mexico." Billy teased his outlaw myth; stating about onlookers: "Well, perhaps some of them will think me half man now; everyone seems to think I was some sort of animal." Wilcox wrote:

> With its customary enterprise, the *Gazette* was the first paper to give the story of the capture of Billy Bonney, who has risen to notoriety under the sobriquet of "the Kid," Billy Wilson, Dave Rudabaugh and Tom Pickett. Just at this time everything of interest about the men is especially interesting, and after damning the men in general and "the Kid" in particular through the columns of this paper we considered it the correct thing to give them a show.
>
> Through the kindness of [San Miguel County] Sheriff Romero, a representative of the *Gazette* was admitted to the jail yesterday morning.
>
> Mike Cosgrove, the obliging mail contractor, who has met the boys frequently while on business down the Pecos, had just gone in with four large bundles. The doors at the entrance stood open, and the large crowd strained their necks to get a glimpse of the prisoners, who stood in the passageway like children waiting for a Christmas tree distribution. One by one the bundles were unpacked disclosing a good suit of clothes for each man. Mr. Cosgrove remarked that he wanted "to see the boys go away in style."
>
> "Billy the Kid," and Billy Wilson who were shackled together stood patiently while a blacksmith took off their shackles and bracelets to allow them an opportunity to make a change of clothing. Both prisoners watched the operation

which was to set them free for a short while, but Wilson scarcely raised his eyes, and spoke but once or twice to his compadres. **Bonney on the other hand, was light and chipper, and was very communicative, laughing, joking and chatting with the bystanders.**

"You appear to take it easy," the reporter said.

"Yes! What's the use of looking at the gloomy side of everything. The laugh's on me this time," he said. Then looking about the placita, he asked: "Is the jail at Santa Fe any better than this?"

This seemed to trouble him considerably, for as he explained, "this is a terrible place to put a fellow in." He put the same question to every one who came near him and when he learned that there was nothing better in store for him, he shrugged his shoulders and said something about putting up with what he had to.

He was the attraction of the show, and as he stood there, lightly kicking the toes of his boots on the stone pavement to keep his feet warm, one would scarcely mistrust that he was the hero of "Forty Thieves," romance which this paper has been running in serial form for six weeks or more.

"There was a big crowd gazing at me wasn't there?" he exclaimed, and then smiling continued: "Well perhaps some of them will think me half a man now; everyone seems to think I was some kind of an animal."

He did look human, indeed, but there was nothing very mannish about him in appearance, for he looked and acted like a mere boy. He is about five feet, eight or nine inches tall, slightly built and lithe, weighing about 140; a frank and open countenance, looking like a school boy, with the traditional silky fuzz on his upper lip, clear blue eyes, with a roguish snap about them, light hair and complexion. He is, in all, quite a handsome looking fellow, the only imperfection being two prominent front teeth, slightly protruding like a squirrels' teeth, and he has agreeable and winning ways.

On December 28, 1880, for the *Las Vegas Gazette*, from inside the train to Santa Fe, for "Interview with the Kid," Billy's steely self-control is evident when one realizes it was detained by a mob, either to lynch or to rescue him. The article stated:

We saw him again at the depot when the crowd presented a really war like appearance. Standing by the car, out of one of the windows from which he was leaning, he talked freely with us of the whole affair:

"I don't blame you for writing of me as you have. You have had to believe others' stories, but then **I don't know as anyone would believe anything good of me, anyway," he said. "I really wasn't the leader of any gang.** I was for Billy all the time. About that Portales business, I owned the ranch with Charlie Bowdre. I took it up and was holding it because I knew that at some time a stage line would run there, and I wanted to keep it for a station. **But I found that there were certain men who wouldn't let me live in the country and so I was going to leave.**

We had all our grub in the house when they took us in, and we were going to a place six miles away in the morning to cook it and then light out. I haven't stolen any stock. I made my living by gambling, but that was the only way I could live. **They wouldn't let me settle down; if they had I wouldn't be here today," and he held up his right arm on which was the bracelet.**

"Chisum got me into all this trouble and then wouldn't help me out. I went up to Lincoln to stand my trial on the warrant that was out for me, but the Territory took a change of venue to Dona Ana, and I knew I had no show, and so I skinned out ...

If it had not been for the dead horse in the doorway I wouldn't be here in Las Vegas. I would have ridden out on my bay mare and taken my chances of escaping. But I couldn't ride over that for she would have jumped back **and I would have got it in the head**. We could have stayed in the house but there wouldn't have been anything gained by that for they would have starved us out. I thought it was better to come out and get a square meal - don't you?"

The prospects of a fight exhilarated him, and he bitterly bemoaned being chained. "If I only had my Winchester, I'd lick the whole crowd" was his confident comment on the strength of the attacking party. He sighed and sighed again for the chance to take a hand in the fight and the burden of his desire was to be set free to fight on the side of his captors as soon as he should smell powder.

As the train rolled out, he lifted his hat and invited us to call and see him in Santa Fe, calling out "*adios.*"

Billy's loyal attorney, Ira Leonard, protectively accompanied him on the train ride to Mesilla, via the Rincón depot. From there, they took the stagecoach to Las Cruces. With them were guards and prisoner, Billy Wilson, also transported to Mesilla. At Las Cruces, a crowd had gathered to see the famous outlaw, Billy the Kid. The arrival was covered in the April 3, 1881 *Santa Fe Daily New Mexican* in: "Something About the Kid." It stated:

An extract of a letter written by W.S. Fletcher from Mesilla to a gentleman in the city reads about as follows: Tony Neis and Francisco Chaves, deputy U.S. Marshals, arrived Thursday night with **Billy, the Kid,** and Billy Wilson. They met an ugly crowd at Rincon, where some threats were made, but Tony's crowd were too much for them. **At Las Cruces an impulsive mob gathered around the coach and someone asked which is "Billy the Kid." The Kid himself answered by placing his hand on Judge Leonard's shoulder and saying "this is the man."** The Kid weakened somewhat at Las Cruces, where he found quite a number of Lincoln County men, who were to appear against him as witnesses.

[AUTHOR'S NOTE: Billy had no defense witnesses. The prosecution had Ringites James Dolan, Saturnino Baca, and Sheriff William Brady's deputy, Billy Matthews; and subpoenaed Lincolnite, Isaac Ellis.]

He says at least two hundred men have been killed in Lincoln County during the past three years, but that he did not kill all of them. I think twenty murders can be charged against him. He was arraigned yesterday (Wednesday) before the United States court for the murder of Roberts, on the Mescalero Apache reservation, in 1878. Judge Leonard was assigned to his defense. Judge Newcomb gave notice that he had three other indictments for murder against him, and it looks as if he had no show to get off. His counsel asked today for time to send to Lincoln, which was granted, so that his trial will not commence for at least ten days. Billy Wilson's case is before the grand jury. He is charged with passing counterfeit money. He has retained Judge Thornton as his counsel. He seems to have friends here while the Kid has none.

No mails between Rincon and Doña Ana for the past week. Mosquitoes and flies abound and weather hot as blazes.

Billy's articulate response to the hanging verdict was in an April 16, 1881 article in the *Mesilla News*. He summarized Santa Fe Ring injustice: "I think it hard that I should be the only one to suffer the extreme penalty of the law." He called his court "mob law;" ending with facetious "personal advice": "If mob law is going to rule, better dismiss judge and sheriff and let all take chances alike." And he said sarcastically: "Advise persons never to engage in killing." About Lew Wallace's pardon, he said curtly: "Don't know that he will do it." The article stated:

> Well I had intended at one time not to say a word on my own behalf because persons would say, "Oh he lied." Newman, editor of the *Semi-Weekly*, gave me a rough deal; he created prejudice against me, and is trying to incite a mob to lynch me. He sent me a paper which showed it; I think it a dirty mean advantage to take of me, **considering my situation and knowing that I could not defend myself by word or act. But I suppose he thought he would give me a kick down hill.** Newman came to see me the other day. I refused to talk to him or tell him anything. But I believe the *News* is always willing to give its readers both sides of a question. **If mob law is going to rule, better dismiss judge and sheriff and let all take chances alike.** I expect to be lynched going to Lincoln. **Advise persons never to engage in killing.**
>
> **Considering the active part Governor Wallace took on our side and the friendly relations that existed between him and me, and the promise he made me, I think he ought to pardon me. Don't know that he will do it.** When I was arrested for that murder he let me out and gave me freedom of the town, and let me go about with my arms. When I got ready to leave Lincoln in June, 1879, I left. **I think it hard that I should be the only one to suffer the extreme penalty of the law.**

For his secret transport to Lincoln for hanging, to prevent his partisans' rescue, at night, on April 17, 1881, Billy was taken by wagon from the Mesilla jail. April 20, 1881's *Newman's Semi-Weekly* reported his departure, with Billy, as usual, joking:

On Saturday night about 10 o'clock Deputy U.S. marshal Robt. Ollinger [sic] with deputy sheriff David Wood and a posse of five men (Tom Williams, Billy Mathews [sic], John Kinney, D.M. Reade and W.A. Lockhart) started for Lincoln with Henry Antrim *alias* the Kid. The fact that they intended to leave at that time had been purposely concealed and the report circulated that they would not leave before the middle of the week in order to avoid any possibility of trouble, it having been rumored that the Kid's band would attempt a rescue. They stopped in front of our office while we talked to them, and we handed the Kid an addressed envelope with some paper and he said he would write some things he wanted to make public. **He appeared quite cheerful and remarked that he wanted to stay until their whiskey gave out, anyway.** Said he was sure that his guard would not hurt him unless a rescue should be attempted and he was certain that it would not be done, unless, perhaps, "those fellows at White Oaks come out to take me," meaning to kill him. **It was, he said, about a stand-off whether he was hanged or killed in the wagon ...** He was hand-cuffed to the back seat of the ambulance. Kinney sat beside him, Olinger on the seat facing him, Mathews on the seat facing Kinney, Lockhart driving, and Reade, Wood and Williams riding along on horseback on each side and behind. The whole party was armed to the teeth and anyone who knows the men of whom it was composed will admit that a rescues would be a hazardous undertaking. Kid was informed that if trouble should occur he would be shot first and the attacking party attended to afterwards.

CONCLUSION

As is obvious from his words, Billy Bonney would not have backed down. The inevitability of his killing, after he refused to flee the Territory like most of the Regulators, is like grand tragedy, with the Coroner's Jury Report its grim conclusion.

PART II

THE "BRUSHY BILL" IMPOSTER HOAX AND ITS FAKED DEATH SCENE AND DENIED CORONER'S JURY REPORT

CHAPTER 1
THE "BRUSHY BILL" IMPOSER HOAX

THE "BRUSHY BILL" HOAX

The most elaborate and enduring Billy the Kid imposter hoax was devised by a deranged mid-twentieth century old-timer named Oliver Pleasant Roberts, self-named "Brushy Bill." He was promoted by two ambitious hoaxers: a con-artist traveling salesman named William Vincent Morrison; and a wannabe historian and English teacher, named Charles Leland Sonnichsen. Their 1955 book advertising "Brushy," titled *Alias Billy the Kid*, became "Brushy's" subsequent believers' bible.

I exposed this hoax in my 2019 books: *Cracking the Billy the Kid Imposter Hoax of Brushy Bill Roberts*, and *The Cold Case Billy the Kid Megahoax: The Plot to Steal Billy the Kid's Identity and Defame Sheriff Pat Garrett as a Murderer*.

The hoaxers were limited by lack of Billy the Kid history books in their day. So they used historical names with made-up events; adding coaching and "sight seeing" trips to Lincoln for "Brushy." It did not work, either in their attempt to get him a modern-day governor's pardon as Billy the Kid; or for their book presenting him as Billy. Nevertheless, his later champions declared the real history as a conspiracy of historians against him!

The "Brushy" hoax's flimflam had two parts: he knew things-not-printed; and, being illiterate, could not read-up on things-printed. Both were lies. **And the bigger lie was hiding that he was born 20 years *after* Billy Bonney**.

But their hoax's biggest obstacle was the existence of William Bonney's Coroner's Jury Report, and its requiring an alternate death scene to explain survival. Obviously, the hoaxers were forced to deny the Report's existence, and to deny the historical death scene. In so doing they revealed their elaborate lies, and how they were constructed, exposing the hoax itself.

THE "BRUSHY BILL" HOAX TRIUMVIRATE

Three men created a Frankensteinian Billy the Kid. There was "Brushy Bill" Roberts, crazy enough to play the character; William V. Morrison, willing to research and coach; and C.L. Sonnichsen, posing as an historical expert vouching for the gambit and writing *Alias Billy the Kid*, claiming "Brushy" as Billy, and rationalizing the failure to get him accepted as such.

Oliver P. Roberts, self-named "Brushy Bill," was mentally disabled, dependent on family care in adulthood; while fabricating multiple name-recognition personas, largely of Old West characters, like Frank James and Billy the Kid. He also had psychopathic tendencies, first adding 10 years to his life and the middle initial "L." to commit Social Security benefits fraud, according to his relative, Roy L. Haws, in his 2015 book: *Brushy Bill: Proof that His Claim to be Billy the Kid Was a Hoax.* "Brushy" proved incapable of remembering Billy the Kid history fed to him by Morrison, and failed ridiculously his November 30, 1950 pardon hearing with New Mexico's Thomas Jewett Mabry.

William Vincent Morrison was a huckster, traveling salesman, with a history of other imposter scams. He himself impersonated an attorney, while flaunting descent from famous Maxwell Land Grant owner, Lucien Bonaparte Maxwell's, brother, Ferdinand. Before "Brushy," he promoted another addled imposter, J. Frank Dalton, claiming to be Jesse James. Morrison's extensive Billy the Kid research to coach "Brushy" included Billy known writings; but broke down when "Brushy" parroted, as "Billy's memories," the errors in the antiquated sources he was being fed.

Charles Leland Sonnichsen was an English teacher in the El Paso, Texas College of Mines and Metallurgy, who had aspirations of being an Old West historian, publishing several semi-fictional takes of minor characters. Morrison introduced him to "Brushy," who parroted some Lincoln County War events (which were erroneous), but convinced Sonnichsen to join their endeavor of promoting him as Billy the Kid. This proved Sonnichsen's ignorance, in not recognizing "Brushy's" fakery. But he proved himself an ambitious hoaxer by working with Morrison to devise needed ploys to deny the existence of the Coroner's Jury Report and to fabricate the death scene; then to devise conspiracy theories to explain "Brushy's" rejection by legitimate historians.

CHAPTER 2
THE MAKE-OR-BREAK DEATH SCENE

REAL "BRUSHY'S FAKE DEATH SCENE

The press excitedly awaited "Brushy's" pardon hearing. On November 25, 1950, beating the gun for the hearing by five days, a Sexton Humphreys wrote " 'Pardon Me, I'm Alive,' Says Billy the Kid" for the *Indianapolis News*; stating: "The 1878 [sic - 1881] death of BILLY THE KID is "nothing but a legend," says an attorney [Morrison impersonating one] who asks New Mexico Governor THOMAS J. MABRY for a pardon for him ... The "legend" is that he was killed in the escape attempt [sic], but the petition says that he was only wounded and got to Mexico, that it was a companion that was killed."

From Indianapolis, Indiana, on the November 30, 1850 day of the hearing, the United Press reported anticipation of the big decision in *The Indianapolis News* under "Pardon My 6-Shooters. Billy the Kid? Governor to Decide." It stated: "The lawyers [representing Morrison] claimed Billy had not really been killed by Sheriff Garrett, but only wounded. He was then nursed back into health by a Mexican woman, and later escaped to old Mexico where he lived up to now, they said."

For his flubbed Governor Thomas Jewett Mabry pardon hearing as "Billy the Kid," the press reported his ludicrous death scene errors (everything else had been wrong too, like saying Billy had killed no one, and forgetting Pat Garrett's name.) He thought Billy's problem was that Fort Sumner's restaurant was out of steak! (This was his garbling of the Maxwell's house's side of beef.) The November 30, 1950 *Santa Fe New Mexican* article by an Art Morgan gave "Brushy's whole death scene fable in "Billy the Kid Only A Phony It Turns Out." The article stated: "His story of that night of July 14, 1881 at Fort Sumner was substantially this:

A restaurant was out of meat. He was asked to go to Pete Maxwell's house and get some. He suspected a trap and declined. However [his friend] **Billy Barlow**, who was "half-shot," volunteered to go.

Roberts heard shooting and ran to Maxwell's yard. Men shot at him and he shot back. A bullet creased his skull, knocking him out. A Mexican woman who, who lived in the back of the yard, dragged him into her house and revived him. Soon afterward he lit out for the Mexican border.

Since someone had to be killed in the fake death scene, "Brushy" had made-up Billy Barlow, mistaken for him as Billy. The front page, November 30, 1950, *El Paso Herald Post's* article by Vernon Smylie, was: " 'Billy the Kid' Flunks in Talk With Governor." Smylie quoted "Brushy": " 'The fellow that was killed was named Billy Barlow,' Roberts said. 'I was with him. We looked like two peas in a pod. Billy Barlow drank a heap. I never drank. Couldn't go for that rotgut beer. I figured it was a trap at the Maxwell house. I stayed away. It was Barlow that went' ... History does not mention Billy Barlow as an associate of the Kid's."

The December 1, 1950 *Albuquerque Journal's* front page had " 'Billy the Kid' Bubble Bursts as Gov. Mabry Rejects Oldster's Claim" with Governor Mabry's statement: "I am taking no action, now or ever, on this application for a pardon for Billy the Kid because I do not believe this man is Billy the Kid." So, it turned out that people were smarter than Morrison had reckoned, and "Brushy" was dumber than he had realized. It took a thick-skinned con-artist, like him, to be undaunted.

And, though not mentioned by the reporters at the Mabry hearing, the Coroner's Jury Report loomed in the background, since on its November 30, 1050 day, the *Alamogordo News* snidely printed: "Sumner Jury Thought The Kid Had Been Killed." It stated: "George Abbott, also of Alamogordo has in his office at the Pioneer Abstract Co., a photostatic copy of the verdict of the coroner's jury which viewed the remains of the late Wm. Bonney. ... As the reader will see from the document, translated below [in entirety], the six men serving on the jury and the Justice of the Peace who empanelled them, seemed convinced that Wm. Bonney, known as "Kid," was quite dead, and that he had been killed by Pat Garrett."

The Report had entered the hearing indirectly through Morrison's fake Affidavits of non-historical people claiming Billy had not been killed by Garrett. November 30, 1850's *The Indianapolis New s* under "Pardon My 6-Shooters. Billy the Kid? Governor to Decide;" stated: "

The latest claimant [to be Billy the Kid] ... has been both verified and denied by elderly Southwesterners who claim to be former companions of "The Kid."

Mrs. Martile Able, of El Paso, Tex., says he "has the same keen blue eyes" as Billy. Fevero [sic - Severo] Gallegos, of Ruidoso, N.M., said he is "still as fast on the draw, despite age."

Both agreed in sworn affidavits that he possesses the same small hands and large wrists, supposedly physical characteristics of the pint-sized outlaw.

RATIONALIZING THE LOST PARDON BY DENIAL OF THE CORONER'S JURY REPORT

Sly salesman, William V. Morrison, turned "Brushy's" lost pardon into martyrdom; hiding his total mismatch with Billy Bonney in the Mabry hearing, while waving the core claim of his hoax: the non-existence of the Coroner's Jury Report; ergo, no proof of the killing of Billy the Kid.

One can see the fabricated claims in a December 3, 1953, El Paso Rotary Club lecture on "Billy the Kid," which Morrison gave, while being introduced by C.L. Sonnichsen (a copy of which was sent to Paul Blazer, a Morrison fan and grandson of Dr. Joseph Blazer, owner of Blazer's Mill site of the "Buckshot" Roberts killing.) Morrison stated: "During my talk I hope to dispose of the two purported coroner's verdicts **[Morrison's fabricated claim]**, and I hope to prove, among other things, That: The Kid was not killed by Garrett or anyone else; No official coroner's verdict was rendered ... the Kid lived for many years before appearing and applying for a pardon in 1950, which was refused by Governor Mabry without considering the indisputable records and evidence." Morrison concluded: "Garrett's posse purportedly killed an unidentified man in July or August, 1881 ... In fact, there is no legal evidence in San Miguel County to prove that they killed anyone at that time."

For this next phase of his scam, Morrison had fabricated an absurd and error-filled plot based on the Santa Fe Ring falsifying documents, and giving Garrett the reward money, to hide that he did not kill the Kid and that "Brushy" was Billy. This fakery can be seen in Morrison's letters to historian Philip J. Rasch, in an ultimately failed attempt to dupe him.

On April 12, 1954, Morrison sent Rasch his fabricated version of the pardon failure, blaming the Santa Fe Ring and claiming the Coroner's Jury Report as "lost." He wrote: "I don't believe there was any secret why the Garrett faction opposed a legal hearing. **They were put on notice that there was no legal record or evidence to support the contention that Garrett's Posse had killed anyone on that memorable July 14, 1881.** And probably, that had acknowledged that I conferred with legal authority in New Mexico in an endeavor to prove up their purported coroner's verdict, or the first verdict - not mentioned by the Ring - in an attempt to file suit to then have it set aside. I was advised that **it would be impossible to prove up the lost instrument at this late date.** Therefore, the idea was abandoned and the Petition for Pardon was the only manner in which to make a declaration. The Santa Fe Ring had failed to make a legal record of the purported killing at the time. However, they did almost everything else in an attempt to collect the $500 reward [presumably for Pat Garrett]."

On May 7, 1954 Morrison wrote to Rasch (with a copy to Paul Blazer): "[Y]ou can understand that little credence can be placed on those papers controlled by the Ring at that time. I am sure you are probably aware **of** the fact that Catron was a dominant figure in the Lincoln County War, even though it might not have been written up. Also that Green, Garrett's attorney [sic - he was not] in the reward issue [for killing the Kid], was editor of Catron's <u>New Mexican</u> that printed the Government publications. And that Thornton, Catron's law partner, was the member of the legislature that pushed the act for relief of Garrett for killing the Kid in August [this was a transcriptionist error seized on by Morrison and Sonnichsen, though

July was also correctly used] and not on that memorable July 14 as Garrett would have you believe. All of this was done in less than a year from the time they claimed the Kid was killed, which they could not prove at the time. And none of it was reported in their paper as it actually happened, Why not? Certainly the Editor, Mr. Greene, knew about it ... In fact, all writers still contend that the killing took place on that memorable July 14, except Sonnichsen and Morrison, who have reproduced the record, the Official Act. Why has it gone untouched all of these years? Certainly they had never intended for old man Roberts to come along seventy years later and dig it out, or did they? ... **Garrett did not kill anybody in the month of July or August 1881.**" **[AUTHOR'S NOTE: Carried away by his lying, Morrison forgot "Brushy's" key Billy Barlow as victim tale!]**

On April 3, 1954, Morrison had sent a letter to a Carl W. Breihan, then writing a Billy the Kid biography (and sent a copy to loyalist Paul Blazer). His meaningless double-talk was that: a Coroner's Jury Report did not exist, so there was no proof Billy the Kid had been killed; so "Brushy" had no legal judgment to contest in a real court; so requesting pardon was his only option. Then Morrison fabricated a catch-22: Governor Mabry could not pardon him without proof of death,! So a legal technicality explained refusal! Morrison wrote: "It was most unfortunate that ["Brushy" and I] did not have the opportunity to prove our case in a court of law for the reason that we could not dig up a cause of action. You know that they never made a legal coroner's verdict. Therefore it was not possible to file an action against the non-existent judgment. So, the Pardon was the only legal declaration that could be made. They had no cause of action against Billy Roberts for the reason that there was no proof that Garrett killed anyone in Fort Sumner on July 14, as contended."

The next step for Morrison and Sonnichsen was putting this rigmarole into a book, in hopes that there existed more dupes than historians as an audience.

IMPROVING ON "BRUSHY"

"Brushy's" dying soon after the Mabry hearing was a boon to hoaxing, since his embarrassing give-away gaffes were eliminated. And rather than throwing in the towel after such a big failure, Morrison and Sonnichsen, took note of the massive publicity their hoax had generated, and wrote 1955's *Alias Billy the Kid.* And, with actual "Brushy" gone (along with his Fort Sumner steak restaurant), they were free to create a better "Brushy."

It took 62 years after *Alias Billy the Kid's* publication, for their fix-ups to be revealed. "Brushy"-believer, W.C. Jameson, in his 2012 book, *Billy the Kid: The Lost Tapes,* stated that Sonnichsen used Morrison's taped interviews to write *Alias Billy the Kid.* (Jameson, Page 29) That should mean "Brushy's" words. But no. Jameson's past co-author, Frederick Bean, had transcribed them in 1989. When Jameson compared that transcript to *Alias Billy the Kid,* he realized, as he stated: "Sonnichsen used a relatively small amount of the information contained therein. It was also apparent that Sonnichsen, a long-time college professor of English literature, **heavily edited** Robert's grammar, even **adding and deleting** words for clarity. In other places, Sonnichsen merely summarized what Roberts said." (Jameson, Page 42) Jameson missed that this meant that Sonnichsen had created a fictional "Brushy."

This fictionalizing was especially important for Billy's death scene, and the Coroner's Jury Report that proved it occurred. The response had been elaborate fakery using misstated period documents, denial of its existence, conspiracy theories, and quoting other lying old-timers' windbag malarkey addressing it.

ALIAS BILLY THE KID'S DEATH SCENE

Alias Billy the Kid's "Publisher's Foreword" features the death scene: "What if Garrett lied about killing Billy, and shot an innocent victim instead?" The rest of the book's errors were fatal and revealing. But it would be decades until "Brushy's" true-believer authors, and "Billy the Kid Case" hoaxers building on the hoax, would reveal Morrison's fatal and revealing mistake - right at the death scene intended to prove "Brushy" was Billy Bonney.

The Fort Sumner death scene had three well known elements: bright moonlight; Billy walking to the Maxwell house to cut himself a steak from the hanging side of beef there; and his going into Peter Maxwell's bedroom where hiding Pat Garrett fatally shot him in ambush. *Alias Billy the Kid's* chapter title is "Death by Moonlight." For his survival, "Brushy" has an "innocent victim" mistaken for himself (as Billy the Kid) by Pat Garrett. That victim was his claimed partner, Billy Barlow.

POSSIBLE SOURCE: Barlow is non-historical. But "Brushy's" family member, Roy L. Haws, in his 2015's *Brushy Bill: Proof That His Claim To Be Billy the Kid Was a Hoax,* found the "Billy Barlow" name in a 1930's song called "Cutty Wren." (Haws, Page 91) It was also in a popular Southwestern ballad called "Billy Barlow," derived from an old English version. (Haws, Page 90)

"Brushy's" killing scene occurs after a Jesus Silva (the dropped name of Peter Maxwell's foreman) was cooking a meal for him and Billy Barlow; and Barlow wanted "fresh beef." (The Mabry hearing's local steak restaurant has been purged!) Sensing a "trap," "Brushy" lets Barlow go alone to the Maxwell house, where his is **shot on the back porch**, not inside the bedroom! (Page 49)

SHOCKING PROMPT SOURCE: First of all, real Billy was alone in the house of Saval and Celsa Gutierrez, when he went to get meat, carrying their butcher knife.

But shockingly revealed accidentally is *why* "Brushy" had Barlow oddly shot on the back porch: "BRUSHY" CREATED HIS BARLOW SHOOTING SCENE FROM SONNICHSEN'S PROMPT, proving Sonnichsen invented the hoax's key lie.

It went like this: Sonnichsen had used a hearsay source stating Barlow was shot *outside the bedroom.* But Sonnichsen wrongly thought Maxwell's bedroom was at the *back porch.* So to be *shot outside the bedroom*, meant being *shot at the back porch.* That is why "Brushy" was coached to put Barlow there.

The footnote for the scene gives Sonnichsen's source as his April 15, 1944 interview of Jack Fountain, the son of Albert Jennings Fountain. Jack gave him windbag malarkey. He claimed Pat Garrett had told him that Billy was at the "house of a woman across the street" and went to get the beef. And the beef was in a "little outer room" beside Peter Maxwell's bedroom. From that spot, Billy asked

Peter, in his bedroom, who was there, and was told, "Nobody." Jack said, "Garrett, in the room, had a perfect target of Billy outside the room. So he shot him dead." (Page 49) Sonnichsen – evidencing his ignorance of the house's layout - added that there are many versions, but this is best, since it "places the victim outside Maxwell's bedroom."

Proved is Sonnichsen's incompetence as an historian. And proved is that he was doing shoddy, conspiracy theory-oriented research about Billy the Kid five years before partnering with Morrison! Jack's fake descriptions are give-aways. The actual side of beef hung on the cool north porch, on the *opposite side of the house* from Maxwell's south-eastern corner bedroom. Neither beef nor bedroom was at a "back porch." And there was no house "across the street." The Maxwell mansion faced a large parade ground with buildings around its perimeter. But, as usual, "Brushy" stuck to his prompts for his tales.

Also, neither the hoaxing team, nor Jack Fountain, knew Fort Sumner's layout. And when "Brushy" and Morrison visited in 1949, there were no buildings left. So "Brushy" made-up that when he heard shots (at Barlow) he ran through a gate into Maxwell's back yard (to stick to the Jack/Sonnichsen back porch fable) and shot at "shadows along the house." He was then shot by unnamed assailants through the mouth, his left shoulder, and across his forehead. He stumbled "into the gallery of an adobe behind Maxwell's yard fence," where a Mexican woman pulled him inside. (Page 49)

Then historical character, Celsa Gutierrez, entered to tell him that Garrett and his deputies were passing-off Barlow's body as his, and "they would not leave Maxwells for the night ... [because] [t]hey were afraid of being mobbed." (Page 50)

PROMPT SOURCE: Celsa's statements would have been unknown to her. They come from John W. Poe's 1933 *The Death of Billy the Kid*": "We spent the remainder of the night on the Maxwell premises, keeping constantly on our guard, as we were expecting to be attacked by friends of the dead man." (Poe, Page 44) Also, "Brushy" had no idea who Celsa was. It was just name-dropping. He had earlier called her his sweetheart and the sister of her actual husband, Saval, because they both had the name Gutierrez.

But the error that would tumble the "Brushy Bill" hoax's house of cards was something hidden here. Following the "**Death by Moonlight**" chapter title, "Brushy" is quoted for the shooting scene: "I ran through the gate into Maxwell's back yard **in the bright moonlight**." (Page 49) The moonlight was correct, and came from a source footnote: Garrett's Deputy, John W. Poe's, 1933 *The Death of Billy the Kid*, which stated: **"[T]he moon was shining very brightly**." (Poe, Page 28) That was also in *The Saga of Billy the Kid*: **"The Kid's figure stood out clearly in the moonlight.**" (Burns, Page 281) It would take 43 years to recognize how fatal to "Brushy's" hoax that night's "moonlight" had been.

FAKING NO CORONER'S JURY REPORT

Having failed at the Mabry pardon hearing, having provided no real evidence in their book that "Brushy" was Billy the Kid, and having belied their own claim of his illiteracy blocking studying-up, Morrison and Sonnichsen descended to rationalizations, hearsay, and conspiracy theories to argue for his being Billy Bonney, in chapters: "The Tangled Web," "Black and White" and "Epilogue." But everything spun-off denying the existence or reality of the Coroner's Jury Report.

"BE HE ALIVE, OR BE HE DEAD": FAKING SURVIVAL EVIDENCE

For this chapter, Sonnichsen and Morrison tried to contradict the Mabry hearing's imposter label by claiming old-timers vouched for "Brushy" as Billy the Kid, obviously meaning he survived the shooting; and the Coroner's Jury Report was fake. But offered are just random rumors that the Kid was not killed by Garrett, and five meaningless Affidavits obtained by Morrison. It was all hearsay junk, discarded by legitimate historians. The alternative is worse: intent to trick readers by faking evidence.

MEANINGLESS SURVIVAL RUMORS

Meaninglessly presented are a woman from Seven Rivers claiming Billy had dinner at her house three days after the Garrett shooting; another living in "Peñasco country" from 1887 to 1889 claiming Billy was known to be hiding there; a man from the Whipple, Arizona, Veterans' Hospital having heard that Garrett had killed a Mexican boy instead in a plot with Billy; and a Manuel Taylor telling someone that Garrett had killed a young cattle detective instead of Billy. (Pages 65-67)

Hearsay articles were cited to fake corroboration. (Pages 67-69) A June 23, 1926 El Paso *Herald* one was quoted to say that someone in Alamogordo heard that George Coe did not believe Billy was killed, and people in Lincoln did not believe it either. Dishonestly omitted is the title: "**Billy the Kid, Alive Is Ridiculed by Oldtimers;**" the actual gist being that the killing was historically verified, and Garrett and the Fort Sumner residents knew Billy and identified him when "the body lay in state for several hours." The parts quoted by Sonnichsen are at its end merely to illustrate claims that had been ridiculed.

Used was a 1938 El Paso *Herald* article about Pawnee Bill in "Frontiersmen Track Reports 'Kid' Is Alive" claiming he and others were searching for Billy as alive, but having nothing to do with "Brushy."

And an article by a Wilbur Smith, in an April of 1933 *New Mexico Magazine*, claimed that Billy's friend, Ygenio Salazar, believed he had not been killed. (Page 69) That is true. But Ygenio, as an old-timer, thought a school teacher from Mexico, who had visited him, was Billy the Kid. But Ygenio was unreliable, sadly being a morphine addict from the pain of the two bullets left in his back from the Lincoln County War Battle.

And Sonnichsen presented any preposterous claim indiscriminately. For example a C.C. McNatt of Alamogordo, "who was in the vicinity of Lincoln when the Kid was supposed to have been killed ... recalls that settlers there at the time doubted the story of the Kid's demise." (Page 67) In fact, Lincoln was 150 miles from the Fort Sumner killing, and the claim is not even McNatt's; it was hearsay from equally fantasizing others.

MEANINGLESS SURVIVAL AFFIDAVITS

An equally dishonest thrust was inducing five people, with no connection to real Billy Bonney, to sign meaningless Affidavits that "Brushy" was Billy the Kid. Three came from Morrison's taking "Brushy" on an April of 1950 trip to New Mexico and Texas; and two were from friends of "Brushy's." They were printed in full in *Alias Billy the Kid's* "Appendix."

AFFIDAVIT OF SEVERO GALLEGOS

Called by Sonnichsen "one of the best prospects" (Page 70), Severo Gallegos was the only affiant from Lincoln County. He was an old-timer Morrison previously interviewed in Ruidoso, New Mexico, on October 11, 1949 to get his apocryphal tale of getting a rope for Billy's escape horse, which was later parroted by "Brushy." (Page 45) Gallegos, living in Lincoln at the time of Billy's escape, was 11 or 12 years younger than Billy (giving birth dates of 1867 or 1868), and had no direct contact with him.

Gallegos proved himself to be a self-aggrandizing windbag in an interview he gave to a Mary Nell Taeger for a two-part article in the *Ruidoso News* titled "Severo Gallegos Tells His Story of His Family's Friend 'Billy the Kid,' " on July 30 and August 6, 1948. It appears that Morrison found the article, then interviewed Gallegos on October 11, 1949 (Page 45) to get prompting information for "Brushy." But the article, which Morrison did not cite, destroyed Gallegos's credibility.

In the July 30th part, Gallegos garbled Walter Noble Burns's *The Saga of Billy the Kid* to claim Billy told him and his family that, at age 13, he was jailed for killing his step-father for abusing his mother. Then Gallegos wildly fabricated, unaware of the Lincoln County War, capture by Pat Garrett, or Billy's Mesilla hanging trial. He had child Billy escape that step-father killing jailing to come to Ruidoso (which did not yet exist), make friends with Frank and George Coe, hide in caves, and befriend his own family. His family then saved Billy from a posse in San Patricio, and he hid Billy's horse. Then Gallegos said his father killed a man, was put in Lincoln's jail, and Billy promised to rescue him.

The August 6th part completed the lies. Gallegos has Billy dressed as a woman get into the jail, tie the jailor, and release his father and all the other prisoners from behind "iron bars" [though the courthouse-jail had no cells]. His Billy, in hiding again for unclear reasons, is captured in the Gallinas Mountains [in the northwest, where Billy never was], escapes by killing a Deputy Sheriff Johnnie Hurley [made up], then is surrounded in a fortress-like stone house in the mountains [garbling of Stinking Springs] where he surrendered and was put in jail in Lincoln. Then Gallegos inserted himself into Billy's escape, first as playing marbles with friends [from the reference to himself in *The Saga of Billy the Kid*] seeing Billy kill "jailor George" [sic-Robert Olinger], and seeing Billy breaking "every one [of the armory guns] over a big rock in the yard." [This is a garbling of Billy smashing Olinger's

Whitney double barrel shotgun after shooting the man, then throwing the pieces out the second floor window at the corpse.]

Then Gallegos gave his horse-rope tall tale, which Morrison fed to "Brushy" to parrot: "Billy yelled to me saying, "Severo ... come help Gus(the cook in the jail) [sic - Gauss] get a horse and saddle from the corral ... I went to the corral ... caught the horse ... a fine big one, black with a white nose [in truth, Gauss brought County Clerk Billy Burt's pony]... took him back to Billy. Right then Billy came out with every gun in the jail ... the one he killed George with too ... he broke every one over a big rock in the yard. [He is confabulating around the fact that, after killing Olinger from the second story, Billy smashed his Whitney double shotgun and threw it down at his body]. [Mounting the horse it] started bucking ... then Billy called to me 'Severo, see that man in the field plowing with the steers ... and the rope around their horns ... go get it.' I ran to the field ... asked for the rope ... brought it back to the Kid ... he threw it around the neck of the horse ... the saddle horn ... [this maneuver makes no sense] and was off across the field into Ventura Canyon." Following this horse lie, Gallegos claimed that "Gus" [sic - Gauss] took him upstairs in the courthouse and found a dead jailor on the steps. [In fact, Deputy Bell got to the back door; from there, Gauss dragged him outside.]"

And Morrison pressured Gallegos to sign the Affidavit. (Pages 70-71) Meeting "Brushy," Gallegos refused, saying correctly that he was too young. So Morrison told the attention-craving old-timer that he could get another visit if he could identify him as Billy. That time, Gallegos - who had never been up close to real Billy or spoken with him - identified him by "small brown spots" in his eyes and talking like Billy. His Affidavit repeated his lies from his *Ruidoso News* interview articles (Pages 117-118), with added ones. He claimed Billy was an expert shootist - though he had no proof that "Brushy" was. He also made up that he brought Billy food in the Lincoln jail. In fact, Gallegos, if legitimate, would have been the obvious person to address "Brushy" in Spanish. He did not. And "Brushy" would have failed that test.

For his 1988 unpublished book, *Brushy Bill Roberts: I Wasn't Billy the Kid*, historian Don Cline stated that Morrison first used this Gallegos's Affidavit in the Governor Mabry hearing, but that Gallegos was discredited by his preposterous *Ruidoso News* interview. (Cline, Pages 145-146)

And concealed was Gallegos's certainty that Billy was killed; stating in his *Ruidoso News* interview: "We always knew he was dead ... he would have come to see my brother Chavez ... they were always such amigos."

AFFIDAVIT OF MARTILE ABLE

Morrison, posing as "Brushy's" lawyer, took him to El Paso, Texas, to meet an 89 year old, bedfast Martile Able, who claimed that she and her husband, John Able, had been the Kid's friends [non-historical]. She gave no historic specifics, stating only that "Billy would come to our house [of indeterminate location] when he was on the dodge." (Pages 71, 119-120) Her affidavit stated that she and her husband were Texans, who lived on a ranch near Carlsbad, New Mexico [no date given, and where Billy never was], then returned to Texas. She also claimed they knew Billy in Pecos, Texas [where he never was], and he visited them [location unstated] up to 1902. She said photos of young "Brushy" looked like her "Billy" in 1880 in Pecos, Texas. Unsurprisingly, "Brushy" then told her tales of Pecos life! This tomfoolery resulted in her meaningless Affidavit.

AFFIDAVIT OF JOSÉ B. MONTOYA

In Carrizozo, New Mexico, Morrison and "Brushy" met with 80 year old José B. Montoya, a non-historical figure, who had been previously interviewed by Morrison; and for his Affidavit claimed he had **seen Billy at a bullfight in Juarez, Mexico, in 1902**. He added that an unnamed man in El Paso had told him Billy had been seen there. (Page 72) Don Cline, in his 1988 unpublished book, *Brushy Bill Roberts: I Wasn't Billy the Kid*, from Roberts family interviews, stated that **in 1902 "Brushy" was "living with his family in west Texas, which is verified by census reports**." (Cline, Page 153)

Like Severo Gallegos, Montoya made up that he knew Billy in Lincoln, that Billy stayed with his family in the Capitan Mountains, and had his own fake tale of throwing quarters in the air while Billy shot them. He added some commonly known Lincoln County history unrelated to Billy. Like the other affiants, he declared "Brushy" to be Billy without any cited examples of proof except that "he looks the same." (Page 122)

AFFIDAVIT OF DEWITT TRAVIS

The last two meaningless affidavits were by people who merely knew "Brushy," and believed his tall tales. An oddity was DeWitt Travis, born in 1889, ten years younger than "Brushy," and was an oilman friend from Longview, Texas. Inexplicably, Travis swore that he knew "Brushy" all his life.

But historian Don Cline, in his 1988 book, *Brushy Bill Roberts: I Wasn't Billy the Kid,* stated that Travis had not met "Brushy until 1930 or 1931 when "Brushy" moved to Gladewater, Texas. Cline also pointed to Travis's claim that his and "Brushy's" fathers fought together in the Civil War, though "Brushy's" father was not in the War, being nine years old when it began. (Cline, Page 165) And Travis merely repeated "Brushy's" tales of multiple personas, and demonstration of shackle-slipping. (Pages 124-125) To make sense of Travis's misinformation, Cline theorized that Travis had signed a document already prepared by Morrison. (Cline, Page 165)

In his affidavit, Dewitt Travis also cited "Brushy's" multiple scars, quoting "Brushy's" tale about being shot by Garrett's posse on July 14, 1881, and while retrieving a gun from Sheriff Brady's corpse. **Travis also claimed that "Brushy" had big "eye teeth" like "tusks," that were removed by a dentist. (Pages 74, 124) But eye teeth are the upper canines. Real Billy had protruding *incisors, the front teeth.* This bit of accidental truth was enough to sink "Brushy!"**

AFFIDAVIT OF ROBERT E. LEE

The last affiant was a 76 year old Robert E. Lee from Baton Rouge, Louisiana. (Pages 126-129) Claiming no knowledge of Billy Bonney, he was acquainted with "Brushy's" social group of Old West impersonators, and merely took "Brushy's" word that he was the Kid. Lee stated the last time he had seen "Brushy" was in "New York City in January, 1950 ... at the Jesse James Press Conference [when Morrison was passing off J. Frank Dalton as Jesse James, and using "Brushy" as witness]." Along with "Brushy," Lee may have also been a "witness" cited by the press, whom Morrison brought along to vouch for Dalton as Jesse James.

Lee's Affidavit summarized "Brushy's" tales and aliases. Giving no Billy the Kid history, Lee claimed that he himself had worked at Buffalo Bill's ranch and at his Wild West Show as his bodyguard; and that "Brushy" had worked there in 1893 as a rider in the show. Lee stated Buffalo Bill had fought Indians with "Brushy's" father, and had known "Brushy's" mother and the Roberts family in Texas. Lee provided his own tall tale that he met "Brushy" in 1889 near Fort Selden, New Mexico, where, as Billy the Kid with his "band of thieves," "Brushy" rescued him from kidnappers. This malarkey proved nothing.

REFUSED AFFIDAVITS

The only people with credible contact with Billy Bonney refused to give Morrison Affidavits. On July 2, 1950, Morrison took "Brushy" to meet Sam and Bill Jones, brothers of John and Jim Jones - who were erroneously claimed to have worked with Billy at Chisum's ranch. When shown a photograph of four Seven Rivers boys, "Brushy" identified Marion Turner as himself. The Jones brothers refused to sign affidavits, stating correctly that "Brushy" gave "no conclusive proof." (Page 72)

"IN BLACK AND WHITE": DEFAMING GARRETT AND DENYING THE CORONER'S JURY REPORT

The obvious make-or-break for the "Brushy" hoax was proving that Pat Garrett had not killed Billy the Kid. But Garrett said he did; and the Coroner's Jury Report proved it. So faked was Garrett's being a liar, and the Report's not existing.

Morrison had heralded their fabrication two years before *Alias Billy the Kid's* publication, on December 3, 1953, by defaming Garrett in his El Paso Rotary Club talk, introduced by Sonnichsen. He stated: "Garrett had made a trip into [San Miguel County] Sheriff Romero's jurisdiction in an attempt to capture the Kid. Garrett's posse purportedly killed an unidentified man there in July or August, 1881. But, did they call in Sheriff Romero and turn the matter over to him? There's no legal evidence that they did. In fact, there is no legal evidence in San Miguel Court to prove they killed anyone at that time."

FAKERY: As a Deputy U.S. Marshal, Garrett had Territory-wide jurisdiction. And saying "there is no legal evidence in San Miguel Court to prove they killed anyone at that time" is lying; since, as Morrison knew, Harold Abbott had located the Coroner's Jury Report three years earlier in San Miguel court records in the Capital Building, as was reported in November 30, 1950's *Alamogordo News* as "Sumner Jury Thought The Kid Had Been Killed." Obviously, it proved Garrett's victim was identified as William Bonney. (See pages 43-46 above)

Blather follows about Garrett's death warrant *after* Billy's jailbreak being useless, and Garrett having "no papers" to arrest

Billy on July 14, 1881; though, admittedly, none were needed. (Page 82) Sonnichsen concluded his meaningless nonsense with: "**THERE IS NO ACTUAL PROOF OF THE DEATH OF BILLY THE KID.**" (Page 82)

HIDING THE CORONER'S JURY REPORT

The fatal "black and white" proof against "Brushy," was obviously the existing July 15, 1881 Coroner's Jury Report, confirming that Garrett killed William Bonney; with its inquest identifying the body and determining the legal status of the homicide as self-defense.

So Sonnichsen lied. He said it never existed, or was "two" invalid versions, or Morrison could not find it, or its irregularity prevented Garrett from getting his reward - for a nonsensical leap that this meant Billy Bonney was not killed; and Billy Barlow was killed instead. Highlighting Sonnichsen's ridiculousness, is that the Coroner's Jury Report for Sheriff William Brady has not been located. So by his illogic, Brady was not dead either!

Alias Billy the Kid's "Appendix" even reprints the translated Coroner's Jury Report (Pages 108-109) labeled: "Report of the Coroner's Jury (translation of a Photostat copy of a **purported original which was never filed in San Miguel County**)."

FAKERY: Typical of Sonnichsen's style is snideness - "like purported original" – instead of giving real evidence to the contrary. And his claim that it was not filed in San Miguel County is typical of his incompetence, since the quoted first line of that report, right below this claim, gives its filed location: "To the attorney of the first Judicial District of the Territory of New Mexico." As discussed above, that meant it was sent to District Attorney/Attorney General William Breeden in Santa Fe. (See pages 8, 14, 29, 43-46)

Concealed also is the November 30, 1950 *Alamogordo News's* "Fort Sumner Jury Thought The Kid Had Been Killed," about Harold Abbott's 1932 finding of the Report in San Miguel County court records. (See pages 44, 112 above)

A copy was also in the Lincoln Museum, which Morrison used for research. Its Spanish photostatic copy was subsequently printed by William Keleher in his 1957 *Violence in Lincoln County: 1869-1881*, along with a translation. (See pages 9-12 above) But Sonnichsen never recanted his lies up to his 1991 death.

THE TWO-CORONER'S REPORTS SCAM

To discredit validity of the Report, Sonnichsen alleged two coroner's juries, generating no "official record." His source was an A.P. Anaya telling a George Fitzpatrick, editor of the *New Mexico Magazine*, that a first report had been lost and that Garrett and another man wrote one with different jurymen's names. (Page 83)

Sonnichsen's motive was to call Garrett a liar, since Garrett had paraphrased the Report in his *The Authentic Life of Billy the Kid*; stating: "On the following morning, the alcade, Alejandro Segura, held an inquest over the body, M. [Milnor] Rudolph of Sunnyside being foreman of the coroner's jury. Their verdict [in the Report] was that William H. Bonney came to his death from a gunshot wound, the weapon being in the hands of Pat F. Garrett; and that the fatal wound was inflicted by the said Garrett in the discharge of his official duty as sheriff and that the homicide was justifiable." (Garrett, Page 219)

FALSE EVIDENCE: Sonnichsen was apparently unaware that Anaya confirmed Billy's death. A.P. "Paco" Anaya, Billy's friend, wrote a manuscript titled *I Buried Billy*. Published posthumously in 1991, it proved Billy's vigil and burial. Anaya wrote: "I, the writer, and my brother, Higinio Garcia, and several others of those that were there, dressed Billy with those clothes then we laid him on a high bed ... [A]nd on the next day we buried him." (Anaya, Page 132) But beyond that, Anaya knew no history, his book being mere windbag malarkey - like his two coroner's juries fable - information to which he would not have been privy, as any legitimate historian would have recognized.

MORRISON'S NOT-FINDING-IT EXCUSE

Sonnichsen also repeated Morrison's scam that not finding the Report (in Las Vegas instead of correct Santa Fe) proved it was never filed. And a footnote about its copy being in the Lincoln Museum is facetiously called a "purported copy of this purported death certificate" (Page 83), and repeated for the Report translation used in the "Appendix." Not to be forgotten is that by the time *Alias Billy the Kid* was published in 1955, the finding of the Report by Harold Abbott, in 1932, and by Maurice Garland Fulton, in 1951, had been reported. And Fulton had certified his copy. Sonnichsen could have even gotten his own copy!

SCAM OF HIDING THE CORONER'S JURY REPORT'S PROPER DISPOSITION BY PAT GARRETT

Sonnichsen hid Pat Garrett's proper legal disposition of the Coroner's Jury Report, to create a fake argument of its not existing, and to call Garrett a liar. But his own footnote of the *Executive Record Book* presented its correct disposition.

THE REAL HISTORY: Countering Sonnichsen's fakery of the Report's not existing, or not being "filed," was Pat Garrett's proper disposition of it to the correct authorities, as discussed above. (See pages 8, 15-17 above)

The immediate issue was that Garrett had killed a man; so he had to establish justification. He was also justifying getting the offered reward.

Both issues were covered in his July 15, 1881 letter to Acting-Governor William Ritch (Governor Lionel Sheldon was then traveling). Garrett made clear his disposition of the Coroner's Jury Report: "I herewith annex a copy of the verdict rendered by the jury called in by the justice of the peace (*ex officio* coroner), the original of which is in the hands of the prosecuting attorney of the first judicial district [William Breeden]."

So, as stated in the Coroner's Jury Report, Alejandro Segura sent its original to the potential prosecutor, District Attorney Breeden, responsible for the First Judicial District, which included San Miguel County's Fort Sumner; and who was also Territorial Attorney General. Breeden needed the jurymen's confirmation that the killing was immune to his prosecution, with their attesting: "*[O]ur verdict is that the action of said Garrett was justifiable homicide.*" So the original was in Breeden's files.

Garrett's letter to the governor had to address another technicality, which had to do with the reward. (And he properly enclosed a copy of the Coroner's Jury Report for him.) And his letter to the Governor was made public in July 23, 1881's *Rio Grande Republican* as "Kid the Killer Killed." (See pages 15-16 above) The reward, as originally promised by Lew Wallace, was not a dead-or-alive offer. The December 22, 1880's Las Vegas *Daily Gazette*, and May 3, 1881's *Daily New Mexican*, had both stated: "I will pay $500 reward to any person or persons who will capture William Bonney, alias The Kid, and deliver him to any sheriff of New Mexico. Satisfactory proofs of identity will be required."

So the fact that there was not a capture, but a killing, had to be addressed. So Garrett did, explaining his self-defense necessity. He wrote: "It was my desire to have been able to take him alive, but his coming upon me so suddenly and unexpectedly leads me to believe that he had seen me enter the room, or had been informed by someone of the fact, and that he came there armed with pistol and knife expressly to kill me if he could. Under that impression I had no alternative but to kill him or to suffer death at his hands."

SCAM OF CLAIMING GARRETT'S REWARD WAS WITHHELD FOR AN IMPROPER REPORT AND NO IDENTIFIED BILLY THE KID

To attack the Coroner's Jury Report from another angle, Sonnichsen faked that Garrett's $500 Billy the Kid reward was withheld **for lack of proof of the killing**. (Pages 84-86) But this just proved Sonnichsen's incompetence in reading primary documents - or his lying. The simple truth was that the Legislature merely had to convert Wallace's personal reward offer to a Territorial reward. That was done. Garrett was paid. (See pages 17-25 above)

But Sonnichsen lied that Acting-Governor William Ritch refused payment **because of no record of the reward on file**, hissing snidely that this was "truly amazing ... strange and wonderful" as he revved-up for a conspiracy theory. (Page 84) For it, he misquoted Acting-Governor Ritch's report of July 21, 1881 in the *Executive Record Book* of July 25, 1867-November 8, 1882 (even though it was his own footnote source!). (Page 84). Sonnichsen's dishonest intent was to manufacture a conspiracy theory that there was something irregular or concealed about the Coroner's Jury Report, then to leap to making-up that the Report did not exist for premeditated concealment that the corpse was not Billy the Kid's – ergo, "Brushy" was surviving Billy!

THE REAL HISTORY: Garrett's meeting with Acting-Governor Ritch on July 20th, was reported by the July 21, 1881 *Santa Fe Daily New Mexican*. Ritch was quoted as "willing to pay the amount, and would be glad to do so," but the delaying issue was that proper procedure had to be followed first. (See pages 18-19 above)

But Sonnichsen, ignorantly or deceptively, called **Attorney Breeden's legal opinion to Ritch**, which Ritch had transcribed into his report of July 21, 1881 in the *Executive Record Book* of July 25, 1867-November 8, 1882, Ritch's words. Then he claimed Ritch had refused the reward! (Page 84)

THE REAL HISTORY: As discussed above with the entire "Executive Records Book" entry (see pages 19-21), the only delay in payment, as Ritch made clear, was converting Wallace's offer from personal to a Territorial one.

So Ritch had sought the legal opinion of Territorial Attorney General William Breeden (also District Attorney of the First Judicial District and recipient of the original Coroner's Jury Report).

Then Ritch quoted Breeden's opinion in his *Executive Record Book* entry. Breeden agreed that the reward was a private offer, claiming Wallace had not filed it with his office or that of the Territorial Secretary, converting it to a Territorial offer. Breeden stated (though Sonnichsen called his words Ritch's, and took them out of context): "*In addition, we will add as fact that there was no record whatever in this [Attorney General's] office or at the Secretary's office of there having been a reward offered as set forth by Attorney General, nor was there any reward or file in said offices of a corresponding reward in any form*." So the issue was just conversion for proper payment. But dishonest Sonnichsen faked that as no reward offered at all, or the reward being withheld on irregularity; which he concluded meant no Report and no corpse!

In fact, as seen in Ritch's *Executive Record Book* entry above (see pages 19-21), Garrett's request was sent for legal opinion to Attorney General Breeden concerning Lew Wallace's reward being a private offer. Breeden's answer was then excerpted by Ritch in his entry. And Breeden saw no problem with the Legislature's eventual approving of reward payment. But Breeden said if Ritch paid the reward himself *before proper procedure of legislative approval*, it could be criticized as Ritch's misappropriating of Territorial funds for Lew Wallace's private reward offer. So Ritch concluded that the reward was justified, but had to be converted to a Territorial reward for payment – as was done; and Garrett was paid. (See pages 22-23 above)

SCAM OF NO PUBLISHED REWARD NOTICES

Sonnichsen next made up that no printed notices of the reward existed. (Page 85) But he had merely checked papers using the wrong dates of December 24, 1880 for the *Las Vegas Gazette*, and May 7, 1881 for the *Santa Fe New Mexican*! He had incompetently missed the correct December 22, 1880 Las Vegas *Gazette* front page notice, and its May 3, 1881 *Daily New Mexican* repeat!

THE REAL HISTORY: On December 22, 1880, nine days after Wallace actually wrote his reward notice in the *Executive Record Book*, he published his reward notice in the *Las Vegas Gazette's* front page. After Billy's escape from the Lincoln courthouse-jail, Wallace reprinted it in the May 3, 1881 *Daily New Mexican*. It stated: "BILLY THE KID $500 REWARD, I will pay $500 reward to any person or persons who will capture William Bonney, alias The Kid, and deliver him to any sheriff of New Mexico. Satisfactory proofs of identity will be required. LEW. WALLACE, Governor of New Mexico."

But Sonnichsen leapt from faking no reward notices to claiming that proved no Coroner's Jury Report - supposedly meaning no corpse's identity. Then using Ritch's same July 21, 1881 *Executive Record Book's* "Response of Acting Governor William Ritch to Pat Garrett's Reward Petition," Sonnichsen made-up that Ritch knew "the shaky character of the purported death certificate ... [which] cannot now be, and perhaps never could never have been produced." (Page 85)

LYING: Sonnichsen, thus, maliciously and willfully hid from the readers the printed reward notices and Coroner's Jury Report, both reported by Ritch in his July 21, 1881 *Executive Record Book* entry: "*As evidence of said [reward] offer having been made the affidavit of publication thereof made by Chas. H. Green [sic – Greene] the editor and manager of the Daily New Mexican was presented with said bill, as also was presented a statement of the proceedings and verdict of a coroner's jury at Fort Sumner in San Miguel County upon the body of the said Bonny, captured as aforesaid, and a statement of Garret directed to this office of his doings in the premises.*" That meant confirmation by the Territory's highest officials of the reward and legal identification of the body as Billy Bonney's.

FAKING A SANTA FE RING CONSPIRACY OF THE LEGISLATURE FOR GARRETT'S REWARD

Still laboring dishonestly in attempt to convert the simple delay in paying Garrett his reward to a conspiracy to conceal that he did not kill Billy the Kid and hid the corpse of Billy Barlow by no Coroner's Jury Report, Sonnichsen next focused on the Legislature as being controlled by the Santa Fe Ring.

In fact, Sonnichsen had no idea of the Ring's role in Billy the Kid history. He was merely name-dropping from Maurice Garland Fulton's footnote about it being a corrupt cabal, in his 1927 annotation of Pat Garrett's *The Authentic Life of Billy the Kid.* (See pages 38-39 above). In fact, the specifics of the Ring, and the Territory-wide grass-roots uprisings against it in the 1870's were not elucidated until my 2017 *The Lost Pardon of Billy the Kid: An Analysis Factoring In the Santa Fe Ring, Governor Lew Wallace's Dilemma, and a Territory in Rebellion*; and my 2018 *The Santa Fe Ring Versus Billy the Kid: The Making of an American Monster.*

But Sonnichsen wrote that Ring bad guys were helping bad guy Garrett get the reward through the Legislature, because the Ring was against good guys Ritch and Wallace, who were Ring opponents trying to stop Garrett getting it. (Pages 85-86)

FAKERY: Sonnichsen was just writing fiction. As seen, the issue of Garrett's reward was merely one of converting Wallace's private offer to a Territorial one by legislative act. But Sonnichsen was lying to build his fake conspiracy.

In fact, Ritch was a Ringite, as Lew Wallace was warned in a 1878 secret notebook listing Ringites, given to him by Investigator Frank Warner Angel. The entry stated: "*Ritch W.G. Santa Fe Sec Territory, Axtel man, otherwise reliable.*" Governor S.B. Axtell was a central Ringite. And Wallace *refused to oppose* the vindictive Ring to protect his own political future. And by the time of Garrett's reward request, Wallace had left the Territory anyway.

Continuing his conspiracy theory, Sonnichsen again misrepresented Acting-Governor William Ritch's July 21, 1881 *Executive Record Book* response to Garrett's reward request, which mentioned Charles W. Greene. Sonnichsen made-up that Greene was **"Garrett's lawyer," and "an important Ring man."** (Page 85) This innuendo was apparently to prove Ring backing of Garrett. So Sonnichsen stated that the Ring's being "opposed to

Billy the Kid ... may explain, at least partly, why Charles W. Greene asked the legislature to do what Ritch would not or could not do. A bill was introduced to afford Garrett 'relief.'" (Page 86)

THE REAL HISTORY: Sonnichsen is lying wildly. In fact, Charles W. Greene was not Garrett's lawyer. He ran a printing company. Ritch had referenced Greene as *giving an Affidavit about having printed Lew Wallace's reward notices.* Ritch was merely establishing proof that the reward notices existed as Garrett had claimed. Ritch stated: "*As evidence of said [reward] offer having been made the affidavit of publication thereof made by Chas. H. Green [sic – Greene] the editor and manager of the Daily New Mexican was presented with said bill.*" Greene also published the *Santa Fe New Mexican*, which ran one of Wallace's two reward notices. It was a Ring-biased paper, but that is irrelevant to the reward issue. (Greene had also printed, for Wallace, reward posters for "the Kid," billing Wallace on May 20, 1881.) Greene had nothing to do with asking the Legislature for a Garrett reward.

And there was nothing sinister about the progress of Garrett's request to the Legislature. As Ritch made clear in his July 21, 1881 response to the request, the body was identified, since he had a copy of the Coroner's Jury Report with "*verdict of a coroner's Jury at Fort Sumner in San Miguel County upon the body of the said Bonney, captured as aforesaid.*" And Ritch paraphrased Attorney General William Breeden's response to the request: "*[I]t is very probable that the Legislature would approve the payment if desired, and that no objection would be raised.*" That meant Breeden too had no doubt about the body being Billy Bonney's.

Then, desperately seeking any supposed irregularity, Sonnichsen stated: "It is interesting to note that the [Legislature's] act credits Garrett with killing William Bonney 'on or about the month of August, 1881.' " (Page 86) So its not saying JULY specifically, is supposed to mean that the killing never happened; rather than a minor vagueness in a pro forma act that had not been passed until February 18, 1882, 218 days after the Coroner's Jury Report recommending reward.

THE REAL HISTORY: The actual "Act for the Relief of Pat. Garrett," of February 18, 1882, made clear the straightforward process, with the delay being a mere "technicality" [the conversion to a Territorial reward];" stating: "Garrett is justly entitled to the above reward, and payment thereof has been refused upon a technicality." (See pages 22-23 above) The issue was not the body identity - there was no doubt it was William Bonney's.

And once back in the Territory, Governor Lionel Sheldon even said, in his February 14, 1882 letter to the Legislature, that *he* would have paid it outright: "*It is a claim which I think I should have paid if it had not been understood that the matter was to be referred to the legislature before it came into my hands.*" (See page 24 above)

So, contrary to Sonnichsen's lies, the Coroner's Jury Report for William Bonney ended up getting additional scrutiny by the Acting-Governor, the Territorial Attorney General, the Governor, and the Legislature; which all agreed that Garrett killed Billy the Kid, and therefore deserved the reward.

THE MISSING HISTORY: Sonnichsen was unaware that the Ring wanted Billy dead as an anti-Ring zealot. From the Ring's angle, Garrett was paid *because* he killed Billy.

CONCLUDING WITH FAKE "DOUBTS"

Sonnichsen concludes ridiculously - based on his own lies about the Coroner's Jury Report and Garrett's reward - that foul play had occurred in 1881 because no one expected "Brushy Bill's" appearance years later to question it! (Page 86) So he concludes that Billy's death and burial are also in doubt! And all his fakery and dumb misreadings, for Sonnichsen, added up to his cry that "Brushy" deserved "his day in court in order that his representatives could produce whatever was down in black and white for or against him." (Page 86)

Omitted is that "Brushy" had his Mabry hearing, and deservedly lost. Proved, however, was that Sonnichsen was trying to insert himself into the famous history of Billy the Kid. And though he failed, his fake claims about the Coroner's Jury Report and Pat Garrett's reward would become gospel to the next generation of "Brushy"-believers, and grist for hoaxers.

"EPILOGUE": "BRUSHY'S" LAST SHOT

The "Epilogue" lumped together Sonnichsen's conspiracy theories, in lieu of any evidence, for the claim of "Brushy" as Billy.

Admitting that the survival claim required a cover-up conspiracy of Fort Sumner residents from July 14, 1881 to the present (Page 89), Sonnichsen backed that, claiming people there would have protected Billy. For irrelevant example of that loyalty, Sonnichsen quoted John W. Poe's 1933 *The Death of Billy the* Kid: "[I]f the object of my visit had been known, I should have stood no chance for my life whatever." (Page 89) But, to support his claim, he hid Poe's stated belief in his book that only a few rough local Americans were in sympathy with the Kid, "while the remainder [of the town of 200-300 people] stood in terror of him" (Poe, Pages 18-19), which removed the 100% needed for Sonnichsen's conspiracy!

More importantly, Sonnichsen omitted Poe's documentation of Billy's corpse being taken for the night vigil, and profuse identifications by townspeople. Poe wrote: "Within a short time after the shooting, quite a number of the native people had gathered around, some of them **bewailing the death of their friend**, while several women **pleaded for permission to take charge of the body, which we allowed them to do**. They carried it across the yard to a carpenter shop, where **it was laid out on a workbench**, the women placing lighted candles around it according to their ideas of properly conducting **a 'wake' for the dead.**" (Poe, Page 41-42)

After hiding Poe's eye-witness quote which was enough to sink *Alias Billy the Kid's* ship of fools, Sonnichsen claimed survival was supported by rumors. (Page 89)

And he repeated his Santa Fe Ring conspiracy theory. His illogic, with fake premises, went like this: If the Ring handled Garrett's reward money claim, then they wanted Billy to go away because he was "the hottest political potato." If so, Garrett fearing "imminent danger of mob violence, went along with a fiction which allowed Billy to get away and start a new life." (Page 90)

FAKERY: As stated above, the Ring wanted Billy dead, and got him dead. And Sonnichsen had lifted the phrase "mob violence," out of context, from Poe's fear of Fort Sumner

residents' reprisal on the night Garrett killed Billy. As Poe stated in *The Death of Billy the Kid:* "We spent the rest of the night on the Maxwell premises, keeping constantly on guard, as we were expecting to be attacked by friends of the dead man." (Poe, Page 44)

SUMMARIZING *ALIAS BILLY THE KID'S* HOAXING OF THE DEATH SCENE AND THE CORONER'S JURY REPORT

Hiding damning evidence of the Coroner's Jury Report and multiple additional eye-witness identifications of dead Billy, the "Brushy Bill" imposter hoax relied on "Brushy's" faked death scene with accidentally shot Billy Barlow, instead of himself as Billy the Kid; relied on lying that the Coroner's Jury Report did not exist; and relied on fabricated conspiracy theories garbling the Santa Fe Ring as somehow involved in hiding corpse identity and rewarding Garrett for unclear reasons.

But it would be another Morrison-Sonnichsen lie about the death scene which would lay bare their hoaxing technique. It would emerge in a later "Brushy"-believers' book; and in the even later "Billy the Kid Case" hoax. Both reprinted "Brushy' Bill's" actual long transcript from his Morrison tapes on the death scene; and both were too historically naïve to forge a fix-up.

CHAPTER 3
TRUE-BELIEVERS CONTINUE THE "BRUSHY BILL" HOAX'S FAKE DEATH SCENE AND CORONER'S JURY REPORT DENIAL

DUPES REPLACE CHARLATANS

Forty-three years after C.L. Sonnichsen's and William V. Morrison's hoax of *Alias Billy the Kid*, its dupes took over. In 1998, "Brushy" got true-believer authors. William Carl "W.C." Jameson, a country music performer, and, now deceased, Frederic Bean, a novelist. They published *The Return of the Outlaw Billy the Kid*, dedicated to Sonnichsen and Morrison. As Jameson said in their book: "This amazing story captivated me such that for the next twenty-eight years I investigated it at every opportunity." (Page vii) Both stated: "We believe the case for William Henry Roberts ["Brushy's" made-up name] as Billy the Kid is stronger than the case against it." (Page 207)

Jameson and Bean, converted by Morrison's knowing-things-not-printed trick; wrote: "Roberts' recollections of people, places, and events were too 'detailed and precise' for a semiliterate man to have come from sources other than from personal experience." (Page 165) This revealed their quirk. Since the hoax's 1950's origin, scholarly books had been written; but their faith was immune to facts. "Brushy" was gospel.

To them, missing was just more "proof." And key to their starry-eyed strategy was letting "Brushy" speak for himself through Morrison's interview tapes. (Page vii) Not till Jameson's 2012 book, *Billy the Kid: The Lost Interviews,* was it explained that Bean had gotten them in 1989 from "Brushy's" last wife's family, made a transcript, then returned them. As Jameson wrote: "I was convinced I was looking at the words of the outlaw, Billy the Kid." (*The Lost Interviews,* Page 43)

Uncensored "Brushy" was bad for their mission, but great for hoaxbusting. As Jameson had guilelessly reported in *Billy the Kid: The Lost Interviews,* Sonnichsen had *"heavily edited"* "Brushy" from those tapes. (*The Lost Interviews,* Page 42) (Sonnichsen knew that "Brushy" in the raw was what Governor Mabry saw in the pardon hearing - along with his Fort Sumner steak restaurant!)

Though role-model Sonnichsen's admitted editing was corrupting, inspiring Jameson's and Bean's secret fix-ups to add historical names - like "Regulators" - unknown to "Brushy," nevertheless, *The Return of the Outlaw Billy the Kid* froze him in largely intact in their adoration, for all to see. And what was revealed, by comparing their text to *Alias Billy the Kid's,* were Sonnichsen's dishonest fix-ups, making their book hoaxbusting treasure.

THE FAKE DEATH SCENE

To Jameson and Bean, the death scene was the holy grail. So their faith in "Brushy's" words, combined with their historical ignorance, give a view of him in the raw, comparable to his Mabry pardon hearing fiasco. This version would not be seen again as Jameson wised-up more and fixed-up more for his later "Brushy"-backing books. But now they opened a can of worms for "Brushy!"

ACCIDENTALLY LETTING "BRUSHY" REVEAL HIS HOAXBUSTING MOON ERROR

The chapter "William Henry Roberts' Story Part I: 1859-1881," just uses *Alias Billy the Kid's* death scene summary, with no quotes; and mindlessly repeats: "Billy, **easily seen in the moonlit yard**, immediately drew return fire from the lawmen." (Page 73)

Hoaxbusting treasure is in the chapter "Quien es? A Reexamination of the Shooting in Fort Sumner" (Pages 101-133) where "Brushy" finally speaks. **And he says July 14, 1881's night was dark!** And, in reality, that night's near-full moon, hovering in moon illusion at the horizon, made it light as day!

Revealingly, "Brushy's" dark night was **not in *Alias Billy the Kid*.** Sonnichsen, as supposedly quoting "Brushy" for the death scene," in the chapter he titled "Death **By Moonlight,**" had written: "I ran through the gate into Maxwell's back yard **in the bright moonlight**." (*Alias Billy the Kid,* Page 49)

So Jameson and Bean had merely copied *Alias Billy the Kid's* "Brushy" being "**easily seen in the moonlit yard**." (Page 73) But unaware of the moon's significance, they left it untampered when quoting "Brushy's" own transcript: "[After hearing the shot from Pete Maxwell's place] I pulled one of my .44's and ran through the door, **trying to see in the dark**. Two more shots came from the shadow beside the Maxwell house. **I couldn't find a target. It was too dark to see**." (Page 112) "Brushy stuck to darkness with: "emptying my six-shooter at the shadow where I saw the muzzleflash." (Page 113) And "Brushy" used the darkness to explain the accidental killing of Barlow: "Garrett knew by now that he'd **killed the wrong man in the dark**." (Page 117) Also, "Brushy" had Celsa Gutierrez say: "They took the body of your friend inside the house and they say it is yours ...**Your partner looks very much like you in the dark."** (Page-117)

CRACKING THE "BRUSHY BILL" IMPOSTER HOAX: **Thus, "Brushy's" dark night moon error, in one fell swoop, proved not only that he was not present in Fort Sumner on the night of July 14, 1881, but that Sonnichsen and Morrison had willfully, dishonestly, and despicably fixed-up and concealed his fatal error to perpetrate their hoax of his being Billy the Kid. And by Jameson's next books, his newly fixed-up bright moonlight would prove his descent into active hoaxing himself.**

ACCIDENTALLY LETTING "BRUSHY" REVEAL THE REST OF HIS DEATH SCENE ERRORS

Jameson and Bean also provided the rest of "Brushy's" hoax-revealing claims; as follows:

"Brushy" said he had been hiding at "the Yerby Ranch." (Page 105) **[Billy was in Maxwell's sheep camps.]**

"Brushy" said: "Pat's wife was a sister to my friend, Saval Gutierrez, and Saval told me that Pat was after me – he heard it from his sister." (Page 106) "She was another of Saval's sisters, named Celsa, and she had been a sweetheart of mine." (Page 116) **[Celsa and Saval were husband and wife.]**

"Brushy" said he and Billy Barlow went to Jesus Silva's house in Fort Sumner. **[Billy was at Celsa and Saval's house; Barlow was fictional; and Silva was name-dropping Maxwell's foreman.]**

"Brushy" said, after hearing three shots, he ran to "Maxwell's back porch." (Page 113) **[The back porch was unrelated; but "Brushy" got it from Sonnichsen's prompt source error claiming the bedroom was there with the side of beef beside it. (See pages 117-118 above)]**

"Brushy" said "too many guns were shooting at me;" and that he emptied his .44. (Page 113) **[There were over 200 residents, and no such gunfire was heard by anyone.]**

Wounded by those unnamed shooters, "Brushy" said: "I ran past a little adobe shack down the alley from Pete Maxwell's" from which a Mexican woman took him in. (Page 114) **[He was unaware that Fort Sumner's buildings were arranged around Fort's original parade ground.]**

"Brushy" quoted Celsa: "They took the body of your friend inside the house." (Page 116) **[He had tried to match the historical scene of the shooting in Peter Maxwell's bedroom.]**

"Brushy" has Celsa present the Barlow hoax with the murdered and concealed innocent victim: "Pat is telling everyone you are dead. They took the body of your friend inside the house and they say it is yours. Some men from the town have already been sent to dig a grave by lantern light ... Your partner looks very much like you in the dark except for his beard ... Pat says they will bury the body in the morning. If the coffin is closed, who will guess that you are not inside it?" (Pages 116-117)

FUTURE HOAXING: This is noteworthy because when this fake omniscient quoting appeared in a future Jameson book, it would be a forgery in the mouth of a new character, and would be an expanded vehicle for using characters to present the hoax's conspiracy theories and to add information to match the hoax's claims! (See pages 277, 289 below)

FAKING DEATH SCENE SUSPICIONS

Having presented their testament with "Brushy's" sacrosanct words, Jameson and Bean attack the philistines who denied their truth, that he was Billy the Kid, by expanding the Morrison-Sonnichsen gospel of explanatory conspiracy theories.

CONSPIRACY OF HISTORIANS

Jameson and Bean acknowledge that historians called "Brushy" an imposter. But the mountain of denials elicits only accusations that historians want to maintain the *status quo*, refuse to admit to being wrong so long, and perpetuate myth and misinformation. (Pages 15, 185-186) They state: "There exists a confederacy of Billy the Kid researchers and writers, an informal alliance composed of a number of adherents to the prevailing and accepted theories regarding the death of the outlaw ... The alliance dismissed Roberts ... The truth is, however, their efforts were never supported by valid scientific and historical research." (Pages 15-16)

CONSPIRACY OF GARRETT

Obviously the key person to denounce is Pat Garrett, who knew Billy and killed him. So Jameson and Bean lie that the only evidence that he killed Billy "was the word of Pat Garrett." (Page 14) "None of the so-called facts relating to the death of Billy the Kid at the hands of Pat Garrett have ever been supported by concrete, or even competent evidence." (Page 125)

FAKING DEATH SCENE SUSPICION

For proof, they make-up discrepancies to claim a conspiracy. So Garrett's seeing two figures in the peach orchard, and later realizing one was Billy on the killing night, is called suspicious because Poe did not have that in his book. (Page 105)

MEANINGLESS: Poe's 1933 *The Death of Billy the Kid* was published 52 years after the event. This minor and insignificant observation was recorded by Garrett right after it for his *Authentic Life of Billy the Kid*, coming out the next year. There is nothing suspicious.

They question Billy's asking Maxwell: "Quien es?" They wrote: "If Billy the Kid, an Anglo, had entered Maxwell's bedroom and encountered the resident, who spoke excellent English, why would he question him in Spanish? It is likely that a person of Mexican heritage would be more inclined to speak Spanish instead of English." (Page 123)

PREPOSTEROUS: This is not only absurd, but contrives to make Billy Barlow match their claim of his Mexican identity. And it hides that bi-lingual Billy, disguising himself, would indeed use Spanish with bi-lingual Maxwell about a stranger in the room. There is no discrepancy.

They question why Billy did not shoot the deputies on the porch since "there was a full moon - light enough for anyone to see" (forgetting that their man "Brushy" said it was a dark night)!

MEANINGLESS: They forget Poe's own statement that strangers could be in town, with him thinking that approaching Billy could be Maxwell's guest. (Page 110) Billy would have been equally uncertain of who they were, which is why he asked Poe: "Quien es?" He would have had no idea that they were deputies, or its being a trap. His walking into it, proved that! There was no discrepancy.

Attempt is made to turn Poe's book's initial disbelief after the shooting ("Pat, the Kid would not come to this place; you have shot the wrong man" (Poe, Page 37)) into proof that he killed the Kid, by claiming that Poe accepting it was Billy Bonney was based "entirely on what he was told by Garrett." (Page 198)

FAKERY: Omitted is Poe's quote of Garrett's response: "I am sure that that was him, for I know his voice too well to be mistaken." (Poe, Page 38) And omitted is that Poe subsequently knew that Peter Maxwell, Deluvina Maxwell, 200 townspeople in the night vigil, and the Coroner's Jurymen, all identified the body as Billy Bonney's; and was left with no doubt himself. There was no discrepancy.

They state that the only witnesses to the shooting were Pat Garrett and Peter Maxwell, with John Poe and "Kip" McKinney, falsely discounted because they were outside the room. They then claim that "Maxwell contributed very little relative to describing what actually took place in the room." (Page 119)

FAKERY: This hides that Maxwell knew, and could identify Billy, and made a definitive Coroner's Jury Report statement on July 15, 1881: "[The jurors] examined the evidence of Pedro Maxwell, which evidence is as follows: "I being in my bed in my room, at about midnight on the 14th day of July, Pat F. Garrett came into my room and sat down. William Bonney came in and got close to my bed with a gun in his hand and asked me "who is it" and then Pat F. Garrett fired two shots at the said William Bonney and the said William Bonney fell near my fire place and I went out of the room and when I came in again about three or four minutes after the shots the said William Bonney was dead."

They state that there was confusion "about whether the body had fallen inside the room or out on the porch." (Page 188)

FAKERY: There is no historical confusion. This is made-up using "Brushy's" "back-porch-body" fabrication, which parroted Sonnichsen's fabrication, which confused the location of the bedroom and side of beef. (See pages 117-118 above) There is no discrepancy.

They claim a discrepancy about immediate disposition of the body by alleging the carpenter's shop vigil contradicted the Coroner's Jury's viewing the body in the Maxwell house. (Page 188)

FAKERY: There was no contradiction. The vigil was at night; the body would have been carried into the house in the morning for the inquest.

They allege that Poe's account of the body being taken to the carpenter's shop was countered by a book by Charles Frederick Rudulph titled "*Los Billitos: The Story of Billy the Kid and his Gang*," published by a Louis Leon Branch in 1980 from Rudulph's 1880 manuscript. They claim that Rudulph **stated that the body was on the floor for the coroner's jury**.

FAKERY: Charles Rudulph did not say that. In his book, he wrote: "Alejandro Segura, justice of the peace, had been happy to see his friend [Milnor] Rudulph, whom he knew was of unquestionable integrity and clear thinking. He appointed him to head the coroner's jury, and together they picked other prominent level-headed leaders of the community to fill the remaining five seats. <u>They met over the Kid's body and with no</u>

argument or dissent unanimously agreed on the following report given below." (Rudulph, Page 252) [The Coroner's Jury Report is then provided in English. (Rudulph, Page 253)] And Rudulph claimed his father, Milnor, brought him along: "Hearing the news, Milnor Rudulph called Charley from his bed, and together they sped through the night to Fort Sumner." (Rudulph, Page 252) In fact, Charles Rudulph fully confirmed, from his being present the morning after the shooting, that the body was identified as Billy's by Garrett, Peter Maxwell, Deluvina Maxwell, Luz Maxwell, townspeople, and the coroner's jury headed by his father - whom he calls "six honorable men [who] affixed their signatures and marks to the post mortem of William Bonney, 'Billy the Kid.'" (Rudulph, Pages 253-254) There was no discrepancy.

Jameson and Bean ruminate about the caliber of the gun carried by Billy, or there being no gun. A hearsay account of Lucien Maxwell's great-granddaughter is used to claim that fear that Billy was alive made the men have Deluvina go in first to check before entering themselves. (Pages 119-123)

MEANINGLESS: That only adds another eye-witness, since Deluvina and Billy were friends! There is no discrepancy.

Then they use "Brushy" for evidence! They state: "William Henry Roberts maintained that the man who went to Maxwell's room was a friend named Billy Barlow."

MIXED-UP: "Brushy's" version was that Barlow was shot on the back porch, not the bedroom. As "Brushy" stated: "From the corner of my eye I saw the body lying on the back porch ... I knew it had to be Barlow." (Page 113) "Brushy" then had the Celsa character describe taking the body to the Maxwell house: "They took the body of your friend inside the house and they say it is yours." (Pages 116-117) And "William Henry" was "Brushy's" made-up name.

But, still trying to make the body Barlow's, Jameson and Bean add fakery unused by Morrison and Sonnichsen, and absent in *Alias Billy the Kid*; writing: "It has been stated by Sonnichsen that Barlow may have been half Mexican." (Page 123)

FAKERY: This is Sonnichsen's hoaxing, building on an article, also cited by Jameson's and Bean, by journalist, Singleton M. Ashenfelter, on July 23, 1881 titled "Exit 'The Kid'" in his Grant County newspaper, *The New Southwest*, in which he made-up an outlaw fantasy that the corpse of Billy the Kid had a beard and "stained his skin to look like a Mexican." Jameson's and Bean's Bibliography cites their interview with Sonnichsen dated June 25, 1991 in Oklahoma City, Oklahoma, when he seems to have told them this. It is mere fable.

Jameson and Bean also forgot that Billy Barlow was *their* victim, and "Brushy" said *they* looked the same – which was how Barlow was passed-off as him. (The November 30, 1950, *El Paso Herald Post's* article by Vernon Smylie, " 'Billy the Kid' Flunks in Talk With Governor," quoted "Brushy": "The fellow that was killed was named Billy Barlow," Roberts said. "I was with him. We looked like two peas in a pod.") And Grant County put Ashenfelter about 250 miles from the fast Fort Sumner burial, so he obviously faked his "outlaw" description for his readership.

Then they claim there was another version of the shooting, and quote Sonnichsen's hearsay interview of April 15, 1944 with Jack Fountain, A.J. Fountain's son. (Page 124)

FAKERY: They are repeating Sonnichsen's use of Jack's interview faking the side of beef beside Maxwell's door, which led Sonnichsen to think the death scene happened at the back porch, resulting in "Brushy's" parroted back-porch-Barlow fable. (See pages 117-118 above) But Jameson and Bean miss that Jack Fountain confirmed that Pat shot Billy. There was no discrepancy.

They use a hearsay claim from Morrison that an unnamed man called the law firm doing "Brushy's" pardon case to say that McKinney told Garrett in a saloon "that he should know that he had not killed anyone that night." (Page 126)

MEANINGLESS: Hearsay is not valid evidence.

This meaningless conglomeration elicits the Jameson-Bean conclusion: "[N]o credible evidence exists to indicate what actually occurred in Pete Maxwell's bedroom around mid-night on 14 July 1881. Or who was killed." (Page 126)

FAKING NO CORONER'S JURY REPORT

Jameson and Bean approach the impassable hurdle of the Coroner's Jury Report by copying Sonnichsen's convoluted lying in *Alias Billy the Kid* that Pat Garrett's reward for killing Billy the Kid was withheld for lack of a Coroner's Jury Report proving the body's identity. (Page 14); instead of the innocuous truth that payment was delayed simply by need to convert Lew Wallace's private reward into a Territorial one by legislative act, since he had already left the Territory. (See pages 17-25 above)

CONSPIRACY OF GARRETT'S REWARD

To claim their conspiracy around Garrett's reward, "Brushy" is quoted as saying: "Garrett realized his mistake and was making a try at collecting the reward that was out on me anyway." (Page 117) And Sonnichsen's fakery is repeated about Acting-Governor Ritch denying the reward; with their added faking that Garrett never got it. (Page 129) They also add that the reward was denied because he had not killed Billy, or "the death certificate was never found" [meaning the Coroner's Jury Report was never found], or the Legislature gave Garrett the money because they were "his henchmen." They add, like Sonnichsen, "suspicion" because the Legislature wrote August, not July, for the killing date in the act granting the reward. (Page 129)

FAKERY: This is repetition of Sonnichsen's fakery, with their added fakery. Noteworthy, is that Jameson, in his later books, would continue to repeat the absurd "August" clerical imprecision in the legislative act for Garrett's reward, as if it was meaningful evidence that something was irregular in the reward. But the truth is that the reward was granted because everything was in order.

CONSPIRACY OF THE CORONER'S JURY

Obviously, William Bonney's Coroner's Jury Report of July 15, 1881 was the bugaboo, with its profuse evidence of existing - with its English translation even in *Alias Billy the Kid* - and its identification of the body as Billy Bonney's. So Jameson and Bean made-up conspiracies to hide all that.

CONSPIRACY OF MILNOR RUDULPH

Jameson and Bean sought suspicion about Coroner's Jury President, Milnor Rudulph. So, for John Poe's July 14, 1881 recognizance to Sunnyside's Postmaster, Milnor Rudulph, about Billy, they portray him as "a friend of the Kid." (Page 102) Poe's observing that Rudulph was "nervous out of fear of the Kid," to them meant Rudulph was "protective of the Kid" against lawmen, and gave misleading information. (Page 189) Or maybe he and Garrett had plotted to make the Kid seem "officially dead." (Page 191) So Jameson and Bean conclude that he was part of a conspiracy to hide Billy's survival to let him go free. (Page 190)

FALSE: As discussed, Rudulph was an Ringite, who in 1872, as Speaker of the House, assisted the Ring's take-over of the Legislature to block anti-Ring bills; thus, precipitating what I named the 1872 Legislature Revolt: the first anti-Ring uprising in the Territory. Rudulph was Billy's *enemy*, and likely feared reprisal from him for betrayal. (See pages 53, 74 above) And Rudulph would not have known that Poe was a lawman. And Rudulph's son, Charles, had ridden on a Garrett posse to capture or kill Billy.

CONSPIRACY OF CORONER'S JURYMEN

Jameson and Bean fabricate that the inquest was "shrouded in confusion and mystery" (Page 126), make-up "suspicions," and conclude: "There is, in fact, no legal proof of the death of Billy the Kid." (Page 129)

But their "proof" of no proof was preposterous and fabricated! They claimed the inquest was fast. (Page 126) **[Why not?]** They claimed Garrett did not put the body on public display. (Page 126) **[For whom? It was an isolated town, and its more than 200 residents had already conducted a vigil for it that night.]** They wanted the body photographed. (Page 126). **[By whom? Rural people in 1881 did not have cameras.]** They recycled Sonnichsen's A.P. Anaya malarkey of two coroner's jury reports. (Pages 126-127) **[But Anaya had no access to knowing about any report at all; and they were apparently unaware that he was real Billy's friend and, in his manuscript, claimed to be an eye-witness preparing dead Billy for burial, in his book published posthumously in 1991 as *I Buried Billy*.]** They claimed: "To date, no one has ever seen the document."

(Page 127) **[The photostatic copy of the original report is in William Keleher's 1957 *Violence in Lincoln County*, cited in their own Bibliography.]** They questioned spelling of the signers' names, and make-up that the report was a forgery by Garrett. (Page 128) **[But Garrett, as the homicide suspect, would have had no access to writing the report.]** They claimed that the Report "never made it to the official records of San Miguel County," and "Justice of the Peace Segura never made an entry regarding the report in his own books." (Page 118) **[As discussed above, the original Report was sent to District Attorney of the First Judicial District William Breeden – as the Report itself stated. It was stored in Santa Fe <u>with his records for the San Miguel County court</u>, and was found in 1932 in the basement of the State Capitol. (See pages 43-46 above) Segura was irrelevant.]** Added is that Morrison was told there was no filed report by an August 14, 1951 letter from District Attorney Jose E. Armijo in Las Vegas. **[That was because it was not filed there! And Morrison must have known, then hid, that on "Brushy's" pardon hearing day of November 30, 1950, the *Alamogordo News* confirmed the Report's finding, almost 20 years earlier, in its Santa Fe filing, and confirming dead Billy Bonney!]**

CONSPIRACY OF BURIAL

Jameson and Bean stated: "There has long been uncertainty relative to whose remains, if anyone's, is buried at the Fort Sumner site." (Page 132) **[But the uncertain gravesite within Fort Sumner's cemetery has nothing to do with Billy Bonney having been killed, indicating instead poor cemetery maintenance and flooding disrupting graves.]**

Claimed is that the body was seen only by Garrett, Poe, McKinney, "and two or three other people." (Page 130) **[This omits Peter Maxwell, Deluvina Maxwell, over 200 townspeople in the night vigil, and the Coroner's Jury.]** Leon Metz, Garrett's biographer, is misrepresented as saying in his *Pat Garrett: The Story of a Western Lawman*, that Garrett could have passed off the body. (Page 130) **[Metz's book confirmed that Garrett killed Billy.]**

They give the fake corpse identity created by Grant County journalist S.M. Ashenfelter in his July 23, 1881 *The New*

Southwest's "Exit 'The Kid', that the corpse was dark-skinned, like a Mexican, and bearded. (Page 119) So they solemnly, preposterously, and with what they call "scientific style," cite a book on sexual maturity (with "SMR's - Sexual Maturity Ratings") to compare Ashenfelter's corpse to fair beardless Billy, to show the impossibility of his transformation from fair and blue-eyed to dark-skinned and bearded. So they conclude that the body could not have been Billy's. (Page 131) **[They forgot that Billy Barlow was *their* victim, and "Brushy" whole death scene was based on their looking identical – fair and unbearded!]**

Hearsay tales follow about non-historical people claiming a Mexican that looked like Billy had been shot, or a Maxwell hired hand was shot, or that the wagon carrying the casket had an "armed guard" so no one could see the body. (Pages 132-133)

And Yginio Salazar of Lincoln is fabricated as being one of Billy's pallbearers and not knowing the gravesite. (Page 133) **[For the future, this uncertain site admission is important, because the "Billy the Kid Case" hoax, which continued the "Brushy Bill" hoax, would fake certainty of its location.]**

MOTHER OF ALL CONSPIRACY THEORIES

By the book's end, Jameson and Bean were out-of-control with death scene conspiracy theories. They claimed:

All Fort Sumner people were in a conspiracy. They tricked Garrett into thinking he had killed Billy, since they were "friendly and sympathetic to the Kid ... [and they perpetuated] the masquerade well into the twentieth century because they knew the Kid was still alive." (Page 189) This scenario is "Brushy's" own, since Jameson and Bean state: "According to Roberts, the two (Jesus Silva and Deluvina) decided to perpetuate a deception, perhaps allowing Garrett to believe the victim was, in fact, the wanted outlaw." (Page 189)

FAKERY: More than absurdity ruins this; it needs Garrett unable to recognize Billy. But Garrett knew him; captured him at Stinking Springs; and transported him by train to Las Vegas, then Santa Fe, for jail. And, as Sheriff, Garrett imprisoned him in his Lincoln jail, awaiting his hanging.

THE JAMESON-BEAN OUTCOME

The whole "Brushy Bill" hoax house of cards was obviously built on his survival. That entailed the Billy Barlow fable of how that occurred by an accidental and covered-up shooting by Pat Garrett, the denial of the existence of the Coroner's Jury Report confirming the corpse as Billy Bonney's, and conspiracy theories to explain why none of this hogwash was accepted as real.

At the end of Jameson's and Bean's meaningless game, the score was still "Brushy" zero. And the Jameson-Bean plan for *The Return of the Outlaw Billy the Kid* to reveal "Brushy's" own words, made clear his chaotic death scene, and let him spout his tale of a dark and moonless night of July 14, 1881 that would expose them all as fakers.

The hoaxing was now obvious, since Morrison and Sonnichsen not only knew about the Coroner's Jury Report's existing, but put its English translation in their book's "Appendix." But most important, was ignorant Jameson's and Bean's inadvertent revealing of "Brushy's" moon error. The "dark night" of July 14, 1881 would become a give-away for "Brushy"-believing hoaxers. Then it would mark Jameson as a convert to active hoaxing when he did its fix-up to the correct "bright moonlight" in his later "Brushy" books.

PART III

THE JOHN MILLER IMPOSTER HOAX AND THE FAKED DEATH SCENE AND DENIED CORONER'S JURY REPORT

CHAPTER 1 JOHN MILLER'S IMPOSTER HOAX'S DEATH SCENE AND CORONER'S JURY REPORT FAKERY

RIDING ON "BRUSHY'S" COATTAILS

Obscure Billy the Kid imposter, John Miller, dead since 1937, with no known believers, only made it to wider public awareness by riding the pretender trail cut by the "Brushy Bill" hoax. In 1993, Miller got an author named Helen Airy for her *Whatever Happened to Billy the Kid?* A lethargic hoaxlet, it kept secret that Miller had been almost a decade older than Billy the Kid - so no "Kid." It used the "Brushy" hoax premise of Pat Garrett's accidental shooting of an innocent victim, and Billy surviving.

It would have remained in obscurity except for a later imposter hoax: the "Billy the Kid Case." Started in 2003, by 2005, it became desperate for any imposter's bones for its fake forensic DNA matchings. So its illegal exhumation of John Miller made the news. And my 2019 book, *Billy the Kid's Pretender John Miller*, debunked his and Helen Airy's hoaxing, and showed his violated remains playing a key role in the "Billy the Kid Case" hoax.

A FAKE DEATH SCENE AND A MINIMIZED CORONER'S JURY REPORT

For posing as Billy the Kid, John Miller needed a survival death scene. So Helen Airy started her book with a tiny sly one: "It was near midnight on July 14, 1881, when Sheriff Pat Garrett shot someone in Pete Maxwell's darkened bedroom in the old officers' quarters in Fort Sumner, where Maxwell lived." (Page 9) Why that "someone" was not Billy is missing; though later, to Miller, is attributed a tale of Pat Garrett's accidental killing of an Indian-friend-dressed-similarly death scene.

Airy added that there was a cover-up of the victim's identity because Pat Garrett and a coroner's jury identified Billy, but there were "doubts." (Page 9) She mentions an unreferenced, heretofore unknown document, and says: "When he was asked to sign an affidavit that it was the Kid he had shot, Garrett refused to sign." (Page 9) She also malingers: "McKinney and Poe accused Garrett of shooting the wrong man" (Pages 9, 13) adding McKinney to her own distortion of John Poe's statement of initial identity concern in his 1933 book, *The Death of Billy the Kid*; and explained by his not knowing Billy.

Airy concluded: "But all through the years since that night, there have been doubts that it really was Billy the Kid's body they buried the next day." (Page 9) Why doubts? Airy says unnamed people "saw Billy" after the death date **[meaningless hearsay]**; some Coroner's Jurymen signed with an X **[so what, they were illiterate]**; there was "irregularity" in filing the Coroner's Jury Report **[untrue]**; and the corpse was seen by only a few people **[untrue]**. For witnesses, she lists Garrett and his deputies, "immediate family members" **[there were none]**, and adds snidely: "supposedly, members of the coroner's jury" **[snideness is no argument]**. Without attempting a conspiracy theory, she declared: "Surely there was reason to wonder."

For the actual scene, she gave "Brushy Bill's(!)" version of first being at a dance! And the historical shooting is called "Garrett's version." Then she tried to manufacture doubts. She says the Kid would not go into a darkened room; makes-up that Poe said Garrett was not a good enough shot to hit the Kid; makes-up that Poe and McKinney accused Garrett of shooting the wrong man; says people saw Billy after the death date; and makes-up that years after the death date rewards were offered for arrest of Billy. (Page 27) The coroner's jury is attacked as "hastily recruited," with illiterate signatures with an X, no one viewing the body, and no official report filed. (Page 27)

MILLER'S PRE-DEATH SCENE SHOOTING

Bizarrely, Miller had added a pre-death scene shooting of himself, backed by his wife, Isadora. To friends and neighbors, she claimed that he, as "the Kid," had been shot "**some days before the shoot-out at Pete Maxwell's house,**" - without elaboration as to why or by whom - and that Isadora tended his wounds and hid him from "officers" [unclear who they were] in her Fort Sumner house's mattress. (Page 9) But, for unstated reason, the Santa Fe Ring of "unscrupulous and treacherous men" and Thomas Benton Catron were after him, as well as Governor Lew Wallace [actually gone from the Territory]. (Pages 11, 13)

Oddly, Airy makes no attempt to reconcile the death scene with John Miller's claim of being shot days before it.

FOR SURVIVAL TALES, OLD-TIMERS SAY MILLER WAS BILLY

Having offered nothing to indicate that Miller was Billy the Kid, Helen Airy used non-historical old-timers. Most merely said he *told them or others they knew* that he was Billy the Kid.

HERMAN TECKLENBURG

A Herman Tecklenburg, made-up that he knew John Miller in Fort Sumner as Billy the Kid; and was later his "most trusted friend." (Page 42) On August 9, 1944, Tecklenburg, then a janitor, but claiming to have been a cowpuncher and Indian hunter, gave an interview for the *Gallup Independent*, to a Wesley Huff, titled: "Did Garrett Kill Billy the Kid? Herman Tecklenburg Says No; Billy Lived on Ranch at Ramah 35 Years Ago and Visited Him." Tecklenburg stated: "They shot somebody over in Fort Sumner, and they buried him there and put an end to the hunt for Billy the Kid. But it wasn't Billy they shot. He and his Mexican wife escaped over into Old Mexico ... [Later] he was ranching it down near Ramath. They all knew of him down there as Billy the Kid, but never spoke of it for fear of getting him in trouble." (Page 43)

Jim Johnson, in his 2006 book, *Billy the Kid, His real Name Was ...* exposed Tecklenburg's lying through family records, showing that he was born in Germany on June 9, 1869, and immigrated to the United States as a teenager, **arriving on**

June 5, 1884. (Johnson, Page 4) Thus, in 1880 and 1881, he was in Germany, not in Fort Sumner as "Billy the Kid's friend."

FRANK BURRARD "BURT" CREASY

Frank Creasy, was a hired ranch hand of John Miller's. He alleged that Miller told him his history as Billy the Kid. It is Helen Airy's only sample of Miller's own fabrications: garbled from Pat Garrett's *The Authentic Life of Billy the Kid* or Walter Noble Burns's *The Saga of Billy the Kid*.

The utterly confused death scene is presented. Creasy claimed that a $10,000 reward had been made for Billy, dead or alive. In 1880, in the company of an Indian boy who looked like him, he **went to Lincoln** to visit his Mexican sweetheart. Hearing that a side of beef hung next door, the Indian went there to steal some meat. "Pat Garrett, who was the marshal of Lincoln at the time, and a well known bounty hunter, heard that Billy was in town and along with two of his deputies laid in waiting near the side of beef. **When the Indian boy stepped up onto the veranda of the house, he was shot down by Pat Garrett, who had apparently mistaken him for Billy**. Billy [Miller] told me once that he and the Indian were dressed alike to confuse people. Pat Garrett was afraid of the reaction of townspeople and immediately buried the body. [And he collected the $10,000 reward.] (Page 92)

Creasy concluded: "Billy [Miller] hearing the shooting, and after finding out what happened he immediately left with the Mexican girl, whom he later married." (Page 92)

Important is not only the total misinformation - including the shooting in **Lincoln instead of Fort Sumner**, 150 miles away in San Miguel County - but that totally ignorant Helen Airy thought it was correct! Creasy's fabrications inspired her to a vehement crescendo of conspiracy theory hoaxing. She wrote: "To date, American historians maintain Sheriff Pat Garrett **killed Billy the Kid in Lincoln County, New Mexico**. But according to Creasy's account Garrett killed the wrong man, concealed the error and collected the reward ... For reasons unknown, historians in the United States failed to follow up on the leads Frank Creasy furnished about John Miller's claim that he was Billy the Kid." (Page 92)

BILL CROCKETT

Bill Crockett, speaking for Miller's adopted son, Max Miller, his friend; stated: "I do believe John Miller was truly William Bonney, alias Billy the Kid ... Max told me many times that Miller had told him ... there was a Mexican shot and buried in the coffin that was supposed to be the Kid." (Page 155) **[But Miller had told Frank Creasy that the victim was his Indian friend dressed like him.]**

OTHER OLD-TIMERS FOR SURVIVAL TALES

Helen Airy's other meaningless interviews with old-timers demonstrated that it was common in their day to fake personal knowledge of Billy the Kid to shine by reflected glory.

An Apollas Boaz Lambson's son, Eugene Lambson, said, when he was a boy, his father knew John Miller in Ramah, and Miller "talked a lot about Billy the Kid." He recalled his father telling him he knew Pat Garrett too, who told him that Billy the Kid was hiding in Pete Maxwell's house, so Garrett knocked on the door and a Mexican youth opened it, and Garrett shot him dead. Then he told Billy the Kid and his girlfriend "to pack up and leave Lincoln County forever." (Page 50) From this fakery, Helen Airy concluded absurdly that when John Miller and his wife went to El Paso for supplies, they were actually socializing with Pat Garrett as friends! (Page 50)

In about 1883, an Emma Tietjen, one of Mormon Earnest Tietjen's wives, was frightened by some rough men who came to the house when she was alone, so she hit one over the head with a bowl of butter. Another man told her she had hit Billy the Kid; though no one said he was John Miller. And nothing was done to her. To Helen Airy, that proved Billy was alive after the 1881 Fort Sumner shooting and was John Miller! (Page 62)

CONCLUDING SURVIVAL FAKERY

Pretending that her nonsense proved something, Helen Airy launched a conspiracy theory that "the testimonies that Billy the Kid had escaped death in Fort Sumner [she forgot that Bernard Creasy said Miller said it was in Lincoln] were silenced [because] the myths surrounding Billy the Kid and Pat Garrett were too overwhelming." (Page 147) She wildly fantasized that maybe Susan McSween, "Cattle Queen of the Pecos," had helped Miller escape New Mexico; or even got money for him from John Tunstall's family. (Pages 159-160)

Airy's small "Afterward" has hearsay claims by non-historical people, like the fake Affidavits in "Brushy Bill's hoax. So a woman whose father lived near Fort Sumner in the early 1900's said a Mexican he worked for told him he saw Billy the Kid in bullfights in Mexico after the death date. Someone from Albuquerque was told by a man who died in 1935 and said he worked for Pete Maxwell, that an Indian who died the night before the supposed shooting of Billy was buried as him. A man told his family that he was Billy the Kid's friend, and helped bury the body, and it was not Billy's. A granddaughter of Sheriff William Brady told someone that someone told her that Garrett had not killed Billy, but had killed a "wanderer" to let Billy escape. And George Coe is claimed as not believing Billy was shot; though he had no way of knowing. (Pages 162-163)

For fake press reports of Billy sightings after his death, Airy presented tabloid-like *El Paso Times* articles from the 1920's to 1960's. For example, the Fort Sumner Billy the Kid grave is said to have been "marked by a rude cross, that was to prove to Billy's sister that he was still alive." (Page 165) **[But Billy had no sister. And he was dead!]**

Airy concluded whimsically: "And so William Bonney, alias Billy the Kid, alias John Miller, alias The Old Man, alias Old Dad, died alone and was buried in the Arizona Pioneer [sic] Home Cemetery in Prescott. But John Miller won the last round. He was not hanged by the lackeys of the Santa Fe Ring." (Page 148)

SUMMARY

Presenting no evidence whatsoever that John Miller was Billy Bonney, Helen Airy's book nevertheless bears striking resemblance to the more labor-intensive "Brushy Bill" hoax: having a death scene of an accidentally shot innocent victim, denying the Coroner's Jury Report, and offering vague conspiracy theories to explain the fables.

PART IV

THE "BILLY THE KID CASE" HOAX AND THE FAKE DEATH SCENE AND DENIED CORONER'S JURY REPORT

CHAPTER 1
THE "BILLY THE KID CASE" FORENSIC DNA HOAX

A HOAX BASED ON THE DEATH SCENE

The "Billy the Kid Case" hoax was arguably the most elaborate and most expensive historic-forensic hoax ever perpetrated. Spawned in 2003 by publicity-seeking, corrupt New Mexico Governor Bill Richardson, it was also an apparent pay-to-play to his major political donor, who was a "Brushy"-believer. Building on William V. Morrison's original scam, its covert goal was to fulfill Morrison's huckster's dream of an attention-grabbing, gubernatorial pardon for imposter "Brushy Bill" Roberts.

Because the 53 years following honest Governor Thomas Jewett Mabry's pardon rejection of "Brushy" had yielded major scholarly Billy the Kid history books, "Brushy's" claim of surviving Pat Garrett's shooting was now even more ludicrous.

So it took special people to take on a re-run: self-serving sociopaths. True-believers, like W.C. Jameson, were rolled out for saccharine sincerity; while the cynical perpetrators were profiteers, hoping to peddle tabloid-level documentaries about "history's mysteries."

The hoax hook was modernizing old-timer Billy the Kid imposters' death scene survival claims by alleged use of forensic DNA matchings from exhumations of Billy Bonney; his mother, Catherine Antrim; "Brushy Bill" Roberts;" and John Miller to prove that the innocent victim, not Billy Bonney, lay in the Fort Sumner Billy the Kid grave. **[The truths that there existed no valid DNA from Billy or his mother for identity matching because of uncertainty of their grave locations, and that New Mexico's Office of the Medical Investigator (OMI) had refused exhumation permits based on the graves being invalid for a DNA quest, was kept secret.]**

I exposed this hoax in my 2014 *Cracking the Billy the Kid Case Hoax: The Strange Plot to Exhume Billy the Kid, Convict Sheriff Pat Garrett of Murder, and Become President of the United States.* And I litigated against the hoaxers from 2003 to 2014; first to block their exhumations of Billy and his mother, then to expose the records showing their DNA frauds.

Master promoter William Morrison had already invented the hook after the failed pardon: digging up Billy the Kid. Right after his *Alias Billy the Kid* came out, he wrote to a William Waters on June 29, 1955 (sending a copy to his fan, Paul Blazer): "You believe that the Kid was killed, but you say, " 'shouldn't we pay a little more attention to the body buried in the grave,' and I agree with you. **We should pay a lot of attention to the body buried.** If we could have found a cause of action to get into court, one of the first orders would have been to exhume the remains. In the absence of a coroner's verdict [his fake claim], **we did not have the necessary cause of action.** I am giving serious thought to a plan that may enable a legal exhumation. **If so, I firmly believe that a scientific investigation would determine that it was not the body of the Kid and that the lead slugs did not pass through the pistol Garrett had claimed he used that night.** This will not prove Roberts' claim, but it will prove that the Kid was not killed by Garrett."

But traveling salesman Morrison was unable to solve the legal obstacle of "[no]necessary cause of action." Human exhumation needs someone with legal standing: the right to make a case in a court - usually kin of the deceased.

The clever solution likely came from Richardson's major donor and potential pay-to-play recipient of "Brushy's" Billy the Kid crown: a law partner in a multi-million dollar law firm named Bill Robins III, who called himself a Billy the Kid historian, and whose hoax productions revealed his "Brushy"-backing. The second category able to conduct exhumations is law enforcement, to solve a crime. That fit the murdered innocent victim, Billy Barlow, being in Billy's grave. SO ALL THAT WAS NEEDED WAS OPENING A REAL MURDER CASE AGAINST GARRETT TO GET IN THE BILLY THE KID GRAVE TO "PROVE" A STRANGER WAS THERE INSTEAD OF BILLY!

So it became a "Brushy Bill" hoax on an astronomical scale, appearing in national and international press and a TV documentary. It became Lincoln County Sheriff's Department murder Case 2003-274 filed against Pat Garrett and named by its promulgators the "Billy the Kid Case."

Of course, non-existence of Billy the Kid's DNA to match with anyone was a potential problem for the scam. Needed was a forensic expert who was a sociopathic profiteer like the perpetrators, and willing to fake claims and results. The perfect match was Dr. Henry Lee, scorned by colleagues as doing "show-biz" forensics: choosing cases for their limelight. He had gotten name recognition by helping O.J. Simpson walk free in his 1996 murder trial. As to reputation for veracity, that was another story.

Prosecutor, Vincent Bugliosi, in his book, *Outrage: The Five Reasons Why O.J. Simpson Got Away With Murder*, called Henry Lee "nothing short of incompetent." Bugliosi was avoiding "liar." An example from *Outrage* was Lee's testifying that "crime-scene" shoe "imprints" on murder victim Nicole Simpson's walkway did not match O.J. Simpson's incriminatory, "size-12 Bruno Magli bloody shoe prints" - also at the scene. But the smaller "prints" Lee used, according to Bugliosi, had been hardened into the concrete during its laying "ten years earlier!"

Helpful Dr. Lee resurfaced for the 2007 murder trial defense for music impresario, Phil Spector; accused, and ultimately convicted, of fatally shooting actress, Lana Clarkson. But Attorney Sara Caplan - in Spector's first defense team - testified to the judge, Larry Paul Fidler, that, at the crime scene, Lee bottled dead Clarkson's torn-off fingernail, which indicated possible struggle - not Spector's defense's claim of her committing suicide. Then that fingernail disappeared. Judge Fidler declared destruction of evidence. The CNN.com AP headline of May 25, 2007 was: "Famed expert's credibility takes a hit at Spector trial."

Lee's involvement in a 2016 documentary, "The Case of JonBenet Ramsey," accusing her nine year old brother, Burke Ramsey of murdering her, resulted in Burke's $750 million defamation suit, which included Lee. On January 5, 2019, Dailymail.com reporter Maxine Shen wrote: "CBS and the brother of JonBenet Ramsey settle their $750m defamation lawsuit to the 'satisfaction of both parties.' " It stated: "Beyond CBS and the documentary production company Critical Content, LLS, Burke's lawsuit named **forensic scientist Henry Lee** and forensic pathologist Werner Spitz among several others who appeared in the broadcast."

So Henry Lee was the right "expert" to hide that no verifiable DNA of Billy the Kid existed on the planet to justify any of the proposed high-tech CSI forensics. He went through all the motions, as if doing a real investigation; when the only reality was intended production of fake TV documentaries.

And all this chicanery came down to the fact that the "Brushy Bill" hoax had now been distilled down to just the innocent victim death scene, denial of the Coroner's Jury Report of William Bonney, and some conspiracy theories fabricating why real historians denied their claims. But to spare head-on ridicule, the "Billy the Kid Case" hoax was presented as merely investigating if old pretenders were telling the truth; while hiding that they were long debunked by wrong ages, and total historical ignorance.

ANNOUNCING THE "BILLY THE KID CASE" HOAX AS A DEATH SCENE ALTERNATIVE

The "Billy the Kid Case" hoax entered public awareness at a stratospheric level. On June 5, 2003, Governor Bill Richardson announced his scam in a front page *New York Times* article titled "122 Years Later, The Lawmen Are Still Chasing Billy the Kid." Its irresponsible reporter, Michael Janofsky, mouthed that Richardson was simply doing an investigation about pardoning Billy the Kid. And Janowsky never researched that Richardson's "experts" were just "Brushy"-believers and the hoax's complicit lawmen. And the Coroner's Jury Report was unmentioned.

So Janofsky wrote that Richardson was seeking **"evidence to a long-held alternative theory that Garrett shot someone other than the Kid and led a conspiracy to cover up his crime;"** and that a Jannay Valdez, owner of a "Billy the Kid ["Brushy Bill"] Museum" in Canton, Texas, said: **"I'm absolutely convinced that Garrett killed someone else and that Brushy Bill was the Kid."** Listed lawmen were Lincoln County Sheriff Tom Sullivan, and his Deputy, Steve Sederwall, filing a murder case against Pat Garrett; as well as a Texas law firm for the case [**Attorney Bill Robins III**]. Richardson's spokesman stated **"the state would assist by clearing any legal hurdles to gain access to the mother's body."** Faking CSI glamour, Janofsky concluded that if "Brushy" was not a match, they could check John Miller. Then pardon would be a possibility. The article stated:

LINCOLN, NEW MEXICO - For more than 120 years, Pat Garrett has enjoyed legendary status in the American West, a lawman on a par with Wyatt Earp, Bat Masterson, even Matt Dillon. As sheriff here in Lincoln County in 1881, Garrett is credited with shooting to death the notorious outlaw known as Billy the Kid, a killing that made Garrett a hero. For years, a patch bearing his likeness has adorned uniforms worn by sheriff''s deputies here.

But now, modern science is about to interrupt Garrett's fame in a way that some say could expose him as a liar who covered up a murder to save his own skin and reputation.

Officials in New Mexico and Texas are working out plans to exhume and conduct genetic tests on the bodies of a woman buried in New Mexico who was believed to be the Kid's mother and a Texas man known as Brushy Bill Roberts, who claimed to be the Kid and died in 1950 at the age of 90. If test results suggest that the two were related, it would add new evidence to a long-held alternative theory that Garrett shot someone other than the Kid and led a conspiracy to cover up his crime.

Such skepticism is hardly uncommon. Disputes over major events in the Old West have engaged historians almost since they happened. The debate over Billy the Kid is one of the longest-running.

Beyond renewing interest in the Kid saga, the possibility that testing could enlarge Garrett's reputation or destroy it has even caught the fancy of Gov. Bill Richardson of New Mexico, who has offered state aid for the investigation and a possible pardon that an earlier New Mexico governor had once promised the Kid for a murder he committed.

"The problem is, there's so much fairy tale with this story that it's hard to nail down the facts," said Steve Sederwall, the mayor of Capitan, N.N., who is working with Lincoln County's current sheriff, Tom Sullivan, to resolve the matter. "All we want is the truth, whatever it is. If the guy Garrett killed was Billy the Kid, that makes him a hero. If it wasn't, Garrett was a murderer, and we have egg on our face, big time."

No matter what the genetic testing may show - and it might not show much of anything - it is hard to overstate the prominence of Garrett and the Kid in Western lore, especially here in southeastern New Mexico where their lives converged during and after the gun battles for financial control of the region that were known as the Lincoln County War. The Kid's notoriety grew after he and friends on one side of the conflict killed several men in an ambush, including Garrett's predecessor, Sheriff William Brady. For that, the Kid was hunted down, captured by Garrett, found guilty of murder and taken to the Lincoln jail, where he was placed in shackles to await hanging. He was only 21.

Today the tiny town of Lincoln, population 38, is a memorial to what happened next. More than a dozen buildings, including one that housed the jail, have been preserved as a state monument that attracts as many as 35,000 visitors a year.

Historians generally agree that the Kid, born Henry McCarty and known at times as William H. Bonney, escaped after it became apparent that Gov. Lew Wallace had reneged on a promise to pardon him in exchange for information about another killing in the county war. On April 28, 1881, the Kid managed to get his hands on a gun, kill the two deputies assigned to watch him and leave the area on horseback.

But then the stories diverge, providing fuel for two major theories of where, when, and how the Kid's life ended.

The version embraced here and supported by numerous books and Garrett relatives is that the Kid made his way to a friend's ranch in Fort Sumner, about 100 miles northeast of Lincoln. The ranch owner, Pete Maxwell, was also a friend of Garrett and somehow got word to Garrett that the Kid was in the area. After arriving, Garrett posted two deputies at the door.

As the Kid approached on the night of July 13 [sic], he spoke a few words in Spanish to the deputies, who did not recognize him. But Garrett, waiting inside, knew the voice. When the Kid walked in, Garrett turned and shot him in the heart.

William F. Garrett of Alamogordo, N.M., who is Garrett's grand-nephew, said years of research, including conversations with his cousin Jarvis, the last of Garrett's eight children, convinced him there is "no question about it" that his great-uncle killed Billy the Kid at Maxwell's. Jarvis died in 1991 at the age of 86.

"He was hired to get the Kid, and he got the Kid," Mr. Garrett said in an interview. "uncle Pat was a person of integrity who did his job. He was a law abider, not a law breaker."

But just as the story of Garrett as hero has flourished over the years, so have others, including the tale of Brushy Bill of Hico, Tex. His trip to New Mexico in 1950 to seek the pardon he said he was denied nearly 70 years before gave new life to an alternative possibility, that Garrett had not killed the Kid at all, but a drifter friend of the Kid's named Billy Barlow.

This story holds that Garrett and the Kid may have been in cahoots for some reason and that Garrett had stashed a gun at the outhouse at the jail that the Kid used to kill the deputies and escape. Even if only part of that is true, it would strongly suggest that Garrett killed the wrong man.

Speaking with the same person as Garrett's great-nephew, Jannay P. Valdez,

curator of the Billy the Kid Museum in Canton, Tex., said he had no doubt that Garrett killed someone else and that Brushy Bill was the Kid. "I'm absolutely convinced," he said here on Monday after meeting with Mr. Sederwall to discuss theories and how to begin the kind of genetic testing that has been used to ascertain lineage of other historical figures like Thomas Jefferson and Jessie James. "I'd bank everything I have on it."

As longtime friends, Mr. Sederwall and Sheriff Sullivan decided they wanted to settle the matter once and for all but could do so only through scientific analysis. To justify the effort that would require much of their time and, perhaps at some point, taxpayer money, they needed an official reason. So in April, they opened the first-ever investigation into the murders of the two deputies shot in the Kid's escape, James W. Bell and Robert Olinger, to examine what happened at the jail and Maxwell's ranch.

[AUTHOR'S NOTE: Janofsky is parroting the hoax. The deputy murders and Garrett's killing of the Kid are unconnected, but the hoaxers made-up that Garrett helped the escape.]

As Mr. Sederwall said, "There's no statute of limitations on murder."

[AUTHOR'S NOTE: This announces the real murder case; but hidden is New Mexico's having had a Statute of Limitations.]

The goal now, he said, is to compare genetic evidence of Catherine Antrim, believed to be the Kid's mother, who died of tuberculosis in 1874 and is buried in Silver City, N.M., and of Brushy Bill, who lived out his life in Texas. A Dallas firm [sic Houston] has agreed to help, and a spokesman for governor Richardson said the state would assist by clearing legal hurdles to gain access to the mother's body.

The Kid was buried at Fort Sumner, N.M., although the whereabouts of the grave are uncertain; he has no known living relatives. Mr. Valdez said he had already secured permission to exhume the body of Brushy Bill, who is buried 20 miles from Hico in Hamilton, Texas.

But solving the mystery might not be so simple. For one thing, Mr. Valdez said he was certain that the woman buried in Silver City was but "a half aunt." And even if tests disqualify Brushy Bill as Billy the Kid, other "Kids" have emerged over the years, including a man named John Miller, who died in 1937 and is buried in Prescott, Ariz. Mr. Sederwall said that efforts would be made to exhume his body as well.

The investigators conceded that much is riding on their quest. Sheriff Sullivan, a tall, strapping man who carries a turquoise-handled .357

magnum on his right hip, said he, like so many others in the West, revered Garrett for gunning down the Kid. The uniform patch with Garrett's likeness was his design. Now, the legend is threatened.

"I just want to get to the bottom of it," said Sheriff Sullivan, who is retiring next year. "My integrity's at stake. So's my department's. So's what we believe in and even New Mexico history. If Garrett shot someone other than the Kid, that makes him a murderer and he covered it up. He wouldn't be such a role model, then, and we'd have to take the patches off the uniforms."

On June 10, 2003, Richardson held a press conference. Present were key hoaxers: Lincoln County's Sheriff Tom Sullivan and Deputy Steve Sederwall; De Baca County's Sheriff Gary Graves; Attorney for exhuming the mother, Sherry Tippett; and University of New Mexico professor Paul Hutton, appointed by Richardson as the hoax's "historical advisor." Richardson revealed that Lincoln County Sheriff's Department murder case against Pat Garrett had been flied as No. 2003-274. The press release promised use of forensic DNA to prove that the Kid deserved a pardon. It stated:

State of New Mexico
Office of the Governor

Bill Richardson
Governor
For immediate release
6/10/03

Contact: Billy Sparks
telephone number

GOVERNOR BILL RICHARDSON ANNOUNCES STATE SUPPORT OF BILLY THE KID INVESTIGATION

SANTA FE – Governor Bill Richardson today outlined how the state of New Mexico will support the investigation efforts to investigate the life and death of Billy the Kid.

Governor Richardson delivered the following remarks during a news conference today in the State Capitol:

This is an important day in the history of New Mexico and the American West. I am announcing my support and the support of the state of New Mexico for the investigation into the life and death of Henry McCarty, also known as William Bonney. To millions around the world, he was called Billy the Kid. How he captured the world's imagination is well worth exploring. His life, though ended at the age of 21, is part of what makes New Mexico and an American West, unique.

My goal is to shed new light on old history.

I am pleased to be joined here by Lincoln County Sheriff Tom Sullivan, Capitan Mayor Steve Sederwall, DeBaca County Sheriff Gary Grays [sic - Graves]. Grant County Attorney Sherry Tippett, University of New Mexico History Professor, Doctor Paul Hutton and State Police Major Tom Branch.

Let me tell you how this all came about.

Last month I was contacted by Lincoln County Sheriff, Tom Sullivan and Capitan Mayor, Steve Sederwall, to support reopening the case. Case number 2003-274 seeks to answer key questions that have lingered for over 120 years surrounding the life and the death of Billy the Kid.

This episode in the history of New Mexico and the history of the old west is both fact and legend and continues to stir the imagination and interest of people all over the world.

By utilizing modern forensic, DNA and crime scene techniques, the goal of the investigation is to get to the truth. In the process, the reputation of Pat Garrett, still a hero in Lincoln County law enforcement, hangs in the balance. **The question is did Sheriff Garrett kill Billy the Kid at Fort Sumner, New Mexico on July 14. 1881?**

This investigation will also seek to shed new light on the events surrounding the escape of Billy the Kid from the Lincoln County Jail on April 28, 1881. The shooting of Deputies J.W. Bell and Bob Olinger by Billy the Kid has never been officially investigated. Where did Billy get his gun and what really happened?

I have contacted the national Labs, Los Alamos and Sandia and have been assured that they will volunteer their support in this effort. Los Alamos Lab can assist us by providing ground penetrating radar, DNA expertise and technical forensic assistance. Sandia Labs will allow their experts to volunteer their time to help us uncover the facts.

The State Police will help supervise the investigation and crime scene analysis of the evidence uncovered in the investigation.

I **have also asked University of New Mexico Professor of History and Executive Director of the Western History Association, Doctor Paul Hutton, to serve as our historical advisor.** Dr. Hutton has served as President of the Western Writers of America and has won several national honors for his works on western history.

I intend to hold hearings at Fort Sumner, Lincoln, Silver City and Mesilla. I will appoint a defense counsel and a prosecutor to present the evidence. **[Never done.]**

As Governor, I will examine the events surrounding the alleged offer of a pardon to Billy the Kid by former New Mexico

Governor Lew Wallace. I will evaluate the evidence uncovered and make a decision.

There is no question that this story deserves our attention and that the history of New Mexico and the American West is important to all of us. If we can get to the truth we will. I have total confidence in the team you see here today to conduct a professional, honest and exhaustive investigation of the facts and report back to me and to the rest of the world what really happened here in New Mexico.

The benefits to our state and to the history of the West far outweigh any cost we may incur. I expect the actual cost to be nominal. Just since this investigation was announced, it has sparked news articles about New Mexico and Lincoln County from New York to London to India. Getting to the truth is our goal. But, if this increases interest and tourism in our state, I couldn't be happier.

I understand that Movie Producer Ron Howard has donated the cabin used in shooting his movie "The Missing", being shot in Santa Fe, to Silver City. The cabin is a replica of a Billy the Kid era home. The cabin will be delivered to Silver City this week.

The potential benefit from this investigation to all of New Mexico is already being felt and is well worth the effort. #30#

But what about the pardon? **The mother's "DNA" (though there was none) would be matched to "Brushy" (though he denied she was his mother, and the matching was for maternal DNA only). If it "matched," then *he* was Billy the Kid; so the Fort Sumner grave must hold the innocent victim. So Pat Garrett was a murderer.** And since there would be no real DNA anyway, any matchings wanted could be claimed.

But what about the pardon? Hoax Attorney, Bill Robins III, gave the link in the Grant County District Court in his January 5, 2004 "Pre-Hearing Brief" petitioning to dig up Catherine Antrim. His fakery began with stating that his client was dead Billy the Kid! (Note that a dead person cannot be a client.) And, speaking for Billy, he claimed "Billy" had and interest in "his legacy." Then Robins slipped in "Brushy." **The diabolically clever hoax, possibly Robins's own brain-child, was to claim the fake "DNA match," and then claim "Brushy" deserved the gubernatorial pardon as Billy the Kid for having led a long and law-abiding life**. So Robins wrote: "**Should the DNA extracted from Ms. Antrim confirm that one of the potential Kids was in fact Billy the Kid, undersigned counsel will be able to make an even stronger argument for pardon by citing to the long years of law abiding life.**"

CHAPTER 2 THE "BILLY THE KID CASE" HOAX'S FAKED DEATH SCENE

NEWLY INVENTED DEATH SCENES

The "Billy the Kid Case" hoax hinged on Sheriff's Departments' filings of a murder case against Pat Garrett to get legal justification to do exhumations to prove he murdered the innocent victim. So the documents required fabrication of a non-historical death scene. Possibly because the "Brushy Bill" hoax was an embarrassment, its death scene was not in the final papers - though an earlier and concealed version did use his Morrison tapes' transcript, possibly provided by W.C. Jameson.

Made-up for the "Billy the Kid Case" hoax was a new death scene scenario: a non-historical bromance between Pat Garrett and Billy Bonney, with Pat first being complicit in Billy's jailbreak by giving him the revolver to murder his own Deputies James Bell and Robert Olinger; then helping Billy escape again by purposefully killing the innocent victim in Fort Sumner as grave-filler. Of course, there was no shooting of Billy the Kid by Garrett. **It should be noted that this is a mismatch with "Brushy's" and John Miller's death scenes which had accidental killings of the innocent victim - with "Brushy's" tale adding Garrett's massive gunfire at him (with wounds claimed) - then with Garrett covering-up his murder mistake by a rushed burial to get the Billy the Kid reward.**

But the hoaxers hit a wall. My litigation blocked their exhumations of Billy and his mother, so there was no way to fake DNA matches to claim the murdered innocent victim lay in the

Fort Sumner grave. So, by 2004, the hoaxers secretly rewrote their hoax, with a Version II death scene so preposterous that it took their sociopathic scorn to foist it on the public.

They claimed to have found the carpenter's bench on which shot Billy Bonney had been laid out. Of course, in Version I, the point was that Billy *was not shot*. But the hoaxers were now desperate for any DNA claim to continue their hoax and the TV cameras. So now claimed was that shot Billy bled on the bench, leaving "blood DNA" to match with "Brushy" and John Miller.

But if there was shot Billy on the bench, it meant he was dead, and defaulted to conventional history. So they lied that "dead men don't bleed," and segued to the preposterous scenario that Garrett shot Billy in a mutual plot, *so Billy could "play dead;"* then Garrett murdered the innocent victim to substitute for Billy on the carpenter's bench (while Billy presumably painfully exited). And presumably the townspeople doing the night vigil on Billy's corpse did not notice all this activity - or a new corpse!

In my book on this hoax, I debunked Version II, as more than just absurd, by using forensic consultants. Confirmed was that dead men *do bleed*, because blood flows out from exit wounds from residual blood pressure, then gravitational seepage. Also, when shot in the chest, one cannot play dead because of involuntary hyperventilation. But the key was that this "bench-blood-DNA" could never be proved as Billy's to match with anyone. **Forensic DNA matching requires "reference DNA," meaning DNA obtained with absolute certainty from the individual in question.** The hoaxers were actually claiming the counterpart of finding a random finger print, and having no finger prints of the individual in question to compare with it to determine its identity. Ultimately, it would emerge that the lab the hoaxers were using for their "forensics," did not even test for blood, so none was ever shown as present on the bench. Then their samples from claimed bench areas (with likely rust stains) yielded no DNA anyway.

Since it was a hoax, these realities fazed none of the participants, including their forensic expert, Dr. Henry Lee. And Lee made blood claims himself. And the hoaxers then claimed to have obtained the bench-blood-DNA-of-Billy the Kid to justify digging up John Miller, and to try to dig up "Brushy Bill" for "DNA identity matching." In fact, they had nothing but psychopathic audacity.

CHAPTER 3
"BILLY THE KID CASE" HOAX LEGAL FILINGS

DOCUMENTS FAKING THE DEATH SCENE TO ACHIEVE EXHUMATIONS

To attain their desired exhumations, the "Billy the Kid Case" hoaxers created legal documents faking the death scene, and concealing the Coroner's Jury Report, to justify their exhumation petitions and to create fake documentaries. Involved were the Lincoln County Sheriff's Department with its murder Case No. 2003-274 against Pat Garrett, created by Sheriff Tom Sullivan and his Deputy, and Mayor of Capitan, Steve Sederwall. In the De Baca County Sheriffs Department, the same investigation was filed as No. 03-06-136-01 under hoax participant Sheriff Gary Graves. An imposter-backing historian in the U.S. Marshals Service, named David Turk, participated in creating the documents, and filed one of his own hoax productions with them. Then the next Lincoln County Sheriff, Rick Virden, deputized Sullivan and Sederwall for the case. And the illegal Arizona exhumation of John Miller (and a random man buried beside him, named William Hudspeth) was done during his tenure.

And the hoaxers' attorneys, Sherry Tippett, Bill Robins III, and Mark Acuña, created exhumation petitions for District Courts with the hoaxed claim of Garrett as a murderer.

CAPITAN "MAYOR'S REPORT" OF STEVE SEDERWALL

Lincoln County Sheriffs Department Deputy Steve Sederwall was first in announcing the "Billy the Kid Case" murder case in his capacity as Capitan Mayor in his May, 2003, *Capitan Village Hall News* "Mayor's Report." His focus was "Brushy Bill;" even claiming that Billy Barlow was in the Fort Sumner grave. Low in hoax hierarchy, Sederwall was hardworking, claiming to have written the major hoax document: the "Probable Cause Statement." And his later association with "Brushy"-backing W.C. Jameson in 2006, would inspire Jameson's continuation of the "Billy the Kid Case" hoax in his 2018 book, *Cold Case Billy the Kid*. As to the death scene, Sederwall's "Mayor's Report" used "Brushy Bill" and Billy Barlow, stating:

> This investigation came about after Sheriff Sullivan and I talked about a man by the name of Brushy Bill Roberts. In 1950 Roberts came to the Governor of New Mexico with his attorney [sic - William Morrison, not an attorney]; saying he was Billy the Kid. He said that Pat Garrett shot a man by the name of Billy Barlow and buried his body claiming to be that of Billy the Kid. Roberts said he lived out a life within the bounds of the law under an assumed name and wanted a pardon that was promised to him by Governor Wallace.
>
> **[AUTHOR'S NOTE: This is the hoax's first known reference connecting the "Billy the Kid" hoax's claim that Garrett did not kill the Kid, to the "Brushy Bill" Roberts hoax.]**
>
> On the surface of this story you would say "so what?" But if you look at this man's claim he is saying our Sheriff Pat Garrett is a murderer. Garrett knew the Kid and killed someone else. **What this says also is that Pete Maxwell who said the body is of The Kid is a co-conspirator in a murder. There is no statute of limitations on Murder**, so the Lincoln County Sheriff''s Office has opened a case to pursue the investigation. If Brushy Bill Roberts is Billy the Kid then history changes. But if he is lying, we need to clear Garrett's name.
>
> **[AUTHOR'S NOTE: Confirmed is the case as a filed murder investigation against Pat Garrett, with a "Brushy" emphasis. Though avoiding mention of the Coroner's Jury Report, it is referenced by claiming that its witness, Peter Maxwell, lied about Billy being the victim. Also, it is untrue that there was no New Mexico Statute of Limitations for murder. For Pat Garrett it had expired in 1891! (See pages 42-43 above) Also, the sly double-talk that would characterize the hoax is used. Here, the absurd claim is made that the murder case against Pat Garrett was being done to clear his name of murder - though the hoaxers were his only accusers, and murder cases are not done to prove someone innocent!]**

I feel this investigation will put a positive light on the county, our town and the state in whole. Tom Sullivan and I have been in touch with the Governor's office and he is behind us. People who are conducting DNA on victims of the World Trade Center have agreed to complete DNA tests for us on remains of persons believed to be Billy the Kid. We have a filmmaker creating a made-for-TV story about this investigation. We have recruited some of the best investigators in the country from other states to assist in this investigation. The Sheriff and I feel this should not only clear up a 122-year-old mystery but also bring money into our village ...

Tom Sullivan and I know it is a crazy idea but won't it be fun.

"PROBABLE CAUSE STATEMENT" FOR PAT GARRETT AS A MURDERER

The key to the "Billy the Kid Case" hoax- and to faking "Brushy Bill's" survival tale - was getting legal access to historic graves to fabricate self-serving DNA matches. That meant filing a real murder investigation with a "Probable Cause Statement" which established, with probability, Pat Garrett's guilt.

That required manufacturing a fake murder motive for Garrett and a fake murder scene. Denied was the William Bonney Coroner's Jury Report, and the multiple additional corpse identifications. Resorted to were hearsay post-death Billy the Kid sightings, as used in the "Brushy Bill" and John Miller hoaxes.

The December 31, 2003 "Probable Cause Statement for Lincoln County Sheriff's Department Case No. 2003-274" is 11 pages of single-spaced footnoted text, combining double-talk, lies, and mock erudition. Though Steve Sederwall claimed to have written it, Attorney Bill Robins III may contributed, since he used the same wording a month before its December signing in reporter Louie Fecteau's November 19, 2003 *Albuquerque Journal's* "No Kidding: Governor Taps Lawyer for Billy." Robins stated: "[I]t was hard to tell who the good guys were." The "Probable Cause Statement" has: "[I]t was hard to tell who the good guys were." Also hoaxer, U.S. Marshals Service Historian David Turk, provided fake research and an Addendum.

The "Statement" had two thrusts to establish Pat Garrett as a murderer of an "innocent victim" on July 14, 1881. The first used fabricated "suspicions," misinformation, and false forensic DNA claims, to claim Garrett's guilt.

The second thrust was fabrication of a murder motive for Garrett by a sub-investigation of Billy Bonney's jailbreak murder of his deputy guards, James Bell and Robert Olinger. Used were meaningless "what-ifs": *If* Garrett gave Billy the revolver used for the jailbreak, he and Billy *might* have been friends. And *if* they were friends, Garrett *might* again have helped Billy escape in Fort Sumner by killing an innocent victim. But the ifs" had no evidence. And there was no historical friendship between Garrett and Billy. So substituted were only old-timers' malarkey of post-death sightings of Billy. In fact, Garrett had no motive to assist Billy's jailbreak, and was not in Lincoln that day.

Subsequently, however, when I was litigating against the hoaxers, this sub-investigation was switched by them as the *total* Case 2003-274 to hide their attack on Garrett, and to hide its connected DNA records. Also, this sub-investigation had its own fake CSI forensics and DNA claims about "Deputy Bell's blood."

But for the "Probable Cause Statement," Sederwall and Sullivan claimed that Garrett was guilty, as would be proven by DNA comparisons of remains of Billy the Kid and his mother (to show Garrett's innocent victim lay in Billy the Kid's grave).

An Addendum of two pages was an affidavit by a Homer Overton, addressed to Sheriff Sullivan, swearing that Garrett had not shot the Kid; but crumbling under Overton's made-up wrong dates. (It was comparable to the fake affidavits of *Alias Billy the Kid*, attesting that "Brushy" was Billy.)

The upshot is that the "Probable Cause Statement" presented no reason to assume that Garrett did not kill the Kid. One can guess that expecting no opposition, the hoaxers had written it for their complicit and beholden judges, just appointed by Richardson, who were supposed to rubber-stamp their exhumation petitions, but might have wanted documentation to bear scrutiny.

Importantly, it would much later emerge, as I pursued the hoaxers with my open records investigations, that there had been a first and rejected "Probable Cause Statement," titled "Lincoln County Sheriff's Office, Lincoln County New Mexico, Case: William H. Bonney, a.k.a. William Antrim, a.k.a. The Kid, a.k.a. Billy the Kid: An Investigation into the events of April 28, 1881 through July 14, 1881 - seventy-seven days of doubt." Its authorship was uncertain. But it overtly promoted "Brushy Bill," gave his quoted murder scene, and was apparently rejected in lieu of Sederwall's and Sullivan's more circumspect treatment. The official "Probable Cause Statement" follows.

LINCOLN COUNTY SHERIFF'S DEPARTMENT

CASE # 2003-274

Probable Cause Statement

In the struggle dubbed the "Lincoln County War" investigators [Sullivan and Sederwall] soon learned that nothing was as seemed.

[AUTHOR'S NOTE: For lack of any evidence, this is the familiar "suspicion" used by Billy the Kid imposters' authors.]

As they poured through the volumes of information, documents, paperwork, reports, county records, books and examined newly discovered evidence, it became apparent no clear lines could be drawn as to who was working with or for whom. What first appeared to be clear quickly became clouded as new information was uncovered,

[AUTHOR'S NOTE: No new evidence is ever presented.]

it's difficult to judge who the "good guys" and the "bad guys" were. One would think that the Lincoln County Sheriff''s Department would be on the side of the law. However, it was a duly sworn posse of Lincoln County Deputies that shot and killed John Tunstall, in what investigators in clean conscience can only cauterize [sic] as an unprovoked murder.

[AUTHOR'S NOTE: Tunstall's murder is irrelevant. It occurred when William Brady was Sheriff of Lincoln County; and was 3½ years before Garrett killed the Kid. Of course, Brady's dishonesty is irrelevant to Garrett as a murderer.]

Evidence shows that posse-men, Hill and Morton

[AUTHOR'S NOTE: Error: Tom Hill was not Brady's official posseman; he was in Jessie Evans's outlaw gang. Brady, in writing, swore he used no known outlaws on that posse.]

committed murder when "*Hill called to him* (Tunstall) *to come up and that he would not be hurt; at the same time both Hill and Morton threw up their guns, resting their stocks on their knees; that after Tunstall came nearer, Morton fired and shot Tunstall through the breast, and then Hill fired and shot Tunstall through the head ...*" [1]([1]Deposition of Albert Howe, Angel Report) Although these deputies were acting under the color off the law they were not acting within the law. This behavior permeates the Lincoln County War and investigators will not make judgments on that behavior but rather uncover the facts and present the facts without varnish.

[AUTHOR'S NOTE: Repeating that lawman can be dishonest, is irrelevant to proving Garrett a murderer.]

No one from the Governor to the District Attorney to the Sheriff of Lincoln County is beyond suspicion of deception and covering up the true facts in this case.

[AUTHOR'S NOTE: Vague "suspicion" is irrelevant to Garrett.]

This can be seen in a number of examples. In a letter to Riley and Dolan of the Murphy-Dolan faction from District Attorney W. L. Rynerson of the 3rd Judicial District, the attorney clearly demonstrates he himself plays a part in the hostile actions when he writes, "*Shake that McSween outfit up until it shells out and squares up and then shake it out of Lincoln. I will aid to punish the scoundrels all I can.*"[2] ([2]Rynerson letter to Riley and Dolan, Feb. 7 [sic], 1878, University of Arizona Special Collection)

[AUTHOR'S NOTE: Error: The letter is dated February 14, 1878; is about murdering Tunstall; and is irrelevant to Garrett.]

When investigators began to look at the murder of Deputy Sheriff J.W. Bell and Deputy Robert Olinger on April 28, 1881, it was found that much of the information we now know as "history" came from Pat F. Garrett's book, "The Authentic Life of Billy the Kid" published in 1882.

[AUTHOR'S NOTE: Error: Bell/Olinger eye-witness murder information was not claimed by Garrett, who was away at White Oaks; but was from, Gottfried Gauss, the caretaker.]

Investigators learned that much of this history is flawed for the reason historian Robert Utley writes: "*Although not many copies of the Authentic Life were sold, it nevertheless had a decisive impact on the Kid's image. More than any other single influence, the Garrett-Upson book fed the legend of Billy the Kid. As the legend blossomed, writers turned to the Authentic Life for details. Ash Upson's fictions became implanted in hundreds of " histories" that followed. For more than a century, only a few students thought to question the wild fantasies that flowed from Ash's imagination. In the evolution of the Kid's image, the Authentic Life is a book of enormous consequence.*"[3] ([3]Robert M. Utley. Billy the Kid a short and violent life. University of Nebraska Press, 1989.)

[AUTHOR'S NOTE: Utley is merely describing evolution of the legend, not history. And Garrett's book confirms his shooting of Billy. All subsequent scholarly historians, including Utley, confirmed that Garrett fatally shot Billy the Kid.]

On March 23 [sic – 17], 1879, Governor Lew Wallace met with William Bonney (Kid) in Lincoln. In this meeting it is demonstrated that Wallace convinced the Kid that it would be to his advantage to work for the government.

[AUTHOR'S NOTE: Wrong. Billy proposed to Wallace, by a letter of about March 13, 1879, to give eye-witness Grand Jury testimony against the murderers of Huston Chapman in exchange for Wallace's annulling his Lincoln County War indictments. But a straw man argument is being set up.]

The Kid becomes, what would be referred to in today's terminology as a "Confidential Informant." In Governor Wallace's hand we read "Statements made by Kid, Made Sunday night March 23, 1879."[4] ([4]Statements by Kid, Lew Wallace Collection, Indiana Historical Society Library) It was through this meeting Wallace devised a plan and attempted to deceive when he and the Kid entered into an agreement where by the Kid would appear to have been arrested.

[AUTHOR'S NOTE: Claiming attempt "to deceive" is a misleading switcheroo. The hoaxers admitted Billy's confidential informant status. The arrest plan was devised by both Wallace and Billy to prevent his being killed before his testimony against Chapman's murderers. But the hoaxers are still pumping the irrelevant claim that everyone was deceptive. Of course, that was irrelevant to Garrett as murderer.]

The Kid later talks of this and says he was allowed to wear his guns and he left when he wanted to leave.

David S. Turk, Historian for the United States Marshals Service has discovered other such deceptions in his study of official records.

[AUTHOR'S NOTE: Referring to "other such deceptions" is fake. Turk's "other deceptions" are never given. And Turk, an active "Billy the Kid Case" hoaxer, contributed his own fake Probable Cause addendum to the hoax. (See pages 226-230 below]

It is commonly believed

[AUTHOR'S NOTE: Misstatement: It is a *known*.]

that Lincoln County Sheriff Pat F. Garrett arrested the Kid in December of 1880 in Stinking Springs near Fort Sumner. But the records show that Garrett was elected in November of 1880 and did not take office until January of 1881.[5] ([5]Lincoln County Commissioners Records, November 8, 1880).

[AUTHOR'S NOTE: This leads to a fake claim that he did not have proper authority to capture Billy.]

He went to Fort Sumner as a Deputy United States Marshall, but even that Commission and authority are now questioned. Secret Service Special Operative Azariah F. Wild of New Orleans writes in his daily logs "*I this day went to Lincoln to meet Capt. Lea & Garrett who are to organize the Posse Comatatus [sic] to make a raid on Fort Sumner to arrest counterfeiters.*"[6] ([6]Report of Azariah F. Wild, November 11, 1880, Record Group 87, National Archives) Garrett shot and killed Charles Bowdre and Tom O'Folliard during the chase and arrested the Kid. Later, Secret Service Special Operative Azariah F. Wild writes to his superior and admits he was deceptive in his commission of Garrett. "*I will respectfully state that I applied to Marshall Sherman to appoint P.F. Garrett as a Deputy Marshall to which he paid no attention. I was in great need of Mr. Garrett [sic – Mr. Garrett's aid] at that time and took one of the Commissions Sherman sent to John Hurley (he having sent two) and substituted P.F. Garrett the very man who has rendered the Government such a valuable service in killing and arresting these men who I was in pursuit.*"[7] ([7]Report of Azariah F. Wild, January 4 [sic -3], 1881, Record Group 87, National Archives)

[AUTHOR'S NOTE: This fakes doubt about Garrett's commission. In fact, Wild, needing Garrett's aid, got paperwork from U.S. Marshal John Sherman; but two commissions were for John Hurley. So he crossed out Hurley's name on one, and added Garrett's. It was not done secretly, since Wild put it in his daily report to Secret Service Chief James Brooks. And it was accepted. Also, Sederwall recycled this fakery in W.C. Jameson's 2018 book titled *Cold Case Billy the Kid.]*

No one in 122 years has been able to speak with clear certainty where the gun came from that William Bonney used to kill Deputy J.W. Bell.

[AUTHOR'S NOTE: A switch to a sub-investigation begins to fake Garrett as Billy's escape accomplice.]

With the information investigators have seen they question Garrett's involvement in the Kid obtaining a weapon.

[AUTHOR'S NOTE: What follows is just fake "what-ifs": *If* Garrett was Billy's friend, he helped him escape. *If* he did that, he would later kill the victim to help Billy escape again.]

It would go to reason that if the body in Fort Sumner is anyone other than William Bonney then Garrett no doubt had a hand in allowing the Kid to escape on July 14, 1881.

[AUTHOR'S NOTE: This is fakery. No one says anyone but Billy was buried. It is just hoaxing.]

If the body at Fort Sumner is anyone other than William Bonney, then Garrett, whether by accident or design, is responsible for homicide of the person resting in that grave.

[AUTHOR'S NOTE: Here are more meaningless "what ifs."]

If it is not Bonney in the grave at Fort Sumner it would also go to reason that Garrett would be looked at as a suspect in furthering the escape of the Kid on April 28, 1881 when the two Lincoln County Sheriffs were murdered.

[AUTHOR'S NOTE: Here is the switcheroo. Now the fake "what-ifs" are used as fact: that Garrett helped Billy escape. THIS FAKERY IS THE HOAXERS' SOLE PROBABLE CAUSE FOR GARRETT AS A MURDERER. In fact, no evidence has been given; and none exists. And Pat and Billy were not friends.

[AUTHOR'S NOTE: What follows next is built on the hoaxers' lying that (1) they established Garrett's murder motive, and that (2) they established need to check Billy's grave for Garrett's "innocent victim."]

Although the investigation will deal with what happened in the Lincoln County court house on April 28, 1881, this writing will deal with the alleged shooting of William Bonney at Fort Sumner on the night of July 14, 1881.

[AUTHOR'S NOTE: Do not let this fast-one slip by. The deputy murders "sub-investigation" at the courthouse consisted merely of: (1) firing a gun inside to test if it could be heard across the street; and (2) bringing in a forensic consultant, Dr. Henry Lee, whose finding of "blood" on the upstairs hallway floorboards was a hoaxer lie. Lying more, the hoaxers said the "blood" was Bell's. Olinger was left out. Also left out is that this "investigation" has nothing to do with the gun used to shoot Bell. And, even if it did, that would have nothing to do with whether Garrett gave it to Billy, or whether Garrett murdered an innocent victim 2 ½ months later. The "upstairs blood," though irrelevant, will be debunked later with the rest of the fake forensic claims.]

[AUTHOR'S NOTE: At this point, the hoaxers abandon the deputy murders and the Garrett murder motive. But they pretend that they: (1) established Garrett's Billy friendship; (2) Garrett's escape weapon involvement; (3) Garrett's murder motive; and (4) Garrett's murder of the innocent victim.]

This writing will set forth probable cause as to why investigators question who is in the grave in Fort Sumner and seek DNA from Catherine Antrim.

[AUTHOR'S NOTE: Probable cause of Garrett as a murderer has not been established. But this double exhumation is the hoaxers' goal.]

[AUTHOR'S NOTE: What follows is the hoaxers' attempt to fake that someone other than William Bonney was shot by Garrett. It is back to "what-ifs": *If* there was any inconsistency in reporting of events around the murder, something is "suspicious;" ergo, Garrett killed someone else. But the hoaxers only fabricate some "inconsistencies."]

The detractors of this investigation hold up the statements of Lincoln County Sheriff Pat F. Garrett, Deputy Sheriff John W. Poe, and the Coroner's Jury report as proof it is William H. Bonney that Sheriff Garrett shot and killed on July 14, 1881 and that the Kid is buried in Ft. Sumner.

[AUTHOR'S NOTE: Hidden are the multiple additional corpse identifications. Later, in this document, in slip-ups, the hoaxers accidentally present more of them!]

Historian Philip J. Rash [sic - Rasch] tells the story history puts forth about the shooting of the Kid in the following manner:

Garrett led them to the mouth of Taiban Arroyo, arriving after dark on 13 July. When Brazil failed to appear, Poe, who was unknown in the area, agreed to ride into fort Sumner the next morning to see what he could learn. Finding the inhabitants suspicious and uncommunicative, he proceeded to Sunnyside, about seven miles north, to visit Milnor Rudulph [sic - Rudulph throughout], the postmaster and an old friend of Garrett's. Rudulph was nervous and evasive. He denied all knowledge of the Kid's whereabouts, but Poe was sure he was concealing something.[8] ([8] Poe, John W. *The Death of Billy the Kid*. New York: Houghton Mifflin Company, 1933) *There is a curious story that while the officer was on the way to Sunnyside, John Collins (Abraham Gordon Graham), a former member of Billy's gang, headed to Lobato's camp to warn the outlaw that officers were in the vicinity. On the way he met the Kid, bound for Fort Sumner. "Billy," he warned, "don't go down there. I just saw Poe, and no doubt Pat Garrett and a posse are around town looking for you."*

[AUTHOR'S NOTE: Recall that Poe was unknown to the locals; so this irrelevant hearsay further lacks credibility.]

The Kid merely laughed and answered, "Oh, that's O.K. I'll be alright," and rode on, leaving Collins badly puzzled."[9] ([9]Ben Kemp. *Dead Men, Who Rode Across the Border*. Unpublished. No date.)

That night Poe rendezvoused with Garrett and McKinney at La Punta de la Glorietta [sic], four miles north of Fort Sumner. Poe's report of both his failure to learn anything definite and his suspicions that there was so much smoke there must be some fire only increased the sheriff's skepticism. After some discussion he commented that the Kid was a frequent visitor to the house of Celsa Gutierrez (sister of Pat's wife Polineria [sic] *Gutierrez) and suggested that they watch her home. Their vigil proved fruitless. As midnight approached Garrett and Poe decided that there was only one other possible source of information - Peter Maxwell, the town's most prominent citizen.*

The officers arrived at his home about 12:30 AM on Friday, the 15th [sic]. *Pat instructed Poe and McKinney to wait outside while he went in to talk to Maxwell. Sitting down on the edge of the bed, he asked in a low voice whether the Kid was on the premises. Maxwell became very agitated, but answered that he was not. At that point a bare headed, bare footed man in his shirt sleeves, carrying a butcher's knife in his left hand and a revolver in his right sprang through the door and asked Maxwell who the two men outside were.*

Maxwell whispered, "That's him."

[AUTHOR'S NOTE: Note the hoaxer slip-ups in presenting this source: (1) *This* Garrett cannot recognize Billy, though they claimed he and Billy were such good friends that Garrett killed for him; and (2) Maxwell identifies the victim as Billy!]

Sensing a third person in the room, the intruder backed toward the door, at the same time demanding, "Quien es? Quien es?"

Pat jerked his gun and fired twice.[10] [11] ([10]*Las Vegas Daily Optic, July 18, 1881.* [11]*Santa Fe Daily New Mexican, July 21, 1881) As the man fell Maxwell plunged over the foot of the bed and out the door, closely followed by the sheriff. Maxwell would surely have been shot by Poe if Garrett had not struck the latter's gun down saying, "Don't shoot Maxwell." He added, "That was the Kid that came in there onto me, and I think I have got him."*

[AUTHOR'S NOTE: This is Peter Maxwell's second dead Billy identification; and is not contradicting Garrett's statement.]

Poe was not so sanguine. "Pat," he answered, "the Kid would not come to this place, you shot the wrong man." All was quiet inside. After some persuasion Maxwell brought a tallow candle and placed it on the outside of the window sill. By its light the body of a man could be seen. Deluvina Maxwell, a Navajo servant, entered the room, examined the body, and found that it was indeed the Kid's.

[AUTHOR'S NOTE: This is a third identification of Billy! And Deluvina knew him, as he hoaxers later confirm themselves. She also reported his killing in a June 24, 1927 interview by J. Evetts Haley. And Poe's quote, in his 1933 book, *The Death of Billy the Kid*, expressed initial disbelief of Billy's coming there – and he did not know him. It does not disprove the victim.]

Garrett's first shot had struck him in the left breast just above the heart; the second had gone wild. Later it was learned that Billy had been staying at the house of Juan Chavez.

[AUTHOR'S NOTE: A fourth Billy identification!]

Becoming hungry, he had gone to Maxwell's to slice a steak from a yearling Pete had killed that morning.

The corpse was taken to a carpenter's shop and laid on the work bench.

[AUTHOR'S NOTE: The carpenter's bench would later became the hoaxers' focus for faking DNA claims.]

Fearing an assault from Billy's friends, the officers remained awake and on guard the rest of the night. However, it passed without incident.

[AUTHOR'S NOTE: The townspeople join the list confirming the body as Billy's, and are called "Billy's friends." Note also that Garrett does not try to conceal the body of the supposed innocent victim of his "murder."]

When morning came, Justice of the Peace Alejandro Segura convened a jury, with Rudulph as president.

[AUTHOR'S NOTE: The Justice of the Peace convened the Coroners Jury. Later the hoaxers will switch this fact.]

They rendered a verdict that William Bonney, Alias "Kid," had been killed by Garrett and were "unanimous in the opinion that the gratitude of the whole community is due the said Garrett for his act and that he deserves to be rewarded".

[AUTHOR'S NOTE: Note that the job of a Coroners' Jury was to identify the body. They did. Billy was known to them. The hoaxers already quoted historian Philip Rasch saying Rudulph was nervous when interviewed by Poe - indicating he knew Billy, and knew he was in the area. Crucial also is that the Coroner's Jury declared the killing justifiable homicide. That closed the case legally. Re-opening it is double jeopardy.]

That afternoon Jesus Silva and Vincente Otero dug a grave for the outlaw in the old military cemetery.[12] ([12]Philip Rasch. *Trailing Billy the Kid* by Philip J. [sic - Rasch] Outlaw-lawman research series Volume 1, University of Wyoming, Laramie, Wyoming, 1993.)

On face value this looks to be the truth. However, if you study the statements of the eye witness [sic] and the documents they do not match up and both can not be true.

[AUTHOR'S NOTE: This is to fake "inconsistencies."]

Deputy John Poe says the following:

It was understood when I left my companions in the morning that in case of my being unable to learn any definite information in Fort Sumner, I was to go to the ranch of Mr. Rudulph (an acquaintance and supposed friend of Garrett's) whose ranch was located some seven miles north of Fort Sumner at a place called "Sunnyside," with the purpose of securing from him, if possible, some information as to the whereabouts of the man we were after. Accordingly I started from Fort Sumner about the middle of the afternoon for Rudulph's ranch,

[AUTHOR'S NOTE: Remember "in the middle of the afternoon." It will later be switched to Poe leaving for Rudulph's <u>at night</u>.]

arriving there sometime before night. I found Mr. Rudulph at home, presented the letter of Introduction which Garrett had given me, and told him that I wished to stop overnight with him.[13] ([13]Poe, John W. Billy the Kid. Privately published by E.A. Brininstool. Los Angeles, CA.)

[AUTHOR'S NOTE: With this unpublished, Brininstool source - and reasonable assumption of its unavailability to readers – the hoaxers are about to construct a fake argument.]

In this part of Deputy Poe's statement he tells us he was sent to Rudulph's ranch by Garrett because Rudulph was "*an acquaintance and supposed friend of Garrett's,*" that the ranch was located seven miles north of Ft. Sumner, at Sunnyside. Poe also tells Rudulph he is going to spend the night at the ranch.

[AUTHOR'S NOTE: The fakery here is leaving out part of the quote. Brininstool information is as follows: There was <u>no</u> "Brininstool book." Poe wrote his account, including the Rudulph episode, for Charles Goodnight in 1917. In 1919; and an Edward Seymour in New York contacted Goodnight for information on the Kid. Goodnight referred him to Poe. Poe sent his account of Billy's death to Seymour, who sent it to Brininstool, who published it in British *Wild World Magazine*, in December of 1919, later making it a brochure. It was also used in in Poe's book, *The Death of Billy the Kid*, which the hoaxers

earlier cited. On its page 22, Poe states he declined the invitation to spend the night. But the hoaxers omitted its pages 25-26. There, Poe states: "Darkness was now approaching, and I said to Mr. Rudulph that inasmuch as myself and my horse were by this time pretty well rested, having had a good meal, I had changed my mind, and instead of stopping with him, would saddle up and ride during the cool of the evening to meet my companions. This I accordingly did, much, I thought, to the relief of Rudulph." So there was no inconsistency]

In Sheriff Garrett's statement he gives about the same facts of where he was headed and how far it was from Ft. Sumner. Garrett differs with Poe in one area when he says he "arranged with Poe to meet us that night at moonrise" rather then spend the night with Rudulph, as can be seen below:

[AUTHOR'S NOTE: This is to fake Garrett as making contradictions. But Poe *did not* spend the night. The hoaxers merely hid Poe's quote saying that he did not spend the night.]

I advised him (Poe) *also, to go to Sunnyside, seven miles above Sumner, and interview M. Rudulph Esq. In whose judgment and discretion I had great confidence. I arranged with Poe to meet us that night at moonrise, at La Puenta de la Glorietta, four miles north of Fort Sumner.*[14] ([14]Garrett, Pat F. The Authentic Life of Billy the Kid. University of Oklahoma Press, Norman. Oklahoma. 2000)

[AUTHOR'S NOTE: That was it: the hoaxers' alleged inconsistency: whether Poe did or did not spend the night at Milnor Rudulph's! But both Poe and Garrett agree that Poe did not. There was no inconsistency. Nevertheless, this hoaxer flimflam is later repeated on the same subject.]

Deputy Poe then gives his account of when he says he first saw the Kid when he writes:

I observed that he was only partly dressed, and was both bare-headed and bare-footed - or rather, had only socks on his feet, and it seemed to me that he was fastening his trousers as he came toward me art a very brisk walk.

As Maxwell's was the one place in Fort Sumner that I considered above suspicion of harboring "The Kid," I was entirely off my guard, that thought coming into my mind that the man approaching was either Maxwell

[AUTHOR'S NOTE: This quote dovetails with Poe's question about the correct man, since he could not identify Billy. Also note Poe's lack of alarm. It will be misstated by the hoaxers.]

or some guest of his who might have been staying there. He came on until he was almost within arm's length of where I sat before he saw me, as I was partly concealed from his view by the post of the gate. Upon his seeing me he covered me with his six-shooter as quick as lightening, sprang onto the porch, calling out in Spanish, "Quien es?" (Who is it?), *at the same time backing away from me toward the door through which Garrett only a few seconds before had passed, repeating his query, "Quien es?" in Spanish several times. At this I stood up and advanced toward him, telling him not to be alarmed: that he should not be hurt, and still without the least suspicion that this was the very man we were looking for.*

This statement raises many questions with investigators. Poe says he sees a man "*partially dressed, and was bare-headed and bare-footed - or rather, had only socks on his feet, and it seemed to me that he was fastening his trousers as he came toward me art a very brisk walk.*" Then the man covers him with his six shooter. Where did the man put the "*six-shooter*" when he was "*fastening his trousers*"?

[AUTHOR'S NOTE: This is an accidentally hilarious hoaxer contrivance of the impossibility of doing two things at once! Actually, one can hold a revolver and button one's pants. And Billy was a gunman and ambidextrous, so even more able! Amazingly, this silliness would be repeated by Sederwall for W.C. Jameson's 2018 book, *Cold Case Billy the Kid.*]

He did not stop and lay it down because Poe says he "*he came toward me art a very brisk walk.*"

[AUTHOR'S NOTE: Triple tasking!]

Another question that investigators struggle with is would it not go without saying Poe would have had a description of the Kid as he ventured into Ft. Sumner to scout around and gather information. It is beyond reason that he would go searching for a man without at least having a description of the man for whom he was searching?

[AUTHOR'S NOTE: It is not beyond reason. Garrett was not an experienced lawman. And Poe's task was not to search for Billy, but to find out from locals about Billy's whereabouts.]

In a town of about 200 people, many of which were Hispanic would Poe be unable to recognize the Kid from this description as he claims?

[AUTHOR'S NOTE: What description? It seems Poe had none. Also, this is racist. Many people of Hispanic background could be as fair as Billy.]

Deputy Poe continues his statement with these words:

As I moved toward him trying to reassure him, he backed up into the doorway of Maxwell's room, where he halted for a moment, his body concealed by the thick adobe wall at the side of the doorway, from whence he put his head out and asking in Spanish for the fourth or fifth time who I was. I was within a few feet of him when he disappeared into the room.

When the Kid asks Poe who he is in Spanish and has his pistol pointed at the deputy, what is Deputy McKinney doing at this time? Why is he not shouldering his rifle, and at least deploying to the side to cover his partner Deputy Poe from this very real threat? Today the shooting policy for police officers is tight and narrow: in 1881 a shooting policy was non-existent. Investigators believe the deputies had to have a description for whom they were searching. With a threat such as Poe describes, a man with a gun, added to the description of the most wanted man in New Mexico, there would have been cause for both deputies to have fired on the suspect.

[AUTHOR'S NOTE: Here comes fakery. Who says Poe had the description, or thought the gun was a threat? Back then, most men were armed. Poe even shows lack of alarm by reassuring the stranger. This fakery was repeated by Sederwall for W.C. Jameson's 2018 book, *Cold Case Billy the Kid.*]

Even if the deputies chose not to fire, would they have allowed the man who was threatening their lives with a gun

[AUTHOR'S NOTE: Note this switcheroo from a fake claim of alarm at "threatening their lives," to making it a fact.]

to walk in on the unaware Sheriff in the dark? If they chose to allow the man with a gun to walk in on the Sheriff would these seasoned lawmen

[AUTHOR'S NOTE: Kip McKinney was just a hog farmer.]

not at least have warned the Sheriff of the danger?

[AUTHOR'S NOTE: No danger is established.]

In Garrett's statement he relates the following:

From his step I could perceive he was either barefooted or in his stocking feet and held a revolver in his right hand and butcher knife in his left.

He came directly towards me. Before he reached the bed, I whispered, "Who is it Pete?"

[AUTHOR'S NOTE: If Garrett cannot recognize Billy, there goes the hoaxers' best-buddies-murder-plot case centerpiece! Note also that Maxwell provides another Billy identification!]

But I received no response for a moment. It struck me that it might be Pete's brother-in-law. Manuel Abrea [sic], who had seen Poe and McKinney and wanted to know their business. The intruder came close to me, leaned both hands on the bed, his right and almost touching my knee, and asked in a low tone: "Who are they, Pete?" At the same moment Maxwell whispered to me, "That's him!" Simultaneously the Kid must have seen, or felt, the presence of a third person at the head of the bed. He raised quickly his pistol, a self cocker, within a foot of my breast. Retreating rapidly across the room he cried: "Quien es? Quien es? (Who's that? Who's that?) All this occurred in a moment. Quickly as possible I drew my revolver and fired, threw my body aside, and fired again. The second shot was useless: The Kid fell dead ..."

Investigators find it hard to believe that Garrett could see a 6 inch knife in the Kid's hand.

[AUTHOR'S NOTE: That night had a bright moon. When Billy opened the door, a held weapon would have been visible.]

Yet the Kid could not see a six foot, five inch man.

[AUTHOR'S NOTE: It was dark in the room. Note that at this half-way point in the Probable Cause Statement, with killing done, nothing indicates the victim was not Billy.]

Deputy Poe talks about what happened after the shooting of the Kid. He writes:

Within a very short time after the shooting, quite a number of the native people had gathered around, some of them bewailing the death of their friend,

[AUTHOR'S NOTE: From Poe's *The Death of Billy the Kid*, comes this hoaxer slip-up: These people, who can recognize Billy, will later be given his body to lay out.]

while several women pleaded for permission to take charge of the body, which we allowed them to do. They carried it to the yard to a carpenter's shop, where it was laid on a workbench, the women placing candles lightened around it, according to their ideas of properly conducting a "wake" for the dead.

[AUTHOR'S NOTE: By this point, there are profuse eye-witness identifications of Billy!]

Investigators keep Deputy Poe's statement in mind as they studied the Coroner's Jury Report:

Greetings:

On this 15th day of July, A.D. 1881, I, the undersigned, Justice of the Peace of the above named precinct, received information that a murder had taken place in Fort Sumner, in said precinct, and immediately upon receiving said information I proceeded to the said place and named Milnor Rudulph, Jose Silva, Antonio Sevedra [sic], Pedro Antonio Lucero, Lorenzo Jaramillo and Sabal Gutierres a jury to investigate the case and the above jury convened in the home of Luz B. Maxwell and proceeded to a room in the said house where they found the body of William Bonney alias "Kid" with a shot in the left breast and having examined the body they examined the evidence of Pedro Maxwell, which evidence is as follows: "I being in my bed in my room, at about midnight on the 14th day of July, Pat F. Garrett came into my room and sat down. William Bonney came in and got close to my bed with a gun in his hand and asked me "who is it" and then Pat F. Garrett fired two shots at the said William Bonney and the said William Bonney fell near my fire place and I went out of the room and when I came in again about three or four minutes after the shots the said William Bonney was dead."

[AUTHOR'S NOTE: This is a definitive Jury, plus Maxwell , making identifications of the victim as William Bonney.]

The jury has found the following verdict: We the jury unanimously find that William Bonney has been killed by a shot on the left breast near the region of the heart, the same having been fired with a gun in the hand of pat F. Garrett and our verdict is that the deed of said Garrett was justifiable homicide and we are unanimous in the opinion that the gratitude of all the community is due to the said Garrett for his deed and is worthy of being rewarded.

M. Rudolph, President *Anto, Sevedra [sic](signature)*
Pedro Anto. m. Lucero (signature)
Jose Silba (x) *Sabal Gutierrez (x)* *Lorenzo Jaramillo (x)*

All said information I place to your knowledge.

Alejandro Segura Justice of the Peace (signature)

[AUTHOR'S NOTE: This is a legally binding document confirming victim identification. To reopen the case is double jeopardy. Further confirmation of jurymen's certainty, is that no murder indictment was later made with the District Attorney of the First Judicial District Attorney against Garrett.]

Investigators remembered Deputy Poe's statement and Sheriff Garrett's statement as to where Poe had been that night.

[AUTHOR'S NOTE: The hoaxers hope the reader believed their faked contention that Poe spent the night at Rudulph's. What follows is more fakery to manufacture "inconsistencies."]

Earlier that evening

[AUTHOR'S NOTE: The time was afternoon, as quoted by the hoaxers earlier, and tagged by me to prepare for this switcheroo where they need night for their fake argument.]

Garrett had dispatched Deputy Poe to interview M. Rudulph in Sunnyside, seven miles north of Fort Sumner. Poe says he left Rudulph and rode to meet Garrett and McKinney. All records show that the shooting took place about midnight and Historian Philip I. Rash [sic] sets the time at 12:30 AM on July 15th. If this were true then the time does not allow for the statement of Poe and the coroner's jury report to both be true.

[AUTHOR'S NOTE: Their hoaxers' time switcheroo is done to discredit the Coroner's Jury Report: their bugbear. But, even if granted them, it does not work because of the length of the ride. Poe could cover the 7 miles to Sunnyside in 1½ hours. Puenta de la Glorietta was 4 miles north of Fort Sumner on the way. So Poe's return journey to meet his companions was only 3 miles, or about 45 minutes: easy to meet them by evening: a fact he and Garrett confirmed. No time inconsistency exists.]

If, after the shooting, Garrett had to get some order to the scene, locate a rider to ride to Sunnyside to get Rudulph,

[AUTHOR'S NOTE: The above Coroner's Jury Report clearly states that the appointment - and contacting - of Rudulph was a legal duty performed by the appropriate official: Justice of the Peace, Alejandro Segura; certainly <u>not</u> Garrett, then a murder suspect awaiting the verdict for Billy Bonney's killing.]

and the rider then had to get his horses [sic] caught, saddled and ready to go all of which would take the better part of an hour,

[AUTHOR'S NOTE: Timing here is faked. Maxwell had a stable and workers. A horse could be readied quickly.]

the time would be 1:30 am.

[AUTHOR'S NOTE: The hoaxers are faking time "inconsistency. Yet they know that the Coroner's Jury met sometime during daytime of the 15th. There was no need for extreme urgency; and no evidence that it occurred.]

It would take a rider who was in shape, on a good horse, and riding fast, an hour and a half to cover the seven miles to Rudulph's ranch, putting the time at 2:30 am. Adding an hour for the rider to wake Rudulph up and for Rudulph to catch his horse and saddle the horse the time would be 3:30 am. If Rudulph was in good shape, on a good horse it would be another hour and a half on the return trip to Fort Sumner putting the time at 4:30 am. Add another hour to put together a jury, and the time is now 5:30 am. This is if everyone worked smoothly.

In the jury's report we find the words:

... a jury to investigate the case and the above jury convened in the home of Luz B. Maxwell and proceeded to a room in the said in said house where they found the body of William Bonney alias "Kid"...

Either the jury found the Kid in the Maxwell's home, or he was not given to the women to put on the carpenters workbench as Poe says, or the jury report is deceptive.

[AUTHOR'S NOTE: The hoaxers hope they convinced readers of that conclusion to fake an inconsistency. But there was enough time to carry the corpse from the Maxwell house, across about 300 yards of parade ground, to the carpenter's shop. In the morning, it could be returned to the Maxwell's house for the jurymen. This fakery was recycled by Sederwall for W.C. Jameson's 2018 book, *Cold Case Billy the Kid.*]

Deputy Poe also says:

The next morning we sent for the justice of the peace,

[AUTHOR'S NOTE: Here is undone the fakery of the night riding by giving this quote about the next morning.]

who held an inquest over the body, the verdict of the jury being such as to justify the killing, and later, on the same day, the body was buried in the old military burying ground at Fort Sumner.

If the Kid's body was taken to the carpenter shop then the jury did not find the body at Maxwell's house as stated and makes investigators wonder why they would lie in the report.

[AUTHOR'S NOTE: This fabrication leads to a "lie" accusation. But nothing indicates that the body was not brought to the house from the carpenter's shop. But the hoaxers are still trying to discredit the Coroner's Jury Report by fake

"contradictions;" though, of course, that is irrelevant to establishing the victim's identity.]

Deputy Poe says something else that raised investigators suspicions when he writes about the shooting itself:

[AUTHOR'S NOTE: This switcheroo distracts from the sly misstatements slipped past. And though the hoaxers never say what is "suspicious" in Poe's quote – which is merely repeating Garrett's description - they are setting the stage for their fake "investigation" to be described next.]

An instant later a shot was fired in the room, followed immediately by what everyone within hearing distance thought was two shots fired, the third report, as we learned afterward, being caused by the rebound of the second bullet which had struck the adobe wall and rebounded against the headboard of the wooden bedstead.

[AUTHOR'S NOTE: Let us take stock now. Nothing so far indicates a victim other than profusely identified Billy Bonney. Nor are there any "contradictions." Later, when exhumations were blocked, the hoaxers contradicted this document: stating Billy *was* shot, laid out on the bench, but played dead to bleed as a source of DNA, before evil Garrett switched him with the murdered innocent victim!]

[AUTHOR'S NOTE: Note that the second bullet hit the headboard. But the hoaxers will do fake forensics on a washstand instead! So next is a faked CSI-style investigation.]

On August 29, 2003, Deputy Sederwall of the Lincoln County Sheriff''s Department

[AUTHOR'S NOTE: Sederwall calls himself a deputy; years later, when hiding the case's DNA documents from my open records case, he would lie that he did the case as his "hobby!"]

located the carpenter bench where the Kid's body was placed on July 14, 1881.

[AUTHOR'S NOTE: Error: earliest morning of July 15th]

On September 13, 2003, investigators located all the furniture that was in Pete Maxwell's bedroom the night of the shooting, July 1881.

[AUTHOR'S NOTE: Though this information is irrelevant to the claim of whether Billy was Garrett's victim, this Maxwell furniture - including the carpenter's bench - became pivotal to the survival of the hoax after exhumations were blocked. But the furniture's connection to the historical scenes is not iron-clad. Maxwell family sold Fort Sumner at public auction on January 15, 1884 to Lonny Horn, Sam Doss, Daniel Taylor and

John Lord in partnership with the New England Cattle Company, which transferred its operations there. The Maxwell house (with the fateful bedroom) was torn down about 1887, and some of the timber was used to build the Pigpen Ranch south of Melrose, New Mexico.

Pete Maxwell died in 1898, Luz Maxwell in 1900. One of their daughters, Odile Maxwell married a Manuel Abreu, and settled outside the town. Odile may have taken family furniture. In about 1925, Odile's and Manuel's then 15 year old daughter, Stella, made a little "Billy the Kid Museum" in a shack to cater to tourists. She labeled some furniture and a carpenter's bench as from that history. It closed in 1936. In about 1940, she and her husband, Kenneth Miller, displayed the furniture in their Santa Rosa, New Mexico gas station. Later in the decade, they moved to Albuquerque, but stored the furniture until bringing what remained to their converted back-yard chicken coop in 1959. Her youngest son, Mannie Miller, showed it to the hoaxers. He died on March 20, 2011, and it was sold to a collector. So all one can say is that about 44 years after Billy's killing, Stella Abreu assembled some alleged Billy the Kid-related furniture for profit.]

Among these items is the headboard of the bed that was in Maxwell's room that night. There is no bullet hole in the headboard.

[AUTHOR'S NOTE: That finding, though irrelevant to the victim, is part of the hoaxers fake forensics and was created to contradict Poe's eye-witness statement that the headboard was hit. The fakery omitted mention that Stella Abreu's museum's headboard was just a thin frame around a huge opening of the missing headboard. There is no place for a bullet hole! This fakery would be recycled by Sederwall in W.C. Jameson's 2018 book, *Cold Case Billy the Kid.*]

In a statement made by Deluvina Maxwell she says the following:

... There was a washstand with a marble top in Pete Maxwell's bedroom, which Garrett had seen in the moonlight and shot at, thinking it was Bonney trying to get up.

[AUTHOR'S NOTE: This is a faked Deluvina quote. Its footnote states: "[15]Deluvina Maxwell's story as related to Lucien B. Maxwell grandchildren, unpublished." This is just hearsay, without even a source. It is being used to fake legitimacy of the hoaxers' claim that the washstand was shot by Garrett.]

It was an old Spanish custom that the night before the burial of a person, people would take turns staying with the body and reciting prayers. William Bonney had a proper funeral. The people took turns and stayed through the night.

[AUTHOR'S NOTE: Another body identification as Billy!]

He was buried in the old government cemetery in Fort Sumner. For many years Deluvina left flowers on his grave in the summer time.[15]

[AUTHOR'S NOTE: This third person statement again shows the quote was not Deluvina. But she did lay flowers for decades, proving the body was Billy's!]

Deluvina lends credibility to the story of the Kid's body being laid on the carpenter bench.

[AUTHOR'S NOTE: Here is a hoaxer slip that ends their case: Billy's corpse on bench! And it ends "Brushy's" hoax too! To get out of that problem, the hoaxers later fabricated that Billy was just "playing dead!"]

In the items investigators located on September 13, 2003 was that wash stand.

[AUTHOR'S NOTE: This washstand is unsubstantiated as from Pete Maxwell's bedroom - as is the rest of the furniture from Stella Abreu's Billy the Kid Museum. And this washstand is implausibly toy-sized. Furthermore, eye-witness Poe said the headboard was hit. But what follows is a fake "crime scene investigation" using the unsubstantiated washstand.]

The was stand was dark in color and 29 1/2 inches wide, with a splash board on the back that measured 5 inch at the middle and tapered down to the ends in a decorative curve. From front to back the wash stand measured 16 inches. It stood 29 inches with three drawers with rusted locks on each drawer. There was what appeared to be a bullet hole through the stand.

Deputy Sederwall removed a .45 caliber pistol round from his deputy weapon and noticed the round was just a little bit bigger than the hole. The night of the shooting Sheriff Garrett was shooting a Colt Single Action Army Revolver, Serial Number 55093, caliber .44/40.[16] ([16]Typed letter from P.F. Garrett dated April 16, 1906. James H. Earl Collection, from County Clerk's office, El Paso, Texas.)

[AUTHOR'S NOTE: Note that there is no bullet, just holes. Claiming .44/40 ammunition is fakery to match Garrett's known weapon's caliber. Actually, there is no link to Garrett or to Maxwell's bedroom. There is even no link to anyone being shot, since accidental discharges happened in New Mexico where owning guns was common from the 19th century to the present – the time frame for "shooting" the tiny washstand!]

The bullet pierced the left side of the washstand, both sides of the drawer and exited out the right side of the stand.

The bullet struck the left side of the stand 22 1/4 inches on the center up from the bottom and 6 1/2 inches on the center of the back of the stand. The bullet exited to the right side 20 1/2 inches on the center up from the bottom and 6 1/2 inches on center from the back of the washstand. On the inside of the left side panel the wood was somewhat splintered indicating that was where the bullet entered the stand. On the right side panel the outside of the panel was splintered indicating the exit of the bullet.

The owner of the washstand, whose name investigators do not wish to release at this time

[AUTHOR'S NOTE: The hoaxers later named Mannie Miller.]

says it was inherited along with the bed from Maxwell's bedroom. The discovery of this evidence makes Deluvina's statement believable.

[AUTHOR'S NOTE: Historically real or not, the furniture examination is irrelevant to Garrett's victim's identity.]

Many questions remain. Why would the coroner's jury report and the eye witness reports be so at odds?

[AUTHOR'S NOTE: They are not at odds. The hoaxers simply made up some "discrepancies." But the hoaxers were heading to additional fakery, once again to attach the hated Coroner's Jury Report that undid their hoaxing.]

A hint can be found in a document discovered in July of 1989 by Joe O. Bowlin.

[AUTHOR'S NOTE: This is a low blow to a dead man. Joe Bowlin, with his wife Marlyn, founded the Billy the Kid Outlaw Gang to "preserve, protect, and promote the history of Billy Bonney and Pat Garrett." This hoax would have been anathema to Joe Bowlin. What follows misstates a book Bolin published posthumously for its old-timer author, A.P. "Paco" Anaya.]

The document is a story, according to Louis Anaya of Clovis, New Mexico as told to his father, Paco Anaya, a friend of Billy the Kid.

[AUTHOR'S NOTE: Note the admitted friendship of Paco Anaya and Billy. It will catch the hoaxers in another slip-up about the victim being Billy.]

This story was translated from Spanish and then printed in book form. In this transcript you will find the following:

Also, I will have to tell you a lot in reference to the reports that Pat Garrett made about the sworn declaration that appears in the records of the Secretary of State and more, concerning what he said about the

Coroners Jury that investigated the death of Billy the Kid when Pat killed Billy.

In this report, I find that the Coroners Jury that investigated the death of Billy the Kid when he was dead is not part of the same report that acted as a Coroners Jury, neither the form or the verdict of the Coroners Jury. The verdict is recorded in the office of the Secretary of State in Spanish, and they (the jury) are not the same men. There are two that did not even live in Fort Sumner.[17] ([17]Anaya, A. P. *I Buried Billy*. Creative Publishing Company. 1991.)

Paco Anaya goes on to list the members of the Jury that he remembered holding the inquest over the body. They are not the same as the jury report as is held up as proof that Garrett killed the Kid.

[AUTHOR'S NOTE: This is the two coroner's jury report claim made-up by windbag "Paco" Anaya, spewing malarkey for his manuscript devoid of historical knowledge. He was used first as an "expert" in the "Brushy Bill" hoax; and subsequently recycled as a staple in all Billy the Kid imposter hoax books to follow – including W.C. Jameson's *Cold Case Billy the Kid*]

One of the differences is Illeginio Garcia [sic - poor legibility - unclear spelling] as the Jury President and not M. Rudulph.

Paco Anaya says that Garrett wrote the first version in English himself. Anaya says that Garrett later came back and wrote another report in Spanish with the help of "Don Pedro Maxwell and Don Manuel Abrea," [sic - Abreu] Maxwell's brother-in-law.

This makes the investigators ask, if Garrett wrote the verdict is that why the words are found, "*...we are unanimous in the opinion that the gratitude of all the community is due to the said Garrett for his deed and is worthy of being rewarded*"?

It should be noted that in the Coroners Jury Report that Garrett puts forth

[AUTHOR'S NOTE: Note the switcheroo. Garrett did not "put forth" the Coroner's Jury Report. It was a legal document done by authority of Justice of the Peace, Alejandro Segura. Garrett was the *subject* of their investigation. The document was available to him after he was cleared of wrongdoing, to send to District Attorney William Breeden. And it surely was not available to humble citizen Anaya. But the hidden punch line is that Anaya's posthumously published manuscript was titled *I Buried Billy*, confirming the body as Billy Bonney's.]

it is interesting to note that two of those listed were in Garrett's wedding, Sabal Gutierrez is his brother-in-law, and Garrett admits in his statement that Rudulph is a close friend.

[AUTHOR'S NOTE: Note the lie. Garrett did not pick the jurymen; the Justice of the Peace did. All the fakery has done nothing to show that Garrett murdered anyone but Billy.]

[AUTHOR'S NOTE: Next is the hoaxer' last try: using fellow hoaxer, David Turk, for useless hearsay and his fancy title.]

David Turk, Historian for the United States Marshal's Service has pointed out other documents

[AUTHOR'S NOTE: Only one document is presented; though Turk came to New Mexico in December of 2003, possibly to assist in writing this Probable Cause Statement.]

bringing into question Garrett's involvement in the Kid's escape.

[AUTHOR'S NOTE: Note the switcheroo. Who said Billy escaped? He was dead.]

Mr. Turk has produced a Works Progress Administration, Federal Writer's Project interview where the following statement was taken:

The people around Lincoln

[AUTHOR'S NOTE: The killing was 150 miles from Lincoln; and Turk's old-timer reports are useless hearsay. He also supplied the hoax with his own slip-shod and pretender-oriented booklet titled "U.S. Marshals Service and Billy the Kid."]

say Garrett didn't kill Billie (sic) the Kid. John Poe was with Garrett the night he was supposed to ... said that he didn't see the man that Garrett killed.

[AUTHOR'S NOTE: Besides the fact that Poe's statements all refer to seeing the victim, Poe did not know Billy.]

I can take you to the grave in Hell's High Acre, an old government cemetery, where Billie (sic) was supposed to be buried and show you the grave.

The cook at Pete Maxwell's was always putting flowers on the grave and praying at it. This woman thought a lot of Billie (sic), but after Garrett killed the man at Maxwell's home her grandson was never seen again

[AUTHOR'S NOTE: No "grandson" was part of this history.]

and Billie (sic) was seen by Bill Nicholi an Indian scout. Bill saw him in Mexico.[18] ([18]Frances E. Tolly [Totty], comp. "Early Days in Lincoln County," Charles Remark Interview. February 14, 1938, Works Progress Administration, Federal Writer's Project, Folklore-Life Histories, Manuscript Division. Library of Congress.)

[AUTHOR'S NOTE: So this sole "evidence" that Garrett did not kill Billy is old-timer malarkey 57 years later, by someone unconnected to the event, and titled as "folklore."]

[AUTHOR'S NOTE: Next comes the conclusion pretending they proved their contentions.]

Discovering the headboard of Maxwell's bed that does not have a bullet hole in it, as Deputy Poe says it did, leads investigators to question if Poe was in fact in the room after the shooting of William Bonney as he said.

[AUTHOR'S NOTE: Omitted is that the headboard is just an empty frame. And claiming if it was not shot, Poe was not in the room" is absurd; and also irrelevant to victim identity.]

However, the discovery of the Maxwell wash stand with the bullet hole through it indicates someone was shot in Maxwell's room on the night of July 14, 18821.

[AUTHOR'S NOTE: Why? A shot washstand does not mean a shot person - or anything at all about who Garrett shot.]

The question remains as to who is in William H. Bonney's grave at Fort Sumner.

[AUTHOR'S NOTE: No question remains. This is all fakery.]

Investigators believe with the conflicts of Sheriff Pat F. Garrett and Deputy John Poe and the fact that these statements are at odds with the Jury Report as shown above,

[AUTHOR'S NOTE: This is fakery. The "conflicts" do not exist; and had nothing to do with whom Garrett shot.]

coupled with the evidence discovered by deputies,

[AUTHOR'S NOTE: There has been no legitimate evidence.]

probable cause exist [sic] to warrant the court to grant investigators the right to search for the truth in criminal investigation 2003-274 through DNA samples obtained from Catherine Antrim.

[AUTHOR'S NOTE: Without any probable cause of a murder, the hoaxers, contrived their objective: exhumation of Billy and his mother.]

[AUTHOR'S NOTE: Signatures follow; typed and written.]

Steven M. Sederwall: Deputy Sheriff, Lincoln County (12/31/03)

Tom Sullivan: Sheriff Lincoln County (12/31/03)

THE OVERTON AFFIDAVIT

Attached to the "Probable Cause Statement" was a two page, typed, old-timer Affidavit prepared for Sheriff Tom Sullivan by a Homer Overton in the mold of the fake identity Affidavits used by William V. Morrison for *Alias Billy the Kid*.. To be noted is that Overton is lying, for whatever reason. It should be noted that Pat Garrett's widow, Apolinaria Gutierrez Garrett, died in 1936, four years *before* Overton's alleged conversation with her in 1940 (b.1861 - d.1936)! She is buried in the Masonic Cemetery in Las Cruces, New Mexico, where Pat Garrett also lies.

Overton's windbag malarkey includes fabrications of a Pat Garrett report to Texas Rangers, a corpse with blasted face, and, of course, Garrett's murder of someone other than Billy the Kid.

Overton's claims also insult Pat Garrett's widow's reverential protection of Garrett's legacy. After Garrett's death in 1908, she even legally fought and reclaimed from a saloonkeeper his revolver used to kill Billy the Kid. She was the last person in the world to tell random, nine year old child, Homer Overton, that Pat had not shot the Kid - even if she had not been four years dead! Homer Overton wrote:

December 22, 2003

Tom Sullivan
Lincoln County Sheriff
P.O. Box 278
Carrizozo, NM 88301

Tom,

It was good talking to you on the phone and, as promised, I am sending this letter as promised to present this Statement of Facts.

Fact: I was born in Pecos, Texas in the year 1931 and lived there until the later [sic] part of 1941. In the summer of 1940, I was invited to spend the summer with Bobby Talbert and his mother, who had moved from Pecos to Las Cruces, New Mexico earlier that year.

[AUTHOR'S NOTE: Time specificity of Overton's age plus the date fixes Overton in Las Cruces in 1940 – not earlier.]

The time I spent there was wonderful, but one thing happened that summer that made the summer unforgettable.

Bobby's next door neighbor was a lady who introduced herself as Mrs. Garrett, the widow of Pat Garrett. Mrs. Garrett would invite us over to have iced tea with mint leaves in it, and told us stories about her life with Pat. I recall her having a parrot that had belonged to Pat which she said was very old. She told us some parrots live to be over 100 years.

That afternoon, she brought out a gun to show us and said it had belonged to Pat. As I recall, the gun appeared to be a Colt single action revolver. At that point I asked her if that was the gun used to kill Billy the Kid. At this point she got an unusual look on her face and stated that she was going to tell us something we would have to promise to keep a secret, and never to tell anyone. We both promised, and until this day I have never told anyone but my immediate family.

Mrs. Garrett proceeded to tell us the following facts concerning her husband and Billy:

Mrs. Garrett said, "Pat did not shoot Billy". She said there was a very close relationship between Pat and Billy, almost like a father and son relationship. She further stated that the night Pat was supposed to kill Billy, that they were in Ft. Sumner and had made a plan to make it look like Pat killed Billy so Billy could go to Mexico and live with no one looking for him any more. She said that Pat had seen a drunk Mexican lying in the street on his way to talk to Billy. So they planned to use the Mexican and claim that he was in fact Billy the Kid. She didn't state if the Mexican was dead or not, but said that they shot him in the face so he couldn't be recognized. They dressed him in Billy's clothes and Pat signed a paper for the Texas Rangers stating that he had killed Billy the Kid and that this was his body. The Mexican was then buried in Fort Sumner and identified as Billy.

Mrs. Garrett struck me as being very sincere when she told us this and she stated that she had never told anyone before. I have kept this secret for sixty-three years and feel it is time to disclose this story. I hope it will be helpful to you in your quest to find the truth about Billy, as I believe what Mrs. Garrett told us that day was the absolute truth.

All that I have told you is as I recall it related to me sixty-three years ago when I was nine years old. It made such an impression on me that I have remembered it in detail these sixty-three years.

Sincerely,
Homer D. Overton
AKA: Homer D. Kinsworthy
CONTACT INFORMATION

Witnessed by: Jerry Raffee, NOTARY
on December 27th 2003

SEAL AFFIXED

THE ABANDONED "SEVENTY-SEVEN DAYS OF DOUBT" DOCUMENT

A unused document which the lawmen hoaxers hid, and I got by my open records litigation against them, revealed the "Brushy Bill" core of the "Billy the Kid Case" hoax. Likely created around April of 2003, it is a draft of a "Probable Cause Statement" for Pat Garrett as the murder suspect. "LATEST" is handwritten on its front page, as if drafts were attempted. It was titled: "Lincoln County Sheriff's Office, Lincoln County New Mexico, Case: William H. Bonney, a.k.a. William Antrim, a.k.a. The Kid, a.k.a. Billy the Kid: An Investigation into the events of April 28, 1881 through July 14, 1881 - seventy-seven days of doubt." I nick-named it the "Seventy-Seven Days of Doubt Document." Typed-in for future signatures are: "Tom Sullivan: Sheriff, Lincoln County Sheriff's Office; and Steven M. Sederwall: Deputy Sheriff, Lincoln County Sheriff's Office."

Its intent was promoting "Brushy" as Billy the Kid. His death scene is used as "survival" "evidence," or probable cause, for accusing Pat Garrett of murdering innocent victim, Billy Barlow. So, according to the fledgling "Billy the Kid Case" hoax, Barlow was in Billy's Fort Sumner grave - and the intended recipient of their hoax's "high-tech, modern, CSI, DNA forensics."

The "Seventy-Seven Days of Doubt" version is pure conspiracy theory where "Brushy" is king; with John Miller fleetingly referenced for "survival suspicion." And with ignorance matching true-believers W.C. Jameson and Frederick Bean, it used "Brushy's" unscreened quotes as proof. **So "Brushy's" fatal mistake of the *dark night* of the July 14, 1881 killing scene appears again, as in *The Return of Billy the Kid*;** after having been slyly fixed-up to "bright moonlight" by the original Sonnichsen-Morrison hoaxing team for *Alias Billy the Kid*.

But its actual author is unclear. The person was unaware of the history, for example, calling Paulita (Peter Maxwell's sister), his "teenage daughter." Mere guesses for authoring are amateur historian Attorney Bill Robins III, since needed was a "Brushy"-believer. Or it could have been W.C. Jameson (since he had the "Brushy" transcript); or David Turk, who contributed his own big "Brushy"-oriented addendum to the case.

Importantly, the "Seventy-Seven Days of Doubt Document" reveals the imposter hoax modus operandi of faking a death scene and concealing the Coroner's Jury Report. The document stated:

LINCOLN COUNTY SHERIFF'S OFFICE LINCOLN COUNTY, NEW MEXICO

Case: *William H. Bonney,* *a.k.a.* **William Antrim,** a.k.a. **The Kid, *a.k.a.* Billy the Kid**

An Investigation into the events of April 28, 1881 through July 14, 1881 - seventy-seven days of doubt.

Just minutes after twelve, noon, on April 28, 1881, two lawmen lay dead, in the yard of the courthouse in Lincoln, New Mexico, from gunshot wounds. In less time then [sic] it took the New Mexico breeze to clear the gunsmoke, history was clouded with the myth of the shooting and escape of William H. Bonney, a.k.a. Billy the Kid from the make-shift jail, where he awaited a date with the hangman.

The following is a thumbnail sketch of the most widely excepted [sic] account of the events of the escape, capture and shooting death of William H. Bonney a.k.a. Billy the Kid.

The Last Days of William H. Bonney

On August 17, 1877, in George Atkin's cantina near Camp Grant, Arizona, William H. Bonney, who answered to "The Kid" found himself in an altercation with Francis P. "Windy" Cahill over cards or Cahill's woman, no one is quite sure as newspapers report both. It's reported that Windy Cahill called The Kid a "pimp", and in response The Kid dubbed Cahill a "sonofabitch". Infuriated, Cahill reportedly grabbed the Kid and The Kid shoved his pistol into Cahill's stomach, sending a hot round into his belly. With Cahill on the floor, The Kid fled on a stolen horse. Cahill died the next day. A coroner's jury headed by Miles Wood found the shooting by The Kid to be "*criminal and unjustifiable*". The Kid now being a bona fide outlaw drifted across the line into New Mexico's Lincoln County where he signed on as a cowboy working for London born rancher John Tunstall.

Tunstall and his lawyer friend Alexander McSween had decided to challenge the chock-hold [sic] monopoly L.G. Murphy & Company had on Lincoln County. Murphy and his associates, with the backing of the "Santa Fe Ring" ran Lincoln County as they pleased and verticality [sic] unchecked until Tunstall's challenge. The Santa Fe Ring, with their powerful political and financial backing and through Murphy controlled the sheriff, maintained a buddy-buddy relationship with the military and appropriated by means both legal and illegal most of the government money out of the Mescalero Apache Indian Agency near Fort Stanton. When Tunstall wouldn't back down and his challenge became to [sic] powerful for the Murphy faction to turn their heads to, Tunstall was killed. His death on February 18, 1878 fanned the spark that raged into the white-hot flame that became the famed and bloody Lincoln County War.

As history goes Bonney was insignificant as a man, but there exist [sic] no better example of how legends of the west are born and continue to grow. By participating in a number of bloody shootouts, included [sic] the assassination of Lincoln County Sheriff William Brady and one of his deputies, on April 1, 1878, Bonney was catapulted from his status of an unknown drifter to the undisputed leader of the Tunstall-McSween faction and into history becoming bigger the [sic] life.

[AUTHOR'S NOTE: Though starting when Bonney was 17 ½ (not his last days!), the intent is to feign "historical knowledge, and fails. Billy was never the leader of the Tunstall-McSween faction. The fakery intentionally blurs history and "legend," to pretend that actual history *was* legend, to segue to the fakery that history was not as written. But all this is irrelevant to any probable cause of Pat Garrett murdering an innocent victim.]

After newly elected Lincoln County Sheriff Pat Garrett captured Bonney at Stinking Springs, east of Fort Sumner, just before Christmas 1880, Bonney was held in the jail in Santa Fe for several months and then taken to La Mesilla, New Mexico for trial.

The Dona Ana County, District Court records reveal on April 13, 1881, William H. Bonney was convicted of the April 1, 1878 murder of Lincoln County Sheriff William Brady. United States District Judge, Warren Henry Bristol, of the Third Judicial District, sentenced Bonney to be confined in Lincoln County until Friday, May 13, 1881. Looking down from the bench, the judge proclaimed, "*between 9 a.m. and 3 p.m., William Bonney, alias Kid, alias William Antrim, be taken from such prison to some suitable and convenient place of execution within said county of Lincoln, by Sheriff of such county and that then and there, on that day and between the aforesaid hours thereof, by the sheriff of said county of Lincoln, he, the said William Bonney, alias Kid, alias William Antrim, be hanged by the neck until his body be dead.*"

On April 21, 1881, Bonney was transported back to Lincoln under heavy guard. Because Lincoln had no adequate jail Bonney was incarcerated in the upstairs of the old Murphy-Dolan store, recently bought by the county to be used as the courthouse. A staircase led up to a hallway that ran north to south across the middle section of the building. The room ahead and to the left of the hallway was being used as the sheriff's office. Off the sheriff's office, with access only through the sheriff's office was the room where Bonney was confined.

With no bars on the windows of this room, Sheriff Garrett had special leg shackles made, and Bonney was chained to the hardwood floor at all times. In addition, Garrett assigned Lincoln County Sheriffs Deputy J.W. Bell and Deputy United States Marshall [sic] Bob Olinger, to guard the prisoner twenty-four hours a day. On the floor Bonney's guards drew a chalk line across the center of the room, a line which Bonney was forbidden to cross or he would be shot by the guards.

On Wednesday, April 27, 1881 Sheriff Pat Garrett left Lincoln on a tax-collecting mission to White Oaks, New Mexico. Just after twelve, noon, the next day, Thursday, April 28, Deputy United States Marshall [sic] Olinger escorted all the prisoners with the exception of Bonney to the Wortley Hotel, across the street from the courthouse, for their midday meal, leaving Deputy Sheriff Bell in charge of Bonney.

No eye witness record can be found of the escape of Bonney with the exception of the following statement made by the courthouse caretaker Gottfried Gauss, published in the *Lincoln County Leader* on January 15, 1890, nearly a decade later.

I was crossing the yard behind the courthouse, when I heard a shot fired then a tussle upstairs in the courthouse, somebody hurrying downstairs, and deputy sheriff Bell emerging from the door running toward me. He ran right into my arms, expired the same moment, and I laid him down, dead. That I was in a hurry to secure assistance, or perhaps to save myself, everybody will believe.

When I arrived at the garden gate leading to the street, in front of the courthouse, I saw the other deputy sheriff Olinger, coming out of the hotel opposite, with the four or five other county prisoners, where they had taken their dinner. I called to him to come quick. He did so, leaving his prisoners in front of the hotel. When he had come up close to me, and while I was standing not a yard apart, I told him that I was just after laying Bell dead on the ground in the yard behind. Before he could reply, he was struck by a well-directed shot fired from a window above us, and fell dead at my feet. I ran for my life to reach my room and safety, when Billy the Kid called to me: "Don't run, I wouldn't hurt you – I am alone, and master not only of the courthouse, but also of the town, for I will allow nobody to come near us." "You go," he said, "and saddle one of Judge (Ira) Leonard's horses, and I will clear out as soon as I have the shackles loosened from my legs." With a little prospecting pick I had thrown to him through the window he was working for at least an hour, and could not accomplish more than to free one leg. He came to the conclusion to wait a better chance, tie one shackle to his waistbelt, and start out. Meanwhile I had saddled a small skittish pony belonging to

Billy Burt (the county clerk), as there was no other horse available, and had also, by Billy's command, tied a pair of red blankets behind the saddle ...

When Billy went down the stairs at last, on passing the body of Bell he said, "I'm sorry I had to kill him but I couldn't help it." On passing the body of Olinger he gave him a tip with his boot, saying, "You are not going to round me up again." And so Billy the Kid started out that evening, after he had shaken hands with everybody around and after having a little difficulty in mounting on account of the shackle on his leg, he went on his way rejoicing.

There are numerous theories about the killing of Deputy J.W. Bell. One is that he was coming up the stairs when shot. Another theory is Bell was running down the stairs and was at the bottom of the stairs and heading to the doorway when Bonney shot him. Garrett's testimony seems to be the most solid. Garrett says, "*Bell was hit under the right arm, the bullet passing through his body and coming out under the left arm. The ball had hit the wall on Bell's right, caromed passed through his body, and buried itself in an adobe (wall) on the left. There was no other proof besides the marks on the walls."*

Garrett later said of Olinger, that he was "*hit in the right shoulder, breast and side. He was literally riddled by thirty-six buckshot.*" Each pellet weighed four grams - nearly a quarter pound of lead in all hit Olinger.

It's hard to determine how many shots were fired at Bell from Bonney's pistol. In the 1920's Maurice G. Fulton saw the building and states there were "*any number of bullet holes"*. Fulton had a photograph taken in the 1930's prior to the restoration, which shows three.

With only two people on the stairway that day numerous versions of what happened have been brought forth, and debated. One theory in the Kid's escape is that he slipped his irons, which were double the usual weight, over his small wrists and hands. He turned on Bell striking the deputy over the head with the irons and grabbing the deputy's pistol. This theory could have come from the following article.

In the *Grand County Herald's*, May 14, 1881 edition an article appeared quoting an "anonymous bystander" as testifying about the Kid's escape. *He had at his command eight revolvers and six guns. He stood on the upper porch in front of the building and talked with the people who were in Wortley's, but he would not let anyone come towards him. He told the people that he did not want to kill Bell but, as he had to. He said he grabbed Bell's revolver and told him to hold up his hands and surrender; that Bell decided to run and he had to kill him. He declared he was "standing pat" against the world; and while he did not wish to kill anybody, if anybody interfered with his attempt to escape, he would kill him.*

In this statement the "anonymous bystander" claims Bonney says he took Bell's pistol from him and used it to kill the deputy. In Garrett's book *The Authentic Life of Billy the Kid,* Garrett writes this about the escape:

From circumstances, indications, information from Geiss (also spelled Gauss – the courthouse caretaker) and the Kid's admissions, the popular conclusion is that:

At the Kid's request, Bell accompanied him down stairs and to the back corral. As they returned, Bell allowed the Kid to get considerably in advance. As the Kid turned on the landing of the stairs, he was hidden from Bell. He was light and active, and with a few noiseless bounds, reached the head of the stairs, turned to his right, put his shoulder to the door of the room used as an armory (thought locked, this door was well known to open by a firm push), entered, seized a six-shooter, returned to the head of the stairs just as Bell faced him on the landing of the staircase, some twelve steps beneath, and fired. Bell turned, ran out into the corral and towards the little gate. He fell dead before reaching it. The Kid ran to the window at the south end of the hall, saw Bell fall, then slipped his handcuffs over his hands, threw them at the body, and said: "Here, damn you, take these, too."

Garrett's account seems to have to [sic] many holes to be taken as truth in this matter. At the beginning of Chapter XXII, where this account is found Garrett begins, *On the evening of April 28, 1881, Olinger took all the other prisoners across the street to supper, leaving Bell in charge of the Kid in the guard room.* It is a known fact that the escape did not happen in the evening as Garrett writes but just after noon.

Frederick Nolan, in his commentary notes at the side of the page in this book, points out the following: *The "popular" conclusion set forth here - that Bell would have allowed the Kid latitude and time he needed to perform these maneuvers - has already been examined. That he could have moved "noiselessly" when wearing manacles and leg irons defies belief. And would Billy have waited until after killing Bell before he "slipped his handcuffs over his hands?" Either the Kid struck Bell over the head with his handcuffs, grabbed Bell's gun and killed him with it, or, far more plausibly, someone hid a pistol in the outhouse privy, which*

Billy retrieved and, when they got inside, killed Bell with it.

When Garrett describes The Kid shooting Olinger he says that ... *Olinger appeared at the gate leading into the yard, as Geiss appeared at the little corral gate and said, "Bob, The Kid has killed Bell." At the same instant the Kid's voice was heard above: "Hello, old boy," said he. "Yes, and he's killed me too," exclaimed Olinger, and fell dead with eighteen buckshot in his right shoulder and breast and side.*

It is doubtful that Olinger would have time to say the words that Garrett contributes [sic] to him before the Kid cut him down, making Garrett's account difficult to be taken as true accounting of the events.

[AUTHOR'S NOTE: Though lacking crafty finesse of the final Probable Cause Statement, this author likewise uses Garrett's ghostwritten, dime-novel-style book to try to discredit him. But it remains irrelevant to Garrett as a murderer.]

Garrett also says about The Kid in his account – *He took deliberate aim and fired the other barrel, the charge taking effect in nearly the same place as the first; then breaking the gun across the railway of the balcony, he threw the pieces at Olinger, saying: "Take it, damn you, you won't follow me any more with that gun."*

This doubtful this happened. [sic] The account of The Kid breaking Olinger's shotgun on the balcony is not found elsewhere. Added to the fact that Olinger's shotgun was a Whitney, serial number SN903, and is now on loan to the *Texas Ranger Hall of Fame* in Waco, Texas from the James H. Earl Collection; the shotgun is in tact [sic].

[AUTHOR'S NOTE: Error. Deputy Bob Olinger's Whitney double-barreled shotgun there is broken at its waist, and repaired, at some unknown time, by a wrapping of copper wire. Its curator at the Texas Ranger Museum, giving its description, was Don Agler. This is another irrelevant attempt to discredit Garrett.]

The version which seems the more popular, is that Bonney, retrieved a pistol that had been hidden in the outhouse by a "friend." History has theories but no firm answers to the identity of the "friend" who put the pistol in the outhouse.

[AUTHOR'S NOTE: Error. This seems to be a confusion of the Bell killing with Olinger's, for which the Whitney was used.]

After the Kid shot and killed both of his guards he gather [sic] weapons, and left Lincoln about 3 p.m. on a stolen horse. The Kid's whereabouts from the date of his escape until just before his death, as nearly every aspect of the case, is still debated. The Kid later showed up in Ft. Sumner, New Mexico. **Pete Maxwell's teenage daughter, Paulita**,

[AUTHOR'S NOTE: Error. Paulita was Peter Maxwell's sister. Also, using Paulita contradicts the "love tales" of "Brushy Bill" (Celsa) and John Miller (Isadora), and eliminates them as Billy contenders!. But revealed is the writer's historical ignorance.]

was supposedly in love with the Kid and he with her, which seems to be the most likely motive for him to return to Ft. Sumner.

On the night of July 14, 1881, after searching the area around Ft. Sumner Lincoln County Sheriff Pat Garrett and his deputies John Poe and Thomas C. "Kip" McKinney were about to ride back to Lincoln. Before leaving they thought it a good idea to check with Pete Maxwell. In Garrett's account of this he takes credit for wanting to check with Maxwell before giving up the chase, Deputy Poe differs with Garrett. In Deputy Poe's account written in 1919 we see the events through his eyes.

Garrett seemed to have but little confidence in our being able to accomplish the object of our trip, but said that he knew the location of a certain house occupied by a woman in Fort Sumner which the Kid had formerly frequented, and that if he was in or about Fort Sumner, he would most likely be found entering or leaving this house some time during the night. Garrett proposed that we go to a grove of trees near the town, conceal our horses, then station ourselves in the peach orchard at the rear of the house, and keep watch on who might come or go. This course was agreed upon, and we entered the peach orchard about nine o'clock that night, stationing ourselves in the gloom or shadow of the peach trees, as the moon was shining very brightly. We kept up a fruitless watch here until some time after eleven o'clock, when Garrett stated that he believed we were on a cold trail; that he had very little faith in our being able to accomplish anything when we started on the trip. He proposed that we leave the town without letting anyone know that we had been there in search of the Kid.

I then proposed that, before leaving we should go to the residence of Peter Maxwell, a man who up to that time I had never seen, but who, by reason of his being a leading citizen and having a large property interest should, according to my reasoning, be glad to furnish such information as he might have aid us [sic] *in ridding the country of a man who was looked on as a scourge and curse by all law-abiding people.*

Garrett agreed to this, and there-upon led us from the orchard by circuitous by-paths to Maxwell's residence, which was a building formerly used as officers' quarters during the days when a garrison of troops had been maintained at the fort. Upon our arriving at the residence (a very long, one-story adobe, standing end to the flush with *the street, having a porch on the south side, which was the direction from which we approached, the premises all being enclosed by a paling fence, one side of which ran parallel to and along the edge of the street up to and across the end of the porch to the corner of the building).\, Garrett said to me, "This is Maxwell's room through the open door (left open on account of the extremely warm weather), while McKinney and myself stopped on the outside. McKinney squatted on the outside of the fence, and I sat on the porch.*

It should be here that up to this moment I had never seen Billy the Kid, nor Maxwell, which fact in view of the events transpiring immediately afterward, placed me at an extreme disadvantage.

It was probably not more than thirty seconds after Garrett had entered Maxwell's room, when my attention was attracted, from where I sat at the little gateway, to a man approaching me on the inside of and along the fence, some forty or fifty steps away. I observed that he was only partially dressed and was both bareheaded and barefooted, or rather had only socks on his feet, and it seemed to me that he was fastening his trousers as he came toward me at a very brisk walk.

As Maxwell's was the one place in Fort Sumner that had considered above suspicion of harboring the Kid, I was entirely off my guard, the thought coming to my mind that the man approaching was either Maxwell or some guest of his who might be staying there. He came on until he was almost within arm's length of where I sat, before he saw me, as I was partially concealed from his view by the post of the gate.

Upon seeing me, he covered me with his six-shooter as quick as lightening, sprang onto the porch, calling out in Spanish "Quien es" (Who is it?) - at the same time backing away from me toward the door through which Garrett only a few seconds before had passed, repeating his query, "Who is it?" in Spanish several times.

At this I stood up and advanced toward him, telling him not to be alarmed, that he should not be hurt; and still without the least suspicion that this was the very man we were looking for. As I moved toward him to reassure him, he backed up into the doorway of Maxwell's room, where he halted for a moment, his body concealed by the thick adobe wall at the side of the doorway, form [sic] *whence he put his head and asked in Spanish for the fourth time who I was. I was within a few feet of him when he disappeared into the room.*

After this, and until after the shooting, I was unable to see what took place on account of the darkness of the room, but plainly heard what was said on the inside. An instant after the man left the door, I heard a voice inquire in a sharp tone, "Pete, who are those fellows on the outside?" An instant later a shot was fired in the room, followed immediately by what anyone within hearing distance thought were two shots. However, there were only two shots fired, the third report, as we learned afterward, being caused by the rebound of the second bullet, which had struck the adobe wall and rebounded against the headboard of a wooden bedstead.

I heard a groan and one or two gasps from where I stood in the doorway, as of someone dying in the room. An instant later, Garrett came out, brushing against me as he passed. He stood by me close to the wall at the side of the door and said to me, "That was the Kid that came in there onto me, and I think I got him". I said, "Pat, the Kid would not come to this place; you have shot the wrong man".

Upon saying this, Garrett seemed to be in doubt himself as to whom he had shot, but quickly spoke up and said, "I am sure it was him, for I know his voice to [sic] *well to be mistaken". This remark of Garrett's relieved me of considerable apprehension, as I had felt almost certain that someone whom we did not want had been killed.*

The next day Billy the Kid was buried in Fort Sumner. Or was it the Kid in the grave?

[AUTHOR'S NOTE: Poe's initial uncertainty about Billy's identity, is this writer's only "evidence" of victim identity doubt. Omitted are all witnesses, the Coroner's Jury, and Poe's acceptance.]

What Happen [sic] to William H. Bonney a.k.a. Billy the Kid?

Soon after the shooting in Maxwell's home on July 14, 1881, the rumor took life that Garrett shot the wrong man and that he knew he shot the wrong man but covered it up.

[AUTHOR'S NOTE: This "Seventy-Seven Days Document" is transparently tailored to fit the pretenders.]

Some even say that Garrett had an empty coffin buried the next day in Fort Sumner. Some say Garrett wrote the book *The Authentic Life of Billy the Kid*, in which he demonizing [sic] Billy the Kid, to prop up his waning popularity that was being eroded by the rumor that he killed The Kid in less than a fair fight or that he did not kill The Kid at all.

[AUTHOR'S NOTE: These contentions, without sources, appear made-up, and are not evidence.]

To this day the rumor still has life that Billy the Kid never died that night.

[AUTHOR'S NOTE: Nothing has been presented to support that "rumor."]

Most everything we know about William H. Bonney a.k.a. Billy the Kid is what is know [sic] about him in during the last three years of his life. The date and place of his birth, who his father was, where he lived, as a child is still a mystery. Most of what we do know and what we call history is flawed by myth. Even where he is buried is the subject of controversy these 122 years later.

[AUTHOR'S NOTE: This "what-if" illogic tries to make Bonney's death uncertain, by manufacturing "uncertainties" in his earlier history.]

In England is a grave with the name William H. Bonney on the headstone, where is it said [sic] Billy the Kid is buried. The story is that the Tunstall family, in apparition [sic] of his help and loyalty to John Tunstall, brought the Kid back to England where he lived a long life dying of old age.

[AUTHOR'S NOTE: This is so bizarre, it seems a delirium, rather than an argument. It does indicate the author lacks ability to sort fact from fiction.]

[AUTHOR'S NOTE: The case for Garrett's murder of an innocent victim ends here without proof; and segues to the pretenders.]

John Miller

[AUTHOR'S NOTE: At this preliminary stage - years before the hoaxers needed John Miller's exhumation to keep their hoax afloat - he was of minimal interest; their focus being "Brushy Bill." This disinterest is reflected in the following cursory text - and its negative presentation was kept secret when the hoaxers headed with backhoe to John Miller's grave, suddenly claiming *he* was Billy the Kid.]

In 1993 Helen Airy published a book by Sunstone Press entitled *What* [sic- Whatever] *Happened to Billy the Kid.* In this book the claim is made that a John Miller who died on November 7, 1937, at six-thirty in the evening, in the Pioneer [sic] Home in Prescott, Arizona and was buried in the Prescott Pioneer home cemetery [sic], was Billy the Kid. In Airy's book Miller is quoted as saying, "*there was a Mexican shot and buried in the coffin that is supposed to be the Kid.*"

In her book *What* [sic- Whatever] *Happened to Billy the Kid* these accounts are found:

Page 162 paragraph 2 - *Ann Storrer of Belen writes: "My father, Charlie Walker, grew up around Fort Sumner during the early 1900's. A Mexican he used to work for told him that he saw Billy the Kid at the bullfights in Mexico long after he was supposed to be dead. The rumor around Fort Sumner was that Pat Garrett and Bill [sic] the Kid were good friends and Garrett tried to stop everyone from killing Billy. My father believed there was never a body in the grave.*

Page 162 paragraph 3 and 4 - *Arleigh Nation of Albuquerque supplied the Following story; "A man by the name of Trujillo, who died in 1935 at the age of ninety-five told Nation he worked for Pete Maxwell at the time Billy the kid was supposed to have been killed. He said the day before the shoot-out they dressed up an Indian, who had died the night before, to look like the Kid. The Indian was buried in the grave that was said to have been the Kid's.*

Nation, who is a Billy the kid Buff, also said a neighbor of his who lived in Lincoln, Mrs. Syd Boykin, told him that the kid stayed as [sic] her home in Lincoln many times after he was supposed to have been dead.

Airy states that a John Collins claimed to have been a friend of Billy the Kid. Collins says that he helped bury the corpse of the man Garrett killed on July 14, 1881, and it was not Billy the kid.

Arley Sanches interviewed Nadine Brady, of Adelino, New Mexico, and whose grandfather was Sheriff William Brady, who was shot by the Kid, for a story, which appeared in the *Albuquerque Journal* on September 8, 1990. Nadine says one old timer told her Garrett didn't shoot Bonney. He told her Garrett and Bonney were friends and Garrett invented a story to help his friend escape. A wanderer was killed and buried, and Garrett told everyone he had shot Billy the Kid.

Airy says Frank Coe, a friend of Billy the Kid during the Lincoln County War, believed to the day of his death that Billy was still alive, and spent a great deal of time tracing reports that he had been seen.

The El Paso Herald Post, June 29, 1926 reported a story that a "government official" re[ported that "Billy the Kid and Garrett framed an escape" from Lincoln, New Mexico. The government official claimed the Kid was still alive in this article.

The El Paso Times, July 26, 1964, reported that retired Immigration and Naturalization Service Inspector, Leslie Traylor of San Antonio, Texas claimed Billy the Kid was a man named Henry Street Smith. Traylor said he traced Smith and believes him to be buried under the name of John Miller who died in 1935 in Prescott, Arizona.

[AUTHOR'S NOTE: Airy's John Miller hoax was debunked above. The writer here, however, does not appear to argue for Miller as Billy. And no death scene is presented, that being the purpose of a probable cause statement for a murder case!]

William Henry Roberts a.k.a. Brushy Bill Roberts

[AUTHOR'S NOTE: Next is the attempt to establish Oliver "Brushy Bill" Roberts as Billy the Kid. Noteworthy is use if his fake "William Henry" from *Alias Billy the Kid.* Though he surfaced throughout the hoax, it was given as "survival suspicion," not the case's goal. The very fact that this "Seventy-Seven Days of Doubt Document" was kept secret, indicated hiding of that motive. Apparently, it was intended to have that conclusion arise from the fake forensic DNA matchings. But the effusions that follow here show the "Brushy" bias as well as access to the transcript of "Brushy's" Morrison interviews. And the contradiction of his non-bench death scene, presented in detail below, was not yet anticipated; since the hoaxers expected the Billy and mother exhumations to go through, followed by a faked match to "Brushy." So switching to the bench scenario for "blood DNA" was unanticipated.]

Before Sheriff Pat Garrett could clean his pistol the bogus Billy the Kid's began to crop up everywhere. Some were too ridiculous to take notice of and some convinced a few people but were forgotten with the passage of time. Out of all the men to come forward to claim they are Billy the Kid the one that caused the most stir and gained national and even worldwide attention was Brushy Bill Roberts.

To this day Roberts' claim is being taken seriously by many. In Hamilton, Texas, where William Roberts is buried there stands a sign that proclaims that his grave is "The Authentic Grave Site of Billy the Kid." A plaque states that he spent the last part of his life attempting to get a "promised pardon" from the New Mexico Governor. Just weeks before Roberts death he and his attorney [sic - William Morrison, not an attorney] approached the Governor of New Mexico and asked for a pardon for the Kid, who Roberts claimed to be. Dubious of Roberts claims the Governor granted no pardon.

[AUTHOR'S NOTE: This "Brushy" pardon focus exposes the otherwise inexplicable linking of DNA to pardon in the hoax. Making "Brushy" Billy by the fake match, would then lead to a pardon for an alleged long law-abiding life as Billy the Kid.]

The story goes that in 1948, William V. Morrison was working as an investigator for a law firm. Morrison was a graduate attorney **[Morrison was not an attorney, but often falsely portrayed himself as such]** and it was said that he had a "good nose for evidence". He was a member of the Missouri Historical Society and a descendant of Ferdinand Maxwell, the brother of Lucien Bonaparte Maxwell and uncle of Pete Maxwell. Because of this, Morrison possessed a keen interest in New Mexico history.

During this time Morrison was sent to Florida to investigate an inheritance claimant by the name of Joe Hines. Hines' brother, in North Dakota, had passed away and Hines claimed to be the sole inheritor of some property. As Morrison interviewed the old man the story did not match with the facts Morrison possessed. After more questions Joe Hines told Morrison his name, Hines, was an alias. Hines claimed his real name was Jesse [sic] Evans and he was a survivor of the Lincoln County War.

[AUTHOR'S NOTE: This is the pure "Brushy" hoax, straight from *Alias Billy the Kid.* Indicated is that the writer was a true-believer, like Bill Robins III or W.C. Jameson, or an opportunistic copier, merely seeking publicity and profit from winning.]

Morrison being proud of his ancestral connection to New Mexico history mentioned to Hines (Evans) that Billy the Kid worked for the Maxwells at one time

[AUTHOR'S NOTE: Morrison's fake claim about Billy.]

and added that the Kid was shot and killed in Maxwell's house on July 14, 1881. To that Hines replied, "Garrett did not kill the Kid on July 14, 1881, or any other time." Hines went on to say, "In fact Billy was still living in Texas last year. The reason that I know is that a friend of mine, now living in California stops over to visit with me here every summer. He and Billy and me are the only warriors left of the old Lincoln County bunch.

[AUTHOR'S NOTE: Besides the total fakery, real outlaw-murderer-rustler Jessie Evans would not have called himself a Lincoln County War "warrior."]

Later that year Morrison became acquainted with another man in Missouri who said he knew who all the parties were and gave Morrison an address of a man named O.L. Roberts who lived in Hamilton, Texas. In June of 1948 Morrison drove to Hamilton, Texas and met Roberts. On their first meeting Roberts told Morrison that the Kid was his half brother and was still alive in Old Mexico. The next day Morrison came back to Roberts home and Roberts sent his wife to a neighbor's house saying he and Morrison had business to discuss.

After Mrs. Roberts left the house Morrison claims Roberts pointed his finger at him and said, "Well, you've got your man. You don't need to look any farther. I'm Billy the Kid. But don't tell anyone. My wife doesn't know who I am. She thinks my half brother is Billy the Kid, but he died in Kentucky many years ago. I want a pardon before saying anything about this matter. I don't want to kill anyone anymore, but I'm not going to hang." Morrison goes on to write that Roberts told his story and tears coursed down his cheeks, as he said, "I done wrong like everyone else did in those days. I want to die a free man. I do not want to die like Garrett and the rest of them, by the gun. I have been hiding so long and they have been telling so many lies about me that I want to get everything straightened out before I die. I can do it with some help. The good Lord left me here for a purpose and I know why He did. Now will you help me out of this mess."

Morrison wanted proof that Roberts claims were true and knew the scars the Kid would have on his body. Morrison had Roberts strip and from the scars on Roberts' body Morrison was convinced that he was talking to the true William H. Bonney.

Roberts tells Morrison in detail how he escaped death at the hands of Sheriff Pat Garrett the night of July 14, 1881. In a statement Roberts records the following:

[AUTHOR'S NOTE: To follow are "Brushy's" words from pages 105-117 of W.C. Jameson's and Frederick Bean's 1998 *The Return of the Outlaw Billy the Kid.* They claimed to have gotten the transcript from "Brushy's" step-grandson, Bill Allison. Thus, indicated is possible participation of W.C. Jameson.]

[AUTHOR'S NOTE: Do not miss the attempted validation of "Brushy" that this document represents. His words are being used as "evidence" in *a real law enforcement case* to show probable cause that Garrett was a murderer, since *he* survived; ergo, Garrett *must have murdered innocent Billy Barlow*.]

I rode into Fort Sumner from Yerby's a few days before Garrett and his posse rode in. When they rode in that day, I had spent the day with Garrett's brother-in-law, Saval Gutierrez. Nearly all the people in this country were my friends and they helped me. None of them liked Garrett. It was dark that night, but there was enough moonlight to make shadows. Me and my partner Billy Barlow, rode up to Jesus Silva's house when we reached Fort Sumner. We had been staying at the Yerby Ranch laying low for a while. Word was all around that Pat Garrett and a posse were after me. Pat's wife was a sister to my friend Saval Gutierrez, and Saval told me that Pat was after me, that he heard it from his sister.

Things were mighty hot in Lincoln County for me right about then, but I wasn't running from it. I meant to have a talk with Pat Garrett and set things straight between us if I could. We used to be friends ... We hid our horses in the barn and walked up to Jesus' back door. Barlow was nervous about being in Fort Sumner with me and I couldn't blame him much. Jesus came to the back door when I tapped on it with the barrel of my six-shooter. When he saw that it was me, he grinned and let us in. I told Jesus we were hungry. We'd been out in the hills all day, scouting around Fort Sumner for any sign of Garrett and his posse. "I have nothing but cold frijoles, compadre," Jesus whispered as he closed the door. Barlow made a sour face. "I want some meat," he said, "we have been living on beans and tortillas all week. Ain't you got any beef?

According to Roberts statement Jesus Silva told Barlow that Pete Maxwell had some meat hanging on his porch. Barlow wanted to get the beef to cook but Roberts told him it was too dangerous and they should not move from the house. Barlow would not listen. According to Roberts statement Barlow took a butcher knife and left the house to head to Maxwell's to get the beefsteak. While Roberts and Jesus were lighting the wood stove they hear [sic] gunfire in the direction of Pete Maxwell's place. Roberts' statement goes on to describe the following events:

I pulled one of my .44's and ran through the door, trying to see in the dark. Two more shots came from a shadow beside the Maxwell house. I couldn't find a target to shoot at. It was too dark to see. *I ran toward Maxwell's back porch. I heard another gunshot and felt something hit me in the jaw. I stumbled and kept on running with a broken tooth rolling around my tongue. I tasted blood and spit the mess out of my mouth as I started emptying my six-shooter at the shadow where I saw the muzzleflash. From the corner of my eye I saw a body lying on the back porch ... I knew it had to be Barlow.*

My partner had walked right into a trap, and the trap had likely been set for me. I pulled my other .44 and ran toward the porch to check on Barlow, but I ran into a wall of gunfire. I knew I wasn't going to make it to my partner. Too many guns were shooting at me. I didn't have a chance. I turned for a fence across the back of Maxwell's yard and dove for it when a bullet caught me in the left shoulder. I jumped over the fence and landed hard on the far side, with the echo of gunshots all around me, ringing in my ears. I staggered into an alley that ran behind the house, firing my .44 over my shoulder until it clicked empty. My mouth and shoulder were bleeding and I lost track of where I was, but I knew I had to get away from Maxwell's before they killed me. I heard a shout and another gunshot. Something passed across my forehead like a hot branding iron. I was stunned. I lost footing and fell on my face in the darkness. I knew I was hurt bad and wondered if I would make it out of this scrape alive.

I forced myself up again, wiping the blood from my eyes with my shirtsleeve as I stumbled headlong down the ally. I didn't know how bad the head wound was, only that it was bleeding and I couldn't see. It wouldn't matter if the found me in the alley just then, they were bent on killing me, to be sure. If I fell again I knew they'd find me and finish the job, so I kept running down the ally as hard as I could, barely able to see where I was going. I heard them shouting to each other behind me, arguing over something, but I was too woozy to think about what they were saying and too frightened to care. The gunshot to my head had knocked me senseless. I kept on staggering and running down the alley, trying to get away. Blood was pouring into my eyes; I couldn't see a thing. I ran past a little adobe shack down the alley from Pete Maxwell's. I supposed all the shooting woke everybody up, because a door opened just a crack when I ran behind the adobe and I could see a lantern light spilling from the doorway across the alley.

I stumbled toward the light not knowing what else to do. I needed help and the open door was the only place I could find, hurt like I was. A Mexican woman pulled me inside. She saw the blood on my face and threw her hands over her mouth. She closed the door quickly and helped me to a chair. I sleeved the blood from my eyes, watching her, loading my Colts.

In Roberts' statement he identifies the woman as Celsa Cutierriz [sic - Gutierrez] who he had known previously. Ms. Cutierriz [sic] helped Roberts and kept him at her home that night. Roberts says that later Ms. Cutierriz [sic] had Frank Lobato saddle his horse and bring it around in the alley so he can [sic] escape. Before Roberts was able to leave Ms. Cutierriz [sic] told him it was rumored about Fort Sumner that Sheriff Garrett was telling everyone he had killed the Kid.

Roberts says, *I started puzzling over what Celsa told me. Garrett was trying to pass off Barlow's body as that of Billy the Kid. I wondered how he figured to get away with it. Garrett knew by now that he'd killed the wrong man in the dark. Billy Barlow looked a lot like me, the same general description, with blue eyes like mine. But in the daylight, a lot of folks who knew me would know they had the wrong body. I couldn't figure it, unless Garrett realized his mistake and was making a try at collection [sic] the reward money that was out on me anyway ...*

Roberts says it was 3 a.m. when Celsa brought his horse up to the house. He says he left with Frank Lobato. Roberts stayed in a camp south of Fort Sumner until his wounds healed and the first of August he rode to El Paso, Texas.

[AUTHOR'S NOTE: "Brushy's" expansive dialogue demonstrates the floridness of his lies and imagination. Noteworthy for the "Billy the Kid Case" hoaxers, however, is that his death scene with back-porch-Barlow points to an early phase of their own faking, where they were not yet concealing the major discrepancies between his "death scene" tale and their own.]

Questions About the Case

There seems [sic] to be problems with every account of the escape of Billy the Kid from the make shift [sic] jail in Lincoln and the shooting at Fort Sumner by Pat Garrett. In every account there remain questions as to what really happened.

[AUTHOR'S NOTE: The above used the hoaxers' fakery of "vague, though unfounded, suspicions" instead of actual evidence - which they lacked. What follows are fake "what-ifs" to make unwarranted leaps to hoaxed conclusions – called by the writer "Questions." It represents the writer's last chance to fake a link of Garrett to a "probable cause" of murder.]

[AUTHOR'S NOTE: For clarity, the illogical transitions are put in boldface. The breath-taking leap of the scam is seen when the "what-ifs" of the outhouse version, lead to a fake, implied accusation that Garrett reported the gun from armory version to hide that *he* was the pistol-giving "friend."]

1. In the historical account of the escape of Billy the Kid, from the courthouse in Lincoln, **it's believed** that a "friend" placed a pistol in the outhouse for Billy to use in his escape. The identity of the "friend" who placed the pistol in the outhouse has gone nearly unasked. **If** this version is true, and a "friend" left a pistol in the outhouse to aid in Bonney's escape that "friend" is a coconspirator to the murder of Bell and Olinger. This "friend" also should have been charged with two counts of homicide but remained at large. **Why** didn't Sheriff Garrett pursue the question of the idenenty [sic] of the "friend" who hid the pistol? Garrett says the Kid took the pistol from the armory. **If** the story of the pistol in the outhouse is true did Garrett have a reason to say it was from the armory?

2. **If** Roberts account and claim about the night of July 14, 1881, is to be believed then Lincoln County Sheriff Pat Garrett was not the hero that history portrays him as. Instead, he becomes a murderer who killed Billy Barlow and covered up that killing and passed off Barlow's body as that of Billy the Kid. With the sign in at [sic] Brushy Bill's grave site claiming to the [sic] grave site of Billy the Kid they are in short saying Pat Garrett lied. Did Garrett lie?

[AUTHOR'S NOTE: This earliest version of the "Billy the Kid Case" hoax relies heavily on "Brushy"; later discrepancies between the evolving hoax and "Brushy's" tales would be concealed by the hoaxers. Here, certainty of winning without bearing scrutiny, apparently yielded a devil-may-care attitude.]

[AUTHOR'S NOTE: This earliest version of the hoax also is unabashedly vicious in accusing Garrett of heinous crimes. Later, under scrutiny, the hoaxers would lie that the case was to protect Garrett's honor against "others" who had accused him!]

3. **If** Roberts claims are believed, it beings up other questions? [sic] He claims in his statement when talking about Pat Garrett, "*we use* [sic] *to be friend*" [sic]. **If** Garrett and Roberts were friends did Garrett and Garrett [sic] allowed The Kid out of friendship to escape from Fort Sumner, *did he also* arrange his escape from Lincoln? Did Garrett question why **his friend, the Kid**, with all the others involved in all the killing was the only one to be convicted and sentenced to hang? The Kid **mentions this** in an interview that was published in the *Mesilla News* on April 15, 1881 when he said, *Think it hard that I should be the only one to suffer the extreme penalties of the law.*"

[AUTHOR'S NOTE: Here, "Brushy" is the authority, with "what-ifs" that fabricate Garrett as Billy's "friend" and "accomplice." In addition, lied is that Billy's mention had anything to do with Garrett, rather than to his own sense of injustice.]

4. **Did** Garrett arrange having the pistol put in the outhouse by the "friend" **and is this** why he did not search for the coconspirator to the murder of the two lawmen? **If this is the case then** Garrett is also a coconspirator in the murder of those two lawmen.

[AUTHOR'S NOTE: More meaningless "what-ifs."]

5. In the Lincoln County Courthouse Caretaker Gauss' statement he quotes Bonney as saying about Bell, "*I'm sorry I had to kill him but couldn't help it.*" This statement must raise the question did Bonney, when he produced the pistol he retrieved from the outhouse

[AUTHOR'S NOTE: Sly switcheroo from "what-ifs" to using the outhouse as a fact.]

order Bell to surrender? Did Bell panic and instead of throwing up his hands, turn and run causing Bonney to shoot him?

[AUTHOR'S NOTE: This parrots the historically accepted version. Later in the hoax, for fake forensics, it would be switched to Billy striking Bell with a shackle to cause "blood" on the hallway.]

6. Other questions come to mind in this investigation, some about Gauss. It should be noted that Gauss had worked with Tunstall, so had Bonney. Gauss and Bonney shared the same table as they took meals, slept on the same floor and spent a great deal of time together when Bonney was in the courthouse under guard. It goes to reason that Gauss was sympathetic towards Bonney. With that in mind it could be pointed out that there

were a number of things missing from Gauss's account. Gauss made no reference to how Bell was killed, and leaves out the fact that Bonney used Olinger's own shotgun to kill him. If Bonney retrieved a pistol from the outhouse it had to be prearranged with Bonney and the "friend" as to what date and where to place the pistol in order for Bonney to find it. Since Gauss spent so much time with Bonney would he not have heard something about the plot?

[AUTHOR'S NOTE: This is failed hoaxing! With Gauss as the accomplice, Garrett is innocent - undoing the scam!"]

7. Since the caretaker Gauss worked outside it is not outside the realm of possibility that he saw who put the pistol in the outhouse?

[AUTHOR'S NOTE: The historical reality of Gauss being the accomplice never made it to the final hoax.]

8. It is known that Bonney ate his meals at the courthouse and the only time he was allowed to leave was to use the outhouse. Bell and Olinger took turns escorting the prisoners to the hotel for lunch, leaving the other in charge of Bonney. Bonney as well as the others would have known that Olinger would be escorting the prisoners to lunch that day. Bonney was aware that out of the two guards Bell was the one to make his escape move on since Bell was easy going and seemed to get along with him. Bonney also knew that Olinger had killed men in the past and had threatened to kill him. **Had Garrett and the Kid discussed this and chose Bell** as the deputy for Bonney to make his move thinking Bell would just give up giving the Kid an hour to escape while Olinger was eating?

[AUTHOR'S NOTE: "What-if" blather with a fake conclusion.]

9. **If** Garrett was part of the plot for the Kid's escape **is that why** he rode to White Oaks on a "tax collecting" trip, to give himself an alibi?

[AUTHOR'S NOTE: More 'what-if" fakery.]

10. **If Garrett were part of the plot to allow the Kid to escape he would have reason to chase the Kid. He could not afford for the Kid to tell of his involvement in the two killings of the lawmen. Garrett also has a weak link in the plot, that being the "friend" who put the pistol in the outhouse. If Roberts' story is true, is Billy Barlow the one who put the pistol in the outhouse under orders of Garrett? In Roberts' accounting he shows up at Fort Sumner with no one but Barlow. Did he meet Barlow after he rode out of Lincoln and move on [sic] to Fort Sumner?**

[AUTHOR'S NOTE: The culmination of "what-if" fakery.]

11. **If** Garrett shot Billy Barlow in the dark, by mistake, on July 14, 1881, and Barlow was the only one who could tell the story of Garrett's involvement other than the Kid, would Garrett not know the Kid would run to keep from hanging?

[AUTHOR'S NOTE: This incoherent reverie, appears to contradict the Pat-Billy friendship on which this hoax relies.]

12. In Deputy John W. Poe's statement as he lays out the shooting in Maxwell's house on July 14, 1881, he says "... Garrett came out, brushing against me as he passed. He stood by me close to the wall at the side of the door and said to me, That was the Kid that came in there onto me, and I think I got him.' I said, "Pat, the Kid would not come to this place; you have shot the wrong man.' Upon my saying this, Garrett seemed to be in doubt himself as to whom had shot ..." Did Garrett kill the wrong man by mistake and cover it up?

[AUTHOR'S NOTE: The writer forgot that backing "Brushy" means no bedroom murder scene – but a Barlow-on-back-porch one. Also forgotten is that "Brushy's" scene had enough gunfire to rival the Alamo.]

[AUTHOR'S NOTE: Similar to the final "Probable Cause Statement," this "question" hides the multiple identifications of Billy, following this moment of doubt in a darkened room.]

13. Most researchers and historians have accepted without much question, the statement that Billy the Kid was born Henry McCarty, in New York on November 23, 1859. It should be noted that the first time this information comes to light is in Pat Garrett's book *The Authentic Life of Billy the Kid.*

[AUTHOR'S NOTE: Error. This was outlaw myth press in Billy's lifetime, while he was pursued by Garrett and Secret Service Agent Azariah Wild. It was in "Outlaws of New Mexico. The Exploits of a Band Headed by a New York Youth. The Mountain Fastness of the Kid and His Followers - War Against a Gang of Cattle Thieves and Murderers." December 27, 1880. *The Sun.* New York. Vol. XLVIII, No. 118, Page 3, Columns 1-2.]

In the book the evidence for this claim is sited [sic] to have come from a birth announcement that appeared in the on November 25, 1859. In 1950 William Morrison the attorney **[AUTHOR'S NOTE: Morrison was not an attorney]** for William (Brushy Bill) Roberts claims he asked the *New York Times* about the announcement and the Times replied that no information about birth announcements appeared in that issue. A ghostwriter by the name of Marshall Asmon [sic - Ashmun] Upson is credited with writing Garrett's book. It might also be worth mentioning the date November 23, is the birth date of Marshall Asmon [sic - Ashmun] Upson. Is it by chance that Upson and the Kid have the same birthday or by design?

[AUTHOR'S NOTE: Irrelevant, but a clumsy manufacturing of fake "suspiciousness," instead of evidence.]

14. As stated above most believe Billy the Kid was born in New York. This information also appeared for the first time in Garrett's book. **[AUTHOR'S NOTE: See *New York Sun* 1880 article reference above.]** It is also believed that Billy the Kid was shot and killed in 1881 at the age of 21. However, according to the United States Bureau of Census, 1880 census, Fort Sumner, San Miguel County, William Bonney says differently. Between June 17 and 19, 1880, while taking census records at the Fort, Lorenzo Labadie, a former Indian Agent, noted the vital statistics of one William Bonney, who was living next to Charlie Bowdre and his wife Manuela, leaving us to believe this to be the William Bonney of Lincoln County fame. What is interesting about the entry is that he gave his age as twenty-five, and his place of birth not New York but Missouri.

[AUTHOR'S NOTE: This fakes" suspicions. Also, it is believed that Manuela Bowdre gave the interview's incorrect information.]

The attorney Morrison asked Roberts why Garrett would say he was born in New York. Roberts told him that is what the told the "Coe boys" when he first came to New Mexico. Roberts went on to say he never saw New York until he was a grown man.

[AUTHOR'S NOTE: Morrison was not an attorney. And this is irrelevant, since "Brushy" was not Billy.]

Conclusion

If history is correct and William H. Bonney a.k.a. Billy the Kid was shot and killed by Lincoln County Sheriff Pat Garrett on July 14, 1881, at the house of Pete Maxwell in Fort Sumner, and was buried the next day in Fort Sumner, then Brushy Bill Roberts is a fake and nothing more than a story teller of the first order.

[AUTHOR'S NOTE: Again, this early document points to "Brushy" as Billy; which would later be more hidden.]

However, if it is not the body of William H. Bonney buried in Fort Sumner then Lincoln County Sheriff Pat Garrett killed the wrong man on July 14, 1881. He covered up that killing with help from others such as Pete Maxwell. If it is not Bonney buried at Fort Sumner then Garrett is a murderer and Maxwell is a knowing coconspirator to that homicide.

[AUTHOR'S NOTE: This is an early hoax attempt at a conspiracy theory. Instead of the "Garrett friendship," is presented "Brushy's" accidental killing of the innocent victim version. And Maxwell is added as a cover-up conspirator, without motive or evidence – or truth.]

If Brushy Bill Roberts were William H. Bonney then one would have to assume that the body in the grave is that of Billy Barlow as Robert's claims. If that is true Sheriff Garrett could quite possibly be a coconspirator of the double murder of two lawmen that occurred during the Kid's escape from Lincoln.

[AUTHOR'S NOTE: This illogical jump even leaves "Brushy" behind, since he never claimed Garrett as a jailbreak accomplice, or a "friendship" with Garrett to explain not being killed on July 14, 1881 to enable escape.]

The Lincoln County Sheriff''s Department believes, with the unanswered question as to who is buried in Fort Sumner

[AUTHOR'S NOTE: This is fakery. The victim is not doubted.]

there remains serious doubt as to what involvement Sheriff Pat Garrett played in the escape of Billy the Kid from Lincoln that resulted I the deaths of two lawmen.

[AUTHOR'S NOTE: This is fakery. There is no evidence that Garrett assisted the jail escape of Bonney, though it is an early version of the final "Probable Cause Statement's" fake Deputy Bell killing investigation.]

If the body of William H. Bonney is buried in Fort Sumner the claims of William Roberts'' and others alleging to have been Billy the Kid are unfounded and the name of Pat Garrett is cleared of any wrong doing in this incident. It is the duty of the Lincoln County Sheriff''s Office to clear this mystery and possible crime off the books of history in a professional manner and to allow the guilt to fall where it belongs.

[AUTHOR'S NOTE: The imposters are easily debunked without exhumations. And no one is accusing Garrett, except imposters and hoaxers – and without basis.]

Billy the Kid's mother is buried in Silver City, New Mexico. To exhume her body could provide the DNA to solve this 122-year-old mystery. Her DNA would hold the key to the true answer as to where William Bonney is buried and if Pat Garrett was a murderer or a Sheriff doing his duty.

If those in Hamilton, Texas believe Roberts is in fact Roberts [sic] this DNA should prove their claim. If he is not the town of Hamilton,

Texas needs to take down the signs that the grave of Roberts is "The Authentic Grave Site of Billy the Kid." However, if Roberts is William Bonney then history should be rewritten showing what really happened in Lincoln County and Fort Sumner.

If Bonney is buried in Fort Sumner the History stands and the name of Sheriff Pat Garrett would be cleared and he did not kill some incendet [sic] person in Fort Sumner and would appear he had no hand in the escape of William Bonney from Lincoln and the death of Olinger and Bell.

Lincoln County Sheriff, Tom Sullivan and the Lincoln County Sheriff''s Office believe it our duty to put this mystery to rest after 122 years of doubt. Since these questions continue to nag at our conscience, and since there is no statute of limitations on Murder we feel this investigation should answer the question of "is Pat Garrett a murderer?" or a Sheriff doing his duty and wrongly accused of a crime?

[AUTHOR'S NOTE: No probable cause has been established to implicate Pat Garrett of murder of the innocent victim - the purpose of this document. But much evidence was revealed that the "Billy the Kid Case" hoax was a modernized version of the "Brushy Bill" hoax. And it is a lie about no Statute of Limitations. New Mexico's Statute of Limitations on murder ended the time for prosecution of Garrett to 1891.]

In Pat Garrett's book *The Authentic Life of Billy the Kid* he pens these words - "*Again I say that the Kid's body lies undisturbed in the grave - and I speak of what I know.*"

It is the intention of the Lincoln County Sheriff''s Office to prove one way or the other if these words are true.

____

Tom Sullivan: Sheriff
Lincoln County Sheriff''s Office

____

Steven M. Sederwall: Deputy Sheriff
Lincoln County Sheriff''s Office

____

Date

U.S. MARSHALS SERVICE HISTORIAN DAVID TURK'S PROBABLE CAUSE ADDENDUM

A secret "Billy the Kid Case" participant was Washington, D.C., based U.S. Marshals Service Historian David Turk, involved in the hoax from its 2003 start, and coming to New Mexico to help the hoaxers destroy Pat Garrett's reputation. To put his participation in perspective, as the Marshals Service Historian, he was attacking its most famous Old West Deputy U.S. Marshal by declaring him a murderer of an innocent victim, with "Brushy Bill" as a possible surviving Billy the Kid.

Turk was the only "historian" backing Case 2003-274 in its "Probable Cause Statement;" with his fake "proof" being an old-timer's hearsay claim about a post-death Billy the Kid sighting. Also, since the "Statement's" footnotes were obscure National Archive documents on microfilm (like Azariah Wild's Secret Service reports), Turk may have provided them.

Later, in the forensic DNA scam being conducted by Dr. Henry Lee with the old carpenter's bench, Turk used his title as expertise to fake its "validation" as the one on which Billy was laid out.

Turk must have known he was a subversive, since he hid his participation in the "Billy the Kid Case;" and I only got his secret Addendum to its "Probable Cause Statement" by my open records litigation against its lawmen promulgators.

Its cover had a galloping Old West rider with a big marshal's badge. Its date was December 2003: the signing date of the actual "Probable Cause Statement." It was titled: "United States Marshals Service Executive Services Division: Research Report, Submitted by David S. Turk." Page one stated: "Research Report: The U.S. Marshals Service and Billy the Kid. **To Be Added in Its Present Entirety, with Exhibits, to Lincoln County, New Mexico Case # 2003-274**." It had nine pages of text; bibliographic "Endnotes;" and "Exhibits" consisting of a Turk article titled "How much did it cost to find Billy the Kid?;" a "National Police Gazette" May 21, 1881 article on Billy's escape; and a May 30, 1881 letter from Attorney Sidney Barnes (one of Billy's Mesilla prosecutors) about Billy's Mesilla trial and his later escape.

So David Turk had added to the "Billy the Kid Case's Probable Cause Statement," using his U.S. Marshals Service Historian title and government money to defame one of the most famous Deputy

U.S. Marshals for a hoax! And he had contributed his own, major hoax document! And its style implied him as possibly assisting the actual "Probable Cause Statement," besides his hearsay old-timer quote. And it indicated that he was supplying National Archive documents for the hoax.

For his own document, providing no historical evidence, Turk backed the "Billy the Kid Case" hoax's faked death scene, with Pat Garrett as the murderer of an innocent victim. William Bonney's Coroner's Jury Report is concealed, as are the multiple other corpse eye-witnesses. For filler, discussed are U.S. Marshals in the Lincoln County War period (including Garrett). But abruptly, based on a few WPA hearsay interviews from the 1930's (of people unconnected to the event), Turk concluded that Billy the Kid's killing "fueled speculation over the precise outcome."

The only parts of Turk's "Research Report" that also appear in the "Probable Cause Statement" are his Frances E. Totty, WPA quote about "Billie" being seen after the death date; and his "Endnote" sources, like Secret Service Operative Azariah Wild's reports. But Turk's report - that he tried so hard to hide - was part of the 2003-274 case file, as "probable cause" of a death scene in which Pat Garrett murdered an innocent victim, instead of killing Billy the Kid. Below is the report that Turk hid (with its irrelevant general U.S. Marshals' history omitted).

Research Report:
The U.S. Marshals Service and Billy the Kid

Submitted by David S. Turk, Historian
December 2003

"Research Report: The U.S. Marshals Service and Billy the Kid. To Be Added in its Present Entirety, with Exhibits, to Lincoln County, New Mexico Case # 2003-274."

Purpose of Research [Page 1]

There is renewed interest in examining the crimes and final resting place of William H. Bonney, also known as Henry Antrim, Henry McCarty, or Billy the Kid.

[AUTHOR'S NOTE: The only "renewed interest" was from the "Billy the Kid Case" hoax and loony conspiracy theorists.]

Two Sheriffs' Offices in New Mexico reopened an investigation, with the approval of the Governor of New Mexico. In September 2003 Steve Sederwall, Mayor of Capitan, and Deputy Sheriff, Lincoln County, New Mexico, contacted me on research matters relating to the Lincoln County War.

[AUTHOR'S NOTE: Turk claims Sederwall as contact.]

Given the integral role of the U.S. Marshals Service, and the dual roles between our two institutions during the time of Billy the Kid, and further that Pat Garrett was a Deputy U.S. Marshal during the pursuit of the Kid, and that another Deputy U.S. Marshal (and Lincoln County officer), Robert Olinger, was shot and killed by the Kid during his escape, it is relevant to the agency's historical interest to research those portions of the case pertinent to it to ensure accuracy.

[AUTHOR'S NOTE: The report gives no information to doubt conventional history. It does not "ensure accuracy!"]

The primary investigation of Lincoln County, New Mexico State No. 2004-274 [sic] is being conducted by Lincoln County Sheriff Tom Sullivan, De Baca County Sheriff Gary Graves, and Steve Sederwall, but the following findings add significantly to the data being collected in revisiting Billy the Kid.

[AUTHOR'S NOTE: No reason is given for "revisiting Billy the Kid," except hearsay death rumors 56 years after the event.]

<u>Overview of Research Focus</u> [Page 1]

The following research relates to the prominent roles of the U.S. Marshals Service in the Lincoln County War ... Finally, there is a study on the deaths of Deputy Marshal Olinger and Lincoln County Officer J.W. Bell, followed by Billy the Kid's subsequent escape. The Works Progress Administration interviewed several Lincoln residents during the late 1930's in this regard ...

[AUTHOR'S NOTE: The oddness of this statement is easy to miss; but each part is irrelevant to the others. Out of nowhere, will come Turk's "suspicions" that the Kid was not Garrett's murder victim.]

<u>Deputy U.S. Marshal Garrett and His Agency Status</u> [Page 4]

[AUTHOR'S NOTE: This page, about Garrett's U.S. Marshal status has Secret Service Agent Azariah Wild's praise of Garrett to his Chief. All is irrelevant to Garrett's murder victim.]

Key Event: Billy the Kid's Escape and the Deaths of Bell and Olinger [Page 8]

On April 28, 1881, [sic - missing word] made his famous escape from Lincoln. Accounts of the events were recalled later by witnesses. A contemporary news account from *The National Police Gazette* dated May 21, 1881, followed a generally accepted recollection pattern with some minor inconsistencies. Deputy U.S. Marshal Olinger and guard J.W. Bell ... were holding the Kid in the jail. Olinger dined at a local establishment, and during his absence the shackled prisoner hit Bell with handcuffs. He then grabbed Bell's revolver and shot him in the chest ... Just as he [Olinger] entered a small gate leading through the jail fence, the Kid shot him with a double-barreled gun, filling his breast of shot and killing him.

[AUTHOR'S NOTE: Note that the *National Police Gazette*, published in New York, was merely a dime novel tabloid, and not a legitimate historical source. Also, Turk presents Billy the Kid's escape without Garrett's participation.]

Differing Accounts on Death of Billy the Kid [Pages 8 - 9.]

Deputy U.S. Marshal and Lincoln County Sheriff Pat Garrett pursued Billy the Kid for several months after the deaths
[AUTHOR'S NOTE: About 2 ½ months.]

of Deputy Olinger and J.W. Bell. The end of the chase appeared to be at Pete Maxwell's ranch on July 15 [sic], 1881.

[AUTHOR'S NOTE: This is "Brushy" hoax-style sly innuendo of "suspicion" without evidence. And the date was July 14, 1881.]

What occurred at the Maxwell Ranch fueled speculation over the precise outcome. There appears [sic] to be many questions to answer.

[AUTHOR'S NOTE: This is full-blown, hoax conspiracy theory, with vague "suspicion." No evidence is given.]

According to the WPA interview of Francisco Trujillo in May 1937, Garrett was negotiating capture of the Kid with Pete Maxwell himself. Josh Brent's father was one of the Sheriff's deputies, stating that Garrett said "that he sure hated to kill the boy, but he knew it was either his life or the boy's life."

[AUTHOR'S NOTE: The "Billy the Kid Case" hoaxers omitted this hearsay from their "Probable Cause Statement."

Yet another resident stated,

> The people around Lincoln say Garrett didn't kill Billie [sic] the Kid. John Poe was with Garrett the night he was supposed to ... [sic] said that he didn't see the man that Garrett killed. Ican [sic] take you to the grave in Hell's Half Acre, a old government cemetry [sic], where Billie [sic] was supposed to be buried to show you the grave.
>
> The cook at Pete Maxwell's was always putting flowers on the grave and praying at it. This woman thought a lot of Billie [sic], but after Garrett killed the man at Maxwell's home her grandson was never seen again and Billie [sic] was seen by Bill Nicoli? And indian scout. Bill saw him in old Mexico.

[AUTHOR'S NOTE: This hearsay was put in the "Probable Cause Statement" with attribution to Turk.]

The recollections took a legendary bent, even extending to events that occurred after those at the Maxwell ranch. Josh Brent stated that Garrett told his father that after he killed the Kid, "that a fellow from the east wrote him and said that he would pay $5000.00 for the trigger finger of the boy."

[AUTHOR'S NOTE: Irrelevant pseudo-historical filler like in the "Probable Cause Statement."]

<u>Other Related Fact</u> [Page 9.]

A sidelight from this period was the debunking of one widely-held story that Billy the Kid killed twenty-one men by the age of twenty-one. U.S. Attorney Barnes stated in a letter to the Attorney General, dated May 30, 1881, that while the Kid "has killed fifteen different men & is only twenty one years of age."

[AUTHOR'S NOTE: This irrelevant hearsay by one of Billy's Mesilla prosecutors, who had no way of knowing; was used to fake historical savvy, as in the "Probable Cause Statement."]

So U.S. Marshals Service Historian David Turk was a "Billy the Kid Case" hoaxer, abusing the prestige of his federal title, to present a fake death scene in Fort Sumner, and to conceal the definitive Coroner's Jury Report.

EXHUMATION PETITIONS

Since the exhumation petitions for Billy the Kid and his mother, Catherine Antrim, required a law enforcement murder case against Pat Garrett, necessitated was the non-historical murder scene in which he murdered an innocent victim. So that is what the hoaxers' attorneys presented, with the petitioners being Sheriff's Tom Sullivan and Gary Graves, and Deputy Sheriff Steve Sederwall. Demonstrating their lawman status and the faked murder scene is their exhumation petition of July 26, 2004 for Billy the Kid. By their attorney, Mark Acuña, it was titled "County of De Baca, State of New Mexico, Tenth Judicial District. In the Matter of William H. Bonney A/K/A 'Billy the Kid.' Cause No. CV-04-00005." Acuña wrote:

PETITIONER'S [sic] RESPONSE TO THE VILLAGE OF FT. SUMNER'S MOTION TO DISMISS

COME NOW Petitioners Sullivan, Sederwall and Graves by and through their attorneys of record The Jaffe Law Firm (Mark Anthony Acuña, Esq.) and for their response to the Village of Fort Sumner's Motion to Dismiss sate as follows:

INTRODUCTION

Tom Sullivan, Steve Sederwall and Gary Graves are law enforcement officers. Prior to the filing of the Petition for Exhumation of the Remains of Billy the Kid, a.k.a. William H. Bonney, Sullivan, Sederwall, and Graves acting in their capacity as law enforcement officers initiated Investigation No. 2004 [sic] –274 filed in Lincoln County and Case No. 03-06-136-01 filed in De Baca County. **The principle purpose of opening the investigation and the case was to determine the guilt or innocence of sheriff Pat Garrett in the death of Billy the Kid**.

Initially, as part of their on-going investigation, Sederwall, Sullivan, and Graves, in their capacity as law enforcement officers petitioned the Sixth Judicial District Court for exhumation of the remains of Billy the Kid's mother, Katherine [sic] Antrim. As a part of the on-going investigation, the Petition to Exhume Katherine [sic] Antrim was intended to obtain DNA samples for purposes of comparing those DNA samples with DNA samples that were hoped to be obtained upon the exhumation of the remains of what are thought to be that of Billy the

Kid. After filing of the Petition to Exhume the remains of Katherine [sic] Antrim, a second petition was filed in the Tenth Judicial Court for purposes of the exhumation of Billy the Kid's remains and for purposes of obtaining DNA samples to compare with those samples obtained from the remains of Katherine [sic] Antrim. Sederwall, Sullivan, and Graves, all joined in on the Petition to Exhume the remains of Billy the Kid as Co-Petitioners and in their capacity as **law enforcement officers** engaged in an on-going investigation.

Petitioners assert that they maintain standing in the instant action as law enforcement officers engaged in the investigation of criminal violations, namely, the alleged killing of Billy the Kid by the legendary Sheriff, Pat Garrett. Moreover, Petitioners assert that as law enforcement officers they are duly authorized to investigate the death of Billy the Kid to determine 1) the guilt or innocence of sheriff Pat Garrett, and 2) to determine whether or not foul play was involved if there were violations of criminal statutes or laws. Acting in their capacity **as law enforcement officers** on behalf of the public and the public's best interest, Petitioners further assert that they are the real parties in interest to this suit and, therefore, maintain proper standing to prosecute these claims.

ARGUMENT

Petitioners are Law Enforcement Officers Currently Conducting Active Investigations Regarding the Death of Billy the Kid and, therefore, they have Standing.

New Mexico Rule of Civil Procedure 1-017 states in pertinent part that "every action shall be prosecuted in the name of the real party in interest ... for a party authorized by statute may sue in that person's own name without joining the party for whose benefit the action is brought; and when a statute of the state so provides, an action for the use or benefit for another shall be brought in the name of the state.

Moreover, Section 29-1-1 states impertinent [sic] part that ...

> "It is hereby declared to be the duty of every Sheriff, Deputy Sheriff, Constable and every other peace officer to investigate all violations of the criminal laws of the state which are called to the attention of any such officer or which he is aware, and it is also declared the duty of every such officer to diligently file a complaint or information, if the circumstances are such to indicate to a reasonably prudent person that such action should be taken, and it is also declared his duty to cooperate with and assist the Attorney General, District Attorney or other prosecutor, if any, if any in all reasonable ways ... Failure to perform his duty in any

material way shall subject such officer to removal from the office and payment of all costs of prosecution."

In the instant case, Petitioners Sullivan, Sederwall, and Graves acting in their capacity as law enforcement officers pursuant to Section 29-1-1, were not only authorized to commence the investigation into the death of William H. Bonney, a.k.a. Billy the Kid, but were duty-bound to fulfill their responsibilities as law enforcement officers to investigate the circumstances surrounding the death of Billy the Kid. Indeed, Petitioners initiated the investigations into the death of Billy the Kid based upon inconsistent and incongruous facts and information surrounding the death of Billy the Kid and raising suspicion as to the truth of the circumstances surrounding the killing of Billy the Kid. Under the circumstances, Petitioners had a duty to investigate or be subject to removal of office subject to Section 29-1-1.

Furthermore, pursuant to Rule 1-017, Petitioners acting in their capacity as law enforcement officers, are real parties in interest to the instant causes of action. Plaintiffs are authorized by statute, that is, Section 29-1-1, to being this action in their own names on behalf of and for the benefit of the public in their capacities of investigating law enforcement officers.

CONCLUSION

Therefore, based upon all the foregoing, it is clear that the Petitioners acting in their capacity as law enforcement officers and engaged in an active investigation regarding the death and alleged killing of Billy the Kid by Sheriff Pat Garrett, and of standing in this case and are real parties in interest.

Wherefore, Petitioners respectfully request that the court issue its order denying the Village of Ft. Sumner's Motion to Dismiss as against Petitioners; that the court allow Petitioners to remain in the instant action and for such other further and proper relief as the Court deems just and proper."

Respectfully submitted by:
The Jaffe Law Firm
Mark Anthony Acuña
Attorneys for Petitioners Sullivan,
Sederwall & Graves

BILLY THE KID AS PETITIONING FOR HIS OWN EXHUMATION FOR A FAKED DEATH SCENE!

The "Billy the Kid Case" hoax's most extreme fake death scene came from the case's likely intended beneficiary, Attorney Bill Robins III. His first public entry in the" Billy the Kid Case" may have been forced: to take-over from the hoaxers' faltering Silver City attorney, Sherry Tippet, who was losing to my attorneys. And Robins was not circumspect about "Brushy Bill." On November 19, 2003, an AP internet article for Silver City, titled "Lawyer Appointed to Represent Dead Outlaw," quoted him: "Robins says he's excited to represent the Kid. His first duty as Billy's lawyer will be to intervene in the Silver City case to exhume the body of Billy's mother, Catherine Antrim. **DNA testing is supposed to show whether Antrim was related to Ollie "Brushy Bill" Roberts. If Antrim is related to Roberts, that would mean Billy the Kid is buried in Hico [sic - Hamilton], Texas – not Fort Sumner**."

After replacing Tippett, Robins led the exhumation attacks on both the mother's and Billy's graves. But an attorney needs a client to appear in a court. The client Robins chose proved his scorn of the law, the public, and the sanctity of graves. **His client was dead Billy the Kid as a "co-petitioner" with the lawmen for his own exhumation!**

This, of course, ignored that a corpse, as a non-existent being, has no legal standing in court of law. But for Governor Bill Richardson's complicit judges - Henry Quintero in Silver City and Ted Hartley in Fort Sumner - Robins channeled "Billy the Kid," and spoke for him (or "Billy" spoke through him) without their objection!

And "Billy the Kid," of course, wanted his mother and himself dug up to protect his "legacy." And the "legacy" dead "Billy the Kid" was "protecting" was the imposter hoaxes' fake death scene: that an innocent victim, not himself, had been killed in Fort Sumner on July 14, 1881 on a "dark and moonless night" (the fatal "Brushy" moon error, likely lifter from W.C. Jameson's and Frederick Bean's *The Return of the Outlaw Billy the Kid*, that gave away Robins's "Brushy" hoax thrust). And "Billy the Kid," through Robins's mouth, claimed he had led a long and law-abiding life, so deserved a pardon (Robins's second give-away for his "Brushy" hoax thrust).

BILLY THE KID'S PRE-HEARING BRIEF

To corrupt Silver City Judge, Henry Quintero, Attorney Bill Robins III presented his January 5, 2004's "In the Matter of Catherine Antrim, Billy the Kid's Pre-Hearing Brief." **[APPENDIX: 1]** It revealed, for the first time, the hoax's attaching DNA matching to the pardon, as linked to the faked death scene and imposter survival claims, themselves linked to denying existence of the Coroner's Jury Report. The plot was for hoaxed DNA matching to claim an innocent victim in Billy's grave, and the mother would match "Brushy." With those fake forensics, Richardson would then pardon "Brushy" as Billy. As Robins wrote: "**Should the DNA extracted from Ms. Antrim confirm that one of the potential Kids ["Brushy"] was in fact Billy the Kid, undersigned counsel will be able to make an even stronger argument for pardon by citing to the long years of law abiding life.**"

So Robins's "Brief" had his client, dead Billy the Kid, as a co-petitioner for exhumation of his own mother, joining Sheriffs Tom Sullivan and Gary Graves, and Deputy Steve Sederwall, and backing the pretenders as legitimate! Robins wrote:

> [T]he very question of [Billy the Kid's] life and death will be impacted by the results of the Petitioners' [lawmen's] investigation [into the Garrett murder and DNA].
>
> B. *The Planned Request For Pardon Confers Standing Here*
>
> Undersigned counsel intends to ask Governor Richardson that he pardon Billy the kid for the murder conviction of Sheriff Brady on several known bases including the fact that then Territorial Governor Lew Wallace reneged on his promise to pardon the Kid. There were at least two individuals that laid claim to Billy the Kid's identity years after his alleged shooting by Garrett. **Both of them apparently led long and peaceful and crime-free lives** ...
>
> The reasons that the exhumation is sought is to disinter the remains of Billy the Kid's mother for the extraction of Mitochondrial DNA.
>
> As such, Ms. Antrim presents the only source of such DNA. Should the exhumation be denied, Billy the Kid will be forever denied the opportunity to make use of modern technology to shed light on his life and death. **Should the DNA extracted from Ms. Antrim confirm that one of the potential Kids was in fact Billy the Kid, undersigned counsel will be able to make an even stronger argument for pardon by citing to the long years of law abiding life.**

Convinced he was above law or decency this smug rogue presented the following examples of fakery in his "Billy the Kid's Pre-Hearing Brief;" writing:

(1) COMES NOW, Bill Robins, III and David Sandoval, of the law firm of Heard, Robins, Cloud, Lubel & Greenwood, LLC, and on the behalf of the estate of William H. Bonney, aka "Billy the Kid."

[AUTHOR'S NOTE: The first claim is representation of Billy's "estate." First of all, Billy had no estate - meaning posthumous property for probate court. Secondly, property has nothing to do with exhuming his mother. Thirdly, this cover of something that sounds legal - like an estate - will next be switched to Billy talking for himself through Robins. Note that Attorney Sandoval was present to provide the New Mexico law license which Robins lacked, making him complicit in the hoax.]

(2) This is an interesting proceeding in that the relief sought here is not exclusively judicial. "[N]ormally a district court would not become involved in such matters unless a protesting relative or interested party files an injunction or takes some other legal action to halt the autopsy or disinterment,"

[AUTHOR'S NOTE: Robins's Brief is not "judicial" at all. It is pseudo-historical rambling with an irrelevant idea of a pardon. And its legal citations are all irrelevant filler.]

(3) Petitioners [Lincoln County Sheriff Tom Sullivan and his Deputy, Steve Sederwall] should thus be commended for bringing this Court into the picture.

[AUTHOR'S NOTE: Robins is trying to legitimize fellow hoaxers. Note also their law enforcement titles.]

(4) As will be shown clearly, Billy the Kid's interests are real, legitimate, proper for consideration, and we respectively ask the Court to recognize them as such.

[AUTHOR'S NOTE: Segueing into speaking for Billy, Robins does a switcheroo from "estate" to "interests." But a dead person has no interests, being dead - meaning legally non-existent.]

(5) To the extent that the Court remains concerned **with the presence of Billy the Kid in this litigation**, it is a matter that can be more properly addressed pursuant to legal requirements of standing and intervention, which the discussion below shows the Kid satisfies.

[AUTHOR'S NOTE: This is now the switcheroo point for Billy himself entering the courtroom. Robins even claims that Billy has "standing," meaning the legal right to be present in court.]

(6) The governor has the "power to grant reprieves and pardons." Undersigned counsel intends on seeking a pardon for Billy the Kid. Certainly Governor Richardson is within his inherent appointment power to hire counsel to advise him on the merits of such a pardon.

[AUTHOR'S NOTE: Tricky Robins omits that pardon advising gives him no legal justification to be in this court seeking exhumation of Catherine Antrim. He has no real client.]

(7) Counsel's appointment here is in the nature of an appointment as a public defender

[AUTHOR'S NOTE: Now cagy Robins makes up that he was appointed by Richardson as a "public defender" for Billy. But only the judge can legally appoint an attorney for an indigent client in court - and, obviously, the client has to be alive.]

(8) Billy the Kid's interest here is his legacy. As noted in previous briefing the very question of his life and death will be impacted by the results of the Petitioners' investigation.

[AUTHOR'S NOTE: Here, dead Billy has "told" channeling Robins that *he* cares about "his legacy." Besides being absurd, that is not what "interest" means: which is legal justification for a case, not sentimentality of an historical nature.]

(9) Undersigned counsel intends to ask Governor Richardson that he pardon Billy the kid for the murder conviction of Sheriff Brady on several known bases including the fact that then Territorial Governor Lew Wallace reneged on his promise to pardon the Kid.

[AUTHOR'S NOTE: The pardon issue, though irrelevant to exhuming Catherine Antrim, is here segueing into "Brushy Bill" territory with "several known bases" that will apply to "Brushy" and not to Billy Bonney.]

(10) There were at least two individuals that laid claim to Billy the Kid's identity years after his alleged shooting by Garrett. Both of them apparently **led long and peaceful and crime-free lives**.

[AUTHOR'S NOTE: Here is the jump to "Brushy." And the "several known bases" for pardon are his long, peaceful, and crime-free life. The second pretender, John Miller, was added by the hoaxers to obscure their "Brushy" focus.]

(11) The reasons that the exhumation is sought is to disinter the remains of Billy the Kid's mother for the extraction of Mitochondrial DNA. As such, Ms. Antrim presents the only source of such DNA. Should the exhumation be denied, Billy the Kid will be forever denied the opportunity to make use of modern technology to shed light on his life and death.

[AUTHOR'S NOTE: Now Billy is himself in court, pleading, through Robins's mouth, for modern technology to help him. But do not miss the greater absurdity: this is a pretender argument by channeled "Brushy," wanting *his* life and death vouched for as Billy the Kid. And "Brushy's" real problem is hidden by Robins: mitochondrial DNA proves a mother relationship; "Brushy" *denied* she was his mother!]

(12) Should the DNA extracted from Ms. Antrim confirm that one of the potential Kids was in fact Billy the Kid, **undersigned counsel will be able to make an even stronger argument for pardon by citing to the long years of law abiding life.**

[AUTHOR'S NOTE: <u>This was the sentence that proved to me that the "Billy the Kid Case was a "Brushy Bill" hoax, along with its plot: claim a match by faking DNA, then pardon "Brushy" as Billy the Kid. Note again the fakery that neither "Brushy" nor John Miller claimed Ms. Antrim was their mother – so mitochondrial DNA matching was meaningless unless the results' claims were faked</u>.]

(13) This Court has allowed the intervention of the Town of Silver City in this matter. The municipal politicians there have apparently authorized the Town's Mayor to oppose the exhumation. Billy the Kid acknowledges the existence of case law that accords standing to the owners of the cemetery concerned in such proceedings.

[AUTHOR'S NOTE: Do not miss that speaking, channeled, dead Billy Bonney even has legal expertise on "case law" about court standing!]

(14) What is of interest here, is that such standing is often given to the cemetery owner because it may be the only entity that can represent the wishes of the deceased, an element typically considered in whether to order an exhumation ...

As expected, the Mayor here opposes the exhumation and is positioned to present evidence in support of its objection. Whether or not that truly represents the interests of Ms. Antrim can never be known. Given the identity of the decedent and the time that has passes since her death, the Mayor cannot possibly have any direct evidence of Ms.

Antrim's wishes. As such, the evidence that is presented by the Mayor can be viewed as best, supposition, or at worst, utterly unreliable.

[AUTHOR'S NOTE: Do not miss the bizarreness of this argument. The Mayor, whose legal duty is to protect remains in a cemetery under his authority, according to Robins, needs to mind-read corpse Catherine to find out if *she* wants to be dug up. But Attorney Robins, the channeler, is about to come to the rescue and speak for the dead woman also!]

(15) One is left to question why such a party with such a remote interest and lack of express knowledge about the decedent's wishes is conferred standing while the interests of Billy the Kid go unheard if this Court denier him standing. Allowing such a party to appear and present evidence while denying the same opportunity to a party that has been appointed to represent the interests of the decedent's son does not seem prudent nor fair

[AUTHOR'S NOTE: This argument is so crazy that a reader might be tempted to rationalize that it cannot be as crazy as it sounds. Attorney Robins is saying that dead Billy has more credibility to let his wishes be known than the live Mayor, whose obligation it is to protect the cemetery. And Robins can speak for the exact wishes of the dead, unlike the more supernaturally limited Mayor.]

(16) 1st Factor Public Interest, Billy the Kid's name is forever tied to New Mexico and to that of another legendary figure of the Old West, Sheriff Pat Garrett. **A commonly held version** of history paints a picture of an ambush in which Garrett killed the Kid in Ft. Sumner where most believe the Kid still lies at rest. **This version has been questioned. It is the investigation into whether Garrett killed the Kid that has prompted these investigators to seek exhumation**.

[AUTHOR'S NOTE: This is pure "Brushy Bill" hoaxing. Only "Brushy's" believers question Pat Garrett's killing of Billy. Since "Brushy" was not Billy, there is no "public interest," meaning public value in the case. There are only the self-serving motives of the hoaxers, and the "Brushy" goal of puppeteer Robins.]

(17) 2nd Factor, the Decedents wishes. In spite of Silver City's position to the contrary, we simply do not know what the decedent's wishes would be. Given the present circumstances, however, where her remains could possibly provide critical evidence to be used by modern day advocates to clear her son's name, one might easily surmise that Silver City's dogged attempt to resist exhumation would not be appreciated by Ms. Antrim.

[AUTHOR'S NOTE: Now Robins is channeling Billy's mother enough to know that Silver City's blocking her exhumation would "not be appreciated" by her! For Robins, she is a "Brushy"-believer too! And she is angry! And corrupt Judge Henry Quintero never objected at all to Robins's making a mockery of his court. He was just basking in his undeserved Richardson appointment for a desired judgeship.]

(18) 3rd Factor, Surviving Relatives Wishes. There are no relatives of Ms. Antrim currently before the Court ... The closest party currently before the Court is in fact Billy the Kid as represented by the undersigned counsel. As is apparent from the arguments set forth in this brief, the kid's [sic] interests would be furthered by the exhumation.

[AUTHOR'S NOTE: Here is Robins channeling dead Billy again to say that he wants his mother dug up as part of his agenda!]

(19) **Billy the Kid believes that the evidence adduced at the exhumation hearing will certainly support an order of exhumation here.**

[AUTHOR'S NOTE: Robins has crossed into the "Exorcist" movie's territory. He has disappeared. Only dead Billy is talking now through Robins's mouth. And *he* is "Brushy." The creepy thought is that Robins might not be faking. He may really think he *is* "Brushy Bill" incarnate.]

20) The foregoing has established that the undersigned counsel may legally and properly appear in these proceedings on behalf of, and to represent the interests of Billy the Kid.

[AUTHOR'S NOTE: Robins has established nothing whatsoever to justify his being in court as a channeler of dead Billy; nor has he established any reason for exhumations. But he has proved New Mexico's intractable corruption of collusive cronyism.]

(21) Respectfully submitted this 5th day of January, 2004.
Heard, Robins, Cloud, Lubel & Greenwood, L.L.P.

Bill Robins III
David Sandoval
Address and Telephone Numbers
ATTORNEYS FOR BILLY THE KID

SPEAKING FOR BILLY IN FORT SUMNER

On February 26, 2004, Attorney Robins, with Attorneys David Sandoval and Mark Acuña, filed the "Tenth Judicial Court of De Baca County Case No. CV-2004-00005, Petition for the Exhumation of Billy the Kid's Remains." **[APPENDIX: 2]** Dead Billy is listed as a co-petitioner with the hoax's lawmen: "Gary Graves, Sheriff of De Baca County, Tom Sullivan, (Sheriff) and Steve Sederwall (Deputy Sheriff) of Lincoln County, New Mexico. (hereinafter the 'Sheriff-Petitioners')."

For digging up Billy, Robins used hoaxer-style of vague suspicion, like: "This was also a time whose history was not accurately nor completely written." Or, as he made-up: "For generations now, the life of Billy the Kid has been the subject of historical debate. Perhaps the most significant lingering question involves whether Billy the Kid was indeed shot by Sheriff Pat Garrett in an ambush."

"Brushy Bill" makes his expected grand entrance under Section "IV. Historical Background." with introduction of the pretenders. Robins stated: "The debate has been sparked at various times in the past by at least two individuals who laid claim to his identity. **Ollie "Brushy Bill" Roberts** resided in Hico, Texas and claimed to be Billy the Kid. John Miller, in Arizona also died still claiming he was Billy the Kid. Co-Petitioners are in the initial phases of pursuing exhumations of these individuals as well."

"Brushy" is emphasized with Robins's ignorant true-believer plug of repeating his "dark night" confabulation for the Fort Sumner murder scene's actual bright moonlight; and by adding the pardon as deserved by "Brushy" for a reformed long life. So Robins stated about the shooting that the "ambush [was on] **one dark night** in Ft. Sumner;" and he claimed that the question that needed to be answered was **"whether the Kid went on to live a long and peace-abiding life elsewhere**."

To justify exhumation, Robins called the July 14, 1881 killing of Billy the Kid an "historical quandary" – but it was only a "quandary" for "Brushy" believers! He stated: "The investigation ["Billy the Kid Case"] has renewed questions as to whether Billy the Kid lies buried at the fabled grave-site in Ft. Sumner. Allowing the exhumation of the remains at Ft. Sumner grave site for extraction of DNA to be compared with that of Ms. Antrim's will likely finally provide definitive answers to this **historical quandary**."

Robins's lying becomes clear when one recalls that the month before, on January 9, 2004, the OMI issued the Affidavits of its forensic experts, Drs. Ross Zumwalt and Debra Komar, stating the graves' DNA was invalid. And Robins himself participated in the Komar deposition of January 20, 2004, in which she said the same thing. Obvious is the intent of the hoax to fake results, since real ones were impossible, as the hoaxers knew.

Also, contemplate this weirdness when contemplating Attorney Bill Robins III's filings: When he was channeling dead Billy the Kid, he was actually channeling dead, talking "Brushy Bill" Roberts! So dead 'Brushy" was seeking *his own* pardon, while *still pretending* to be real Billy Bonney, by using demon-possessed Attorney Bill Robins's tongue in Silver City and Fort Sumner courts to fake a death scene with Garrett killing an innocent victim, namely Billy Barlow!

So Robins now had Billy the Kid (secretly as "Brushy") request his own exhumation from Richardson's pocket-judge, Ted Hartley based entirely on the imposter hoax death scene and the concealed Coroner's Jury Report.

CHAPTER 4
"BILLY THE KID CASE" HOAX TV DOCUMENTARY WITH THE FAKE DEATH SCENE AND CORONER'S JURY REPORT DENIAL

HOAX HISTORIAN, PROFESSOR PAUL HUTTON, MAKES A TV DOCUMENTARY

University of New Mexico history professor, Paul Hutton, was appointed by Governor Bill Richardson as the hoax's official historian. He fulfilled his role by making the hoax's key media contacts: Bill Kurtis of Bill Kurtis Productions, and forensic expert, Dr. Henry Lee. And he wrote, narrated, and co-produced, with Bill Kurtis, the "Billy the Kid Case" hoax's 2004 TV documentary titled "Investigating History, Billy the Kid."

"INVESTIGATING HISTORY: BILLY THE KID" ON TV

The first, in the hoaxers' anticipated TV series of "Billy the Kid Case" fake forensics with exhumations, was Paul Hutton's 2004 History Channel documentary titled "Investigating History: Billy the Kid." It preserved, like in a chunk of amber, all the major hoaxers as its talking-head participants. They declared the "Billy the Kid Case" hoax's tenets: the historical death scene was untrue; Pat Garrett assisted Billy the Kid's jailbreak because they were friends; Garrett murdered an innocent victim, not Billy the Kid in Fort Sumner; the body was kept secret; there was no Coroner's Jury Report; and tourist interests blocked truth-seeking exhumations for DNA. Stressed was that "Brushy Bill" Roberts was plausibly Billy the Kid. Added was that the "investigation" was to assist Governor Bill Richardson's decision as to pardoning Billy, with "Brushy" implied as the recipient.

HUTTON'S PROFITEERING PLOT

From the start, Hutton saw the program as his cash cow: the first in his series. He boastfully confirmed it to a *University of New Mexico Campus News* reporter, Carolyn Gonzales, for her February 16, 2004 article titled "Hutton Writes Wild Frontier Stories for History Channel." Gonzalez wrote: "His role has evolved into fulltime scriptwriting for "Investigating History" ... Hutton pitched **the idea of the series** to the History Channel after working with Governor Bill Richardson to try to verify the Kid's identity through a DNA comparison with his mother ... Richardson, who dubbed Hutton "Doc," appointed him historian on the Billy the Kid issue."

For it, Hutton also created a hoax mantra: "the mystery of Billy's murder." When interviewed on April 24, 2004 by a Rick Nathanson for the *Albuquerque Journal* weekly television guide, "Entertainer," Hutton was quoted: "[P]eople are always intrigued by mystery, and this has always been one of the great mysteries of the Old West. **The great mystery in this case is, of course, who is buried in Billy the Kid's grave in Fort Sumner**." Setting up Garrett as murder of an innocent victim, Hutton called him "Billy's good friend." He also straddled the fence, stating: "I'm pretty sure that Pat Garrett shot Billy the Kid that night at Pete Maxwell's house." Left out was that his program claimed the opposite.

HUTTON'S PROGRAM'S OVERVIEW

In his error-filled, "Brushy"-backing program, proving his ignorance of real history, Hutton had Richardson as an "historical investigator" assembling "experts" as a "pardon team" for Billy the Kid. They were fellow hoaxers: Sheriff Tom Sullivan, Deputy Steve Sederwall, *True West* magazine Editor-in-Chief Bob Boze Bell; and "Brushy"-believers, Bill Robins III and W.C. Jameson. In the credits, Hutton listed "Frederick Nolan;" though, Nolan told me it was without his participation or knowledge.

Hutton narrates, as *Alias Billy the Kid's* cover looms: "Over the years that story has gained some credence." W.C. Jameson states that the "Coroner's Jury Report was never found," and there was "no evidence jurymen saw the body." Steve Sederwall adds, "If "Brushy Bill" is Billy the Kid, it comes down to this ... Garrett had to have let him escape in Fort Sumner."

As to the pardon, Hutton states: "New Mexico Governor Bill Richardson is ready to make things right." Then, Richardson himself says: "I might pardon him." But *that* will be based on [Attorney Bill] Robins's "investigation."

Since I had been exposing their exhumation-seeking hoax in District Courts, Hutton switched the "Billy the Kid Case" from Pat Garrett murdering the innocent victim, to an investigation" to see if Billy the Kid "deserved" a pardon for his own killings.

Faking hoaxers' expertise, Hutton has Sheriff Sullivan "discover" that Billy was promised a pardon; has himself and Bob Boze Bell as "historians" on the "Governor's pardon team;" and has Bill Robins III doing pardon legalities. Deputy Sederwall is a Capitan Mayor wondering if "Brushy" was Billy. And Richardson declares his commitment to "science," "tourism," and New Mexico.

RE-ENACTING THE FAKE DEATH SCENE

Hutton's presentation, relying on "Brushy Bill" and "Billy the Kid Case" hoaxes, seeks to cast doubt on the Fort Sumner death scene; to make Pat Garrett a liar; and to denigrate legitimate historians. The film starts with Billy approaching a dark Maxwell house (no bright moonlight), while Hutton intones: "This is one of the most controversial moments in the history of the Old West: history's version of the last seconds of Billy the Kid ... Pat Garrett fires into the darkness ... Billy the Kid is dead when he hits the floor - or is he?" He then doubts a successful shot in the dark; and sneers: "The story is almost too good ... that the Kid ... would come strolling into this room unarmed and right into the hands of the law enforcement official ... is just too bizarre." **[But Billy was armed; and was likely sent to the ambush, since he was just going to the opposite side of the house to cut a steak.]**

Concealing all corpse identifications, Hutton calls the killing "a mystery;" quotes Poe's initial doubt, as if denying corpse identity; calls the killing "Garrett's version;" and lies that eye-witness, Pete Maxwell, never gave his version." He concludes that it was "unlikely" that Billy the Kid was shot.

Alias Billy the Kid is then backed by Hutton. Jameson denies the Coroner's Jury Report. And Sederwall declares that Garrett let Billy "escape in Fort Sumner."

Hutton proclaims: "Some suggested that it was more likely that Pat Garrett, Billy's friend, let him go ... burying someone else in his place" **[hoaxing friendship and innocent victim]**. Bob Boze Bell (subtitled as "Editor, True West Magazine") sneers that: "Friends of Pat Garrett conducted what they called an autopsy. But there were no photographs." He adds that they said Garrett deserved the reward. **[Jurymen were not Garrett's friends; they identified the body as Billy's; and nobody had a camera.]** Boze Bell says Garrett did the killing in "secrecy," and buried the body the next day. **[There was no secrecy. The body had a vigil and legal inquest.]**

Hutton calls history "Garrett's version;" says that the only eye-witness was Pete Maxwell, "who was never interviewed" **[hiding Maxwell's Coroner's Jury testimony, and the townspeople's corpse vigil]**, and lies that Poe "contradicted" Garrett's statement. **[Poe was merely initially unsure that Garrett had shot Billy, whom he could not recognize.]**

But the most egregious and most damaging part of Hutton's TV fraud is his "Billy the Kid Case" hoax re-enactment scene with Garrett, as Billy's friend and deputy murder accomplice, himself placing the revolver in the courthouse-jail's outhouse to enable Billy's killing of the deputy guards. No one, before this "Billy the Kid Case" hoax, had accused Garrett of this horrific crime of assisting murder of his own deputies and assisting escape of his condemned prisoner. And Paul Hutton contaminated public awareness irrevocably by this faked scene.

In conclusion, "Investigating History: Billy the Kid" was "Billy the Kid Case" hoaxing, with its covert "Brushy" pardon thrust.

CHAPTER 5
"BILLY THE KID CASE" HOAX FAKE FORENSICS WITH DR. HENRY LEE

DR. LEE WAS THE PERFECT DNA MATCH

After I had legally blocked the exhumations of Billy Bonney and his mother, Dr. Henry Lee entered the "Billy the Kid Case" in 2004, at its Version II of the hoax, with playing-dead-shot-Billy-bleeding-on-the-carpenter's-bench-for-DNA.

Deputy Steve Sederwall had contacted him through the "Billy the Kid Case's" official historian, Paul Hutton; as Sederwall testified in his June 26, 2012 deposition for my open records litigation against the lawmen: "Paul Hutton wanted me to be on some investigative history … I said, "You know, I'm looking at bringing Henry Lee out here … Tell Kurtis I'll let him film it if he wants to, or whatever, if he can get Henry out here." So [Hutton] jumped on it." Sederwall had also alluded to Hutton's setting up the "deal" with Bill Kurtis; stating in my litigation's January 21, 2011 Evidentiary hearing that: "I got a call from Paul Hutton, a historian up in Albuquerque, teaches at the University. He was writing a deal for Bill Curtis [sic]. He wanted us [Sederwall and Sullivan] to interview with Bill Curtis [sic] … Paul and I were friends … So Curtis [sic] contacted us and wanted to know if he could follow the investigation … That's when Bill Curtis [sic] got involved, and **Curtis [sic] paid to bring Dr. Lee to New Mexico**." [Transcript 1/21/11, pp. 164, 168]. It soon emerged that Lee and Kurtis were partners in producing TV documentaries.

As forensic expert, Lee brought in his lab, Orchid Cellmark. On August 9, 2004, I had contacted its then director, Mark Stolorow, explaining the "Billy the Kid Case" hoax. He was amused. On August 18th, we spoke again. He was defensive. Orchid Cellmark, he told me, was under a "gag order" on the case.

Dr. Lee was in charge! Three months later, Orchid Cellmark was caught faking DNA computer data on another case. That scandal appeared on November 18, 2004, in "TalkLeft.com," as "Fraud alleged at Cellmark, DNA Testing Firm." It stated: "This is shocking to the forensic community which has always believed that raw data cannot be electronically manipulated." It concluded: "Bottom line: A lot of defendants will be seeking retesting by an independent lab when the prosecution is relying on results by Cellmark."

Orchid Cellmark was reduced to one lab in Farmers Branch, Texas. And Mark Stolorow was replaced as director by Dr. Rick Staub. Unlike Stolorow, he seemed indifferent to scandal. And, as will be seen, though *his lab found no DNA at all* in Henry Lee's eventual carpenter's bench specimens, it did not stop Staub and the hoaxers from exhuming John Miller, with the claim of having Billy the Kid DNA from that bench for identity matching!

Also, Lee would be seeking blood - as the only DNA source the hoaxers could think of after exhumations were blocked. So it was kept secret that **Orchid Cellmark does not test for blood**!

Thus, Henry Lee was the perfect "expert" to hide that no verifiable DNA of Billy the Kid was available as "reference DNA" - and to find "some." He sham-tested for "blood" wherever he was pointed; and made up crime scene scenarios however he was directed - as long as Bill Kurtis Productions kept filming.

One can even surmise that Lee and his lab would also have participated in Version I one of the hoax, and claimed DNA from the likely empty gravesites of Billy and his mother, and presented whatever results were desired - with "Brushy" added in.

Lee's joining the "Billy the Kid Case" was announced by hoax-backing *Albuquerque Journal* reporter, Rene Romo. On August 2, 2004, Romo splashed, "Forensic Expert on Billy's Case: Questions Remain on Outlaw's Fate" Romo declared: "Dr. Henry Lee, one of the nation's leading forensic scientists ... has added the Billy the Kid slaying to his case files ... "This is an extremely interesting case of some historical importance,' Lee said in an interview ... 'That's why I agreed to spend some of my own time to work with them ... **It's basically a worthwhile project and legitimate**."

So famous Dr. Lee called the "Billy the Kid Case" "a worthwhile project and legitimate." What else was the public to think? And Romo confirmed: "Lee's expenses were paid by Illinois-based Kurtis Productions, headed by Bill Kurtis, host of the History Channel series 'Investigating History.' "

Lee's profit motive was further elucidated in the August 12, 2004 *Lincoln County News* article by Doris Cherry: "Forensics 101 for 'Billy." She quoted Sheriff Tom Sullivan: "Along with Sullivan and Lee were a crew from Curtis [sic] Production Company filming for the History Channel and Court T.V. **Dr. Lee also has a show produced by Curtis [sic] Production**."

So Billy the Kid DNA exhumations and "matchings" were to be churned out by Henry Lee and Bill Kurtis for their enterprise. No wonder Lee called the project "worthwhile." He was intending an exhumation franchise.

But the public was fed a different bill of goods via the hoaxers. By April 13, 2006, deceived reporter, Leo W. Banks of the *Tucson Weekly*, in "The New Billy the Kid?" had Lee pleading; as in: "Everybody wants a piece of the Kid, even a celebrity like Henry Lee ... when he heard about the Kid dig-up efforts, **he called Sederwall to volunteer his services**."

The "Billy the Kid Case" hoaxers plugged Lee extravagantly. Rene Romo's August 2, 2004 *Albuquerque Journal* article even used their "Probable Cause Statement's" fellow hoaxer: "You're getting the top guy ... I think that will go a long way to finding out what happened in Lincoln," said **David S. Turk**, historian with the U.S. Marshals Service ... who is cooperating on the case."

DR. LEE AND THE FAKE BENCH "BLOOD"

When presented with the carpenter's bench, a legitimate forensic expert would have wanted to know its verification as a "crime scene" object, and if "reference DNA" of Billy the Kid existed for identity matching if DNA was found.

As to validity, the answer is: it had none. It first appeared in 1926, 45 years after Billy's shooting, when a teenaged Maxwell relative named Stella Abreu made a Fort Sumner Billy the Kid Museum in a shack. And, knowing Billy had been laid out on one, she asked around for a bench for her display. (Historian Jerry Richard Weddle told me she got it from a local man.) After her museum closed in 1937, its storage was nil for preserving blood. As stated in the "Probable Cause Statement," the hoaxers found it in the Albuquerque converted chicken coop of Stella's descendant, with her other alleged Maxwell family furniture.

But claiming "blood" - not necessarily *real* blood - was the hoaxers' only bench concern. So they faked it. On August 14, 2004, for the *Lincoln County News*, reporter Doris Cherry's "Forensics 101 for 'Billy," quoted Sederwall: "The bench has been in the Maxwell family descendents since 1881 and has been stored out of weather, protecting the blood evidence ... **Only once was the blood**

exposed to the elements, when a family member who took the bench without family approval returned it to the Maxwell family home in Fort Sumner and left it outside to get rained on once. So the odds of finding blood evidence were very good."

The "rained on" part was not good for blood! It got worse. For an October 6, 2005 *RuidosoNews.com* article, hoax loyalist, Julie Carter, wrote "Follow the Blood: In the Billy the Kid Case, Miller Exhumed." She stated: "The Maxwell compound and everything in it was reportedly washed away in a flood of 1906. The photo of the bench was taken in 1926 by historian Maurice Fulton ... Since 1959, they [Maxwell family] had stored the historical furniture and household items in an old chicken coop." The "washed away" in a 1906 flood, and unknown location from 1881 to 1926 were also bad! And added was the gap from its being photographed in Stella's Museum in 1926, to the 1959 transport to the Albuquerque, back yard, chicken coop.

For its "validation," fellow hoaxers were used. On April 19, 2006, hoax-backing reporter, Julie Carter, in *RuidosoNews.com*, reported in "Digging up Bones": "UNM History professor Paul Hutton and U.S. Treasury [sic - Marshals Service] historian Dave Turk have both authenticated the bench."

And the hoaxing lawmen lied wildly. Julie Carter, for her October 6, 2005, *RuidosoNews.com* article "Follow the Blood: In the Billy the Kid Case, Miller Exhumed," quoted Deputy Steve Sederwall: "Whoever was laid on that [bench], whether it was Billy the Kid or not," said Sederwall, "he left his DNA." The investigators said the amount of blood found on the bench indicated that whoever was on that bench must have been still alive. **"Dead men don't bleed," explained Sederwall. "and we witnessed a large amount of blood."** The hoaxers were back in business with their hoax Version II and new exhumation hopes.

When Henry Lee examined the bench, he, of course, found "blood" too. Rene Romo's August 2, 2004, *Albuquerque Journal's* "Forensic Expert on Billy's Case" stated: "Lee, assisted by Calvin Ostler [his assistant] ... performed tests on the bench that Sederwall believes to be the one on which the Kid's body was laid out after Garrett gunned him down. Preliminary results indicated **trace evidence of blood**, but, without further testing, it is not certain whether the blood was human, Lee said."

In fact, there was no certain blood at all! Since I too had seen the bench; it just had a few rust-like discolorations - like expected on a carpenter's bench.

By August 12th, reporter Doris Cherry, for her *Lincoln County News*, "Forensics 101 for 'Billy,' " wrote: "Dr. Lee proved the good odds by utilizing a laser to bore into the wood of the bench to take samples and he took scrapings from the top and underneath of the bench. '**Then he swabbed it with the chemical that changes color to indicate the presence of blood,' Sullivan said**."

The hoaxers were just hoaxing. Lee stated in his report - which I got after years of open records litigation against the record-hiding lawmen – that the had tested with Luminol, a non-specific chemical that fluoresces with any iron-containing substance - like rust, more likely on a carpenter's bench than blood. **And no other testing would *ever be done* to verify blood, or to connect it to Billy (which was impossible).**

Next the hoaxers got carried away. Romo's original **"trace,"** in his August 2, 2004, "Forensic Expert on Billy's Case," started bleeding like stigmata. In Doris Cherry's "Forensics 101 for Billy," **Sullivan stated that Lee "found a lot of blood**." For Julie Carter's "Follow the Blood," **Sederwall said: "We witnessed a large amount of blood;" and he creatively lied that it proved "an upper chest wound**." By April 13, 2006, "blood" was almost dripping off the bench. Leo Banks of the *Tucson Weekly*, in "The New Billy the Kid," reported that **Sederwall said the bench was "saturated**!"

I got Lee's February 25, 2005 report on January 31, 2012 in my open records litigation. It was titled "Forensic Research & Training Center Forensic Examination Report," as ""Requested by: Lincoln County Sheriff's Office, New Mexico; Investigation History Program, Kurtis Production." "Local Case No." was "2003-274." The "Report To:" was Steve Sederwall, Lincoln County Sheriff's Office, New Mexico." The "forensic investigation team" had: "Calvin Ostler, Forensic Consultant, Riverton, Utah;" "Tom Sullivan, Sheriff, Lincoln County, New Mexico;" "Steve Sederwall, Deputy Sheriff, Lincoln County;" and "David Turk, US Marshall [sic], United States Marshall [sic] Service." The carpenter's bench was reported under "Item # 1 Workbench." Lee concluded:

> After a detail examination of the evidence and review of all the results of field testing, the following conclusion was reached.
>
> 1. Brownish dark stains were observed on different areas of the workbench. These areas were subjected to chemical presumptive blood tests. Some of those samples give a positive reaction. These results indicate the presence of Heme or Peroxidase like activity with those stains testing positive, **which suggest that those stains could be bloodstains**. Further DNA testing could reveal the nature and identity of these blood-like stains.

Lee proved his own hoaxing by hiding more likely rust, or that Orchid Cellmark does not test for blood. And finding DNA would not even connect it to the stains, since he did no controls from non-stained areas. Nor were controls taken from everyone present at his testing to check for *their* contaminating DNA (think sneeze!). Lastly, he was lying that "[f]urther DNA testing could reveal the nature and identity of these blood-like stains," since there was no "reference DNA" of Billy the Kid to test their "identity."

But Orchid Cellmark Lab was hyped. Reporter, Doris Cherry, in her August 12, 2004, "Forensics 101 for 'Billy' " stated: "Each swab and all scrapings from the bench were sealed in preparation to shipping to the Orchard Selmark [sic - Orchid Cellmark] Lab in Dallas. Sullivan said Dr. Lee uses the lab for most of his work."

Ultimately, by open records litigation and subpoena of Orchid Cellmark Lab, on April 20, 2012, I got Lee's carpenter's bench DNA results. October 15, 2004's "Laboratory Report, Forensic Identity, Mitochondrial Analysis, Results and Conclusions" for its Case 4444-001B-004B (for Case 2003-274) **SHOWED LEE'S SPECIMENS HAD NO DNA! THE HOAXER'S CLAIM TO HAVE BENCH-BLOOD-DNA OF BILLY THE KID FOR DNA MATCHINGS WAS A LIE!** And they knew it by October 15, 2004. There was no justification to dig up anyone at all in their fake "investigation!" But they did anyway!

DR. LEE ATTACKS SHERIFF PAT GARRETT WITH A WASHSTAND, A HEADBOARD, AND A FABRICATED DEATH SCENE

What the hoaxers really wanted was a death scene incriminating Garrett as a bad guy capable of killing the innocent victim, then lying that the victim was Billy the Kid.. So they must have told Dr. Henry Lee. With no Maxwell house in existence since about 1887 to investigate for a "crime scene," and with the uncertain bedroom furniture of Peter Maxwell's bedroom from Stella Abreu's Museum, he, of course, obliged with his fake forensics and flaunted expertise as cover for being a crook.

Lee started with a washstand from Stella's Museum, which was not part of the historical death scene, and which further lacked credibility as being the size of a toy, not an actual washstand. (Its eventual measurements by Lee were: 28¾" x 16", x 30" high.) **[FIGURE: 7]**

But it had two bullet holes in it; though there was no bullet, and no record as to when it was shot! But, at least, the lawmen had it, as stated in the "Probable Cause Statement": "On September 13, 2003, investigators located all the furniture that was in Pete Maxwell's bedroom the night of the shooting, July 1881. In the items investigators located on September 13, 2003 was that wash stand."

Their "Probable Cause Statement" had used it to fabricate Garrett as a liar, since he claimed his second shot hit Maxwell's **headboard, and never mentioned a washstand**. In his 1933 *The Death of Billy the Kid*, Poe had reported that: "[A] shot was fired in the room, followed immediately by what everyone within hearing distance thought were two other shots. However, there were only two shots fired, the third report, as we learned afterward, being caused by the rebound of the second bullet, which had struck the adobe wall and **rebounded against the headboard of a wooden bedstead**." So, by their fake "what-if" reasoning, the lawmen had made-up that *if* Garrett lied about not hitting the washstand, he lied about the corpse's identity!

So obliging Dr. Lee recycled their washstand-headboard scam as a "forensic investigation" to incriminate Garrett as a liar, by faking a crime scene for them, then saying Garrett must have lied because it was not the shooting scene he gave! Hoax-helping reporter, Rene Romo, presented Lee's "washstand" fakery in his August 2, 2004 *Albuquerque Journal*'s "Forensic Expert on Billy's Case." stating:

> Lee and the investigators [Sullivan, Sederwall, and Calvin Ostler] also examined a washstand that was purportedly struck by a bullet when Garrett shot the Kid in a bedroom of the outlaw's friend, Pete Maxwell, in Fort Sumner ... Lee and the investigators used laser technology Saturday to determine the trajectory of the bullet as it entered the left side of the washstand and exited the right at a downward angle. Given the washstand's likely location in the room, the investigation has already cast some doubt on Garrett's account of the fatal shooting, Sederwall and [Calvin] Ostler said.
>
> 'The evidence we are seeing does not corroborate the popular legend,' Ostler said. 'Something's askew' ...
>
> **One simple explanation that Lee offered is that Garrett may have shot defensively at the Kid as he fled and struck the washstand from the side instead of head on. Garrett's official story may have omitted that embarrassing detail. "You don't want to paint yourself as a chicken," Lee suggested**.

Item # 2 Washstand

This Washstand measures approximately 28 ¾" long by 16" deep by 30" tall. Figure 6 is a sketch diagram of the washstand. This washstand is made of wood with a black color finish on it.

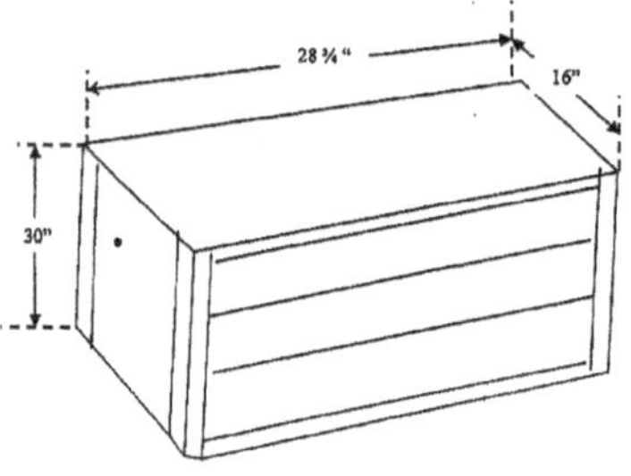

Figure 6, Washstand

Photograph # 3 shows the left side panel of the washstand and photograph # 4 depicts a view of the
Visual examination of the external s
holes, one single hole in each end of
examination of these holes indicates
bullet holes.

Page 10 of

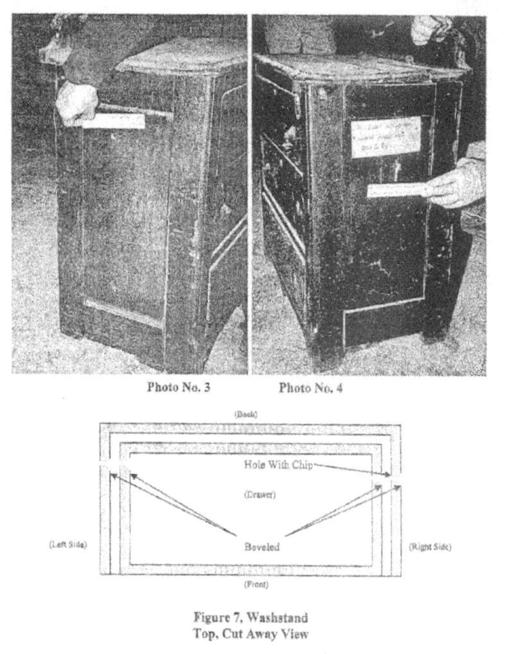

Figure 7, Washstand
Top, Cut Away View

Figure 7 is a cut away diagram of the washstand. This diagram depicts the relative locations of the two holes on the side panels of the washstand.

The hole on the left side panel is round and well defined. The hole on the right side panel is chipped and beveled. The left side panel hole is consistent with a bullet entrance hole.

Page 11 of 25

FIGURE: 7. "Washstand" from Stella Abreu's Fort Sumner Billy the Kid Museum, 1926-1936

So Lee made-up this scene with no bullet for dating, and no provable relationship of the washstand to Garrett or to Billy or to Peter Maxwell or to the shooting. And Lee fabricated his groveling Garrett from the little box being toy-sixed, so being near the floor.

For his February 25, 2005 report titled "Forensic Research & Training Center Forensic Examination Report" - which I got during my open records litigation against the hoaxing lawmen - under "Item # 2 Washstand," Lee babbled his fabrication:

> The angles produced in the examination tell us two things: First, the bullet was fired from no more than 41" from the floor given the reported limitations of the room. The room was reported to be 20' by 20'; the maximum distance is assumed to be 20'. If the firearm was a maximum of 41" off the floor it is unlikely that the shooter was standing. It is more likely the shooter was kneeling, squatting, or close to the floor. Second, the horizontal angle is such that if the Washstand was positioned so that the back was against the wall, the shot could not have been fired from more than approximately 40 inches from the Washstand, because the wall would have been in the way. The angle of trajectory intersects the back plane of the Washstand at approximately 45 3/16", and no more than 46". Lee's conclusion reflected his well-known caution about putting his lies in writing: "Two bullet holes were located on the side panels of the Washstand. The hole on the left side panel is consistent with a bullet entrance hole while the hole on the right side panel is consistent with a bullet exit hole. However, it is not possible to determine when those bullet holes were produced at this time.

The lawmen also gave Dr. Lee Stella's Museum's headboard to "investigate." Important for their fake argument of Garrett as a liar, was claiming it had no bullet hole, as claimed by him and Poe. So that is what Lee gave them.

Lee's February 25, 2004 "Forensic Research & Training Center Forensic Examination Report," under its topic, **"Item # 2 Headboard;"** stated:

> **No bullet hole and no observable damage, no sign of bullet ricocheted type of defects were found on the Headboard. No blood or biological materials were observed on the Headboard.**

FIGURE: 8. Headboard lacking a center from Stella Abreu's Fort Sumner Billy the Kid Museum, 1926-1936 (Courtesy of Kenny Miller)

But Lee slyly omitted that the "headboard" is just a rim around empty space **[Figure: 8]**, *with no place for a bullet hole!* So Lee and his assistant, Calvin Ostler, had lied to Rene Romo for his August 2, 2004 *Albuquerque Journal*'s "Forensic Expert on Billy's Case" by stating: "The evidence we are seeing does not corroborate the popular legend" [what Lee called actual history].

Deputy Steve Sederwall was soon spouting Dr. Lee's Garrett-is-a-liar fable in Julie Carter's October 2005, "Follow the Blood": "Using high-tech lasers and other modern crime scene methods, investigators learned that the shooting of the Kid in Pete Maxwell's bedroom was not in the way history has portrayed it. Tests indicate that Garrett fired his second shot from the doorway while on his knees and with his left hand on the floor, firing back over his shoulder ... Being blinded by his first shot, it appears he was in a great hurry to get out of the room and fell to the floor.' [Sederwall] added: 'To find the furniture from Maxwell's bedroom was great. But to have Dr. Lee recover usable evidence was truly a historical find.' "

In fact, this Garrett-washstand-headboard fabrication merely illustrates hoaxers' collusion to fake a death scene defaming Garrett as a murderer of an innocent victim.

HIDING LEE'S RECORDS AND LAB RESULTS

Dr. Henry Lee, though hoaxing, was circumspect enough for the hoaxers to fear his that his forensic report would reveal their lies. And they knew that his Orchid Cellmark results showing no DNA extracted from his carpenter's bench samples proved their lie of having gotten "bench-DNA-of-Billy-the-Kid," which they claimed they would use for identity matchings for exhumed Billy the Kid identity claimants.

So they hid these records in my open records litigation against them. Furthermore, Steve Sederwall forged Lee's reports to trick the District Court Judge, George Eichwald, that the case was his hobby, while deleting Lee's conclusions. This forging was punitively sanctioned in Eichwald's May 15, 2014 "Findings of Fact and Conclusions of Law and Order of the Court": "At an Evidentiary Hearing conducted on December 21 [sic – 18], 2012 and February 4, 2013 ... [w]itness Seterwall [sic], still calling [law enforcement] Case 2003-274 his private hobby, admitted to altering the first Lee report's header to remove Case 2003-274 information; and admitted to creating the other report versions given to the Court and lacking law enforcement information ... Defendants' conduct in providing altered records ...is wanton, willful, and in bad faith."

BIG PICTURE FOR DR. HENRY LEE'S FAKE FORENSICS

In fact, Dr. Henry Lee's so-called forensic investigation was just his own fictions built on the hoaxers' fictional death scene.

And even if the hoaxers had gotten DNA from Lee's specimens, they had no "reference DNA" of Billy Bonney to prove it was his.

But the hoaxers' lie that they had Billy the Kid's carpenter's bench "blood-DNA" would become the basis for digging-up John Miller (with added William Hudspeth) for matching to it, and for trying to dig up "Brushy Bill" - all based on the imposters' faked death scenes of the killing of an innocent victim, and the denial of the existence of the Coroner's Jury Report that put an end to their tomfoolery.

CHAPTER 6
ILLEGAL EXHUMATIONS OF JOHN MILLER AND WILLIAM HUDSPETH BASED ON THE FAKE DEATH SCENE AND NO CORONER'S JURY REPORT

DESCENT INTO CRIMINALITY

Since the "Billy the Kid Case" was a publicity stunt, its drive was for *any* publicity. "Brushy Bill" as Billy the Kid may have been its covert goal, but any exhumation keeping the TV cameras rolling sufficed. And the Arizona grave of John Miller, in the Arizona Pioneers' Home Cemetery, was available for desecration because it was state-owned and under the auspices of corrupt Governor Janet Napolitano, apparently willing to do a favor for her corrupt New Mexico counterpart, Bill Richardson. Once again, the crux of the endeavor was a faked death scene (this time John Miller's), with hiding of the Coroner's Jury Report.

Since the hoaxers knew by the May 19, 2005 exhumation that they had no "DNA of Billy the Kid" from Dr. Henry Lee's carpenter's bench specimens, it was mere felonious wanton desecration of Miller's grave, and grave-robbing to give his bones for Orchid Cellmark Director Rick Staub - present to get in the footage Bill Kurtis Productions was filming. But there was worse. The cemetery had unmarked graves. So uncertain of John Miller's location, and out-of-control, the hoaxers dug up an adjoining man named William Hudspeth, and took his bones too!

SHERIFF RICK VIRDEN LEADS THE EXHUMATIONS

After Lincoln County Sheriff Tom Sullivan's term ended in 2004, his Undersheriff, Rick Virden, a "Billy the Kid Case" peripheral participant, was elected Sheriff. He immediately deputized Sullivan and Sederwall to continue Case No. 2003-274.

From the 2003 start of their "Billy the Kid Case," the hoaxers had John Miller half-heartedly in their sights, as was seen in their already-cited "Seventy-Seven Days of Doubt" initial draft of a "Probable Cause Statement" for their Lincoln County Sheriff's Department Case No. 2003-274. There, Miller's brief presence was for "survival suspicion," and as a foil for "Brushy Bill." (See pages 202, 212-213 above)

By 2005, with their faltering hoax, John Miller looked better to the hoaxers. They hid his 10-years-too-old death certificate proof from the Arizona Pioneers' Home. They also hid that he had no playing-dead-on-the carpenter's-bench scene - and *even denied being present* on July 14, 1881, for his fabricated Garrett-killing-an-Indian tale. Nonetheless, scorning their audience as idiots, the hoaxers waved their flag of bleeding-playing-dead-Billy-on-the-bench-DNA from famous forensic expert Dr. Henry Lee - though there was none for matching with anyone. So there was no basis, by history or by DNA, to justify his exhumation. So the hoaxers hid that too, but proceeded with paranoid secrecy.

FAKING JOHN MILLER BELIEVERS: FELLOW HOAXERS, DALE TUNNELL AND TOM SULLIVAN

A hoaxer problem with John Miller was that he had no believers. So fellow hoaxer, Dale Tunnell, became his fan, via Helen Airy's 1993 *Whatever Happened to Billy the Kid?*

A March 13, 2006 Internet article about Tunnell, on helenair.com, by a Robert Struckman, was "Bitterroot man hopes to uncover the truth about Billy the Kid." A major hoax document, it was another hoax rewrite apparently in response to my open records requests to the lawmen hoaxers as public officials. So they now switched to being "amateur historians" with private records, immune to the open records act. For Struckman, Tunnell became an "amateur historian" too. Struckman wrote: "[Tunnell] would like to confirm the story put forth by Airy. Like him, she was an amateur historian who bucked the official story. Academics scoffed at her account. **'I'd like to prove her correct,' he said.**"

Also calling himself a "forensic criminologist," Tunnell tried to upgrade imposter, John Miller. Struckman recorded:

> Tunnell's interest in the famous outlaw was piqued when he read a 1993 book by Helen Airy entitled, "Whatever Happened to Billy the Kid" ...
>
> "Even if it [DNA matching] comes back positive, there will be more work to do," Tunnell said. He hopes to find conclusive documentation placing Miller at or near Fort Sumner in July of 1881 or connecting his wife, Isadora, to a relationship there ...
>
> Tunnell has found enough material to poke holes in the official histories, he said ...
>
> "I want to set the record straight. If Billy the Kid , from 1881 to 1937, lived the life of an honest man, a hardworking fool, then I say he paid his debt to society," Tunnell said.

A credibility gap remained. Hiding their Garrett murder case, made exhumation seem like just a favor to Miller: setting *his* record straight! So hapless Tunnell became confused by the tangled fakery and made an unintentionally funny comment to Struckman: ""It's possible," Tunnell said, "that Garrett conspired with Billy to fake the death. Maybe **Billy never laid, wounded, on the carpenter's bench**. Maybe another body was buried in Billy's place." Oops, "Doctor" Tunnell! Without Billy on the bench, there goes Lee's blood-DNA-of-Billy-the-Kid." There goes digging up John Miller solely for a DNA match to it!!!

Struckman ended with hoaxing Deputy Tom Sullivan, who had also just become a John Miller believer:

> After getting permission [no legitimate permit for exhumation for DNA matching was obtained] to exhume Miller's body, DNA samples were taken. The DNA analysis will be done by Dr. Henry Lee, founder of the Forensic Science Program at the University of New Haven and chief emeritus of the Connecticut State Police, Sullivan said.
>
> What if the DNA matches the wooden bench?
>
> "We'll change history. I don't know. Arizona would have the real Billy the Kid," Sullivan said.

Amusingly, Tunnell was also the hoaxers' patsy. When they were investigated for the criminality, they blamed him! It did not matter, since Napolitano and Richardson did a cover-up anyway.

THE SECRET FRENZIED DIG

John Miller's eternal rest ended on May 19, 2005, when the hoaxers secretly and violently backhoed his grave and coffin, frenetically grabbing bones into the night, and handing them to on-site Orchid Cellmark Lab Director, Dr. Rick Staub, who, along with them, was being filmed by Bill Kurtis Productions.

Present with the hoaxers was moonlighting, Maricopa County, forensic anthropologist, Dr. Laura Fulginiti, who had been nervously added by them to feign forensic credibility. She, however, ultimately presented a problem by being honest, and dutifully recording everything they did!

Feigning a legitimate investigation (and before they got caught for its illegalities, and lied that they were not involved in the digging), the lawmen prepared the "Lincoln County Sheriff's Department Supplemental Report for Case No. 2003-274 for the Exhumation of John Miller." I got it from Prescott Police Department. Signed by Steve Sederwall on Sheriff Rick Virden's official form, it began like this:

LINCOLN COUNTY SHERIFF'S DEPARTMENT SUPPLEMENTAL REPORT

Case # : 2003-274
Date: Thursday, May 19, 2005
Subject: Exhumation of John Miller
Location: Arizona Pioneers' Cemetery, Prescott, Arizona
Report By: Steven M. Sederwall

On Thursday, May 19, 2005, at approximately 1:00 pm the following met at the Arizona Pioneers' Cemetery at Prescott, Arizona.

Investigators:

Steven M. Sederwall, Lincoln County Deputy Sheriff

Following Sederwall, was Tom Sullivan as "Sheriff of Lincoln County, Retired," then Dale Tunnell as an "Arizona State Investigator." In line was "**Dr. Rick Staub, Orchid Cell Mark** [sic], DNA," proving the lab head himself was there for the bones.

The remaining "Investigators" were listed as: "Mike Poling, Yavapai County Sheriff''s Deputy [a random lawman who merely arrived to give forensic expert, Laura Fulginiti, specimens from another case, but was slyly added to fake presence of Arizona authority; and was later faked by the hoaxers as responsible for the exhumation!]; Laura Fulginiti, Forensic Scientist - Anthropologist; Kristen Hartnett, Forensic Scientist - Archeologist; Misty Rodarte, Arizona Pioneers' Administration."

Then came "Others Present," mostly Arizona Pioneers' Home staff, with addition of Deputy Tom Sullivan's wife, Pat.

Lastly, under "Bill Kurtis Productions," were cameraman, Joel Sapatori; and the soundman, Greg Gricus.

And Steve Sederwall posed for a trophy photo holding John Miller's (or William Hudspeth's) skull for hoax-backing reporter, Julie Carter's, October 6, 2005 *RuidosoNews.com* article, "Follow the Blood: In the Billy the Kid Case, Miller Exhumed."

Subsequently, the Case 2003-274 lawmen perpetrators denied any participation in the exhumation.

EXPOSED IN THE PRESS

Besides risk of Dr. Fulginati's honesty, the hoaxers got their first skeptical reporter: the *Tucson Weekly's* Leo W. Banks. In his April 13, 2006 article "The New Billy the Kid?" he noted that the graves were unmarked; so, unsure of Miller's location, they simply guessed. But after digging up one grave, they felt uncertain, and dug up the adjoining one and took its remains too - just to be safe! The secret of William Hudspeth was out. Banks wrote:

> The Miller exhumation began about 1 p.m. on May 19 last year, and didn't end until about 7:30 that night, with investigators examining the last of the remains by flashlight. A backhoe did most of the heavy labor, after which the diggers worked by hand to avoid damaging the coffins or the remains.
>
> But they soon learned that the coffins had already collapsed with age, which had also made the bones extremely fragile. Each piece was carefully photographed, measured and cleaned, then placed on a white sheet on the ground.
>
> Dr. Laura Fulginiti, a well-known forensic anthropologist from Phoenix, supervised the dig. She describes the atmosphere as collegial and charged with excitement as they removed the tobacco-colored bones from the ground.
>
> "At one point, they were holding up the skull and comparing it with pictures of Billy," Fulginiti says. "They recited the story to each other, and when we found something that matched, like the scapula (shoulder) fracture, they were like little kids. They were really invested in this, and that added to the enthusiasm."
>
> But the effort was anything but clear-cut.

In the first place, Miller's grave held no marker or headstone, and neither did the grave closest to his. To determine where Miller's plot should be, the investigators used a map provided by the Pioneers' Home, which pinpointed the location to within 20 square feet.

As Tunnell acknowledges, ground shift and weather patterns can sometimes move bodies underground, and Miller had been 6 feet under almost 70 years. How certain were they of digging in the right place? "Probably upwards of 90 percent," says Tunnell.

PILTDOWN MAN HOAX REDUX

The hoaxers were inadvertently rerunning the most famous skeleton hoax of all: Piltdown man. Between 1908 and 1912, an amateur anthropologist named Charles Dawson, claimed to have found Charles Darwin's coveted "missing link" between apes and men in and near Piltdown gravel quarry in East Sussex, England. Possible, though unproved, hoaxer, Dawson, hoped his discovery would yield him a fellowship in the British Royal Society. He had "discovered" parts of a human-like skull, an ape-like jawbone, a hominid-seeming canine tooth; plus an ivory tool and Stone Age animal teeth - for a Stone Age touch. "Museum experts" assembled the skull and jawbone into a creature they named *Eanthropus dawsoni*, to honor Dawson. Popularly called "Piltdown Man," it held its spot in humans' family tree for over 40 years.

In 1953, Sir Kenneth Oakley, using a new fluorine absorption test, proved Piltdown Man was a fake composite of a medieval human skull and an antique orangutan's jawbone - all stained to match. And the ape's jawbone's teeth were filed to fit the skull.

For their own Piltdown Man hoax, the "Billy the Kid Case" hoaxing lawmen had turned to reporter, Leo Banks, and tried to seduce him by: "We're giving Arizona Billy the Kid!"

For Banks's April 14, 2006 *Tucson Weekly* article, "The New Billy the Kid?" Deputy Tom Sullivan took over for fake Miller fan, Dale Tunnell, to be the Helen Airy convert, and was quoted: "Helen Airy's book triggered it for me ... It made a lot of sense. I read it and thought, 'We have another Billy the Kid.' "

And Sederwall and Sullivan performed their "high-tech forensic" routine, flaunting famous Dr. Lee and the carpenter's bench - now "saturated with blood." Banks quoted: "When we found the bench and the other evidence, we thought, 'Let's forget about these other bodies,' " says Sullivan, referring to Catherine Antrim and the Kid. "Let's do Miller. And if that doesn't work, we'll go down to Texas and do Brushy Bill."

But Banks had researched the "Billy the Kid Case," and had discovered their digging up of the random man (later identified as William Hudspeth). So he called their roving extravaganza "airship Billy." And he exposed that Sullivan's and Sederwall's "Billy the Kid" skeleton claims were made by mixing-up Miller's and the random man's bones! Banks had interviewed Dr. Laura Fulginiti. She denied their skeletal claims! Banks wrote:

> Fulginiti says the first body she studied had buck teeth and the scapula fracture that caused such a commotion with investigators.
>
> As Sederwall told the *Weekly,* "We were shocked when we got him up. He had buck teeth just like the Kid and a bullet hole in the upper left chest that exited the shoulder blade."
>
> Sullivan made a similar statement, suggesting this might be the man Garrett shot the morning of July 14, 1881.
>
> **But when contacted by the *Weekly*, Fulginiti didn't support their enthusiasm. "There was evidence of trauma on the scapula, but I couldn't tell whether it was from a gunshot wound or not," she said.**

She also said the buck teeth were from what Banks named "Scapula Man" [Hudspeth] from his non-shot *right* scapula! And Miller's skull *had no teeth*! Fulginiti had researched Miller as dying of a broken hip. So Banks called him "Hip Man."

Banks also contacted Orchid Cellmark Lab, discovering: "**The DNA expert present at the exhumation, Dr. Rick Staub, of Orchid Cellmark Labs in Dallas, <u>was unable to extract useable DNA from Hip Man [Miller]</u>. But he did get a usable sample from Scapula Man [Hudspeth]**." This was Staub's admission that John Miller's bones had yielded no DNA at all.

When confronted by Banks, Sullivan and Sederwall were left clumsily lying that Dr. Laura Fulginiti - their forensic expert hired specifically to validate the exhumation - was wrong.

Nevertheless, it was now obvious that, for their own Piltdown Man hoax, the hoaxers had assembled a "John Miller as a Billy the Kid" from William Hudspeth's bones (Banks's "Scapula Man"). That was how random man, William Hudspeth - his coffin smashed and corpse dismembered, with Dr. Rick Staub of Orchid Cellmark stealing his bones to grind to oblivion for meaningless DNA extraction - became part of Billy the Kid history.

THE INCRIMINATING FULGINITI REPORT

Dutiful Dr. Laura Fulginiti had reported it all. Duped into thinking Dale Tunnell was a forensic expert conducting the exhumation, as "Dr. Tunnell," she titled her June 2, 2005 report: "Re: Exhumation, Pioneer Home Cemetery, Prescott, Arizona for "Dale L. Tunnell, Ph.D. [sic – no evidence of a Phd.], Forensitec." I got its copy from the Prescott Police Department.

In her official report, Fulginiti described the scene, while the hoaxers feverishly dug before they were caught. She had written:

On May 19, 2005 at approximately 1230 hours I am asked to assist in the exhumation of the remains of an individual known as Mr. John Miller by Dr. Dale Tunnell, President, Forensitec. The purpose of my involvement is to aid in the exhumation process as well as to assess any skeletal remains recovered. The exhumation takes place at the Arizona Pioneer [sic] Home Cemetery, Iron Springs Road in Prescott Arizona in the presence of Dr. Tunnell, several of his associates, members of the Arizona Pioneer Home staff and Kristen Harnett M.A., AMSU graduate student.

[AUTHOR'S NOTE: The unmarked grave first exhumed was later called the South Grave, and was John Miller's.

Dr. Tunnell located the alleged gravesite of Mr. Miller prior to our arrival on the scene ... At approximately 1400 hours, a backhoe began to remove the sod overlying the alleged grave, which was oriented in an East-West direction, with the head to the West. When fragments of wood began to be removed, the grave was excavated using a shovel ... The left femoral shaft, minus the head, was removed, examined, and packaged for DNA analysis [the role of Rick Staub, Director of Orchid Cellmark].

[AUTHOR'S NOTE: Tunnell then changed his mind, and they dug up the adjacent, North Grave of William Hudspeth]

Dr. Tunnell, in consultation with the cemetery staff and his other associates determined that the adjacent grave to the North was likely that of Mr. Miller and excavation shifted to that gravesite ... The backhoe removed the overlying sod until fragments of wood began to be unearthed. The excavation shifted to shovels and the top of the casket was identified. Excavation proceeded using trowels and hand tools until various aspects of the skeleton were identified and cleared ... Skeletal elements were measured for depth and location, removed from the grave and examined ... **There were extensive healed traumata on the right**

scapula … The remains were photographed, samples were harvested for DNA (tooth and femur) [Note and the skull had teeth] remains were returned to the grave and reburied.

[AUTHOR'S NOTE: Fulginiti then had doubts about the North Grave's remains being John Miller's.]

Anecdotal historical information suggested that Mr. John Miller had died from complications of a fractured hip while recuperating in the Arizona pioneer Home. The individual in the north grave, while having extensive pathological conditions, particularly in the upper body, did not have discernible pathology of the *os coxae* [pelvis].

[AUTHOR'S NOTE: The North Grave's body had no pelvic damage to go with John Miller's broken hip. So they ravished the South Grave again.]

The south grave was excavated by shovel to the point where the remnants of the casket lid were identified. Excavation resumed using trowels and hand tools until the left femoral head was identified.

The head of the femur was misshapen with bony remodeling, suggesting an **antemortem injury** … The ischium [part of the pelvis] tapered to a point with lack of union to the pubis [another part of the pelvis], suggesting a healing fracture of the ischiopubic ramus. **This evidence led the team to believe that the individual in the south grave was, in fact, more consistent with the known facts regarding the Medical history of Mr. John Miller and additional DNA samples were recovered (femur, scalp [?], matter from inside the braincase).**

[AUTHOR'S NOTE: The South Grave was confirmed as Miller's because of its broken hip.]

The maxillae and mandible were recovered but were edentulous [had no teeth at all].

[AUTHOR'S NOTE: So Miller had NO TEETH. Random man Hudspeth had the "buck teeth" claimed as Billy the Kid's!"]

This was how Fulginiti revealed that the body in the North Grave its the bad scapula and alleged buck teeth was not Miller's! That was how she revealed that William Hudspeth had been dug up also. And the bad scapula and buck teeth were his! And his damaged scapula was the right one, not the left! And its damage was not from a bullet! So the hoaxers were switching "Scapula Man" (William Hudspeth) for John Miller ("Hip Man") for their fables to the press; a well as switching his right scapula as a left one!

THE CRIMINAL INVESTIGATION

Great effort went into blocking the criminal investigation for desecration of graves and grave-robbing begun by an Arizona citizen named David Snell. Yavapai County's Prescott City Prosecutor Glenn Savona had honestly pointed out that the "internal management" statute of the Pioneers' Home did not apply; nor did any law allow carrying off the remains to Texas. Also, he said there had been no necessary court order from Yavapai County Community Health Services Department or family permission. He indicated commission of felonies.

So the hoaxers got out of Yavapai County. They lied that Deputy Mike Poling, who had delivered to Dr. Fulginiti specimens from another case, then lent his metal detector at their request, was responsible for the exhumation! That meant that Yavapai County might have to prosecute *him*: making a conflict of interest. So the case was transferred to Maricopa County!

Since I was providing information at each stage, I was informed of the other ploy used by the hoaxers. They also claimed that Arizona Pioneers' Home Supervisor Jeanine Dike and Dale Tunnell were responsible for the exhumations. So Maricopa County opened Case No. 2006020516 against Dike and Tunnell! But I was told the names were just a filing formality.

In actuality, it would emerge that Governor Bill Richardson and Governor Janet Napolitano were pressuring Maricopa County's Chief Prosecutor Andrew Thomas to stop the case.

Unaware, from June 9, 2006 to October 17, 2006, I supplied the assigned Maricopa County Prosecutor, Deputy Attorney Jonnell Lucca, with hoax information, hoaxer names, and lack of DNA to justify any exhumation. Nevertheless, this corrupt official wrote to me on October 17, 2006: "Dear Dr. Cooper: This letter is to inform you that the Maricopa County Attorney's Office has **declined to file charges against Jeanine Dike and Dale Tunnell** as there is no reasonable likelihood of conviction in this case. There is no further information regarding the decision. Thank you for your interest in the case." So she pretended they were the only suspects. And she hid the felonious desecration and grave-robbing of William Hudspeth.

She had folded under Richardson's Santa Fe Ring-style racketeering. I owned a telling e-mail (obtained from its Lincoln County public official recipient), dated May 16, 2006, by gloating Steve Sederwall, feeling immune. It was signed with a smiley face symbol and "Steve." He stated:

Well **we have the governor reaching out to the Arizona [sic- missing word, Prosecutor?]** to stop this investigation. They thought we had the DNA [sic - illegible word follows] and they tried to get the FBI to get John Millers bones back with a warrant and get the DNA. They think we are going to announce that John Miller is the kid in France [an upcoming secret trip promoting the hoax]. We will not give them a break. They are now trying to get is [sic - us?] worked up about grave robbery charges. But being good cops we have all the docs that show the state of Arizona did the dig not us. How funny. if [sic] they do something stupid and file on us we sue and Arizona well [sic] be the state of Tom and Steve.

THE RAVAGED GRAVES

Not until my open records litigation, with subpoena of Orchid Cellmark Lab's records, was the extent of the graves' ravishment made apparent. Its Case No. 4444 (for Case 2003-274) January 26, 2009's "Laboratory Report, Forensic Identity, Mitochondrial Analysis: Evidence Received," confirmed the dismemberment of John Miller in the "South Grave," and William Hudspeth in the "North Grave." Torn from their bodies and destroyed for no reason for Dr. Rick Staub's bone-bags for transport back to Texas were: Miller's "skull and mummified brains," Miller's "pelvis," Miller's "left femur," Hudspeth's "mandible and teeth," and Hudspeth's "right femur." Even part of Miller's shattered casket had been taken. There was not much left in the graves.

And DNA extraction destroys much of the bones to get results. And the hoaxers would have known all along that they had no DNA of Billy the Kid to compare with anything. And they all had to know that one of the two bodies represented straightforward wanton desecration and grave-robbing of a random man (since there could not be two John Miller's)!

And Bill Kurtis Productions was filming all along. But this time he documented a crime scene. I was told the rumor that he subsequently destroyed or hid his footage.

THE DNA TRAVESTY

Of course, the Orchid Cellmark records were hidden by the hoaxers and Dr. Rick Staub. But my open records litigation, with subpoena of Orchid Cellmark Lab's records, gave the results they had obtained from their horror show exhumations.

Dr. Rick Staub, hiding that there was no Billy the Kid DNA for matching to justify exhumations, had told reporter Leo Banks, for his April 13, 2006 *Tucson Weekly* article "The New Billy the Kid?" that no DNA had been obtained from the John Miller specimens, and the only DNA came from random man, William Hudspeth! Nevertheless, by 2009, Orchid Cellmark claimed DNA extracted from John Miller's *and* William Hudspeth's femurs; meaning, by then, there had been a possible fix-up - like Orchid Cellmark's other DNA faking case: its scandal as reported in November 18, 2004's "TalkLeft.com," as "Fraud alleged at Cellmark, DNA Testing Firm," with illegal manipulation of data.

The Orchid Cellmark results of DNA testing from the Miller/Hudspeth exhumations were in January 26, 2009's "Laboratory Report - Forensic Identity – Mitochondrial Analysis," using the subsets of its in-house Case 4444 (for its Case No. 2003-274 specimens). Under its Case 4444-011, John Miller's left femur from the South Grave was reported as having "a mitochondrial DNA profile obtained." For pulverized William Hudspeth, Case 4444-012 from his North Grave's mandible and teeth indicated a useless mixed sample: "Consequently no sequence data are reported ... [P]rofiles are therefore inconclusive." However, **Hudspeth's Case 4444-013 North Grave's right femur yielded the "mitochondrial DNA profile obtained**," as originally admitted by Dr. Staub to reporter Leo Banks. Of course, there was no Billy the Kid DNA anyway for determining identity by matching (since the carpenter's bench yielded none, and could not be "reference DNA" anyway). So they had nothing.

Nevertheless, to Governor Napolitano, the hoaxers made-up a DNA match for John Miller. It was a double-talk lie, claiming a match of 80%; which has no forensic meaning - a match is 100%, meaning identical. And it was merely submitted to her office; and I got it by open records request. It was not publicized.

The hoaxers were hedging their bets, and hoping against convictions. And they really had not wanted to make Miller Billy the Kid anyway.

CHAPTER 7
TRYING TO DIG UP "BRUSHY BILL"

HEADING TO TEXAS WITH SHOVELS

In 2007, Governor Bill Richardson, seemed to have no adequately corrupt Texas contact; because Hamilton's mayor and town council refused exhumation of "Brushy Bill."

That Texas onslaught, like the Arizona one, was under Sheriff Rick Virden, using his Deputies, Tom Sullivan and Steve Sederwall. And they had another hurdle, compliments of me. In 2006, was my American Academy of Forensic Sciences Ethics Complaint against Dr. Henry Lee for hoaxing. Though the unethical Ethics Committee covered-up, Lee apparently stopped the hoaxer's using his name for the carpenter's bench DNA scam. So they could not claim having DNA to match with "Brushy's."

Nevertheless, Virden tried, writing in 2007 on his official stationery to Mayor Roy Rumsey, misspelling his name, but using lawman clout to try and get the job done. Virden wrote:

> Hamilton Texas
> Mayor Roy Ramsey
>
> Mayor Ramsey,
>
> This letter will inform you that Tom Sullivan and Steve Sederwall are both commissioned deputies with the Lincoln County New Mexico Sheriff's Department.
>
> They have been investigating case # 2003-274. Their investigation has been funded by them personally and has been conducted on their own time.
>
> Mr. Mayor, should you have any questions please do not hesitate to contact me.
>
> R.E. Virden
> Lincoln County Sheriff

Virden's double-talk was trying to cover all hoax bases. The "funded by them personally," came from my years of open records exposure of their tax-dollar squandering. And, "their own time" was part of their new switcheroo that it was not a law enforcement case at all, but their private hobby! That scam was to hide the DNA records from me, since turn-over was only legally demanded of public officials, not private citizens. That left Virden absurdly telling Rumsey that he was sending his deputies for his New Mexico murder case - which was really a hobby - but those deputies could dig up "Brushy," though his jurisdiction was Lincoln County, New Mexico; and certainly not Texas!

Mayor Rumsey did not have to decipher this craziness, since I had already told him that the circus was coming to town. Deputy Steve Sederwall met with him. Rumsey told me that he told Sederwall: "If 'Brushy Bill' is Billy the Kid, I'm Pancho Villa."

Rumsey added for the press in a May 5, 2007 *Houston Chronicle* article titled "DNA could solve the mystery of Billy the Kid": "Roberts was 'just a big windbag who went around telling stories. Few people, if anybody, believed him."

Sederwall had floated the hoax's new spin. The *Roswell Daily Record*, using a Stephenville, Texas, article, wrote on May 2, 2007, "Billy the Kid Exhumation a Possibility." "Sederwall said if DNA is allowed to be obtained from Roberts, investigators will pursue exhuming the body of Catherine McCarty Antrim, who researchers have confirmed was Billy the Kid's mother." (Omitted is that "Brushy" had said she was not his mother.)

On May 4th, for the hoax-backing *Albuquerque Journal's* "Manhunt for Real Billy the Kid Goes On: Deputy hopes DNA will finally reveal outlaw's true identity." Sederwall again blew smoke. "Those (Hamilton City) people want to know, they are not afraid ... You talk to Fort Sumner and they want to pull pistols on us. You talk to Hamilton City and they're like, 'Sure, we'd like to know.' "

On May 10, 2007, Hamilton's Town Council unanimously opposed exhumation; even though Texas's own "Brushy Bill" believer, Jannay Valdez - still pitching after his stint for Richardson for the June 5, 2003 *New York Times* - spoke for it.

But what if the hoaxers had gotten "Brushy's bones? Even Henry Lee might have returned with that lure. (Some old-timer could claim: "Didn't Gramps say that Billy the Kid had vomited on his saddle?"). And Orchid Cellmark's Dr. Rick Staub, could have "matched" Billy-vomit-DNA to "Brushy"-bones-DNA. Then there could be another TV show, and Bill Robins III could get the faked "Brushy" pardon. But I had kept the hoaxers at bay.

PART V

THE RETURN OF THE "BRUSHY BILL" HOAX'S FAKE DEATH SCENE AND DENIED CORONER'S JURY REPORT WITH FIX-UPS

CHAPTER 1
RETURN OF FAKERY IN *BILLY THE KID: BEYOND THE GRAVE*

ALLIANCE WITH "BILLY THE KID CASE" HOAXERS

"Brushy"-backing author, W.C. Jameson, had participated in the "Billy the Kid Case" hoax's 2004 Discovery Channel program: "Investigating History: Billy the Kid." Jameson's transcript of "Brushy's" Morrison tape recordings was quoted for the hoax's earliest "Probable Cause Statement" for Case 2003-274: the "Seventy-Seven Days of Doubt Document."

The hoaxers' chicanery apparently influenced him. By his 2005 *Billy the Kid: Beyond the Grave*, he was less the innocent who had co-authored 1998's *The Return of the Outlaw Billy the Kid.* He was emboldened to slip-in historical information "Brushy" had lacked. So he hid his *The Return of the Outlaw Billy the Kid*, with its starry-eyed accidental exposures, and proceeded to contradict his old self, hoping to go unnoticed and better sell "Brushy."

THE HOAXBUSTING DEATH SCENE MOON OF JULY 14, 1881

Despite his many dishonest fix-ups of "Brushy" in *Billy the Kid: Beyond the Grave*, Jameson was still ignorant "Brushy's" fatal moon error proving he was not in Fort Sumner on the night of July 14, 1881 for his fake death scene. Jameson used "Brushy's" original construct of an accidental killing of Billy Barlow mistaken as "Brushy" **because the moonless night was so dark**.

Thus, for this book, still honestly portraying "Brushy's" original transcript, Jameson wrote: "**William Henry Roberts**

recalled that the night was dark but there was enough moonlight to make shadows." (Page 57) And after "Brushy was shot, Jameson quoted from "Brushy's" transcript: "**I lost my footing and fell on my face in the darkness**." (Page 61) And from the transcript came "Brushy's" stating: "**Garrett knew by now that he killed the wrong man in the dark.**" (Page 64)

This dark night matched Jameson's *The Return of the Outlaw Billy the Kid*, which had "Brushy" say: **"[After hearing the shot from Pete Maxwell's place] I pulled one of my .44's and ran through the door, trying to see in the dark. Two more shots came from the shadow beside the Maxwell house. I couldn't find a target. It was too dark to see."** (*The Return of the Outlaw Billy the Kid*, Page 112) That dark night was repeated in that book in "Brushy's" quote explaining Billy Barlow's killing: **"Garrett knew by now that he'd killed the wrong man in the dark."** (*The Return of the Outlaw Billy the Kid*, Page 117)

"Brushy's transcript of the death scene was also used in the "Seventy-Seven Days of Doubt" Probable Cause Statement by "Billy the Kid Case" hoaxers, Lincoln County Sheriff Tom Sullivan and his Deputy, Steve Sederwall. Like Jameson, they were still unaware of "Brushy's" fatal error. So they quoted him: "*I had spent the day with Garrett's brother-in-law, Saval Gutierrez. Nearly all the people in this country were my friends and they helped me. None of them liked Garrett.* ***It was dark that night, but there was enough moonlight to make shadows.*** *Me and my partner Billy Barlow, rode up to Jesus Silva's house when we reached Fort Sumner.*" Sullivan and Sederwall continued: "While Roberts and Jesus [Silva] were lighting the wood stove they hear [sic] gunfire in the direction of Pete Maxwell's place. Roberts' statement goes on to describe the following events: "***I pulled one of my .44's and ran through the door, trying to see in the dark. Two more shots came from a shadow beside the Maxwell house. I couldn't find a target to shoot at. It was too dark to see.*** *I ran toward Maxwell's back porch. I heard another gunshot and felt something hit me in the jaw. I stumbled and kept on running ... I tasted blood and spit the mess out of my mouth as* ***I started emptying my six-shooter at the shadow where I saw the muzzleflash****. From the corner of my eye I saw a body lying on the back porch ... I knew it had to be Barlow ... My mouth and shoulder were bleeding and I lost track of where I was, but I knew I had to get away from Maxwell's before they killed me. I heard a shout and another gunshot. Something passed across my forehead like a hot branding iron. I was stunned.* ***I lost footing and fell on my face in the***

darkness. *I knew I was hurt bad and wondered if I would make it out of this scrape alive.*"

But, as stated above, Morrison and Sonnichsen had caught "Brushy's" error, likely from reading John William Poe's 1933 *The Death of Billy the Kid*, which stated about July 14, 1881: **"[T]he moon was shining very brightly."** (Poe, Page 28) For *Alias Billy the Kid*, taking no chances, they even titled the death scene chapter "**Death by Moonlight**;" and dishonestly changed "Brushy's" words to: "I ran through the gate into Maxwell's back yard **in the bright moonlight**." (*Alias Billy the Kid*, Page 49)

That confused Jameson, who forgot "Brushy's" words, which he had himself quoted, so he added the Sonnichsen-Morrison text to *Billy the Kid: Beyond the Grave's* death scene; writing: "Roberts, **easily seen in the moonlit yard,** drew return fire from the lawmen." (Page 41)

But Jameson, next allying with "Billy the Kid Case" hoaxers, for subsequent books, would never again reveal the moon error. But it was too late. **Every time he lied about "Brushy's" death scene by adding bright moonlight," it branded his hoaxing.**

OTHER DEATH SCENE FIX-UPS

Jameson, however, did other fix-ups to "Brushy's" death scene to mold "Brushy" into a better Billy the Kid.

CELSA GUTIERREZ AS OMNISCIENT NARRATOR

Claiming "Brushy's" quote, Jameson faked Celsa Gutierrez's omniscient description of the death scene aftermath; one she would not know. Pseudo-Celsa stated that Garrett and his deputies feared to leave Maxwell's house because Billy's friends would shoot them; Garrett set a trap expecting Billy's visit; Garrett killed bearded Barlow but passed him off as Billy; Garrett had the grave dug by lantern light; and Deluvina was crying to pretend Billy was shot. So "Brushy" realized that Garrett was hiding the corpse identity to collect the reward. (Pages 63-64)

A clairvoyant narrator would get even weirder in seven years in Jameson's 2012's *Billy the Kid: The Lost Tapes*; when he created a new character - Frank Lobato - for pseudo-"Brushy" to quote about information from Garrett's and Poe's books, plus the "Brushy" hoax's conspiracy theories! (See page 289 below)

CLAIMING KIP McKINNEY DENIED THE CORPSE AS BILLY BONNEY'S

Jameson tried to contradict the historical death scene by stating that John William Poe and "Kip" McKinney denied the corpse was Billy Bonney's. (Page 109) First of all, Poe and McKinney were irrelevant, since the July 15, 1881 Coroner's Jury Report confirmed William Bonney as killed; as did Pat Garrett, Peter Maxwell, Deluvina Maxwell, and about 200 townspeople. And Poe did not know Billy. As to McKinney, Jameson recycled William V. Morrison's double hearsay account in a June 29, 1855 letter to a William Waters, claiming that McKinney's cousin had said that McKinney had told relatives that *he* McKinney had "killed the man in Maxwell's bedroom 'by mistake and that the Kid got away.' " (Pages 70-71) Jameson ignored or forgot that this McKinney fakery did not match "Brushy's" own fake back-porch-Barlow death scene.

CLAIMING BILLY BARLOW AS HISTORICAL

Jameson states that Billy Barlow was the innocent victim. And the fact that he was discredited as being non-historical is explained by his name being an alias – which leaves out that the whole death scene is fake! (Pages 109-110)

CLAIMING THE DEATH SCENES OF GARRETT AND POE DO NOT AGREE

Jameson used the original "Brushy" hoax's faked "discrepancies" (as also seen in the "Billy the Kid Case's Probable Cause Statement" to claim disagreement between the Garrett and Poe accounts), in hopes of "proving" they were lying, and Billy's killing did not occur. This fabrication also concealed the Coroner's Jury Report and profuse identification of the body as Billy's. Conversely, where Garrett's and Poe's accounts concurred, Jameson accused them of conspiring to hide truth!

OUTCOME

All that W.C. Jameson proved in *Billy the Kid: Beyond the Grave* was his cross-over to hoaxing as best he could with his historical ignorance.

CHAPTER 2
FURTHER FAKERY IN *BILLY THE KID: THE LOST INTERVIEWS*

FAKING "BRUSHY'S" WORDS

By his 2012 *Billy the Kid: The Lost Interviews*, Jameson had descended to active hoaxing, possibly explained by his new alliance with past "Billy the Kid Case" hoaxers for creating his books. In his 2018 book, *Cold Case Billy the Kid*, he described making a relationship with Steve Sederwall in 2006; stating that he knew "by reputation," from newspapers and TV, that "his aggressive investigations into a variety of Billy the Kid-related events ... were based on solid police work, and they differed, sometimes dramatically, from established history." Jameson added that Sederwall "irritated" "self-anointed experts," but ignored them. (*Cold Case*, Page v) For *The Lost Interviews*, Jameson enthused in his "Preface" about Sederwall as a "retired federal investigator ... separating truth from legend ... who treated ... Billy the Kid-related events as historic cold cases ... and got "information and facts heretofore unknown." Of course, the "Billy the Kid Case" went unmentioned. But adulating Jameson had added Sederwall to his pantheon of "Brushy," Morrison, and Sonnichsen. I exposed this hoaxing in my 2019 *The Cold Case Billy the Kid Megahoax: The Plot to Steal Billy the Kid's Identity and to Defame Sheriff Pat Garrett as a Murderer*.

For the flagrantly hoaxed *The Lost Interviews* book, even the title is misleading by implying newly found, convincing, "lost interviews" of "Brushy Bill."

In fact, they were just the taped 1949-1950 Morrison interviews that Sonnichsen had used to write *Alias Billy the Kid*; and that Jameson's original co-author, Frederick Bean, had located in 1989, and were quoted in their *The Return of the*

Outlaw Billy the Kid from Bean's transcript of them. What was new was that Jameson now secretly re-wrote "Brushy's" words from them to create a pseudo-"Brushy" stating updated information (with modern Billy the Kid history books listed in a Bibliography), correcting his past errors, and himself mouthing the hoax's conspiracy theories.

FIXING-UP THE DEATH SCENE

The key death scene is now rewritten - without informing the readers. Jameson makes-up that impressive evidence had accumulated since "Brushy's" day proving that he was Billy the Kid; that only Garrett identified the Fort Sumner corpse; that there was no "inquest;" that the dark-skinned bearded body in the casket proved it was not Billy Bonney **[using uncited Grant County newspaperman Singleton Ashenfelter's fake description first floated by Sonnichsen]**; that the burial was hurried to hide the body's identity; and that people saw live Billy after the burial. And the now hoaxing Jameson lies that Morrison introduced "Brushy" to "veterans of the Lincoln County War" who "immediately recognized" him as Billy the Kid. (Page 11) **[There were none. He is faking the fake Affidavits of non-War participants in *Alias Billy the Kid*. And, this time around, they are hidden to block checking.]**

"Brushy's" confabulated Billy Barlow killing scene is given, but with a clumsy attempt to make sense of the Ashenfelter swarthy bearded corpse, by calling Barlow looking so much like fair unbearded Roberts to be mistaken for him, except for dark skin and beard! Barlow is now killed in a vague location "near Pete Maxwell's bedroom," instead of "Brushy's" give-away-for-faking with his back-porch-Barlow. He then has "Brushy" rushing to the scene and getting some gunshot wounds, then being helped by two women and a Frank Lobato.

The major weakness in the original "Brushy Bill" hoax, had been its threadbare death scene, lacking explanation for why his Billy Barlow was killed on the back porch (it having been fed to "Brushy" from Sonnichsen's fake Jack Fountain interview), and omitting the Maxwell bedroom scene.

Jameson's solution was having his pseudo-"Brushy" himself present Sonnichsen's conspiracy theories against Pat Garrett. And, apparently feeling above detection, Jameson also had his pseudo-"Brushy" insert "Billy the Kid Case" hoax claims, coming either from his own involvement with that hoax, or from "Billy the Kid Case" hoaxer, Steve Sederwall's, input.

All this exposes active hoaxing and a forged transcript; with forgery defined by *Duhaime Legal Dictionary* as "[t]he making of a false document knowing it to be false with intent that it should be used or acted on as genuine to the prejudice of another." These are examples:

1) "Brushy" has a long passage before the Fort Sumner shooting saying he wanted to "have a talk with Mr. Pat Garrett" to set things "straight between us" because "[w]e used to be friends before the Lincoln County War." (Page 121)

FAKING THE TRANSCRIPT: This was not in *Alias Billy the Kid.* But it fabricates a friendship between "Brushy" and Pat Garrett like in the "Billy the Kid Case" hoax. "Brushy's" version merely had an accidental killing of Billy Barlow, when Garrett was trying to kill *him.*

2) "Brushy" says about the shooting: "I pulled one of my .44's and ran through the door, trying to see in the dark. I ran through the gate into Maxwell's back yard **into the bright moonlight**. Two more shots came from a shadow beside the Maxwell house. I started shooting at the shadows along the house." (Page 124)

EXPOSING JAMESON AS A HOAXER BY HIS FAKED TRANSCRIPT: "Brushy's" fatal error had been making-up that July 14, 1881 had a dark night. In fact it had unusually intense moonlight. That moonlight was the hoaxers' undoing, as they fraudulently rewrote his words to hide his fatal mistake. One should, however, note that "Brushy's fable was well thought out. His tall tale was that Billy Barlow was mistaken for him *because* the night was so dark, making the killing accidental. Bright moonlight was incompatible with his fabrication!

In *Alias Billy the Kid*, Morrison and Sonnichsen, taking no chances with "Brushy's" bad mistake, titled the death scene chapter "Death by Moonlight." (*Alias Billy the Kid,* Page 48) So "Brushy" is quoted: "I ran through the gate into Maxwell's back yard in the bright moonlight." (*Alias Billy the Kid,* Page 49)

But for their 1998, *Return of the Outlaw Billy the Kid,* Jameson and Frederick Bean were just naïve true-believers, quoting from Bean's transcript of "Brushy's" tapes, as the gospel words of Billy the Kid. So they were accidentally honest, presenting "Brushy's" dark and moonless night.

But first, they had copied equally idolized Sonnichsen's fixed-up text for: "Billy, easily seen in the moonlit yard, immediately drew return fire from the lawmen." (*Return of the Outlaw,* Page 73) Then, unaware that the moonlight was fatal, they honestly quoted "Brushy" from the transcript: "[After hearing the shot from Pete Maxwell's place] I pulled one of my .44's and ran through the door, trying to see in the dark. Two more shots came from the shadow beside the Maxwell house. I couldn't find a target. It was too dark to see." (*Return of the Outlaw,* Page 112) And they repeated his dark night quote as his explanation for the killing of Barlow: "Garrett knew by now that he'd killed the wrong man in the dark." (*Return of the Outlaw,* Page 117) Thus, they accidentally proved the dishonest Morrison-Sonnichsen fix-up.

But a more debased Jameson now hid "Brushy's" error. To trick readers, as Morrison and Sonnichsen had intended, he deleted "Brushy's" disastrous quote in his own book, *The Return of the Outlaw Billy the Kid,* stating: "I pulled one of my .44's and ran through the door, trying to see in the dark. Two more shots came from the shadow beside the Maxwell house. I couldn't find a target. It was too dark to see." (*Return of the Outlaw,* Page 112)

For *Billy the Kid: The Lost Interviews,* all Jameson used was: "I pulled one of my .44's and ran through the door, trying to see in the dark. I ran through the gate into Maxwell's back yard into the bright moonlight" – adding "bright moonlight," which "Brushy" never said. This is despicable and willful forgery to hide that "Brushy" could not have been in Fort Sumner on the night of July 14, 1881.

Nevertheless, hoaxing Jameson still seemed unaware of just how dangerous to the hoax the error was, since he was careless in "cleaning up" all "Brushy's quotes. Later in the text, he fabricated "Brushy" ruminating to Morrison about the Billy Barlow killing (adding "half-Mex" to Barlow's

background to go with S.M. Ashenfelter's newspaper article's swarthy corpse). Here Jameson has "Brushy" repeat the darkness: **"Barlow looked a little like me but he was half-Mex. I could imagine Garrett couldn't tell us apart in the real dark, except Barlow had a beard."** (Page 133)

3) "Brushy" is quoted about the location of the side of beef at Maxwell's house: "Silva said if one of us would go over to Maxwell's and get beef, he would cook it for us. He said Maxwell had one on his back porch hanging from a rafter hook, killed on the day before ..." (Page 123) "[After hearing shots] [f]rom the corner of my eye I saw a body lying on the back porch. A candle was lit in the alcove where the beef was hung and I knew it had to be Barlow." (Page 124)

EXPOSING JAMESON AS A HOAXER BY HIS FORGED TRANSCRIPT: In *Alias Billy the Kid* and *The Return of the Outlaw Billy the Kid*, "Brushy" says only: **"One of their shots had killed my partner on the back porch."** (*Alias Billy the Kid,* Page 49; *The Return of the Outlaw*, Page 113)

Revealed in Jameson's made-up "Brushy" quote is even more extreme hoaxing: fabricating these scenes as "Brushy's" words. He was trying to fix-up "Brushy's" - and Sonnichsen's and Morrison's - fatal ignorance about the lay-out of Fort Sumner and the Maxwell house. So the "back porch" is a clue to hoaxing going back to Sonnichsen's and Morrison's prompting by sources that revealed themselves by fatal errors when "Brushy" used then for his fables.

The problem these first liars had, was not knowing the location of Maxwell's bedroom or the side of beef. So Sonnichsen got that from a provided footnote. It was an apocryphal tale told to him by Jack Fountain (Albert Jennings Fountain's son) in an April 15, 1944 interview. Jack said that Garrett said the beef hung beside Maxwell's bedroom from which Garrett saw Billy and killed him outside the room. This is Jack's made-up Garrett quote: **"The beef was hanging in a little outer room from the vigas. There was a candle and materials for making a light in the niche in the wall. [Billy] made a light and held it up while he cut.**

I was in Pete's room, talking. Billy heard something and asked Pete who was there. Pete said, 'Nobody.' I looked out at a perfect target - Billy lighting himself up with a candle ... I thought if he ever got his gun it was him or me. My conscience bothers me about it now." (*Alias Billy the Kid,* Page 49)

When given to "Brushy" as a prompt, he simply made-up that the connected bedroom and beef were at the "back porch." And, using the rest of Jack Fountain's fable, he put the shot victim (Billy Barlow) outside that room. So this explained "Brushy's" weird death scene's ignoring the shooting inside the Maxwell bedroom.

But equally ignorant Jameson, accepting "Brushy's" fable and Sonnichsen's fake footnote, fixed-up by putting the footnote into "Brushy's" mouth to make sense of the absurd scene. Instead, he merely proved that he had faked the transcript.

4) "Brushy" is "quoted" for a two page description of being shot and running down a long "alley" behind the Maxwell house to an "adobe shack." (Pages 125-126)

FAKING THE TRANSCRIPT: This is not in *Alias Billy the Kid*; which only stated: "I stumbled into the gallery of an adobe behind Maxwell's yard fence." (*Alias Billy the Kid,* Page 49) Morrison-Sonnichsen may have omitted it as too revealing of "Brushy's" utter ignorance of the Maxwell property and Fort Sumner buildings; or Jameson may have added it to justify "Brushy's" claims of being shot there, since he quotes him saying about one of his faked head wounds: "That's this scar here." (Page 125)

5) "Brushy" says about his rescue that when he came to he saw "another woman in the room ... She was another of Saval's sisters, named Celsa, and she had been a sweetheart of mine at one time." (Page 127)

FAKING THE TRANSCRIPT: This is not in *Alias Billy the Kid* at this location, but was "Brushy's" Celsa-Saval-sibling mistake which he made earlier in that book.

Fortunately, Jameson's utter historical ignorance limited his fix-ups of "Brushy's" fatal errors. In fact, Celsa was Saval Gutierrez's wife, with "Brushy" and his original hoaxing team misled by Saval's being called Garrett's

brother-in-law by being married to one of Celsa's sisters, Apolinaria. But that did not make Apolinaria Saval's sister. It made Garrett his brother-in-law by marriage.

6) "Brushy" quotes Celsa telling him that Garrett and his men stayed at Maxwell's house after the shooting: "She said, 'They are afraid to come out in the dark, afraid of being mobbed. They think some of your friends may try to shoot them. You have many friends here, Billy. Pat and his men say they won't leave the house until early daylight." (Page 128)

FAKING THE TRANSCRIPT: This fixed-up *Alias Billy the Kid's*: "She said they would not leave Maxwell's house for the night. They were afraid of being mobbed." (*Alias Billy the Kid*, Page 50) It was lifted from John W. Poe's 1933 *The Death of Billy the Kid*; which stated: "We spent the remainder of the night on the Maxwell premises, keeping constantly on our guard, as we were expecting to be attacked by friends of the dead man." (Poe, Page 44) Noteworthy is that real Celsa would not have known this information.

7) "Brushy" says: "Celsa confirmed what I had guessed. Garrett and a posse had been laying for me over at Maxwell's. They knew Pete and I were friends and that I'd stop by to see him if I was in this country. Me and Barlow rode into town late and I figured Mrs. Maxwell was already in bed by the time we got there. I aimed to talk to Pete in the morning." (Page 128)

FAKING THE TRANSCRIPT: This is not in *Alias Billy the Kid*. It appears to be a made-up quote by Jameson to explain why "Brushy" went to Peter Maxwell's room. But Jameson's historical ignorance made him unaware that real Billy had been hiding-out, since his jailbreak, on Maxwell's property's sheep camps; so Jameson had "Brushy" merely visiting "the country."

8) "Brushy" says: "Celsa said, 'Don't worry, Billy. Pat is telling everyone that you are dead. They took the body of your friend inside the house and they say it is yours. Some of the men in town have already been sent to dig a grave by lantern light. Jesus is building a coffin in the carpenter's shop. Deluvina Maxwell is crying and carrying on, but she knows Pat killed the

wrong man ... Your partner looks very much like you in the dark except for his beard. His eyes are blue like yours, Billy. Pat says they will bury the body in the morning. If the coffin is closed, who will guess that you are not inside it?' I couldn't figure it right then, hearing what Celsa was saying about Garrett. Was he trying to pass off Barlow's body as mine? We were friends. He knew the body was not mine, so why was he telling everybody that he had killed me?" (Page 129)

FAKING THE TRANSCRIPT: This is not in *Alias Billy the Kid*, which merely stated: "Celsa came running in and said they had killed Barlow and they were passing off his body as mine." (*Alias Billy the Kid*, Page 50) Jameson appears to be making-up "Brushy's" dialogue to encompass the entire hoax: the body taken into the house (to correspond with history); Deluvina Maxwell being in on the conspiracy to hide the body's identity; the burial rushed by dishonest Garrett to hide corpse identity; and a resemblance of Barlow to "Brushy," with even the "beard" from S.M. Ashenfelter's fake article on the body. But amusingly, Jameson forgets the "bright moonlight," and has Celsa to say: "Your partner looks very much like you in the dark."

Important to note is that even in Jameson's expanded death scene, there is no match to the "Billy the Kid Case" hoax, with which he was allying. The latter had Billy's super-friend, Garrett, purposefully shoot *him* for playing dead on the carpenter's bench (to leave "blood" for Dr. Henry Lee's future DNA fakery); then had Billy sneak off while evil Garrett *replaced him on the bench* with the murdered innocent victim - not necessarily Billy Barlow. Desperate Jameson had climbed in with incompatible bed-fellows, but now matched them in his scornful intent to trick his reader-dupes.

9) "Brushy" says in answer to a Morrison question about Garrett's claim of killing Billy the Kid: "I wondered how he figured to get away with it. I had lots of friends in town. Would they go along with Garrett's ploy. Garrett knew by now he had killed the wrong man in the dark ... [Barlow looked like me] [b]ut in daylight, a lot of folks who knew me would know they had the wrong body. I couldn't figure it, unless Garrett was making a try at collecting the reward ... [He] was out of his

bailiwick in San Miguel County. Hilario Romero was sheriff there ... Sheriff Romero would have to appoint a coroner's jury to sign the death certificate, not Garrett ... [T]hey would have trouble rounding up a coroner's jury that didn't know what I looked like." (Pages 130-131)

FAKING THE TRANSCRIPT: This is not in *Alias Billy the Kid.* It appears made-up by Jameson to put his and Sonnichsen's fake conspiracy theories in pseudo-"Brushy's" mouth: Garrett hid the corpse identity to collect the Billy the Kid reward; Garrett was out of his jurisdiction; and no Coroner's Jury had been called, since it was Sheriff Romero's responsibility.

10) "Brushy" states that there was another reason for Garrett being in trouble: that Barlow had a .41 double action revolver, which he himself would not use because they jam. (Page 131)

FAKING THE TRANSCRIPT: This is not in *Alias Billy the Kid.* It appears to be Jameson's fiction to set-up his future claim that Garrett lied about the gun with Billy's body. It is also wrong, since the .41 caliber, double action Colt Thunderer was used by Billy and others as a back-up hide-away, preferable to a single shot derringer; and it did not cast doubt on Garrett's claim of its being with Billy.

11) "Brushy" ruminates about Garrett digging a grave the night of the killing to hide that the body was Barlow's, since killing Billy the Kid would have made him famous and he would have showed off the body. And he claims gravedigger Jesus Silva, who knew him, kept secret the body's identity. (Pages 131-132)

FAKING THE TRANSCRIPT: This is not in *Alias Billy the Kid.* It appears to be Jameson's fiction to set up his and Sonnichsen's conspiracy theorizing about Garrett hiding the corpse's identity for personal gain.

12) "Brushy" says: "**It crossed my mind that Garrett might be trying to help me. We'd been friends once,** back when he first came to this country." (Page 132) "Brushy" continues that, as Lincoln County Sheriff, Garrett had to pursue him, but wonders if "he saw his chance to let me get away clean and make a fresh start for myself'" by killing Billy Barlow. (Pages 132-133)

EXPOSING JAMESON AS A COMPLICIT "BILLY THE KID CASE" HOAXER BY HIS FAKED TRANSCRIPT: This is not in *Alias Billy the Kid.* This shockingly appears to be Jameson's making-up quotes to make "Brushy" fit the "Billy the Kid Case" hoax - which relied on a fake Garrett friendship motive for the innocent victim killing to let Billy go free.

It should be noted that this book first came out in 2012, and Jameson was a participant in the latter hoax since 2004; and hoaxer, Steve Sederwall, was also participating with him for this book. As will be seen, Jameson's unwieldy fusing that hoax, and its hoaxers, to his "Brushy" hoaxing culminated six years later in his *Cold Case Billy the Kid.*

Used here, however, it contradicts original "Brushy's" own description of Garrett's effort to kill him as Billy the Kid. As Jameson's own "Brushy" text quoted: "My partner walked right into the trap, and the trap had likely been set for me ... I knew I had to get away from Maxwell's before they killed me." (Pages 124-125) And Jameson himself had first stuck to the theme of Garrett's intent to kill "Brushy" as Billy, by the quote: "Barlow looked a little like me but he was half-Mex. I could imagine Garrett couldn't tell us apart in the real dark, except Barlow had a beard." (Page 133) That meant Garrett intended to kill the Kid in the world according to "Brushy." Jameson could not keep his hoaxing straight.

13) "Brushy" is quoted that Garrett could keep the corpse identity secret because the only people who knew it was not him were Celsa, Jesus Silva, the Mexican woman who took him in, and a Frank Lobato; and they would keep a secret.

FAKING THE TRANSCRIPT: This is not in *Alias Billy the Kid.* It appears to be Jameson's fiction to have pseudo-"Brushy" mouth conspiracy theories of Sonnichsen and himself. Of course, this maintains the "Brushy" hoax's key lies of hiding both the night vigil over Billy's body and his Coroner's Jury Report.

14) "Brushy" states a flashback of a **Frank Lobato** having checked Fort Sumner and reporting to him that Barlow's body had been taken to the carpenter's shop wrapped in a sheet to hide its identity; Poe could not recognize him, so could not identify the

body; Garrett sealed the house to prevent viewing of the body; and a "coroner's jury was appointed to sign the death certificate so Garrett could file for the reward." "Brushy" adds that there were two coroner's jury reports, with the first lost and Garrett making people sign a second with different signers; that Milnor Rudulph was not the real president, and never viewed the body. And he says Garrett succeeded by burying Barlow in the Billy the Kid grave, and by taking the fake coroner's jury report to Santa Fe to get his reward. (Pages 134-135)

EXPOSING JAMESON AS AN ACTIVE HOAXER AND COMPLICIT WITH THE "BILLY THE KID CASE" HOAX BY HIS FAKED TRANSCRIPT: This obviously fabricated flashback quote, is not in *Alias Billy the Kid;* and adds omniscient Lobato to omniscient pseudo-Celsa in *Billy the Kid: Beyond the Grave.* (See page 277 above) It is an awkward fix-up to match the "Brushy" hoax to the "Billy the Kid Case" hoax's faking DNA from the carpenter's bench by putting Barlow's body on it, hiding the body with a sheet to counter the townspeople's viewing in the vigil, and announcing a fake coroner's jury merely to shield Garrett. For the "Brushy" hoax, it puts into pseudo-"Brushy's" mouth Sonnichsen's fake conspiracy theory of two coroner's jury reports derived from the windbag malarkey of A.P. "Paco" Anaya.

This is now brazenly out-of-control hoaxing and forging of "Brushy's" transcript. But it ridiculously requires sheepherder, Frank Lobato, to know insiders' information about a cover-up of the innocent victim. And, if real non-insider Lobato had found it out, it would prove general gossip among townspeople, and no postulated conspiracy of them all to keep the secret that Pat Garrett did not kill Billy the Kid!

DISCUSSION

Jameson's give-away for intentional and premeditated trickery was his altering his own rendition of "Brushy's" quoting the death scene in his 1998 *The Return of the Outlaw Billy the Kid.* There "Brushy" confabulated the night of July 14, 1881 as dark and moonless - eliminating any chance of his having been there.

(And even Morrison and Sonnichsen had fixed that up for *Alias Billy the Kid* as "bright moonlight.")

But Jameson undoes his earlier honesty to add "bright moonlight" for this *Billy the Kid: The Lost Interviews.* And, as if that chicanery broke the dam for honesty, out poured his fictionalized "Brushy" quotes supporting his own and Sonnichsen's conspiracy theories, as well as the main elements of the "Billy the Kid Case" hoax!

Jameson had apparently crossed-over to no-holds-barred flimflam to attain his goal of "Brushy" as Billy. And this book ends with Jameson stating: "Steve Sederwall's ongoing research and investigative work applied to Billy the Kid and the Lincoln County war continues to yield new and exciting results." (In "Acknowledgments") Sederwall would now be in the driver's seat for Jameson's books.

CHAPTER 3 ACCUSING GARRETT IN *PAT GARRETT: THE MAN BEHIND THE BADGE* OF A FAKED DEATH SCENE AND NO CORONER'S JURY REPORT

THE GARRETT CASE HOAX

W.C. Jameson's 2016 *Pat Garrett: The Man Behind the Badge*, focuses character assassination on Pat Garrett, in illogical hope that if he was unpleasant enough, it meant he killed the innocent victim and "Brushy was surviving Billy the Kid! Added was a fake death scene and claim of no Coroner's Jury Report.

And, though not a co-author, Steve Sederwall was Jameson's acknowledged source; as he wrote: "Intrepid investigator Steve Sederwall turned over more stones and found more pertinent information and evidence regarding Pat Garrett ... Billy the Kid, and others than all the so-called experts put together." (Page 223) So the "Billy the Kid Case" hoax's forensic fakery now is added, with sly alterations to "Brushy's" hoax for match-ups. And adding to the ridiculousness, is that a quoted authority, contradicting Garrett's version of events, will now be "Brushy" himself – with his made-up name of "William Henry Roberts aka Billy the Kid!"

As sneaky, Jameson now also relied for "evidence" on his own forged transcripts of "Brushy's" Morrison tapes from his 2012 *Billy the Kid: The Lost Interviews.*, Jameson was well on his way to his 2018 megahoax book: *Cold Case Billy the Kid.*

THE FAKE DEATH SCENE

Amusingly, right from the start, wised-up and hoaxing Jameson was taking no more chances with "Brushy's" fatal error of the "dark night," which the more honest version of himself had put in his 1998 *The Return of the Outlaw Billy the Kid*, and repeated in his 2005 *Billy the Kid: Beyond the Grave.* He now officiously announced July 14, 1881's moon was full three nights earlier, in waning phase, with 87 percent brightness! (Page x)

And the defamation of Pat Garrett characterizing this book, concludes that he was famous for an act he "did not perform": killing Billy the Kid. Resistance to this "truth," was attributed to a "reigning clique" of historians. (Pages 200-201) The ghostwritten *The Authentic Life of Billy the Kid* is unsurprisingly claimed as not an authoritative. (Pages 98-100) This leads to the usual fake reasoning: *if* Garrett had fiction in it, he also made-up the killing; so "Brushy" was Billy the Kid, and the body was Billy Barlow's!

So the key Fort Sumner shooting event gets much attention, it being make-or-break for both the "Brushy" and "Billy the Kid Case" hoaxes. A fix-up is adding Paulita Maxwell as Billy's girlfriend to explain why Billy returned to Fort Sumner (Page 66); though that was unknown to "Brushy," with his made-up Celsa Gutierrez girlfriend. Information from Pat Garrett's *The Authentic Life of Billy the Kid* and John W. Poe's *The Death of Billy the Kid* is manipulated to fabricate discrepancies, from the stake-out of the Maxwell house, to the shooting scene in Peter Maxwell's bedroom. Faked by a Steve Sederwall "investigation," is that **Peter Maxwell's bedroom had no door to the outside**, so a door's being in accounts of Garrett, Poe, and Maxwell, meant they were all liars, and the death scene never happened!

FAKERY: The no outside door fakery came with an undated, unreferenced, untitled sketch in the glossy print section, claiming to be the Maxwell house. It was reused when this fakery was repeated in *Cold Case Billy the Kid*. It is debunked there. (See pages 306-312 below) But the diagram was of the 1860's Fort Sumner Commanding Officer's quarters. And ignored was that Lucien Maxwell rebuilt it as his home in 1870, adding the door.

Of course, the identification of the body is claimed as in doubt. (Pages 69-70) To cast doubt on the historical version, fabricated are "discrepancies," "contradictions," no "inquest," Poe doubting the identity of the body, and a questionable "burial." (Pages 71-97)

"William Henry Roberts aka Billy the Kid" as the expert, provides his alternative version with shot-back-porch-Billy-Barlow, though expanded from his original fable with Jameson's forged transcripts of his words from *Billy the Kid: The Lost Interviews*! (Page 72)

And for doubting the bedroom scene, used are fake hearsay accounts of Charles Frederick Rudulph, from his reprinted manuscript in 1980's *Los Billitos: The Story of Billy the Kid and His Gang*; and of a Bundy Avant (misspelled as "Bud Avants," from his unreferenced old-timer malarkey in a 1978 *True West* article: "The Bundy Avant Story"); and C.L. Sonnichsen's hearsay interview with Jack Fountain. (Pages 80, 83) Jameson's conclusion is: "[T]here is little corroborative, logical evidence on which to base the claim that Billy the Kid was shot and killed by Sheriff Pat Garrett on the night of July 14, 1881." (Page 84) And this means to Jameson that "Brushy" survived as Billy, with proof being William V. Morrison's original fake Affidavits. (Page 85) Concluded is that "no shred of evidence" proves Billy the Kid was killed on July 14, 1881, and "Pat Garrett lied about the entire incident." (Page 86) Jameson adds: "[C]ompelling evidence suggests the body was that of Billy Barlow." (Page 96)

FAKERY: This Charles Rudulph and Bundy Avant fakery, apparently by Sederwall, was repeated in two years in Jameson's culminating "Brushy" plus "Billy the Kid Case" megahoax: *Cold Case Billy the Kid*. For it, I debunked these claims in detail. (See pages 316-319 below)

The "Billy the Kid Case's" hoaxed forensics with Dr. Henry Lee's fake washstand investigation is first slipped in for the Maxwell bedroom death scene to ruminate about where Garrett's second shot ended up, while hiding that it hit the wall and bed's headboard. So Lee's fabricated washstand scenario is presented as if fact; saying that Garrett must be lying about his position in the shooting, since his bullet perforated a washstand "fifteen feet" away "at an angle that indicted he was on his knees in the far corner of the room when he fired." As to the search by Garrett, Poe and McKinney for the second bullet strike, it was claimed Garrett would have hidden the washstand holes, because they proved a different positioning than his lie. (Page 76)

FAKERY: This brazen hoaxing is intended to dupe readers into thinking it is accepted history. They are not informed that the "washstand" was an unsubstantiated little box with two holes, from a teenaged girl's 1920's amateur tourist museum in a Fort Sumner shed, and alleging to have Peter Maxwell's bedroom furniture. Nor are readers told that the Maxwell house no longer exists, and the placement of that made-up "washstand" was also made-up by complicit "Billy the Kid Case" hoaxer, Dr. Henry Lee. The intent is defaming Garrett as a liar by fabricating a different shooting scenario. But it is still irrelevant to the body being Billy Bonney's, or to "Brushy" being Billy.

This washstand hoaxing is continued in the book's glossy print section, with an unattributed diagram of the alleged Maxwell bedroom, with a washstand positioned to go along with the hoax (as well as no outside door, to go with that other hoaxed claim).

The washstand hoax is continued in "Appendix II" as "Crime Scene Investigation: The Washstand." (Pages 206-207) Hidden is that it was part of Lincoln County Sheriff's Department Case No. 2003-274, "Billy the Kid Case." Instead, as mere "investigators," are listed , Steve Sederwall (first, with "Deputy" hidden), Tom Sullivan (with "Sheriff" hidden), Kim [sic – Calvin] Ostler, Dr. Henry Lee, David Turk (as from the U.S. Marshals Service, but with "Historian" hidden to fake him as a Marshal), and Mike Haag (as a firearms examiner). They are to examine the washstand, claimed as from Peter Maxwell's bedroom on July 14, 1881. Its measurements and two holes are presented, with Lee's laser as showing a "bullet path." The conclusion is that Garrett "shot the holes in the washstand ... from a position that likely involved being on both knees with one hand on the floor for support while the opposite hand fired the revolver."

FAKERY: The exposé of Dr. Henry Lee's washstand hoax for Case 2003-274 is on pages 252-257 above. And Steve Sederwall's forgery of Lee's report to make the case seem like his private hobby is presented on pages 257 and 326 above. In fact, the non-historical washstand was mere hoaxed fiction by Lee to make-up Pat Garrett as a liar about the death scene, for the hoaxers to make their leap to his lying about the innocent victim.

FAKING NO CORONER'S JURY REPORT

The Coroner's Jury Report is faked as "subsequent inquests" serving to "generate doubt as to whom [he] actually shot and killed that night." (Page 71) 33) The actual document is concealed; and the claim of no certain report is made. (Pages 87-92) "Paco" Anaya's malarkey of two reports is used, plus Sonnichsen's fake conspiracy theories about Garrett's problem collecting his reward being based on no corpse identification. And the burial is claimed to have hidden the body, with "only a handful" of witnesses; along with the fake swarthy bearded body from fabricating newspaperman S.M. Ashenfelter. (Page 93)

FAKERY: This flim-flam is debunked under *Alias Billy the Kid's* fakery by Sonnichsen (see pages 125-134 above); and under *Cold Case Billy the Kid* (see pages 321-322 below).

FAKING NO REWARD

Garrett is claimed as being so poor that he depended on collecting the Billy the Kid award; but it was denied; indicating he was a liar about Billy the Kid's killing. (Page 50)

FAKERY: This fabrication jumps the gun to the post-killing, with Sonnichsen's fake conspiracy theories and lies that Garrett was denied the reward because the body was not identified as Billy's since there was no legitimate Coroner's Jury Report. In fact, the Coroner's Jury Report was used as proof of justifiable homicide; the delay was in converting Wallace's personal reward offer to a Territorial one; and Garrett was paid. (See pages 16-25 above)

RETURN OF THE "BILLY THE KID CASE"

Case 2003-274's Billy the Kid exhumation attempt is shape-shifted by duped Jameson as: "An attempt by investigator and researcher Steve Sederwall to examine the space beneath the stone in order to learn the truth was rejected by the Fort Sumner city council. Clearly they did not want to take the chance of the result indicating there was nothing there. In this case, tourism dollars were more important than truth." (Page 97)

FAKERY: Jameson's confusion about the "Billy the Kid Case" is evident. Before he was pushing the conspiracy theory that tourism interests blocked truth, he had himself confirmed that the exact gravesite of Billy the Kid was unknown, and that flooding had destroyed remains. (*The Return of the Outlaw*, Pages 132-133) That was before the "Billy the Kid Case" hoax occurred and depended on faking that valid DNA *was* available from that tourist-marked grave – which Jameson now flip-flopped to back.

STAGE SET FOR A MEGAHOAX

Pat Garrett: The Man Behind the Badge, represented another step downward for W.C. Jameson into active hoaxing. Having at least some awareness of the "Billy the Kid Case," and having been a participant, he willfully kept it secret from his readers; instead portraying one of its perpetrators, its erstwhile Sheriff's Deputy, Steve Sederwall, as a random investigator of Billy the Kid history.

So hidden by Jameson was that hoaxes' agenda of hijacking Billy the Kid history for an imposter, as linked to defamation of Pat Garrett as a willful and never-punished murderer of an innocent victim, and a criminal accomplice of Billy the Kid both in his jailbreak murders of his deputy guards, and in his Fort Sumner "escape."

But Jameson was poised to give the "Billy the Kid Case" hoaxers a book to flaunt their fakery yet again: his 2018 *Cold Case Billy the Kid,* in an apparent notion that their fake claims that "history was not as written" would translate into "Brushy" being Billy the Kid - since "history" definitely did not write that!

But all that Jameson was about to achieve was becoming the author of a megahoax; once again a dupe for the same kind of charlatans as lying huckster, William V. Morrison, and fake conspiracy-theorist-historian-wannabe, C.L. Sonnichsen.

PART VI

"COLD CASE BILLY THE KID" MEGAHOAX WITH FAKED DEATH SCENES AND DENIED CORONER'S JURY REPORT

CHAPTER 1
FUSING OF ALL THE IMPOSTER HOAXES AS A MEGAHOAX WITH A FAKE DEATH SCENE

AN UNEASY UNION OF HOAXES

Sixty-eight years after "Brushy Bill" Roberts and William V. Morrison failed to trick honorable Governor Thomas Jewett Mabry with their Billy the Kid imposter hoax, and 15 years after corrupt Governor Bill Richardson tried to trick the public with his "Billy the Kid Case" rerun of that imposter hoax, W.C. Jameson fused them, while adding more hoaxing, to create a megahoax.

His "Acknowledgements" lists many of the "Billy the Kid Case" hoaxers as assisting him: Gary Graves, Dr. Henry Lee, Lonnie Lippman (hoax photographer of Steve Sederwall holding John Millers, or William Hudspeth's, skull), Rick Staub, Tom Sullivan, Dale Tunnell, and Dave Turk. (Page 181) Lippman's 2007 death, and Sullivan's in 2013, prove Jameson's long association with these men.

Jameson, acting as their narrator for his book, in particular show-cased Steve Sederwall; writing: "His tenacity and thoroughness when taking on the study of historical topics is exceeded by no one I have ever encountered." Impressed by his cowboy costuming and 6'5" height, Jameson advertised Sederwall vaguely as a "cop," a U.S. government investigator, and a worker of crime scenes; having his own "investigative agency" for "western cold cases." (Page vi) At last, Jameson had found a partner for the Morrison-Sonnichsen history-is-not-as-written trick, originally floated with "Brushy."

But even his title was a hoax based on the faked death scene that characterized the "Brushy" and "Billy the Kid Case" hoaxes. *Cold Case: Billy the Kid* had no cold case! There was just "Brushy's" fable that Pat Garrett murdered Billy Barlow; and the "Billy the Kid Case's" lie that Garrett killed an innocent victim to save Billy Bonney from the fatal bullet.

SETTING THE STAGE WITH FAKERY

Jameson plays narrator to Steve Sederwall's "crime scene investigations" to claim no past historian "possessed much insight"(Page 11); but Sederwall uses "tells" - a "cop term" to find "suspicious discrepancies" - in Pat Garrett's 1882 *The Authentic Life of Billy the Kid* and John W. Poe's *The Death of Billy the Kid.* (Page xvi) So Sederwall's history-is-not-as-written trickery is the backbone of *Cold Case Billy the Kid.*

Important to recognize is that the two hoaxes formulated their bad guy Garrett differently. In the "Brushy" hoax, he was a tool of the Santa Fe Ring trying to kill Billy, and dishonestly collected a reward while hiding that he had accidentally murdered Billy Barlow instead. In the "Billy the Kid Case" hoax, Garrett was in a bromance with Billy, was an accomplice to Billy's jailbreak murder of his own deputy guards, and intentionally killed an innocent victim (risking his own life to future hanging) so Billy could live free (after he helpfully shot Billy for playing-dead-on-the carpenter's-bench-to-bleed-for-Dr. Lee's-future-"blood-DNA").

As to Fort Sumner, the duo claim Billy was there because of Paulita Maxwell, Peter Maxwell's teenaged sister. (Page 127) This is important to note because it is a fix-up unknown to "Brushy," who fabricated Celsa Gutierrez there as his sweetheart.

Also cited is known history that Garrett did not believe Billy was in Fort Sumner, and that his Deputy, John W. Poe, convinced him to go there. But, to fake Garrett as unmotivated to capture Billy, Poe is portrayed as having to take the initiative.

HIDING EVIDENCE: Omitted is Garrett's explanation, in *The Authentic Life of Billy the Kid*, about using Poe for recognizance: "Poe was a stranger in the country, and there was little danger he would meet anyone at Sumner who might know him. So, after an hour or two spent in the hills, I sent him to Fort Sumner to take observations. I advised him to go to

Sunnyside, seven miles above Sumner, and interview M. Rudulph, in whose judgment and discretion I had great confidence. It was understood that Poe would meet with us that night at moonlight." (Garrett, Pages 212-213)

Then, to portray Garrett as a liar, the approach to the Maxwell house is garbled from *The Authentic Life of Billy the Kid*, about his seeing two figures in the peach orchard. Stated is: "As Garrett, Poe, and McKinney approached the houses, Garrett said, they 'heard the sound of voices conversing in Spanish,' though they were too far away to hear words distinctly. As they watched from hiding, 'a man rose from the ground in full view, but too fat away to recognize. He wore a broad-brimmed hat, dark vest and pants, and was in his shirt sleeves.' This man, claimed Garrett, was Billy the Kid, even though he previously stated he was too far away to recognize.' A few lines later, however, Garrett again wrote, 'The Kid by me unrecognized.' Did Garrett recognize the Kid or not?" This faked "discrepancy leads the duo to claim the incident never happened because Poe did not mention the scene in his own book. So Garrett lied. (Page 129)

FAKING EVIDENCE: What Garrett *actually* stated in *The Authentic Life of Billy the Kid* is that he, Poe, and McKinney, on foot, secretly entered the Maxwell's peach orchard which extended to some houses "occupied by Mexicans, not more than sixty yards from Maxwell's house. We approached these houses cautiously, and when within ear-shot heard the voices of people conversing in Spanish [i.e., they heard the Spanish voices of the people in the houses]. We concealed ourselves quickly and listened, but the distance was too great to hear words or even distinguish voices [i.e., referring to a couple at a distance in the orchard, too far to make out their words]. Soon a man arose from the ground, close enough to be seen but too far away to be recognized [i.e., the distant man, whose words could not be made out, rose]. He wore a broad-brimmed hat, dark vest and pants, and was in his shirt sleeves ... [H]e went to the fence, jumped it, and walked toward the Maxwell house. Little as we suspected it, this man was the Kid." (i.e., it would only be later, that Garrett would realize, likely by the outfit of the corpse he had shot, that it had

been Billy). (Garrett, Page 214) Garrett makes clear he did not recognize Billy in the orchard: "When the Kid, who had been thus unrecognized by me, left the orchard, I motioned to my companions." (Page 215) And Poe merely left out this insignificant scene in his book, written decades later. Jameson and Sederwall were faking a "discrepancy."

FAKING DEATH SCENE DOUBTS

The Jameson-Sederwall duo (presumably assisted by the acknowledged additional "Billy the Kid Case" hoaxers) present their "Cold Case Billy the Kid" hoax's make-or-break July 14, 1881 death scene in chapters "Shooting at Fort Sumner" (Pages 131-134) and "Discrepancies." (Pages 135-163)

Concealed is that "Brushy's" tale is totally different from the "Billy the Kid Case's." "Brushy" had Billy Barlow accidentally killed in a dark July 14, 1881 night on the back porch of the Maxwell house. The "Billy the Kid Case" hoax had Version I with super-friend Pat Garrett shooting the innocent victim instead of Billy. Its rewritten Version II had willing Billy shot, at unspecified location, by Garrett to play dead on the carpenter's bench (to bleed for future fake DNA); with Garrett then murdering the innocent victim to switch with playing-dead Billy for burial.

Concealed also, is no evidence for either hoax; and profuse evidence debunking them. Relied on for this megahoax are only fake "discrepancies," fake "investigations," and Dr. Henry Lee's fake carpenter's bench and washstand forensics.

The duo's hoaxed claim is that "researchers never noted the obvious and glaring discrepancies" in Pat Garrett's and John W. Poe's accounts of the shooting. There were none, but the Jameson-Sederwall duo propose to show them by breaking the death scene shooting to parts: arrival of participants to Maxwell's room, shooting, post-shooting removal of body, the "inquests" [sic - there was just one] and burial. (Page 135)

Since the key relevant facts in the death scene are the Coroner's Jury Report and the added profuse identifications of the body as Billy Bonney's - as was obviously omitted by these charlatans - the meaninglessness of their scam is obvious. Important, however, for hoax evolution are the additions to the original hoaxes of this magahoax's new fake "cop investigations."

FAKING DISCREPANCIES

Discrepancies are faked using Pat Garrett's 1882 *Authentic Life of Billy the Kid* and John W. Poe's *The Death of Billy the Kid,* to pretend they proved events did not occur. So the duo conclude that this "incident [shooting in the bedroom] as the two lawmen described it never took place." (Page 141) Examples follow:

1) DEPUTIES OUTSIDE: The duo claim it was suspicious for Garrett to enter the Maxwell's bedroom, while leaving his deputies outside, because it was too careless for searching for "the most dangerous outlaw in New Mexico." (Page 138)

FAKING EVIDENCE: Omitted is that Garrett did not believe that Billy was in Fort Sumner, and was merely checking with Maxwell. Omitted is another possibility, that a trap was being set, with Billy being sent to Maxwell's bedroom for ambush. In that case, it was strategic to have the deputies outside in case Billy escaped from the room.

2) IN SOX AND BUTTONING PANTS: The approach of the stranger, in sox and buttoning his pants, is tackled by "cop" Sederwall, recycling this absurdity from his (concealed) Case No. 2003-274's "Probable Cause Statement" about it being too hard to hold a gun and a knife and button your pants; plus gravel would hurt your sensitive stockinged feet! (Page 139)

FAKING EVIDENCE: Billy apparently could multi-task! And apparently he could tackle gravel too! Sederwall's silliness in the "Probable Cause Statement" stated:

> **[Poe stated] *At this I stood up and advanced toward him, telling him not to be alarmed ... and still without the least suspicion that this was the very man we were looking for.***
>
> **This statement raises many questions with investigators. Poe says he sees a man "*partially dressed, and was bare-headed and bare-footed - or rather, had only socks on his feet, and it seemed to me that he was fastening his trousers as he came toward me art a very brisk walk.*" Then the man covers him with his six shooter. Where did the man put the "*six-shooter*" when he was "*fastening his trousers*"?**
>
> **He did not stop and lay it down because Poe says he "*he came toward me art a very brisk walk.*"**

3) SPEAKING SPANISH: Sederwall cogitated that if approaching Billy said, "Quien es?" and non-Spanish-speaking Poe responded in English to reassure him, then bi-lingual Billy would have reverted to English. So Sederwall concludes that left just two possibilities: it was not Billy, or Poe lied! (Page 140)

FAKING EVIDENCE: Omitted is that Billy was the most hunted man in the Territory. Speaking Spanish to a stranger was his disguise. Furthermore, he probably used the language commonly, as he would with bi-lingual Peter Maxwell in the next a moment. And the disguise worked! Poe assumed he was a Maxwell worker. Sederwall's two "possibilities" are absurd.

Noteworthy is ongoing demolition of "Brushy" as Billy; here arguing based on being bi-lingual. "Brushy" was not.

4) LETTING BILLY ENTER THE BEDROOM: Sederwall claimed it was unimaginable that two deputies let a man with a knife and a gun walk into the bedroom with Garrett, without shouting a warning. And he imagines that Billy would have been more cautious, or even shot the deputies. (Pages 140-141)

FAKING EVIDENCE: Fantasizing is not evidence.

In fact, neither Poe nor McKinney knew Billy, and thought he was a Maxwell worker. Billy's gun was attributed to strangers alarming him, and could as easily be construed as a worker being protective of Maxwell, and rightly asking them in Spanish, "Who are you?" And none of the lawmen were expecting Billy to turn up at Maxwell's house, so were not alarmed. As Poe stated in his book: "As Maxwell's was the one place in Fort Sumner I considered above suspicion of harboring the Kid, I was entirely off my guard." (Poe, Page 34)

As to Billy being incautious, he was known for fearlessness. That is how he ended up in Fort Sumner, instead of hightailing it to Old Mexico after his jailbreak. And Fort Sumner had strangers passing through. It is absurd to think that he would automatically shoot them!

5) ENTERING THE BEDROOM: Garrett's statement that the person "sprang quickly into the door" is contrasted with Poe describing Billy backing towards the door, to claim Billy never entered the room! (Page 132)

FAKING EVIDENCE: Actually, the manner of entering is merely vantage point. In his 1933 book, Poe described Billy as "backed up into the doorway of Maxwell's room, where he halted for a moment, his body concealed by the thick adobe wall at the side of the doorway." (Poe, Page 35) So Poe could not have seen Billy's final turn to enter the room face-forward as Garrett saw. There is no discrepancy.

6) THE VICTIM'S IDENTITY: After the shooting, Maxwell is presented as running out; Garrett as doubtful, saying, "I think I have got him;" and Poe being doubtful. (Page 133)

FAKING: Garrett did not say, "I think I have got him." In his book, he was certain: "I told my companions that I had got the Kid. They asked if I had not shot the wrong man. I told them I made no mistake, for I knew the Kid's voice too well." He explained the Deputies' doubt: "Seeing a bareheaded, bare-footed man, in his shirt sleeves, with a butcher knife in his hand, and hearing his hail in excellent Spanish, they naturally supposed him to be a Mexican and an attaché of the establishment, hence their suspicion that I had shot the wrong man." (Garrett, Page 217)

As to Poe, *he* is the one who gave quote the duo called Garrett's: " 'I think I have got him' ... I said, 'Pat, the Kid would not come to this place; you have shot the wrong man ...' Upon my saying this, Garrett seemed to be in doubt himself as to whom he shot, but quickly spoke up and said, 'I am sure that was him, for I know his voice too well to be mistaken.' " (Poe, Pages 37-38) And Poe confirmed: Upon examining the body, we found it to be that of Billy the Kid." (Poe, Page 41) There was no discrepancy.

7) POST-SHOOTING SCENES: The scene is given of "native people" taking the body "to a carpenter shop where it was laid out on a workbench." Poe is quoted about staying in Maxwell's house for fear of attack by "friends of the dead man." (Page 134) Then appears "cop" Sederwall to say it all seemed suspicious to him that Garrett would let women take the body of such a famous outlaw, or that he would "cower" in Maxwell's house. To him that means Garrett was a bad leader - or worse. (Page 134)

FAKING DOUBT: Sederwall's fantasies are not evidence.

FAKING A MAXWELL BEDROOM DOOR DISCREPANCY

This new hoax of Maxwell's bedroom having no outside door - first in *Pat Garrett: The Man Behind the Badge* (see page 292 above) - is to destroy the historical death scene in one fell swoop, since all participants recounted it. A diagram is given and labeled "Floor plan of the Maxwell house," and has no door. And the building is called a one-story adobe. (Page 137) **[FIGURE: 9]**

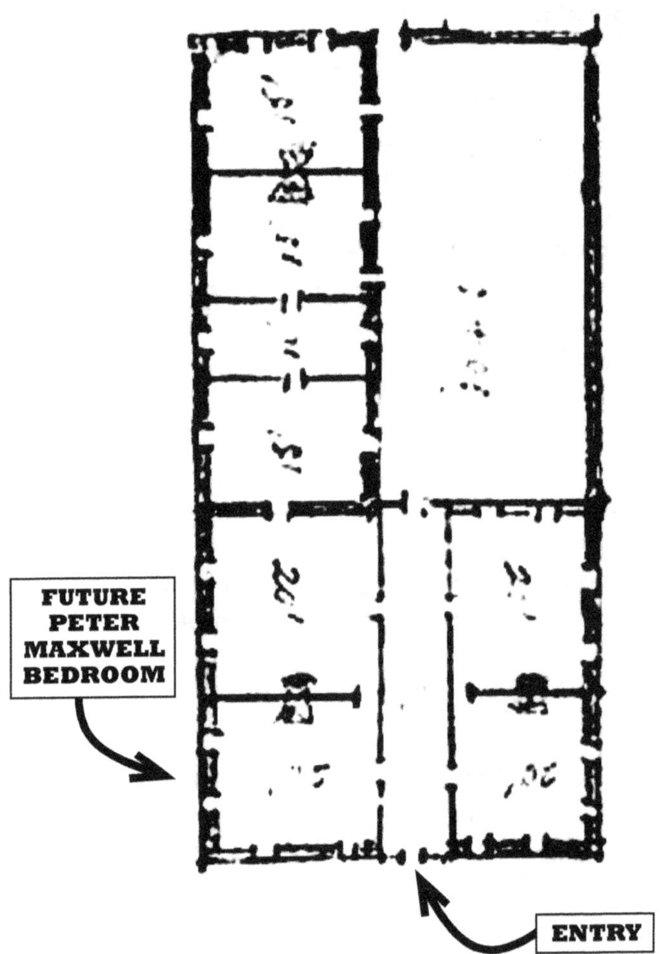

FIGURE: 9. Falsely used by the hoaxers as "Floor plan of Maxwell house" from the "National Archives" (Page 137); this diagram is actually from the National Archives as "Commanding Officer's Quarters, Fort Sumner, New Mexico Territory;" and its copy, so labeled, is at the Fort Sumner State Monument

To indicate that Garrett lied about the door, the hoaxers state: "**Garrett wrote, '[Billy] 'stepped onto the porch and entered Maxwell's room through the open door left open on account of the extremely warm weather**.' " (Page 131) And Poe's witnessing Billy enter through that door is cited as to his lying also. (Page 140) Added is that if there was a door, it was not open, as Garrett said, because scary animals could get in. (Page 138) So the duo conclude that Garrett and Poe were lying about the entire scene to conceal that Billy the Kid was never shot.

FAKED INVESTIGATION: The claimed "floor plan" is not Maxwell's bedroom, but is the original Fort Sumner Commanding Officer's quarters for the Bosque Redondo Indian Reservation from 1863 to 1868. Since its sources in the National Archives and at Fort Sumner State Monument label it as such, the hoaxers are faking its identification.

Omitted is that in 1870, when Lucien Maxwell bought Fort Sumner, he rebuilt it as his family home. As Robert Mullin wrote on the back of the Maxwell house photo: "*Pete Maxwell's House Fort Sumner ... Originally 1 Story Flat Roof, Officers Quarters. 2nd Floor Added By Maxwell.*"

The actual Maxwell house floor plan shows the outside door. [Figure: 10] And the Maxwell house photograph, also shows that door in Maxwell's bedroom. [Figure: 11]

And to claim, as did the hoaxing duo, that the door was not left open, is meaningless fantasizing.

And the Garrett quote is faked. He actually wrote: "When we reached the porch in front of the building, I left Poe and McKinney at the end of the porch, and about twenty feet from the door of Pete's bedroom, while I myself entered it." (Garrett, Page 215) The quote is actually distorted from Poe's book; stating: "'You fellows wait here while I go in to talk to [Maxwell].' Thereupon he stepped onto the porch and entered Maxwell's room through the open door (left open on account of the extremely warm weather), while McKinney and myself stopped on the outside." (Poe, Page 31)

Also, **Poe described that door when he almost shot Maxwell: "A moment after Garrett came out of the door, Pete Maxwell rushed squarely onto me in a frantic effort to get out of the room." (Poe, Page 38) This contradicts the hoaxers' walking-through-the-house-to-get-out fakery.**

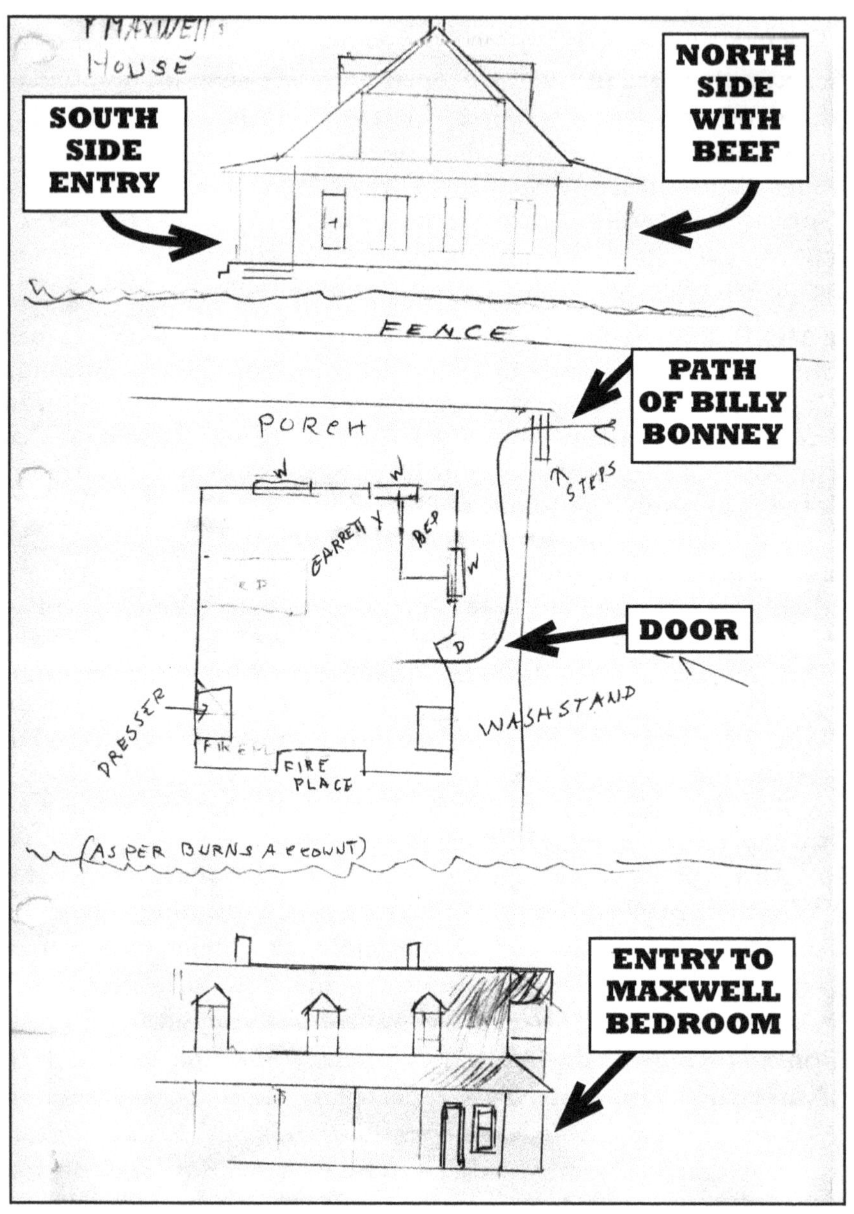

FIGURE: 10. Diagrams by Maurice Garland Fulton of the Maxwell's house, with Peter Maxwell's bedroom, and Billy Bonney's entry through its outside door. From the Midland, Texas, Haley Library, Robert N. Mullin Collection.

FIGURE: 11. Photograph of the Maxwell house showing Peter Maxwell's bedroom with a door to the outside. From the Midland, Texas, Haley Library, Robert N. Mullin Collection.

SOURCE FOR FAKE DOOR INVESTIGATION: This "investigation's" no door claim was lifted from an undated article by an unknown author (erroneously named as Gregory Scott Smith) titled "The Death of Billy the Kid: A New Scenario?" now in the Fort Sumner State Monument files. It used John L. McCarty papers of an October 22, 1942 interview titled "Kid Dobbs Interviews: An Interview with Garrett H. 'Kid' Dobbs at Farmington, New Mexico," on September 12, 1942, with Mel Armstrong and John McCarty, Thursday Morning, October 22, 1942, In the Presence of Mrs. Dobbs and Pat Flynn. J.D. White, Amarillo, Heard Part of the Final Statements of this Interview Re. Billy the Kid's Death."

Garrett H. "Kid" Dobbs merely spouted old-timer windbag malarkey. His fabrication, with the usual claim of knowing Billy the Kid, began with: "Billy told me ... he came from San Francisco, California, and had killed a chinaman out there for insulting his mother." Here is Dobbs's Lincoln County War Battle: "Once when a friend of Billy the Kid was killed, Billy went to Chisholm [sic] and volunteered to lead the Chisholm party at war ... They made a fight and Murphy's men set fire to McSwain's [sic] house ... Billy had killed four of Murphy's men during the fight ... [During the escape] McSwain [sic] was killed by Murphy. Mrs. McSwain [sic] yelled for her trunk in the house and Tom O'Folliard went back in and got it but burnt his whiskers."

For the death scene, Dobbs's fakery continued:

> Billy was hiding out in Pete Maxwell's house ...
>
> Maxwell wrote Garrett a letter saying he would turn over Billy to him. Garrett thought it might be a trick to trap him for Billy. <u>Pat had Frank Poe and Jim McIntosh, two deputies with him</u>. [Note ignorance of even of the famous deputies.] He told them he was afraid this was a trap and wasn't going up there until he spoke with Maxwell ... Garrett wrote a note to Maxwell and sent it to him by a Mexican boy telling him to meet them at the Mexican plaza 6 miles below Fort Sumner ...
>
> Garrett told Pete if it was a trap he would kill him too. He told Pete he was coming up that night.
>
> They arrived ay Maxwell's early before Billy came in from his daylight hiding and [Pat] told his deputies to bed down in one corner of Maxwell's yard. Pat went in to the house and waited in Maxwell's bedroom.

When Billy came in that night he saw the men in the yard and asked the cook who they were. The cook said they were some of Pete's sheepherders ...

In the meantime Maxwell had told the cook not to save any cold meat ... so the Kid would have to fix his own supper.

Billy asked the cook where the knife was ... Garrett could hear every word in the bedroom.

Then the Kid asked where the meat was and the cook said he guessed it was in the meat box. The Kid told him it wasn't. The cook told Billy it must be in Pete's bedroom then as Pete had brought some new meat out from town. [Note that Dobbs did not even know that Fort Sumner *was* the town.]

The Kid had the knife in his left hand and started to the bedroom to get some meat. [Note that Billy walks through the house to get to the bedroom.] There was a broken-rock walk way just large enough for two to pass in the hall way from the kitchen to the bedroom. There was a dining room between the kitchen and bedroom. Garrett could hear the Kid coming on those rocks. He was sitting on the foot of the bed [The interviewer here explains that the hall "ran east and west; and Pete's room was on the west] ...

It was warm weather and the bedroom window was open ... The door opened and Billy saw Pat move off the bed. Billy said: Como estes? (What's that) ...

Garrett ... fired and as Billy fell he fired over Pat's head and the bullet went in the ceiling ... Pat's shot went under Billy's heart ...

Pat and Pete ... told me how it happened many times as did the deputies.

For "The Death of Billy the Kid: A New Scenario?" the ignorant unknown author used this junk and added the National Archives floor plan. It was called "the original layout of the officers' quarters buildings, one of which became the Maxwell house [provided to show no outside door]. It stated: "Taken in conjunction with the Dobbs interview [Billy going through the house], it raises a whole new series of questions as to exactly how Billy the Kid was killed on that July night in 1881." This author was unaware that Lucien Maxwell had rebuilt the house as two stories and added the outside door to what would be Peter's bedroom. And the ignorant or lying hoaxers used that diagram for *Cold Case Billy the Kid.* (Figure 4 above). So the incompetent author concluded:

"We can posit an alternative scenario, based partly on what Dobbs said and partly on common sense. If the Kid was really after a hunk of steak he would have gone to the kitchen or the 'cool box' either in the storage or dining area or even outside in the courtyard, because it beggars belief that Maxwell would have a side of beef hanging in his bedroom. However, if the Kid was either going to or just leaving [his lover] Paulita either from the room next to Dona Luz - which would then require him to use the hallway just as Dobbs describes it – or alternatively from one of the two rooms on the northern side of the house, he would as he reached the front (eastern) doorway [believed by Smith, and used by the hoaxers, as the only entrance] – either from the inside or out – have seen the two strangers and acted just as Poe and Garrett described – skipping through the door [here an inside door] into Pete's bedroom to find out who they were – and Garrett was there waiting for him."

HOAXERS' PAST FAKE DOOR GAMBIT": Sederwall had provided this fakery for the no door scam to fellow "Billy the Kid Case" hoaxer and editor, Bob Boze Bell, for Bell's August, 2010's *True West's* "Caught with his Pants Down? Billy the Kid vs Pat Garrett, One Door Closes."

For it, Sederwall was a "**retired lawman**" giving "CSI" evidence that Billy was in Paulita's bedroom, "**across from Pete's, when he heard two men (Poe and McKinney) talking outside.**" Using Dobbs's no outside door, Sederwall has Billy enter the bedroom from the hall. And his "CSI" proof is none other than hoaxing Dr. Henry Lee's Case 2003-274 fake washstand forensics, with Sederwall making-up his own version that "**laser lines up perfectly with the hole [sic] in the washstand**" if Garrett shot Billy, then ran out the inside door, and on his knees fired back in, hitting the washstand!

So Bob Boze Bell concluded: "**[C]onventional wisdom is often misinformed, which I found out when Gregory Smith [the erroneously listed author of the article] discovered the original 1863 floor plans ... Apparently, windows, not doors, were located alongside these rooms. Lucien ... might have created doorways when he and his family moved in. Yet if Pete's room did not have an outside door, historians will certainly be forced to look at the event with new eyes.**"

To be noted is that opportunistic Sederwall here backed the victim being Billy Bonney!

FAKING SHOOTING SCENE DOUBTS

The historical shooting scene is given, with Garrett's sitting on Peter Maxwell's bed when Billy entered; with Maxwell identifying him; and with Garrett shooting twice. Doubts are presented about Garrett's claim that Billy had a gun and knife, and the possibility that Billy was unarmed. (Pages 142-143)

OMITTED EXPLANATIONS: Omitted are historically postulated explanations for Garrett's description of the shooting. His telling of a surprise encounter with Billy was likely to shield Maxwell from accusation of complicitness. It was possible that Peter Maxwell played traitor, setting up the ambush with Garrett, who was hiding in the dark room, with his deputies outside to shoot in case Billy escaped. With Billy's popularity in the town, it would have been a great risk to Maxwell if this had been revealed. This is supported by Poe's book, in which he described almost shooting Maxwell when he ran out the door; which would have only occurred if Poe was anticipating an escaping Billy, and was prepared to shoot him. (Poe, Page 39) And Poe reported the danger from Billy's partisans: "We spent the remainder of the night on the Maxwell premises, keeping constantly on our guard, was we were expecting to be attacked by friends of the dead man." (Poe, Page 44)

A further possibility is presented in Frederick Nolan's 1992 *The Lincoln County War: A Documentary History.* "Garrett found the Kid in bed with Paulita Maxwell and shot him *in flagrante delictu*; the authored version [given by Garrett] ... was then cooked up to protect the girl's reputation." (Nolan, Page 425)

Obviously, Garrett's possible need to protect other killing participants, has nothing to do with an unwarranted leap that the corpse was not Billy's.

Questioned are whether two or three shots were fired.

OMITTED EVIDENCE: Poe provided the explanation for the sound of three shots in his book: "An instant later a shot was fired in the room, followed immediately by what everyone within hearing distance thought were two other shots. However, <u>there were only two shots fired</u>, the third report, as

we learned afterward, being caused by the rebound of the second bullet, which had struck the adobe wall and rebounded against the headboard of a wooden bedstead." (Poe, Pages 36-37) Garrett also addressed it in his book as first thinking Billy had fired one shot to his two. But Billy's revolver showed no shot fired. Garrett stated: "We searched long and faithfully – found both my bullet marks but no other." (Garrett, Page 218) And eye-witness Peter Maxwell testified on July 15, 1881 for the Coroner's jurymen: "*Pat F. Garrett fired two shots at the said William Bonney and the said William Bonney fell near my fire place.*"

Then, added as "evidence" is the "Brushy" hoax's claiming Garrett had "high political ambitions": Sonnichsen's faked motive for hiding the shooting of an unarmed man. Added, while that Billy Barlow fakery was being given, is: "there is disagreement on whether the body of the slain man was inside or outside the room." (Page 143; and *Alias Billy the Kid*, Page 49)

FAKING EVIDENCE: Garrett was not politically ambitious, and the corpse was in Maxwell's bedroom. Using the "Brushy" hoax's back-porch-dead-Billy-Barlow for this hoax is obviously not evidence.

Omitting that the actual second strike involved Maxwell's headboard, given is Dr. Henry Lee's fake washstand forensics, with his positioning of Garrett on the floor and shooting.

Then, like Jameson's silly "Sexual Maturity Ratings," a Homeland Security "expert" is used to claim physiologic alterations in a shooter causing "fight or flight mode" and flinching, supposedly as confirmation of Lee's positioning to claim Garrett lied by reporting it differently. Also claimed is that he lied additionally by leaving out the washstand. (Pages 144-146)

MAJOR HOAXING: This fakery uses the "Billy the Kid Case" hoax as evidence to call Garrett a liar, by its substitution of the unsubstantiated washstand for the shot headboard; and use of Dr. Henry Lee's fraudulent crime scene reconstruction based on it. (See pages 252-257 above) And Poe had confirmed that: "[T]he second bullet, which had struck the adobe wall ... [had] rebounded against the headboard of a wooden bedstead." (Poe, Pages 36-37)

FAKING THE BODY'S REMOVAL

To avoid the townspeople's identifications of Billy, little is said about taking Billy's body to the carpenter's shop.

Instead, a quote is taken from Garrett's July 15, 1881 "letter to the territorial governor": "It was my desire to have been able to take him alive, but his coming upon me so suddenly and unexpectedly led me to believe that he had seen me enter the room, or had been informed by someone of the fact, and that he had come there armed with pistol and knife expressly to kill me if he could." (Page 147) Trying to fake a discrepancy, there followed a convoluted rendition of Poe's stating that the room was too dark to make things out. And Poe is claimed to have had to go through the house to get to the doorless bedroom. (Page 147)

FAKING EVIDENCE: Hiding the numerous identifications of the corpse as Billy Bonney's, shows that the other blather about Garrett's description, and Poe's blocking entry based on no outside door is just filler.

But Garrett's quoted letter of July 15, 1881 to Acting-Governor William Ritch (as reprinted in the Las Cruces *Rio Grande Republican* as "Kid the Killer Killed, Wm. Bonney alias Antrim, alias Billy the Kid, Fatally Meets Pat Garrett, the Lincoln County Sheriff" (see pages 15-16 above)) debunked the Jameson-Sederwall duo's fakery by giving the shooting scene, and reprinting the Coroner's Jury report's identifying the body and confirming justifiable homicide. Written to initiate his receiving the promised reward, Garrett apparently added his necessity of killing to address Lew Wallace's offers on December 22, 1880's Las Vegas *Daily Gazette*, and May 3, 1881's *Daily New Mexican*, which had both stated: "I will pay $500 reward to any person or persons who will capture William Bonney, alias The Kid, and deliver him to any sheriff of New Mexico. Satisfactory proofs of identity will be required." It was not a dead-or-alive notice. So killing, instead of capture, had to be addressed. So Garrett did. Noteworthy is that this was also the letter confirming he had sent the original Coroner's Jury Report to First Judicial District Attorney William Breeden. And Breeden agreed to the justifiable homicide, and assisted in processing the reward through the Legislature. This alone destroyed the hoaxing duo's lies.

Next was quibbling about the body lying on its back or front, with Jesus Silva, Maxwell's foreman, quoted from Miguel Otero's **1936** book, *The Real Billy the Kid*, as the body being face down. So the duo questioned if Silva entered first (Page 148) (with Jameson forgetting "Brushy" had no bedroom scene!).

FAKING EVIDENCE: Poe, in his *The Death of Billy the Kid*, stated that looking through the window: "[W]e saw a man lying stretched upon his back dead" (Poe, Page 40); which matches Garrett's bullet's impact hitting Billy from the front. And the hoaxers admit the room was next lit, and the body examined. And it could have been turned over then.

The Jesus Silva story was an *Alias Billy the Kid* prompt footnote: a July, 1936 *Frontier Times* interview of a Leslie Traylor of Galveston, Texas, titled "Facts Regarding the Escape of Billy the Kid." History buff Traylor interviewed old-timers in Lincoln and Fort Sumner in 1933 and 1935; including Silva about Billy's shooting. He wrote: "Silva said he was at home when he heard the shot, and they sent for him, that when he arrived they were afraid to go into the room, and as he knew the Kid well and was not afraid, he went in with a light and found him dead, lying face downward with a pistol in one hand and a butcher knife in the other." So the real issue was not face-up or down, but that Jesus Silva was yet another witness identifying the corpse as Billy Bonney's!

And Miguel Otero was a meaningless hearsay source, who wrote his book 55 years after the shooting!

There was no discrepancy.

And, by now, the hoaxers had presented multiple body identifications as Billy: Garrett, Peter Maxwell, Jesus Silva, the townspeople's vigil, and the Coroner's Jury Report in the Garrett article's letter. Thus Garrett killed Billy. Thus, "Brushy" was not Billy. End of story.

FAKING A "PETER MAXWELL"

A key witness was Peter Maxwell, stating to the Coroner's Jury: *"Pat F. Garrett fired two shots at the said William Bonney and the said William Bonney fell near my fire place and I went out of the room and when I came in again about three or four minutes after the shots the said William Bonney was dead."*

So Sederwall tried to discredit Maxwell's fatal testimony by citing a 1978 article by a Bundy Avants [sic] (in an unreferenced publication) titled "The Bundy Avants [sic] Story," claiming to have spoken to Maxwell years after the shooting, with Maxwell telling him: Billy was not shot; Poe was not there; the body was of a Mexican; and Garrett kept it all secret. (Page 136)

FAKE EVIDENCE: The article is from a May-June, 1978 *True West* interview with old-timer Bundy Avant, spouting windbag malarkey. In 1894, as a child, he came with his ranching family from Texas to Roswell, New Mexico; and moved to Capitan, when he was eight; then White Oaks in 1905 for farming. His Billy the Kid fakery begins with a fictional George Coe wrongly telling him he had retrieved murdered John Tunstall's body. Name-dropping Avant also faked John Chisum's brand as the "Long S," when it was the "Long Rail." He also said "Colonel Henry Fountain" was a family friend; when Fountain's name was Albert, and his little son, murdered with him, was Henry.

For his Peter Maxwell fabrication, Avant had himself meeting an old man named "Pete," a cook at a ranch near the San Andres Mountains. This pseudo-Pete says: "I've taken a likin' to you" ... I sensed he had something on his mind which had bothered him for a long time and he felt he had found someone to confide in." Avant says the man told him he was Pete Maxwell, and would tell Avant a secret, if he promised not to tell it "to a living sole as long as I'm alive." Pete then tells him, "Billy is not dead; I can take you to where he lives and has a nice family ... I'll tell you how it was ... There was no light in the house and Pat and I were in the dark when we heard someone come in. We both thought it was Billy. So when the man came in and sensed someone else was there beside me, he said, 'Quien es?' and Pat just fired. We heard the man fall. But when we struck a match and looked at him, we saw it was not the Kid ... Pat was pretty well shook up, as he didn't want it said he had killed the wrong man. It was a Mexican and we decided he was a drifter who would never be missed ... I agreed to keep quiet, too, as I could see it would give Billy a chance to slip away and start a new life, which he had been talking of doing."

Avant says it must be true, because Maxwell would know.

In fact, Peter Maxwell lived near Fort Sumner until his death on June 21, 1898. [FIGURE: 12] His death, as a "Las Vegas" item, in June 28, 1898's *The Albuquerque Citizen*; stated: "**By parties arriving from Fort Sumner it was learned Saturday that Peter Maxwell died at his home near that place , an the morning of the 21 st, and was buried on the following day. He leaves a wife and one child. Peter Maxwell was the son of Lucien B. Maxwell, the original owner of the celebrated Maxwell land grant lying in Colorado and New Mexico. Peter Maxwell is well remembered in Las Vegas, where he was a frequent visitor in years past.**" Also, the coarse vernacular Bundy Avant invented for his pseudo-Pete is unlike that of the bi-lingual man born to Luz Trotier de Beaubien of Hispanic aristocracy, and Lucien Bonaparte Maxwell, of the prosperous and political Menard family.

Avant continued his Billy the Kid period lies with meeting John W. Poe at Roswell at a later date. Poe asks him what he thought of Garrett, and Avant "**didn't think too highly of him.**" This pseudo-Poe, who was not present at the killing scene, tells Avant that he had been Garrett's deputy when Garrett killed Billy in Fort Sumner, but since "**Pat, Billy, and I were good friends at one time,**" he wanted to pay his last respects [with Avant unaware that Poe had never met Billy until moments before the killing]. So Poe used two horses to ride to Fort Sumner that night. Avant says Garrett then refused to let Poe see the body; so Poe suspected foul play and turned in his badge. Avant concluded: "**This made the second time in a period of three years that I had been told by two men, who of all people should know the facts, that Billy was not killed by Pat Garrett.**" (Avant, Pages 47-48)

This Bundy Avant-style fakery had been repeatedly used as evidence in the imposter hoaxes. In the "Brushy" hoax was old-timer Severo Gallegos, used for his fake jailbreak scene and as an affiant for Morrison's collection of fake Affidavits that "Brushy" was Billy the Kid. In the "Billy the Kid Case" hoax was old-timer Homer Overton's fake Affidavit used as evidence in 2003 by then "Billy the Kid Case" hoaxer, Sheriff Tom Sullivan, for an addendum to Case No. 2003-274's "Probable Cause Statement" for Overton's fake claim that Pat Garrett's widow, Apolinaria, had told him that Pat never shot Billy (though she was four

years dead at the time of the supposed confession). (See pages 200-201 above) And it revealed the current fakery of the Jameson-Sederwall duo by using the same kind of junk as "evidence."

An interesting aside is that old-timer Bundy Avant described owning "a little white pony called Billy Barlow" (Avant, Page 12), showing the prevalence of the name "Brushy Bill" picked for his own death scene fable.

FIGURE: 12. Peter Maxwell's house near Fort Sumner, where he lived after the town was sold; discrediting Bundy Avant's claim that he lived as a cook in a San Andres Mountains cow camp; from Midland, Texas, Haley Library, Robert N. Mullin Collection

NOTHING BUT FAKING

The Jameson-Sederwall fakery, though adding more hoaxing to the original chicanery, added not a stitch of evidence to prove Pat Garrett did not kill Billy the Kid. And abandoning "Brushy's" back-porch-Billy-Barlow-shot-fetching-meat contrivance actually ended "Brushy's" run. One is left wondering what the hoaxers were trying to accomplish, besides the well-worn, hollow, meaningless, and failed history-is-not-as-written mantra of their respective hoaxes; along with Sederwall showing off his fake "investigations" and hijacking the Billy the Kid Case" as his own.

CHAPTER 2
FAKING NO INQUEST

HOAXERS VERSUS CORONER'S JURY REPORT

To attack the July 15, 1881 Coroner's Jury Report, the Jameson-Sederwall duo had only faked discrepancies, fake "investigations," and fake conspiracy theories.

Hiding its source, recycled was Steve Sederwall's "Billy the Kid Case" hoax's "Probable Cause Statement," with his made-up time discrepancies for Justice of the Peace Alejandro Segura's contacting Sunnyside's Milnor Rudulph to fabricate that the Jury never even convened. (See pages 185-186 above)

As in that "Probable Cause Statement," the body's location is questioned because the Report said: "*[T]he above jury convened in the home of Luz B. Maxwell and* ***proceeded to a room in the said house where they found the body of William Bonney alias "Kid."*** But because the body was taken to the carpenter's shop, the location is called a lie. (Page 149)

FAKERY: It is obvious that, after that wake, the body was returned to the Maxwell house for the inquest.

It is claimed that Justice of the Peace Segura "instructed Rudulph to assemble a coroner's jury and serve as foreman." (Page 149)

WRONG: Segura appointed Rudulph and the other five jurymen, as he stated in the Coroner's Jury Report: "*I, the undersigned, Justice of the Peace ... immediately upon receiving said information I proceeded to the said place and named Milnor Rudulph, Jose Silva, Antonio Saavedra, Pedro Antonio Lucero, Lorenzo Jaramillo and Sabal Gutierres a jury to investigate the case.*"

The Report, involving Rudulph, about "gratitude of the community" being owed to Garrett, is called "suspicious" to "cop"

Sederwall, because it praises; while Fort Sumner people were angry at the killing, not grateful. (Pages 150-151)

FALSE INTERPRETATION: Sederwall seems unaware that Rudulph was a Ringite. (See pages 53, 74, 147 above) Rudulph would have praised Garrett for stamping-out the last anti-Ring rebel. And the jurymen, presumably terrified by this ambush killing, would not have dared to object.

The Report's existence is next "doubted" by saying it was not filed in San Miguel County; by using "Paco" Anaya's two reports fable; by a fast inquest; by William Keleher's photocopy in Spanish [in his 1957 *Violence in Lincoln County*] being a "second coroner's report," and his English translation meaning the victim spoke English; and by some signers' having misspelled names. So denied is that jurymen even saw the body. (Pages 150-151)

HOAXING EVIDENCE: This rewrites the "Brushy" hoax's C.L. Sonnichsen fakery (see pages 126-134 above), with a bit more added. As discussed, the original Report was sent by Pat Garrett to First Judicial District Attorney William Breeden. It was, in fact, filed with his San Miguel County court records; and was found, in 1932 by, State Land Office employee, Harold Abbott, in the Capitol Building's basement. (See pages 43-46 above) Abbott made copies, eventually reproduced by historians, like William Keleher.

Windbag "Paco" Anaya's "two reports" was his fabrication, as was the rest of his posthumous book's Billy the Kid history. But, as stated, he did know one thing: Billy was killed by Pat Garrett; hence the title, *I Buried Billy*.

As to viewing the body, the Coroner's Jury Report confirmed it performed the inquest's legal duties: interviewing witness Peter Maxwell, identifying the body as Billy Bonney's, examining the wound, and concluding that the homicide did not require prosecution since it was justifiable self-defense.

For their conclusion, the Jameson-Sederwall duo rely on their own fakery as proof; and, of course, state that Garrett killed an innocent man, rushed through the inquest process to hide the body of the non-Billy victim by burial, and wrote the "second" [i.e., real and only] Coroner's Jury Report himself. And 'cop" Sederwall intones that "somebody (or somebodies) are lying" to hide the truth. (Pages 151 -152)

CHAPTER 3
THE RETURN OF FAKE FORENSICS

THE "BILLY THE KID CASE'S" HOAXED FORENSICS

Jameson and Sederwall, pretending they proved the corpse was unidentified (Pages 153-154), recycled Dr. Henry Lee's fake "Billy the Kid Case" forensics, while shape-shifting it as Sederwall's personal investigation - of course, hiding that he had forged Lee's reports for my open records case. So Sederwall calls Fort Sumner an active crime scene (Page 154), echoing the fake title of the book as a "cold case" involving Billy the Kid.

HOAXING: **Fort Sumner was not Pat Garret's shooting's "crime scene" after the Coroner's Jury decision of July 15, 1881; stating: "*[O]ur verdict is that the deed of said Garrett was justifiable homicide.*"**

FAKING CARPENTER'S BENCH FORENSICS

Steve Sederwall, as sole "investigator," of the pretend crime scene, presents the "Billy the Kid Case's" carpenter's bench hoax, with some additions. The bench is called an **important source of "bloodstains from the slain intruder"** - a new name for the innocent victim - **as a source of DNA**. (Page 155)

Research is claimed on the Maxell house history (Pages 155-159), though it was never bench's location. Admitted is that the town was sold in 1884, and its buildings no longer stand. A new claim is that the Maxwell house's floorboards are in a house built by a Charlie Floor, and they could have blood DNA too (which accidently refuted "Brushy's" back-porch-Barlow!).

The furniture (bed, washstand, with added carpenter's bench) is traced to Peter Maxwell's sister Odelia, married to Manuel Abreu. Hilariously inserted is Bundy Avant's old-timer malarkey of meeting "Pete" in the San Andres mountains. (See pages 316-319 above) So Peter Maxwell is portrayed as giving away his furniture after being reduced to "cooking for 'wagon outfits!' " It is then is traced to Odelia's and Manuel's daughter, Stella Abreu, for her "Museum" (with a photograph of that shed-like building). The carpenter's bench photo by an unknown photographer from the Robert Mullin Collection is cited, but its date of about 1926 - 46 years after the shooting - is omitted. Given is Sederwall's tracing the bench to the Albuquerque home of Stella Maxwell's son, Mannie Miller, in his converted chicken coop. (Pages 158-160) [Oddly, a photo of the bench, labeled as in the "Steve Sederwall Collection" (Page 160) does not match the Mullins Collection photo, or the bench I saw in 2010 with Kenny Miller at deceased Mannie's chicken coop. The Sederwall one, is falling apart, with one of the top boards cracked. It may have been repaired, with possible board replacement, to become the one later photographed by Dr. Lee - adding to its invalidity for his "forensics."]

Dr. Henry Lee is introduced as contacted by Sederwall; who lies that "**a number of locations" on the bench's top and bottom tested positive for blood** by "presumptive blood test reagents phenolphthalein and o-tolidine." **He attributes the "blood" to "two different human beings;" claiming future separation to presumably identify the "slain intruder."** (Page 163) A Lee report is not cited, but one is in the Bibliography as: "Lee, Dr. Henry. Forensic Examination Report (Examination of Furniture From Pete Maxwell's of July 15, 1881) 22 May 2004." (Page 187)

HOAXING: Sederwall is lying. No blood was identified. Lee's sole report of February 25, 2005 merely hoaxed "blood-like" stains; and Orchid Cellmark Lab got no DNA from the bench. The mixed sample was from floorboards.

The cited Lee report appears to be one of Sederwall's forged ones, with the date changed to May 22, 2004. The one he gave to the Court was titled "Forensic Research and Training Center Forensic Examination Report: "Examination of furniture from Pete Maxwell's of July 15, 1881," and dated February 25, 2005.

Sederwall's "bloodstains from the slain intruder" were his fiction, repeating the "Billy the Kid Case" hoax's lie

about the bench having "mixed DNA" of two people bleeding on the bench: first playing-dead-Billy; next, switched shot innocent victim (possibly Billy Barlow).

IRRELEVANT: Not only did this fakery give no proof that Garrett did not kill Billy, it contradicted "Brushy's" death scene with shot-Billy-bleeding-on-the-bench-for-DNA.

FAKING "MAXWELL FURNITURE" FORENSICS

Sederwall, as sole "investigator," next had Dr. Henry Lee examine the headboard and the washstand *for him.*

HOAXING THE HEADBOARD

Sederwall reminds the reader that Deputy Poe had said Garrett's second shot rebounded from the wall and hit the headboard of Maxwell's bed. But he states that Lee found "nothing resembling the impact of a bullet, even a scratch." So Poe is called a liar. (Pages 160-161) No mention is made of Lee's report, but the Bibliography cites "Lee, Dr. Henry. Forensic Examination Report (Examination of Furniture From Pete Maxwell's of July 15, 1881) 22 May 2004." (Page 187)

HOAXING: Sederwall is tricking readers, since the "headboard" is just a big empty hole with a frame, missing the place for the bullet hit. But scorning readers' intelligence, he gives its photo. (Wily Dr. Lee had omitted a photo of it for his February 25, 2005 section on it.)

The Lee report in the Bibliography appears to be one of Sederwall's forged ones, with the date changed to May 22, 2004. The one Sederwall first presented to me was his fake "Forensic Research and Training Center Forensic Examination Report: "Examination of furniture from Pete Maxwell's of July 15, 1881," dated February 25, 2005. Its second forged version, with different font and deleted "Results and Conclusions," went to the Court as Exhibit E.

Lee's, actual report of February 26, 2005 had stated dishonestly: "No bullet hole and no observable damage, no sign of bullet ricocheted type of defects were found on the Headboard. No blood or biological materials were observed on the Headboard."

This is pure hoaxing by both Sederwall and Lee; as well as records forgery, as found by the Court, for Sederwall.

IRRELEVANT: All this fakery had nothing to do with Garrett not killing Billy, or "Brushy" being Billy.

HOAXING THE WASHSTAND

Sederwall also repeated Dr. Henry Lee's fake washstand forensics. (Pages 161-163) A photo of it (Page 162) differs from the one photographed and diagramed by Lee in his February 25, 2005 report, by having a raised back rim - with Lee's picture being only a box. Described are the washstand's two holes. Lee's bullet trajectory is presented, with his fake claim of Garrett shooting from the floor. No report is mentioned, but the Bibliography cites: "Lee, Dr. Henry. Forensic Examination Report (Examination of Furniture From Pete Maxwell's of July 15, 1881) 22 May 2004." (Page 187)

HOAXING: The toy-sized washstand used, is implausible as being one from Maxwell's bedroom; or he would have had to wash himself crouched on the floor - like Lee's faked shooting Garrett!

And neither Garrett nor Poe reported a washstand as struck by a bullet of Garrett's. So the alleged bullet trajectory is meaningless hoaxing of Garrett as shooting it, and of his position in the room.

The Lee report cited in the Bibliography appears to be one of Sederwall's forged ones, with date changed to May 22, 2004. It was given to me with a "Results and Conclusions" section absent.

Lee's actual report of February 25, 2005 was just non-committal; stating: "Two bullet holes were located on the side panels of the Washstand. The hole on the left side panel is consistent with a bullet entrance hole while the hole on the right side panel is consistent with a bullet exit hole. However, it is not possible to determine when those bullet holes were produced at this time [meaning any time from the 1870's to the 1900's!]."

IRRELEVANT: All this was irrelevant to Garrett not killing Billy, or "Brushy" being Billy.

CHAPTER 4
RETURN OF THE "BILLY THE KID CASE'S" EXHUMATION FAKERY

THE RETURN ATTACK ON JOHN MILLER'S BONES

In his desperate attempt to attain credibility, W.C. Jameson even let Steve Sederwall flaunt the "Billy the Kid Case's" fake forensics of the John Miller exhumation, with the misguided hope that any denial of the historic death scene would help "Brushy Bill's" cause. So unleashed Steve Sederwall proclaimed that John Miller matched Billy the Kid! (To hell with "Brushy!") And Case 2003-274's exhumation became, in Sederwall's telling, just part of his personal "ongoing investigation" (Page 165) - with dug up random man, William Hudspeth, obviously concealed!

FAKING THE JOHN MILLER EXHUMATION

Reflecting Sederwall's audacity, no background is given for John Miller: like being born in 1950, almost ten years before Billy; like knowing no Billy the Kid history at all; like dying soon after breaking a hip; and like being toothless. His exhumation is claimed to have been done on May 9, 2005 [sic – May 19] by an unnamed "forensic anthropologist" and "authorized by the state of Arizona."(Page 165)

HOAXING: Hidden is the report for that exhumation: "Lincoln County Sheriff's Department Supplemental Report," listing "Case # 2003-274, Date: Thursday, May 19, 2005, Subject: Exhumation of John Miller, Location: Arizona Pioneers' Cemetery, Prescott, Arizona, Report By: Steven M. Sederwall, On Thursday May 19, 2005,

at approximately 1:00 pm the following met at the Arizona Pioneers' Cemetery at Prescott, Arizona. Investigators: Steven M. Sederwall, Lincoln County Deputy Sheriff."

Hidden is that the hired Maricopa County forensic anthropologist was Dr. Laura Fulginiti, who denied all the hoaxers claims. Hidden is that the hoaxers had no Billy the Kid DNA to justify any exhumation for identity matching. Hidden is the wanton desecration of random man, William Hudspeth, buried beside Miller.

Sederwall shamelessly repeated his and Tom Sullivan's Piltdown man-style hoax, originally used in 2005 after the exhumation to claim that Miller had buck teeth and a shot left scapula; when they were using *Hudspeth's skeleton* with non-bullet damaged *right* scapula.

Sederwall lied: "**The right scapula of John Miller manifested a round hole. The anthropologist observed that it appeared to be a bullet hole that had healed" and the bullet entered the upper chest and exited his back.** He added that **Miller's right front incisor was placed somewhat in front of his left front incisor." So he concluded that this was Pat Garrett's bullet killing buck-toothed Billy the Kid.** (Page 165)

HOAXING: Sederwall is recycling his fakery to reporter, Rene Romo, in his November 6, 2006's *Albuquerque Journal's* "Billy the Kid Probe May Yield New Twist." Romo wrote: "Sederwall ... said Miller's skeletal remains were intriguing. He said Miller had buck teeth, like the Kid, and an old bullet wound that entered his upper left chest and exited through the scapula." Hidden, is that forensic expert, Dr. Laura Fulginiti, reported Miller having no teeth, and no damaged scapula. Hidden is that Sederwall was faking the results from random man, William Hudspeth, who had a damaged *right*, not *left* scapula, with Dr. Fulginiti denying a bullet wound. (See pages 265, 267 above)

Sederwall then claimed he got DNA from Miller's remains "sufficient to conduct a test." (Page 165)

HOAXING: Hidden was having no Billy the Kid DNA to compare with Miller's. Hidden was no need for DNA matching, since Miller had no historical match to Billy.

Jameson was apparently unaware of the "Billy the Kid Case's" publicity, in which the conscienceless, profiteering hoaxers were willing to claim any remains as Billy the Kid's to keep Bill Kurtis's cameras rolling. For Julie Carter's October 6, 2005 "Follow the Blood," Sederwall had plugged Miller as Billy; crowing: ""In the light of the evidence, we see that the history of Billy the Kid will change. Those with monied interest in history remaining the same will not be happy ... As a cop I know when people fight to keep you from looking at something, they are always trying to hide something. The Lincoln County War is still going on."

For reporter Rene Romo's November 6, 2006's *Albuquerque Journal's* "Billy the Kid Probe May Yield New Twist," hoaxing Sederwall plugged Miller, as well as faking having DNA from the carpenter's bench; stating: "If that [John Miller] DNA matches the work bench, I think the game is over."

RETURN TO "BRUSHY" FOR "DNA FORENSICS"

Finally, after 165 pages, Jameson got to extol his man. "Brushy" is described as dying in Hico, Texas, on December 27, 1950, "two days shy of his ninetieth birthday." He is praised for the knowing-things-not-printed trick, with "revelations" beyond knowledge of historians. He is claimed to have more credibility than Pat Garrett. (Pages 165-167)

TRUE-BELIEVER BEFUDDLEMENT: **It will remain a mystery as to what Jameson thought he was accomplishing with this *Cold Case Billy the Kid* book, as he mouthed Steve Sederwall's out-of-control fakery, which had practically nothing to do with "Brushy;" which invented alternative events not dreamed of by "Brushy," which demolished "Brushy's" knowing-things-not-printed trick; which showcased the "Billy the Kid Case" hoax which mismatched "Brushy;" and which even pushed imposter John Miller, not "Brushy," as Billy the Kid.**

WISHING FOR "BRUSHY'S" DNA

Sederwall's fake forensics, however, inspired Jameson's focus on "Brushy's" DNA. Jameson had a pathetic wish: if only Steve Sederwall had been allowed to get DNA from the Fort Sumner grave, and compared it to the carpenter's bench, the "controversy" would have been settled. (Page 167)

TRUE-BELIEVER BEFUDDLEMENT: Jameson appeared unaware that the "Billy the Kid Case" hoax claimed that Billy Bonney's playing-dead-blood-DNA was alleged to be on the carpenter's bench. That claim alone canceled out "Brushy," who had no such tale. And Jameson seems to have forgotten his own claim in *The Return of the Outlaw Billy the Kid* that the Fort Sumner Billy the Kid grave was just a fake tourist marker. As he and Frederick Bean wrote: "Billy the Kid's gravesite is not even authentic ... the original wooden marker ... disappeared ... Furthermore, because the majority of bodies in the cemetery were soldiers [and] were disinterred when the army removed them to the Santa Fe National Cemetery. There is more. On a number of occasions the Pecos River flooded ... carrying ... coffins ... The current marker is a tourist attraction, nothing more, and it is estimated it lies several yards from the original burial site. The truth is, no one is actually buried under the stone." (*The Return of the Outlaw Billy the Kid*, Pages 132-133)

Jameson may also have been hoodwinked by Sederwall's tall tale of DNA of two people on the bench (when no DNA at all had been recovered), and concluded that one of those people must have been Billy Barlow. So Jameson wished *that DNA* could have been compared to the bones in the Fort Sumner grave to show Barlow was buried there as the innocent victim. He did not understand that even if a DNA match had been found, the mitochondrial DNA used by Orchid Cellmark has coincidental matches; and worse, without the proven "reference DNA" of Billy Barlow, no DNA from the bench or the grave can be called his. And Barlow did not exist!

CHAPTER 5
FOREGONE FAKE CONCLUSION

WHEN HOAXERS FOOL THEMSELVES

Having been convinced himself by the fake forensics of the "Billy the Kid Case" hoaxers, and impressed by the flimflam "investigations" of "cop" Steve Sederwall, Jameson apparently believed that, in this rerun with his *Cold Case Billy the Kid*, "Brushy" was finally home free, as he depicted in his "Conclusion." (Pages 178-180) Smugly, he declared, "The historians got it wrong" because they believed legends instead of truth. But he despaired of convincing historians, because they refused to admit being wrong. He was certain that the state of New Mexico suppressed the truth. (Page 180)

In fact, neither Jameson, Sederwall, nor the back-up team of other "Billy the Kid Case" hoaxers in the wings, had offered any evidence whatsoever in *Cold Case Billy the Kid* to indicate that "Brushy" had been Billy Bonney, or that history was not as written. In that book, the "Billy the Kid Case" hoax had fared no better; though Steve Sederwall had repeated its lies as truths - while audaciously absconding with that case as his own!

OUTCOME: By firing all the ammunition he had, and showing it was all blanks, W.C. Jameson inadvertently discredited the Billy the Kid pretender hoaxes, as well as the hucksters who had sought to profit from riding the coattails of famous Billy the Kid.

PART VII

SUMMARY AND CONCLUSIONS

CHAPTER 1
IMPASSABLE HURDLES ARE IMPASSABLE

THE POWER OF REALITY

With labor-intensive efforts spanning 70 years, Billy the Kid imposters and their charlatan promoters battered themselves to no avail against impassable hurdles of Billy the Kid's real death scene, his Coroner's Jury Report confirming it and his corpse, and the profuse additional identifications of his body. Left only is their massive heap of junk, created in greedy hopes of hijacking famous history to which they had no connection.

To relegate them to history's trash heap, needed was just William Bonney's July 15, 1881 Coroner's Jury Report.

One could add two birthdays and one almost-full moon. Oliver Pleasant "Brushy Bill" Roberts was born on August 26, 1879, twenty years after Billy Bonney; making him a baby on July 14, 1881. John Miller was born in December of 1850, nine years before Billy; making him no Kid on July 14, 1881. The near-full moon of the light-as-day night of July 14, 1881, undid the "Brushy" and "Billy the Kid Case" hoaxes by their use of his faked dark and moonless night; then their forging of his transcripts to hide it.

In the end, hoaxing reduced to pathetic peddling of antiquated outlaw mythology that even Billy Bonney had ridiculed six days after his Stinking Springs capture, in a December 28, 1880 interview with city editor, Lucius "Lute" Wilcox, for J.H. Koogler's Las Vegas *Gazette*, for an article titled "The Kid. Interview with Billy Bonney The Best Known Man in New Mexico." Brilliant Billy had simply teased and taunted any future hangman and his own fate. The reporter had commented: "You appear to take it easy." Billy had answered: "Yes! What's the use of looking on the gloomy side of everything. The laugh's on me this time."

ANNOTATED APPENDIX

APPENDIX: 1: Attorney Bill Robins III and Attorney David Sandoval [present for a New Mexico law license which Robins lacked]. "Sixth Judicial District Court, State on New Mexico, County of Grant. Case No. MS-2003-11." "Billy the Kid's Pre-Hearing Brief." January 5, 2004.

IN THE MATTER OF CATHERINE ANTRIM,
BILLY THE KID'S PRE-HEARING BRIEF

COME NOW, Bill Robins, III and David Sandoval, of the law firm of Heard, Robins, Cloud, Lubel & Greenwood, LLC, and on the behalf of the estate of William H. Bonney, aka "Billy the Kid",

[AUTHOR'S NOTE: The Kid had no estate: posthumous property settled in a probate court. This fakery segues to Robins's calling dead Billy as his client as exhumation petitioner!]

file this Pre-Hearing Brief and state as follows:

I. INTRODUCTION

The Court asks the undersigned counsel to brief several questions as follows:

1. The Governor's right to assign an Attorney to Represent the Interests of Billy the Kid and the Associated Zone of Public Interest;
2. Who is the Real Party in Interest Represented by Counsel;
3. What Stake Does that Party Have in Intervening in This Cause;
4. Billy the Kid's Interest as Defined in the Law Relating to Standing; and
5. The Effect of *In Re: Application of Lois Telfer, for the Removal of the Body of William H. Bonney*

[AUTHOR'S NOTE: These questions by corrupt Judge Quintero are a parody. He well knows that Governor Richardson had no right to appoint an attorney to his court, knows that Robins has no "real party" as a client; knows that the dead do not appear in court and have no standing; and knows that the Fort Sumner Telfer exhumation case blocked all future exhumation attempts there by stating that the grave location was uncertain and contiguous remains would be disturbed.]

The Points and Authorities section below does so as follows: **Point One** provides introductory legal analysis, **Point Two** addresses Question 1, **Point Three** addresses Questions 2, 3, and 4, and **Point Four** addresses Question 5. **Point 5** supports the merits of the Petition for Exhumation.

II. POINTS AND AUTHORITIES

Point One
Initial Discussion as to the Nature of This Proceeding

This is an interesting proceeding in that the relief sought here is not exclusively judicial.

[AUTHOR'S NOTE: That is true. The following is just hoaxing.]

New Mexico allows the state registrar or state medical examiner to issue permits for disinterment. 1978 NMSA §24-14-23D. The statute does not identify who may make such a request nor specify the showing that needs to be made in order to obtain the permit. Rather than proceeding with this simple and non-adversarial process, Petitioners here have invoked this Court's equity jurisdiction for an order allowing the exhumation of Billy the Kid's mother, Catherine Antrim. See, *Hood v. Spratt,* 357 So.2d 135 (Miss. 1978) (request for disinterment "is particularly one for a court of equity") citing *Theodore v. Theodore*, 57 N.M. 434, 259 P.2d 795 (1953).

"[N]ormally a district court would not become involved in such matters unless a protesting relative or interested party files an injunction or takes some other legal action to halt the autopsy or disinterment," *In Re Johnson*, 94 N.M. 491, 494, 612 P.2d 1302 (1980). Petitioners should thus be commended for bringing this Court into the picture and in doing so, offering the town of Silver City, a relative of another descendent buried in the cemetery, and the legal interests of Billy the Kid, an opportunity to participate in the process.

[AUTHOR'S NOTE: This implies the hoax is a favor to Silver City - in court opposing exhumation - and a favor to dead Catherine Antrim. Also, Billy has no "legal interests," being dead!]

The questions the Court asked briefed, however, suggest the possibility that the court may not allow Billy the Kid to be heard.

[AUTHOR'S NOTE: At this point, the hoaxers were going through the motions, believing the judge was in their pocket.]

As will be shown clearly, Billy the Kid's interests are real, legitimate, proper for consideration, and we respectively ask the Court to recognize them as such.

[AUTHOR'S NOTE: This is audacious lying.]

A challenge to a governor's appointment power is made in a *quo warranto* proceeding.

[AUTHOR'S NOTE: Robins is faking legitimacy of his appointment as dead Billy's attorney. In fact, only the judge can appoint an attorney for a client. This appointment was an example of Richardson's illegal abuse of power.]

New Mexico Judicial Standards Commission v. Governor Bill Richardson and Espinoza, 134 N.M. 59, 73 P.2d 197 (2003); see also, 1978 NMSA. §§44-3-1 *et. seq.* (*quo warranto* action proper when "any person shall usurp, intrude into or unlawfully holds or exercise any public office, civil or military, or any franchise within this state.")

The *quo warranto* statute contains specific procedures that the Town has not properly followed, nor could follow because the Town is not a "private person."

[AUTHOR'S NOTE: This fact demonstrates that Robins is misapplying the law to the town with his false argument.]

Standing to bring such a proceeding lies first with the attorney general or district attorney. 1978 NMSA, §44-3-4; *Beese v. District Court,* 31 N.M. 82, 239 P. 452 (1925). Those public officials do not present any challenge here.

A private person can bring a *quo warranto* action only when he has requested the aforementioned public officials to bring action and they have refused. 1978 NMSA, §44-3-4. The only private person in this matter is Ms. Amos-Staadt [sic] and she has not challenged the Governor's appointment, much less shown compliance with the procedural requisites of the *quo warranto* statute.

As noted, the challenge to the Governor comes from the Town of Silver City. It simply has no standing to bring a *quo warranto* proceeding. 1978 NMSA, §44-3-4. The validity of Governor Richardson's appointment of the undersigned counsel is thus not before this Court.

[AUTHOR'S NOTE: In fact, a legitimate judge would have made it his/her matter and kicked an inappropriately appointed lawyer representing a dead client out of court.]

To the extent that the Court remains concerned with the presence of Billy the Kid in this litigation,

[AUTHOR'S NOTE: Robins here switches from the "estate" of Billy the Kid to the dead Kid as client.]

it is a matter that can be more properly addressed pursuant to legal requirements of standing and intervention, which the discussion below shows the Kid satisfies.

[AUTHOR'S NOTE: Robins now fakes that dead Billy had court standing to justify his intervening.]

(Given the express direction to brief the question, however, the discussion below sets forth the proper gubernatorial powers at play here.)

C. *The Governor's Powers*

As noted above, the governor is the supreme executive officer of the state. There can be no question that in that capacity Governor Richardson has authority to engage the services of professionals to assist him in accomplishment of those duties. Lawyers are certainly within that group, as is witnessed by Geno Zamora, the Governor's chief legal counsel.

[AUTHOR'S NOTE: Robins is here making a false argument by omission. The governor can engage an attorneys services. But the matter here is not services, it is the illegal nature of Robins's appointment to this court.]

The source of power behind such appointments is likely found in the "inherent general power of appointment in the executive." *Matheson v. Ferry*, 641 P.2d 674, 682 (Ut 1982); *Hadley v. Washburn*, 67 S.W. 592 (Mo. 1902) (appointment of election commissioners is an inherent executive power); *Application of O'Sullivan*, 158 P.2d 306, 309 (Mont. 1945) ("the power of appointment is an executive function which cannot be delegated to the judiciary); *State v. Brill*, 111 N.W. 294, (1907) (legislature prohibited from requiring judges at appoint members to a board of control unrelated to the judiciary on a separation of powers theory grounded in the presumption that the power of appointment is inherently executive).

[AUTHOR'S NOTE: Robins, spewing irrelevant cases, is omitting that the Constitution guarantees separation of powers: executive branch Richardson could not appoint him to a court!]

This inherent power must also allow the Governor to appoint attorneys to address his concerns and/or further his interests outside his immediate circle.

[AUTHOR'S NOTE: Robins gives dramatic proof that the "Billy the Kid Case" was Richardson's baby. Then he leaps to the motive of the publicity-seeking hoax: the Billy the Kid pardon.]

The governor has the "power to grant reprieves and pardons." N.M. Const. Art. V Sec. 6. Undersigned counsel intends on seeking a pardon for Billy the Kid. Certainly Governor Richardson is within his inherent appointment power to hire counsel to advise him on the merits of such a pardon.

[AUTHOR'S NOTE: Robins omits that pardon advising gives no standing for this court seeking exhumation.]

That the power extends to pardons of long-dead individuals is clear because our Constitution extends that power to pardon offences under the Territorial Laws of New Mexico. N.M. Const. Art. XXII Sec 5. (Footnote: Posthumous pardons are not unusual. In fact, Lenny Bruce was pardoned by Governor Patake in New York just last month.)

[AUTHOR'S NOTE: Robins omits that pardon was at the discretion Governor's discretion. Richardson could pardon Billy if he wanted to. The rest was just a publicity stunt.]

That the appointment is consistent with the statutorily granted powers is shown by consideration of two different status. Counsel's appointment here is in the nature of an appointment as a public defender; a portion of their work effort will go towards exposing the merits of a pardon. 1978 NMSA §§31-15-1, *et. seq.* The public defender department is within the executive branch and is headed [sic-by] an appointee of the governor. 1978 NMSA §§31-15-4A. The duty and function of the department is to have attorneys serve as defense counsel "as necessary and appropriate." 1978 NMSA §§31-15-7B(10).

[AUTHOR'S NOTE: Robins is preposterously saying he is in an exhumation court to decide on a pardon.]

The Governor has apparently deemed it necessary and appropriate to seek guidance from undersigned counsel on matters related to the Kid and potential pardon.

Similarly, the Governor has authority to request the appointment of prosecutorial attorneys. 1978 NMSA, Section 8-5-2B provides that a governor may request the attorney general to appoint counsel in "all actions civil or criminal" in which the governor believes the state is "interested." The governor's pardon power gives the state an interest [sic-in] legal matters involving a potential candidate for pardon and Governor Richardson could rely on Section 8-5-2B's power at the appropriate time. This should not be read to mean that Governor Richardson is assuming power to appoint attorneys to act on behalf of the State, a power that lies exclusively with the Attorney General. It is referenced here as another example of how the governor is authorized in several instances to procure the assistance of attorneys.

[AUTHOR'S NOTE: Faking Robins has given no justification for his being in this court, a travesty which only a corrupt judge, like Henry Quintero, would have permitted.]

Point Three
What Interests Are of Importance Here

A. *The Law of Standing*

As has been established, this is an action in equity. New Mexico's Supreme Court wrote: "The equity right of intervention in proper cases has always been recognized. The equitable test is, 'Does the intervener stand to gain or lose by the judgment.' " *Stovall v. Vesely*, 38 N.M. 415, 34 P.2d 862, 864 (1934)

[AUTHOR'S NOTE: The actual test here is that Robins has no existing client to have an interest, since Billy is dead.]

Billy the Kid's interest here is his legacy.

[AUTHOR'S NOTE: Robins is out-of-control faking that dead Billy, for whom he can speak, is after a "legacy."]

As noted in previous briefing the very question of his life and death will be impacted by the results of the Petitioners' investigation.

[AUTHOR'S NOTE: Robins's fake argument reveals the thrust to make "Brushy Bill" Billy the Kid - and pardon him.]

B. *The Planned Request For Pardon Confers Standing Here*

Undersigned counsel intends to ask Governor Richardson that he pardon Billy the kid for the murder conviction of Sheriff Brady on several known bases including the fact that then Territorial Governor Lew Wallace reneged on his promise to pardon the Kid.

[AUTHOR'S NOTE: Now comes Robins's leap that cracked the hoax for me. He seemed to be talking about pardoning Billy Bonney, but segues to the pretenders - as if one *is* Billy, who deserves pardon. This is to be a rerun of the Governor T.J. Mabry hearing, with "Brushy" winning!]

There were at least two individuals that laid claim to Billy the Kid's identity years after his alleged shooting by Garrett. **Both of them apparently led long and peaceful and crime-free lives.** [author's boldface]

As was recently recognized by the court in *Mestiza v. DeLeon,* 8 S.W. 3d 770 (Tx. Ct. App. - Corpus Christi - (1999) this interest is sufficient to properly confer standing. There an inmate imprisoned on murder conviction sought the exhumation of the victim's body on the basis that the exhumation could lead to new evidence to support a habeas corpus claim. While not deciding the merits, the Texas court determined that the inmate's interest in showing the improper conviction was sufficient to confer standing. That certainty is an analogous situation here.

The reasons that the exhumation is sought is to disinter the remains of Billy the Kid's mother for the extraction of Mitochondrial DNA.

As such, Ms. Antrim presents the only source of such DNA. Should the exhumation be denied, Billy the Kid will be forever denied the opportunity to make use of modern technology to shed light on his life and death.

[AUTHOR'S NOTE: Do not miss that this is just a Billy the Kid pretender argument: namely that Billy's death is in question, and Pat Garrett's innocent victim may lay in his grave. Hidden is the historical certainty of Billy's killing by Garrett.]

Should the DNA extracted from Ms. Antrim confirm that one of the potential Kids was in fact Billy the Kid, undersigned counsel will be able to make an even

stronger argument for pardon by citing to the long years of law abiding life.

[AUTHOR'S NOTE: THIS IS THE SENTENCE THAT CRACKED THE "BILLY THE KID CASE" HOAX. And here is the full-blown plot: prove a pretender by faking DNA, then pardon him; ergo, Oliver "Brushy Bill" Roberts - as Billy the Kid!]

C. A Comparison of Interests

This Court has allowed the intervention of the Town of Silver City in this matter. The municipal politicians there have apparently authorized the Town's Mayor to oppose the exhumation. Billy the Kid acknowledges the existence of case law that accords standing to the owners of the cemetery concerned in such proceedings.

[AUTHOR'S NOTE: Do not miss Robins's sly and crazy switch from "Billy the Kid's estate" to channeling dead Billy, who is now speaking along with him - in apparent legal agreement!]

What is of interest here, is that such standing is often given to the cemetery owner because it may be the only entity that can represent the wishes of the deceased, an element typically considered in whether to order an exhumation. *Theodore*, 57 N.M. at 438, *Estate of Conroy*, 530 A2d 212, 530 N.Y. S.2d 668 (N.Y.Super. 1988)

As expected, the Mayor here opposes the exhumation and is positioned to present evidence in support of its objection. Whether or not that truly represents the interests of Ms. Antrim can never be known. Given the identity of the decedent and the time that has passes since her death, the Mayor cannot possibly have any direct evidence of Ms. Antrim's wishes. As such, the evidence that is presented by the Mayor can be viewed as best, supposition, or at worst, utterly unreliable.

[AUTHOR'S NOTE: Do not miss the bizarreness of this argument. In the real world, the Mayor is has to protect remains in a cemetery under his authority. But Robin is saying the Mayor actually needs to mind-read corpse Catherine to find out if she wants to be dug up. Or better, Robins implies, the Mayor should channel her, so she could speak in Court!]

One is left to question why such a party with such a remote interest and lack of express knowledge about the decedent's wishes is conferred standing while the interests of Billy the Kid go unheard if this Court denier him standing. Allowing such a party to appear and present evidence while denying the same opportunity to a party that has been appointed to represent the interests of the decedent's son does not seem prudent nor fair.

[AUTHOR'S NOTE: This argument is so crazy that a reader might be tempted to rationalize that it cannot be as crazy as it sounds. Robins is saying that dead Billy the Kid has more credibility to let his wishes be known, than the live Mayor whose obligation it is to protect his city's cemetery. And, by the way, Robins makes clear that he himself can tell the wishes of the dead, unlike the limited Mayor. And also, Robins claims, this speaking for the dead adds up to corpse Billy the Kid having standing in court - in fact, better justification to speak in Court than the Silver City Mayor himself!]

Point Four
The *Telfer* Case and Impact on This Case

The *Telfer* case is of no major consequence here.

[AUTHOR'S NOTE: This statement is evidence that Robins has nerve as well as nuttiness. The *Telfer* case was fatal to the Catherine Antrim exhumation. The 1962 blocked exhumation on the Billy the Kid grave by Lois Telfer established precedent that remains were in uncertain location, and exhumation could disturb contiguous bodies. Catherine Antrim was to be exhumed to match with Billy the Kid's DNA. But it was unattainable. So there was no reason to exhume her. In what follows, Robins hides all that.]

First, since neither of the parties here were parties there, the doctrines of res judica and collateral estoppel cannot possibly apply against the current litigants. *Brantley Farms v. Carlsbad Irrigation District,* 124 N.M. 698, 702, 954 p.2d 763 (1998).

Second, the body sought to be exhumed there was the purported body of Billy the Kid and not the subject of this request, his mother. Third, the basis for the request was that the Ft. Sumner burial site had been abandoned and not maintained for years. The petitioner's desire was to re-inter the body in a "decent and respectable burial place" in Lincoln, New Mexico. The factual and legal matters there are thus distinct to those here. That one was denied cannot serve to prohibit the exhumation of the other.

The opponents of exhumation may rely on the *Telfer* court's finding that "it is no longer possible to locate the site of the grave of the said William H. Bonney" as a means to argue that the exhumation of Ms. Antrim for DNA would be futile. Even if such a factual finding was true and correct the technology available now as opposed to 1962 is such that a new factual inquiry would be likely to yield different results.

[AUTHOR'S NOTE: This argument about "new technology" is fakery. Technology cannot show where Billy Bonney himself rests in Fort Sumner's cemetery, or prevent disturbing contiguous remains.]

Even if the body buried in Ft., Sumner cannot possibly be exhumed for comparable DNA, a denial here is not called for. As has been mentioned there are at least two other individuals who claim to have been the Kid. Surely *Telfer* would not be a binding precedent to deny exhumations of grave sites in Texas or Arizona.

[AUTHOR'S NOTE: Robins is arguing for exhuming pretenders, when they fail just based on invalid history.]

Point Five
Exhumation is Proper

The Sheriffs invoke the jurisdiction of this Court in an attempt to exhume the remains of Catherine Antrim. The Court has express statutory authority to so order. It is a crime in New Mexico to knowingly and willfully disturb or remove remains of any person interred in a cemetery. 1978 NMSA, § 30-12-12. The criminal statute, however, recognizes three exceptions. Disinterment is allowed "pursuant to an order of the district court, the provisions of Section 24-14-23 NMSA 1978 or as otherwise permitted by law." This request falls into the first and last exceptions.

[AUTHOR'S NOTE: Robins must know that the OMI was blocking exhumation and that Attorney Sherry Tippett lied about its permission. He is, thus. trying to get the court to act independently of the OMI.]

The leading exhumation case in New Mexico is *Theodore*, 57, N.M. 434 and sets forth as follows:

[AUTHOR'S NOTE: The irrelevant *Theodore* case, which follows, is simply about digging up and relocating a body.].

> In determining whether authority to disinter a body **and bury it elsewhere** should be granted, controlling consideration seems generally to be given by the courts to the following factors, (1) the interest of the public; (2) wishes of the decedent; (3) rights and feelings of those entitled to be heard by reason of relationship; (4) the rights and principles of religious bodies or other organizations which granted the right to inter the body in the first place of burial, and (5) the question of whether or not consent was given to the burial in the first place of interment by the one claiming the right of removal.(emphasis added).

The bolded language is important because it shows that *Theodore* is not directly on point.

[AUTHOR'S NOTE: Robins even admits the Theodore case is irrelevant. In fact, his whole document is just fake filler.]

The exhumation there was for the purpose of moving remains from one grave site (preferred by the decedent's brother) to another site (preferred by the plaintiff's widow). That is not the case here. Petitioners asking for an exhumation that is of importance in their investigation surrounding the Lincoln County Wars [sic] and the shooting of Billy the Kid.

The distinction renders some of the *Theodore* factors of no consequence and the others of limited precedential value. Since the Ms. Antrim remains will be replaced in the same burial site, the 4th and 5th factor, which involves the decedent's ties to the "first place of burial" sought to be abandoned are of no consequence here. The first three factors remain.

1st Factor Public Interest, Billy the Kid's name is forever tied to New Mexico and to that of another legendary figure of the Old West, Sheriff Pat Garrett. A commonly held version of history paints a picture of an ambush in which Garrett killed the Kid in Ft. Sumner where most believe the Kid still lies at rest. This version has been questioned. It is the investigation into whether Garrett killed the Kid that has prompted these investigators to seek exhumation.

[AUTHOR'S NOTE: This is pure hoaxing The only ones to "question" history are the hoaxers themselves for their stunt. There is no "public interest" - meaning value - there is only the self-serving motives of the hoaxers - and definite "lack of public interest" by destroying New Mexican's iconic Old West history and its tourist sites.]

2nd Factor, the Decedents wishes. In spite of Silver City's position to the contrary, we simply do not know what the decedent's wishes would be. Given the present circumstances, however, where her remains could possibly provide critical evidence to be used by modern day advocates to clear her son's name, one might easily surmise that Silver City's dogged attempt to resist exhumation would not be appreciated by Ms. Antrim.

[AUTHOR'S NOTE: This is Robins at his most slippery. First of all, he is now near-channeling Catherine Antrim to express "her wishes." Secondly he is misstating Silver City's position. The Mayor has standing not to guess "wishes," but to protect the sanctity of her grave from exactly the groundless publicity stunt that this hoax represents. Thirdly, Robins is still faking "public interest." Fourthly, is his most outrageous thrust: that Catherine Antrim would want to be dug up to "prove" that her son was "Brushy Bill."]

3rd Factor, Surviving Relatives Wishes. There are no relatives of Ms. Antrim currently before the Court. This Court can take judicial notice from the *Telfer* case, that at least one of her claimed relatives was not adverse to the concept of exhumation since the disinterment of Billy the Kid was sought in 1962 [sic - 1961, denied in 1962]

[AUTHOR'S NOTE: Robins hid that Lois Telfer had no proven kinship to Billy the Kid, so had no true standing. And no opinion was expressed by her as the exhuming Catherine Antrim anyway.]

The closest party currently before the Court is in fact Billy the Kid as represented by the undersigned counsel. As is apparent from the arguments set forth in this brief, the kid's [sic] interests would be furthered by the exhumation.

[AUTHOR'S NOTE: Here again is Robins is channeling dead Billy to say that HE, BILLY THE KID (meaning more bizarrely: he "Brushy Bill" Roberts) wants his mom dug up!]

The "limitation of "currently before the Court" was used above because of undersigned counsel is aware of certain individuals who claim to be related to Ms. Antrim who at worst will likely testify in support of exhumation and may even attempt to intervene in this matter.

[AUTHOR'S NOTE: Robins is apparently referring to Elbert Garcia, a Santa Rosa, New Mexico, resident who wrote a book claiming to be Billy the Kid's grandson. Since his kinship was unproven, he was soon abandoned by the hoaxers.]

Billy the Kid believes that the evidence adduced at the exhumation hearing will certainly support an order of exhumation here.

[AUTHOR'S NOTE: Oops, Robins has crossed into the "Exorcist" movie's territory. He has "disappeared" as an entity; only dead Billy is talking now. The creepy thought is that Robins not be faking. He may really think he IS "Brushy Bill" incarnate.]

As such, Billy the Kid's mother's name, will forever be tied with other famous names and legendary figures: Czar Nicholas II of Russia and his family, John Paul Jones, President Zachary Taylor, Jesse James, Butch Cassidy and the Sundance Kid. All these individuals were themselves exhumed for various reasons. Other lesser known, or perhaps less colorful figures, have also been exhumed. They include Samuel Mudd (conspirator in the assassination of Abraham Lincoln), Haile Selassie (former emperor of Ethiopia), Czar Lazar (14th century Serbian monarch), Medgar Evers (civil rights leader, Carl A. Weiss (alleged assassin of Huey Long). Those whose exhumation has been proposed at various times in the past include, Meriwether Lewis. John Wilkes Booth, John F. Kennedy, Lee Harvey Oswald and J. Edgar Hoover.

[AUTHOR'S NOTE: Exhumation of other famous people does not lend any justification to this exhumation attempt.]

Clearly, exhumation as a truth seeking device has been used throughout history. Exhumation has also been the subject of case law and legal discourse. See, 61 U. Colo.L.Rev. 567, Evidentiary Autopsies,

1990; 21 A.L.R.2d. 538, *Annotation*, Power of a Court to Order Disinterment and Autopsy or Exhumation for Evidential Purpose in a Civil Case."

[AUTHOR'S NOTE: Robins is using irrelevant cases. First of all, this is allegedly a criminal murder case, not a civil one. More important, the murder case is a hoax, since Pat Garrett killed Billy Bonney not an innocent victim.]

The current state of knowledge and technology, and its expected refinement and expansion, will likely make it even more of a common occurrence in the future. It is proper to allow such an inquiry here.

III. CONCLUSION

The foregoing has established that the undersigned counsel may legally and properly appear in these proceedings on behalf of, and to represent the interests of Billy the Kid. They are ready to present testimony and evidence to further support their interests that the exhumation of the Kid's mother, Ms. Catherine Antrim be allowed to proceed.

[AUTHOR'S NOTE: Robins established nothing to justify his being in this Court, or to channel dead Billy. One is left with the creepy "They are ready ..." and wondering if "they" are Robins and his dead buddy Ollie Roberts, or just Robins and his co-counsel, David Sandoval - present with his New Mexico law license because Robins had just a Texas one.]

Respectfully submitted this 5th day of January, 2004.

Heard, Robins, Cloud, Lubel & Greenwood, L.L.P.

By: David Sandoval

Bill Robins III

David Sandoval

Address and Telephone Numbers

ATTORNEYS FOR BILLY THE KID

[AUTHOR'S NOTE: Really, in boldface, Robins and Sandoval are listed as Billy's lawyers! And New Mexico taxpayers footed the district court bills in Grant and De Baca Counties for these hoaxing charlatans.]

APPENDIX: 2: Attorneys Bill Robins III, David Sandoval, and Mark Acuña. "Tenth Judicial Court of De Baca County. Case No. CV-2004-00005, In the Matter of William H. Bonney, aka 'Billy the Kid.' " February 26, 2004.

PETITION FOR THE EXHUMATION OF BILLY THE KID'S REMAINS

COME NOW, Co-Petitioners, and respectfully request that this Court order that the body of William H. Bonney, aka "Billy the Kid" be exhumed, and in support of the Petition state:

I. The Petitioners

1. The Co-Petitioners are Gary Graves, Sheriff of De Baca County, Tom Sullivan, (Sheriff) and Steve Sederwall (Deputy Sheriff) of Lincoln County, New Mexico. (hereinafter the "Sheriff-Petitioners").

2. Co-Petitioner Billy the Kid is one of the subjects of an investigation being conducted by the Sheriff-Petitioners. Bill Robins III and David Sandoval have been appointed by the Honorable Bill Richardson, Governor of the State of New Mexico, to represent the interests of Billy the Kid in the investigation.

II. Jurisdiction and Venue

3. Jurisdiction is proper with this Court on the basis of 1978 NMSA Statute 30-12-12.

4. Venue is proper in this County on the basis that the remains that are the subject of this exhumation are located in deBaca [sic] County.

III. Procedural Background

5. The Sheriff-Petitioners initiated investigation in their respective counties to set the historical record straight as to the guilt or innocence of the legendary Sheriff Pat Garrett in the death of Billy the Kid. The investigative files bear the numbers 03-06-136-01 (*deBaca* [sic] *County*) and 2003-274 (*Lincoln County*).

[AUTHOR'S NOTE: During my open records case from 2007 to 2015, its law enforcement officers would lie, claiming the "Billy the Kid Case" was their "private hobby," and/or it was just the investigation of the deputy murders by Billy the Kid – to hide their Garrett murder case as Sheriffs and Deputies.]

6. The remains of Billy the Kid's mother, Catherine Antrim, currently lie in a marked grave located in Silver City, New Mexico. The Sheriff-Petitioners previously filed a Petition to Exhume the remains of Catherine Antrim (hereinafter the "Antrim Petition") which is currently pending before the Honorable District Court Judge Quintero in the Sixth

Judicial District. Counsel for Billy the Kid filed a Petition to Intervene in support of that exhumation.

[AUTHOR'S NOTE: Robins's client is dead Billy!]

7. The purpose of the Antrim Petition is to disinter her remains to extract vital mitochondrial DNA to then be used to compare with the DNA sought to be extracted from the purported remains of Billy the Kid. Those purported remains of Billy the Kid lie in a cemetery in Ft. Sumner, New Mexico. A hearing on the merits of the Antrim exhumation is scheduled for August 16-18, 2004.

8. Exhumations, DNA extractions and comparisons have become an increasingly common and accepted investigatory method and tool in forensic criminology and historical investigation ...

IV. Historical Background

[AUTHOR'S NOTE: This section confirms the "Billy the Kid Case" as a "Brushy Bill" hoax, and another attempt at the lost Governor Mabry pardon.]

9. Billy the Kid is New Mexico's best known Old West figure. He has even been called the best known New Mexican ever. The Kid is no doubt the stuff of legend, myth, and continuing popular attention.

10. The Kid lived during a complex and violent time in New Mexico history which included the "Lincoln County War." It was a time when the distinction between "outlaw" and "lawman" was blurred due to rival political factions having deputized their respective supporters. Billy the Kid himself was deputized during these times.

11. This was also a time whose history was not accurately nor completely written.

[AUTHOR'S NOTE: This is hoaxer-style fake "suspicion," which is ultimately the fake "proof" used for "survival suspicion" and accusing Garrett of murdering the innocent victim, not Billy.]

For generations now, the life of Billy the Kid has been the subject of historical debate. Perhaps the most significant lingering question involves whether Billy the Kid was indeed shot by Sheriff Pat Garrett in an ambush **one dark night** in Ft. Sumner **or whether the Kid went on to live a long and peace-abiding life elsewhere**.

[AUTHOR'S NOTE: THIS IS THE DARK NIGHT GIVE-AWAY OF A "BRUSHY"-BELIEVER, LIKE ROBINS. Faking that "historical debate" exists, he is quoting "Brushy's" confabulation about the "dark night" as fact, ignorant of July 14, 1881's full moon. His motive, however, is to validate intended pretender exhumations.]

12. The debate has been sparked at various times in the past by at least two individuals who laid claim to his identity. **Ollie** "Brushy Bill" Roberts [author's boldface] resided in Hico, Texas and claimed to be Billy the Kid. John Miller, in Arizona also died still claiming he was Billy the Kid. Co-Petitioners are in the initial phases of pursuing exhumations of these individuals as well.

[AUTHOR'S NOTE: Amusingly and revealingly, Robins affectionately and familiarly calls Roberts "Ollie."]

13. The Sheriff-Petitioners' investigation has certainly fueled debate as to whether or not Pat Garrett's version of events surrounding his claimed killing of Billy the Kid is in fact historically accurate. The investigation has renewed questions as to whether Billy the Kid lies buried at the fabled grave-site in Ft. Sumner. Allowing the exhumation of the remains at Ft. Sumner grave site for extraction of DNA to be compared with that of Ms. Antrim's will likely finally provide definitive answers to this historical quandary.

[AUTHOR'S NOTE: As discussed, these DNA claims are fake, and were the basis of the Office of the Medical Investigator's refusal of exhumation permits.]

IV. Claim for Relief, *Exhumation of Remains*

14. Co-Petitioners repeat and re-allege the foregoing paragraphs 1-13 as if fully set herein.

15. Section 30-12-12 of the New Mexico Statutes grants district courts power and discretion to order the exhumation of remains at a grave site.

16. This Court's power and discretion should be exercised and the exhumation be allowed to proceed for purposes of examining the purported remains of Billy the Kid. And for the extraction of DNA samples from the same.

WHEREFORE, Petitioners request that this Court issue an order allowing the exhumation of William H. Bonney, and all such further relief as the Court deems just and proper.

Respectfully submitted this 24th day of February, 2004.

Heard, Robins, Cloud, Lubel & Greenwood L.L.P.
Bill Robins III, David Sandoval
Attorneys for Co-Petitioner BILLY the KID

[AUTHOR'S NOTE: Do not miss that Bill Robins's *client* is still the dead Billy the Kid - requesting his own exhumation!]

ANNOTATED BIBLIOGRAPHY

RELEVANT 19th CENTURY HISTORY

COMPREHENSIVE REFERENCES

Nolan, Frederick. *The War: A Documentary History*. Norman: University of Oklahoma Press. **1992.**

__________. *The West of Billy the Kid*. Norman: University of Oklahoma Press. **1998.**

HISTORICAL ORGANIZATIONS (PERIOD)

SANTA FE RING, 19th CENTURY

MODERN SOURCES

Brown, Richard Maxwell. *Strain of Violence: Historical Studies of American Violence and Vigilantism*. New York: Oxford University Press. 1975. (**New Mexico unique for assassination as part of political system**)

Caffey, David L. *Chasing the Santa Fe Ring: Power and Privilege in Territorial New Mexico*. Albuquerque, New Mexico: University of New Mexico Press. 2014.

__________. *Frank Springer and New Mexico: From the Colfax County War to the Emergence of Modern Santa Fe*. Texas A and M. University Press. 2007.

Cleaveland, Agnes Morley. *No Life for a Lady*. Boston: Houghton Mifflin. 1941.

__________. *Satan's Paradise: From Lucien Maxwell to Fred Lambert*. Boston: Houghton Mifflin Company. 1952.

Cleaveland, Norman, *Colfax County's Chronic Murder Mystery*. Santa Fe: New Mexico. The Rydel Press. 1977.

__________. *A Synopsis of the Great New Mexico Cover-up*. Self-printed. 1989.

__________. *Some Comments Norman Cleveland May Make to the Huntington Westerners on Sept. 19, 1987*. Unpublished.

__________. *Some Highlights of William R. Morley's Contribution to the Pioneer Development of the Southwest*. Self-printed. No Date.

__________. *The Great Santa Fe Cover-up*. Based on a Talk given Before the Santa Fe Historical Society on November 1, 1978. Self-printed. 1982.

Cleaveland, Norman and George Fitzpatrick. *The Morleys - Young Upstarts on the Southwest Frontier*. Albuquerque, New Mexico: Calvin Horn Publisher, Inc. 1971.

Cooper, Gale. *The Santa Fe Ring Versus Billy the Kid: The Making of An American Monster*. Albuquerque, New Mexico: Gelcour Books. 2018.

Klasner, Lilly. Eve Ball. Ed. *My Girlhood Among Outlaws*. Tucson, Arizona: The University of Arizona Press. 1972. Klasner, Lilly. Eve Ball. Ed. *My Girlhood Among Outlaws*. Tucson, Arizona: The University of Arizona Press. 1972. (**John Chisum's in jail write-up about Santa Fe Ring injustices to himself**)

Lamar, Howard Robert N. *The Far Southwest 1846 – 1912: A Territorial History*. New Haven and London: Yale University Press. 1966. (**Chapter 6 covers the Santa Fe Ring)**)

Meinig, D. W. *The Shaping of America. A Geographical Perspective on 500 Years of History. Vol. 3. Transcontinental America 1850 - 1915*. New Haven and London: Yale University Press. 1998. (**Pages 127 and 132 are on the Santa Fe Ring.**)

Montoya, María E. Translating Property. The Maxwell Land Grant and the Conflict Over Land in the American West, 1840-1900. Berkeley and Los Angeles: University of California Press. 2002.

Naegle, Conrad Keeler. *The History of Silver City, New Mexico 1870-1886.* University of New Mexico Bachelor of Arts thesis. Pages 30-60. Unpublished. 1943. Collection of the Silver City Museum, Silver City, New Mexico. **(Grant County rebellion)**

__________. "The Rebellion of Grant County, New Mexico in 1876." *Arizona and the West: A Quarterly Journal of History.* Autumn, 1968. Volume 10. Number 3. Tucson, Arizona: The University of Arizona Press. 1968. Pages 225-240. **(Grant County rebellion against Santa Fe Ring)**

Newman, Simeon Harrison III. "The Santa Fe Ring." *Arizona and the West.* Volume 12. Autumn 1970. Pages 269-288.

Otero, Miguel A. *My Life on the Frontier, 1882-1897: Incidents and Characters of the period when Kansas, Colorado, and New Mexico were Passing Through the Last of their Wild and Romantic Years.* New York: The Press of the Pioneers. 1935. Pages 232-233. (Quoted by Victor Westphall, *Thomas Benton Catron and His Era.* Page 188) **(Quote: "the 'Santa Fe Ring,' the real machine controlling the political situation in New Mexico.")**

Pearson, Jim Berry. *The Maxwell Land Grant.* Norman: University of Oklahoma Press. 1961.

Taylor, Morris F. *O.P. McMains and the Maxwell Land Grant Conflict.* Tucson, Arizona: The University of Arizona Press. 1979. **(Traces origins of the Santa Fe Ring)**

Theisen, Lee Scott. "Frank Warner Angel's Notes on New Mexico Territory, 1878." *Arizona and the West: A Quarterly Journal of History.* Winter 1976. Volume 18. Number 4. Pages 333-370. **(About the Angel notebook given to Lew Wallace and listing names of Santa Fe Ring members)**

Westphall, Victor. *Thomas Benton Catron and His Era.* Tucson, Arizona: University of Arizona Press. 1973. **(Ring-denier, who cites sources exposing the Ring)**

CONTEMPORARY SOURCES (CHRONOLOGICAL)

A.C.L. Editorial. "New Mexico, A Sorry Showing for a Would-be State, Tweed's Disciples Preying on the Populace, How the Territorial Ring is Run, Why the Territory Should Not Be Made a State. **March 13, 1876.** *The Boston Daily Globe.* Volume IX, Number 62. Newspaperarchive.com.

No Author. "A Contemplated Political Change." Grant County *Herald.* **September 16, 1876**. Quoted by Conrad Keeler Naegle in *The History of Silver City, New Mexico 1870-1886* doctoral thesis. Pages 39-40. **(Listing reasons to escape the Ring by annexing to Arizona Territory)**

Wallace, Lew. "Our mutual friend, M. Hinds, who will hand you this ..." Letter to A.H. Markland. **November 14, 1878**. Indiana Historical Society. Lew Wallace Collection. M0292. Box 3. Folder 17. **(Ring tries to remove him as governor)**

Leonard, Ira E. "When you left here I promised to write you concerning events transpiring here ..." Letter to Lew Wallace. **May 20, 1878 [sic - 79]**. Indiana Historical Society. Lew Wallace Collection. M0292. Box 4. Folder 10. **(Quote: "Santa Fe ring ... so long an incubus on the government.")**

Wallace, Lew. "I have the honor to inform you that the Legislature of this Territory adjourned ..." **February 16, 1880**. Letter to Carl Schurz. Indiana Historical Society. Lew Wallace Collection. M0292. Box 4. Folder 14. **(Key documentation of Catron as head of the Santa Fe Ring, and Wallace's Ring opposition)**

No Author. "White Cap's Proclamation." *Las Vegas Optic.* March 12, 1880. **(Manifesto against land-grabbing Catron and the Ring)**

No Author. "The Santa Fe Ring is the most corrupt combination that ever cursed any country or community." Las Cruces *Thirty-Four Newspaper.* **October 27, 1880**. From Victor Westphall, *Thomas Benton Catron and His Era.* Page 186. **(Article on Santa Fe Ring abuses urging voters to oppose Ring candidates)**

No Author. "The Ring must soon discover that the time has passed in New Mexico when men can be herded like so many sheep ..." *Albuquerque Daily Democrat.*

March 4, 1884. (Quoted by Victor Westphall, *Thomas Benton Catron and His Era*. Page 191.) (**About Santa Fe Ring control of appointments to legislature**)

No Author. *Santa Fe Weekly New Mexican Review*. **March 13, 1884.** *Santa Fe Weekly New Mexican Review*. (**Accusation of Catron and the Ring of controlling grand juries and** bribery)

No Author. *Albuquerque Daily Democrat*. **March 15, 1884**. (**Oscar P. McMains "Memorial" against land-grabbing Ring**)

Valdez, Jose and Enrique Mares. "Scorching Letter, The Knights of Labor Send a Communication to Powderly! Politicians Arraigned! The Boldest Document Ever Issued in the Territory." **August 18, 1890.** *Las Vegas Democrat*. Volume 1. Center for Southwest Studies. Thomas B. Catron Papers, MSS 29, Series 102, Box 8, Folder 4. (**Gives history of Santa Fe Ring with T.B. Catron as head**)

No Author. *Los Angeles Times*. **1899**. Undated clipping, Laughlin Papers, State Records Center, Santa Fe, New Mexico. Quoted by Victor Westphall, *Thomas Benton Catron and His Era*. Page 285. (**Joking article about the Santa Fe Ring**)

EXPOSÉS Of (CONTEMPORARY)

COMPLAINT ABOUT TO PRESIDENT RUTHERFORD B. HAYES

Matchett, W.B. and Mary E. McPherson. " W.B. Matchett and Mary E. McPherson 'Make certain charges against the U.S. Officials in the Territory of New Mexico.' " Letter to President Rutherford B. Hayes. Received and filed **May 1, 1877**. Interior Department Papers 1850-1907; Appointments Division and Subsequent Actions. Microfilm File Case Number 44-4-8-3. Record Group 48. Microfilm No. M750. Roll 1. National Archives and Records Administration. U. S. Department of Justice. Washington, D.C. (**Sent to President Rutherford B. Hayes and Secretary of the Interior Carl Schurz**.)

McPherson, Mary and W.B. Matchett. "To the President. Please make the enclosed a part of the evidence in the case of "Charges Against New Mexican Officials" Letter to President Rutherford B. Hayes. **May 3, 1877**. McPherson, Mary E. Letters and Petitions to President Rutherford B. Hayes re: Removal Governor Axtell and the Santa Fe Ring. Interior Department Papers 1850-1907; Appointments Division and Subsequent Actions. Microfilm File Case Number 44-4-8-3. Record Group 48. Microfilm Roll M750. National Archives and Records Administration. U.S. Department of Justice. Washington, D.C. (**Addendum to their May, 1877 "Certain Charges Against U.S. Officials in New Mexico Territory."**)

__________. "The Secretary of the Interior, Sir – Accompanying please find <u>copy</u> of charges, &c., against S.B. Axtell, Governor, and Other New Mexican Officials ..." "Charges Against New Mexican Officials." Letter to Secretary of the Interior Carl Schurz. **May 5, 1877**. McPherson, Mary E. Letters and Petitions to President Rutherford B. Hayes re: Removal Governor Axtell and the Santa Fe Ring. Interior Department Papers 1850-1907; Appointments Division and Subsequent Actions. Microfilm File Case Number 44-4-8-3. Record Group 48. Microfilm Roll M750. National Archives and Records Administration. U.S. Department of Justice. Washington, D. C.

__________.*"In the Matter of Charges vs. Gov. S.B. Axtell and Other New Mexico Officials. Submitted to the Departments of the Interior and Justice.* **August, 1877.** Printed as a 31 page booklet. No publisher listed. Indiana Historical Society. Lew Wallace Collection. M0292. Box 3. Folder 20. (**About the Santa Fe Ring, Catron, and Elkins; in Lew Wallace's personal possession**)

McPherson, Mary. "Please place before the Attorney General ..." Letter to President Rutherford B. Hayes. **August 23, 1877.** Interior Department Papers 1850-1907; Appointments Division and Subsequent Actions. Microfilm File Case Number 44-4-8-3. Record Group 48. Microfilm No. M750. Roll 1. National Archives and Records Administration. U. S. Department of Justice. Washington, D.C.

Springer, Frank. Deposition to Investigator Frank Warner Angel for the Departments of Justice and the Interior. **August 9, 1878**. Frank Warner Angel report titled *In the Matter of the Investigation of the Charges Against S.B. Axtell Governor of New Mexico*. October 3, 1878. Interior Department Papers 1850-1907; Appointments Division and Subsequent Actions. Microfilm Case File No. 44-4-8-3. Record Group 48. Microfilm Roll M750. National Archives and Records Administration. U.S. Department of Interior. Washington, D.C.

(SEE: Thomas Benton Catron; Frank Warner Angel, Legislature Revolt, Grant County Rebellion, Colfax County War, Lincoln County War)

LINCOLN COUNTY REGULATORS, 19th CENTURY

Regulator. "Mr. Walz. Sir ..." Letter to Edgar Walz. July 13, 1878. Adjutant General's Office. File 1405 AGO 1878. (Quoted in Maurice Garland Fulton, *History of the Lincoln County War*. Tucson: University of Arizona Press. 1975. pages 246-247, and Frederick Nolan, *The Lincoln County War: A Documentary History*, page 310.) **(Likely by Billy Bonney)**

SECRET SERVICE, 19th CENTURY (CHRONOLOGICAL)

Bowen, Walter S. and Harry Edward Neal. *The United States Secret Service.* Philadelphia and New York: Chilton Company Publishers. **1960**.

Brooks, James J. *1877 Report on Secret Service Operatives.* (**September 26, 1877**). "On Azariah Wild." Page 392. Department of the Treasury. United States Secret Service. Washington, D.C.

Johnson, David R. *Illegal Tender. Counterfeiting and the Secret Service in Nineteenth Century America.* Washington and London: Smithsonian Institution Press. **1995**.

(SEE: Azariah F. Wild)

NEW MEXICO TERRITORY REBELLIONS AGAINST THE SANTA FE RING (CHRONOLOGICAL)

LEGISLATURE REVOLT (1872)

No Author. *Journal of the House of Representatives of the Territory of New Mexico, Session of 1871-1872.* Santa Fe: A.P. Sullivan. **1872.** Pages 144-154. (**Confirms troops used by Ring to suppress the Legislature Revolt of 1872**)

No Author. "Our Own Dear Steve, How Elkins Made His Influence Felt in New Mexico – The Ring in Which a Judge Figured – Politics in 1870. *Las Vegas Daily Optic.* **September 2, 1884.** (Reprinted from the *Omaha Herald*) Front Page. Volume V, Number 258, Column 4. Newspaperarchive.com. **(Exposing the Ring in the 1872 Legislature Revolt)**

GRANT COUNTY REBELLION (1876)

MODERN SOURCES

Naegle, Conrad Keeler. *The History of Silver City, New Mexico 1870-1886.* University of New Mexico Bachelor of Arts thesis. Pages 30-60. Unpublished. 1943. Collection of the Silver City Museum, Silver City, New Mexico.

__________. "The Rebellion of Grant County, New Mexico in 1876." *Arizona and the West: A Quarterly Journal of History.* Autumn, 1968. Volume 10. Number 3. Tucson, Arizona: The University of Arizona Press. 1968. Pages 225-240. **(Rebellion against Santa Fe Ring)**

CONTEMPORARY SOURCES (CHRONOLOGICAL)

No Author. "Diario del Consejo der Territorio de Neuvo Mejico, Session de 1871-1872." *Santa Fe New Mexican*. **January 8, 1872**. Santa Fe: A.P. Sullivan. 1872. Pages 144-154. New Mexico Supreme Court Library. Santa Fe, New Mexico. (**A Ring expurgated document, with a copy found in 1942 by Conrad Naegle; confirming troops used by Ring to suppress Territorial legislature**)

No Author. "Diario del Consejo der Territorio de Neuvo Mejico, Session de 1871-1872. Las Cruces *Borderer*. **January 24, 1872**. Pages 110-113. (**Don Diego Archuleta, President of the Council, gives speech objecting to troops in legislature**)

No Author. "Ring influence [in the Territorial legislature is] being actively used against every measure that tends to do justice" [in Grant and Doña Ana Counties]." *Grant County Herald*. **August 8, 1875.** Quoted by Conrad Keeler Naegle in *The History of Silver City, New Mexico 1870-1886*, doctoral thesis. Page 39.

No Author. "A Contemplated Political Change." Grant County *Herald*. **September 16, 1876**. Quoted by Conrad Keeler Naegle in *The History of Silver City, New Mexico 1870-1886* doctoral thesis. Pages 39-40. (**Listing reasons to escape the Ring by annexing to Arizona Territory**)

No Author. [Grant County should not] "sort o' wait and hear from Santa Fe ... before taking action." Tucson *Arizona Citizen*. **September 23, 1876.** Quoted by Conrad Keeler Naegle in *The History of Silver City, New Mexico 1870-1886* doctoral thesis. Page 41. (**Arizona encourages escape from Santa Fe Ring**)

No Author. Grant County *Herald*. **September 30, 1876**. (**"Annexation Meeting" announced**)

No Author. "Proceedings of Grant County Annexation Meeting." Grant County *Herald*. **Saturday October 7, 1876**. Page 2. Columns 1 and 2. Collection of the Silver City, New Mexico, Museum. (**Anti-Santa Fe Ring "Grant County Declaration of Independence" published**)

No Author. Grant County *Herald*. " 'Petition to Remove Judge Bristol. We the undersigned citizens of the Third Judicial District of the Territory of New Mexico, without regard to party, would respectfully request and petition for the removal of Judge Warren Bristol ...' " No date. **1876 or 1877**.(Quoted in "W.B. Matchett and Mary E. McPherson 'Make certain charges against the U.S. Officials in the Territory of New Mexico.' " Letter to President Rutherford B. Hayes. Received and filed May 1, 1877. Interior Department Papers 1850-1907; Appointments Division and Subsequent Actions. Microfilm File Case Number 44-4-8-3. Record Group 48. Microfilm No. M750. Roll 1. National Archives and Records Administration. U.S. Department of Justice. Washington, D.C.) (**Anti-Santa Fe Ring article**)

(SEE: Santa Fe Ring; Thomas Benton Catron; Stephen Benton Elkins)

COLFAX COUNTY WAR (1877)

MODERN SOURCES

Caffey, David L. *Frank Springer and New Mexico: From the Colfax County War to the Emergence of Modern Santa Fe*. Texas A and M. University Press. 2007.

Cleaveland, Norman. *The Morleys - Young Upstarts on the Southwest Frontier*. Albuquerque, New Mexico: Calvin Horn Publisher, Inc. 1971.

Dunham, Harold H. "New Mexican Land Grants with Special Reference to the Title Papers of the Maxwell Grant." *New Mexico Historical Review*. (January 1955) Vol. 30, No. 1. pp. 1 - 23.

Keleher, William A. *The Maxwell Land Grant. A New Mexico Item*. Albuquerque, New Mexico: University of New Mexico Press. 1964.

Lamar, Howard Roberts. *The Far Southwest 1846 - 1912. A Territorial History*. New Haven and London: Yale University Press. 1966.

Montoya, María E. *Translating Property. The Maxwell Land Grant and the Conflict Over Land in the American West, 1840-1900.* Berkeley and Los Angeles, California: University of California Press. 2002.

Murphy, Lawrence R. *Lucien Bonaparte Maxwell. Napoleon of the Southwest.* Norman: University of Oklahoma Press. 1983.

Pearson, Jim Berry. *The Maxwell Land Grant.* Norman: University of Oklahoma Press. 1961.

Poe, Sophie. *Buckboard Days.* Albuquerque, New Mexico: University of New Mexico Press. 1964.

Taylor, Morris F. *O.P. McMains and the Maxwell Land Grant Conflict.* Tucson, Arizona: The University of Arizona Press. 1979.

CONTEMPORARY SOURCES (CHRONOLOGICAL)

No author. "Anarchy at Cimarron." *Santa Fe Weekly New Mexican.* **November 16, 1875. (Ringite backing of Axtell's use of troops in the Colfax County War)**

Dawson, Will. Editorial. *Cimarron News and Press.* **December 31, 1875. (Ring-biased editorial by temporary editor blaming citizens for unrest)**

No Author. Report on murder trial for Franklin Tolby. Pueblo, *Colorado Chieftain.* **May 25, 1876**. Quoting *Daily New Mexican,* May 1, 1876. From Morris F. Taylor. *O.P. McMains and the Maxwell Land Grant Conflict.* Tucson, Arizona: The University of Arizona Press. 1979. Page 49. **(Ring-biased jury instructions by Judge Henry Waldo to protect Ring murderers of Tolby)**

No Author. "Rejoicing at Cimarron," "Axtell's Head Falls at Last," "General Lew. Wallace Appointed Governor." *Cimarron News and Press.* **September 6, 1878.**

No Author. *Santa Fe Weekly New Mexican.* **September 21, 1878 and October 19, 1878. (Ring-biased accolades for removed Gov. Axtell)**

(SEE: Regulators, Santa Fe Ring; Thomas Benton Catron; Stephen Benton Elkins, Colfax County War, Lincoln County War)

LINCOLN COUNTY WAR (1878)

MODERN SOURCES

Cramer, T. Dudley. *The Pecos Ranchers in the Lincoln County War.* Orinda, California: Branding Iron Press. 1996.

Fulton, Maurice Garland. Robert N. Mullin. Ed. *History of the Lincoln County War.* Tucson, Arizona: The University of Arizona Press. 1997.

Jacobsen, Joel. *Such Men as Billy the Kid. The Lincoln County War Reconsidered.* Lincoln and London: University of Nebraska Press. 1994.

Keleher, William A. *The Fabulous Frontier: Twelve New Mexico Items.* Albuquerque, New Mexico: The University of New Mexico Press. 1962.

__________. *County 1869-1881.* Albuquerque, New Mexico: University of New Mexico Press. 1957.

Mullin, Robert N. Re: Frank Warner Angel Meeting with President Hayes. August, 1878. Binder RNM, VI, M. Midland, Texas: Nita Stewart Haley Memorial Library and J. Evetts Haley History Center. (Unpublished).

Nolan, Frederick W. *The Life and Death of John Henry Tunstall.* Albuquerque, New Mexico: The University of New Mexico Press. 1965.

__________. *The Lincoln County War: A Documentary History.* Norman: University of Oklahoma Press. 1992.

__________. *The West of Billy the Kid.* Norman: University of Oklahoma Press. 1998.

Rasch, Philip J. *Gunsmoke in Lincoln County.* Laramie, Wyoming: National Association for Outlaw and Lawmen History, Inc. with University of Wyoming. 1997.

__________. Robert K. DeArment. Ed. *Warriors of Lincoln County.* Laramie: National Association for Outlaw and Lawmen History, Inc. with University of Wyoming. 1998.

Utley, Robert M. *High Noon in Lincoln. Violence on the Western Frontier.* Albuquerque, New Mexico: University of New Mexico Press. 1987.

Wilson, John P. *Merchants, Guns, and Money: The Story of Lincoln County and Its Wars.* Santa Fe, New Mexico: Museum of New Mexico Press. 1987.

No Author. "Disturbances in the Territories, 1878 - 1894. Lawlessness in New Mexico." Senate Documents. 67th Congress. 2nd Session. December 5, 1921 - September 22, 1922. pp. 176 - 187. Washington, D.C.: Government Printing Office. 1922.

CONTEMPORARY SOURCES (CHRONOLOGICAL)

No Author. "Brady Inventory McSween Property." **February, 1878**. Herman B. Weisner Papers, ca. 1957-1992. New Mexico State University Library at Las Cruses. Rio Grande Historical Collections. Accession No. Weisner Ms 0249. Box 10. Folder M15. Folder Name. "Will and Testament A. McSween."

No Author. "Amnesty for Matthews and Long in the Third Judicial Court April Term 1879." **April, 1879**. Herman B. Weisner Papers, ca. 1957-1992. New Mexico State University Library at Las Cruces. Rio Grande Historical Collections. Accession No. Ms 0249. Box 1. Folder 4. Folder Name. "Amnesty."

No Author. "Charges against Jessie Evans and John Kinney." Doña Ana County Civil and Criminal Docket Book. **August 18, 1875 to November 7, 1878**. Herman B. Weisner Papers, ca. 1957-1992. New Mexico State University Library at Las Cruces. Rio Grande Historical Collections. Accession No. Ms 0249. Box 13. Folder V 3. Folder Name. "Venue, Change Of."

No Author. "Dismissal of Cases Against Dolan, Matthews, Peppin, October 1879 District Court." **October, 1879**. Herman B. Weisner Papers, ca. 1957-1992. New Mexico State University Library at Las Cruces. Rio Grande Historical Collections. Accession No. Ms 0249. Box 13. Folder V3. Folder Name: "Venue, Change Of."

No Author. "Killers of Tunstall. February 18, 1879." Herman B. Weisner Papers, ca. 1957-1992. New Mexico State University Library at Las Cruses. Rio Grande Historical Collections. Accession No. Ms 0249. Box 12. Folder T1. Folder Name: "Tunstall, John H."

No Author. "Lincoln County Indictments July 1872 - 1881." Herman B. Weisner Papers, ca. 1957-1992. New Mexico State University Library at Las Cruces. Rio Grande Historical Collections. Accession No. Ms 0249. Box 8. Folder L11. Folder Name. "Lincoln Co. Indictments."

(SEE: William H. Bonney, John Henry Tunstall, Alexander McSween, Samuel Beach Axtell, Frank Warner Angel, Nathan Augustus Monroe Dudley)

HISTORY OF WILLIAM HENRY BONNEY (WILLIAM HENRY McCARTY, HENRY ANTRIM, AKA BILLY THE KID)

BIOGRAPHICAL SOURCES

Abbott, E.C. ("Teddy Blue") and Helena Huntington Smith. *We Pointed Them North: Recollections of a Cowpuncher.* Norman, Oklahoma: University of Oklahoma Press. 1955. (**Billy the Kid's multi-culturalism, Page 47.**)

Anaya, Paco. *I Buried Billy.* College Station, Texas: Creative Publishing Company. 1991.

Ball, Eve. *Ma'am Jones of the Pecos.* Tucson, Arizona: The University of Arizona Press. 1969.

Bell, Bob Boze. *The Illustrated Life and Times of Billy the Kid.* Cave Creek, Arizona: Boze Books. 1992. (Frank Coe quote about the Kid's cartridge use, Page 45.)

Bell, Bob Boze. *The Illustrated Life and Times of Billy the Kid.* Second Edition. Phoenix, Arizona: Tri Star-Boze Publications, Inc. 1996.

Burns, Walter Noble. *The Saga of Billy the Kid.* Stamford, Connecticut: Longmeadow Press. 1992. (Original printing: 1926, Doubleday.)

__________. *"I also know that the Kid and Paulita were sweethearts."* Unpublished letter to Jim East. June 3, 1926. Robert N. Mullin Collection. File RNM, IV, NM, 116-117. Nita Stewart Haley Memorial Museum, Haley Library. Midland, Texas.

Coe, George with Doyce B. Nunis, Jr. Ed. *Frontier Fighter. The Autobiography of George Coe Who Fought and Rode With Billy the Kid.* Chicago: R. R. Donnelley and Sons Company. 1984.

Cooper, Gale. *Billy the Kid's Writings, Words, and Wit.* Gelcour Books: Albuquerque: New Mexico. 2012.

__________. *Billy and Paulita: The Saga of Billy the Kid, Paulita Maxwell, and the Santa Fe Ring.* Gelcour Books: Albuquerque: New Mexico. 2012.

__________. *The Lost Pardon of Billy the Kid: An Analysis Factoring in the Santa Fe Ring, Governor Lew Wallace's Dilemma, and a Territory in Rebellion.* Gelcour Books: Albuquerque: New Mexico. 2017.

__________. *The Santa Fe Ring Versus Billy the Kid: The Making of an American Monster.* Gelcour Books: Albuquerque: New Mexico. 2018.

Garrett, Pat F. *The Authentic Life of Billy the Kid The Noted Desperado of the Southwest, Whose Deeds of Daring and Blood Made His Name a Terror in New Mexico, Arizona, and Northern Mexico.* Santa Fe, New Mexico: New Mexico Printing and Publishing Co. 1882. (Edition used: Edited by Maurice Garland Fulton. New York: The Macmillan Company. 1927)

Hendron, J. W. *The Story of Billy the Kid. New Mexico's Number One Desperado.* New York: Indian Head Books. 1994.

Hoyt, Henry. *A Frontier Doctor.* Boston and New York: Houghton Mifflin Company. 1929. **(Describes Billy's superior abilities. Pages 93-94, including fluency in Spanish.)**

Jacobsen, Joel. *Such Men as Billy the Kid. The Lincoln County War Reconsidered.* Lincoln and London: University of Nebraska Press. 1994.

Kadlec, Robert F. *They "Knew" Billy the Kid. Interviews with Old-Time New Mexicans.* Santa Fe, New Mexico: Ancient City Press. 1987.

Keleher, William A. *The Fabulous Frontier: Twelve New Mexico Items.* Albuquerque, New Mexico: The University of New Mexico Press. 1962.

__________.*Violence in Lincoln County 1869-1881.* Albuquerque, New Mexico: University of New Mexico Press. 1957.

McFarland, David F. Reverend. *Ledger: Session Records 1867-1874. Marriages in Santa Fe New Mexico. "Mr. William H. Antrim and Mrs. Catherine McCarty." March 1, 1873.* (Unpublished). Santa Fe, New Mexico: First Presbyterian Church of Santa Fe.

Meadows, John P. "Billy the Kid to John P. Meadows on the Peñasco, May 1-2, 1881." *Roswell Daily Record.* February 16, 1931. Page 6.

__________. Ed. John P. Wilson. *Pat Garrett and Billy the Kid as I Knew Them: Reminiscences of John P. Meadows.* Albuquerque: University of New Mexico Press. 2004.

Mullin, Robert N. *The Boyhood of Billy the Kid.* Monograph 17, Southwestern Studies 5(1). El Paso, Texas: Texas Western Press. University of Texas at El Paso. 1967.

Poe, John W. *The Death of Billy the Kid.* (Introduction by Maurice Garland Fulton). Boston and New York: Houghton Mifflin Company. 1933.

__________. "The Killing of Billy the Kid." (a personal letter written at Roswell, New Mexico to Mr. Charles Goodnight, Goodnight P.C., Texas) July 10, 1917. Earle Vandale Collection. 1813-946. No. 2H475. Center for American History. University of Texas at Austin.

Rakocy, Bill. *Billy the Kid.* El Paso, Texas: Bravo Press. 1985.

Rasch, Phillip J. *Trailing Billy the Kid.* Laramie, Wyoming: National Association for Outlaw and Lawman History, Inc. with University of Wyoming. 1995.

Russell, Randy. *Billy the Kid. The Story - The Trial.* Lincoln, New Mexico: The Crystal Press. 1994.

Scanland, John M. (Foreword) using Patrick F. Garrett, Patrick F. *Billy the Kid: The Outlaw. Authentic Story of Billy the Kid by Pat F. Garrett. Greatest Sheriff of the Old Southwest.* New York: Atomic Books Inc. **1946**. Oberlin College Library Special Collections, Pop Culture. Walter F. Tunks Collection. Number 2344. (**Pirated edition of Pat Garrett's *Authentic Life of Billy the Kid* featuring apocryphal outlawry of Billy the Kid**)

Siringo, Charles A. *The History of Billy the Kid.* Santa Fe: New Mexico. Privately Printed. 1920.

Tuska, Jon. *Billy the Kid. His Life and Legend.* Westport, Connecticut: Greenwood Press. 1983.

Utley, Robert M. *High Noon in Lincoln. Violence on the Western Frontier.* Albuquerque, New Mexico: University of New Mexico Press. 1987.

__________. *Billy the Kid. A Short and Violent Life.* Lincoln and London: University of Nebraska Press. 1989.

Weddle, Jerry. *Antrim is My Stepfather's Name. The Boyhood of Billy the Kid.* Monograph 9, Globe, Arizona: Arizona Historical Society. 1993.

No Author. "The Prisoners Who Saw the Kid Kill Olinger." April 28, 1881. Herman B. Weisner Papers, ca. 1957-1992. New Mexico State University Library at Las Cruces. Rio Grande Historical Collections. Accession No. Ms 0249. Box 30 T. Folder 8.

WORDS OF (CHRONOLOGICAL)

SPENCERIAN PENMANSHIP OF

Spencer, Platt Rogers. *Spencerian Penmanship.* New York: Ivison, Phinney, Blakemont Co. **1857.**

__________________. *Spencerian System of Practical Penmanship.* New York: Ivison, Phinney, Blakemont Co. **1864.** (Reprinted by Milford, Michigan: Mott Media, Inc. 1985.)

Spencer, H.C. (Prepared for the "Spencerian Authors) *Spencerian Key to Practical Penmanship.* New York: Ivison, Phinney, Blakemont, Taylor & Co. **1874**.

__________________. (Prepared for the "Spencerian Authors) *Theory of Spencerian Penmanship for Schools and Private Learners Developed by Questions and Answers with Practical Illustrations: Designed to Be Used by Pupils in Connection With the Use of Spencerian Copybooks.* New York: Ivison, Phinney, Blakemont, Taylor & Co. **1874**.

Spencerian Authors. *Theory of Spencerian Penmanship for Schools and Private Learners Developed by Questions and Answers with Practical Illustrations: Designed to Be Used by Pupils in Connection With the Use of Spencerian Copybooks.* (New York: Ivison, Phinney, Blakemont, Taylor & Co. 1874.) Reprinted and modified by Milford, Michigan: Mott Media, Inc. **1985**. (**Page 30 describes forming "the capital stem;" pages 2-7 describe "position" and "hand-arm movements;" and page 45 describes the pen and "shading;" all used by Billy Bonney**)

Sull, Michael, *Spencerian Script and Ornamental Penmanship.* Prairie Village: Kansas. (Unpublished, undated, modern manual).

Cooper, Gale. *Billy the Kid's Writings, Words, and Wit.* Albuquerque, New Mexico: Gelcour Books. **2012**.

HOYT BILL OF SALE BY

Bonney, W H. "Know all persons by these presents ..." Thursday, **October 24, 1878.** Collection of Panhandle-Plains Historical Museum, Canyon, Texas. Item No. X1974-98/1. (**Hoyt Bill of Sale**)

LETTERS TO LEW WALLACE

Bonney, W H. "I have heard you will give one thousand $ dollars for my body which as I see it means alive ..." **March 13(?), 1879**. Fray Angélico Chávez Historical Library, Santa Fe, New Mexico. Lincoln County Heritage Trust Collection. (AC481).

__________. "I will keep the keep the appointment ..." **March 20, 1879**. Indiana Historical Society. M0292.

__________. "... on the Pecos." ("Billie" letter fragment). **March 24(?), 1879**. Indiana Historical Society. Lew Wallace Collection. M0292. Box 4. Folder 7.

__________. "I noticed in the *Las Vegas* Gazette a piece which stated that 'Billy the Kid' ..." **December 12, 1880**. Indiana Historical Society. Lew Wallace Collection. M0292.

__________. "I would like to see you ..." **January 1, 1881**. Indiana Historical Society. Lew Wallace Collection. M0292.

__________. "I wish you would come down to the jail and see me ..." **March 2, 1881**. Fray Angélico Chávez Historical Library, Santa Fe, New Mexico. Lincoln County Heritage Trust Collection. (AC481).

__________. "I wrote you a little note day before yesterday ..." **March 4, 1881**. Indiana Historical Society. Lew Wallace Collection. M0292.

__________. "For the last time I ask ..." **March 27, 1881**. Indiana Historical Society. Lew Wallace Collection. M0292.

(SEE: Lew Wallace response letters to)

LETTER TO SQUIRE WILSON

Bonney, W H. "Friend Wilson ..." **March 18, 1879**. Indiana Historical Society. Lew Wallace Collection. M0292. (**For pardon negotiation with Lew Wallace**)

LETTER TO EDGAR CAYPLESS

Bonney, W H. "I would have written before ..." **April 15, 1881**. Copy in William Kelleher's *Violence in Lincoln County;* originally reproduced in Griggs *History of the Mesilla Valley*. (**Original lost**)

REGULATOR MANIFESTO LETTER

Regulator. "Mr. Walz. Sir ..." Letter to Edgar Walz. **July 13, 1878**. Adjutant General's Office. File 1405 AGO 1878. (Quoted in Maurice Garland Fulton, *History of the Lincoln County War*. Tucson: University of Arizona Press. 1975. Pages 246-247.)

DEPOSITION OF

Bonney, William Henry. Deposition to Frank Warner Angel. **June 8, 1878**. Frank Warner Angel report, Pages 314-319 from *In the Matter of the Examination of the Causes and Circumstances of the Death of John H. Tunstall a British Subject.* Report filed October 4, 1878. Angel Report. Records of the Justice Department. Record Group 60. Class 44 Litigation Files. Container 21. National Archives and Records Administration. U.S. Department of Justice. Washington, D.C. or Angel Report in Interior Department Papers 1850-1907; Appointments Division and Subsequent Actions. Microfilm File Case Number 44-4-8-3. Record Group 48. Microfilm No. M750. Roll 1. National Archives and Records Administration. U.S. Department of Justice. Washington, D.C.

COURT TESTIMONIES OF

Rynerson, William. "The Grand Jurors for the Territory of New Mexico taken from the body of the good and lawful men of the County of Lincoln ..." Indictments of the April, Lincoln County Grand Jury. **April 28, 1879**. Herman B. Weisner Papers, ca. 1957-1992. New Mexico State University Library at Las Cruces. Rio Grande Historical Collection. Accession No. Ms 0249. Box 4/39. Folder E-Z. Folder Name: "Jessie Evans Accessory to Murder." (**Billy's testimony for pardon bargain**)

Bonney, William Henry. Testimony in Court of Inquiry for N.A.M. Dudley. **May 28-29, 1879**. *Proceedings of a Court of Inquiry in the Case of Lt. Col. N.A.M. Dudley (May 2,1879 – July 5, 1879).* File No. QQ1284. (Boxes 3304, 3305, 3305A); Court Martial Files 1809-1894. Records of the Office of the Judge Advocate General - Army. Record Group 153. Old Military and Civil Branch. National Archives and Records Administration. Washington, D. C.

Waldo, Henry. "Then was brought forward William Bonney, alias "Antrim," alias "the Kid," a known criminal of the worst type ..." Closing argument on Billy Bonney's testimony in Court of Inquiry for N.A.M. Dudley. **July 5, 1879**. *Proceedings of a Court of Inquiry in the Case of Lt. Col. N.A.M. Dudley (May 2,1879 – July 5, 1879).* File No. QQ1284. (Boxes 3304, 3305, 3305A); Court Martial Files 1809-1894. Records of the Office of the Judge Advocate General – Army. Record Group 153. Old Military and Civil Branch. National Archives and Records Administration. Washington, D. C.

INTERVIEW WITH LEW WALLACE OF

Wallace, Lew. "Statements by Kid, made Sunday night **March 23, 1879**." (Cover sheet reads: "Fort Stanton, March 20, 1879. William Bonney ("Kid") relative to arrangement with him." Indiana Historical Society. Lew Wallace Collection. M0292. Box 4. Folder 6.

NEWSPAPER INTERVIEWS BY

Wilcox, Lucius "Lute" M. (city editor, owner, J.H. Koogler). "The Kid. Interview with Billy Bonney The Best Known Man in New Mexico." *Las Vegas Gazette.* **December 27, 1880**.

__________. Interview, at train depot. *Las Vegas Gazette.* **December 28, 1880. (Has Billy Bonney's "adios" quote.)**

No Author. "Something About the Kid." *Santa Fe Daily New Mexican.* **April 3, 1881. (With quotes Billy Bonney's "this is the man" and "two hundred men have been killed ... he did not kill all of them.")**

No Author. "I got a rough deal ..." *Mesilla News.* **April 15, 1881**.

Newman, Simon N. Ed. Interview with "The Kid." *Newman's Semi-Weekly.* **April 15, 1881**.

__________. Departure from Mesilla. *Newman's Semi-Weekly.* **April 15, 1881**.

No Author. "Advise persons never to engage in killing." *Mesilla News.* **April 16, 1881. (Billy Bonney's quote)**

FEDERAL INDICTMENT OF

Catron, Thomas Benton. "Case No. 411. The United States vs. Charles Bowdry [Bowdre], Doc Scurlock, Henry Brown, Henry Antrim alias "Kid," John Middleton, Stephen Stevens, John Scroggins, George Coe and Frederick Waite." **June 21, 1878**. Herman B. Weisner Papers, ca. 1957-1992. New Mexico State University Library at Las Cruces. Rio Grande Historical Collections. Accession No. Ms 0249. Box 1. B-Folder 4. Name: Andrew Roberts Indictment.

GENERAL LETTERS ABOUT

Kimbrell, George. "I have the honor to request that you will furnish me a posse ..." Letter to Lieutenant Millard Filmore Goodwin. **February 20, 1879**. Indiana Historical Society. Lew Wallace Collection. Box 4, Folder 3. (**For pursuit of William Bonney and Yginio Salazar**)

Goodwin, Millard Filmore. ""I have the honor to submit the following report regarding my duties performed ..." Letter to Fort Stanton Post Adjutant John Loud. **February 23, 1879**. Indiana Historical Society. Lew Wallace Collection. Box 4. Folder 3. (**Assisting pursuit of William Bonney and Yginio Salazar**)

Dudley, Nathan Augustus Monroe. "I enclose herewith report of 2nd Lieut. M.F. Goodwin ..." Letter to Acting Assistant Adjutant General at Headquarters. **February 24, 1879**. Indiana Historical Society. Lew Wallace Collection. M0292. Box 4, Folder 3. (**Documents military pursuit of William Bonney**)

Leonard, Ira. "The air is filled tonight with 'rumors of wars ... Letter to Lew Wallace. **April 20, 1879**. Indiana Historical Society. Lew Wallace Collection. M0292. Box 4. Folder 9. (**About DA Rynerson: "He is bent on going for the Kid"**)

Hoyt, Henry F. "This time it is me who is apologizing for the long delay in answering ..." (Letter to Lew Wallace Jr.) **April 27, 1927**. Indiana Historical Society. Lew Wallace Collection. M0292. Box 14, Folder 11.

__________. "Copy of a bill of sale written by Wm H. Bonney ..." Letter to Lew Wallace Jr. **April 27, 1927**. Indiana Historical Society. Lew Wallace Collection. M0292. Box 14, Folder 11. (**Calls Billy Bonney "a natural leader of men"**)

SECRET SERVICE REPORTS ABOUT

Wild, Azariah F. "Daily Reports of U. S. Secret Service Agents, Azariah F. Wild." Microfilm T-915. Record Group 87. Rolls 308 (July 1, 1879 - June 30, 1881) National Archives and Records Department. Department of the Treasury. United States Secret Service. Washington, D. C.

LEW WALLACE WRITINGS TO AND ABOUT

WALLACE'S LETTERS TO (CHRONOLOGICAL)

Wallace, Lew. "Come to the house of Squire Wilson ..." Letter to W H. Bonney. **March 15, 1879**. Indiana Historical Society. Lew Wallace Collection. M0292. Box 4. Folder 6.

__________. "The escape makes no difference in arrangements ..." Letter to W.H. Bonney. **March 20, 1879**. Indiana Historical Society. Lew Wallace Collection. M0292. Box 4. Folder 6.

WALLACE'S LETTERS ABOUT (CHRONOLOGICAL)

Wallace, Lew. "I have just ascertained that 'The Kid' is at a place called Las Tablas ..." Letter to Edward Hatch. **March 6, 1879**. Indiana Historical Society. Lew Wallace Collection. Box 9, Folder 10. (**Written on dead John Tunstall's stationery**)

__________. "I beg to submit to you a list of persons whom it is necessary, in my judgment, to arrest ..." Letter to Henry Carroll. **March 11, 1879**. Indiana Historical Society. Lew Wallace Collection. M0292. Box 4. Folder 5. (**Sherman outlaw list with "The Kid" – William Bonney**)

__________. "I enclose a note for Bonney." Letter to John "Squire" Wilson. **March 20, 1879**. Indiana Historical Society. Lew Wallace Collection. M0292. Box 4. Folder 6.

__________. "My time has been so constantly occupied in getting my work into operation ..." Letter to Carl Schurz. **March 21, 1879**. Indiana Historical Society. Lew Wallace Collection. M0292. Box 4. Folder 7. (**Listing "The Kid -William Bonney in anti-outlaw campaign "taking the head off the evil."**)

__________. "To day I forwarded a telegram to you, with another to the President ..." Letter to Carl Schurz. **March 31, 1879**. Indiana Historical Society. Lew Wallace Collection. M0292. Box 4. Folder 7. (**Mention of "precious specimen nicknamed 'The Kid' "**)

REWARD NOTICES FOR

Wallace, Lew. "Be good enough to prepare a draft of proclamation of reward $500 for the capture and delivery of William Bonney, alias the Kid ..." Letter to Territorial Secretary William Ritch. **December 13, 1880**. Herman B. Weisner Papers, ca. 1957-1992. New Mexico State University Library at Las Cruces. Rio Grande Historical Collections. Accession No. Ms 0249. Box W3. Folder 13. Folder Name: "Wallace, Gov. N.M." From Lew Wallace Papers. New Mexico State Records Center. Santa Fe, New Mexico. (**Wallace's first reward for Billy the Kid**)

__________. "Billy the Kid: $500 Reward." *Las Vegas Gazette*. **December 22, 1880**.

__________. "Billy the Kid. $500 Reward." **May 3, 1881**. *Daily New Mexican*. Vol. X, No. 33. Page 1, C 3.

REWARD POSTERS FOR

Greene, Chas. W. "To the New Mexican Printing and Publishing Company." **May 20, 1881**. Indiana Historical Society. Lew Wallace Collection. M0292. Box 4, Folder 17. (**Printer's bill to Lew Wallace for Reward posters for "Kid"**)

__________. "I enclose a bill ..." Letter to Lew Wallace for "Kid" wanted posters. **June 2, 1881**. Indiana Historical Society. Lew Wallace Collection. M0292. Box 4, Folder 18.

DEATH WARRANT FOR

Wallace, Lew. "To the Sheriff of Lincoln County, Greeting ..." **April 30, 1881**. Indiana Historical Society. Lew Wallace Collection. M0292. Box 9, Folder 11.

CORONER'S JURY REPORT FOR, AND LATER LOCATION OF (CHRONOLOGICAL)

Segura, Alejandro. Coroner's Jury Report for William Bonney alias "Kid." **July 15, 1881**. Original in Spanish. Indiana Historical Society. Lew Wallace Collection. M0292. Box 9. Folder 11. (**Certified photocopy donated by Maurice Garland Fulton in 1951 of Spanish Coroner's Jury Report, July 15, 1881 - matches photo in William Kelleher's *Violence in Lincoln County*, Pages 306-307**)

__________. Coroner's Jury Report for William Bonney alias "Kid." **July 15, 1881**. English translation. The Mullin Collection, RNM, VI, J - Legal Papers and Documents. Midland, Texas: Nita Stewart Haley Memorial Library and J. Evetts Haley History Center.

__________. Coroner's Jury Report for William Bonney alias "Kid." **July 15, 1881**. English translation. William A. Keleher. *Violence in Lincoln County 1869-1881*. Pages 343-344.

Ritch, William G. "In the matter of the application by Patrick F. Garrett for a reward claimed to have been offered May-1881 for the capture of Wm Bonney alias "the Kid." *Executive Record Book Number 2*. July 25, 1867-November 8, 1882. **July 21, 1881**. Pages 533-535. New Mexico Secretary of State Records. Collection 1971-001, Series 1; Records of the Secretary of the Territory. (Accessed from Albuquerque Public Library Microfilm, Territorial Archives of New Mexico, Roll 21.) (**Presentation of Garret's bill for the reward and demonstrating that Acting-Governor Ritch agreed with the reward, and citing the Coroner's Jury Report's identification of William Bonney**)

No Author. *Executive Record Book Number 2*. July 25, 1867-November 8, 1882. **July 21, 1881.** Pages 533-535. New Mexico State Records Center and Archives, Santa Fe. New Mexico Secretary of the State Records Series 1. Records of the

Secretary of the Territory. (**About granting Garrett's reward, citing copy of Coroner's Jury Report**)

No Author. "Kid the Killer Killed, Wm. Bonney alias Antrim, alias Billy the Kid, Fatally Meets Pat Garrett, the Lincoln County Sheriff." Las Cruces *Rio Grande Republican.* **July 23, 1881**. Page 2. Volume 1, Number 10. NewspaperArchive.com. (**Copy of Pat Garrett's letter to Acting Governor William Ritch confirming that the original Coroner's Jury Report was sent to District Attorney of the First Judicial District, and copy of it was included in this letter to the Governor; this was later found in 1932 with the papers of the Secretary of State in the state Capitol Building**)

Prince, L. Bradford, Ed. *The General Laws of New Mexico; Including All the Unrepealed Laws From the Promulgation of the 'Kearney Code' in 1846, to the End of the Legislative Session of 1880. With Supplement, Including the Session of 1882.* Albany, New York: W.C. Little & Co., Law Publishers. **1882.**

No Author. The Western Survey Company. *New Mexico: The Last Great West.* Chicago: Rand McNally & Co. **1917**. (**States that the State Land Office was housed in the Capital Building – the future Bataan Memorial Building**)

No Author. "Call for Bids." *Santa Fe New Mexican.* **May 26, 1932.** Page 6, Column 4. (**Showing that the Secretary of State's office was in the state Capitol Building, where Pat Garrett's letter to Acting-Governor Ritch was found**)

No Author. "Local Items." *Alamogordo News.* **February 12, 1933.** Volume 37, Number 8. Page 4. Column 1. (**Harold Abbott, finder of the original Report in state capitol basement while working for the State Land Office)**

King, Frank M. *Wranglin' the Past: Reminiscences of Frank M. King.* "Chapter xix, The Kid's Exit." Pasadena, California: Trail's End Publishing Company. **1935 and 1946**. (**Describes recent location of Pat Garrett's report to the Governor about the killing of Billy the Kid, which had a copy of the Coroner's Jury Report, Page 171**)

Anderson, Clinton P. "The Adobe Palace." *New Mexico Historical Review.* **1944.** Volume 19, Number 2. Pages 97-122. (**Diagram showing that William Breeden's office was later used by the State Land Office, Pages 110-111**)

No Author. "Fort Sumner Jury Thought the Kid Had Been Killed." *Alamogordo News.* **November 30, 1950.** Volume 53, Number 48. .NewspaperArchive.com. (**Harold Abbott's finding the Coroner's Jury Report in 1932**)

No Author. "Glimpses of History." **February, 1951**. *New Mexico Magazine.* Volume 29, Number 2, Pages 26, 54. (**Reprinting the Harold Abbott Coroner's Jury Report copy**)

Keleher, William A. *Violence in Lincoln County 1869-1881.* Albuquerque, New Mexico: University of New Mexico Press. **1957**. (**Photocopy of Spanish Coroner's Jury Report, July 15, 1881. Pages 306-308; Keleher's English translation, Pages 343-344; Harold Abbott's finding it, Page 343.**)

Nusbaum, Rosemary. *The City Different and the Palace, The Palace of the Governors: Its Role in Santa Fe History.* Santa Fe: Sunstone Press. **1978**.

No Author. "Obituaries." *Alamogordo Daily News.* **January 22, 2006**. Page 7A. (**Death announcement for George Abbott, who got a copy of the Coroner's Jury Report from his brother, Harold Abbott, in 1932**)

No Author. *Texas, Death Certificates. 1903-1982.* Provo, Utah. Ancestry.com. Operations, Inc. **2013**. (**Death certificate of Harold Abbott, who located the Report in 1932 in the State Land Office basement in the Capitol Building**)

Stangl, Karin. Ed. "New Mexico State Land Office." *State Land Office 2011-2012 Annual Report.* Santa Fe. 2013. nmstatelands.org. (**Function of Office**)

Taylor, Aaron. Expert consultation on the orthography of the Coroner's Jury Report. Consultation with author, April, 2020. (**Confirming the Report was written with stylistic idiosyncrasies of the later 1880's and by a native Spanish speaker like Alejandro Segura**)

CERTIFIED COPY OF

Segura, Alejandro, Milnor. Coroner's Jury Report for William Bonney alias "Kid." **July 15, 1881.** Indiana Historical Society. Lew Wallace Collection. M0292. Box 9. Folder 11. Accession Number 1951.0104 from Maurice G. Fulton. (**Photostatic copy of original Spanish Coroner's Jury Report, certified on January 18, 1951, donated by Maurice Garland Fulton - matches photo in William Kelleher's *Violence in Lincoln County* copy; identifying the body of Billy Bonney**)

No Author. "Coroner's Report Proves Billy the Kid is Dead, Historian Asserts, Researcher Discovers Document." **August 5, 1951**. *The El Paso Times.* Number 217, Page 13. (**M. G. Fulton finds and publishes its certified copy**)

CONFIRMING SIGNERS OF REPORT

Rudulph, Milnor. " I beg your indulgence for ..." Letter to William G. Ritch. **May 18, 1879.** Albuquerque and Bernalillo County Public Library. Genealogical Center. MS. Territorial Archives of New Mexico Microfilm. Roll 99. Image 10. (**Rudulph's signature matches his signature on the Coroner's Jury Report.**)

No Author. **Census 1880 for Alejandro Segura and Sabal Gutierrez**. Place: *Cabra Arenoso, Fort Sumner, San Miguel, New Mexico*; Roll: *803*; Page: *434B*; Enumeration District: *037*. Ancestry.com and The Church of Jesus Christ of Latter-day Saints. *1880 United States Federal Census* [database on-line]. Lehi, UT, USA: Ancestry.com Operations Inc, 2010. 1880 U.S. Census Index provided by The Church of Jesus Christ of Latter-day Saints © Copyright 1999 Intellectual Reserve, Inc. Original data: Tenth Census of the United States, 1880. (NARA microfilm publication T9, 1,454 rolls). Records of the Bureau of the Census, Record Group 29. National Archives, Washington, D.C. (**Confirmed as local residents**)

No Author. **Census 1880 for Milnor Rudulph and Jose Silva**. Place: *Sunnyside, Fort Sumner, San Miguel, New Mexico*; Roll: *803*; Page: *435C*; Enumeration District: *037*.Ancestry.com and The Church of Jesus Christ of Latter-day Saints. *1880 United States Federal Census* [database on-line]. Lehi, UT, USA: Ancestry.com Operations Inc, 2010. 1880 U.S. Census Index provided by The Church of Jesus Christ of Latter-day Saints © Copyright 1999 Intellectual Reserve, Inc. Original data: Tenth Census of the United States, 1880. (NARA microfilm publication T9, 1,454 rolls). Records of the Bureau of the Census, Record Group 29. National Archives, Washington, D.C. (**Confirmed as local residents**)

No Author. **Census 1880 for Lorenzo Jaramillo and Antonio Saavedra**. Place: *Fort Sumner, San Miguel, New Mexico*; Roll: *803*; Page: *436A*; Enumeration District: *037*. Ancestry.com and The Church of Jesus Christ of Latter-day Saints. *1880 United States Federal Census* [database on-line]. Lehi, UT, USA: Ancestry.com Operations Inc, 2010. 1880 U.S. Census Index provided by The Church of Jesus Christ of Latter-day Saints © Copyright 1999 Intellectual Reserve, Inc. Original data: Tenth Census of the United States, 1880. (NARA microfilm publication T9, 1,454 rolls). Records of the Bureau of the Census, Record Group 29. National Archives, Washington, D.C. (**Confirmed as local residents**)

No Author. **Census 1880 for Pedro Antonio Lucero**. Place: *San Miguel, New Mexico*; Roll: *803*; Page: *381B*; Enumeration District: *035*. Ancestry.com and The Church of Jesus Christ of Latter-day Saints. *1880 United States Federal Census* [database on-line]. Lehi, UT, USA: Ancestry.com Operations Inc, 2010. 1880 U.S. Census Index provided by The Church of Jesus Christ of Latter-day Saints © Copyright 1999 Intellectual Reserve, Inc. All rights reserved. Original data: Tenth Census of the United States, 1880. (NARA microfilm publication T9, 1,454 rolls). Records of the Bureau of the Census, Record Group 29. National Archives, Washington, D.C. (**Confirmed as local resident**)

(SEE: William Breeden)

OUTLAW MYTH ARTICLES ABOUT (CHRONOLOGICAL)

No Author. Grant County *Herald*. **May 10, 1879**. Results of the Lincoln County Grand Jury. (**Also published in the Mesilla *Thirty Four*. Confirmation of Billy Bonney's testimony and indictments of James Dolan and Billy Campbell , Page 224 of William Kelleher, *Violence in Lincoln County*.**)

Koogler, John H. Editorial. "Desperadoe's Stronghold, An Organized Gang Assisted by Nature and Defiantly Reckless, Who Terrorize the Country to the East of Us." *Las Vegas Morning Gazette*. **December 3, 1880**. Volume 2, Number 120. https://chroniclingamerica.loc.gov. (**Calling Billy Bonney an outlaw leader; motivating his denial letter of December 12, 1880 to Governor Lew Wallace.**)

No Author. "Outlaws of New Mexico, The Exploits of a Band Headed by a New York Youth, The Mountain Fastness of the Kid and His Followers - War Against a Gang of Cattle Thieves and Murderers - The Frontier Confederates of Brockway, the Counterfeiter." *The Sun*. New York. **December 22, 1880**. Vol. XLVIII, No. 118, Page 3, Columns 1-2.

No Author. "A Big Haul! Billy Kid, Dave Rudabaugh, Billy Wilson and Tom Pickett in the Clutches of the Law." *The Las Vegas Daily Optic*. Monday, **December 27, 1880**. Volume 2, Number. 45. Page 4, Column 2. chroniclingamerica.loc.gov.

No Author. "A Bay-Mare. Everyone who has heard of Billy 'the kid' has heard of his beautiful bay mare." *Las Vegas Morning Gazette*. Tuesday, **January 4, 1881**.

No Author. "The Kid. Billy 'the Kid' and Billy Wilson were on Monday taken to Mesilla for Trial." *Las Vegas Morning Gazette*. Tuesday, **March 15, 1881**.

Newman, Simon. "In the Name of Justice! In the Case of Billy Kid." *Newman's Semi-Weekly*. Saturday, **April 2, 1881**.

No Author. "Billy the Kid. Seems to be having a stormy journey on his trip Southward." *Las Vegas Morning Gazette*. Tuesday, **April 5, 1881**.

No Author. "The Kid." *Santa Fe Daily New Mexican*. **May 1, 1881**. Volume X, Number 32, Page 1, Column 2.

No Author. "Billy Bonney. Advices from Lincoln bring the intelligence of the escape of 'Billy the Kid.' " *Las Vegas Daily Optic*. Monday, **May 2, 1881**.

No Author. "The Kid's Escape." *Santa Fe Daily New Mexican*. Tuesday Morning, **May 3, 1881**. Volume X, Number 33, Page 1, Column 2.

No Author. "The above is the record of as bold a deed ..." *Santa Fe Daily New Mexican*. **May 4, 1881**. (**About Billy's great escape jailbreak**)

No Author. "Dare Devil Desperado. Pursuit of 'Billy the Kid' has been abandoned." *Las Vegas Daily Optic*. **May 4, 1881**.

No Author. "More Killing by Kid, When But a Short Distance From Lincoln, He Meets one of His Old Enemies, and Kills Him and His Companion. Two More Victims." Editorial. *Santa Fe Daily New Mexican*. **May 4, 1881**. Volume X, No. 34, Page 1, Column 2. Newspaperarchive.com. (**Claims Kid killed Billy Matthews**)

No Author. No headline. "Anything that the imagination can concoct ..." *Santa Fe Daily New Mexican*. **May 5, 1881**. Volume X. Page 4, Column 1. Newspaperarchive.com. (**Claims Kid was in Albuquerque**)

No Author. No headline. Mr. Richard Dunham says ..." *Santa Fe Daily New Mexican*, **May 5, 1881**, Volume X. Page 4, Column 3. Newspaperarchive.com.

No Author. "Richard Dunham's May 2, 1881 encounter with Billy the Kid.", *Santa Fe Daily New Mexican*, **May 5, 1881**, Page 4, Column 3. (private collection)

No Author. "The question if how to deal with desperados who commit murder has but one solution - kill them." *Las Vegas Daily Optic*. Tuesday, **May 10, 1881**.

No Author. "Billy 'the Kid.' " *Las Vegas Gazette*. Thursday, **May 12, 1881**.

No Author. "The Kid was in Chloride City ..." *Santa Fe Daily New Mexican*. **May 13, 1881**. Page 4, Column 3.

No Author. "Billy 'the Kid' is in the vicinity of Sumner." *Las Vegas Gazette*. Sunday, **May 15, 1881**.

No Author. "The Kid is believed to be in the Black Range ..." *Santa Fe Daily New Mexican*. **May 19, 1881**. Page 4, Column 1.

No Author. "Billy the Kid was last seen in Lincoln County ..." *Santa Fe Daily New Mexican*. **May 19, 1881**. Page 4, Column 1.

No Author. (O.L. Houghton's Conversation with Lew Wallace, before May 26, 1881), *The Las Vegas Daily Optic*, **May 26, 1881**, p.4, c.4. Indiana Historical Society. Lew Wallace Collection. M0292.

No Author. " 'Billy the Kid' has been heard from again." *Las Vegas Daily Optic*. Friday, **June 10, 1881**.

No Author. " 'Billy the Kid,' He is Reported to Have Been Seen on Our Streets Saturday Night." *Las Vegas Daily Optic*. Monday Evening, **June 13, 1881**. Vol. 2, No. 188, Page 4, Column 2.

Wilcox, Lute, Ed. "Billy the Kid would make an ideal newspaper-man in that he always endeavors to 'get even' with his enemies." *Las Vegas Daily Optic*. Monday Evening, **June 13, 1881**. Volume 2, Number 188, Page 4, Column 1.

No Author. "Land of the Petulant Pistol, "Scenes" where Life and Land are Cheap ... 'Billy the Kid' as a Killer." *Las Vegas Daily Optic*. Wednesday Evening, **June 15, 1881.** Front Page. 1, Volume 2, Number 190, Columns 1-2. (Possibly contributed to by Lew Wallace, who published with a similar title in the Crawfordsville *Saturday Evening Journal* on June 18, 1881)

No Author. "Barney Mason at Fort Sumner states the 'Kid' is in Local Sheep Camps." *Las Vegas Morning Gazette*. **June 16, 1881.**

No Author. "The Kid." *Santa Fe Daily New Mexican*. **June 16, 1881**. Volume X, Number 90, Page 4, Column 2.

No Author. "Billy the Kid." *Las Vegas Daily Optic*. Thursday, June 28, 1881.

No Author. " 'The Kid' Killed." *Las Vegas Daily Optic*. **July 18. 1881**.

No Author. "Account of the Manner in Which 'Billy the Kid' Was Killed, The Kid Killed." *The Chicago Daily Tribune*. **July 20, 1881**. Volume XL. Page 2. Column 5. ChroniclingAmerica.loc.gov/.

No Author. "Billy the Kid, At Last the Bullet Finds its Billet, New Mexico's Noted Outlaw Shot by a Sheriff." *The Weekly Gazette (Colorado Springs Gazette)*. **July 23, 1881**. Volume XI, Number 33. Page 5. Column 4. NewspaperArchive.com. **(Killing of Billy the Kid)**

No Author. "Kid the Killer Killed, Wm. Bonney alias Antrim, alias Billy the Kid, Fatally Meets Pat Garrett, the Lincoln County Sheriff." Las Cruces *Rio Grande Republican*. **July 23, 1881**. Volume 1, Number 10. Page 2. NewspaperArchive.com. **(Copy of Pat Garrett's letter to Acting Governor William Ritch with copy of Coroner's Jury Report)**

No Author. "Billy the Kid, A Youth With Nineteen Murders to His Account – The Inhabitants of New Mexico Overawed by a Boy of Twenty-One, Who Was Killed at Sight." *Savannah Morning News*. **July 26, 1881.** Front Page. Column 7. ChroniclingAmerica.loc.gov/. **(Killing of Billy the Kid)**

No Author. "Champion Murderer." *Fort Wayne Daily Gazette*. **July 26, 1881**. Volume XVIII, Number 11. Page 6. NewspaperArchive.com. **(Killing of Billy the Kid)**

No Author. No title. **Thursday, July 28, 1881.** Pueblo, Colorado, Col*orado Chieftain*. 9?". **(Quoting from the New York *Tribune* on killing of "Tiger in human form known as "Billy the Kid")**

No Author. "Billy the Kid, His Name Was Billy McCarthy and He was Born in New York, Murdering a Man at the Age of Sixteen – Made a Deputy Constable – Gen. Lew Wallace's Admiration for the Youthful Desperado, Under Sentence of Death – Killing Two Men in Thirty Seconds – The Kid Killed." *The Lancaster Intelligencer*. **August 12, 1881.** Volume XVII, Number 295. Front Page. Columns 3-5. ChroniclingAmerica.loc.gov/.

Gauss, Gottfried. Interview with *Lincoln County Leader*. **November 21, 1889. (About Billy Bonney's Lincoln jailbreak)**

LEW WALLACE'S OUTLAW MYTH ARTICLES

Koogler, John H. "Interview with Governor Lew Wallace on 'The Kid.'" *Las Vegas Gazette*. **April 28, 1881**.

No Author. "The Thug's Territory. Stage Robbers and Cut-Throats Have Things Their Own Way in New Mexico. Gen. Lew Wallace Anxious to Punish the Crime That is So Prevalent – A Chapter About 'Billy the Kid' – The Governor has a Narrow Escape From Being Spanked." *St. Louis Daily Globe-Democrat*. Monday Morning, **May 16, 1881**. Page 2, Columns 5 and 6. (private collection)

No Author. (Lew Wallace interview) "Billy the Kid. General Wallace Tells Why the Young Desperado of New Mexico Wanted to Kill Him, A Dashing and Daring Career in the Land of the Petulant Pistol." (Lew Wallace interviewed on June 13, 1881), Crawfordsville *Saturday Evening Journal*, **June 18, 1881**. Indiana Historical Society. The Papers of Lew and Susan Wallace. Microfilm Edition. Indianapolis, Indiana: Indiana Historical Society Press. 2008.

No Author. (Lew Wallace interview) "Lew Wallace's Foe. Threatened by 'Billy the Kid.' The Writing of 'Ben Hur' Interrupted. An Incident of the Soldier-Author's Career in New Mexico. *San Francisco Chronicle*. December 10, 1893. Indiana Historical Society. Lew Wallace Collection. M0292. Box 14. Folder 11. (Lew Wallace creating outlaw myth of outlaw Billy the Kid")

No Author. "Street Pickings," Weekly *Crawfordsville Review - Saturday Edition*, **January 6, 1894**. Indiana Historical Society. The Papers of Lew and Susan Wallace. Microfilm Edition. Series I. Reel 27. Indianapolis, Indiana: Indiana Historical Society Press. 2008.

No Author. "An Old Incident Recalled." Crawfordsville *Weekly News-Review*. **December 20, 1901**. Indiana Historical Society. The Papers of Lew and Susan Wallace. Microfilm Edition. Series I. Reel 27. Indianapolis, Indiana: Indiana Historical Society Press. 2008.

Lewis, E.I. "Gen. Wallace's Feud with Billy the Kid, When the General Was Governor of New Mexico and Billy Bonne Was the Most Dangerous Western Outlaw. He Was a Waif and Was Reared in Indiana. *The Indianapolis Press*. Saturday, **June 23, 1900**. Page 7. Lew Wallace Collection. Indiana Historical Society. M0292. Box 14. Folder 11. (photocopy) (Original article is in OMB 23, Box 1. Folder 5) (**Creating self-serving myth of outlaw Billy the Kid"**)

Wallace, Lew. "General Lew Wallace Writes a Romance of 'Billy the Kid' Most Famous Bandit of the Plains: Thrilling Story of the Midnight Meeting Between Gen Wallace, Then Governor of New Mexico, and the Notorious Outlaw, in a Lonesome Hut in Santa Fe." *New York World Magazine*. Sunday, **June 8, 1902**. Lew Wallace Collection. Indiana Historical Society. M0292. . Box 14. Folder 11.

OTHER HISTORICAL FIGURES (PERIOD)

ANGEL, FRANK WARNER

PRESIDENT HAYES MEETING BY

Mullin, Robert N. Re: Frank Warner Angel Meeting With President Hayes August, 1878. Binder RNM, VI, M. (Unpublished). Midland, Texas: Nita Stewart Haley Memorial Library and J. Evetts Haley History Center. (Undated).

LETTERS BY

Angel, Frank Warner. "I am in receipt of your favor of the 12th ..." Letter to Samuel Beach Axtell. **August 13, 1878**. Interior Department Papers 1850-1907; Appointments Division and Subsequent Actions. Microfilm Roll M750. National Archives and Records Administration Record Group 48. Microfilm Case Number 44-4-8-3. U.S. Department of Interior. Washington D.C.

__________. "I enclose copies of letters received by me from Gov Axtell ..." Letter to Secretary of the Interior Carl Schurz. **August 24, 1878**. (Enclosing copy of letter to him from Governor S.B. Axtell of August 12, 1878; and Angel's response to Axtell of August 13, 1878.) Microfilm File Case Number 44-4-8-3. Record Group 48. Microfilm No. M750. Roll 1. National Archives and Records Administration. U.S. Department of Justice. Washington, D.C.

__________. "I have just been favored by a call from W.L. Rynerson ..." Letter to Secretary of Interior Carl Schurz. **September 6, 1878**. Microfilm File Case Number 44-4-8-3. Record Group 48. Microfilm No. M750. Roll 1. National Archives and Records Administration. U.S. Department of Justice. Washington, D.C.

REPORTS BY

Angel, Frank Warner. *Examination of charges against F. C. Godfroy, Indian Agent, Mescalero, N. M.* **October 2, 1878**. (Report 1981, Inspector E.C. Watkins; Cited as Watkins Report). M319-20 and L147, 44-4-8. Record Group 075. National Archives and Records Administration. U.S. Department of Justice. Washington, D. C.

__________. *In the Matter of the Investigation of the Charges Against S.B. Axtell Governor of New Mexico. Report and Testimony.* **October 3, 1878.** Angel Report. Interior Department Papers 1850-1907; Appointments Division and Subsequent Actions. Microfilm Case File No. 44-4-8-3. Record Group 48. Microfilm Roll M750. National Archives and Records Administration. U.S. Department of Interior. Washington, D.C. (**Mentions Santa Fe Ring**)

__________. *In the Matter of the Examination of the Causes and Circumstances of the Death of John H. Tunstall a British Subject.* Report filed **October 4, 1878**. Angel Report. Interior Department Papers 1850-1907; Appointments Division and Subsequent Actions. Microfilm File Case Number 44-4-8-3. Record Group 48. Microfilm No. M750. Roll 1. National Archives and Records Administration. U.S. Department of Justice. Washington, D.C.

__________. *In the Matter of the Lincoln County Troubles. To the Honorable Charles Devens, Attorney General.* **October 4, 1878**. Angel Report. Microfilm Case File No. 44-4-8-3. Record Group 48. Microfilm Roll M750. National Archives and Records Administration. U.S. Department of Justice. Washington, D.C.

NOTEBOOK ON SANTA FE RING MEMBERS BY

Angel, Frank Warner. "To Gov. Lew Wallace / Santa Fe, N. M., 1878." Notebook. **1878**. Indiana Historical Society. Lew Wallace Collection. M0292. Microfilm No. F372. (**Original missing, copy on microfilm; Notebook prepared for Lew Wallace listing names of Santa Fe Ring members**)

Theisen, Lee Scott. "Frank Warner Angel's Notes on New Mexico Territory, 1878." *Arizona and the West: A Quarterly Journal of History*. Winter 1976. Volume 18. Number 4. Pages 333-370. (**About the Angel notebook**)

ASHENFELTER, SINGLETON M.

BIOGRAPHICAL SOURCE

Twitchell, Ralph Emerson. *The Leading Facts of New Mexico History*. Volume III. Cedar Rapids: The Torch Press. 1917.

XATELL, SAMUEL BEACH

CONTEMPORARY SOURCES (CHRONOLOGICAL)

No author. "Anarchy at Cimarron." *Santa Fe Weekly New Mexico*. **November 16, 1875**. (**Ring-biased article about Axtell calling in troops in Colfax County War**)

Axtell, Samuel B. "The Legislature to Assess Property. *Message of Gov. Samuel B. Axtell to the Legislative Assembly of New Mexico, Twenty-second Session.* Page 4. Manderfield & Tucker, Public Printers: Santa Fe, New Mexico. **1875 or 1876**. Interior Department Papers 1850-1907; Appointments Division and Subsequent Actions. Microfilm File Case Number 44-4-8-3. Record Group 48. Microfilm No. M750. Roll 1. National Archives and Records Administration. U.S. Department of Justice. Washington, D.C.

Elkins, Stephen B. "I trouble you to say a word in behalf of Gov. Axtell ..." Letter to President Rutherford B. Hayes. **June 11, 1877**. Interior Department Papers 1850-1907; Appointments Division and Subsequent Actions. Microfilm Roll M750. National Archives and Records Administration Record Group 48. Microfilm Case Number 44-4-8-3. U. S. Department of Interior. Washington D. C. (**Trying to prevent Axtell's removal as governor**)

Axtell, Samuel B. "I have today mailed to you a reply to the charges on file in your Dept against me." Letter to Secretary of the Interior Carl Schurz. **June 15, 1877**. Interior Department Papers 1850-1907; Appointments Division and Subsequent Actions. Microfilm Roll M750. National Archives and Records Administration Record Group 48. Microfilm Case Number 44-4-8-3 U.S. Department of Interior. Washington D.C. (**Refuting charges made in Colfax County**).

Isaacs, I. and G.N. Coe. "Charges Against S.B. Axtell, Governor of New Mexico." **June 22, 1878**. Interior Department Papers 1850-1907; Appointments Division and Subsequent Actions. Microfilm File Case Number 44-4-8-3. Microfilm No. M750. Roll 1. National Archives and Records Administration. Record Group 48. U.S. Department of Justice. Washington, D.C.

Routt, John C. "I am here on a visit to my daughter and have more by accident than otherwise heard statements ..." Letter to President Rutherford B. Hayes. **August 29, 1878**. Interior Department Papers 1850-1907; Appointments Division and Subsequent Actions. Microfilm File Case Number 44-4-8-3. Microfilm No. M750. Roll 1. National Archives and Records Administration. U.S. Department of Justice. Washington, D.C. (**Ringite letter opposing removal of Governor Axtell and U.S. Attorney Catron.**)

Schurz, Carl. "I transmit herewith an order from the President ..." **September 4, 1878**. Letter to Lew Wallace. Indiana Historical Society. Lew Wallace Collection. M0292. Box 3. Folder 14. (**Suspension of Governor S.B. Axtell and Wallace's appointment as new Governor**)

Elkins, Stephen Benton. "To the President. Referring to a conversation had with you last week ..." Letter to President James Abram Garfield. **March 17, 1881**. (Received Executive Mansion April 6, 1881). Interior Department Papers 1850-1907; Appointments Division and Subsequent Actions. Microfilm Roll M750. National Archives and Records Administration Microfilm Roll M750. National Archives and Records Administration Record Group 48. Microfilm Case Number 44-4-8-3. U.S. Department of Interior. Washington D.C. Microfilm Case Number 44-4-8-3. U.S. Department of Interior. Washington D.C. (**Request for re-appointment of Axtell as Territorial New Mexico Governor**)

Bradstreet, George P. "Referring to the nomination of Sam'l B. Axtell of Ohio to be Chief Justice of the Supreme Court of New Mexico ... he is alleged to have been removed by President Hayes ..." Letter to Judiciary Committee of the U.S. Senate. **June 22, 1882**. Interior Department Papers 1850-1907; Appointments Division and Subsequent Actions. Microfilm Roll M750. National Archives and Records Administration Microfilm Roll M750. National Archives and Records Administration Record Group 48. Microfilm Case Number 44-4-8-3. U.S. Department of Interior. Washington D.C.

No Author. " 'Chief Justice Axtell' is a bitter pill for the Raton *News and Press.*" *Santa Fe New Mexican.* **July 18, 1882**. (**Santa Fe Ring instatement of S.B. Axtell as Chief Justice**)

BONNEY, WILLIAM HENRY

(See History of William Henry Bonney)

BOWDRE, CHARLES

CONTEMPORARY SOURCES (CHRONOLOGICAL)

Wallace, Lew. "Please select ten of your Rangers ..." Letter to Juan Patrón. **March 3, 1879**. Indiana Historical Society. Lew Wallace Collection. M0292. Box 4. Folder 4. **(To arrest "Scurlock and Bowdre")**

__________ "I have reliable information that J.G. Scurlock and Charles Bowdre are now at a ranch called Taiban ..." Letter to Edward Hatch. **March 6, 1879**. Indiana Historical Society. Lew Wallace Collection. Box 4, Folder 4.

BRADY, WILLIAM

BIOGRAPHICAL SOURCE

Lavash, Donald R. *Sheriff William Brady. Tragic Hero of the Lincoln County War.* Santa Fe, New Mexico: Sunstone Press. 1986.

CONTEMPORARY SOURCES (CHRONOLOGICAL)

Brady, William. Affidavit of **July 2, 1876** concerning appointment as Administrator for the Emil Fritz Estate. Copied from the original District Court Record. (private collection)

__________. Affidavit of **August 22, 1876** documenting business debts to L. G. Murphy and Co. pertaining to the Emil Fritz Estate. Copied from the original District Court Record. (private collection)

__________. Affidavit of **July _, 1876** of Resignation as Emil Fritz Estate Administrator. Copied from the original District Court Record. (private collection.)

__________. Affidavit of **August 22, 1876** confirming giving Alexander McSween the books of the L.G. Murphy Company for the purpose of making business debt collections. Copied from the original District Court Record. (private collection)

Tunstall, John Henry. "A Taxpayer's Complaint ... January 18, 1878." Mesilla *Independent*. **January 26, 1878. (Exposé of William Brady embezzling tax money to buy cattle for "The House;" and Catron then paid that bill)**

Dolan, James J. "Answer to A Taxpayer's Complaint." Mesilla *Independent*. **January 29, 1878. (Response to J.H. Tunstall's exposé)**

Bristol, Warren. "Action of Assumpsit to command Sheriff Brady of Lincoln County to attach goods of Alexander A. McSween." **February 7, 1878**. District Court Record. (private collection).

__________. Preprinted form for "Writ of Attachment" (Printed and sold at the office of the Mesilla News) filled out to command the Sheriff of Lincoln County to attach goods of Alexander McSween for a suit of damages for ten thousand dollars. **February 7, 1878**. District Court Record. (private collection).

Brady, William. "List of Articles Inventoried by Wm Brady sheriff in the suit of Charles Fritz & Emilie Scholand vs A.A. McSween now in the dwelling house belonging to A.A. McSween." (undated, but in **February of 1878**) (private collection)

BREEDEN, WILLIAM (CHRONOLOGICAL)

BIOGRAPHICAL SOURCES

No Author. *Acts of the Legislative Assembly of the Territory of New Mexico, Twenty-Second Session, Convened at the Capitol, at the City of Santa Fe on Monday the 6th day of December, 1875, and adjourned on Friday the 14th day of January, 1876. Santa Fe: Manderfield & Tucker.* **1876. (Breeden is listed under**

"Territorial Officers" as both Attorney General and District Attorney for the First Judicial District, Page 13)

Speer, William S. and John Henry Brown, eds. *The Encyclopedia of the New West, Containing Fully Authenticated Information of the Agricultural, Mercantile, Commercial, Manufacturing, Mining and Grazing Industries, and Representing the Character, Development, Resources and Present Development of Texas, Arkansas, Colorado, New Mexico and Indian Territory, Also Biographical Sketches of Their Representative Men and Women.* Marshall, Texas: The United States Biographical Publishing Company. **1881.**

No Author. *Acts of the Legislative Assembly of the Territory of New Mexico, Twenty-Sixth Session, Convened at the Capitol, at the City of Santa Fe on Monday the 18th day of February, 1884, and adjourned on Thursday, the 3rd day of April, 1884.* Santa Fe: New Mexican Printing Co. **1884. (The Attorney General is listed as performing as *ex officio* District Attorney for the First Judicial District, as did Breeden since 1881)**

Prince, L. Bradford, Ed. *The General Laws of New Mexico; Including All the Unrepealed Laws From the Promulgation of the 'Kearney Code' in 1846, to the End of the Legislative Session of 1880. With Supplement, Including the Session of 1882.* Albany, New York: W.C. Little & Co., Law Publishers. "Article VI, Chapter X, Attorney General, District Attorneys, and Attorneys." **1882.** Pages 56-57. **(Inquest law for writing a Coroner's Jury Report, as followed by Alejandro Segura)**

Ritch, William. Ed. *The Legislative Blue-Book of the Territory of New Mexico.* Santa Fe. Charles W. Greene Publisher. **1882. (With listing of Breeden as Attorney General in the "Official Register")**

Ayer, N.W. and Son. eds. *N.W. Ayer & Son's American Newspaper Annual Containing a Catalogue of American Newspapers.* Philadelphia: N.W. Ayer & Son. **1888. (Listing Breeden's and Henry Waldo's New Mexico Printing Company as publishing *The Santa Fe New Mexican*)**

No Author. "Obituary Notes." *The New York Times.* **January 29, 1913**. Page 11, Column 5. Newspaperarchive.com.

Twitchell, Ralph Emerson. *The Leading Facts of New Mexico History.* Volume III. Cedar Rapids: The Torch Press. 1917. (**Breeden biography**)

Anderson, Clinton P. "The Adobe Palace." *New Mexico Historical Review.* **1944.** Volume 19, Number 2. Pages 97-122.

Nusbaum, Rosemary. *The City Different and the Palace, The Palace of the Governors: Its Role in Santa Fe History.* Santa Fe: Sunstone Press. **1978**.

BRISTOL, WARREN HENRY

CONTEMPORARY SOURCES (CHRONOLOGICAL)

Bristol Warren. "From sources of information that I deem perfectly reliable I am satisfied that there are public disorders in Lincoln County ..." Letter to Governor Marsh Giddings. **January 10, 1874**. Herman B. Weisner Papers, ca. 1957-1992. New Mexico State University Library at Las Cruces. Rio Grande Historical Collections. Accession No. Weisner Ms 0249. Box 4/39. Folder D-4. Folder Name: "Judge Bristol's letter." (**Creating Ring's outlaw myth and proposing military intervention**)

__________. "Writ of Embezzlement." **December 21, 1877**. Herman B. Weisner Papers, ca. 1957-1992. New Mexico State University Library at Las Cruces. Rio Grande Historical Collections. Accession No. Ms 0249. Box 10. Folder M-13. Folder Name. "Will and Testament A. McSween." (**Emilie Fritz Scholand's sworn complaint against Alexander McSween**)

__________. "Action of Assumpsit to command Sheriff Brady of Lincoln County to attach goods of Alexander A. McSween." **February 7, 1878**. District Court Record.

__________. Preprinted form for "Writ of Attachment" (Printed and sold at the office of the Mesilla News) filled out to command the Sheriff of Lincoln County to attach goods of Alexander McSween for a suit of damages for ten thousand dollars. **February 7, 1878**. District Court Record. (private collection).

__________. *Instructions to the Jury*. District Court 3rd Judicial. District Doña Ana. Filed **April 9, 1881**. Writ of Embezzlement. New Mexico State University Library at Las Cruces. Rio Grande Historical Collection. Accession No. Ms 0249. Box 1. Folder 14C. Folder Name: "Billy the Kid Legal Documents."

CATRON, THOMAS BENTON

BIBLIOGRAPHICAL SOURCES

Cleaveland, Norman, *A Synopsis of the Great New Mexico Cover-up*. Self-printed. 1989.

__________. *The Great Santa Fe Cover-up. Based on a Talk given Before the Santa Fe Historical Society on November 1, 1978*. Self-printed. 1982.

__________. *The Morleys - Young Upstarts on the Southwest Frontier*. Albuquerque, New Mexico: Calvin Horn Publisher, Inc. 1971. (**Page 93 gives Catron's vindictive indictment of Cleaveland's grandmother, Ada Morley, for mail theft as revenge denying him use of a Maxwell Land Grant buggy.**

Dodge, Andrew R., and Betty K. Koed, eds. *Biographical Directory of the United States Congress 1774-2005*. Washington, D.C.: United States Government Printing Office. 2005

Dunham, Harold H. "New Mexican Land Grants with Special Reference to the Title Papers of the Maxwell Grant." *New Mexico Historical Review*. (January, 1955) Vol. 70. No. 1. pp. 1 - 23.

Hefferan, Vioalle Clark. *Thomas Benton Catron*. Albuquerque, New Mexico: University of New Mexico. Zimmerman Library. Unpublished Thesis for the Degree of Master of Arts. 1940. .(**In praise of Catron; includes railroad involvement, Page 35; First National Bank stockholder from 1871 to 1907, Page 28**)

Keleher, William A. *The Maxwell Land Grant. A New Mexico Item*. Albuquerque, New Mexico: University of New Mexico Press. 1964.

Klasner, Lilly. Eve Ball. Ed. *My Girlhood Among Outlaws*. Tucson, Arizona: The University of Arizona Press. 1972.

Lamar, Howard Robert N. *The Far Southwest 1846 – 1912: A Territorial History*. New Haven and London: Yale University Press. 1966. (**Chapter 6 covers the Santa Fe Ring)**)

Montoya, María E. *Translating Property. The Maxwell Land Grant and the Conflict Over Land in the American West, 1840-1900*. Berkeley and Los Angeles: University of California Press. 2002.

Mullin, Robert N. "A Specimen of Catron's Dirty Work. Sworn Affidavit of Samuel Davis." October 1, 1878. Binder RNM IV, EE. (Unpublished). Midland, Texas: Nita Stewart Haley Memorial Library and J. Evetts Haley Historical Center.

__________. "Catron Embarrassed Throughout His Life by an Affliction." (Date Unknown). Binder RNM, IV, M. (Unpublished). Midland, Texas: Nita Stewart Haley Memorial Library and J. Evetts Haley Historical Center. Robert Mullin Papers. Binder RNM IV, EE (Unpublished).

__________. "Prior to Lincoln County War Catron Had Defended Colonel Dudley." (No Date). Notes from "Lincoln County War Cast of Characters." Midland, Texas: Nita Stewart Haley Memorial Library and J. Evetts Haley Historical Center.

Murphy, Lawrence R. *Lucien Bonaparte Maxwell. Napoleon of the Southwest*. Norman: University of Oklahoma Press. 1983.

Otero, Miguel A. *My Life on the Frontier, 1882-1897: Incidents and Characters of the period when Kansas, Colorado, and New Mexico were passing through the last of their Wild and Romantic Years*. New York: The Press of the Pioneers. 1935. Pages 232-233. (Quoted by Victor Westphall, *Thomas Benton Catron and His Era*.

Page 188) **(Quote: "the 'Santa Fe Ring,' the real machine controlling the political situation in New Mexico.")**

Pearson, Jim Berry. *The Maxwell Land Grant.* Norman: University of Oklahoma Press. 1961.

Sluga, Mary Elizabeth. *Political Life of Thomas Benton Catron 1896-1912.* Albuquerque, New Mexico: University of New Mexico. Zimmerman Library. Unpublished Thesis for the Degree of Master of Arts. 1941. **(Thesis in praise of Catron for an M.A.)**

Taylor, Morris F. *O.P. McMains and the Maxwell Land Grant Conflict.* Tucson, Arizona: The University of Arizona Press. 1979. **(Traces origins of the Santa Fe Ring with T.B. Catron and S.B. Elkins)**

Westphall, Victor. *Thomas Benton Catron and His Era.* Tucson, Arizona: University of Arizona Press. 1973.

__________. "Fraud and Implications of Fraud in the Land Grants of New Mexico." *New Mexico Historical Review.* 1974. Vol. XLIX, No. 3. 189 - 218.

Wooden, John Paul. *Thomas Benton Catron and New Mexico Politics 1866-1921.* Albuquerque, New Mexico: University of New Mexico. Zimmerman Library. Unpublished Thesis for the Degree of Master of Arts. 1959. **(M.A. thesis praising Catron)**

GENERAL CONTEMPORARY EXPOSÉS OF(CHRONOLOGICAL)

Middaugh, Asa F. Deposition. **March 31, 1876**. "Exhibit B" in the August 9, 1878 deposition of Frank Springer to Investigator Frank Warner Angel. Frank Warner Angel report titled *In the Matter of the Investigation of the Charges Against S.B. Axtell Governor of New Mexico.* October 3, 1878. Interior Department Papers 1850-1907; Appointments Division and Subsequent Actions. Microfilm Case File No. 44-4-8-3. Record Group 48. Microfilm Roll M750. National Archives and Records Administration. U.S. Department of Interior. Washington, D.C. **(About Catron's malicious prosecution of Ada McPherson Morley)**

Springer, Frank. Deposition to Investigator Frank Warner Angel. **August 9, 1878**. Frank Warner Angel report titled *In the Matter of the Investigation of the Charges Against S.B. Axtell Governor of New Mexico.* October 3, 1878. Interior Department Papers 1850-1907; Appointments Division and Subsequent Actions. Microfilm Case File No. 44-4-8-3. Record Group 48. Microfilm Roll M750. National Archives and Records Administration. U.S. Department of Interior. Washington, D.C. **(Mentions Catron, Elkins, and the Santa Fe Ring, and provided Exhibits of letters exposing Catron's evil.)**

No Author. "The Santa Fe Ring is the most corrupt combination that ever cursed any country or community." Las Cruces *Thirty-Four Newspaper.* **October 27, 1880**. From Victor Westphall, *Thomas Benton Catron and His Era.* Page 186. **(Article summarizing Ring abuses in urging voters to oppose Ring candidates)**

No Author. "The Ring must soon discover that the time has passed in New Mexico when men can be herded like so many sheep ..." *Albuquerque Daily Democrat.* **March 4, 1884**. Quoted by Victor Westphall, *Thomas Benton Catron and His Era.* Page 191. **(About Santa Fe Ring control of appointments to legislature)**

Valdez, Jose and Enrique Mares. "Scorching Letter, The Knights of Labor Send a Communication to Powderly! Politicians Arraigned! The Boldest Document Ever Issued in the Territory." **August 18, 1890.** *Las Vegas Democrat.* Volume 1. Center for Southwest Studies. Thomas B. Catron Papers, MSS 29, Series 102, Box 8, Folder 4. **(Gives history of Santa Fe Ring with T.B. Catron as head)**

No Author. "Catron and the Laboring Men." Unknown newspaper. **1892?** University of New Mexico Library. Center for Southwest Studies. Thomas B. Catron Papers, MSS 29, Series 401, Box 1, Folder 3. **(Opposition to Catron as Delegate to Congress as "the biggest corporation man in New Mexico")**

Victory, John P. "No Consistent Democrat Should Vote for T.B. Catron, John P. Victory in Forcible and Cogent Language Gives Answerable Reasons." **No month, 1895.** Printed broadside. University of New Mexico Library. Center for Southwest Studies. Thomas B. Catron Papers, MSS 29, Series 409, Box 1, Folder 3.

Wallace, Lew. "I have your several letters, including the last one of the 3rd inst." Letter to Eugene Fiske. **November 6, 1897**. Indiana Historical Society. Lew Wallace Collection. AC233. Box 1. Folder 7. (part of 1981 addition) (**About Catron's control over New Mexicans**)

Cutting, Bronson. "Catron was the boss of the Territory ..." Letter to James Roger Addison. **December 11, 1911**. Cited by Victor Westphall in *Thomas Benton Catron and His Era* from his citation: Lincoln County Manuscripts Division. Box 12. Courtesy of David Stratton. (**Catron as head of the Santa Fe Ring**)

Johnson, E. Dana. "[H]e ruled with a rod of iron ..." Editorial. *Santa Fe New Mexican.* **May 16, 1921**. Catron Papers 801, Box 1. Quoted by Victor Westphall, *Thomas Benton Catron and His Era.* Pages 394-395. (**Tactics of "boss" Catron without using the words Santa Fe Ring**)

(SEE: Santa Fe Ring; Frank Warner Angel)

FEDERAL INDICTMENT OF REGULATORS BY

Catron, Thomas Benton. "Case No. 411. The United States vs. Charles Bowdry [Bowdre], Doc Scurlock, Henry Brown, Henry Antrim alias "Kid," John Middleton, Stephen Stevens, John Scroggins, George Coe and Frederick Waite." **June 21, 1878**. Herman B. Weisner Papers, ca. 1957-1992. New Mexico State University Library at Las Cruces. Rio Grande Historical Collections. Accession No. Ms 0249. Box 1. Folder B-4. Folder Name: Andrew Roberts Indictment. (**Catron's plot to keep control over prosecution of Regulators, including Billy Bonney**)

RESIGNATION AS TERRITORIAL U.S. ATTORNEY BY

Elkins, Stephen Benton. "Asking delay of action upon charges against U.S. Atty. Catron ..." **September 24, 1878**. Angel Report. Microfilm File Case No. 44-4-8-3. Record Group 48. National Records and Archives Administration. Microfilm No. M750. Roll 1. U.S. Department of Justice. Washington, D. C.

__________. "Regarding Attorney General's decision on T.B. Catron." Letter. **September___, 1878**. Angel Report. Microfilm File Case No. 44-4-8-3. Record Group 48. National Records and Archives Administration. Microfilm No. M750. Roll 1. U.S. Department of Justice. Washington, D.C.

Catron, Thomas Benton. "In accordance with a purpose long entertained ...." Letter to Charles Devens. **October 10, 1878.** Angel Report. Microfilm File Case No. 44-4-8-3. Record Group 48. National Records and Archives Administration. Microfilm No. M750. Roll 1. U.S. Department of Justice. Washington, D.C. (**Resignation as U.S. Attorney**)

Devens, Charles. "Your resignation of the office of United States Attorney ..." Letter to T.B. Catron. **October 19, 1878**. Angel Report. Microfilm File Case No. 44-4-8-3. Record Group 48. National Records and Archives Administration. Microfilm No. M750. Roll 1. U.S. Department of Justice. Washington, D. C.

Catron, Thomas Benton. "Please change my resignation ...." **November 4, 1878.** Telegram to Charles Devens. Angel Report. Microfilm File Case No. 44-4-8-3. Record Group 48. National Records and Archives Administration. Microfilm No. M750. Roll 1. U.S. Department of Justice. Washington, D. C. (**Resignation as U.S. Attorney**)

Devens, Charles. "Your resignation of the office of United States Attorney ..." Letter to T.B. Catron. **November 12, 1878**. Angel Report. Microfilm File Case No. 44-4-8-3. Record Group 48. National Records and Archives Administration. Microfilm No. M750. Roll 1. U.S. Department of Justice. Washington, D.C.

lkins, Stephen Benton. "Relative to resignation of T. B. Catron U. S. Attorney." Letter to Charles Devens. **November 10, 1878**. Angel Report. Microfilm File Case No. 44-4-8-3. Record Group 48. National Records and Archives Administration. Microfilm No. M750. Roll 1. U.S. Department of Justice. Washington, D.C.

Barnes, Sidney M.. "I Sidney M. Barnes do solemnly swear ..." Swearing in as U.S. Attorney. **January 20, 1879**. Angel Report. Microfilm File Case No. 44-4-8-3. Record Group 48. National Records and Archives Administration. Microfilm No. M750. Roll 1. U.S. Department of Justice. Washington, D.C. (**Catron replaced by Ringite attorney Sidney Barnes**)

Elkins, Stephen Benton. "I have waited some time to reply to your lengthy letter ..." Letter to T.B. Catron. **August 15, 1879**. West Virginia & Regional History Center. West Virginia University Libraries, Morgantown, W. Va. Stephen B. Elkins Papers (A&M 53). Box 1. Folder 1. (**Reveals he prevented Catron's dismissal and indictment from Angel's report**)

PECOS RIVER COW CAMP OF (CHRONOLOGICAL)

Riley, John H. Letter to N.A.M. Dudley. **May 19, 1878. (Fabricated Regulator theft of Catron's cattle from the Dolan Pecos Cow Camp**) Cited by Victor Westphall, Page 87.

Catron, Thomas Benton. Catron letter to Governor S. B. Axtell to intervene in Lincoln County. **May 30, 1878**. Midland, Texas: Nita Stewart Haley Memorial Library and J. Evetts Haley Historical Center. Robert Mullin Papers. Binder RNM IV, EE (Unpublished). (**Fabricated attack of Regulators on his cow camp workers**) Cited by Victor Westphall, Page 89-90.

OWNERSHIP FILING ON CARRIZOZO CATTLE COMPANY BY

Catron, Thomas Benton.. Statement of Sole ownership of Carrizozo Ranch in Tax Dispute Case. No date. Herman B. Weisner Papers, ca. 1957-1992. New Mexico State University Library at Las Cruces. Rio Grande Historical Collections. Accession No. Ms 0249. Box. 2. Folder C-8. Folder Name "T.B. Catron Tax Troubles." (**One of Catron's Lincoln County holdings**)

CHAPMAN, HUSTON INGRAM

CONTEMPORARY SOURCES (CHRONOLOGICAL)

Wallace, Lew. "I enclose you a copy of a letter from Las Vegas ..." Letter to Edward Hatch. **October 28, 1878**. Indiana Historical Society. Lew Wallace Collection. M0292. Box 3. Folder 16. (**Forwards Chapman's letter to Hatch**)

__________. "In a communication, dated October 28. inst., I requested, for reasons stated, a safe-guard for Mrs. McSween ..." Letter to Edward Hatch. **November 9, 1878**. Indiana Historical Society. Lew Wallace Collection. M0292. Box 3. Folder 17.

No Author. (signed E.). "Death of Chapman." *Las Vegas Gazette.* **March 1, 1879**. From *Proceedings of a Court of Inquiry in the Case of Lt. Col. N.A.M. Dudley (May 2,1879 – July 5, 1879).* File No. QQ1284. (Boxes 3304, 3305, 3305A); Court Martial Files 1809-1894. Records of the Office of the Judge Advocate General – Army. Record Group 153. Old Military and Civil Branch. National Archives and Records Administration. Washington, D. C.

No Author. "Wallace and Lincoln County." Grant County *Herald.* **March 1, 1879**. Indiana Historical Society. The Papers of Lew and Susan Wallace. Microfilm Edition. Indianapolis, Indiana: Indiana Historical Society Press. 2008. (**Ridicule about Huston Chapman's murder**)

Chapman, W.W. "Yours of the 1st inst. came ..." Letter to Ira E. Leonard. **March 20, 1879**. Indiana Historical Society. Lew Wallace Collection. M0292. Box 4. Folder 6.

Rynerson, William. "The Grand Jurors for the Territory of New Mexico taken from the body of the good and lawful men of the County of Lincoln ..." Indictments of the April, Lincoln County Grand Jury. **April 28, 1879**. Herman B. Weisner Papers, ca. 1957-1992. New Mexico State University Library at Las Cruces. Rio Grande Historical Collection. Accession No. Ms 0249. Box 4/39. Folder E-Z. Folder Name: "Jessie Evans Accessory to Murder." (**Billy's testimony indicts J.J. Dolan, Billy Campbell, and Jessie Evans fulfilling his pardon bargain**)

Chapman, W.W. "Since receiving yours of the 1st March ..." Letter to Ira Leonard. **May 8, 1879**. Indiana Historical Society. Lew Wallace Collection. M0292. Box 4. Folder 10.

LETTERS BY

Chapman, Huston I. "You will please pardon me for presuming so much upon your kindness ..." Letter to Lew Wallace. **October 24, 1878**. Indiana Historical Society. Lew Wallace Collection. M0292. Box 3. Folder 16. (**Makes clear N.A.M. Dudley's danger to Susan McSween**)

__________. '*You attach much importance to the awe-inspiring influence of the military* ..." Letter to Lew Wallace. **November 25, 1878**. From Frederick Nolan, *The Lincoln County War*, p. 359.

__________. "You must pardon me for so often presuming upon your kindness ..." Letter to Lew Wallace. **November 29, 1878**. Indiana Historical Society. Lew Wallace Collection. M0292. Box 3. Folder 18.

CHISUM, JOHN SIMPSON

Hinton, Harwood P., Jr. "John Simpson Chisum, 1877-84." *New Mexico Historical Review* 31(3) (July 1956): 177 - 205; 31(4) (October 1956): 310 - 337; 32(1) (January 1957): 53 - 65.

Klasner, Lilly. Eve Ball. Ed. *My Girlhood Among Outlaws*. Tucson, Arizona: The University of Arizona Press. 1972. (**Contains John Chisum's in jail write-up about Santa Fe Ring injustices to himself**)

COE FAMILY

BIOGRAPHICAL SOURCES

Coe, George. Doyce B. Nunis, Jr. Ed. *Frontier Fighter. The Autobiography of George Coe Who Fought and Rode With Billy the Kid*. Chicago: R. R. Donnelley and Sons Company. 1984.

Coe, Wilbur. *Ranch on the Ruidoso. The Story of a Pioneer Family in New Mexico, 1871 - 1968*. New York: Alfred A. Knopf. 1968.

DEDRICK BROTHERS

BIOGRAPHICAL SOURCES

Upham, Elizabeth. (Related by marriage to Daniel Dedrick). Personal interviews. 1998.

Upham, Marquita. (Relative by marriage to Daniel Dedrick). Personal interview. 1998.

CONTEMPORARY SOURCES (CHRONOLOGICAL)

Dedrick, Dan. "I have been under an arrest for six days ..." **April 5, 1879**. Letter to Lew Wallace. Indiana Historical Society. Lew Wallace Collection. M0292. Box 4. Folder 8. (**Says he was not told his arrest charges**)

No Author. "Arrests of Dedricks. Legal Documents." Herman B. Weisner Papers, ca. 1957-1992. New Mexico State University Library at Las Cruces. Rio Grande Historical Collections. Accession No. Ms 0249. Box 1. Folder B-8. Folder Name: "Lincoln County Bonds."

DOLAN, JAMES JOSEPH

BIOGRAPHICAL SOURCE

Slates, Thomas. "The James J. Dolan House, Lincoln New Mexico." *New Mexico Architecture* 11. 8/9 (1969). pp. 17-20.**(With Dolan biography)**

CONTEMPORARY SOURCES BY AND ABOUT (CHRONOLOGICAL)

Tunstall, John Henry. "A Tax-payer's Complaint, Office of John H. Tunstall, Lincoln, Lincoln Co., N.M., January 18, 1878, 'The Present Sheriff of Lincoln County Has Paid Nothing During His Present Term of Office.' Governor's Message for 1878." Mesilla *Independent.* **January 26, 1878**. Volume 1, Number 32. NewspaperArchive.com. **(Exposé of William Brady and John Riley for embezzling tax money to buy cattle; T.B. Catron then paid that bill)**

Dolan, James J. "Answer to A Taxpayer's Complaint." Mesilla *Independent.* **January 29, 1878. (Response to J.H. Tunstall's exposé of embezzlement of tax money to buy cattle)**

McSween, Alexander. "It looks as though the agent were the property of J.J. Dolan & J.H. Riley, known here as Dolan & Co." Letter to Secretary of Interior Carl Schurz. **February 11, 1878**. From Frederick Nolan. *The Life and Death of John Henry Tunstall.* Albuquerque, New Mexico: The University of New Mexico Press. 1965. Page 266.

Rynerson, William. "Friends Riley & Dolan, Lincoln N.M. I have just received letters from you mailed 10th inst." **February 14, 1878.** Letter to James Dolan and John Riley. Copy as Exhibit B in June 6, 1878 deposition of Alexander McSween. Frank Warner Angel report. *In the Matter of the Examination of the Causes and Circumstances of the Death of John H. Tunstall a British Subject.* Report filed October 4, 1878. Frank Warner Angel report. Interior Department Papers 1850-1907; Appointments Division and Subsequent Actions. Microfilm File Case Number 44-4-8-3. Record Group 48. Microfilm No. M750. Roll 1. National Archives and Records Administration. U.S. Department of Justice. Washington, D.C. (James J. Dolan Deposition. June 20, 1878. Pages 235-247.) **(Implying planned killing of J.H. Tunstall)**

Wilson, John, George B. Barker, Robert M. Gilbert, John Newcomb, Samuel Smith, Benjamin Ellis. "We the undersigned Justice of the Peace and Coroners Jury who sat upon the inquest held this 19th day of February 1878 on the body of John H. Tunstall ..." Coroner's Jury Report for John Tunstall. **February 19, 1878. (Naming as murderers, among others, James Dolan, Frank Baker, Jessie Evans, William Morton, and George Hindman)**

Rynerson, William. "The Grand Jurors for the Territory of New Mexico taken from the body of the good and lawful men of the County of Lincoln ..." Indictments of the April, Lincoln County Grand Jury. **April 28, 1879**. Herman B. Weisner Papers, ca. 1957-1992. New Mexico State University Library at Las Cruces. Rio Grande Historical Collection. Accession No. Weisner MS 249. Box 4/39. Folder E-Z. Folder Name: "Jessie Evans Accessory to Murder." **(Billy Bonney's testimony indicts J.J. Dolan, Billy Campbell, and Jessie Evans for pardon bargain)**

Purington, George Augustus. "The District Court adjourned on Thursday ..." **May 3, 1879**. Indiana Historical Society. Lew Wallace Collection. M0292. Box 4. Folder 10. **(Letter to Adjutant General on Grand Jury indictments, including Dolan for the H.I. Chapman murder)**

Wild, Azariah F. "Daily Reports of U. S. Secret Service Agents, Azariah F. Wild." Microfilm T-915. Record Group 87. Rolls 307 (January 1,1878 - June 30, 1879) and 308 **(July 1, 1879 - June 30, 1881)**. National Archives and Records Department. Department of the Treasury. United States Secret Service. Washington, D. C. **(Dolan as an informer against "the Kid gang")**

DUDLEY, NATHAN AUGUSTUS MONROE

BIOGRAPHICAL SOURCES

Heitman, Francis B. *Historical Register and Dictionary of the United States Army, From Its Organization, September 29, 1789, to March 2, 1903.* (Entry for Galusha Pennypacker, Pages 782-7830.) Washington, D.C.: Government Printing Office. 1903.

Kaye, E. Donald. *Nathan Augustus Monroe Dudley: Rogue, Hero, or Both?* Parker, Colorado: Outskirts Press, Inc. 2007.

Oliva, Leo E., *Fort Union and the Frontier Army in the Southwest.* Southwest Cultural Resource Center, Professional Papers No. 41, National Park Service, 1993, Pages 488-489, 550, 574, 624-626, 656-659 are on Dudley. (**Quoted to E. Donald Kaye from the now-lost letter of Amos Kimball: "I guess you heard that Dudley made Colonel. The army bureaucracy is like a giant cesspool, where the biggest chunks rise to the top."**)

MILITARY COURT OF INQUIRY FOR

Leonard, Ira E. "*Charges and specifications against Lieutenant Colonel N.A.M. Dudley, Commander at Fort Stanton, New Mexico.*" **March 4, 1879**. Letter to Secretary of War George McCrary. *Proceedings of a Court of Inquiry in the Case of Lt. Col. N.A.M. Dudley (May 2,1879 - July 5, 1879).* File No. QQ1284. (Boxes 3304, 3305, 3305A); Court Martial Files 1809-1894. Records of the Office of the Judge Advocate General - Army. Record Group 153. Old Military and Civil Branch. National Archives and Records Administration. Washington, D. C. (**Charges against Dudley for murders of A.A. McSween and H.I. Chapman and arson of McSween's house**)

No Author. *Proceedings of a Court of Inquiry in the Case of Lt. Col. N.A.M. Dudley* ***(May 2,1879 – July 5, 1879)***. File No. QQ1284. (Boxes 3304, 3305, 3305A); Court Martial Files 1809-1894. Records of the Office of the Judge Advocate General - Army. Record Group 153. Old Military and Civil Branch. National Archives and Records Administration. Washington, D. C.

ELKINS, STEPHEN BENTON

BIOGRAPHICAL SOURCES (CHRONOLOGICAL)

Lambert, Oscar Doane. *Stephen Benton Elkins. American Foursquare.* Pittsburgh, Pennsylvania: University of Pittsburg Press. **1955**.

Cleaveland, Norman, *The Morleys - Young Upstarts on the Southwest Frontier.* Albuquerque, New Mexico: Calvin Horn Publisher, Inc. **1971**.

Westphall, Victor. *Thomas Benton Catron and His Era.* Tucson, Arizona: University of Arizona Press. **1973.**

Taylor, Morris F. *O.P. McMains and the Maxwell Land Grant Conflict.* Tucson, Arizona: The University of Arizona Press. **1979**. (**Traces origins of the Santa Fe Ring with T.B. Catron and S.B. Elkins**)

Cleaveland, Norman. *The Great Santa Fe Cover-up. Based on a Talk given Before the Santa Fe Historical Society on November 1, 1978.* Self-printed. **1982.**

__________. *A Synopsis of the Great New Mexico Cover-up.* Self-printed. **1989**.

ARTICLE ABOUT

No Author. " 'The Territory of Elkins.' Assassination of Supposed Sun Correspondent. The Murder of the Rev. F.J. Tolby in New Mexico. A Probate Judge Accused of Complicity in the Crime. Indignation Meeting." *New York Weekly Sun*. **December 22, 1875**. Interior Department Papers 1850-1907; Appointments Division and Subsequent Actions. Microfilm Roll M750. National Archives and Records

Administration. Record Group 48. Microfilm Case File Number 44-4-8-3. U. S. Department of Interior. Washington, D.C. (**In May 1, 1877 complaint to President Hayes as "Mary E. McPherson and W.B. Matchett 'Make certain charges**)

(SEE: Santa Fe Ring, Thomas Benton Catron)

EVANS, JESSIE

BIOGRAPHICAL SOURCE

McCright, Grady E. and James H. Powell. *Jessie Evans: Lincoln County Badman.* College Station, Texas: Creative Publishing Company. 1983.

CONTEMPORARY SOURCES (CHRONOLOGICAL)

Wilson, John, George B. Barker, Robert M. Gilbert, John Newcomb, Samuel Smith, Benjamin Ellis. "We the undersigned Justice of the Peace and Coroners Jury who sat upon the inquest held this 19th day of February 1878 on the body of John H. Tunstall ..." Coroner's Jury Report for John Tunstall. **February 19, 1878. (Naming as murderers, among others, James Dolan, Frank Baker, Jessie Evans, William Morton, and George Hindman**)

Wallace, Lew. "I have information that William Campbell, J.B. Matthews, and Jesse Evans were of the party engaged in the killing ..." Letter to Edward Hatch. **March 5, 1879**. Indiana Historical Society. Lew Wallace Collection. M0292. Box 4, Folder 4. (**Murder of Huston Chapman**)

Rynerson, William. "Indictments of the April, Lincoln County Grand Jury." **April 28, 1879**. Herman B. Weisner Papers, ca. 1957-1992. New Mexico State University Library at Las Cruces. Rio Grande Historical Society Collection. Accession No. Ms 0249. Box 4/39. Folder E-Z. Folder Name: "Jessie Evans Accessory to Murder." (**Billy's testimony indicts Dolan, Campbell, and Evans for his pardon**)

Purington, George Augustus. "The District Court adjourned on Thursday ..." **May 3, 1879**. Indiana Historical Society. Lew Wallace Collection. M0292. Box 4. Folder 10. (**Letter to Adjutant General on Grand Jury indictments of the Murphy-Dolans - including Evans for the H.I. Chapman murder**)

FOUNTAIN, ALBERT JENNINGS

BIBLIOGRAPHICAL SOURCE

Gibson, A. M. *The Life and Death of Colonel Albert Jennings Fountain.* Norman: University of Oklahoma Press. 1965.

CONTEMPORARY SOURCE

Fountain, Albert Jennings, Attorney and J.D. Bail. "Instructions Asked for by Defendants Counsel. April 9, 1881. Herman B. Weisner Papers, ca. 1957-1992. New Mexico State University Library at Las Cruces. Rio Grande Historical Society Collection. Accession No. Ms 0249. Box 1. Folder 14-D. Folder Name: "Billy the Kid Legal Documents."

FRITZ FAMILY (EMIL AND CHARLES FRITZ AND EMILIE FRITZ SCHOLAND)

Fritz, Charles. Affidavit of **September 18, 1876** claiming that Emil Fritz had a will. Probate Court Record. (private collection)

__________. Affidavit of **September 26, 1876** Authorizing Alexander McSween to Receive Payments for the Emil Fritz Estate. Probate Court Record. (private collection)

Scholand, Emilie and Charles Fritz. Affidavit of **September 26, 1876** appointing McSween to collect debts for the Emil Fritz Estate. Copied from the original District Court Record. (private collection)

Fritz, Charles. Affidavit of **December 7, 1877** to order Alexander McSween to pay the Emil Fritz insurance policy money. Probate Court Record. (private collection)

Scholand, Emilie. Affidavit of **December 21, 1877** Accusing Alexander McSween of Embezzlement. Copied from the original District Court Record. (private collection)

Bristol Warren. "Writ of Embezzlement." **December 21, 1877**. Herman B. Weisner Papers, ca. 1957-1992. New Mexico State University Library at Las Cruces. Rio Grande Historical Collections. Accession No. Ms 0249. Box 10. Folder M-13. Folder Name. "Will and Testament A. McSween." (**Emilie Fritz Scholand's sworn complaint against Alexander McSween**)

Fritz, Charles. Affidavit sworn before John Crouch, Clerk of Doña Ana District Court, for Writ of Attachment issued against property of Alexander A. McSween. Probate Court Record. **February 6, 1878**. (private collection)

__________ and Emilie Scholand. Attachment Bond sworn before John Crouch, Clerk of Doña Ana District Court, against Alexander A. McSween for indebtedness to them. **February 6, 1878**. (private collection).

No Author. Diagram showing parcels of land to each of the heirs of Emil Fritz. Herman B. Weisner Papers, ca. 1957-1992. New Mexico State University Library at Las Cruces. Rio Grande Historical Collections. Accession No. Ms 0249. Box P1. Folder 11. Folder Name. "Charles Fritz Estate."

GARRETT, PATRICK FLOYD

BIBLIOGRAPHICAL SOURCES

Metz, Leon C. *Pat Garrett. The Story of a Western Lawman.* Norman: University of Oklahoma Press. 1974.

Mullin, Robert N. "Killing of Joe Briscoe." Letter to Eve Ball. January 31, 1964. (Unpublished). Binder RNM, VI, H. Nita Stewart Haley Memorial Museum. Haley Library. Midland, Texas.

__________. "Pat Garrett. Two Forgotten Killings." *Password.* X(2) (Summer 1965). pp. 57 - 65.

__________. "Skelton Glen's Manuscript Entitled 'Pat Garrett As I Knew Him on the Buffalo Ranges.'" (1890, Unpublished). Binder RNM, III B, 20. Nita Stewart Haley Memorial Museum. Haley Library. Midland, Texas. (**The killing of Joe Briscoe is recounted**)

Thomas, David G. *Killing Pat Garrett, Wild West's Most Famous Lawman – Murder or Self-Defense?* Las Cruces, New Mexico: Doc45 Publishing. 2019. (**With circumstances of Garrett's killing by Wayne Brazel**)

Thomas, David. Personal communication. April 23, 2020. (**Stating that Garrett could not speak Spanish at the 1881 time of the writing of the Coroner's Jury Report**)

AUTOBIOGRAPHICAL SOURCES

Garrett, Pat F. *The Authentic Life of Billy the Kid The Noted Desperado of the Southwest, Whose Deeds of Daring and Blood Made His Name a Terror in New Mexico, Arizona, and Northern Mexico.* Santa Fe, New Mexico: New Mexico Printing and Publishing Co. 1882. (Edition used: Edited by Maurice Garland Fulton. New York: The Macmillan Company. 1927)

__________. Letter to Apolinaria Garrett. **December 13, 1901**. Courtesy of David G. Thomas. (**Demonstrating no match to penmanship of the Pat Garrett name in the Coroner's Jury Report of William H. Bonney**)

REWARD FOR KILLING BILLY THE KID

No Author. No title. *Santa Fe Daily New Mexican.* **July 21, 1881.** Volume X, Number 120, Page 4. Column 1. NewspaperArchive.com. (**Pat Garrett's meeting with Acting Governor Ritch about the Billy the Kid reward.**)

Ritch, William G. "In the matter of the application by Patrick F. Garrett for a reward claimed to have been offered May-1881 for the capture of Wm Bonney alias "the Kid." *Executive Record Book Number 2.* July 25, 1867-November 8, 1882. **July 21, 1881**. Pages 533-535. New Mexico Secretary of State Records. Collection 1971-001, Series 1; Records of the Secretary of the Territory. (Accessed from Albuquerque Public Library Microfilm, Territorial Archives of New Mexico, Roll 21.) (**Presentation of Garret's bill for the reward, showing that Acting-Governor Ritch agreed with the reward, but legal opinion from Attorney General William Breeden necessitated getting a legislative act to convert Wallace's private reward to Territorial**)

No Author. "Kid the Killer Killed, Wm. Bonney alias Antrim, alias Billy the Kid, Fatally Meets Pat Garrett, the Lincoln County Sheriff." Las Cruces *Rio Grande Republican.* **July 23, 1881**. Page 2. Volume 1, Number 10. NewspaperArchive.com. (**Copy of Pat Garrett's letter to Acting Governor William Ritch confirming that the original Coroner's Jury Report was sent to District Attorney of the First Judicial District, and copy of it was included in this letter to the Governor**)

Sheldon, Lionel. "In the Matter of the Claim of Sheriff Pat Garrett." Letter to the Legislature. **February 14, 1882**. Territorial Archives of New Mexico. Microfilm Roll 5, Frame 765. (**As Governor, approving Garrett's reward and stating he would have granted it outright had it not already been sent to the Legislature by Acting-Governor Ritch for an act**)

No Author. "An Act for the Relief of Pat. Garrett." *1882 Acts of the Legislative Assembly of the Territory of New Mexico, Twenty-Fifth Session. Convened at the Capitol, at the City of Santa Fe, on Monday, the 2d day of January, 1882, and adjourned on Thursday, the 2d day of March, 1882.* **February 18, 1882**. Chapter 101. Page 191. (**Granting Pat Garrett's reward for Billy the Kid, confirming it had been withheld on a technicality**)

Fulton, Maurice Garland. "I think I have solved the puzzle of the reward offers ..." October 28, 1951. Letter to Robert N. Mullin. Nita Stewart Haley Memorial Library and J. Evetts Haley History Center, Midland, Texas. Mullin Collection. Series RNM, VI, J, Legal Papers and Documents. "William Bonney, Reward for Death, Lincoln Notes." (**Confirming Attorney General's opinion to Acting Governor William Ritch about conversion of reward by legislative act**)

__________. "The rewards for the Kid give a clue to Catron's participation ..." **November 26, 1951.** Letter to Robert N. Mullin. Nita Stewart Haley Memorial Library and J. Evetts Haley History Center, Midland, Texas. Mullin Collection. Series RNM, VI, J, Legal Papers and Documents. "William Bonney, Rewards." (**Contemplating Catron's participation for the reward**)

__________. "Ritch was governor for the time-being ..." **March 15, 1953.** Letter to Robert N. Mullin. Nita Stewart Haley Memorial Library and J. Evetts Haley History Center, Midland, Texas. Mullin Collection. Series RNM, VI, J, Legal Papers and Documents. "William Bonney, Rewards." (**Confirming Attorney General's opinion to Acting Governor William Ritch about conversion of reward by legislative act**)

OTHER CONTEMPORARY SOURCES (CHRONOLOGICAL)

No Author. "Garrett Exonerates Maxwell." *Santa Fe Daily New Mexican.* **July 21, 1881**. Volume X, Number 120. NewspaperArchive.com. (**Confirming Pat Garrett's killing of Billy the Kid**)

Wild, Azariah F. "Daily Reports of U. S. Secret Service Agents, Azariah F. Wild." Microfilm T-915. Record Group 87. Roll 308 (**July 1, 1879 - June 30, 1881**). National Archives and Records Administration. Department of the Treasury. United States Secret Service. Washington, D. C. (**Using Garrett**)

GAUSS, GOTTFRIED

Gauss, Gottfried. Interview with *Lincoln County Leader*. **November 21, 1889.** (**About Billy Bonney's Lincoln jailbreak**)

HOYT, HENRY F.

AUTOBIOGRAPHICAL SOURCE

Hoyt, Henry. *A Frontier Doctor*. Boston and New York: Houghton Mifflin Company. 1929. (**Describes Billy Bonney's superior abilities, pp. 93-94.)**

CONTEMPORARY SOURCES (CHRONOLOGICAL)

Bonney, William H. Bill of Sale to Henry Hoyt. **October 24, 1878**. Collection of Panhandle-Plains Historical Museum. Canyon, Texas. (Item No. X1974-98/1)

Hoyt, Henry F. "This time it is me who is apologizing ..." Letter to Lew Wallace Jr. (Lew Wallace's grandson) **April 27, 1927**. Indiana Historical Society. Lew Wallace Collection. M0292. Box 14, Folder 11.

__________. "Copy of a bill of sale written by W[m] H. Bonney ..." Letter to Lew Wallace Jr. **April 27, 1927**. Indiana Historical Society. Lew Wallace Collection. M0292. Box 14, Folder 11.

LEONARD, IRA E.

BIOGRAPHICAL SOURCE

Nolan, Frederick. Biography and photograph of Ira Leonard. Unpublished. personal communication. July 29, 2005.

COURT OF INQUIRY OF N.A.M. DUDLEY BY (SEE: Nathan Augustus Monroe Dudley Court of Inquiry)

LETTERS TO AND FROM

LEW WALLACE TO AND FROM

Leonard, Ira E. "Dear Gov. You have undoubtedly learned ere this of the assassination ..." Letter to Lew Wallace. **February 24, 1879**. Indiana Historical Society. Lew Wallace Collection. M0292. Box 4. Folder 3. (**On Chapman murder.**)

Wallace, Lew. "It is important to take steps to protect the coming court ..." Letter to Ira Leonard. **April 6, 1879**. Indiana Historical Society. Lew Wallace Collection. M0292. Box 4. Folder 8.

Leonard, Ira. "The air is filled tonight with 'rumors of wars ... Letter to Lew Wallace. **April 20, 1879**. Indiana Historical Society. Lew Wallace Collection. M0292. Box 4. Folder 9. (**About District Attorney Rynerson: "He is bent on going for the Kid"**)

__________. "When you left here I promised to write you concerning events transpiring here ..." Letter to Lew Wallace. **May 20, 1878 [sic - 79]**. Indiana Historical Society. Lew Wallace Collection. M0292. Box 4. Folder 10. (**Has quote on the Murphy-Dolan party as: "part and parcel of the Santa Fe ring that has been so long an incubus on the government of this territory.")**

__________. "I write to you with pencil because I am laboring for breath ..." Letter to Lew Wallace. **May 23, 1879**. Indiana Historical Society. Lew Wallace Collection. M0292. Box 4. Folder 11. (**With quote "we are pouring the 'hot shot' into Dudley." (With enclosed letter of May 20, 1879**)

__________. "Dudley commenced on the defense Thursday afternoon ..." Letter to Wallace. **June 6, 1879**, Indiana Historical Society. Lew Wallace Collection. M0292. Box 4. Folder 11. (**About disgust at corrupt Court.**")

__________. "Yours of the 7th inst reached me ..." Letter to Lew Wallace. **June 13, 1879**. Indiana Historical Society. Lew Wallace Collection. M0292. Box 4. Folder 11. (**about Court of Inquiry corruption**)

MAXWELL, DELUVINA

Maxwell, Deluvina. "I came here after Lucien Maxwell was already here...." Letter to J. Evetts Haley. June 24, 1927. Nita Stewart Haley Memorial Library and J. Evetts Haley History Center, Midland, Texas. J. Evetts Haley Collection, JEH, J-I – Maxwell, Deluvina. (**Debunking "Billy the Kid Case" hoax and *Cold Case Billy the Kid* claims that Peter Maxwell's bedroom had no door to the outside, and that Pat Garrett did not kill Billy the Kid**)

MAXWELL FAMILY

Cleaveland, Agnes Morley. *No Life for a Lady*. Boston: Houghton Mifflin. 1941.

__________. *Satan's Paradise: From Lucien Maxwell to Fred Lambert*. Boston: Houghton Mifflin Company. 1952.

Cleaveland, Norman. *The Morleys - Young Upstarts on the Southwest Frontier*. Albuquerque, New Mexico: Calvin Horn Publisher, Inc. 1971.

Dunham, Harold H. "New Mexican Land Grants with Special Reference to the Title Papers of the Maxwell Grant." *New Mexico Historical Review*. (January 1955) Vol. 30, No. 1. pp. 1 - 23.

Freiberger, Harriet. *Lucien Maxwell: Villain or Visionary*. Santa Fe, New Mexico: Sunstone Press. 1999.

Keleher, William A. *The Maxwell Land Grant. A New Mexico Item*. Albuquerque, New Mexico: University of New Mexico Press. 1964.

Lamar, Howard Roberts. *The Far Southwest 1846 - 1912. A Territorial History*. New Haven and London: Yale University Press. 1966.

Miller, Kenny. Descendant of Lucien Bonaparte Maxwell. Personal communication. 2011 to 2012.

Montoya, María E. *Translating Property. The Maxwell Land Grant and the Conflict Over Land in the American West, 1840-1900*. Berkeley and Los Angeles, California: University of California Press. 2002.

Murphy, Lawrence R. *Lucien Bonaparte Maxwell. Napoleon of the Southwest*. Norman: University of Oklahoma Press. 1983.

Pearson, Jim Berry. *The Maxwell Land Grant*. Norman: University of Oklahoma Press. 1961.

Poe, Sophie. *Buckboard Days*. Albuquerque, New Mexico: University of New Mexico Press. 1964.

Taylor, Morris F. *O. P. McMains and the Maxwell Land Grant Conflict*. Tucson, Arizona: The University of Arizona Press. 1979. (**Origins of Santa Fe Ring**)

No Author. "Mrs. Paula M. Jaramillo, 65 Died Here Tuesday." *The Fort Sumner Leader*. Official Newspaper County of De Baca. December 20, 1929. No. 1158, Page 1, Column 1. (**Billy Bonney's sweetheart, Paulita Maxwell**)

COMMANDING OFFICER'S QUARTERS BEFORE MAXWELL FAMILY CONVERSION

Diagram. "Commanding Officer's Quarters Fort Sumner, New Mexico Territory." National Archives, Microfilm RG 98, Consolidated Files Quartermaster General; with copy in Fort Sumner, New Mexico, State Monument. (**Faked in *Cold Case Billy the Kid* as being the Maxwell house itself**)

MAXWELL FAMILY HOUSE IN FORT SUMNER

Drawing. "As per Burns account." Maxwell family house, and diagram of Peter Maxwell's bedroom with external door. Nita Stewart Haley Memorial Library and J. Evetts Haley History Center, Midland, Texas. Mullin Collection. Series RNM, IV, Y, Notebook: Places and Events, A-O. (**Debunking *Cold Case Billy the Kid* hoax that Peter Maxwell's bedroom had no door to the outside**)

Photograph. "Pete Maxwell's House Fort Sumner." Annotated on back by Robert N. Mullin. **Undated.** Nita Stewart Haley Memorial Library and J. Evetts Haley History Center, Midland, Texas. Mullin Collection. Series RNM, IV, A, 161.0. (**Maxwell family house showing external door in Peter Maxwell's bedroom debunking *Cold Case Billy the Kid* that the Maxwell house was one story and that Maxwell's bedroom had no door to the outside**)

Mullin, Robert N. "Pete Maxwell's House Fort Sumner, Prior to Erection of New Home 2 ½ Mi. S.E.[after sale of town]; Originally 1 Story Flat Roof, Officers Quarters. 2nd Floor Added By Maxwell." Annotation on back of photograph of Maxwell house. **Undated.** . Nita Stewart Haley Memorial Library and J. Evetts Haley History Center, Midland, Texas. Mullin Collection. Series RNM, IV, A, 161.0. (**Making clear the distinction between the Officer's Quarters and the later Maxwell house**)

PETER MAXWELL'S HOUSE OUTSIDE OF FORT SUMNER

Photograph. "Peter Maxwell's home near Fort Sumner, post Lincoln County War, presented to Robert N. Mullin by Maurice Garland Fulton, who obtained it from Mrs. Susan McSween Barber. Nita Stewart Haley Memorial Library and J. Evetts Haley History Center, Midland, Texas. Mullin Collection. Series RNM, IV, A-161. (**For debunking *Cold Case Billy the Kid* hoax that Peter Maxwell lived as a cook in a San Andres Mountain cow camp because he moved from Fort Sumner**)

No Author. "Las Vegas." Death Notice of Peter Maxwell. **June 28, 1898**. *The Albuquerque Citizen*. Page 2, Column 3. NewspaperArchive.com. (**Peter Maxwell death notice about Fort Sumner area residence and death**)

MAXWELL FAMILY FURNITURE

Blythe, Dee. "Billy the Kid Landmarks Fast Vanishing: Historic Spots Hard to Find; Markers Needed." *Clovis, New Mexico Evening News-Journal*. **May 31, 1937** Volume 9. Number 2. Section E. Monday,. (**Photo and article about Maxwell family furniture**)

Weddle, Jerry. "The Kid at Old Fort Sumner." *The Outlaw Gazette: Billy the Kid Outlaw Gang New Mexico*. **December, 1992**. (**Louisa Beaubien Barrett, Luz Maxwell's niece, error-filled history as recorded by her daughter Marian Barrett, including the claim that Pat Garrett's second shot went through a washstand; later used in the "Billy the Kid Case" hoax**)

__________. Statement that he interviewed Stella Abreu Maxwell in Albuquerque in her old age, and she stated she got the carpenter's bench from a man in Fort Sumner for her 1925 Billy the Kid Museum. Author's interview. February 5, 2018. (**The bench had not been kept by the family**)

McSWEEN, ALEXANDER

Bristol Warren. "Writ of Embezzlement." **December 21, 1877**. Writ of Embezzlement. New Mexico State University Library at Las Cruces. Rio Grande Historical Collections. Lincoln County Papers. New Mexico State University Library at Las Cruces. Rio Grande Historical Collections. Accession No. Ms 0249. Box No. 10. Folder M-13. "Will and Testament A. McSween." (**Emilie Fritz Scholand's sworn complaint against Alexander McSween**)

Fritz, Charles. Affidavit sworn before John Crouch, Clerk of Doña Ana District Court, for Writ of Attachment issued against property of Alexander A. McSween. Probate Court Record. **February 6, 1878**. (private collection).

Bristol, Warren. Action of Assumpsit to command Sheriff of Lincoln County to attach goods of Alexander A. McSween. **February 7, 1878**. District Court Record. (private collection).

__________. Preprinted form in his name for "Writ of Attachment" (Printed and sold at the office of the Mesilla News) filled out to command the Sheriff of Lincoln County to attach goods of Alexander McSween for a suit of damages for ten thousand dollars. **February 7, 1878**. (private collection).

McSween, Alexander. "It looks as though the agent were the property of J.J. Dolan & J.H. Riley, known here as Dolan & Co." Letter to Secretary of Interior Carl Schurz. **February 11, 1878**. From Frederick Nolan. *The Life and Death of John Henry Tunstall.* Albuquerque, New Mexico: The University of New Mexico Press. 1965. Page 266.

__________. "Will and Testament A. McSween." **February 25, 1878**. Herman B. Weisner Papers, ca. 1957-1992. New Mexico State University Library at Las Cruces. Rio Grande Historical Collections. Accession No. Ms 0249. Box 10. Folder M15. Folder Name. "Will and Testament A. McSween."

__________. and B.H. Ellis. Secretaries. "The undersigned have the Honor of transmitting you, as requested, a copy of the proceedings of a meeting held by the citizens of Lincoln County ..." Letter to President Rutherford B. Hayes; with attached proceedings of the April 1878 Lincoln Grand Jury. **April 26, 1878**. Microfilm File Case Number 44-4-8-3. Record Group 48. Microfilm No. M750. Roll 1. National Archives and Records Administration. U.S. Department of Justice. Washington, D.C.

__________. Deposition to Frank Warner Angel. **June 6, 1878**. Pages 5-183 of Frank Warner Angel report *In the Matter of the Examination of the Causes and Circumstances of the Death of John H. Tunstall a British Subject.* Report filed **October 4, 1878**. Angel Report. Microfilm File Case Number 44-4-8-3. Record Group 48. Microfilm No. M750. Roll 1. National Archives and Records Administration. U.S. Department of Justice. Washington, D.C. (**Reports secret**

Angel, Frank Warner. *In the Matter of the Lincoln County Troubles. To the Honorable Charles Devens, Attorney General.* **October 4, 1878**. Angel Report. Microfilm File Case Number 44-4-8-3. Record Group 48. Microfilm No. M750. Roll 1. National Archives and Records Administration. U.S. Department of Justice. Washington, D.C.

McSWEEN, SUSAN

BIOGRAPHICAL SOURCE FOR

Chamberlain, Kathleen P. *In the Shadow of Billy the Kid: Susan McSween and the Lincoln County War.* Albuquerque: University of New Mexico Press. 2013.

CONTEMPORARY SOURCES ABOUT (CHRONOLOGICAL)

Dudley, Nathan Augustus Monroe. "I am in receipt of a copy of letter written by one H.I. Chapman, calling himself the Attorney ..." **November 9, 1878**. Letter to Lew Wallace. From *Proceedings of a Court of Inquiry in the Case of Lt. Col. N.A.M. Dudley (May 2,1879 – July 5, 1879).* File No. QQ1284. (Boxes 3304, 3305, 3305A); Court Martial Files 1809-1894. Records of the Office of the Judge Advocate General - Army. Record Group 153. Old Military and Civil Branch. National Archives and Records Administration. Washington, D.C. (**Answer to charges, with attached defamatory affidavits against Susan McSween**)

McSween, Susan. Testimony in Court of Inquiry for Lieutenant Colonel N.A.M. Dudley. **May 23-24, 26, 1879**. *Proceedings of a Court of Inquiry in the Case of Lt. Col. N.A.M. Dudley (May 2,1879 – July 5, 1879).* File No. QQ1284. (Boxes 3304, 3305,

3305A); Court Martial Files 1809-1894. Records of the Office of the Judge Advocate General – Army. Record Group 153. Old Military and Civil Branch. National Archives and Records Administration. Washington, D.C.

No Author. Verdict on Civil Cause 298 for arson of Susan McSween's house. *Mesilla News*. **December 6, 1879**. Unpublished. personal communication from Frederick Nolan. July 29, 2005. (**Dudley exonerated**)

MEADOWS, JOHN P.

Meadows, John P. "Billy the Kid to John P. Meadows on the Peñasco, May 1-2, 1881." *Roswell Daily Record*. February 16, 1931. Page 6.

Meadows, John P. Ed. John P. Wilson. *Pat Garrett and Billy the Kid as I Knew Them: Reminiscences of John P. Meadows*. Albuquerque: University of New Mexico Press. 2004.

PATRÓN, JUAN

Wallace, Lew. "Be good enough to send word to all your men to turn out soon as possible ..." Letter to Juan Patrón. **March 19, 1879**. Indiana Historical Society. Lew Wallace Collection. M0292. Box 4. Folder 6. (**Reports escape of Jessie Evans and Billy Campbell from Fort Stanton**)

Patrón, Juan. First letter to Lew Wallace on **March 29, 1879**. Indiana Historical Society. Lew Wallace Collection. M0292. Box 4, Folder 7.

__________. Second letter to Lew Wallace on **March 29, 1879**. Indiana Historical Society. Lew Wallace Collection. M0292. Box 4, Folder 7.

PEPPIN, GEORGE

No Author. "Old Citizen Gone." *Capitan News*. **September 23, 1904.** Volume 5. Number 29. Page 4. Center for Southwest Research. Microfilm AN2.L52a.

POE, JOHN WILLIAM

Poe, John W. "The Killing of Billy the Kid." (a personal letter written at Roswell, New Mexico to Mr. Charles Goodnight, Goodnight P.C., Texas) July 10, 1917.

__________. *The Death of Billy the Kid*. (Introduction by Maurice Garland Fulton). Boston and New York: Houghton Mifflin Company. 1933.

RILEY, JOHN HENRY

CONTEMPORARY SOURCES ABOUT

Tunstall, John Henry. "A Tax-payer's Complaint, Office of John H. Tunstall, Lincoln, Lincoln Co., N.M., January 18, 1878, 'The Present Sheriff of Lincoln County Has Paid Nothing During His Present Term of Office.' Governor's Message for 1878." Mesilla *Independent*. **January 26, 1878**. Volume 1, Number 32. NewspaperArchive.com. (**Exposé of William Brady and John Riley for embezzling tax money to buy cattle; and T.B. Catron then paid that bill**)

Dolan, James J. "Answer to A Taxpayer's Complaint." Mesilla *Independent*. **January 29, 1878**. (**Response to J.H. Tunstall's exposé**)

RUDULPH, CHARLES

Rudulph, Charles. "Allow me to congratulate you on your recent great victory. **November 5, 1895.** Letter to T.B. Catron. University of New Mexico Library. Center for Southwest Studies. Thomas B. Catron Papers, MSS 29, Series 102, Box 27, Folder 2. (**Son of Milnor Rudulph, Billy Bonney's Ringite President of his Coroner's Jury who apparently influenced its Report praising Pat Garrett's killing of Billy Bonney**)

RUDULPH, MILNOR

Rudulph, Milnor. " I beg your indulgence for ..." Letter to William G. Ritch. **May 18, 1879.** Albuquerque and Bernalillo County Public Library. Genealogical Center. MS. Territorial Archives of New Mexico Microfilm. Roll 99. Image 10. (**Rudulph's signature matches his signature on the Coroner's Jury Report.**)

Keleher, William A. *Violence in Lincoln County 1869-1881.* Pages 350-351. Albuquerque, New Mexico: University of New Mexico Press. 1957.

(SEE: Legislature Revolt, Coroner's Jury Report)

RYNERSON, WILLIAM LOGAN

BIOGRAPHICAL SOURCES

Miller, Darlis A. "William Logan Rynerson in New Mexico. 1862-1893." *New Mexico Historical Review* 48 (April 1973) pp. 101-131.

No Author. "A Brief History of the Rynerson House." Las Cruces: Del Valle Design & Imaging. No copyright. https://delvalleprintinglc.com/rynerson-house/.

CONTEMPORARY SOURCES BY AND ABOUT (CHRONOLOGICAL)

Rynerson, William L "Indictments of the April, Lincoln County Grand Jury." **April 28, 1879**. Herman B. Weisner Papers, ca. 1957-1992. New Mexico State University Library at Las Cruces. Rio Grande Historical Society Collection. Accession No. Ms 0249. Box 4/39. Folder E-Z. Folder Name: "Jessie Evans Accessory to Murder." **(Indictments of Dolan, Campbell, and Evans)**

__________. "Friends Riley & Dolan, Lincoln N.M. I have just received letters from you mailed 10th inst." Letter to James Dolan and John Riley. **February 14, 1878.** Copy as Exhibit B in June 6, 1878 deposition of Alexander McSween. Frank Warner Angel report. *In the Matter of the Examination of the Causes and Circumstances of the Death of John H. Tunstall a British Subject.* Report filed October 4, 1878. Interior Department Papers 1850-1907; Appointments Division and Subsequent Actions. Microfilm File Case Number 44-4-8-3. Microfilm No. M750. Roll 1. National Archives and Records Administration. U.S. Department of Justice. Washington, D.C. (James J. Dolan Deposition. June 20, 1878. Pages 235-247.) **(Planned killing of J.H. Tunstall)**

Rynerson, William. Venue Change. **April 21, 1879**. Herman B. Weisner Papers, ca. 1957-1992. New Mexico State University Library at Las Cruces. Rio Grande Historical Collection. Accession No. Ms 0249. Box 1. Folder 14-D. Folder Name: "Billy the Kid Legal Documents." **(Change of Billy Bonney's trial venue from Lincoln County to Doña Ana County to insure a hanging trial by prevent Lincoln County citizens knowledgeable about the War being jurors)**

SALAZAR, YGINIO

Wallace, Lew. "I beg to submit to you a list of persons ... to arrest ..." Letter to Henry Carroll. **March 11, 1879**. Indiana Historical Society. Lew Wallace Collection. M0292. Box 4. Folder 5. **(Lists Ygenio Salazar and "the Kid)**

Salazar, Joe. (Grandson of Yginio Salazar). Personal Interviews 1999-2001. **(My interviews about Ygenio)**

TUNSTALL, JOHN HENRY

BIOGRAPHICAL SOURCES

Nolan, Frederick W. *The Life and Death of John Henry Tunstall.* Albuquerque, New Mexico: The University of New Mexico Press. 1965.

CONTEMPORARY SOURCES (CHRONOLOGICAL)

Tunstall, John Henry. "A Tax-payer's Complaint, Office of John H. Tunstall, Lincoln, Lincoln Co., N.M., January 18, 1878, 'The Present Sheriff of Lincoln County Has Paid Nothing During His Present Term of Office.' Governor's Message for 1878." Mesilla *Independent*. **January 26, 1878**. Volume 1, Number 32. NewspaperArchive.com. (**Exposé of William Brady and John Riley for embezzling tax money to buy cattle; and T.B. Catron then paid that bill**)

Dolan, James J. "Answer to A Taxpayer's Complaint." Mesilla *Independent*. **January 29, 1878**. (**Response to J.H. Tunstall's exposé of embezzlement of tax money to buy cattle**)

Rynerson, William. "Friends Riley & Dolan, Lincoln N.M. I have just received letters from you mailed 10th inst." Letter to James Dolan and John Riley. **February 14, 1878**. Copy as Exhibit B in June 6, 1878 deposition of Alexander McSween. Frank Warner Angel report. *In the Matter of the Examination of the Causes and Circumstances of the Death of John H. Tunstall a British Subject.* Report filed October 4, 1878. Interior Department Papers 1850-1907; Appointments Division and Subsequent Actions. Microfilm File Case Number 44-4-8-3. Record Group 48. Microfilm No. M750. Roll 1. National Archives and Records Administration. U. S. Department of Justice. Washington, D.C. (James J. Dolan Deposition. June 20, 1878. pp. 235-247.) (**Planned killing of J.H. Tunstall**)

Wilson, John, George B. Barker, Robert M. Gilbert, John Newcomb, Samuel Smith, Benjamin Ellis. "We the undersigned Justice of the Peace and Coroners Jury who sat upon the inquest held this 19th day of February 1878 on the body of John H. Tunstall ..." Coroner's Jury Report for John Tunstall. **February 19, 1878**. (**Naming Tunstall's murderers**)

Springer, Frank. "I hope you have received a full account of the Troubles in Lincoln County from your nephew ..." Letter to Senator Rush Clark. **April 9, 1878**. Herman B. Weisner Papers, ca. 1957-1992. New Mexico State University Library at Las Cruces. Rio Grande Historical Collections. Accession No. Ms 0249. Box 4/39. Folder D-6. Folder Name "Frank Springer Letter to Rush Clark." (**Links Santa Fe Ring to murder of J.H. Tunstall**)

(SEE: Frank Warner Angel)

WALLACE, LEW

AUTOBIOGRAPHICAL AND BIOGRAPHICAL SOURCES

Governor of Territorial New Mexico. 1878-81." *New Mexico Historical Review. 59(1)* (January, 1984).

Morsberger, Robert E. and Katherine M. Morsberger. *Lew Wallace: Militant Romantic.* New York: McGraw-Hill Book Company. 1980.

Wallace, Lew. *An Autobiography. Vol. I.* New York and London: Harper and Brothers Publishers. 1997.

__________. *An Autobiography. Vol. II.* New York and London: Harper and Brothers Publishers. 1997.

COLLECTED PAPERS OF

Wallace, Lew. Collected Papers. Microfilm Project Sponsored by the National Historical Publications Commission. Microfilm Roll No. 99. Santa Fe, New Mexico: State of New Mexico Records Center and Archives. 1974.

__________. Lew and Susan Wallace Collection. Indiana Historical Society. M0292.

__________. Collected Papers. Lilly Library. Bloomington, Indiana.

SECRET ANGEL NOTEBOOK ON SANTA FE RING FOR

Angel, Frank Warner. "To Gov. Lew Wallace, Santa Fe, N. M., 1878." Notebook. **1878**. Indiana Historical Society. Lew Wallace Collection. M0292. Microfilm No. F372. **(Original missing, copy on microfilm; secret notebook prepared for Lew Wallace listing names for Lincoln County and the Santa Fe Ring)**

Theisen, Lee Scott. "Frank Warner Angel's Notes on New Mexico Territory, 1878." *Arizona and the West: A Quarterly Journal of History*. Winter 1976. Volume 18. Number 4. Pages 333-370. **(About the Angel notebook)**

AMNESTY PROCLAMATION OF

Wallace, Lew. "Proclamation by the Governor." **November 13, 1878**. Indiana Historical Society. Lew Wallace Collection. M0292. Box 3. Folder 17. **(Amnesty Proclamation for Lincoln County War fighters, but excluding those already indicted, like Billy Bonney)**

DUDLEY COURT OF INQUIRY TESTIMONY BY

Wallace, Lew. Testimony in Court of Inquiry for Lieutenant Colonel N.A.M. Dudley. **May 12-15, 1879**. *Proceedings of a Court of Inquiry in the Case of Lt. Col. N.A.M. Dudley (May 2,1879 – July 5, 1879)*. File No. QQ1284. (Boxes 3304, 3305, 3305A); Court Martial Files 1809-1894. Records of the Office of the Judge Advocate General – Army. Record Group 153. Old Military and Civil Branch. National Archives and Records Administration. Washington, D.C.

INTERVIEW NOTES ON BILLY BONNEY BY (SEE: William H. Bonney)

REWARD NOTICES AND POSTERS FOR WILLIAM BONNEY BY (SEE: William H. Bonney)

LETTERS BY AND TO

TO AND FROM WILLIAM BONNEY

(SEE: History of William H. Bonney)

TO SHERIFF PATRICK F. GARRETT

Wallace, Lew. "To the Sheriff of Lincoln County, New Mexico, Greeting ..." **April 30, 1881**. Indiana Historical Society. Lew Wallace Collection. M0292. Box 9. Folder 11. **(Death Warrant for William Bonney after his Mesilla trial and before his Lincoln jailbreak)**

TO AND FROM IRA E. LEONARD (SEE: Ira Leonard)

TO AND FROM JUSTICE OF THE PEACE JOHN B. WILSON

Wallace, Lew. "I hasten to acknowledge receipt of your favor of the 11th Jan. ult. ..." **January 18, 1879**. Indiana Historical Society. Lew Wallace Collection. M0292. Box 4. Folder 1. **(Lincoln County as carrying on a revolution)**

Wallace, Lew. "I enclose a note for Bonney." Letter to John "Squire" Wilson. **March 20, 1879.** Indiana Historical Society. Lew Wallace Collection. M0292. Box 4. Folder 6. **(The pardon negotiation for Billy Bonney)**

Wilson, John B. Signed JBW. **April 8, 1879**. Indiana Historical Society, Lew Wallace Collection. M0292. Box 4, Folder 8. **(Notes on rustling)**

__________. Letter to Lew Wallace. **May 18, 1879**. Indiana Historical Society. Lew Wallace Collection. M0292. Box 4, Folder 5.

ARTICLES ABOUT WILLIAM BONNEY BY (SEE: William H. Bonney)

WALZ, EDGAR A.

No Author. *The American Book of Biography: Men of 1912.* Chicago: American Publishers Association. 1913. Page 614.

No Author. "Edgar A. Walz Dead: Expert on credit, Founder of The Travelers Hotel Credit Corporation – Managed New Mexico Ranch in Youth." *The New York Times.* **April 5, 1935.** Volume LXXXIV, Number 28,195. Page 24.

WILD, AZARIAH

Nolan, Frederick. "Biography of Azariah Wild." Unpublished and personal communications, June 11, 2005 and October 9, 2005.

Wild, Azariah F. "Daily Reports of U. S. Secret Service Agents, Azariah F. Wild." Microfilm T-915. Record Group 87. Rolls 308 (July 1, 1879 - June 30, 1881) National Archives and Records Department. Department of the Treasury. United States Secret Service. Washington, D. C.

WILSON, JOHN B. "SQUIRE"

CORONER'S JURY REPORT FOR JOHN H. TUNSTALL BY

Wilson, John, George B. Barker, Robert M. Gilbert, John Newcomb, Samuel Smith, Benjamin Ellis. "We the undersigned Justice of the Peace and Coroners Jury who sat upon the inquest held this 19th day of February 1878 on the body of John H. Tunstall ..." Coroner's Jury Report for John Tunstall. **February 19, 1878.** (**Naming as murderers, among others, James Dolan, Frank Baker, Jessie Evans, William Morton, and George Hindman**)

LETTERS FROM

Wilson, John B. Letter to Lew Wallace. Unsigned but noted as from "Sqr. Wilson by Wallace. Undated, but likely **March, 1879**. Indiana Historical Society. Lew Wallace Collection. M0292. Box 4, Folder 7. (**On Lady Liberty stationery**)

__________. Affidavit of John Wilson. **March ?, 1879**. Indiana Historical Society. Lew Wallace Collection. M0292. Box 4, Folder 7.

__________. Signed JBW. **April 8, 1879**. Indiana Historical Society, Lew Wallace Collection. M0292. Box 4, Folder 8. (**Notes on rustling**)

__________. Letter to Lew Wallace. **May 18, 1879**. Indiana Historical Society. Lew Wallace Collection. M0292. Box 4, Folder 5.

LETTERS TO

Bonney, W H. "Friend Wilson ..." **March 18, 1879**. Indiana Historical Society. Lew Wallace Collection. M0292. (**For mediating his pardon negotiation with Lew Wallace**)

Wallace, Lew. "I enclose a note for Bonney." Letter to John "Squire" Wilson. **March 20, 1879.** Indiana Historical Society. Lew Wallace Collection. M0292. Box 4. Folder 6. (**The pardon negotiation for Billy Bonney**)

OLIVER "BRUSHY BILL" ROBERTS BILLY THE KID IMPOSTER HOAX

SOURCES TO DEBUNK CLAIMS IN "BRUSHY BILL" HOAX, IN ADDITION TO CITED SOURCES FOR WILLIAM BONNEY'S REAL HISTORY (CHRONOLOGICAL)

THE HOAX BOOK

Sonnichsen, C.L. and William V. Morrison. *Alias Billy the Kid.* Albuquerque, New Mexico: University of New Mexico Press. **1955**. (**Presenting "Brushy Bill" Roberts as Billy the Kid**)

THE WILLIAM V. MORRISON PAPERS

IN BLAZER FAMILY PAPERS 1864-1965 AT NEW MEXICO STATE UNIVERSITY, LAS CRUCES

Morrison, William V. "Regarding Billy the Kid." Correspondence. **October 28, 1949-August 4, 1955**. New Mexico State University Library, Archives and Special Collections Department. Blazer Family Papers, 1864-1965. MS 0110, 15:12 and MS 0110, 15:13, William Vincent Morrison Correspondence, Billy the Kid, regarding and General, August 18, 1952-April 24, 1956, March 31, 1962. (**Using the historical papers of the Joseph Blazer family**)

WILLIAM VINCENT MORRISON CORRESPONDENCE, BILLY THE KID, MS 0110, 15:12

Morrison, William V. "I certainly enjoyed talking with you ..." Letter to Paul A. Blazer. **August 18, 1952**. (**Getting information on Billy being ambidextrous and using single action pistols**)

__________. "First, I want to thank you for taking me through the cemetery ..." Letter to Paul A. Blazer. **April 27, 1953**. (**Getting information on the graves of "Buckshot" Roberts and Dick Brewer.**)

__________. "I wish to thank you for your time ..." Letter to Paul A. Blazer. **June 26, 1953**. (**Trying to convince people that Garrett did not kill the Kid**)

__________. "Your winter issue, 1953, Volume 1, No. 3, was handed to me ..." Letter to Fred Gipson. **April 17, 1954**. (**Informing editor of *True West* magazine that Garrett did not kill the Kid**)

__________. "Your letter of the first arrived here ..." Letter to Paul A. Blazer. **April 6, 1955.** (**Announcing publication of *Alias Billy the Kid***)

WILLIAM VINCENT MORRISON CORRESPONDENCE, BILLY THE KID, MS 0110, 15:13

Olyanova, Nadya. "I have your letter of May 13th in which you throw out the challenge ..." Letter to William V. Morrison. **May 18, 1953.** (**Contact with a handwriting analyst about a Billy the Kid letter**)

Morrison, William V. "I have your letter of the 13th ..." Letter to Carl W. Breihan. **March 17, 1954. (About J. Frank Dalton being Jesse James, that historians, like William Keleher, accepted that "Brushy" was Billy the Kid, that he sought movie and television rights for his work, and that he had sought exhumations**)

__________. "Your comment in the March issue with reference to Corle's 'Billy the Kid' ..." Letter to Raymond Carlson. **March 17, 1954. (Boasting to *Arizona Highway* editor, Carlson, that he knew that Ira Leonard did not**

grepresent Billy in Mesilla – even though Leonard did – revealing where "Brushy" got that error from coaching Morrison)

Autry, Gene. "Your letter of March 23rd regarding information on Billy the Kid ..." Letter to William V. Morrison. **March 31, 1954. (Trying to sell his "Brushy" tale to Gene Autry)**

Morrison, William V. "I have your letter of March 24, and wish to thank you ..." Letter to Carl W. Breihan. **April 3, 1954. (Faking reasons for why "Brushy" lost the Governor Mabry pardon)**

__________. "Thanks for your most interesting letter ..." Letter to Philip J. Rasch. **April 19, 1954. (Trying to convince Rasch that "Brushy" matched Billy physically, and the Mabry hearing was affected by the Santa Fe Ring)**

__________. "Thanks for your letter of the first ..." Letter to Philip J. Rasch. **May 7, 1954. (Comparing C.L. Sonnichsen with Billy the Kid historians, trying to convince Rasch that "Brushy" was Billy because the Santa Fe Ring made up the Coroner's Jury Report)**

Truman, Harry S. "I can't tell you how very much I appreciate the Number 1 copy ..." Letter to William V. Morrison. **May 19, 1955. (Past President Truman as duped by *Alias Billy the Kid*)**

Morrison, William V. "I am very grateful for your kind letter ..."Letter to William Waters. **June 29, 1955. (About wanting to exhume Billy the Kid')**

__________. "I have a letter from Doc. Sonnichsen ..." Letter to Robert N. Mullin. **(Claiming "Brushy" could not read)**

WILLIAM VINCENT MORRISON ROTARY CLUB LECTURE, CORRESPONDENCE BILLY THE KID, MS 0110, 15:12

Morrison, William V. "Billy the Kid." Talk to the El Paso, Texas, Rotary Club. **December 3, 1953**. Text of talk sent to Paul A. Blazer. **(Presenting the full-blown "Brushy Bill" hoax, with introduction by C.L. Sonnichsen)**

ADDITIONAL DEBUNKING SOURCES

No Author. Roberts family members. Federal Census for Arkansas, Sebastian County, Bates Township. **June 1, 1880.** Lines 27-33. **(Cited in Don Cline's *Brushy Bill Roberts: I Wasn't Billy the Kid* to show "Brushy" was 10 months old at the census – 20 years too young to be Billy Bonney)**

Wilcox, Lucius "Lute" M. (city editor, owner, J.H. Koogler). "The Kid. Interview with Billy Bonney The Best Known Man in New Mexico." *Las Vegas Gazette.* **December 27, 1880. (Mentions that Billy Bonney has squirrel-like incisors; that contradicts "Brushy's" tusk-like extracted canine teeth)**

Rudulph, Milnor. Coroner's Jury Report for William Bonney alias "Kid." **July 15, 1881.** Indiana Historical Society. Lew Wallace Collection. M0292. Box 9. Folder 11. Accession Number 1951.0104 from Maurice G. Fulton. **(Photostatic copy of original Spanish Coroner's Jury Report, certified on January 18, 1951, donated by Maurice Garland Fulton - matches photo in William Kelleher's *Violence in Lincoln County* copy; identifying body of Billy Bonney)**

Ritch, William G. "In the matter of the application by Patrick F. Garrett for a reward claimed to have been offered May-1881 for the capture of Wm Bonney alias "the Kid." *Executive Record Book Number 2.* July 25, 1867-November 8, 1882. **July 21, 1881**. Pages 533-535. New Mexico Secretary of State Records. Collection 1971-001, Series 1; Records of the Secretary of the Territory. (Accessed from Albuquerque Public Library Microfilm, Territorial Archives of New Mexico, Roll 21.) **(Presentation of Garret's bill for the reward with Ritch seeking legal advice on converting it from private to Territorial; with Charles Greene being the printer of the reward notice, not Garrett's attorney as C.L. Sonnichsen wrongly claimed)**

No Author. "Kid the Killer Killed, Wm. Bonney alias Antrim, alias Billy the Kid, Fatally Meets Pat Garrett, the Lincoln County Sheriff." Las Cruces *Rio Grande Republican.* July 23, 1881. Page 2. Volume 1, Number 10. NewspaperArchive.com. (Copy of Pat Garrett's letter to Acting Governor William Ritch confirming that the original Coroner's Jury Report was sent to District Attorney of the First Judicial District, and copy of it was included in this letter to the Governor)

No Author. " 'The Kid' Killed! He Meets His Death at the Hands of Sheriff Pat Garrett, of Lincoln County. The Particulars of the Affair as Poured into the Ears of Eager Reporters. *The Las Vegas Daily Optic.* **July 18, 1881**. Volume 2, Number 217. NewspaperArchives.com. (**Confirming Pat Garrett's killing of Billy the Kid**)

No Author. *Executive Record Book Number 2.* July 25, 1867-November 8, 1882. **July 21, 1881.** Pages 533-535. New Mexico State Records Center and Archives, Santa Fe. New Mexico Secretary of the State Records Series 1. Records of the Secretary of the Territory. (**About granting Garrett's reward; source used by Sonnichsen to fabricate irregularity**)

No Author. "Garrett Exonerates Maxwell." *Santa Fe Daily New Mexican.* **July 21, 1881**. Volume X, Number 120. NewspaperArchives.com. (**Confirming Pat Garrett's killing of Billy the Kid**)

No Author. No title. *Santa Fe Daily New Mexican.* **July 21, 1881.** Volume X, Number 120, Page 4. Column 1. (**Pat Garrett's presentation to Acting Governor Ritch of his reward request, with Ritch willing to pay but needed to go through procedures.**)

No Author. "Words of Commendation and Encouragement." *Las Vegas Daily Gazette.* **July 22, 1881.** Volume 3. Number 15. Newspapers.com. (**Confirming Pat Garrett's killing of Billy the Kid**)

Ashenfelter, Singleton M. "Exit 'The Kid', The Fugitive Murderer Hunted Down and Killed by Sheriff Garrett." *The New Southwest, And Grant County Herald.* **July 23, 1881.** Number 30. University of New Mexico. Zimmerman Library. Microfilm AN2 G71. (**Ashenfelter's apocryphal description of Billy the Kid's body, but confirmation of the killing**)

No Author. "The Life of Billy the Kid. His Name Was Billy McCarthy, and He was Born in New York." *The New York Sun.* (From *The St. Louis Globe-Democrat*) **August 10, 1881.** Volume XLIII, Number 314. Newspapers.com. (**Confirming Pat Garrett's killing of Billy the Kid**)

Glen, Skelton. "Pat Garrett As I Knew Him on the Buffalo Ranges." (**1890**, Unpublished). Binder RNM, III B, 20. Nita Stewart Haley Memorial Museum. Haley Library. Midland, Texas. (**The killing of Joe Briscoe is recounted, but was unknown to "Brushy" who garbles it from a John Meadows article**)

Taeger, Mary Nell. "Severo Gallegos Tells His Story and of His Family's Friend, 'Billy the Kid.' " *Ruidoso News.* **July 30, 1948.** Front page, Page 6. Volume II, Number 11. NewspaperArchive.com. (**A Billy the Kid history confabulator, used by Morrison as a prompt for "Brushy's" jailbreak tale. Gallegos was then used give a fake affidavit that "Brushy" was Billy**)

__________. No Author. "Severo Gallegos Tells His Story and of His Family's Friend, 'Billy the Kid.' " (continued) *Ruidoso News.* **August 6, 1948.** Page 3. Volume II, Number 12. NewspaperArchive.com. (**A Billy the Kid history confabulator, with this part 2 article used by Morrison as a prompt for "Brushy's" jailbreak tale; then used for a fake affidavit that "Brushy" was Billy**)

Roberts, Oliver Pleasant. ("Brushy" writing as O.L. Roberts) "Dear Uncle Kit Carson, We got here O.K. ..." Letter to Oran Ardious Woodman. **April 1, 1949.** From Roy L. Haws, *Brushy Bill: Proof His Claim to Be Billy the Kid Was a Hoax.* 2015. (Pages 113-117) (**"Brushy Bill's" possibly modeling himself as Billy the Kid based on this Kit Carson imposter**)

No Author. "Cornering Jesse James." *Hico News Review.* **February 3, 1950.** Front Page. Volume LXIV, Number 38. Texas Tech University Library. Southwest

Collections/Special Collections Library. Microfilm H626 Hico (Texas) News Review 1929-1974 Reel 8. (**"Brushy" claiming to identify J. Frank Dalton as Jesse James**)

Holford, Carolyn. " 'Brushy Bill' Is Back From Gotham." *Hico News Review*. **February 20, 1950.** Front Page. Volume LXIV, Number 36. Texas Tech University Library. Southwest Collections/Special Collections Library. Microfilm H626 Hico (Texas) News Review 1929-1974 Reel 8. (**Reporting on Morrison-backed radio show on January 3, 1950 with J. Frank Dalton as Jesse James and "Brushy" backing him and having "wild west" tales**)

No Author. "Fort Sumner Jury Thought the Kid Had Been Killed." *Alamogordo News*. **November 30, 1950.** Volume 53, Number 48. .NewspaperArchive.com. (**Finding the Coroner's Jury Report; ignored in *Alias Billy the Kid***)

No Author. Will A. Keleher, History Student, Sure Kid Was Shot." *Albuquerque Journal*. **December 1, 1950**. Volume illegible, Number 61. Newspaperarchive.com. (**Debunking "Brushy's" claim to be Billy the Kid**)

No Author. "Notorious Character is Buried." *Hico News Review*. **January 5, 1951.** Front Page. Volume LXV, Number 34. Texas Tech University Library. Southwest Collections/Special Collections Library. Microfilm H626 Hico (Texas) News Review 1929-1974 Reel 8. (**Obituary of "Brushy Bill" Roberts**)

Morrison, William V. Letter to Carl Breihan. **March 17, 1954. (Cited in Don Cline's *Brushy Bill Roberts: I Wasn't Billy the Kid* to show Morrison's attempt to sell "Brushy's" story for movies or TV**)

__________. Letter to Philip Rasch. **April 12, 1954.** Rio Grande Historical Collections./Hobson Huntslinger University Archives. New Mexico State University, Las Cruces. (**Lying that he was being backed for "Brushy" by many people, including William Keleher**)

Keleher, William A. *Violence in Lincoln County 1869-1881*. Albuquerque, New Mexico: University of New Mexico Press. **1957**. (**Photocopy of Spanish Coroner's Jury Report, July 15, 1881. Pages 306-308; Kelleher's English translation, Pages 343-344.**)

Walker, Dale L. *C.L. Sonnichsen: Grassroots Historian*. El Paso: Texas Western Press. **1972**. (**About co-author of Roberts in the Billy the Kid hoax**)

Pittmon, Geneva Roberts. "Dear Sir: the reason you are not finding my family ..." **December 16, 1987.** Letter to Joe Bowlin. In collection of Old Fort Sumner Museum, Fort Sumner, New Mexico. (**Roberts's niece using family Bible to prove Roberts was not Billy the Kid**)

__________. "I don't know of any job he held ..." Letter to Don Cline. **April 27, 1988. (Cited in Don Cline's *Brushy Bill Roberts: I Wasn't Billy the Kid* to show "Brushy" was a mentally disabled farm hand in his real life.**)

Sonnichsen, C.L. "I believe, without evidence, that Bill Morrison had a law degree ..." Letter to Don Cline. **June 30, 1988.** (**About believing that Morrison was a lawyer**)

Metz, Leon. "I met William V. Morrison in the early 1970's ..." Letter to Don Cline. **July 2, 1988.** (**Cited in Don Cline's *Brushy Bill Roberts: I Wasn't Billy the Kid* to show that Morrison denied being a lawyer**)

Tunstill, William A. *Billy the Kid and Me Were the Same: A Documentary on the Life of Billy the Kid*. Roswell, New Mexico: Western History Research Center. 1988. (**"Brushy"-backer faking a genealogy using duped Eulaine Emerson Haws's approval, and debunked by "Brushy's" relative Roy L. Haws, Eulaine Emerson Haws's son, in his 2015 *Brushy Bill: Proof That His Claim to Be Billy the Kid Was a Hoax***)

Cline, Don. *Brushy Bill Roberts: I Wasn't Billy the Kid*. **Undated [1988 or 1989?].** Unpublished manuscript. New Mexico Commission of Public Records. State Records Center and Archives. Santa Fe. MS Donald Cline Collection. Subseries 5.2, Folder 138. Box 10421. Serial No. 9560 Santa Fe NMSRCA. (**Debunking "Brushy's" Billy the Kid claims**)

__________. Interview with "Brushy's" brother, Tom's daughter, Mary June Roberts. January 28, 1988. **(Denying "Brushy's" genealogical claims)**

Anaya, Paco. *I Buried Billy.* College Station, Texas: Creative Publishing Company. 1991. **(Eye-witness claim of burying Billy Bonney)**

Jameson, W.C. and Frederic Bean. *The Return of the Outlaw Billy the Kid.* Plano, Texas: Republic of Texas Press. **1998. (Backing Roberts as Billy the Kid)**

Walker, Dale L. *Legends and Lies: Great Mysteries of the American West.* New York: A Tom Doherty Associates Book. **1997. (Backing Roberts as Billy the Kid)**

Nolan, Frederick. *The West of Billy the Kid.* Norman: University of Oklahoma Press. **1998. (See Page 7 for quote on the Eugene Cunningham hoaxed photo of Catherine Antrim, which "Brushy" confabulated as his aunt, Kathleen Bonney)**

Johnson, Jim. *Billy the Kid: His Real Name Was ...*" Denver, Colorado: Outskirts Press, Inc. **2006. (Debunking Roberts as Billy the Kid)**

Haws, Roy L. *Brushy Bill: Proof That His Claim to Be Billy the Kid Was a Hoax.* Santa Fe: Sunstone Press. **2015. (Roberts relative debunking him as Billy the Kid)**

Jameson, W.C. *Cold Case Billy the Kid: Investigating History's Mysteries.* Guilford, Connecticut: Twodot. **2018. (Recycling the "Billy the Kid Case" hoax to argue for Roberts as Billy the Kid)**

No Author. "Memorials." *El Paso Post-Herald.* **September 9, 1977.** Volume XCVII, Number 216. Page 24, Column 5. Newspaperarchive.com **(Obituary for William V. Morrison, showing he was not an attorney)**

Caperton, Thomas J. *Historic Structure Report. Lincoln State Monument. Lincoln New Mexico.* Santa Fe, New Mexico: Office of Cultural Affairs, Department of Finance and Administration, Historic Preservation Division. **1983. (With floor plan of the Lincoln court-house proving "Brushy's" faked armory location)**

Nolan, Frederick. *The West of Billy the Kid.* Norman: University of Oklahoma Press. **1998. (Seven Rovers boy's tintype with Marion Turner identified by Eve Ball, but claimed to be himself as 17 as Billy the Kid by "Brushy Bill;" Page 157)**

Salazar, Joe. (Grandson of Yginio Salazar). Interviews **1999-2001. (My interviews about Ygenio Salazar, cited by the hoaxers as believing Billy had survived the Garrett shooting)**

Cox, Jim. *The Great Radio Soap Operas.* Jefferson, North Carolina: McFarland & Company, Inc. Publishers. **1999. (About "We the People" radio show, in which "Brushy" appeared to vouch for J. Frank Dalton as Jesse James)**

No Author. "We the People." https://www.otrcat.com/p/we-the-people. 2019. **(**About "We the People" radio show, in which "Brushy" appeared to vouch for J. Frank Dalton as Jesse James**)**

Cooper, Gale. *The Cold Case Billy the Kid: Megahoax: The Plot to Steal Billy the Kid's Identity and Defame Sheriff Pat Garrett as a Murderer.* . Albuquerque, New Mexico: Gelcour Books. **2019.**

__________. *The Billy the Kid Imposter Hoax of Brushy Bill Roberts.* Albuquerque, New Mexico: Gelcour Books. **2019.**

(See William H. Bonney's Coroner's Jury Report)

ARTICLES ON REJECTED PARDON (CHRONOLOGICAL)

Humphreys, Sexton. "Pardon Me, I'm Alive," Says Billy the Kid." *Indianapolis News.* **November 25, 1950**. Page 9. Indiana Historical Society. Lew Wallace Collection. M0292. Box 14. Folder 12.

Morgan, Art. "Billy the Kid Only a Phony It Turns Out." *Santa Fe New Mexican.* **November 30, 1950**. Issue 6. Front page, Page 3. NewspaperArchive.com.

No Author. "Mabry Terms "Billy" Outright Imposter." *Clovis News Journal.* **November 30, 1950.** Volume 22, Number 208. Newspaperarchive.com. **(Thursday, when interview was held)**

Smylie, Vernon. "Billy the Kid Flunks in Talk With Governor." *El Paso Herald Post.* **November 30, 1950.** Volume LXX, Number 285. Front Page, Page 13. Newspaperarchive.com. (**Thursday, when interview was held**)

United Press. "Pardon Mt 6-Shooters. Billy the Kid? Governor to Decide." *The Indianapolis News.* **November 30, 1950.** Indiana Historical Society. Lew Wallace Collection. M0292. Box 14. Folder 12.

No Author. " 'Billy the Kid' Bubble Bursts as Gov. Mabry Rejects Oldster's Claim." *Albuquerque Journal.* **December 1, 1950.** Volume [illegible], Number 61. Front Page, Page 4. Newspapers.com.

No Author. "Will A. Keleher, History Student, Sure Kid Was Shot." *Albuquerque Journal.* **December 1, 1950.** Volume [illegible], Number 61. Front Page. Newspaperarchive.com. (**Supports Governor Mabry calling "Brushy Bill" a Billy the Kid imposter**)

No Author. "Billy the Kid is Called Imposter by New Mexico Chief." *Lubbock Morning Avalanche.* **December 30, 1950.** Page 12. Newspaperarchive.com.

WILLIAM V. MORRISON'S PROMPTING RESEARCH FOR PARROTING BY "BRUSHY" FOR INTERVIEW TAPING AND FOR THE PARDON INTERVIEW (CHRONOLOGICAL)

BILLY THE KID'S WRITINGS FROM LEW WALLACE COLLECTION AT THE INDIANA HISTORICAL SOCIETY

Morrison, William V. "Urgent need of photostatic copies correspondence ..." **October 6, 1950.** Telegram to Indiana Historical Society, The William Henry Smith Memorial Library. Indiana Historical Society. Collection Number RG6. Box 17, Folder 11.

Dunn, Caroline. "We have microfilm of Bonney-Wallace correspondence ..." Letter to William V. Morrison. **October 7, 1950.** Letter to William V. Morrison. Indiana Historical Society, The William Henry Smith Memorial Library. Collection Number RG6. Box 17, Folder 11.

Morrison, William V. "Upon my return from Lincoln, N.M., today I have your telegram ..." **October 9, 1950. Letter** to The William Henry Smith Memorial Library. Collection Number RG6. Box 17, Folder 11.

Dunn, Caroline. "Your letter of the 9th received ..." **October 13, 1950.** Letter to William V. Morrison. Indiana Historical Society. Collection Number RG6. Box 17, Folder 11.

Morrison, William V. "Your letter of the 13th received ..." **October 17, 1950.** Letter to Caroline Dunn of The William Henry Smith Memorial Library. Indiana Historical Society. Collection Number RG6. Box 17, Folder 11.

No Author. Bill for $9.78 for "17 sheets photostats, Lew Wallace Collection. **October 25, 1950.** Telegram to Indiana Historical Society Memorial Library. Indiana Historical Society. Collection Number RG6. Box 17, Folder 11.

Dunn, Caroline. "Enclosed are the photostats of the documents in the Lew Wallace collection, with certification ..." **October 25, 1950.** Letter to William V. Morrison. Indiana Historical Society. Collection Number RG6. Box 17, Folder 11.

Morrison, William V. "This will serve to acknowledge receipt ..." **October 28, 1950.** Letter to Caroline Dunn of The William Henry Smith Memorial Library. Indiana Historical Society. Collection Number RG6. Box 17, Folder 11.

No Author. Bill for $2.61 for "6 Pstat neg." **October 30, 1950.** Telegram to Indiana Historical Society Memorial Library. Indiana Historical Society. Collection Number RG6. Box 17, Folder 11.

Wallace, Lew Jr. "A photostatic copy is being prepared of the letter in my possession from William H. Bonney ..." **October 30, 1950 .** Letter to William V. Morrison. Indiana Historical Society. Lew Wallace Collection. M0292. Box 8. Folder 3. (**Received a copy of actual Billy Bonney pardon plea letter of March 13, 1879**)

__________. "Your letter of November 2 confuses me ..." **November 10, 1950.** Letter to William V. Morrison. Indiana Historical Society. Lew Wallace Collection. M0292. Box 8. Folder 3. (**Expressing suspicion about a Billy the Kid imposter**)

Unnamed Archivist. "Copy of transcript sent by Wm V. Morrison ..." **November 10, 1950.** Indiana Historical Society. Lew Wallace Collection. M0292. Box 8. Folder 3. (**Seeking a copy of original of Billy Bonney's first pardon request letter**)

Dunn, Caroline. "In my letter to you of November 5 I said I was returning the transcripts ..." **November 14, 1950.** Letter to William V. Morrison. Indiana Historical Society. Collection Number RG6. Box 17, Folder 11.

(SEE: William V. Morrison papers)

ALIAS BILLY THE KID'S PROMPT FOOTNOTES' SOURCES OF WILLIAM V. MORRISON AND C.L. SONNICHSEN (CHRONOLOGICAL)

BOOKS CITED

Walter Noble Burns's 1926 *The Saga of Billy the Kid.* (**fictionalized account using Pat Garrett's 1882 edition of *The Authentic Life of Billy the Kid***)

Garrett, Pat F. *The Authentic Life of Billy the Kid The Noted Desperado of the Southwest, Whose Deeds of Daring and Blood Made His Name a Terror in New Mexico, Arizona, and Northern Mexico.* Santa Fe, New Mexico: New Mexico Printing and Publishing Co. 1882. (Edition used: Edited by Maurice Garland Fulton. New York: The Macmillan Company. 1927)

Coe, George with Doyce B. Nunis, Jr. Ed. *Frontier Fighter. The Autobiography of George Coe Who Fought and Rode With Billy the Kid.* Chicago: R. R. Donnelley and Sons Company. 1934. (**multiple references**)

Siringo, Charles A. *History of Billy the Kid.* Printed by Charles A. Siringo. 1920. Page 32. (**largely fictionalized, using Garrett's *The Authentic Life of Billy the Kid*, by a Garrett posseman not involved in capturing Billy, for claim that Billy worked for Murphy and Dolan. Also, it contained the Jim East letter used by "Brushy" to confabulate a story about giving an "Indian girl" the Billy the Kid tintype**)

Poe, John W. *The Death of Billy the Kid.* Boston and New York: Houghton Mifflin Company. **1933**. Page 21. [sic- Page 31 in *Alias Billy the Kid*]. (**cited by Sonnichsen for fake argument that Fort Sumner residents would have hidden Billy's survival of the Garrett shooting**)

Miguel Otero. *The Real Billy the Kid.* Rufus Rockwell Wilson, Inc. 1936. Page 37. (**for Pat Garrett's statement that Billy tried to shoot Billy Matthews at Sheriff Brady's ambush, then repeated verbatim by "Brushy"**)

Hudson, Bell. Ed. Mary Hudson Brothers. *Billy the Kid.* Farmington, New Mexico: The Hustler Press. **1949**. Page 47. (**for Billy staying in sheep camps near Fort Sumner and a scene of encountering Barney Mason in one**)

LETTERS CITED

Jim East. "At the time of the capture of Billy, the Maxwell family were living at Fort Sumner ..." Letter to W.H. Burgess. **May 20, 1926.** (**source for the Jim East name, but its key mention of Paulita Maxwell as Billy's love was missed; identified as copy from Burgess supplied by Sonnichsen, who also had a copy of Walter Noble Burns's June 3, 1926 reply to Burgess that Paulita was Billy's "sweetheart"**) (Page 38)

Roberts, Oliver P. "Brushy Bill." "She said she had three affidavits that people knew me in 1887 ..." **May 24, 1949**. Letter to William V. Morrison. Footnote in *Alias Billy the Kid.* (Page 59)

JOURNAL/MAGAZINE ARTICLES CITED

Adams, Ramon F. "Billy the Kid's Lost Years: Cyclone Denton Tells of Bonney's Life as a Cowboy in Arizona." *The Texas Monthly.* 4.2. (**August-December, 1929**). Pages 205-211. (Scan courtesy of Cornette Library at West Texas A&M. (**source for claiming falsely that Billy worked at the Gila Ranch in Arizona**)

Smith, Wilbur. Interview. "The Amigo of 'Billy the Kid': The Man Who Fought Side by Side With Lincoln County's Outlaw Character Tells About the Days of 'Judge Colt's Rule.' " *New Mexico Magazine* article interview of **April, 1933**. Pages 26-49. University of New Mexico, Albuquerque. Zimmerman Library. Center for Southwest Research Anderson. Call Number F 791 N45. (**gives names of people hoping that Billy was alive, including Ygenio) Salazar**)

Traylor, Leslie. "Facts Regarding the Escape of Billy the Kid." *Frontier Times*. **July, 1936.** Pages 506-513 (on Page 509). FrontierTimesMagazine.com. (**About Billy the Kid's jailbreak being aided by Sam Corbett placing a gun in the latrine, based on a hearsay interview by Traylor in Lincoln in 1933 and 1935; also in article are his Jesus Silva interview on identifying Billy's body and his confirming the erroneous identification of Billy's gravesite in the Fort Sumner cemetery in 1935**)

Ball, Eve. "Billy Strikes the Pecos." *New Mexico Folklore Record,* IV. **1949-50.** Pages 7-10. University of New Mexico, Albuquerque. Zimmerman Library. Call Number GR 1 N 47, Volume 4. (**source for Billy Bonney's crossing the Guadalupe Mountains on foot to the Seven Rivers Jones family**)

Fulton, Maurice Garland. "Billy the Kid in Life and Books." *The New Mexico Folklore Record.* Volume IV, **1949-1950**. Pages 1-6. University of New Mexico, Albuquerque. Zimmerman Library. Call Number GR 1 N 47, Volume 4. (**source for the Greathouse shooting of Jim Carlyle, for the Mesilla trial being unjust,, for alleged photo of Billy's mother as "Mrs. Antrim"**)

NEWSPAPER ARTICLES CITED

Hunter's Frontier Times Magazine. "A Story of 'Billy the Kid.' " July, 1943, Pages 217-218. (quoting *Laredo Times* for **August 10, 1881).** frontiertimesmagazine.com/. (**source for claiming falsely Billy's demanding $5 per day payment from John Chisum**)

No Author. *Las Vegas Gazette* December 24, 1880, and the *Santa Fe New Mexican* of May 7, 1881. (**straw man argument for no reward made by Sonnichsen by citing editions with wrong dates for Lew Wallace's Billy the Kid reward notices**)

Wallace, Lew. *New York World Magazine.* "General Lew Wallace Writes a Romance of 'Billy the Kid' Most Famous Bandit of the Plains: Thrilling Story of the Midnight Meeting Between Gen Wallace, Then Governor of New Mexico, and the Notorious Outlaw, in a Lonesome Hut in Santa Fe." **June 8, 1902**. Lew Wallace Collection. Indiana Historical Society. M0292. . Box 14. Folder 11.(**"Brushy's" source for pardon bargain misinformation and for "pardon in your pocket" quote**) Cited by Sonnichsen, but identified as from the Indiana Historical Society, meaning Morrison's research.

No Author. "Billy the Kid, Alive Is Ridiculed by Oldtimers." El Paso *Herald.* **June 23, 1926**. Page 7. Newspapers.com. (**contradicting hearsay reports that Garrett had not killed the Kid, but used by hoax to quote those hearsay reports**)

John Meadows "John Meadows Tells of His Association With Pat Garrett." [sic - "My Association With Pat Garrett, Peace Officer of New Mexico."] *Alamogordo News,* **March 8, 1936**. Pages 1, 4. University of New Mexico, Albuquerque. Zimmerman Library. Zimmerman New Mexico Microfilm AN2, A46. (**source of error for Garrett killing his buffalo hunter partner, when he actually killed Joe Briscoe**)

No Author. "Frontiersmen Track Reports 'Kid' Is Alive." El Paso *Herald-Post*. **June 22, 1938.** NewspaperArchive.com. and El Paso *Times*. **November 10, 1937. (article about Pawnee Bill's planned to search for Billy the Kid as being alive as dishonestly misstated by Morrison and Sonnichsen to mean Pawnee Bill was searching for "Brushy")**

COURT, MILITARY, AND LEGISLATIVE RECORDS CITED

U.S. District Court Minute Book B, Third Judicial District, Indictment 411 for killing "Buckshot" Roberts **[1878,]**, Page 76, quashed.

Lincoln County Grand Jury Minute Book B for **April, 1879**, for Indictments 243, 244; Pages 92-93, 298-299 **(misread and confused with Billy's 1880 Mesilla hanging trial)** (Page 34)

Adjutant General's files from the State Library in Austin, Texas, about Jessie Evans's **July 7, 1880** capture near Fort Stockton, Texas. **(about Jessie Evan's 1880 capture in Texas)**

Doña Ana County Court Minutes, "Instructions to the Jury," Cause No. 532. Pages 100-103; **(indictment for Brady ?)**

Doña Ana County Court Minute Book D for Cause No. 532 (verdict and sentence), killing of William Brady. **[1881]** Page 406. **(listing attorney as Simon B. Newcomb)**

No Author. *Executive Record Book Number 2*. July 25, 1867-November 8, 1882. **July 21, 1881.** Pages 533-535. New Mexico State Records Center and Archives, Santa Fe. New Mexico Secretary of the State Records. Records of the Secretary of the Territory. **(About granting Garrett's reward; used by Sonnichsen to fabricate irregularity)**

INTERVIEWS CITED

Mullin, Robert N. cited as having copies of reminiscences of Louis Abraham about Silver City and Billy. No date. **(noted by Sonnichsen as showing the murder at 12 as fictitious, but rest of information was ignored)** (Page 77)

Anaya, A.P. "Paco." Interview given to a George Fitzpatrick. Undated. **(Used to claim that he claimed two coroner's jury reports, but not knowing that he also claimed in a manuscript, published in 1991, that he buried Billy Bonney)**

Sonnichsen, C.L. Interview With Jack Fountain. April 15, 1944. **(A.J. Fountain's fake hearsay account of Garrett telling him he killed Billy to get a $10,000 reward, and that the side of beef was beside Maxwell's bedroom)**

Morrison, William V. Interviews with Oliver "Brushy Bill" Roberts. 1949-1950. (Unpublished)

Morrison, William V. Miscellaneous hearsay interviews of non-historical people for claims of Garrett not killing Billy, or identifying "Brushy" as Billy.

APPARENT SOURCES USED BUT NOT CITED (CHRONOLOGICAL)

No Author. *Proceedings of a Court of Inquiry in the Case of Lt. Col. N.A.M. Dudley* ***(May 2,1879 – July 5, 1879)***. File No. QQ1284. (Boxes 3304, 3305, 3305A); Court Martial Files 1809-1894. Records of the Office of the Judge Advocate General - Army. Record Group 153. Old Military and Civil Branch. National Archives and Records Administration. Washington, D. C. **(A page of Billy Bonney's testimony about escaping the burning McSween house, with a quote)**

Newman, Simon. No title. *Newman's Semi-Weekly*. **April 20, 1881**. Pages 1, 3. InfowebNewsBank.com, America's Historical Newspapers.

Lewis, E.I. "Gen. Wallace's Feud with Billy the Kid, When the General Was Governor of New Mexico and Billy Bonne Was the Most Dangerous Western Outlaw. He Wa s a Waif and Was Reared in Indiana. *The Indianapolis Press*. Saturday,

June 23, 1900. Page 7. Lew Wallace Collection. Indiana Historical Society. M0292. Box 14. Folder 11. (**available to Morrison**)

Roberts, Dan W. *Rangers and Sovereignty*. San Antonio: Wood Publishing & Engraving Co. **1914**. (**Referenced by Don Cline in *Brushy Bill Roberts: I Wasn't Billy the Kid* to show source of his "grandfather" Dan Roberts fabrication**)

Twitchell, Ralph Emerson. *The Leading Facts of New Mexico History*. Vol. I-II. Santa Fe: Sunstone Press. 2007. (Reprinted from a **1912 edition**) (**misstates the Lincoln County War as a cattle feud**)

Hoyt, Henry F. "This time it is me who is apologizing for the long delay in answering ..." (Letter to Lew Wallace Jr.) **April 27, 1927**. Indiana Historical Society. Lew Wallace Collection. M0292. Box 14, Folder 11.

__________. "Copy of a bill of sale written by W[m] H. Bonney ..." Letter to Lew Wallace Jr. **April 27, 1927**. Indiana Historical Society. Lew Wallace Collection. M0292. Box 14, Folder 11. (**Provided a copy of the Bill of Sale of October 24, 1878**)

King, Frank M. *Wranglin' the Past: Reminiscences of Frank M. King*. "Chapter xix, The Kid's Exit." Pasadena, California: Trail's End Publishing Company. **1935 and 1946**. (**Describes recent location of Pat Garrett's report to the Governor about the killing of Billy the Kid, with confirmation of Coroner's Jury Report, Page 171**)

Taeger, Mary Nell. "Severo Gallegos Tells His Story and of His Family's Friend, 'Billy the Kid.' " *Ruidoso News*. **July 30, 1948.** Front page, Page 6. Volume II, Number 11. NewspaperArchive.com. (**A Billy the Kid history confabulator, used by Morrison as a prompt for "Brushy's" jailbreak tale. Gallegos was then used give a fake affidavit that "Brushy" was Billy**)

__________. No Author. "Severo Gallegos Tells His Story and of His Family's Friend, 'Billy the Kid.' " (continued) *Ruidoso News*. **August 6, 1948.** Page 3. Volume II, Number 12. NewspaperArchive.com. (**A Billy the Kid history confabulator, with this part 2 article used by Morrison as a prompt for "Brushy's" jailbreak tale. Gallegos was then used give a fake affidavit that "Brushy" was Billy**)

ADDITIONAL SOURCES CITED IN THE RETURN OF THE OUTLAW BILLY THE KID (CHRONOLOGICAL)

Ashenfelter, Singleton M. "Exit 'The Kid', The Fugitive Murderer Hunted Down and Killed by Sheriff Garrett." *The New Southwest, And Grant County Herald*. **July 23, 1881.** Number 30. University of New Mexico. Zimmerman Library. Microfilm AN2 G71. (**Ashenfelter's apocryphal description of Billy the Kid's body as dark and bearded**)

Morrison, William V. Letter to Robert N. Mullin. **July 12, 1955**. (**Claiming "Brushy" could not read, so could not have studied sources**)

Branch, Louis Leon. From manuscript of Charles Frederick Rudulph. *"Los Billitos": The Story of "Billy the Kid" and His Gang: As Told by Charles Frederick Rudulph – a Member of Garrett's Historical Posse*. New York: Carleton Press. **1980**. (**Hearsay claim that the body of Billy the Kid was left in the Maxwell bedroom overnight for the coroner's Jury**)

Haws, Eulaine Emerson. Genealogical papers provided to Martha Vada Roberts Heath. Tyler, Texas. No date. Unpublished. (**Fake "Brushy Bill" genealogy debunked by Eulaine Roberts's son, Roy L. Haws**)

Tunstill, William A. *Billy the Kid and Me Were the Same: A Documentary on the Life of Billy the Kid*. Roswell, New Mexico: Western History Research Center. 1988. (**"Brushy"-backer faking a genealogy using duped Robert's family member and debunked by Roy L. Haws in his 2015 *Brushy Bill: Proof That His Claim to Be Billy the Kid Was a Hoax***)

Acton, Scott. Unpublished results of computerized pattern recognition system comparing facial images of William Henry Roberts and Billy the Kid. **1990. (Fake photo-matching of "Brushy Bill" and Billy Bonney)**

Kyle, Thomas G. "Computers, Billy the Kid, and Brushy Bill: The Verdict Is In." *True West.* **July, 1990.** Pages 16-19. **(No "Brushy" photo-match)**

Sonnichsen, Charles Leland. Interview. Oklahoma City, Oklahoma. **1991. (With Sonnichsen's unrepentant claim that there was not a "shred of evidence" that "Brushy" was not Billy Bonney)**

JOHN MILLER BILLY THE KID IMPOSTER HOAX

No Author. Obituary of John Miller. *Prescott Courier.* **November 8, 1937. (Gives date of birth as December, 1850)**

Huff, J. Wesley. "Did Pat Garrett Kill Billy the Kid? Herman Tecklenburg Says No; Billy Lived on Ranch at Ramah 35 Years Ago and Visited Him. *The Gallup Independent.* **August 9, 1944.** Volume 55, Number 185. Newspapers.com. **(Tecklenburg's Billy the Kid confabulations)**

Airy, Helen L. *Whatever Happened to Billy the Kid?* Santa Fe, New Mexico: Sunstone Press. **1993. (John Miller as Billy the Kid)**

Johnson, Jim. *Billy the Kid: His Real Name Was ...* Denver, Colorado: Outskirts Press, Inc. **2006. (Debunking evidence for John Miller as Billy the Kid, and providing his dates of arrival and death at the Arizona Pioneers' home cemetery, and his obituary)**

Sams, Dale. Arizona Pioneers' Home and Cemetery Administrator. Personal communication. January 12, 2010. **(Confirmed that records list John Miller's DOB as December – 1850; and birthplace as Fort Sill, Texas)**

"BILLY THE KID CASE" HOAX (LINCOLN COUNTY SHERIFF'S DEPARTMENT CASE NO. 2003-274)

RELEVANT BOOKS

Althouse, Bill. *Frozen Lightening: Bill Richardson's Strike on the Political Landscape of New Mexico.* Buckman, New Mexico: Thinking Out Loud Press. **2006.**

Bugliosi, Vincent. *Outrage: The Five Reasons Why O.J. Simpson Got Away With Murder.* New York and London: W.W. Norton & Company. **1996. (Exposé of Dr. Henry Lee faking forensics in legal cases, Pages 47-49)**

Cline, Donald. *Alias Billy the Kid: The Man Behind the Legend.* Santa Fe: New Mexico: Sunstone Press. **1986. (Historian cited by the hoaxers as backing them; apparently unaware of his 1988 manuscript: *Brushy Bill Roberts: I Wasn't Billy the Kid*)**

Cooper, Gale. *Billy the Kid's Pretenders: Brushy Bill and John Miller.* Albuquerque, New Mexico: Gelcour Books. **2012.**

__________. *Billy the Kid's Writings, Words, and Wit.* Albuquerque, New Mexico: Gelcour Books. **2012.**

__________. *MegaHoax: The Strange Plot to Exhume Billy the Kid and Become President.* Albuquerque, New Mexico: Gelcour Books. **2012.**

__________. *Cracking the Billy the Kid Case Hoax: The Strange Plot to Exhume Billy the Kid, Convict Sheriff Pat Garrett of Murder, and Become President of the United States.* Albuquerque, New Mexico: Gelcour Books. **2014**.

__________. *The Cold Case Billy the Kid: Megahoax: The Plot to Steal Billy the Kid's Identity and Defame Sheriff Pat Garrett as a Murderer.* . Albuquerque, New Mexico: Gelcour Books. **2019**.

__________. *The Billy the Kid Imposter Hoax of Brushy Bill Roberts.* Albuquerque, New Mexico: Gelcour Books. **2019**.

__________. *Billy the Kid's Pretender John Miller.* Albuquerque, New Mexico: Gelcour Books. **2019**.

__________. *The Famous Coroner's Jury Report of Billy the Kid: An Inquest That Made History.* Albuquerque, New Mexico: Gelcour Books. **2019**.

Garcia, Elbert A. *Billy the Kid's Kid 1875-1964, The Hispanic Connection.* Santa Rosa, New Mexico: Los Products Press. **1999**. (**Early participant in "Billy the Kid Case" as unsubstantiated kin of Billy the Kid**)

Garrett, Pat F. *The Authentic Life of Billy the Kid The Noted Desperado of the Southwest, Whose Deeds of Daring and Blood Made His Name a Terror in New Mexico, Arizona, and Northern Mexico.* Santa Fe, New Mexico: New Mexico Printing and Publishing Co. **1882**. (Edition used: Edited by Maurice Garland Fulton. New York: The Macmillan Company. 1927)

Metz, Leon C. *Pat Garrett. The Story of a Western Lawman.* Norman: University of Oklahoma Press. **1974**.

Nolan, Frederick. *The West of Billy the Kid.* Norman: University of Oklahoma Press. **1998**. (**Page 7 for quote on the Eugene Cunningham hoaxed photo of Catherine Antrim**)

Palast, Greg. *Armed Madhouse.* New York: Penguin Group USA. **2007**. (**Bill Richardson exposé**)

Poe, John W. *The Death of Billy the Kid.* (Introduction by Maurice Garland Fulton). Boston and New York: Houghton Mifflin Company. **1933**. (**Pages 22 and 25-26 have Milnor Rudulph quote with the part omitted by hoaxers' from their Probable Cause Statement**)

Richardson, Bill, with Michael Ruby. *Between Worlds: The Making of an American Life.* New York: G.P. Putnam's Sons. **2005**. (**Bill Richardson autobiography**)

Siringo, Charles. *The History of Billy the Kid.* Santa Fe: New Mexico. Privately Printed. **1920**. (**Reproduces the Jim East letter on pages 96-107**)

(SEE: William H. Bonney; Oliver "Brushy Bill" Roberts Billy the Kid Imposter Hoax; John Miller Billy the Kid Imposter Hoax; *Cold Case Billy the Kid* Megahoax

CORONER'S JURY REPORT FOR WILLIAM H. BONNEY (SEE WILLIAM H. BONNEY)

PAT GARRETT'S PROSECUTION IMMUNITY FOR "BILLY THE KID CASE" BY STATUTE OF LIMITATIONS

No Author. "An Act to Provide the Limitation of Criminal Actions." *Acts of the Legislative Assembly of the Territory of New Mexico, Twenty-Second Session, Convened at the Capitol. at the City of Santa Fe on Monday the 6th Day of December, 1875, and Adjourned on Friday the 14th day of January, 1876.* Santa Fe, New Mexico: Manderfield & Tucker, Public Printers. **1876**. Hathitrust Digital Library. (**Providing for a 10 year statute of limitations on murder; so Garrett could not be prosecuted in 2003 for the 1881 killing of Billy Bonney, since that expired in 1891**)

No Author. Ed. L. Bradford Prince. *The General Laws of New Mexico.* "Limitations of Criminal Actions. "Limitation of Criminal Actions, Acts of the Legislative Assembly of the Territory of New Mexico, Twenty-Second Session, Convened at the Capitol, at the City of Santa Fe on Monday the 6th day of December, 1875, and Adjourned on Friday the 14th day of January, 1876." Chapter 13, Section 1. **1882. (Providing for a 10 year statute of limitations on murder; so Garrett could not be prosecuted in 2003 for the 1881 killing of Billy Bonney)**

PAMPHLETS FOR (CHRONOLOGICAL)

Turk, David S. Historian U.S. Marshals Service. "Research Report: The U.S. Marshals Service and Billy the Kid. To Be Added in its Present Entirety, with Exhibits, to Lincoln County, New Mexico Case # 2003-274." U.S. Marshals Service Executive Services Division." **December, 2003. (a major hoax document by "Billy the Kid Case" participant as an addendum to the "Probable Cause Statement")**

Madrid, Patricia A. Attorney General. *Inspection of Public Records Act Compliance Guide. Fourth Edition. The "Inspection of Public Records Act" NMSA 1978, Chapter 14, Article 2: A Compliance Guide for New Mexico Public Officials and Citizens.* Santa Fe: Office of the Attorney General. **January, 2004. (For open records compliance and litigation)**

PRESS RELEASE FOR (GOVERNOR BILL RICHARDSON)

Richardson, Bill. "Governor Bill Richardson Announces State Support of Billy the Kid Investigation." **June 10, 2003. (Announcement at State Capitol of state backing of case # 2003-274 and listing of the participants: Tom Sullivan, Steve Sederwall, Gary Graves, Sherry Tippett, and Paul Hutton)**

LETTERS ABOUT

Kurtis, Bill. "This letter is provided as official verification ..." Letter to Steve Sederwall. **October 4, 2010.** Entered by Sederwall's Defense Attorney as Exhibit A in Sandoval District Court Case No. D-1329-CV-2007-1364 Hearing on January 17, 2012. (**Paying for Dr. Henry Lee's forensics**)

BLOGS ABOUT

No author. "Fraud Alleged at Cellmark, DNA Testing Firm. TalkLeft: The Politics of Crime. http://www.talkleft.com./new_archives/008809.html. **November 18, 2004.**

WEBSITE FOR:

Sederwall, Steve. "billythekidcase.com" Website. From **October (?) 2010 to 2012(?). (For $25.00 membership selling Case 2003-274 records)**

TELEVISION DOCUMENTARIES PERPETRATING

History Channel. "Investigating History: Billy the Kid." Week **of April 24, 2004 and May 2, 2004.(Co-Producer, writer, narrator was "Billy the Kid Case" hoaxer Paul Hutton)**

ARTICLES ABOUT (CHRONOLOGICAL)

Humphreys, Sexson. "Pardon My 6-Shooters: Billy the Kid? Governor to Decide; 'Pardon Me, I'm Alive,' Says Billy the Kid." *The Indianapolis News*. Thursday, **November 30, 1950**. Indiana Historical Society. Lew Wallace Collection (M292). Box 14. Folder 12.

Hutton, Paul Andrew. "Dreamscape Desperado." *New Mexico Magazine*. Volume 68. Number 6. Pages 44-58. **June, 1990.**

Janofsky, Michael. "122 Years Later, the Lawmen Are Still Chasing Billy the Kid." *The New York Times*. **June 5, 2003**. Vol. CLII, No. 52,505. Pages 1 and A31.

No Author. "Lincoln County deputy sheriff sends his own letter to governor." *Silver City Daily Press*. **June 25, 2003**. Pages 1, 13.

DellaFlora, Anthony. "State Not Kidding Around: Governor won't mind if probe of the notorious 19th century N.M. outlaw boosts tourism." *Albuquerque Journal.* **June 11, 2003**. No. 162. Pages 1 and A1. **(First big New Mexico announcement of Billy the Kid Case)**

Bommersbach, Jana. "Digging Up Billy: If Pat Garrett didn't kill the Kid, who's buried in his grave?" *True West.* **August/September 2003**. Volume 50. Issue 7. P. 42-45.

No Author. AP. "Authorities call for exhumation of Billy the Kid's mother to solve mystery." *Silver City Sun News.* **October 11, 2003**.

Bommersbach, Jana. "From Shovels to DNA: The inside story of digging up Billy." *True West.* **October/November, 2003.** Volume 50. Issue 7. Pages 42-45.

Jameson, W.C. and Leon Metz. "Was Brushy Bill Really Billy the Kid? Experts face off over new evidence." *True West.* **November/December, 2003**. Volume 50. Issue 10. Pages 32-33.

Murphy, Mary Alice. "Billy the Kid 'Hires' a Lawyer." *Silver City Daily Press Internet Edition.* http://www.thedailypress.com/NewsFolder/11.17.2.html. **November 17, 2003**.

Boyle, Alan. "Billy the Kid gets a lawyer: 122 years after shootout, attorney to gather information for a pardon." msnbc.com. **November 18, 2003**.

Fecteau, Louie. "No Kidding: Governor Taps Lawyer For Billy." *Albuquerque Journal.* Page 1, A6. **November 19, 2003**.

No Author. AP. "Lawyer Appointed to Represent Dead Outlaw." *Silver City Sun News.* http://www.krqe.com/expanded.asp?RECORD_KEY%5bContent. **November 19, 2003**. **(Bill Robins III's appointment by Richardson)**

No Author. "Lawmakers Consider Posthumous Pardon for Billy the Kid." *abqtrib.com News.* **November 21, 2003**.

Boyle, Alan. "Billy the Kid's DNA Sparks Legal Showdown: Sheriffs and mayors face off over digging up remains from the Old West." *msnbc.com.* **November 21, 2003**.

Romo, Rene. "Kid's Mom May Stay Buried: Silver City wins round to block exhumation for outlaw's DNA." *Albuquerque Journal.* **December 9, 2003**. Section D3.

Janna Bommersbach. "Breaking Out More Shovels: Fort Sumner's Sheriff Gary Graves commits to digging up Billy the Kid's Grave." *True West.* **January/February, 2004**. Volume 51. Issue 1. Pages 46-47. **(Hoax-backing article)**

Benke, Richard. AP. "N.M. Re-Opens Case of Billy the Kid." Yahoo! News. **January 13, 2004**.

__________. "Billy the Kid's Life and Death May Be Put to DNA Test: Officials want to examine the body of the outlaw's mother to test a Texas man's claim that he was Bonney. If so, Pat Garrett didn't kill the Kid." *The Nation.* **January 18, 2004. (Uses fake Overton Affidavit given by Attorney Sherry Tippett)**

No Author. AP. "Billy the Kid hearing delayed for months: Sheriffs need more time to prepare arguments for exhuming remains of outlaw's mother." **January 23, 2004**.

Miller, Jay. "Digging Up the Latest on Billy the Kid." *Las Cruces Sun-News.* **February 3, 2004**.

Gonzales. Carolyn. "Hutton writes wild frontier stories for History Channel." *University of New Mexico Campus News.* **February 16, 2004**. Volume 39. No. 12. **(Hoaxer Hutton's TV program announced)**

Miller, Jay. "The Billy the Kid Code." *Las Cruces Sun-News.* **March 29, 2004**.

Nathanson, Rick. "Grave Doubts: 'Investigating History' series tries to clear up the mysteries surrounding Billy the Kid." *Albuquerque Journal Weekly TV Guide: Entertainer.* **April 24, 2004**. Pages 3, 5.

Garrett, Wm. F. "Letters to the Editor." *De Baca County News.* Page 4. **May 6, 2004. (Garrett family member objects to hoax)**

Murphy, Mary Alice and Melissa St. Aude. "Sederwall, Sullivan uninvited to ball." *Silver City Daily Press Internet Edition.* **June 10, 2004**.

Hill, Levi. "Billy the Kid Stirring Up Dust in Silver City." *Las Cruces Sun-News.* **June 12, 2004**. Section 5A. Pages 1, A2.

No Author. "Attorney Refuses Judge's statements concerning exhumation." *thedailypress.com*. **June 15, 2004**. **(Attorney Tippett lies about the OMI)**

Richardson, Bill. "Verbatim: I have to decide whether to pardon him. But not right away – after the investigation, after the state gets more publicity." *Time*. **June 21, 2004**. Vol. 163. No. 25. Page 17.

Romo, Rene. "Back off on Billy, Gov. Asked: Silver City says inquiry into death of Kid would harm state tourism. *Albuquerque Journal*. **June 23, 2004**. Section B-1, B-5.

No Author. "Lincoln county deputy sheriff sends his own letter to governor." *Silver City Daily Press*. **June 25, 2004**. Pages 1, 13. **(Letter from Steve Sederwall)**

No Author. "Editorials: New Racing Schedule Tramples Horseman." *Albuquerque Journal*. **June 26, 2004**.

Miller, Jay. "Inside the Capitol. Bizarre case of Billy the Kid." *Roswell Daily Record*. **July 2, 2004**. Page A4.

Romo, Rene. "Forensic Expert on Billy's Case: Questions Remain on Outlaw's Fate." *Albuquerque Journal*. **August 2, 2004.** Page 1. **(Falsely claims blood on bench; says "trace blood")**

No Author. "Forensic expert joins Billy the Kid inquiry in New Mexico." *AP SignOnSanDiego.com*. **August 2, 2004**. **(Announcing Dr. Henry Lee)**

Miller, Jay. "Inside the Capitol. Sheriffs slippery on Billy the Kid Case." *Roswell Daily Record*. **August 9, 2004**. Page A4.

Cherry, Doris. "Forensics 101 for 'Billy'." *Lincoln County News*. **August 12, 2004**. Pages 2, 10. **(Quotes Sullivan's lie: "a lot" of blood on bench)**

Miller, Jay. "Inside the Capitol. Expert questions Kid probe." *Roswell Daily Record*. **August 20, 2004**. Page A4.

__________. "Inside the Capitol. Hat dance on probe funding." *Roswell Daily Record*. **September 1, 2004**. Page A4.

__________. "Inside the Capitol. Three sheriffs push Kid Case." *Roswell Daily Record*. **September 5, 2004**. Page A4.

__________. "Inside the Capitol. Sheriffs hoax is world-class." *Roswell Daily Record*. **September 8, 2004**. Page A4.

__________. "Inside the Capitol. Kid gets day in court Sept. 27." *Roswell Daily Record*. **September 12, 2004**. Page A4.

__________. "Inside the Capitol. Kid probe making us think." *Roswell Daily Record*. **September 13, 2004**. Page A4.

Stinnett, Scot. "De Baca County Citizens' Committee Files Petition for Recall of Sheriff Gary Graves." *De Baca County News*. **September 14, 2004**.

Miller, Jay. "Inside the Capitol. Who is Attorney Bill Robins?" *Roswell Daily Record*. **September 15, 2004**. Page A4.

Green, Keith. "Mountain Asides: Billy's restless bones are stirred up once again. *RuidosoNews.com*. **September 16, 2004**.

Miller, Jay. "Inside the Capitol. Kid Case: David fights Goliath." *Roswell Daily Record*. **September 17, 2004**. Page A4.

__________. "Inside the Capitol. Many reasons to dig up Kid." *Roswell Daily Record*. **September 19, 2004**. Page A4.

__________. "Inside the Capitol. Nothing to worry about." *Roswell Daily Record*. **September 20, 2004**. Page A4.

Stallings, Dianne. "Showdown in the County Seat." *RuidosoNews.com* **September 21, 2004. (Commissioner Leo Martinez's meeting threatening recall of Sheriff Sullivan for perpetrating a hoax)**

Miller, Jay. "Inside the Capitol. Who speaks for Pat Garrett?" *Roswell Daily Record*. **September 22, 2004**. Page A4.

Stallings, Dianne. "Showdown in the County Seat: shouting match erupts at County Commissioners meeting Tuesday over investigation of Billy the Kid." *Ruidoso News*. **September 22, 2004**.

Cherry, Doris. "Lincoln County 'War' Heats Up Over 'Billy: Capitan Mayor Tracks His Kind of '---' To County Commission Meeting. Tells Jay Miller where to go: wonders why commissioner has his panties in a wad." *Lincoln County News.* **September 23, 2003**. Vol. 99. No. 38. Pages 1-3. (**Commissioner Martinez stops the hoaxers' exhuming Billy the Kid**)

Miller, Jay. "Inside the Capitol. Is there a new Santa Fe Ring?" *Roswell Daily Record.* **September 24, 2004**. Page A4.

Stinnett, Scott. "Rest in Peace, Billy! Exhumation case dismissed." *De Baca County News.* **September 30, 2004**. Vol. 104. No. 2. Pages 1, 5, 6.

Miller, Jay. "Inside the Capitol. Fort Sumner celebrates win." *Roswell Daily Record.* **October 1, 2004**. Page A4.

No author. "Fraud Alleged at Cellmark, DNA Testing Firm. TalkLeft: The Politics of Crime. http://www.talkleft.com./new_archives/008809.html. **November 18, 2004**. (**Dr. Henry Lee's lab commits DNA faking**)

Jana Bommersbach. "Kid Exhumation Nixed: Billy and his mom to rest in peace. *True West.* **January/February 2005**. Volume 52. Issue 1. Pages 68-69.

Carter, Julie. "Follow the Blood: In the Billy the Kid Case, Miller Exhumed." *RuidosoNews.com.* **October 6, 2005**. (**Sederwall lies about blood on bench; gives "dead men don't bleed" quote; has the Lonnie Lippman photo of him holding John Miller/William Hudspeth skull**)

Sullivan, Tom. "Letters: Your Opinion." *RuidosoNews.com.* **October 21, 2005**. (**Sullivan letter to the editor: "Why are they so afraid of the truth?"**)

Carter, Julie. "Billy the Kid in Prescott? *New Mexico Stockman.* **November, 2005**. Pages 38, 39, 76.

Romo, Rene. "Billy the Kid Probe May Yield New Twist. *Albuquerque Journal. ABQ Journal.com.* **November 6, 2005**. (**Claims Sullivan and Sederwall have John Miller's DNA**)

Struckman, Robert. "Bitterroot man hopes to uncover truth about Billy the Kid." http://www.helenair.com/articles/2006/03/13/montana/a05031306_01.txt (Missoulian) **March 13, 2006**. (**Dale Tunnell backing John Miller)**

Dodder, Joanna. "Officials could face charges for digging up alleged Billy the Kid." *The Daily Courier of Prescott Arizona.* **April 12, 2006**. (**Sullivan claims DNA in "two months," and fakes Hudspeth skeleton as John Miller's and makes up a left scapula bullet wound**)

Banks, Leo W. "The New Billy the Kid? The mad search for the bones of an American outlaw icon has come to Arizona." *Tucson Weekly.* http://www.tucsonweekly.com/gbase/Currents/Content?oid=oid:81013 **April 13, 2006**. (**Sullivan lies that bench is "saturated with blood; Dr. Rick Staub says DNA extracted from William Hudspeth not John Miller**)

Carter, Julie. "Digging up bones, Arizona may protest Miller exhumation." jcarter@tularosa.net. **April 19, 2006**.

Dodder, Joanna. "Officials could face charges for digging up alleged Billy the Kid." *The Daily Courier of Prescott Arizona.* **April 12, 2006**. (**Sullivan claims DNA in "two months," and fakes Hudspeth skeleton as John Miller's with buck teeth and a left scapula bullet wound**)

Banks, Leo W. "The New Billy the Kid? The mad search for the bones of an American outlaw icon has come to Arizona." *Tucson Weekly.* http://www.tucsonweekly.com/gbase/Currents/Content?oid=oid:81013 **April 13, 2006**. (**Sullivan lies that bench is "saturated with blood; Dr. Rick Staub says DNA extracted from William Hudspeth not John Miller**)

Carter, Julie. "Digging up bones, Arizona may protest Miller exhumation." jcarter@tularosa.net. **April 19, 2006**.

Carter, Julie. "Culture Shock: The cowboys and the Kid go to France. jcarter@tulerosa.net. **May 5, 2006**. (**Sullivan worked on movie 9 months**)

Shafer, Mark. "N.M. pair may face charges in grave case." **May 13, 2006**. markshafer @ArizonaRepublic.com. http://www.azcentral.com/arizonarepublic/local/articles/0513billythekid0513.html

Myers, Amanda Lee. "New Mexicans Dig Up Trouble in Arizona." *Albuquerque Journal, New Mexico and the West.* **May 14, 2006**. Page B4. (**Also in gulfnews.com; states Dallas lab" is doing DNA comparisons**)

__________."Billy the Kid Still 'Wanted.' " **May 16, 2006**. gulfnews.com. http://archive.gulfnews.com/articles/06/05/16/10040234.html.

Valdez, Jannay. "Digging Up the Truth About Billy." *RuidosoNews.com.* http://ruidosonews.com/apps/pbcs.dll./article?AID=/2006069/OPINION03/606090351/101 **June 9, 2006**.

Dodder, Joanna. "Back at Rest: Bones of Billy the Kid return to Prescott." *The Daily Courier.* **July 9, 2006**. http://prescottdailycourier.com/print.asp?ArticleID=40353&SectionID=1&SubSectionID=1

No Author. AP. "Prescott, Ariz. - Prosecutors won't seek charges against two men who exhumed the remains of a man who claimed to be the outlaw Billy the Kid." AOL News. **October 23, 2006**.

__________. AP. "Billy the Kid Case Dropped." *Albuquerque Journal. Metro.* D3. **October 24, 2006**.

__________. AP. "Men Who Exhumed Billy the Kid Won't Be Charged." **October 24, 2006.** *New York Sun.* http://www.nysun.com/article/42176. (**Claims Sullivan and Sederwall did Arizona exhumation, have Miller DNA, and sent to Orchid for matchings to bench DNA**)

__________. AP. "Arizona: No Charges Sought for Exhuming Remains." *New York Times.* A-26. **October 24, 2006**. http://www.nytimes.com/2006/10/24/us/24brfs-002.html?r=1&oref=slogin. (**Cover-up of illegal John Miller/William Hudspeth exhumations**)

Turk, David S. "Billy the Kid and the U.S. Marshals Service." *Wild West.* **February, 2007**. Volume 19. Number 5. Pages 34 – 41. (**Turk's expurgated "U.S. Marshals Service and Billy the Kid"**)

Jason Strykowski. "A Tale of Two Governors ... And one Kid." *True West.* **May, 2007**. Vol. 54. Issue 5. Page 64.

No Author. AP. "Billy the Kid Exhumation a Possibility." *Roswell Daily Record.* **May 2, 2007**. **From Stephenville, Texas AP on "Brushy Bill" exhumation attempt; Sederwall claims has John Miller's DNA**)

Carter, Julie. "Brushy Bill targeted for DNA testing; Billy the Kid workbench goes on display." *Ruidoso News.* **May 3, 2007**.

__________. AP. "Manhunt for Real Billy the Kid Goes On: Deputy hopes DNA will finally reveal outlaw's true identity." *Albuquerque Journal.* **May 4, 2007**. B3.

Zorosec, Thomas. "DNA could solve mystery of Billy the Kid." Chron.com - Houston Chronicle. **May 5, 2007**. (**From Hamilton, Texas; "Brushy Bill" exhumation attempt**)

Carter, Julie. AP. "Texas town denies request to exhume Billy the Kid claimant." *Houston Chronicle.* **May 11, 2007**.

__________. "Evidence Hidden in Spector Trial." BBC Internet News. May 24, 2007. (**Dr. Henry Lee alleged as destroying evidence**)

__________. AP. "Famed experts credibility takes a hit at Spector trial." CNN.com law center. **May 25, 2007**. (**Dr. Henry Lee allegedly destroyed evidence**)

Stallings, Dianne. "Billy the Kid case straps county for insurance." *RuidosoNews.com.* **August 13, 2008**.

Carter, Julie. "Lincoln County deputies resign commissions for Kid case." *Ruidosonews.com.* **August 16, 2007**.

Romo, Rene. "Seeking the Kid, Minus Badges. Deputies Resign to Hunt for Billy." *Albuquerque Journal.* **August 18, 2007**. No. 230. pp. 1-2.

Concerned Citizens of Lincoln County. "Should Lincoln County Have Grave Concerns Over A Person Like Steve Sederwall Running for Sheriff? *Lincoln County News.* **October 16, 2008**. Page 6.

Romo, Rene. "Fight Won, Questions Remain: Billy the Kid DNA Report Released." *Albuquerque Journal*. Front Page and Page B1. **April 29, 2012.**

Sandlin, Scott. "Billy the Kid case costs taxpayers nearly $200K: Billy the Kid lives on in battle of public records." *Albuquerque Journal*. Front Page, Page A2, Page A8. No. 162. **June 11, 2013. (Fakes blood on carpenter's bench)**

Cherry, Doris. "Modern Billy the Kid 'Cases' Cost Public Plenty: County Shells Out Bucks for Failing to Release Information." *Lincoln County News*. **June 27, 2013.** Volume 109. Number 6. Front Page and Pages 7-8. **(Based on my June 18, 2013 letter to the Lincoln County Commissioners)**

Stallings, Dianne. "Former Lincoln County sheriff dies in Texas: Tom Sullivan died Saturday in Texas." **October 22, 2013.** ruidosonews.com.

"BILLY THE KID CASE" LEGAL DOCUMENTS (BY LOCATION)

CAPITAN, NEW MEXICO (FIRST ANNOUNCEMENT OF CASE NO. 2003-274)

Sederwall, Steve, "Mayor's Report, **May 5, 2003.**" *Village of Capitan: Capitan Village Hall News*. Capitan, New Mexico. **(Announces filed Case 2003-274)**

ALBUQUERQUE, NEW MEXICO (OPPOSITION OF THE OMI TO EXHUMATIONS)

Zumwalt, Ross E. "Affidavit of Ross E. Zumwalt, MD. In the Matter of Catherine Antrim. Case No. MS 2003-11 Sixth Judicial Court, County of Grant, State of New Mexico. **January 9, 2004. (Exhumation refused based on invalid DNA)**

Komar, Debra. "Affidavit of Debra Komar, PhD. In the Matter of Catherine Antrim. Case No. MS 2003-11 Sixth Judicial Court, County of Grant, State of New Mexico. **January 9, 2004. (Exhumation refused based on invalid DNA)**

Snead, William E. Attorney for Office of Medical Investigator." "In the Matter of Catherine Antrim: Response of Office of Medical Investigator to Petition to Exhume Remains of Catherine Antrim." Case No. MS 2003-11. Sixth Judicial Court, Grant County. **January 13, 2004. (Opposition of OMI to exhumation)**

Komar, Debra. "Deposition of Debra Komar, Ph.D. In the Matter of Catherine Antrim. Case No. MS 2003-11." Sixth Judicial Court, County of Grant, State of New Mexico. Taken by Adam S. Baker, Attorney for Town of Silver City. Signed: Debra Komar, Ph.D. **January 20, 2004. (Exhumation refused based on invalid DNA in Billy the Kid's and mother's graves)**

LINCOLN COUNTY, NEW MEXICO (LINCOLN COUNTY SHERIFF'S DEPARTMENT CASE NO. 2003-274, "BILLY THE KID CASE")

Virden, R.E. Lincoln County Undersheriff report. "I participated in the investigative reconstruction ..." **April 28, 2003. (Participation in Case # 2003-274.)**

Sullivan, Tom. Lincoln County Sheriff. "Lincoln County Sheriffs Department is currently conducting an investigation ..." Letter to Charles Ryan, Director Arizona Department of Corrections. **April 30, 2003. (Describes Garrett as murderer and planned exhumations of John Miller and "Brushy Bill" Roberts)**

__________. "Denial Letter." Pre-printed form to my attorney, Randall M. Harris. **October 8, 2003. (Denial based on ongoing law enforcement case.)**

Sullivan, Tom. Sheriff, Lincoln County Sheriff's Office, and Steven M. Sederwall. Deputy Sheriff, Lincoln County Sheriff's Office. "Lincoln County Sheriff's Office, Lincoln County, New Mexico, Case: William H. Bonney, a.k.a. William Antrim, a.k.a. The Kid, a.k.a. Billy the Kid: An Investigation into the events of April 28, 1881 through July 14, 1881 – seventy-seven days of doubt." **No Date. (Rejected**

Probable Cause Statement for Case No. 2003-274. In Lincoln County Sheriff's Department case file for 2003-274.)

__________. "Lincoln County Sheriff's Department Case #2003-274 Probable Cause Statement." Filed in Lincoln County Sheriff's Department. Carrizozo, New Mexico. **December 31, 2003. (Became publicly available as "Plaintiff Exhibit 1 in Petitioner's Attorney Sherry Tippett's Silver City "Brief in Chief in Support of the Exhumation of Catherine Antrim." Case No. MS 03-011." Sixth Judicial Court, County of Grant, State of New Mexico." January 5, 2004)**

Overton, Homer D. aka Homer D. Kinsworthy. "Affidavit for Lincoln County Sheriff's Department Case #2003-274 Probable Cause Statement." **December 22, 2003. (Fake swearing that Garrett's widow –dead in 1936 - told him in 1940 that Garrett did not kill the Kid. Became publicly available as "Plaintiff Exhibit 1 in Petitioner's Attorney Sherry Tippett's Silver City "Brief in Chief in Support of the Exhumation of Catherine Antrim." Case No. MS 03-011." Sixth Judicial Court, County of Grant, State of New Mexico." January 5, 2004)**

No Author. "Contact List, William H. Bonney Case # 2003-274, Lincoln County Sheriff's Office & Investigators." No Date. **Probably 2003. (In Lincoln County Sheriff's Department Case file for 2003-274)**

Virden, Rick, Lincoln County Sheriff. "Deputy Sheriff Commission [Card] to Tom Sullivan." **January 1, 2005.**

__________. "Deputy Sheriff Commission [Card] to Steven Sederwall." **February 25, 2005.**

Sederwall, Steven M., Lincoln County Sheriff's Deputy Investigator. "Lincoln County Sheriff's Department Supplemental Report, Case #2003-274. Subject: Exhumation of John Miller. Location: Arizona Pioneers' Cemetery, Prescott, Arizona." **May 19, 2005. (Arizona exhumations John Miller and William Hudspeth)**

Virden, R.E. Lincoln County Sheriff. letter to Jay Miller. "We are interested in the truth surrounding Billy the Kid and are continuing the investigation ..." **November 28, 2005. (Virden confirms continuing Billy the Kid case and deputizing Sullivan and Sederwall for it.)**

Virden, R.E. Lincoln County Sheriff. To Hamilton, Texas, Mayor Roy Ramsey [sic]. "This letter will inform you that Tom Sullivan and Steve Sederwall are both commissioned deputies ..." **No date, but around May 2007. (Virden's attempt to exhume "Brushy" with Sullivan and Sederwall as the Deputies)**

Lee, Henry, Dr. Letter to Jay Miller. "In response to your letter dated March 27, 2006 ..." **May 1, 2006. (Lee confirms sending his carpenter's bench and floorboard report to Lincoln County Sheriff's Department.)**

Sederwall, Steve. "billythekidcase.com." Sederwall's pay for view website with Case 2003-274 records. **October, 2010. (Selling public records online.**

SILVER CITY, NEW MEXICO (EXHUMATION ATTEMPT ON CATHERINE ANTRIM)

Tippett, Sherry. Attorney. To Richard Gay, Assistant to the Chief of Staff, Governor Richardson's Office. "Memorandum, RE: Exhumation of Catherine Antrim." **July 11, 2003. (Tippett's lie of OMI backing exhumation.)**

Tippett, Sherry. Attorney for Petitioners Sullivan, Sederwall, and Graves. "In the Matter of Catherine Antrim: Petition to Exhume Remains." Case No. MS 03-011. Sixth Judicial Court, County of Grant, State of New Mexico. **October 3, 2003. (Start of exhumation attempts; perjury about permission from OMI)**

Kennedy, Paul J., Adam S. Baker, Thomas F. Stewart, Robert L. Scavron, Attorneys for Mayor Terry Fortenberry on Behalf of the Town of Silver City. "In the Matter of Catherine Antrim: Motion to Intervene." Case No. MS 03-011. Sixth Judicial Court, County of Grant, State of New Mexico. **October 31, 2003. (Opposition)**

__________. "In the Matter of Catherine Antrim: Response in Opposition to the Petition to Exhume Remains." Case No. MS 03-011. Sixth Judicial Court, County of Grant, State of New Mexico. **October 31, 2003.**

Tippett, Sherry J. Attorney for Petitioners. "State of New Mexico, County of Grant, Sixth Judicial District Court, In the Matter of Catherine Antrim, No. MS. 2003-11. Petitioner's Response in Opposition to the Town of Silver City's Motion to Intervene." (Unfiled) **No Date.**

Baker, Adam S. Attorneys for Mayor Terry Fortenberry on Behalf of Silver City. "In the Matter of Catherine Antrim: Request for Hearing." Case No. MS 03-011. Sixth Judicial Court, County of Grant, State of New Mexico. **November 4, 2003.**

Miranda, Velia C., District Court Clerk. "In the Matter of Catherine Antrim: Notice of Assignment/Designation of District Judge H.R. Quintero." Case No. MS 03-011. Sixth Judicial Court, County of Grant, State of New Mexico. **November 14, 2003. (Entry of Richardson appointee judge)**

Tippett, Sherry J. Attorney for Petitioners Sullivan, Sederwall and Graves. "In the Matter of Catherine Antrim: Petitioner's Response in Opposition to the Town of Silver City's Motion to Intervene." No. MS. 2003-11. State of New Mexico, County of Grant, Sixth Judicial District Court. (Unfiled) **No Date.**

Robins, Bill III and David Sandoval, Attorneys for Billy the Kid. "In the Matter of Catherine Antrim: Billy the Kid's Unopposed Motion for Intervention and Request for Expedited Disposition." Case No. MS 2003-11. Sixth Judicial Court, County of Grant, State of New Mexico. **November 26, 2003. (First petition with dead Billy the Kid as co-Petitioner to Sullivan, Sederwall, and Graves.)**

Kennedy, Paul J., Adam S. Baker, Thomas F. Stewart, Robert L. Scavron, Attorneys for Mayor Terry Fortenberry on Behalf of the Town of Silver City. "In the Matter of Catherine Antrim: Reply in Support of the Town of Silver City's Motion to Intervene." Case No. MS 2003-11. Sixth Judicial Court, County of Grant, State of New Mexico. **December 8, 2003. (Justifying need to protect Antrim grave)**

Tippett, Sherry J. Attorney for Petitioners Sullivan, Sederwall and Graves. "In the Matter of Catherine Antrim: Petitioners Response in Opposition to the Town of Silver City's Motion to Intervene." Case No. MS 2003-11. Sixth Judicial Court, County of Grant, State of New Mexico. **December 8, 2003. (Tippett lies by saying town has no "legal interest" to intervene)**

Quintero, H.R. District Judge. "In the Matter of Catherine Antrim: Order." Case No. MS 03-011. Sixth Judicial Court, County of Grant, State of New Mexico. **December 9, 2003. (Rescheduling hearing from January 6, 2004 to January 27, 2004.)**

Baker, Adam S. Attorneys for Mayor Terry Fortenberry on Behalf of the Town of Silver City. "In the Matter of Catherine Antrim: Intervenor Town of Silver City's Brief on Petition to Exhume." Case No. MS 03-011. Sixth Judicial Court, County of Grant, State of New Mexico. **January 5, 2004. (Arguing 1962 Lois Telfer case as blocking exhumation)**

Tippett, Sherry J. Attorney. To Mayor Steve Sederwall, Sheriff Tom Sullivan, Sheriff Gary Graves. "In the Matter of Catherine Antrim: Petitioners Brief in Chief in Support of Exhumation." Case No. MS 2003-11. Sixth Judicial Court, County of Grant, State of New Mexico. **January 5, 2004. (Using Probable Cause Statement and Homer Overton Affidavit as Plaintiff exhibits)**

Robins, Bill III and David Sandoval. Attorneys for Billy the Kid. "In the Matter of Catherine Antrim: Billy the Kid's Pre-Hearing Brief." Case No. MS 2003-11. Sixth Judicial Court, Grant County. **January 5, 2004. (Linking exhumation and pardon with "Brushy Bill" Roberts as Billy – CRACKED THE HOAX as a "Brushy Bill" scam by using "Brushy's" dark night for July 14, 1881)**

Tippett, Sherry. Attorney for law enforcement Petitioners Tom Sullivan, Steve Sederwall, Gary Graves. "In the Matter of Catherine Antrim: Petitioner's [sic] Brief in Chief in Support of Exhumation." Case No. MS 2003-11. Sixth Judicial Court, Grant County. **January 5, 2004.**

Kennedy, Paul J., Adam S. Baker, Thomas F. Stewart, Robert L. Scavron, Attorneys for Mayor Terry Fortenberry on Behalf of the Town of Silver City. "In the Matter of Catherine Antrim: Response in Opposition to Petitioners' Brief in Chief." Case No. MS 2003-11. Sixth Judicial Court, County of Grant, State of New Mexico. **January 21, 2004.**

__________. "In the Matter of Catherine Antrim: Silver City's Response in Opposition to Petitioners' Motion for Continuance." Case No. MS 2003-11. Sixth Judicial Court, County of Grant, State of New Mexico. **January 21, 2004.**

Tippett, Sherry J. Attorney. To Mayor Steve Sederwall, Sheriff Tom Sullivan, Sheriff Gary Graves. "Attached is a copy of Judge Quintero's Order of December 9, 2003, ruling on our Hearing ..." **December 17, 2003. (States that they will win on January 27, 2004; urges completing the Probable Cause Statement)**

Quintero, H.R. District Judge, Division 1. "Order of Continuance. In the Matter of Catherine Antrim. Case No. MS 03-011." Filed **January 23, 2004**. Sixth Judicial Court, County of Grant, State of New Mexico. Filed January 23, 2004. (**Tippett sanctioned to pay airfare for witness, Frederick Nolan**)

Robins, Bill III and David Sandoval. Attorneys for Billy the Kid. "In the Matter of Catherine Antrim: Billy the Kid's Brief on the Question of Ripeness." Case No. MS 2003-11. Sixth Judicial Court, Grant County. **February 24, 2004**. (**Setting up Quintero's sending the exhumation to Fort Sumner**)

Acúna, Mark Anthony and Sherry J. Tippett. Attorneys for Petitioners Sullivan, Sederwall and Graves. "In the Matter of Catherine Antrim: Petitioners' Brief on the Question of Ripeness." Case No. MS 2003-11. Sixth Judicial Court, Grant County. **February 24, 2004**.

Baker, Adam S. and Thomas F. Stewart, Robert L. Scavron, Attorneys for Silver City and Joani Amos-Staats. "In the Matter of Catherine Antrim: Silver City's and Joani Amos-Staats' [sic] Joint Motion to Dismiss on Grounds of Ripeness." Case No. MS 2003-11. Sixth Judicial Court, County of Grant, State of New Mexico. **February 24, 2004**.

Acúna, Mark Anthony. Attorney for Petitioners Sullivan, Sederwall and Graves. "In the Matter of Catherine Antrim: Entry of Appearance." Case No. MS 03-011. Sixth Judicial Court, County of Grant, State of New Mexico. **February 26, 2004**. (**Replacing Tippett for law enforcement Petitioners**)

Robins, Bill III and David Sandoval. Attorneys for Billy the Kid. "In the Matter of Catherine Antrim: Response to Motion to Dismiss." Case No. MS 2003-11. Sixth Judicial Court, Grant County. **March 10, 2004**.

Quintero, Henry R. "In the Matter of Catherine Antrim: Decision and Order." Case No. MS 03-011." Sixth Judicial Court, County of Grant, State of New Mexico. **April 2, 2004**. (**Stipulation that case is not ripe, and requires DNA from Fort Sumner Kid grave first before trying to exhume Catherine Antrim**)

Fortenberry, Terry D, Mayor; Thomas A. Nupp Councilor District 2; Steve May, Councilor District 4; Gary Clauss, Councilor District 3; Judy Ward, Councilor District 1; Alex Brown, Town Manager; Cissy McAndrew, Executive Director Chamber of Commerce; Frank Milan, Director Silver City Mainstreet Project; Susan Berry, Director Silver City Museum. "Open Letter to Governor Bill Richardson." **June 21, 2004**. (**Request to cease "Billy the Kid Case" exhumations**)

FORT SUMNER, NEW MEXICO (EXHUMATION ATTEMPT ON WILLIAM H. BONNEY)

De Baca County Commissioners Special Meeting." Minutes. (Powhatan Carter III, Chairman; Joe Steele; Tommy Roybal; Nancy Sparks, County Clerk. To whom it may concern. "The De Baca County Commissioners are in full support of Village of Fort Sumner's stand against exhuming the body of Billy the Kid." **September 25, 2003**. (**Voted against exhumation of Billy the Kid**)

Robins, Bill III and David Sandoval, Mark Acuña, Attorneys for Co-Petitioner Billy the Kid and Sheriff-Petitioners. "In the Matter of William H. Bonney, aka 'Billy the Kid': Petition for the Exhumation of Billy the Kid's Remains." Case No. CV-04-00005. Tenth Judicial District, County of De Baca, State of New Mexico. **February 26, 2004. (Robins joins Acuña to exhume the Kid)**

Robins, Bill III and David Sandoval, Attorneys for Co-Petitioner Billy the Kid. "In the Matter of William H. Bonney, aka 'Billy the Kid': Notice of Excusal." Case No. CV-2004 [sic]-00005. Tenth Judicial District, County of De Baca, State of New Mexico. **March 5, 2004. (Petitioners' removal of honest Judge Ricky Purcell from hearing the case.)**

Jimenez Maes, Petra, Chief Justice. "In the Matter of William H. Bonney, aka 'Billy the Kid': Order Designating Judge." Case No. CV-2004-00005. Tenth Judicial District, County of De Baca, State of New Mexico. **April 1, 2004. (Richardson's corrupt judge appointee, Ted Hartley, is appointed to case)**

Baker, Adam S. and Herb Marsh, Jr., Attorneys for the Village of Fort Sumner. "In the Matter of William H. Bonney, aka 'Billy the Kid': Village of Fort Sumner's Unopposed Motion to Intervene." Case No. CV-04-00005. Tenth Judicial District, County of De Baca, State of New Mexico. **April 12, 2004.**

__________. "In the Matter of William H. Bonney, aka 'Billy the Kid': Response in Opposition to the Petitioners for the Exhumation of Billy the Kid's Remains. In the Matter of William H. Bonney, aka 'Billy the Kid.' " Case No. CV-04-00005. Tenth Judicial District, County of De Baca, State of New Mexico. **April 12, 2004.**

Hartley, Teddy L. "In the Matter of William H. Bonney, aka 'Billy the Kid': Order." Case No. CV-04-00005. Tenth Judicial District, County of De Baca, State of New Mexico. **April 20, 2004. (Intervention of Village of Fort Sumner granted)**

Baker, Adam S. and Herb Marsh, Jr., Attorneys for the Village of Fort Sumner. "In the Matter of William H. Bonney, aka 'Billy the Kid': Response in Opposition to the Petition for the Exhumation of Billy the Kid's Remains." Case No. CV-04-00005. Tenth Judicial District, County of De Baca, State of New Mexico. **May 6, 2004.**

__________. "In the Matter of William H. Bonney, aka 'Billy the Kid': Village of Fort Sumner's Motion For Proof of Attorneys' Authority To Act On Behalf Of William H. Bonney." Case No. CV-04-00005. Tenth Judicial District, County of De Baca, State of New Mexico. **June 24, 2004. (Confronting Attorney Bill Robins III's fakery of representing Billy the Kid based on dead Billy not being real so he cannot have a lawyer)**

__________. "In the Matter of William H. Bonney, aka 'Billy the Kid': Village of Fort Sumner's Motion to Dismiss Against Petitioners Sullivan, Sederwall, and Graves for Lack of Standing." Case No. CV-04-00005. Tenth Judicial District, County of De Baca, State of New Mexico. **June 24, 2004. (Invalid murder case because Pat Garrett properly killed Billy the Kid)**

Hartley, Teddy L. District Judge. "Notice of Hearing. "In the Matter of William H. Bonney, aka 'Billy the Kid': Notice of Hearing." Case No. CV-04-00005. Tenth Judicial District, County of De Baca, State of New Mexico. **July 6, 2004. (Hearing set for September 27, 2004)**

Acuña, Mark Anthony, Attorney for the Petitioners Sullivan, Sederwall and Graves. "In the Matter of William H. Bonney, aka 'Billy the Kid': Petitioner's Response to the Village of Ft. Sumner's Motion to Dismiss." Case No. CV-04-00005." Tenth Judicial District, State of New Mexico, County of De Baca. **July 29, 2004.(Acuña argues Sheriff-petitioners' Sullivan, Graves, and Sederwall's standing based on law enforcement as Sheriffs and Deputy Sheriff; later Sullivan and Sederwall would lie that they had done the case as private hobbyists to avoid the open records act for public officials to hide their fake DNA documents)**

Robins, Bill III and David Sandoval; Attorneys for the Billy the Kid; and Adam S. Baker and Herb Marsh, Jr., Attorneys for the Village of Fort Sumner. "In the Matter of William H. Bonney, aka 'Billy the Kid': Stipulation of Dismissal." Case

No. CV-04-00005. Tenth Judicial District, County of De Baca, State of New Mexico. **August 23, 2004. (Fake dead Billy the Kid petition dismissed with prejudice)**

Acuña, Mark Anthony and Adam S. Baker, Attorneys for Petitioners Graves, Sullivan and Sederwall; and the Village of Fort Sumner. "In the Matter of William H. Bonney, aka 'Billy the Kid': Stipulation of Dismissal With Prejudice." Case No. CV-04-00005. Tenth Judicial District, County of De Baca, State of New Mexico. **September 24, 2004. (Petitioners withdraw with prejudice.)**

ARIZONA: YAVAPAI (PRESCOTT) AND MARICOPA COUNTIES (EXHUMATIONS OF JOHN MILLER AND WILLIAM HUDSPETH)

Sederwall, Steven M., Lincoln County Sheriff's Deputy Investigator. "Lincoln County Sheriff's Department Supplemental Report, Case #2003-274. Subject: Exhumation of John Miller. Location: Arizona Pioneers' Cemetery, Prescott, Arizona." **May 19, 2005. (Arizona exhumations John Miller and William Hudspeth)**

Cahall, Anna, Detective Prescott Police Department. "CASE REPORT 0600012767." **April 5, 2006. (Concerning the John Miller exhumation)**

Tunnell, Dale. To Jeanine Dike. "Subject: RE: Disinterment of Wm Bonney." **May 3, 2005.**

Sederwall, Steven M., Lincoln County Sheriff's Deputy Investigator. "Lincoln County Sheriff's Department Supplemental Report, Case #2003-274. Subject: Exhumation of John Miller. Location: Arizona Pioneers' Cemetery, Prescott, Arizona." **May 19, 2005. (Arizona exhumations John Miller and William Hudspeth)**

Fulginiti, Laura C. Ph.D., D-ABFA. Forensic Anthropologist. To Dale L. Tunnell, Ph.D. "RE: Exhumation, Pioneer Home Cemetery, Prescott, Arizona." **June 2, 2005. (Report of the Miller-Hudspeth exhumations revealing fake hoaxer claims of buck teeth and bullet wound to left scapula of John Miller.)**

Snell, David. To Shiela Polk. Yavapai County Attorney. "I feel it is my duty to report to you that graverobbers are plying their trade ..." **March 11, 2006. (Arizona citizen starting criminal investigation of Miller/Hudspeth exhumations.)**

Cahall, Anna, Detective Prescott Police Department. "CASE REPORT 0600012767." **April 5, 2006. (Concerning the John Miller exhumation; interviews with Sullivan, Sederwall, Tunnell)**

Savona, Glenn A. Prescott City Prosecutor. To Shiela Sullivan Polk, Yavapai County Attorney. "Re: Police Department DR# 2006-12767 Arizona Pioneers' Home Cemetery." **April 13, 2006. (Calls exhumations potential felonies)**

Cooper, Gale. To Detective Anna Cahall. Prescott Police Department. "Re: Exhumation of John Miller and adjacent grave for pursuing the New Mexico Billy the Kid Case." **April 13, 2006.**

__________. To Detective Anna Cahall. Prescott Police Department. "Re: Pertinent articles regarding exhumation of John Miller and remains from adjacent grave for alleged promulgation of the New Mexico Billy the Kid Case, a murder investigation." **April 17, 2006.**

__________. To Deputy County Attorney Steve Jaynes and County Attorney Dennis McGrane. (via fax) "Re: Information on the New Mexico Billy the Kid Case pertinent to the Arizona John Miller exhumations." **May 2, 2006.**

Sederwall, Steve. To confidential recipient. "Well we have the governor reaching out to the Arizona to stop this investigation." **May 16, 2006.**

Cooper, Gale. To Attorney Jonell Lucca (via fax). "Re: Case # CA20006020516. Follow-up to our telephone conversation of June 9, 2006, to address the issue of Permit for the exhumations of John Miller and the remains from an adjacent grave for promulgation of the New Mexico Billy the Kid Case, a murder investigation." **June 12, 2006.**

__________. To Attorney Jonell Lucca (via fax). "Re: Case # CA20006020516. Follow-up to my fax of June 12, 2006, to address additional issues pertinent to the exhumations of John Miller and William Hudspeth, done for promulgation of the New Mexico Billy the Kid Case, an alleged murder investigation." July 11, 2006.

Sams, Dale. Arizona Pioneers' Home Administrator. To Gale Cooper. Confirming approximate date of John Miller's birth as 1850. **August 8, 2006**.

Cooper, Gale. To Attorney Jonell Lucca (via fax). "Re: Case # CA20006020516. Follow-up to my fax of July 11, 2006, to address issues pertinent to the promulgators of the New Mexico Billy the Kid Case (which resulted in the exhumations of John Miller and William Hudspeth)." **August 11, 2006**.

__________. To Attorney Jonell Lucca. "Re: Enclosed reference copy of Freedom of Information Act (FOIA) to Governor Janet Napolitano regarding her possible participation in the Prescott, Arizona exhumations of John Miller and William Hudspeth, and their legal issues related to Maricopa County Prosecutor's Office Case # CA20006020516." **September 22, 2006**.

__________. To Attorney Jonell Lucca. "Re: Information pertaining to Case # CA20006020516 (exhumations of John Miller and William Hudspeth) - American Academy of Forensic Science Ethics and Conduct Complaint against Dr. Henry Lee." **October 2, 2006**.

Lucca, Jonell L. To Dr. Gale Cooper. "This letter is to inform you that the Maricopa County Attorney's Office has declined to file charges ..." **October 17, 2006**. **(Corrupt claim that the only suspects were Jeanine Dike and Dale Tunnell to shield Sullivan and Sederwall)**

HAMILTON, TEXAS (EXHUMATION ATTEMPT ON "BRUSHY BILL" ROBERTS)

Cooper, Gale. "Billy the Kid Case in a Nutshell." Faxed letter to Hamilton, Texas, Mayor Roy Rumsey. **May 3, 2007**. **(About hoax to dig up "Brushy Bill")**

Virden, R.E. Lincoln County Sheriff. To Hamilton, Texas, Mayor Roy Ramsey [sic]. "This letter will inform you that Tom Sullivan and Steve Sederwall are both commissioned deputies ..." **No date, but around May 2007**. **(Virden's attempt to exhume "Brushy Bill" Roberts.)**

Cooper, Gale. "RE: Lincoln County Sheriff's Department's 2007 attempt to exhume Oliver "Brushy Bill" Roberts. Faxed letter to Hamilton, Texas, Mayor Roy Rumsey. **September 11, 2008**.

Rumsey, Roy. Hamilton Mayor. "RE: Lincoln County Sheriff's Department's 2007 attempt to exhume Oliver Roberts." Faxed letter to Gale Cooper. **September 12, 2008**. **(Confirmation that the case is closed)**

PAST ATTEMPT TO EXHUME WILLIAM H. BONNEY

"Motion to Intervene. In Re Application of Lois Telfer, Petitioner for the Removal of the Body of William H. Bonney, Deceased, From the Ft. Sumner Cemetery in Which He is Interred for Reinterment in the Lincoln, New Mexico, Cemetery. Case No. 3255." **December 5, 1961**. In the District Court of the Tenth Judicial District Within and For the County of De Baca. Signed: Victor C. Breen and John Humphrey, Jr., Attorneys for Louis A Bowdre. **(Louis Bowdre was the relative of Charles Bowdre whose grave is contiguous to William Bonney's.)**

Breen, Victor C. and John Humphrey, Jr., Attorneys for Louis A Bowdre. "Motion to Intervene. In Re Application of Lois Telfer, Petitioner for the Removal of the Body of William H. Bonney, Deceased, From the Ft. Sumner Cemetery in Which He is Interred for Reinterment in the Lincoln, New Mexico, Cemetery." Case No. 3255. In the District Court of the Tenth Judicial District, County of De Baca. **December 5, 1961**. **(Louis Bowdre was the relative of Charles Bowdre whose grave is contiguous to William Bonney's.)**

Kinsley, E.T. District Judge. "Decree. In Re Application of Lois Telfer, Petitioner for the Removal of the Body of William H. Bonney, Deceased, From the Ft. Sumner Cemetery in Which He is Interred for Reinterment in the Lincoln, New Mexico, Cemetery." Case No. 3255." In the District Court of the Tenth Judicial District Within and For the County of De Baca. **April 6, 1962. (Petition for exhumation Billy the Kid denied on basis that his grave could not be located and the search would disturb Bowdre's remains. That precedent was ignored by the current Petitioners and their attorneys.)**

OPEN RECORDS LITIGATION FROM 2007-2014: Sandoval County District Cause No. D-1329-CV-2007-1364, Gale Cooper and De Baca County News, a New Mexico Corporation, PLAINTIFFS, vs. Rick Virden, Lincoln County Sheriff and Custodian of Records; and Steven M. Sederwall, Former Lincoln County Deputy Sheriff; and Thomas T. Sullivan, Former Lincoln County Sheriff and Former Lincoln County Deputy Sheriff, DEFENDANTS.

WITH STEVE SEDERWALL'S FORGED DR. HENRY LEE REPORTS

Brown, Kevin. "I am enclosing the document Mr. Sederwall received from Dr. Lee ..." Letter. **February 18, 2010. (Unrequested Lee floorboard report which was a forgery)**

Lee, Henry and Calvin Ostler. "Forensic Research and Training Center Forensic Examination Report: "Examination of Lincoln County Court House." February 25, 2005. **(Given to me on February 18, 2010 by Kevin Brown and on April 6, 2010 by Nicole Werkmeister as a requested Lee report – but was Version I (9 pages) of an unrequested and forged floorboard report)**

Threet, Martin E. "I am returning the Lee report ..." Letter to Brown. (Rejecting and returning the Lee floorboard report) **February 25, 2010. (Not knowing it was a forgery, I returned it merely as unrequested)**

"Presentment Hearing." Transcript. **March 9, 2010. (Defendants gave the judge the unrequested (forged) Lee floorboard report as fulfilling records turn-over; and lied that was the only record in Sederwall's possession)**

Werkmeister, Nicole. "Attached is the Forensic Examination Report From Dr. Henry Lee ..." Fax cover letter. **April 6, 2010. (Copy faxed of same unrequested (forged) Lee floorboard report from Brown)**

Brown, Kevin. "Enclosed please find a copy of another report dated February 25, 2005 which deals with the examination of furniture by Dr. Lee." Letter to Threet. **November 10, 2010. (Sending Lee's (forged) bench report; different font than the (forged) floorboard report)**

Lee, Henry and Calvin Ostler. "Forensic Research and Training Center Forensic Examination Report: "Examination of furniture from Pete Maxwell's of July 15, 1881." February 25, 2005. **(Given to me on November 10, 2010 as Lee bench report (16 pages) – but was forged)**

"Evidentiary Hearing on Plaintiff's Motion for Mandatory Order of Disclosure and Production." Transcript. **January 21, 2011. (Defendants gave forged Lee Floorboard report (9 pages) Version II as Exhibit F; and forged Lee bench report (16 pages) as Exhibit E)**

Lee, Henry and Calvin Ostler. "Forensic Research and Training Center Forensic Examination Report: "Examination of furniture from Pete Maxwell's of July 15, 1881." February 25, 2005. **(Given to Court on January 21, 2011 as Lee bench report (16 pages), Exhibit E – but was a forgery)**

Lee, Henry and Calvin Ostler. "Forensic Research and Training Center Forensic Examination Report: "Examination of Lincoln County Court House." February 25, 2005. **(Given to Court on January 21, 2011 as Lee floorboard report (9 pages), Exhibit F – but was its forged Version II)**

"Presentment Hearing." Transcript. September 23, 2011. **(I realized forgery was taking place and presented discrepancies in the Lee reports)**

Hearing on "Plaintiffs' Motion to Supplement the Record and a Request for Sanctions, and Co-Plaintiff's Motion For Attorney Fees." January 17, 2012 **(Sanctions against Defendants requested for forged reports; and co-plaintiff requested fees for past attorneys. Judge granted 100% fees)**

Eichwald, George P., District Judge. "Order on Plaintiffs Motion to Supplement the Record and Request for Award of Sanctions against Defendants." February 23, 2012. **(Ordered Sederwall to produce authentic Lee report)**

Lee, Henry and Calvin Ostler. "Forensic Research and Training Center Forensic Examination Report." February 25, 2005. **(Court-ordered turn-over to Plaintiffs on January 31, 2012 as "original," authentic, sole Lee report (25 pages) combining bench, floorboards, and wash stand)**

Hearing on "Plaintiffs' Second Motion to Supplement the Record and a Request for Sanctions." **May 31, 2012 (Sanctions requested for forged Lee reports)**

__________.Hearing for Plaintiff Gale Cooper's Motion to Request Award of Her Costs and Damages From Defendants and to Request Award of Sanctions Against Defendants." Transcript. December 18, 2013. **(I won!)**

Eichwald, George P. Judge. "Findings of Fact and Conclusions of Law and Order of the Court." **May 15, 2014. (Plaintiff Gale Cooper prevailed, Sederwall was punitively sanctioned for forging the forensic records of Dr. Henry Lee)**

__________ "Final Judgment." **March 8, 2017. (Plaintiff Gale Cooper prevailed)**

"COLD CASE BILLY THE KID" MEGAHOAX OF W.C. JAMESON'S 21st CENTURY BOOKS

THE JAMESON BOOKS (CHRONOLOGICAL)

Jameson, W.C. *Billy the Kid: Beyond the Grave*. Boulder, Lanham, Maryland: Taylor Trade Publishing. **2005. (A repeat of the "Brushy Bill" imposter hoax)**

__________. *Billy the Kid: The Lost Interviews*. Clearwater, Florida: Garlic Press Publishing. **2012.** (Reprint 2017). **(Forged rewriting of the 1949 Morrison transcript of "Brushy" to fake dialogue to update the hoax)**

__________. *Pat Garrett: The Man Behind the Badge*. Boulder, Colorado: Taylor Trade Publishing. **2016. (Defamation of Pat Garrett, "Brushy Bill" as a quoted authority, and "Billy the Kid Case" hoaxing as evidence to claim Garrett murdered an innocent victim instead of Billy the Kid)**

__________. *Cold Case Billy the Kid: Investigating History's Mysteries*. Guilford, Connecticut: Twodot. **2018. (Fusing the "Brushy" hoax and "Billy the Kid Case" hoax to argue for "Brushy" as Billy the Kid)**

SOURCES FOR DEBUNKING CLAIMS (CHRONOLOGICAL)

(SEE: sources debunking "Brushy Bill" Roberts; see "Billy the Kid Case" hoax)

RELEVANT TO DENYING WILLIAM H. BONNEY'S CORONER'S JURY REPORT'S EXISTENCE

(SEE: William H. Bonney, Coroner's Jury Report; and Patrick F. Garrett, Reward)

RELEVANT TO FAKING FACE DOWN CORPSE

Traylor, Leslie. "Facts Regarding the Escape of Billy the Kid." *Frontier Times.* **July, 1936.** Pages 506-513 (on Page 509). FrontierTimesMagazine.com. **(About his Jesus Silva interview on identifying Billy's body)**

Otero, Miguel, *The Real Billy the Kid.* New York: Rufus Rockwell Wilson. **1936. (Claim that Jesus Silva saw shot Billy Bonney face down.)**

RELEVANT TO FAKING OLD PETER MAXWELL AS A COOK DENYING GARRETT SHOT BILLY

Avant, Bundy. (Told to Arthur Clements). "The Bundy Avant Story: New Mexico in the days when a thin population was intent on bettering itself and each man could devise his own method for 'getting' while getting' was good.' " (Part One) *True West.* **May-June, 1978**, Volume 25, Number 5. **(Old-timer malarkey about a "Peter Maxwell" in the San Andres Mountains telling Avant that Garrett did not kill Billy the Kid)**

No Author. "Las Vegas." *The Albuquerque Citizen.* **June 28, 1898.** Page 2, Column 3. NewspaperArchive.com. **(Peter Maxwell death notice about Fort Sumner area residence and death)**

KEY SOURCES CITED BY HOAXERS (CHRONOLOGICAL)

(SEE: "Brushy Bill" Robert's hoax sources; Secret Service Operatives in Historical Organizations; and counterfeiting framing of Billy Bonney)

Garrett, Pat F. *The Authentic Life of Billy the Kid.* Santa Fe, New Mexico: New Mexico Printing and Publishing Co. **1882.** (Edition used by me: Edited by Maurice Garland Fulton. New York: The Macmillan Company. 1927)

Poe, John W. *The Death of Billy the Kid.* (Introduction by Maurice Garland Fulton). Boston and New York: Houghton Mifflin Company. **1933.**

Otero, Miguel, *The Real Billy the Kid.* New York: Rufus Rockwell Wilson. **1936. (Claim that Jesus Silva for shot Billy Bonney face down. But Otero had no first-hand knowledge, and the book was 55 years after the event.)**

Poe, Sophie. *Buckboard Days.* Albuquerque, New Mexico: University of New Mexico Press. **1964.**

Avant, Bundy. (Told to Arthur Clements). "The Bundy Avant Story: New Mexico in the days when a thin population was intent on bettering itself and each man could devise his own method for 'getting' while getting' was good.' " (Part One) *True West.* **May-June, 1978**, Volume 25, Number 5. **(Old-timer malarkey about a "Peter Maxwell" in the San Andres Mountains telling Avant that Garrett did not kill Billy the Kid; plus other apocryphal Billy the Kid tales)**

Anaya, Paco. *I Buried Billy.* College Station, Texas: Creative Publishing Company. **1991.(Cited as claiming counterfeiting for Billy)**

Lee, Henry and Calvin Ostler. "Forensic Research and Training Center Forensic Examination Report: "Examination of Lincoln County Court House." February 25, 2005. **(Apparently the forged "Billy the Kid Case's floorboard report)**

Lee, Henry. "Forensic Examination Report (Examination of Furniture From Pete Maxwell's of July 15, 1881) 22 May 2004." From W.C. Jameson, *Cold Case Billy the Kid.* Page 187. **(Apparently the forged "Billy the Kid Case's" carpenter's bench, washstand, and headboard report)**

INDEX

www.ingramcontent.com/pod-product-compliance
Lightning Source LLC
Chambersburg PA
CBHW020905100426
42737CB00043B/130

9781949626292